Irwin Allen's *Voyage to the Bottom of the Sea*: The Authorized Biography of a Classic Sci-Fi Series

ALSO BY MARC CUSHMAN

Irwin Allen's Voyage to the Bottom of the Sea: The Authorized Biography of a Classic Sci-Fi Series, Vol. 1
(with Mark Alfred)

I SPY: A History and Episode Guide of the Groundbreaking Television Series
(with Linda J. LaRosa)

Long Distance Voyagers: The Story of the Moody Blues
(2 volumes; Volume 2 forthcoming)

These Are the Voyages – Star Trek: The Original Series
(3 volumes; with Susan Osborn)

These Are the Voyages: Gene Roddenberry and Star Trek in the 1970s
(3 volumes)

Irwin Allen's Lost in Space: The Authorized Biography of a Classic Sci-Fi Series
(3 volumes)

Irwin Allen's *Voyage to the Bottom of the Sea*:
The Authorized Biography of a Classic Sci-Fi Series

Volume 2

Marc Cushman

and Mark Alfred

Jacobs/Brown Press

Los Angeles and Frazier Park, California.

...

LIBRARY OF CONGRESS CATALOGUING-IN-PUBLICATION DATA
Cushman, Marc
Irwin Allen's *Voyage to the Bottom of the Sea*: The Authorized Biography of a Classic Sci-Fi Series, Vol. 2
Marc Cushman and Mark Alfred
Editorial team: Mike Clark, Bill Cotter, Mark Phillips, and Thomas C. Tucker
Publisher: Matthew Williams Brown
Includes bibliographical reference and index

ISBN 978-1-7355673-0-3 (softback)

First Edition – October 2020

©2020 Marc Cushman. All rights reserved

Voyage to the Bottom of the Sea® and its characters and designs are © 20th Century-Fox Television and Legend Pictures, LLC, and licensed by Synthesis Entertainment. All rights reserved.
All photographs, script excerpts, artwork, contractual information, and transcripts taken from the Irwin Allen Archives are ©LegendPictures, LLC, and used with permission, except where otherwise noted.

This book is a work of journalism, protected under the First Amendment, with information presented under "fair usage" guidelines.

Queries regarding rights and permissions, and notifications of errors or omissions may be addressed to Jacobs Brown Press,
P.O. Box 6141, Los Angeles, CA 91603

No part of this book may be reproduced or transmitted in any form or by any means, electronic or mechanical, including photocopying or recording, or by any information storage and retrieval system, without permission in writing from the publisher.

Cover design: Deb Santo
Interior Design: Marc Cushman

First Edition softback manufactured in the United States of America

Jacobs/Brown Press
An imprint of Jacobs/Brown Media Group, LLC
Los Angeles and Frazier Park, California
www.JacobsBrownMediaGroup.com

Marc Cushman says thank you:

To Irwin Allen

for daring to open the door for science fiction and fantasy on television; for winning the space race in TV; for opening eyes and minds everywhere.

To Kevin Burns

for supplying images, as well as information, interviews, and connections that made much of what follows possible.

To Mark Phillips, Mike Clark, Bill Cotter, and Mike Bailey

for their helpful and insightful contributions to this book.

* * *

Mark Alfred says thank you:

To all who provide for those to come.

Acknowledgments

Beyond Kevin Burns, Mike Clark, Bill Cotter, Frank Garcia, Mark Phillips, and the late Mike Bailey, who contributed to this project with their research and interviews, and, after reading the pre-print manuscript, their notes, our further appreciation to those who gave encouragement, guidance, and support:

Our gratitude to the staff of the UCLA Performing Arts Library (since absorbed into the UCLA Special Collections Library), for their help during research in the Irwin Allen Papers Collection and *Voyage to the Bottom of the Sea* show files.

To Ron Hamill for joining the author in digging through the "Private" Irwin Allen Papers, archived by Legend Pictures; and to Derek Thielges of Legend Pictures / Synthesis Entertainment, for his invaluable aid. All the memos, shooting schedules, budgets, and the lion's share of the pictures found in this book (and the previous volume) are presented courtesy of these companies and individuals.

For many of the Nielsen ratings for the original broadcasts of *Voyage to the Bottom of the Sea*, and other science-fiction series from that era, we are indebted to Kate Barnett at Nielsen Media Services, as well as Derek Thielges of Synthesis Entertainment.

A special "Thank You" to those who kindly granted interviews: Michael Allen, Roger C. Carmel, Angela Cartwright, Mike Clark, Paul Comi, Joe D'Agosta, Kevin Burns, James Darren, Barbara Eden, Harlan Ellison, David Hedison, Allan Hunt, Lew Hunter, Sean Kenney, Walter Koenig, Marta Kristen, Derek Lewis, Barbara "BarBra" Luna, Vitina Marcus, Steve Marlo, Bruce Mars, Don Marshall, Lee Meriwether, Lawrence Montaigne, Sean Morgan, Bill Mumy, Herman Rush, Malachi Throne, and Francine York.

Sadly, many of those who helped to make *Voyage to the Bottom of the Sea* possible are no longer with us. To include their voices in this work, we relied on hundreds of newspaper and magazine articles, as well as dozens of books. A full list of these sources can be found in the Bibliography, but here we give special mention to the following books and their authors: *Irwin Allen Television Productions, 1964-1970*, by Jon Abbott; *Seaview: A 50th Anniversary Tribute to Voyage to the Bottom of the Sea*, by William E. Anchors, Jr. and Frederick Barr, with Lynne Holland; *Seaview: The Making of Voyage to the Bottom of the Sea*, by Tim Colliver; and *Science Fiction Television Series*, by Mark Phillips and Frank Garcia.

David Hedison had agreed to write the foreword for this book but, alas, that was not to be. We mourn his passing, and celebrate his life and career.

For those who have given their support and encouragement in other meaningful ways: James Alexander, Doug Diamond, Mike Makkreel, and, from Jacobs/Brown Media Group: Sondra Burrows, Jessica Eynon, Andrew Johnson, Steven Kates, Deb Santos, Susan Templeton, Thomas C. Tucker, and Rebecca Varga.

TABLE OF CONTENTS

Introduction *by Mark Alfred*	xiii
Preface *by Marc Cushman*	xv
01: Fathoming Irwin Allen	1
02: Casting Off for Season Two	21
03: Fall 1965	27
04: Season Two / ABC's Initial Order of 16	35
4.1: "Jonah and the Whale" (Episode 33)	37
4.2: "… And Five of Us Are Left" (Episode 34)	61
4.3: "Time Bomb" (Episode 35)	74
4.4: "Escape from Venice" (Episode 36)	87
4.5: "The Cyborg" (Episode 37)	95
4.6: "The Deadliest Game" (Episode 38)	106
4.7: "The Left-Handed Man" (Episode 39)	117
4.8: "The Death Ship" (Episode 40)	129
4.9: "The Silent Saboteurs" (Episode 41)	143
4.10: "Leviathan" (Episode 42)	152
4.11: "The Peacemaker" (Episode 43)	166
4.12: "The Monster from Outer Space" (Episode 44)	175
4.13: "The X Factor" (Episode 45)	184
4.14: "The Machines Strike Back" (Episode 46)	192
4.15: "Killers of the Deep" (Episode 47)	201
4.16: "Terror on Dinosaur Island" (Episode 48)	210
05: Season Two / ABC's Back Order of 10	219
5.1: "Deadly Creature Below!" (Episode 49)	221
5.2: "The Phantom Strikes" (Episode 50)	229
5.3: "The Sky's on Fire" (Episode 51)	240
5.4: "Graveyard of Fear" (Episode 52)	249
5.5: "The Shape of Doom" (Episode 53)	257
5.6: "Dead Man's Doubloons" (Episode 54)	264
5.7: "The Monster's Web" (Episode 55)	269
5.8: "The Menfish" (Episode 56)	277
5.9: "The Mechanical Man" (Episode 57)	291
5.10: "The Return of the Phantom" (Episode 58)	297
06: Fall 1966: Welcome to the Monster Mash	305
07: Season Three / ABC's Initial Firm Order of 16	319
7.1: "Monster from the Inferno" (Episode 59)	321

7.2: "Werewolf" (Episode 60)	333
7.3: "Day of Evil" (Episode 61)	343
7.4: "Night of Terror" (Episode 62)	352
7.5: "The Day the World Ended" (Episode 63)	359
7.6: "The Terrible Toys" (Episode 64)	365
7.7: "Deadly Waters" (Episode 65)	371
7.8: "Thing from Inner Space" (Episode 66)	378
7.9: "The Death Watch" (Episode 67)	385
7.10: "Deadly Invasion" (Episode 68)	391
7.11: "The Lost Bomb" (Episode 69)	399
7.12: "The Brand of the Beast" (Episode 70)	407
7.13: "The Plant Man" (Episode 71)	414
7.14: "The Creature" (Episode 72)	425
7.15: "The Haunted Submarine" (Episode 73)	435
7.16: "Death from the Past" (Episode 74)	443
08: Season Three / ABC's Back Order of 10	453
8.1: "The Heat Monster" (Episode 75)	455
8.2: "The Fossil Men" (Episode 76)	465
8.3: "The Mermaid" (Episode 77)	472
8.4: "The Mummy" (Episode 78)	479
8.5: "The Shadowman" (Episode 79)	485
8.6: "No Escape from Death" (Episode 80)	493
8.7: "Doomsday Island" (Episode 81)	498
8.8: "The Wax Men" (Episode 82)	507
8.9: "The Deadly Cloud" (Episode 83)	513
8.10 "Destroy Seaview!" (Episode 84)	517
09: Season Four / ABC's Initial Order of 16 – Damage Control	521
9.1: "Man of Many Faces" (Episode 85)	531
9.2: "Time Lock" (Episode 86)	540
9.3: "The Deadly Dolls" (Episode 87)	550
9.4: "Fires of Death" (Episode 88)	560
9.5: "Cave of the Dead" (Episode 89)	571
9.6: "Sealed Orders" (Episode 90)	580
9.7: "Journey with Fear" (Episode 91)	585
9.8: "Fatal Cargo" (Episode 92)	596
9.9: "Rescue" (Episode 93)	603
9.10: "Terror" (Episode 94)	609
9.11: "Blow Up" (Episode 95)	617
9.12: "The Deadly Amphibians" (Episode 96)	623

9.13: "The Return of Blackbeard" (Episode 97)	628
9.14: "A Time to Die" (Episode 98)	635
9.15: "Edge of Doom" (Episode 99)	642
9.16: "Nightmare" (Episode 100)	648
10: Season Four / ABC's Back Order of 10	653
10.1: "The Lobster Man" (Episode 101)	655
10.2: "Terrible Leprechaun" (Episode 102)	662
10.3: "The Abominable Snowman" (Episode 103)	667
10.4: "Man-Beast" (Episode 104)	673
10.5: "Savage Jungle" (Episode 105)	678
10.6: "Secret of the Deep" (Episode 106)	685
10.7: "Flaming Ice" (Episode 107)	690
10.8: "Attack!" (Episode 108)	699
10.9: "No Way Back" (Episode 109)	708
10.10: "The Death Clock" (Episode 110)	713
11: Submarine Down – The End of the Voyage	719
Appendices	725
APPENDIX A: Voyage to the Toy Store	727
APPENDIX B: Episode Lists	739
APPENDIX C: Bibliography	747
Notes	749

Introduction:
Small Screens, Big Dreams, and Happy Endings
by Mark Alfred

When the preteens and adolescents of the 1960s were able to connive control of the TV dial from their parents, a huge variety of larger-than-life adventure was available. The kid-friendly dramas of the day (as opposed to adult-oriented hospital shows or soap operas) often fell into three broad categories: law enforcement, Westerns, and sci-fi.

Many straddled the categories. A tough hero bringing justice to the frontier? That could be Captain Kirk of **Star Trek** or Lucas McCain of **The Rifleman**. The good guy catching bank robbers might be **Gunsmoke**'s Marshall Dillon or **The F.B.I.**'s Inspector Erskine.

These shows featured something perhaps incomprehensible fifty years or more later: the uncorrupted, non-ironic hero. While you'd be hard-pressed to find such a character "played straight" nowadays, this role is a key to the worldview of a 1960s kid.

We came to idealism naturally. It was part of our environment, from comic books to TV shows, from sports to movies. Our parents had fought the Good War and come home to the good life. In mainstream entertainments, at least, families were unbroken; virtue triumphed; and the wonders of the universe could be tamed by the triple threats of Truth, Justice, and the American Way.

Sure, this good-always-wins depiction of the world was wishful thinking on our parents' part. But it also played into the emotional needs of a generation or two of youngsters.

While we were comforted by virtue's victories, like all kids we liked a little subversion – hence the likes of **MAD** magazine and the Chipmunks, who could make even the Beatles sound silly. No one can deny that one of the best rumblers of the status quo was Irwin Allen.

Whether in space, underwater, or tumbling through time, every week his TV shows featured something silly or dangerous (or both) to threaten the heroes and their surroundings. Before he became the 1970s Master of Disaster, the 1960s Irwin Allen was a Wizard of the Weird. The heroes might face aliens, lobster men, or even alternate versions of themselves. But no matter how far the story careened around narrative corners on two wheels, things always righted themselves in time for the end credits.

Youngsters that we were, we didn't understand that the rules of TV demanded these ritual re-impositions of normality. We just thought that this was the way things were supposed to work out.

The happy endings of our sheltered childhoods seem trite nowadays. Still, there's something in the wacky adventures presented by Irwin Allen that still beckons to our imaginations. A big part of that charm lies in the very outlandishness of the stories. The left turns taken in the plots of **Lost in Space** or **Voyage** rival anything a sugar-crazed eight-year-old might concoct. Another undeniable attraction is the aforementioned, now-implausible restoration of the status quo at the end of each tale – the show's family group reaffirmed, all disturbing influences exiled.

The worlds of adventure dished out by Irwin Allen were thrilling and exotic. But they were anchored by the solidity and uprightness of heroes that stood up to evil. Nowadays, those victories come across as farfetched or improbable. But don't we *still* yearn to have our troubles solved by a little derring-do? The finality of those weekly resolutions makes us wish that our grown-up lives could be so easily resolved. Who wouldn't like to beat up the bully, or lock up the transgressor, and make everything happy-ever-after again? When I watched these shows, in my naiveté I never considered that no matter how safely this week's story ended, next week another bad guy or emergency would ripple the waters again.

Come to think of it, take a broader view. Aren't the way-out twists of the Allen imagination allegories for the unexpected crises of adulthood? "The allegories of Irwin Allen" – what a concept!

Even though we grown-up Allen fans will never end up on the Titanic's maiden voyage or be shanghaied to a space circus, let's face it – nowadays I'd settle for one solid victory a week – wouldn't you?

Mark Alfred,
June 2020

Preface
by Marc Cushman

Researching and writing this two-book set on *Voyage to the Bottom of the Sea* has been a revelation for me. I'd always wondered what Irwin Allen was thinking when he altered the course of his 1960s TV series, particularly his two greatest successes, *Voyage* and *Lost in Space*. These changes were curious, to say the least. *Voyage* began with mostly espionage and adventure stories, with a smattering of science-fiction and horror tales. However, by the latter half of its 110-episode history, the series evolved – devolved, some say – into a monster-of-the-week format. That's what people came to call it – those of us watching and the members of the media (newspaper columnist, TV critics, etc.). It was really more like every other week, alternating with the overused premise of either Admiral Nelson or Captain Crane acting strangely, and then turning on the other, often with murderous intent. The reliance on stock footage became increasingly obvious by the middle of the third season. Beginning about this time, some episodes seemed created just to make use of effects shots or even entire scenes from past episodes. The show suffered.

The same question nagged me regarding *Lost in Space*. That series also started as serious science fiction – something aimed at kids, youthful-minded adults, and fans of the genre – but, upon switching to color for its second season, made an abrupt turn toward silliness, juvenile comedy, and pure fantasy. Again, what was Allen thinking?

I had to know. So when the opportunity presented itself for access to the show files for both series, as well as the Irwin Allen Private Papers collection, I was quick to sign aboard. It had been more than 50 years since I had sat before the family TV set, as a wide-eyed pre-teen, watching *Voyage* and *Space* during their network runs in the 1960s. Now I could satisfy my musings. So, I took the plunge. The answers are here – in these *Voyage* volumes, and in the three-volume set covering *Lost in Space*.

The answers had to do with the dreaded family hour and its censorship constraints, restrictive budgets, and Allen's instincts regarding what his audience wanted to see. This theory of viewership was based on fan letters, ratings, and the inner voice of the small boy who thrilled at Saturday morning serials in the movie houses. Allen's inclinations had helped make him one of the two most successful producers of hour-long TV of that era. (The other was Quinn Martin, the only other producer to have three series running concurrently.)

There is a second reason why researching and writing these two volumes about *Voyage* turned out to be a revelation – I finally had an excuse, and the time, to watch the entire series, from pilot to final episode, in the order in which they were produced. Many of these episodes I was discovering for the first time. You see, *Voyage* was not a show that my family watched regularly when I was a boy. I was the youngest, and only boy, of four siblings. Often my preferences were overruled. I saw maybe one out of three episodes during *Voyage*'s four-year run on ABC-TV, and only caught it sporadically after it went into syndicated repeats. My opinion of the series, based on such limited viewing, was that it was entertaining, imaginative, and sometimes silly. So, with this work project, I began watching the show in full, in proper sequence, with a curious and mostly open mind.

I was surprised and happy to find that the first season (covered in Volume 1, along with Irwin Allen's early life and career, the 1961 *Voyage* movie, and the 1963-64 pilot film) was quite good for its time. Espionage/sabotage episodes like "The Fear Makers," "Hail to the Chief," and "No Way Out" come close to excellence. So did some of the sci-fi offerings, such as "The Sky Is Falling," "Mutiny," "The Invaders," and "The Indestructible Man." And the more standard adventure tales ("The Mist of Silence"), or sub-in-destress tales ("Submarine Sunk Here") are truly gripping. Some episodes fall to the level of "mere" adventure tales, but most were much better than I expected.

This second volume covers the making of the 78 color episodes. Again, I was struck by the variety of the stories which were spun, from espionage, to sci-fi, to possession, to monster and horror tales. Season Two, in particular, offers a full buffet of different taste treats. Again, some work better than others, and a few fall flat on their faces, but most are worthy entries. Seasons Three and Four are less varied; by this point, Irwin Allen was sure of what his audience wanted: cheap thrills (as Big Brother and the Holding Company's 1968 album title put it). Budget restrictions were limiting the series, as well. The success-to-failure ratio was closer to 50/50 for these two seasons. But for me, the 50% that worked did so wonderfully. Most of the other half are still fun, in a non-filling, barbequed pork rinds sort of way.

My revelation, therefore, is three fold: 1) *Voyage* is better than I had realized when watching infrequently during my youth and early adulthood; 2) the cast, led by Richard Basehart and David Hedison, was remarkably talented, never phoning their performances in, despite less-than-challenging material; 3) Irwin Allen wasn't as crazy as I had suspected. He was a producer trying to make the best of the limited funding and time he was given; who was imaginative and playful; and who wasn't interested in subtext. Did Allen make mistakes; did he misread a large portion of his audience; did his judgment contribute to torpedoing *Voyage*? Absolutely. But who else could have produced half a science-fiction movie each week, times 26 or more weeks, times three concurrent series? No one else was willing to try, because no one else would have survived the work, or succeeded. There was only one Irwin Allen. Likewise, only one *Voyage to the Bottom of the Sea*.

I believe I have done Irwin Allen and *Voyage* justice in these two volumes, with the help of my editor and collaborator, the very bright, very talented (and very funny) Mark Alfred, and the guidance of *Voyage* aficionados Mark Phillips, Mike Clark, and Mike Bailey, and the generosity of *Voyage*'s caretaker, Kevin Burns and his staff. If you're reading this, then you know *Voyage*, and you love it. I hope you will love this book, as well. It has been our pleasure to bring it to you – with no subtext.

Marc Cushman,
June 2020

1

Fathoming Irwin Allen

**Irwin Allen, surrounded by eye candy for the boys in the press, while promoting the big-screen *Voyage to the Bottom of the Sea* in 1961.
(Courtesy Synthesis Entertainment)**

Staff changes and realignments were always part of the preparation for a TV show's new season. In the spring of 1965, one of these new members of the *Voyage* family was Joe D'Agosta. He was assigned to work under Cliff Gould in the casting department of 20th Century-Fox. D'Agosta had held a similar position at MGM, where he handled the casting for producer Gene Roddenberry's pre-*Star Trek* series, *The Lieutenant*. At Fox, his responsibilities were much greater. Among the series assigned to him were *Voyage to the Bottom of the Sea* and *Lost in Space*... later followed by the pilot film for *The Time Tunnel*. Interviewed for this book, Joe D'Agosta said of Irwin Allen, "He was not as much a producer as he was an emperor. He worked me from 7 in the morning till 11:30 at night. I didn't mind. I loved my work. I was the same as Irwin in that regard. I loved

Casting Director Joseph D'Agosta in his studio office, circa 1967. (Courtesy: Joe D'Agosta)

Monday mornings and hated Friday afternoons. I didn't like *not* going to the studio. And I understood that about Irwin. That's what I respected. The fact that he was a little rigid, I didn't care about. And I didn't care that he was a bit of an emperor, for lack of a better term, with his Napoleonic way. I didn't mind that. I like tough guys; you know what you're dealing with. It's the nice guys that criticize you behind your back that you have to worry about. So, I always liked working with him."

There was a stumbling block, however. D'Agosta recalled, "One thing Irwin wanted from his employees, other than that they agree with him, was absolute exclusive loyalty. When I went to Fox, my deal was that I would cast features as well as television. So, I was assigned *Stagecoach* by my boss, Cliff Gould, the head of casting. And Irwin saw me on the grounds of Fox with the script. He said, 'What's that?' I said, 'I'm casting a movie; it's a remake of the John Wayne movie.' I was very proud when I said it. But he walked away off that comment, and the next thing I get is a call from my boss. I was asked into his office, and he said, 'Irwin wants to meet with us.'"

D'Agosta was about to see how the emperor tested his subjects. He said, "We went into this meeting, and there was this long table – probably 10 to 15 feet long – and on one end sat Irwin, and on the other end sat my boss. And on one side of the length of the long table sat Frank La Tourette, an associate producer who I always had casting sessions with, and Harry Harris, a director who worked on many of the episodes. I sat on the other long side. Irwin proceeded to talk about how he wasn't getting enough of my time, and then turned to the associate producer and said, 'You tell Cliff Gould what it is like to work with Joe.' And this guy went on with a bunch of complaints about my unavailability, how it took me a little longer to get the interviews set up. I don't remember the arguments, but he had a whole list of things that he was programmed to complain about. Then Irwin turned to director Harry Harris and said, 'Tell Cliff about how it is to work with Joe,' and a similar list was presented."[1]

Director Harry Harris.
(Source: *The Los Angeles Times*)

Harris was hoping to pacify Allen, who might send further directing assignments his way. But he certainly understood the difficult situation D'Agosta was in. He told interviewer Kevin Burns, "The experience of working with Irwin did a lot for me, because you have to have a tremendous amount of patience to keep from blowing your stack. Getting through that kind of experience over all those years working with him, that's what I think about. I don't think about *Lost in Space* or *Voyage to the Bottom of the Sea* – the product doesn't mean anything to me; the fact that I worked with him stays with me. I think about him all the time. ... Sometimes it was a love-hate relationship. But I learned a lot from him, and I learned to keep my mouth shut, and I learned to have patience and how to go about my business and do my work and not do anything to hinder my relationship with him."[2]

Joe D'Agosta was still learning that lesson. He told us, "I was a young man at the time, around 26. I sat there and I just started shaking, and my lip was tightening, and my anger was building. And Irwin just sat there, very superior like. Finally, I got up and I stared out the window. I tried to hold my temper, but, when Irwin started to speak again, I verbally attacked him. I put my finger right up to his nose, and said, 'Let me tell you something, *you*! I come here; I work with you till 11:30 at night; I've got a family at home, but I'm *here* at 7 o'clock in the morning, pulling your casting together.' He just sat there; he froze, and he wouldn't meet my stare. He knew that I was ready to explode. I was scary; I scared *myself*. And it was all because I was hurt. I was *hurt* that I'd been set up – with that table and the way he placed us and then presided over that kangaroo court. I just attacked him verbally, then I walked right out the door. As I passed Cliff, I said, 'I'm sorry, Cliff, I couldn't keep it in,' because Cliff was a gentleman; a truly nice guy, and I felt bad for whatever trouble this would create for him."

Those who knew Joe D'Agosta, and this author has talked to many, consistently describe him as friendly and even-tempered. But Irwin Allen had pushed the young casting director's buttons and evoked a response that even surprised D'Agosta. He said, "I went back to my office, and I was shaking. I thought, 'That's it; I'm done here,' because Irwin Allen had more shows on the air than any company in town. I was doing three shows with him. So, the phone rings, and Cliff says, 'Can you come to my office?' I went into his office and said, 'Just fire me. Don't worry about it, Cliff. I'm sorry; I just couldn't hold it in.' He said, 'Boy, you sure can get mad.' I told him, 'Cliff, I worked my ass off for that guy, blah, blah, blah, blah.'"

After apologizing to Gould for losing his temper, D'Agosta braced himself for the worst. He expected to be fired, and wondered if his career in television was over. To his surprise, Gould said, "Well, can you work with him again?"

"I said, 'What are you talking about?' Then, Cliff says, 'He wants nobody but you.' I said, 'What about the feature?' He says, 'You can keep the feature.' 'Really?!'

"Now, if Irwin was the emperor that I thought he was, he could have had my head chopped off. I would have been finished in the business, not just at Fox. So, I went back to Irwin and, from that point on, he never made a casting decision based on the director's or the associate producer's opinions, but only on my opinion. He'd say, 'What do you think, Joe?' And we had this father/son relationship that was just amazing. It always remained a professional relationship; we didn't hang out; it was within the walls of the office, but when I say father/son, I'm saying he treated me kindly, with respect, and he wouldn't make a move in casting without getting my approval." [3]

Another Season Two change, introducing two more people to the complexity of Irwin Allen, involved the control ABC exercised over *Voyage to the Bottom of the Sea*. During Season One, Adrian Samish had been the primary liaison between the series and the network, and Samish was a hands-on production manager. Since the series was not then a hit (with nearly half the first-season episodes filmed before the series premiered), the network had mandated many of the elements within the series and its various episodes. But, as ratings came in which showed *Voyage* was winning its time slot and bringing in well above a 30 percent audience share, Irwin Allen started listening less to the requests of the network and more to his own narrative instincts. At first, this change was not a dramatic one, with Samish attempting to keep a firm hand on the show. By Season Two, however, Samish had moved up at the network. Harve Bennett was now in charge of overseeing the numerous details for many of ABC's series, including *Voyage*. Bennett soon learned that he wasn't going to make much headway in influencing Allen's decisions. He took a step back and assigned one of his junior executives the headache of trying to hold the reins. Handed this touchy job was Lew Hunter.

ABC-TV Production Manager Lew Hunter.

Interviewed for this book, Hunter said, "Harve Bennett was the one that hired me and got me into programming. And I jumped up in pay from an $8,000 annual gig – being the Director of Broadcast Promotions – to $35,000. And, my God, I thought I'd died and gone to heaven. He says over the phone, 'I'm going to give you $35,000 a year.' I gulped and said, 'That will be fine, Harve.'" [4]

Irwin Allen admired Hunter. The two had much in common. Both were tireless workers, and both achieved what they had the hard way.

Hunter said, "I started in television back in 1952 when I was a floor manager at KOLN, Lincoln, Nebraska. I was a self-confessed farm boy, way back then, and I went to Chicago to attend Northwestern. I also did some work in advertising there. So, I think Irwin had an identification with my own background, because when I was going to Hollywood from Chicago, I knew *nobody* in Hollywood. I had an aunt and uncle that lived in Long Beach, and that was it.

"I'd been in town for three weeks, and I was a failure. Particularly when I was at the gas company, trying to sign up for gas service, and the form said, 'Occupation?' I put down 'Producer.' The woman who was dealing with me put a line through 'producer' and she wrote, 'unemployed.' I laughed then, but was shook up at the same time. So, I wrote 95 letters – and that was back in the time when you typed up each letter, because you didn't have the ability to copy them or to readjust the heading. Ninety-five letters to 95 different people at the studios and networks, and at advertising agencies, and I got 15 responses. Of those, five people agreed to meet with me. One was this wonderful man named Ed Cashman, and Ed said, 'You need to get in the door; whether it's the 'Page Cap' or the mail room, you just get in the door, and from then on you can fly.' He was absolutely right. I worked as a page at ABC, starting in 1956, and did that for two weeks, then five months in the mail room, then I went into music clearance, and up the ladder, and up, up, up, and I got into broadcast promotions, where I did the trailers. I won an award for one of those trailers, and that led to me being transferred to work under Harve Bennett. Somehow, Irwin got hold of that information, and that gave him a little more respect for me. The energy that Irwin saw in me, from how I came out with no contacts and then worked my way up from the bottom, was something that he admired."[5]

Allen had done the same when he first arrived in Hollywood. Like Hunter, Allen had no advantages to speak of, no foot up toward his goal. It was a classic rags-to-riches tale.

Born Irwin Grinovit in New York City on June 12, 1916, Allen was the youngest of four brothers – after Rubin, George, and Fred – to begin life in the modest home of a Russian Jewish immigrant who worked as a tailor. The family struggled to survive in the midst of the Great Depression. Allen escaped the bleak period through his keen interest in books. He took night-time classes at Columbia University, including courses in advertising and journalism. He also took free community-college classes at City College of New York. During the day, between classes, he earned money writing publicity material for nightclubs in Greenwich Village and on 52nd Street. Also – emulating one of his role models, P.T. Barnum – he worked as a barker at a carnival.

Allen's cousin, Al Gail, said, "Somehow, it seemed to be a dead end. There was really nothing happening. We had a cousin in Los Angeles, and one day we're sitting around and [Irwin] said, 'What the hell, let's go to California and see what's doing.' Within a week or so, we were on our way. We were hopeful to land something either in the movie industry or advertising, or one of the allied arts, and make our own way. We really had no specific target – just to get a job; start working and see where it goes from there."[6]

Sheila Mathews Allen, Irwin Allen's future wife, said, "He always wanted to be associated with the circus in some way. So, I guess when he came out here, he was running away to *join* the circus."[7]

According to Al Gail, it was on the trip to California that Irwin Grinovit decided to change his name.

"Grinovit was an old family name, and it was a difficult name," said Gail. "It was a harsh name, and people had trouble remembering it. So, when we came out here, we decided to change it to something that's more easily spoken and remembered, and we came up with 'Allen.' ... I said, 'Well, it's a good name, and easy to say, and easy to remember.' So, he liked it. He decided on *Irwin Allen*." [8]

Nephew Michael Allen knew the origin of the name. "He came to Boston to visit my father, and we lived on Allen Street in the West End of Boston. And he thought he would change his name to help him in his profession and he liked the sound of Allen." [9]

Once in Los Angeles, the newly christened Irwin Allen and cousin Al found jobs with a magazine called *Key*, which served as an entertainment directory and nightclub guide. "He had a very agile mind," Al Gail said, "And he was a great salesman. So, we came out and we started to work for a local entertainment magazine. We were always a team. He did what he did best and I did what I did best. I was basically a writer; he was a presenter, a talker, a salesman, and very creative on his own." [10]

Above: On the airwaves with Irwin Allen, over KMTR.
Next page: KLAC-TV's *Hollywood Merry-Go-Round*, with Allen in the center box, as Master of Ceremonies.
(Courtesy Synthesis Entertainment)

Compulsively driven to succeed, Allen ventured into other areas of media, first as an all-night disc jockey at local radio station KMTR. Then, with uncanny speed, he had his own radio program – *Hollywood Merry-Go-Round* – a quarter-hour-long celebrity gossip show heard six nights a week at 9:45 p.m. Cousin Al served as producer.

From 1940 through 1949, Allen made countless contacts throughout the industry by means of newsprint, radio, and video versions of his breathless showbiz reports. He also wrote a column, "On the Set," for Hollywood Features Syndicates. Allen worked tirelessly, rising before the sun and toiling long after it had set. And, like the sun, he never took a day off.

In the fall of 1948, Allen's *Hollywood Merry-Go-Round* radio program began broadcasting to a national audience. A short time later, KLAC-TV, Channel 13 in Los Angeles, launched a video version of the show, with Allen again front and center. Even with this early incarnation of an Irwin Allen Production, high concepts and speed were emphasized over substance.

In May 1949, Allen shifted to a new video series in August, *Irwin Allen's Hollywood Party*. He later boasted that, with this program, he pioneered the TV panel show.

In 1947, while still appearing regularly on radio and TV, Allen branched out even further by becoming a Hollywood agent. This too was only a stepping stone for the ambitious and tireless Allen, as the ravenous reader began searching out potential screen properties which he could shop to the studios. With all the connections he had made, Allen had little trouble getting responses from the movie moguls of Hollywood. One was Howard Hughes, who had recently acquired RKO Pictures. Allen pitched his stories to Hughes and soon jockeyed himself into the position of associate producer for the 1952 comedy *Double Dynamite*, starring Hughes' contract gal, Jane Russell, and Frank Sinatra, along with Allen's soon-to-be lifelong friend, Groucho Marx. A second project, released before *Double Dynamite* in 1951, was the film noir thriller *Where Danger Lives*, starring Hughes' discovery Faith Domergue, cast opposite Robert Mitchum. Another comedy, 1952's *A Girl in Every Port,* with Groucho Marx, William Bendix and Marie Wilson, followed. This film marked Allen's first time as a full-fledged movie producer – the top man behind the camera.

The next step up for Allen – and it was a big one – was to launch himself as a writer-producer-director. To accomplish this, he optioned a most unlikely screen property, Rachel Carson's non-fiction best-seller, *The Sea Around Us*. This provoked snickers from the Hollywood crowd. How was this curious, bespectacled urbanite, who had never written a screenplay, and never directed a film, going to turn a book of natural science, by a marine biologist, into a moneymaking motion picture? Allen sought collaborators, and looked for stock footage. He told Hollywood correspondent Aline Mosby, "I wrote to 2,341 institutions of oceanography…. I kept four secretaries busy for fourteen months, with 6,000 pieces of correspondence.

"About 75 percent of the movie was shot just for us, and the rest was scientific film these institutions had in their vaults. Some was 16mm film that had to be enlarged. The film was shot in every color process known, and some we hadn't heard of, so our laboratory had to fix it so the colors in the different sections matched."

Belying his reputation as a man with no sense of humor, Allen told Mosby, "This is the first time a textbook was made into a movie. I've got a hot script working on an algebra book, too." [11]

Released in 1953 by RKO, *The Sea Around Us* – Irwin Allen's first journey to the bottom of the sea – brought him an Oscar for Best Documentary.

With Oscar in hand, the doors to Tinseltown swung wide open for Allen. He followed up with a thriller for RKO – this time in 3-D. 1954's *Dangerous Mission* starred Victor Mature, Piper Laurie, William Bendix, and someone who would later guest star in TV's *Voyage to the Bottom of the Sea*, Vincent Price.

A move from RKO to Warner Bros. increased Allen's Hollywood ranking and earning potential. In the mode of *The Sea Around Us*, he made 1956's *The Animal World*, another splashy documentary designed to be as much fun for the kids as it was interesting for the adults.

Interviewed by United Press for an April 1955 wire-service article, Allen said of *The Sea Around Us*, "It was the biggest financial success RKO had – *twice as big as Jane Russell* – and *it* won an Oscar! So, I decided to make another picture without actors – a documentary on animals. … *I love to make pictures without actors*. No temperament and [animals are] always on time in the morning because they're the only actors you can lock away at night." [12]

The Animal World, which dispensed with human actors in favor of four-legged ones, included dinosaurs fashioned by Ray Harryhausen.

9

With 1957's *The Story of Mankind*, also for Warner Bros., Allen dared to undertake turning Hendrik Van Loon's history book, which was the second best-selling book of all time (under The Bible) into an "All-Star" pseudo epic. The "stars" included many who had seen their best days a decade or two earlier, but still had – when heralded in a TV commercial for the film – name value. Among them: Ronald Colman, Hedy Lamarr, the Marx Brothers, Virginia Mayo, Vincent Price, Charles Coburn, John Carradine, and Edward Everett Horton. Also present for the first of three films with Allen was Peter Lorre, later to be seen in the big-screen *Voyage to the Bottom of the Sea*. More importantly, *The Story of Mankind* marked Allen's first foray into science fiction.

Irwin Allen turns to fantasy to tell *The Story of Mankind*.

Explaining his curious approach in adapting a straightforward, albeit juvenile, history book to the big screen, Allen told a correspondent for the Associated Press, "Van Loon had a rare ability to put history into popular terms, to make it understandable to children. But with all due respect to van Loon, history is still something like hearing a joke for the second time. The punch is gone out of it. So, we have added a gimmick. We start out with two stars in the sky. They pulsate as they talk to each other and tell how the people on Earth have developed the gamma bomb, which with one blow could destroy the world. Should it be exploded? Now, we go to someplace in outer space. It's not heaven, because we wouldn't want to offend any religious groups. Here, a trial is held to determine whether Earth should be destroyed. Many of the heroes and the villains of history appear to testify, and we flash back to see their deeds." [13]

Flashing back often involved stock footage from old Hollywood movies, a technique Allen would often employ in TV's *Voyage to the Bottom of the Sea* and *The Time Tunnel*.

Despite *The Story of Mankind* being savaged by the critics, the box-office was respectable, and Allen's big-screen career continued to evolve.

With a move to Allied Artists, for 1959's *The Big Circus*, Allen indulged the boy in himself, and assembled another all-star cast, with Victor Mature, Red Buttons, Rhonda Fleming, Vincent Price, Gilbert Roland, Peter Lorre, and David Nelson. And monkeys, lions, and elephants.

This was the movie for which Paul Zastupnevich joined Irwin Allen's team as a wardrobe designer and general all-around factotum.

Zastupnevich created a "presentation" folder with watercolor illustrations of his designs. He declared, "Irwin loved it! He looked at me and said I had 'showmanship.' I was on Cloud Nine, because it was unheard of at the time for an unknown to walk in and get a picture." [14]

"The job was supposed to be for only three weeks. I ended up staying approximately thirty-two years. I'm like the proverbial man who came to dinner – *I never left!* A lot of people say to me, 'Why did you put up with him? Why did you stay if you were so unhappy at times?' And I said, 'Well, you know, after all, I had been in Hollywood for nine years knocking on the doors; I'd been at the Pasadena Playhouse doing things; I'd been an actor and whatnot, and this was the first time

Irwin Allen with Vincent Price, on the set of 1959's *The Big Circus*. (Courtesy Synthesis Entertainment)

that I got a chance to do a picture. He gave me a three [sic] million-dollar picture! I hadn't done any movie work up till this time. But, on the basis of that presentation of mine, he gave me the chance." [15]

Allen began his tenure at 20th Century-Fox with 1960s, *The Lost World*, his second excursion into science fiction and fantasy, which, besides hitting at the box office, became a stockpile of dinosaur footage to be harvested time and again for TV's *Voyage to the Bottom of the Sea*. The use of clips from *The Lost World* in *Voyage* was made all the easier by the inclusion of David Hedison in the cast. Also on hand to fight the monsters were Claude Rains, Jill St. John, Fernando Lamas, Richard Haydn, and, in her first work for Allen, Vitina Marcus.

Interviewed for this book, Marcus said, "He wanted me to test for *The Lost World*. That was fine with me, until I saw the costume he wanted me to wear! As it turned out, Irwin used that costume I wore in *The Lost World* in three different shows. The first three times I worked for him I wore the same outfit!" [16]

Allen, when dealing with restrictive TV budgets in the

1960s, was the master of recycling. With all the special effects, and scary creatures, he was also like a kid in a candy store. Irwin Allen was having the time of his life.

David Hedison told Mike Clark, "I read the script and it was funny at the beginning, with Claude Rains and what he had to do, and I was a photographer, a journalist, all of that. It was nice; it took on something good. But then, once we get on the helicopter, it became a kids' show." [17]

"It was terrible," Hedison lamented. "The alligators with horns and the rhinoceros iguanas were the stars of that picture. Irwin totally wasted the top-notch cast: Michael Rennie, Claude Rains, Fernando Lamas, Jill St. John. We spent the whole film running around from one

Above: David Hedison, in 1959, having fun ... at first ... in *The Lost World*.
Below: Allen (in the highest chair), holding court with his stars on the Fox backlot during filming.

contrived disaster to another. None of the relationships were thought out or even that conflicted." [18]

When Hedison walked away, he was certain he would never deal with anything quite like this again. "When I finished *The Lost World*, I said I will never work with Irwin again – he's impossible! All he knows is photo effects and banging up against the furniture and fights and everything else [of that type]. He doesn't know anything about character, or simple little moments; nothing. He didn't know anything about that. It was just horrific and very hard. And he was a bit of a crazy man." [19]

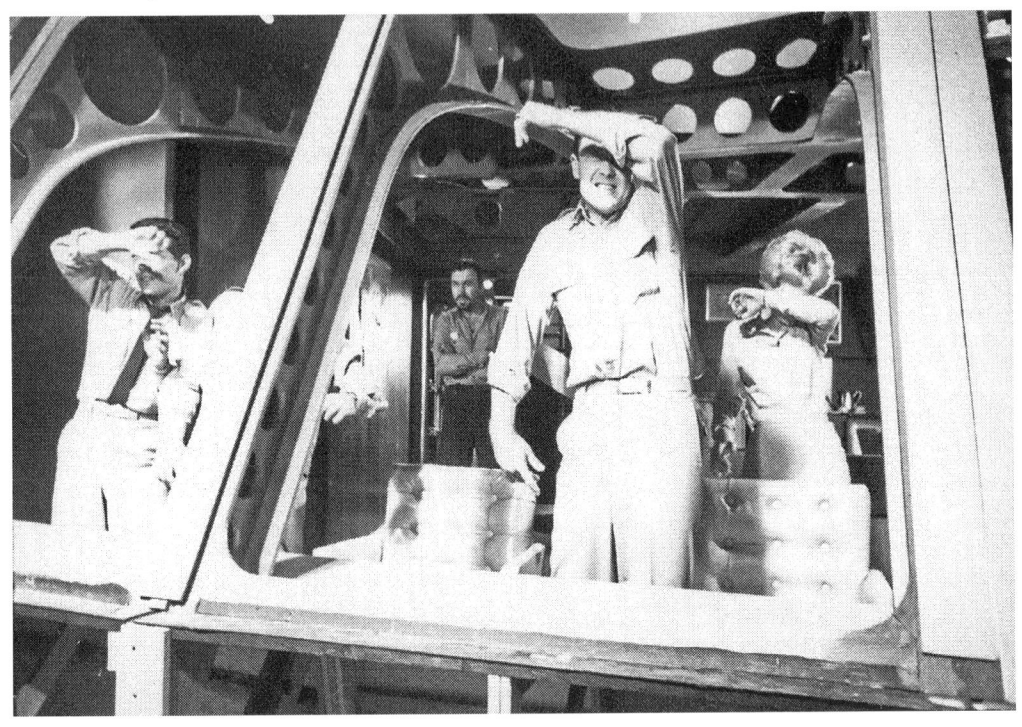

Irwin Allen's biggest bang yet! Frankie Avalon, Michael Ansara, Robert Sterling, and Barbara Eden get an eyeful of special effects on the observation nose set, for 1961's *Voyage to the Bottom of the Sea*. (Courtesy Synthesis Entertainment)

For his next picture with 20th Century-Fox, Allen borrowed a page from another favorite childhood book, Jules Verne's *Twenty Thousand Leagues Under the Sea*. For that film – 1961's *Voyage to the Bottom of the Sea* – Allen knew who he wanted to play the submarine's skipper, Captain Crane, right away – David Hedison. The actor felt differently.

"[1960] was the most depressing time of my life," Hedison recalled. "I was very low; went home every night depressed, because I was working with Irwin Allen in a film called *The Lost World*. It was one of those pictures that the studio wanted me to do and I felt I had to do, [because] I didn't want to go on suspension. ... I was on that film for about eight weeks or so, and I was truly, really, really depressed. So, about a year later, I wasn't depressed anymore, but Irwin called, and he wanted me to do a film called *Voyage to the Bottom of the Sea*. And, after my experience on the *Lost World*, I just couldn't face it, because it was basically the same thing." [20]

Robert Sterling got the job. But Allen never forgot Hedison, and would pursue him again when it came time to move *Voyage* to TV.

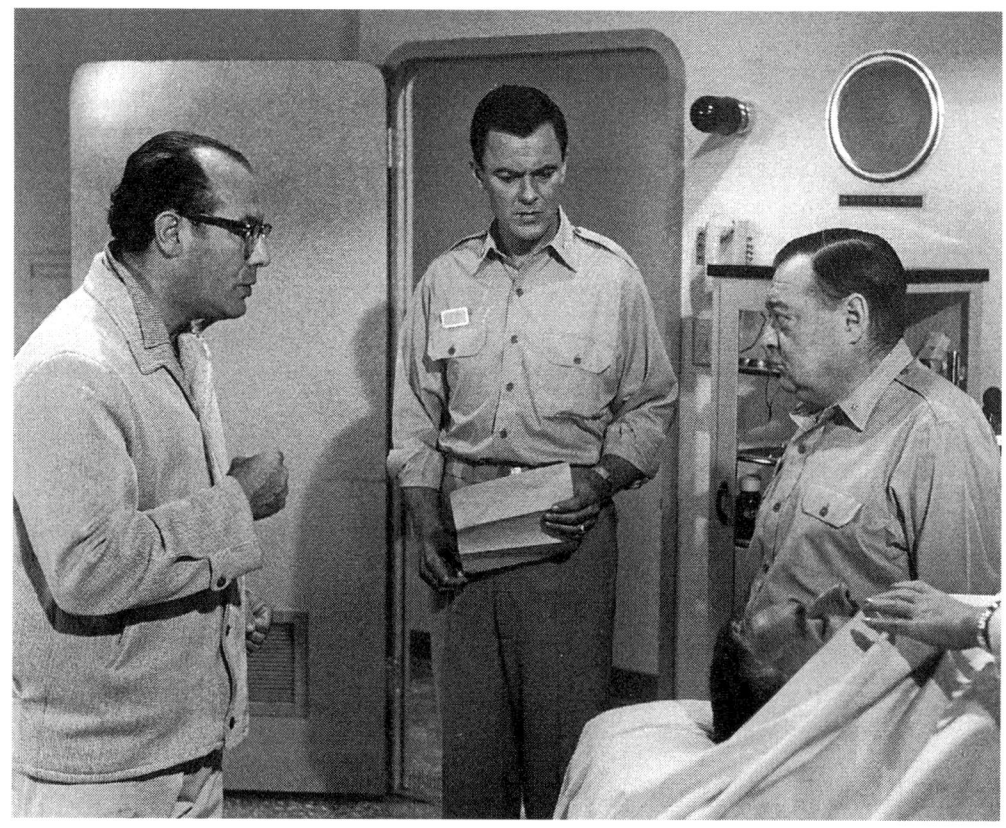

Allen with Robert Sterling and Peter Lorre during production of 1961's *Voyage to the Bottom of the Sea*. (Courtesy Synthesis Entertainment)

Also in the film: Joan Fontaine, Barbara Eden, Peter Lorre, Frankie Avalon, a giant squid, and, as Admiral Nelson, Walter Pidgeon. In skivvies were a couple of actors who would stay onboard for the TV series – Del Monroe and Mark Slade. And, making his first of many appearances in Irwin Allen films and TV shows, Michael Ansara. Also appearing in the TV series were many stock shots from the film. In fact, having access to footage, as well as props, costumes, and detailed miniatures, made Allen's sale of the series to ABC-TV possible.

Allen gives direction to Mark Slade and Del Monroe for 1961's *Voyage to the Bottom of the Sea*. (Courtesy Synthesis Entertainment)

Allen promised to keep costs down, and harvesting materials from the movie enabled him to stay true to his word.

Allen made one more film for Century-Fox before returning to TV – 1962's *Five Weeks in a Balloon*, based on another Jules Verne tale. This one starred Red Buttons, Fabien, Barbara Eden, Peter Lorre, Richard Haydn, BarBara Luna, and Chester the Chimp.

In 1963, 20th Century fell on hard times with numerous problems and cost overruns on *Cleopatra*, and Marilyn Monroe's final, unfinished film, *Something's Got to Give*. Another expensive one, although not problematic, *The Sound of Music*, was in pre-production and would begin filing in early 1964. The studio had to cut back on other film development, and Allen, the workaholic, needed to keep himself busy, busy, busy. So, he proposed *Voyage to the Bottom the Sea* to the television division of Fox, and ABC-TV, as a weekly series. No one thought it possible, not with what little TV paid, and its appetite for a new program every seven days. If anyone were going to pull it off, he would have to be a self-made workaholic. Allen was in the right place at the right time with the right qualifications. By late Fall 1964, *Voyage* was a ratings hit. The critics didn't seem to mind it either. And the kids loved it.

Allen, the poor kid from the Bronx with big dreams, who'd arrived in Hollywood with no introductions, was a true American success story. But that success often seemed surreal to him.

Vitina Marcus said, "Irwin told me he had a recurring dream that he was in a strange city without any money. There was no one he could go to; nowhere for him to turn. And no money to get home. This was a recurring nightmare; he was always telling me about that dream. He had it often. So, this had been a big fear for him." [21]

Allen was quick to discover talent, and to offer support to those who reminded him of himself, like Joe D'Agosta, Paul Zastupnevich, and now the new kid at ABC, Lew Hunter.

Even with his work ethic of long days, Hunter was in awe of the even longer days Irwin Allen put in. He said of Allen, "He worked 18 hours a day. I can't imagine how he had time for anything else. I never got the impression that he had personal friends; only business friends. He wasn't married at that time, and he never did have children. His movies and television shows *were* his children. He was so consumed with what he did that it almost cut out everything else in his life. It was a seven-day-a-week gig. He just loved to work. And I did the same thing." [22]

Despite liking Hunter, Allen wasn't about to put himself in another situation where an ABC man would have control over him, especially a network man who had far less experience in the business than he did. Hunter recalled, "I was going over the notes on this particular script with Irwin one day, and I said, 'We have to have this scene in the middle of the script moved toward the beginning of it, rather than so far back.' Irwin said, 'I'm not going to do it.' I said, 'Now, Irwin, you don't understand, I am the authority here; I am representing ABC, who funds your series.' 'No,' he says, 'I'm not going to do it.' He said, 'Let me tell you, Lew, I was dealing once with Columbia Pictures, and I was preparing a movie called *The Big Circus*, and I sat in a chair in [Columbia Head] Harry Cohn's office, and Cohn taught me a very important lesson.' Now, to Irwin's thinking, part of that lesson was how Cohn had set the stage for the meeting. He told me that Harry Cohn's desk was on a riser about a foot or a foot-and-a-half tall, so that people who sat in a chair across from the desk would be on the lower level. Not only on a lower level, but there was a spotlight aimed at their chair! So, Irwin was sitting there, and Harry Cohn lifted up the script and said, 'Allen, this is a piece of shit!' He threw the script at Irwin, then looked at him and said, 'You

Everyone looked up to studio mogul Harry Cohn – because his desk was on risers! (Source: Alchetron)

17

know how that asshole [character played by Gilbert Roland] walks across fucking Niagara Falls on a tightrope on Page 6?' And Irwin said, 'Yes, Mr. Cohn.' And Harry Cohn said, 'Put him on Page 45 and you got a deal.' Well, I broke out and laughed, because I knew exactly what he meant. Because, on Page 6, you don't give a shit if this character falls into Niagara Falls. You don't know this guy. But on Page 45, the audience is terrified, because they've invested themselves in the character. That was the kind of thinking that Irwin had. He was outrageous and wonderful."

What Allen *did* want to put on Page 6 was something that would grab his youthful audience. Hunter said, "Irwin did not want to do Hitchcock. He wanted to show the monster – 'Pow!' – right up front. Hitchcock liked to play with the audience, and then put the reveal of whoever it is that's the biggest threat as deep into the movie as possible. But Irwin wasn't that way. He was very frontal in his work. There was nothing subtle about him. And, when it came to the TV shows, Irwin would say, 'I'm not serving caviar; I'm serving popcorn!' And it was hard to challenge that when you consider the content of *Voyage*. It was all action and stayed clear of philosophical statements. He'd say, 'You want to send a message, call Western Union. Now get out of the office.'" [23]

"I realized he was a tough man," Joe D'Agosta said. "Everybody in his company, meaning his associate producers and his directors, were, in my observation, 'yes men.' ... There was a certain protocol, because, after all, he *was* the emperor. I'd never met a man like him. I'd heard that expression about other people in this business, Louie B. Mayer, especially, but Irwin was the only emperor I had dealings with." [24]

"There was definitely an imperial air about him," Lew Hunter said. "And every time he'd go someplace, he'd have about six people moving around the lot with him. He'd have Arthur Weiss, who was the Story Editor on one of his shows, and he had Jerry Briskin, who was one of his associate producers, and Frank La Tourette, who used to be at UCLA as one of the professors there. But they were all afraid of him. And they all knew exactly the breaking point with him, and they would back off the minute that was coming up. They all had love/hate for him. The love was the fact that they all knew that they were working for a very different sort of human being, and if they wanted to stick around, they had to love him. Before I came along, in his producing period, he probably fired a number of people in a much more flamboyant way, so they all knew the risk in displeasing him. The best way to put it is they were 'yes men.' But they did it in such a way that he respected them. He would say to me, 'Well, my associate producer here is one of the best men for the job.' He would praise them when he wanted to give them strength with the network. But they all wanted their jobs, so they did what he wanted. And they really knew how to handle him." [25]

D'Agosta added, "Everyone would shut up when he entered the room, or came onto the set. They were afraid he was going to criticize them. I mean, we're all very insecure, aren't we? 'Oh my God, he's going to see right through me.'" [26]

Lew Hunter said, "He had a way of teasing people that was more of a threat than a tease. He would tease you in a negative way. 'You're out of the will.' And 'You just got yourself back in the will.' He wasn't profane, like some of those other guys, but he did intimidate people.

"Irwin's desk was on a riser, too. I don't think it was as high up as Harry Cohn's desk, but it was enough so it certainly made him seem bigger. He was probably about five-foot-eight. And I was six foot at the time. So, he would find ways of rising above you." [27]

D'Agosta said, "I think he knew everybody's job. And he knew how to suck the last piece of energy out of you, and to get the best idea out of you. I think that was his talent, really. You knew Irwin Allen had a great mind. He was a determined, creative man. I might compare him to Orson Welles; he exuded that sense of command, and brilliance. You definitely got a sense of his creativity. And maybe he was always testing us as to what we would take and what we wouldn't take. The thing about men like that is they attract two kinds of people – strong people and weak people. The weak can be manipulated. And the strong people will make you look better. Anyone in between is just going to go away." [28]

Allen tested everybody to one extent or another. Lew Hunter recalled, "The only time I ever heard Irwin use profanity was during a screening. Clay Daniels, an editor friend of mine, and I were watching a rough cut with Irwin, and Irwin was screaming about the different things he thought were wrong. Clay was sitting there, just as an assistant editor; he didn't have anything to do with the cutting of this particular episode, but he saw how Irwin kept yelling at the screen, 'You're fucking me; you're fucking me!', in terms of whoever the editor was that made the cut. Finally, the lights came up, and the producer of the show – Jerry Briskin was his name – said, 'Hey, I want you to meet our new editorial assistant, Clay Daniels.' Irwin looked at Clay and said, 'Clay Daniels, huh? When are *you* going to fuck me?!'"

When asked how the executives at ABC felt about Allen, Hunter said, "We got a kick out of him. I loved him because of his flamboyance, and I think all the people around him were entertained by it. We of course would *never* give him that impression." [29]

The flamboyant Irwin Allen in 1965, with composer-conductor John Williams during a recording session for *Lost in Space*.

2

Casting Off for Second Season

More changes for the second season:

After the sudden death of Henry Kulky, the Chief of the Seaview, the role of a new Chief was offered to actor James Doohan. However, he had just signed aboard another ship – *Star Trek*'s U.S.S. Enterprise. The role of Chief Starkey then went to Terry Becker. David Hedison said, "Henry had a great heart and was a good friend – and the role of the Chief fit him like a glove. After Henry passed on, Terry Becker took on the role and he was perfect. A solid performer." [1]

Becker was born in New York and began acting when but a teen, as a regular on the juvenile radio show, *Rainbow House*, as well as numerous New York City stage productions, including some that played on Broadway. His early work in television was on live shows aired out of New York in the early 1950s, such as *Danger* and *The Philco-Goodyear Playhouse*. In the late 1950s, Becker relocated to Los Angeles and was turning up in episodes of *Gunsmoke*, *M Squad*, and *Perry Mason*. By the 1960s, he was appearing often in episodes of *The Asphalt Jungle*, *Sea Hunt*, and *Rawhide*. He appeared as a condemned man in the notable *Twilight Zone* episode "I Am the Night – Color Me Black," and had appeared twice on *No Time for Sergeants*. He also performed onstage in prominent

Goodbye Chief Curly Jones (Henry Kulky); hello Chief Francis Sharkey (Terry Becker).

roles, garnering positive reviews in Los Angeles. Becker was 43 when cast as Chief Francis Ethelbert Sharkey.

Also added to the cast was Allan Hunt as a hip-talking crew member. With more than a hint of sarcasm, series writer William Read Woodfield said, "To get the young kids, Irwin thought it would be great to get a boy aboard the Seaview. Irwin didn't think he had kids watching *Voyage*." [2]

Hunt told a convention audience, "When I first heard of *Voyage*, I was told by an agent that [associate producer] Frank La Tourette was casting out at 20th Century-Fox; they were looking for an additional character named Riley who, at that time, was being called Stu Casey. He was supposed to be a surfer. I went up for it, along with everyone else, and Mr. La Tourette

Permission to come aboard ... Allan Hunt as Seaman Riley.
(Courtesy Synthesis Entertainment)

didn't seem very impressed or interested…. He thanked me and said they would be calling me back, and so forth. About two months later… everybody else – all my actor friends – tried out, including one Walter Koenig, believe it or not, who was later on *Star Trek*. He was also up for the part of Stu Casey…. [and then] I got a call to come back and meet on *Voyage* again. I said to my agent, 'Great, but you know I went on this before.' The agent said to go back. By now, casting was in the hands of a fellow called Joe D'Agosta. He met me in his office, but he was in a real hurry and said, 'Come on, we're going to see Irwin Allen.'" [3]

By this time, D'Agosta had learned that one never kept Irwin Allen waiting. The two men walked briskly to Allen's office.

Interviewed for this book, Hunt recalled, "So, we started walking, and we're walking very, very quickly, and he says, 'Do you know what's happened?' And I said, 'No; just that I was called back.' And he says, 'Well, I'm telling you, I thought I'd seen it all, but this really happened.' And what he was telling me was that they had viewed some film from a series called *Mr. Novak*, with James Franciscus. And *Mr. Novak* was a great show for all of us of a young age because

James Franciscus played a high school teacher, and there were always good roles for young actors who could pass for students. So, we all had taken turns doing them, and it turned out that there was a kid that they had all but settled on named Bob Random – a really good actor who had done his share of work. Joe said that Bob was the one Irwin wanted, and now it came down to network approval. So, they asked for some film on Bobby to show ABC, and were sent this episode he had just done this episode of *Mr. Novak*, which I was also in. In the episode, he was a bad kid who didn't have a good home life, or something like that, and the whole episode was about him; it was one of those dreams come true for an actor. But he was very brooding and kind of solemn in this part, which is what the role called for. Well, I happened to be his best friend in this episode, and I'm quite the other thing; I'm just kind of jumping around and saying, 'Hey, man, everything's cool!' So, Irwin and Joe were screening it for ABC. They were supposed to be looking at Bobby, but they were looking at me, because what I was doing was so Stu Riley. According to Joe, all these guys said to Irwin, 'Oh, right! He's perfect; you got it!' And Irwin, caught off guard, said, 'Oh, alright, good; I thought you'd like that boy.' Then he leans over to Joe and whispers, 'Who is that?' Joe says, 'He came in about a month and a half ago but Frank didn't think he was right.' And, believe it or not, that's how I got that second meeting!

Bob Random in the early 1970s, in Orson Welles' *The Other Side of the Wind.*

"So, Joe takes me up to Irwin Allen's office, and, just as we're approaching the door, it opens, and Irwin steps out. Now, Irwin was a very *individual* individual; you never knew what was going to come out. So, he looks at me, and he didn't say 'hello,' he didn't say, 'How do you do?', he just looks, then he looks at Joe and says, 'He's too tall.' Joe says, 'Irwin, it's okay.' 'No, he's too tall,' Irwin says again, with me standing right there, then says, 'Richard is going to kill me.'

"Now, David Hedison is a six-footer, and so am I, but Richard Basehart was maybe 5'7", and Irwin was more concerned than anything that Richard was going to have to stand on a lot of apple boxes. And, I'm thinking, 'Oh shit, suddenly I have the part, and just as suddenly, now, I don't.' Joe kept telling Irwin that it would be alright, and Irwin would look at me and shake his head. So, I just stood there, and tried to be funny and said, 'Well, I can slouch beautifully.' And Irwin gave me a blank look, then repeated, 'He's so tall; he's so tall.' And he turned and walked away.

"And that's how I got the job." [4]

"It was explained to me that I was supposed to appeal to the teenagers, and I was delighted," Hunt told Mark Phillips for an article in *Starlog*. "I realized, even then, what my part was, and I didn't expect much meat from the role. Irwin was trying to appeal to a complete circle audience. It was a family show, and 7 p.m. Sunday was a great primetime 'sit down to the TV dinner' kind of hour, and that's why the show continued with the monsters….

"[My character] Riley reminded me of what Ed Byrnes did earlier on *77 Sunset Strip*. I would say, 'This is Kookie Byrnes on a submarine. I should be combing my hair all the time!' I thought it was funny that Riley was always tagging along on these dangerous missions. He was the kid of the ship, yet he was always sent off with Admiral Nelson, and these really salty old guys stayed behind. The character was fairly one-dimensional – sometimes I was the comic relief and sometimes I was just there to add some youth."

As for his new boss, Hunt said, "The stories about Mr. Allen are legendary, and they're *all true*. His office was like a little Disneyland. He had toy airplanes and submarines hanging from the ceiling. He had a very special, almost childlike enthusiasm for toys and gadgets. He was a true eccentric with a wonderful imagination. But he was also a very nervous, very manic man." [5]

"Manic" in a medical way? No. Over-the-top enthusiastic? Absolutely! Temperamental? Sometimes. Down in the dumps? Never.

Allen exuded excitement towards everything he did. He attacked life with determination and energy. If his productions leaned toward the frenetic, so did the way he talked, his work ethic, and his gestures of affection. He would pinch pennies in some areas, in response to restrictive TV budgets, but then splurge with the style of a grand showman when sentiment struck him. An example is on the next page, what Richard Basehart and David Hedison found waiting for them on their return to the studio to begin work on Season Two – new dressing rooms, gift-wrapped by a man who emulated B.T. Barnum.

Such schmaltziness, too, was Irwin Allen. He was unrelenting, controlling, commanding, infuriating, but also brilliant and outlandish. Some loved him; some feared him; some hated him; some misunderstood him; but no one found him boring.

Hunt had pictures taken of him on the first day, too. They included the picture seen earlier in this chapter, and the group shot on the next page.

"So, the first day of work was to shoot a photograph with the entire cast. That's the day I met Terry Becker, who was starting the series at the same time as me, and Richard and David, and Bob Dowdell. Terry Becker and I were the *real* new kids on the block – just having met in the dressing trailer moments earlier, before being introduced to Richard, David, and Bob Dowdell." [6]

You might think a cast would be able to get familiar with one another, and with their roles, before having promotional pictures taken. But that's not always how Hollywood works.

"What's really funny," Hunt said, "is *that* photo was to become the official 'fan card,' with our signatures printed on the reverse side. So, of course, we were asked to look like 'old pals.'" [7]

"Old pals" who had just met? That's where the acting comes in.

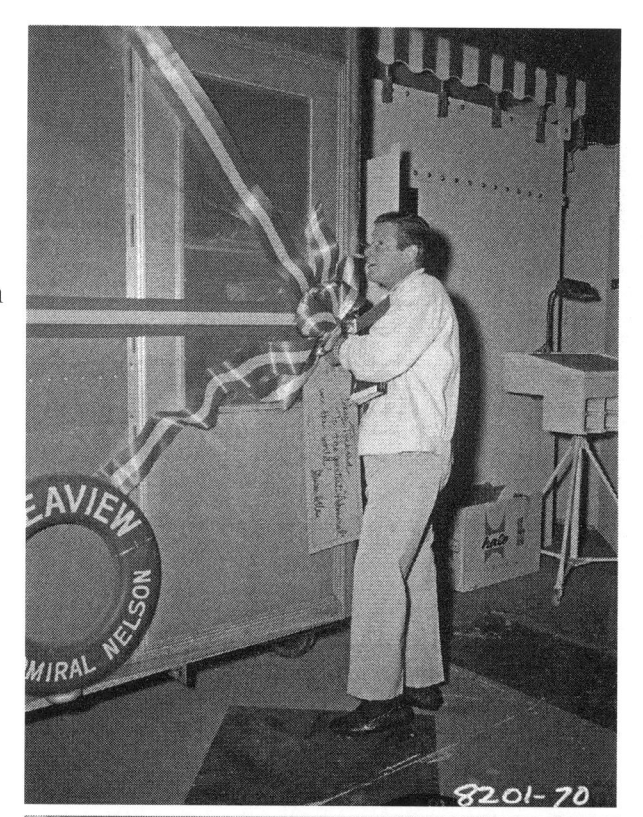

Publicity shot for Season Two. L-R: Basehart and Hedison, newcomers Allan Hunt and Terry Becker, and Bob Dowdell.

3

Fall 1965

VOYAGE TO THE BOTTOM OF THE SEA -- Richard Basehart, left, and David Hedison straddle the fantastic atomic-powered submarine-of-the-future, the Seaview, as they paddle off on a mission leading to high adventure and danger in producer Irwin Allen's exciting 20th Century-Fox Television series, "Voyage to the Bottom of the Sea" (seen in color each Sunday evening over ABC-TV). Lurking in wait beneath the ship is a contingent of deadly denizens of the deep complemented by a lovely mermaid. Overhead shoots the Seaview's flying submarine at remarkable speeds.

Fall 1965. The pop-art world of 1960s American culture was exploding in every direction. And *Voyage* was part of that big bang.

ABC-TV had renewed *Voyage* early, in the first week of February, while first-season episodes were still filming. The plan was to keep the series on Monday nights. After all, it had won its time slot for the first half of the season. This in spite of the audience becoming compromised when, at midseason, NBC moved *The Man from U.N.C.L.E.* opposite *Voyage*. The ratings remained good enough to ensure renewal. [1]

Then, the ABC programmers had a better idea – they'd ditch a series previously ordered for the Fall – *Hercules* – and move *Voyage* into its planned early Sunday-night time slot, to go head-to-head with CBS's *Lassie* and *My Favorite Martian* and NBC's *The Wonderful World of Disney*. All three series, popular with the kids, had given ABC and its current Sunday-evening show, *Wagon Train*, a bloody nose. The network had thought it would take a hero of myth to stand up to them, but perhaps sci-fi would deliver a stronger punch. Supporting this line of thinking was a survey report from TvQ, placing *Voyage* in the Top 10 of series most preferred by teens. Other high-rankers on that list were *Bewitched, Gomer Pyle, The Man from U.N.C.L.E., Gilligan's Island, Shindig, The Addams Family*, and *The Munsters. Lassie, My Favorite Martian*, and *Disney* hadn't even made the Top 40 in teen popularity! [2]

And adults without kids seemed to like *Voyage*, too. At least, adult women without children. A 20th Century-Fox press release boasted that David Hedison, who averaged 1,500 fan letters each month prior to *Voyage*, now was drawing 9,000! [3]

Critics also had warmed up to *Voyage*. In the February 24, 1965 edition of *Daily Variety*, "Daku" reviewed the newest episode, raving:

> Already assured of another voyage next season, Voyage demonstrates in "The Saboteur" the qualities that have made this Irwin Allen-20th-Fox TV series a marked success. Teleplay by William Read Woodfield and George Reed is a bizarre one, true to the spirit of series' futuristic vein.
>
> *Voyage* is one of the more imaginative, ingenious and provocative series in a medium unfortunately lacking in these qualities. ... [4]

And now, for its sophomore year, *Voyage* would be in color!

By the end of February, ABC had decided – *Voyage* would set sail for Sunday nights, 7 to 8 p.m. on the two Coasts, and from 6 to 7 p.m. in the middle of the nation (Central Time).

So confident was Madison Avenue that *Voyage* would make mincemeat of Uncle Martin that the sponsors of *My Favorite Martian* got cold feet. *Variety* reported:

> Those revamped Sunday night lineups for next season appear at least partly responsible for sponsor resistance to CBS-TV's *My Favorite Martian*. One of the incumbent alternate bankrollers, Toni [hair products], has decided not to renew, instead buying into the web's *Lucy* and *My Three Sons*. Co-sponsor Kellogg, meanwhile, is being coy about another *Martian* ride.
>
> Sundays at 7:30 this season the race has been between *Martian* and NBC's Disney hour, with the latter usually on top in the Nielsens. Both entries are stet [unchanged] for '65-'66, but ABC plans to open with its sci-fi *Voyage to the Bottom of the Sea* instead of *Wagon Train*, which could narrow the numbers gap. It's this move, apparently, that helped cue Toni's defection from *Martian*, and which seems to be causing Kellogg second thoughts. [5]

Neither Toni nor Kellogg's could get a piece of *Voyage*; Bristol-Meyers (Clairol, Windex) had it sewn up.

Those creating *Voyage*, however, had their doubts if the move was a good idea. Ray Didsbury, the lighting double for Richard Basehart, said, "We thought we were dead with that competition." [6]

Trying to find a brighter perspective, David Hedison told the *Los Angeles Times*, "We should be able to capture the adult audience which won't be watching *Lassie* or *Walt Disney*. I know I usually turn the TV set on earlier on Sundays to watch *Meet the Press* or *20th Century*. After that, there isn't much for adults, so maybe they'll try our show." [7]

Regardless, *Voyage* would need all the help it could get in its new time period. Irwin Allen, former entertainment reporter, certainly knew the benefits of publicity.

In an April 26, 1965 memo to Bob Suhosky at 20th Century-Fox, Irwin Allen wrote:

> I heartily agree with your recent suggestion to secure two top-notch senior publicists for *Voyage to the Bottom of the Sea* and *Lost in Space*. Both CBS-TV and ABC-TV have already

> assigned their unit men for next season and have started the ball rolling in what I feel is the right direction for a lucrative publicity showing even before the shows go on the air.
>
> I assume that I will be hearing from you very shortly regarding your unit assignments for next year, but, in the meantime, we should still be concerned with an entire summer of weekly ratings for *Voyage to the Bottom of the Sea*. *Voyage* has run a poor second to *Man from U.N.C.L.E.* in the past two Nielsen ratings. A continued publicity push during the summer months would help to hypo the ratings and assist us in finishing our initial full season strongly. I'd like to send weekly telegrams to TV critics throughout the country and continue working with you on any other publicity ideas which you might have to keep our rerun ratings high....
>
> I'd like to sit down with you as soon as possible to discuss plans for a Richard Basehart-David Hedison tour of all 30 key Nielsen areas just prior to the *Voyage* fall debut in the new Sunday timeslot. Basehart and Hedison are enthused with the planned tour. ...
>
> I hope that we can work together during the next year to make *Voyage to the Bottom of the Sea*'s second season even more successful than the first, and launch *Lost in Space* as the most successful of the new fall shows. [8]

Allen remembered the example of P.T. Barnum: The best way to ensure a big audience is with spectacle. With this in mind, and with the enhancement of color photography, Allen scrubbed the idea of filming underwater sequences off the coast of California's Catalina Island. The murky waters in that region were fine for black-and-white, but color photography needed brighter, bluer, surroundings.

On June 17, 1966, *Daily Variety* reported:

> Exec producer Irwin Allen today sends a 23-man crew to the Bahamas for 30 days of location on 20th-Fox's *Voyage to the Bottom of the Sea* TV series...

Unit, under the supervision of John Lamb, will film underwater sequences for inclusion in *Voyage* segments. Series goes color next season on ABC-TV. [9]

In the interest of further spectacle, Allen came up with a new toy. Talking with Dave Kaufman of *Daily Variety*, Allen said, "This flying sub – we call a 'flying fish' at the moment – comes out of the belly of the Seaview, the big sub. It goes underwater, on the water's surface, and flies at 2,000 miles an hour. We're no longer sea-bound. A 'flying fish' project was actually announced by the Navy two weeks ago, but we've been working on ours for six/seven months. Now there are no limitations storywise; we have more scope, and our action can take place anywhere!"

Agent Herman Rush (left) and client Irwin Allen, with Allen's latest toy – the Flying Sub.
(Courtesy Herman Rush)

Allen added that Nelson and Crane, "who did everything by the book last season, will unbend a bit. We are humanizing the military men." [10]

Richard Basehart and David Hedison doubtless hoped that some of the unbending would involve the feminine persuasion.

A press release from the same time read:

> Richard Basehart and David Hedison, actors by trade, are a pair of typical red-blooded American males who, while not professing to be on the same par with a Don Juan or Casanova, do enjoy feminine companionship, both on and off the screen. Furthermore, as is man's wont and prerogative in life, Richard and David receive the same kick from viewing a trim ankle, a shapely figure and a pretty face as do a hundred million of their kind and number. Throughout Basehart's distinguished twenty-year career as a top motion picture personality, he has made "on screen" love to a myriad of filmdom's most beautiful and glamorous leading ladies. As for David, although relatively new to the Hollywood film scene, he nevertheless is no slouch when it comes to femme film fraternization. Between them, they have cut a wide romantic swath across millions of feet of celluloid.
>
> In recent times, however, the boys' respective love-making proclivities have fallen on lean times. The axiom, "All things good must come to an end," has proved a truism in the screen lives of the romantically-inclined pair. If a "heavy" in the case be needed, he is television and motion picture producer Irwin Allen…. As Hedison tells it, "Irwin Allen is a 'bug' for coming up with far-out Jules Verne-type gimmicks in his screenplays. Nothing is too weird or outlandish for his imagination. He believes there are enough producers doing the boy-meets-girl soap operas and doesn't want to clutter up his action with a bevy of beautifully-gowned, gorgeously-coiffured screen beauties. With Irwin, it's move, move, move; action, action, action!" [11]

For Basehart, the desire was always for meatier material. He wanted the bar raised for the new season, a topic discussed when he and Hedison had the cover of *TV Guide* for the magazine's June 19, 1965 issue, with a picture taken in the Seaview's Control Room during early production for the second season. The article within, a feature on Basehart, was appropriately titled, "Well, Of Course, It Isn't Exactly *Hamlet*…"

Marian Dern wrote:

> Fortunately for Basehart, his series doesn't require literal submersion. However, *Voyage* holds some subtler forms of

claustrophobia for a man whose primary focus has always been on serious acting and classical theater. For such an actor, the tightly enclosed observation nose of the Seaview, and the dialog that often reads like a seagoing Buck Rogers, must sometimes feel stifling. [12]

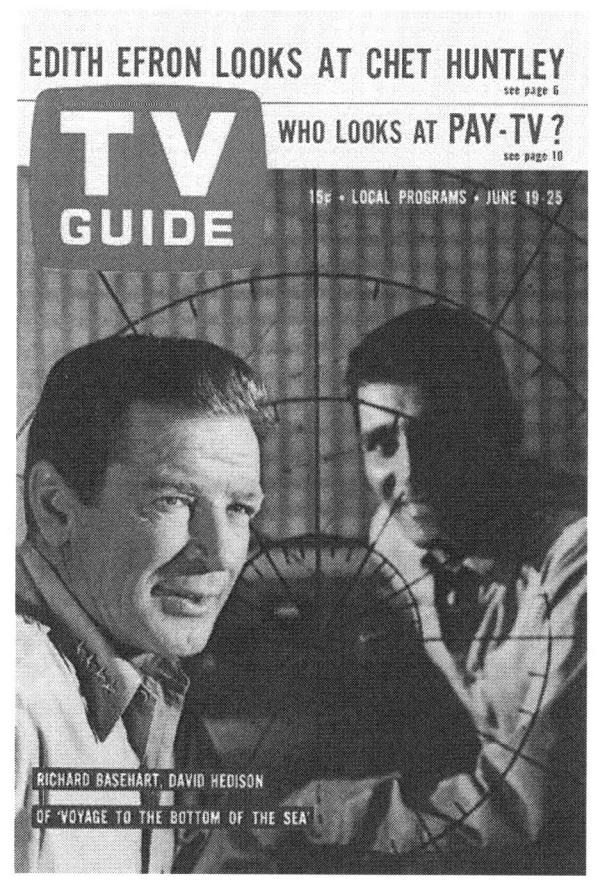

Dern asked Irwin Allen why he chose Basehart, "the self-professed Shakespearean, to go scuba-diving with your giant jellyfish, to battle with your colossal octopi, and to fight off every other kind of robot, monster, or mysterious enemy of mankind that your writers could dream up?" Allen answered: "Because he's a consummate actor. Y'see, we knew that, being such a great actor, he could make all the derring-do believable." [13]

When it was suggested to Basehart that the role he was playing on television wasn't exactly Hamlet, he retorted, "Of course not. With Shakespeare, there's more character than an actor can even plumb. But there's no greater challenge than making something out of nothing. I mean, you take an undeveloped character, and you have to make him alive. You take what's there, and you round him out. You see, the lack of time [in TV production] sharpens an actor's tools to razor-sharp edges. There's no time to study. You're on, and it's up to you to create the man, the mood, instantly." [14]

Television indeed was instant entertainment – written quickly, filmed quickly, aired quickly, and, more often than not, just as quickly forgotten. But the TV shows of Irwin Allen would not be forgotten. Some remembered them as good, some as bad, but never forgettable.

Set course for adventure! Basehart and Hedison prepare to navigate the
treacherous waters of Season Two.
(Courtesy Synthesis Entertainment)

4

Season Two / ABC's Initial Order of 16

Alternate cast photo taken on the day Allan Hunt and Terry Becker met veterans Richard Basehart, David Hedison, and Robert Dowdell.

A teaser article in the *Dayton Daily News* gave a hint of what viewers could look for in Season Two. The unidentified writer discussed the stars' hope for more interactions with the ladies this season:

> David [Hedison] lists some of the "attractive" co-stars with whom he played vis-à-vis in *Voyage*'s freshman year: a gigantic Archeoceti whale; a giant electric eel; a prehistoric sea monster; a man-eating shark; a 100-pound squid; a Coelacanth ancient fossil; a behemoth octopus; a 300-pound tortoise; a killer whale; a giant sea serpent; and a school of man-eating piranha.

Word of Basehart's and Hedison's discontent reached Allen. Calling his actors into his office for a brief meeting prior to the stat of the second season of filming, Irwin began, "I understand you're complaining about the scarcity of female companions in the show last year. I have good news for you. This year I have a scene, Richard, where you receive your first *Voyage* kiss from lovely Ina Balin.

"And I have similar romantic interludes for you with actresses Gia Scala, Susan Flannery, Barbara Bouchet, Audrey Dalton, Nancy Hsueh, Delphi Lawrence, and Francoise Ruggieri. How does that strike you?"

Basehart and Hedison registered delight.

"Now, then," continued the producer, "I want to tell you about the next segment of the series. It's called 'Jonah and the Whale,' and we open the story with you, David, rescuing Richard from the stomach of a whale. You like it?" [1]

4.1

"Jonah and the Whale" (Episode 33)
(Prod. #8201; first aired Sunday, September 19, 1965)
Written by Shimon Wincelberg
Directed by Sobey Martin
Produced by Irwin Allen and Frank La Tourette;
Story Editor: Sidney Marshall
Guest Star Gia Scala

IN THE BELLY OF A WHALE--"Voyage to the Bottom of the Sea" makes its return in color, Sunday, Sept. 19 over ABC-TV, with "Jonah and the Whale" David Hedison (R) and Allan Hunt prowl stomach of giant whale to rescue Richard Basehart and Gia Scala.

From the *Voyage* show files (Irwin Allen papers collection):

> When a Russian scientist inside a bathysphere is killed in a collision with a migrating whale, his female partner insists on another immediate dive in spite of the still-present danger. Nelson accompanies her, and the bathysphere containing them both is swallowed whole by another whale.

While Nelson contends with the scientist and the seemingly hopeless situation, Crane leads a rescue party into the belly of the whale in a desperate attempt to rescue them before their oxygen supply is exhausted. [1]

Assessment:

It was a spectacular one-hour program for 1965. No one had ever seen anything like this since Disney's *Pinocchio* – and *that* had been animation, not live action.

The first change apparent to eager viewers of Season Two wasn't just that *Voyage to the Bottom of the Sea* was now in color, but that it seemed to redefine color. Most of the audience back then, though, had black-and-white TVs. According to an NBC-sponsored survey at the time, only around 10% of American households had color TV sets by January 1966 (four months after the premiere broadcast).

If ever a series were destined for color, it was *Voyage*. Irwin Allen and his technical team made good use of it, with splashes of primary color throughout the ship and even on the seamen, now wearing red and blue (along with a few gray) coveralls. Footage of the animatronic whale, built by the Fox mechanical-effects department for the first season's "Ghost of Moby Dick," was seen in a handful of recycled shots, given a blue tint. Most of the footage featuring the whale, however, was new, and therefore filmed in color.

Richard Basehart, interviewed by columnist Glen Graham while promoting the premiere of the second season, said, "Going to color this year is another great advantage. Our show *is* a color show. It's wild and fantastic." [2]

Chief Sharkey made his debut as a member of the crew. Terry Becker is immediately appealing in the role: energized, strong in the grim moments and yet capable of adding a dash of humor when needed. Also new but less effective is Seaman Riley, played by Allan Hunt. It's not Hunt's fault; it's just that a hipster surfer dude seems a bit out of place on the Seaview. "Kookie," as played by Edd Byrnes, may have seemed a natural on *77 Sunset Strip* (1958-66), but a slang-slinging hepcat as part of a highly-trained team of specialists on a nuclear submarine seemed more implausible than the plot. The writers would eventually lighten up on the lingo in episodes to follow, increasing the effectiveness of the character.

Regardless, 20th Century-Fox and ABC-TV were pushing the new character. A press release circulated to newspapers put it this way:

> Teenagers who enjoy confounding their elders with a jargon that can be understood only by their contemporaries can get an idea of the lingo that will be confusing them 10 years from now by watching ABC-TV's *Voyage to the Bottom*

> *of the Sea*. ... In this second season of the series set in 1975, executive producer Irwin Allen has come up with a hip-talking surfer with a penchant for deep-sixing the King's English. ...
>
> Allen's staff of writers have come up with a circa 1975 space-age lexicon that may help the viewers of the mid-'60s get a 10-year jump on tomorrow's jargon. A few examples:
>
> Statue of Liberty – A girl who lights her own cigarette. ...
>
> Toast – "Bread" after deductions.
>
> A Face Saver – A girl who won't kiss a boy on the first date. ...
>
> Dietetic Date – A girl who acts like she believes kisses contain calories. ... [3]

You get the cringeworthy idea.

Richard Basehart is far less somber this season. Basehart seems to be enjoying himself, at least in proximity of Gia Scala in the diving bell.

Also new: the reconfiguration of the Seaview. The observation nose is now on the same deck as the Control Room, and the two are connected. Admiral Nelson has a lab, with fish tanks. And the bottom of the sub now has hangar doors for the Flying Sub. The "FS1" will make its TV debut in "Time Bomb," the next episode to air.

Another plus: The story has a theme to its adventure, encompassing trust, courage, and self-sacrifice. Russian scientist Dr. Katya Markova is cynical about Western culture's claims that every life is valuable. In her mind, an individual is only valuable in relation to their utility to "the people," or "the system." She doesn't believe a rescue party from the Seaview would risk their necks to do something as crazy as swim into a whale's stomach to liberate her and Admiral Nelson. He has faith that his crew will try. Guess who's right.

Now, about the premise: Despite the common phrase used as the episode title, the Bible *doesn't* say that Jonah was swallowed by a whale, but by a "great fish." However, here are the facts about the seagoing mammal at the center of the tale:

The sperm whale is the largest toothed predator on Earth. It can grow to lengths of nearly 70 feet and weigh more than 45 tons. It is the deepest-diving marine mammal in the world and, when hunting for food, can submerge to depths in excess of 6,000 feet. Sperm whales eat colossal squid, octopus, demersal rays, and a variety of other sea life. Their esophagus is large enough to accommodate an average-sized man, as is their three stomachs. Their digestive tract can hold over 500 gallons. And, since this episode depicts a whale that is, in essence, a freak of nature, perhaps a diving bell could slip down its gullet. At any rate, the outlandish idea made entertaining television, both in 1965 and today.

Script:
Shimon Wincelberg's writers' contract: December 31, 1964.
3rd Rev. Shooting Final (beige): June 25, 1966.
Page revisions (pink paper): June 30.
Page revisions (blue paper): June 28.

Shimon Wincelberg was 40. He had written the screenplay for a 1953 war film starring Sterling Hayden, *Fighter Attack*. In 1956, he did the final rewriting on the low-budget jet-age pseudo-sci-fi, *On the Threshold of Space* (primarily about test pilots). Next, he moved into writing for TV, including 24 episodes of the Western *Have Gun – Will Travel*, and six for the gritty hour-long cop show, *Naked City*. Then Irwin Allen hired him to write the pilot for *Lost in Space*. More than merely providing a single script, Wincelberg's work also established the framework for the new series, with various

Writer Shimon Wincelberg, ready for a ride with Irwin Allen, on the set of the *Lost in Space* pilot film, 1965.

story treatments that were used as springboards for future episodes. He also wrote one additional *LiS* script, "Invaders from the Fifth Dimension." As Wincelberg was finalizing all this work, he asked Allen for an assignment on *Voyage*. He had a whale of a tale in mind.

Wincelberg said, "I reread the biblical narrative and, during some research, I came across the supposedly true story of a sailor who had been swallowed by a whale and came out alive, bleached white!" [4]

The story appeared often in newspapers in the decades to follow the alleged event. One such story, "The Man Who Was Jonah," from writer David Gunston, was published in 1960 in Australia's *The Age*. Gunston told how, in 1890, James Bartley, a young whaler, was assigned to the English vessel "The Star of the East." In February 1891, the ship was cruising off the Falkland Islands when a sperm whale estimated to be between 60 and 70 feet in length was spotted. Bartley was in one of two longboats dispatched to close in on the quarry. Gunston wrote:

> ... The first boat's marksman pierced the whale with his lance, and the enraged beast swung half out of the sea, its 15-ft. tail splintering the second boat and hurtling its little crew into the water. One man was drowned, and when the first whaleboat checked the survivors it had rescued, Bartley was found to be missing…. Bartley's presumed loss by drowning was duly recorded in the ship's log. But not before the first boat had finally killed the troublesome sperm.
>
> In a few hours its great limp carcass was lying alongside the Star of the East, whose crew began at once their unsavory task of flensing it for blubber and flesh. They worked all the day and part of the same night, and next morning had laid bare the whale's vast paunch. Lifting tackle was fixed, and the whole organ hoisted on the deck for cutting up – when one of the whalemen gave a shout. He had noticed a slight spasmatic movement within. The flensers fell to with their scimitar-blades, bent on revealing what gastronomic enormities their prize had earlier committed.
>
> Sperms are whales with eight-foot swallows, and ten-foot chunks of squid and fish, including sharks, half as big again, had often been found inside their bellies. Perhaps there was a fish here still alive, the men thought. But curiosity turned to instant horror as the blades leapt back from the doubled up, drenched, but still living body of their missing comrade.

Bartley was deeply unconscious, and within seconds was being crudely but effectively doused with cold water. Laid on the deck, he slowly began to show signs of returning life.

He was installed in a bed in the captain's own cabin, and gradually regained consciousness. He did not at first recover his reason. He was gibbering with horror and in spite of all the officers and crew could do for him he remained thus for two weeks, during which time he was kept under lock and key in the captain's quarters – for his own and the ship's safety. ...

Wherever his body was not covered with clothes, the merciless acid of the whale gastric juices had eaten deeply into his skin, with the result that his face, neck and hands were bleached a deadly white, dried, shriveled and tautened like a piece of old parchment. ...

Once able to talk coherently of his ordeal, Bartley said he clearly remembered being thrown into the sea. Then... as he himself put it, "encompassed by a great darkness." He felt he was slipping along a smooth passage that itself seemed to carry him onward. Shortly after this he realized the movement had stopped and he had more room.

The poor fellow groped about in the stench and the darkness to find the walls of the prison slimy and yielding to the touch. ... To add to his anguish there was the intense heat of the whale's inside, an oppressive heat he described as opening up every pore in his body and sucking out all his vitality. ... Inevitably he fainted at last, chiefly from shock, and remembered nothing more until he came round in the captain's cabin....

As the monster was itself killed soon after swallowing the man, its stomach secretions probably ceased – and saved Bartley's life. ...

This fantastic case was attested for in separate accounts by the captain and an officer of the ship on its return to England, and later the whole amazing incident was thoroughly investigated and proved to be fully authentic by

the noted French scientist de Parville, who published a full
report in the Paris *Journal des Debats* in 1914. ... [5]

Many children of the sixties, like us, may have encountered Bartley's "whale of a tale" in Frank Edwards' 1956 anthology of gosh-wow "true" stories, *Strangest of All*. It had several paperback printings. When this episode of *Voyage* aired, we could tell our parents that it wasn't made up – such a thing had really happened!

When Wincelberg suggested his version of the idea to Irwin Allen, another whale story, "The Ghost of Moby Dick," had already been put into production. Allen, seeing the potential for an effects-driven episode to outmatch anything attempted on television before – and perhaps hoping to harvest some of the footage already shot for "Ghost of Moby Dick" – immediately sold ABC on the idea of the story and put Wincelberg to work. David Hedison said, "[Irwin] was a great salesman. He liked things done the way he wanted them done; everything was black and white – explosions; the Seaview getting swallowed by the whale." [6]

Wincelberg began work in December 1964, while *Voyage* was still buying scripts for its first season. In fact, "Jonah," as the story and first-draft script were originally called, was originally planned to be filmed in black-and-white.

In the early drafts of the scripts, it was Crane, not Nelson, in the diving bell with the woman scientist named Alexa.

January 20, 1965. ABC's Adrian Samish gave the first round of notes on the "Jonah" story, saying, first and foremost:

> Overall, the use of humor is incongruous in this story and should not be used in the series. [7]

Many have blamed Irwin Allen for being humorless, and keeping *Voyage* a bit too serious and grim. These complainers ignore the fact that Allen was also the producer of *Lost in Space*, which welcomed humor to the point of making an abrupt left-hand turn into semi-comical situations and dialogue before its first season had even ended. This was due to CBS's push for comedy to make the series less frightening for children during the "family hour." Back on ABC, however, Adrian Samish had given the word that *Voyage* would steer clear of the funny stuff.

He continued:

> This is a scientific expedition studying the habits, behavior patterns of migrating whales. You will use stock footage to

> establish large numbers of whales.... Nelson should not be skeptical. He is a scientist and should be as vitally interested in the data as the others.... Eliminate the philosophy about the world dying, etc....
>
> No one [depicted in the script] mentions the fact that the bell has been carried off by the whale. Make something of the reaction to this calamity. It must be a serious reaction – astonishment, concern, etc. There should be a radio contact with Crane and Alexa in the bell for a time. The bell is starting to crack, etc. It is lodged in the whale's throat, not his stomach. If the bell kills the whale or if Seaview should harpoon and kill the whale, it would [drown] and the people in the bell would die. It becomes a delicate maneuver as well as a race against time....
>
> When the expedition enters the whale's mouth, this should be done underwater – 2nd unit. Perhaps the purpose of the expedition is to hook a new cable to the bell. The whale now becomes, in effect, a hooked fish. The whale regains consciousness and fights. [Those] aboard Seaview must play out cable as though fighting a game fish. The whale tries to ram the sub. The sub evades, etc. Eventually, in the climax, they should decide to risk killing the whale now that they are hooked to it. They torpedo it. The bell is disgorged and hauled in. Crane and the scientist don't step jauntily out [as now written]. They are unconscious and near death from the ordeal.[8]

Wincelberg wrote a new draft, and, per Allen's request, the Seaview officer now in the bell with Alexa was Admiral Nelson, not Captain Crane.

Adrian Samish read the latest draft, then wrote to Allen and his people. As you might infer from Samish's notes for "Jonah," sometimes he seemed bent on rewriting the story himself.

ABC executive Lew Hunter said, "Adrian Samish was involved at the beginning of it. He was the West Coast Vice President for ABC Programming. At that early point in the series, he probably felt a little power, and Irwin might have been a little more intimidated by him because this was Irwin's first foray into television. So, when a tiger sees a wounded cow, it will wound the cow even more. And, probably, Samish could see that he could get away with it. But I'll bet you a nickel to a dime that Irwin was probably very adversarial after the success of the show." [9]

Samish's notes to Allen continued:

> This can be a good show. The automated lab is too phony. They should be testing a new type of bell for deep exploration work. They are in the path of migrating whales. Nelson wants to call off the mission because of this but Alexa wants one more chance.... Page 1: Set up stock of migrating whales. Plant [the fact that] they are in vicinity. ...

Regarding Alexa's line, "He was more than my partner. We were engaged," Samish wrote: "Unnecessary. Omit."

He told Allen:

> Page 5: Get rid of the lab notion.... Page 6: Omit lab references.... Page 9: Alexa: "My laboratory, etc." Forget lab. Change to "These experiments ... etc."

Elsewhere, Samish insisted:

> Page 7: "A whale!" Arrive at too pat a conclusion.... Alexa: "8,000 miles underwater..." sounds like it was 8,000 miles deep. [Replace with] "8,000 miles journey underwater." ...
>
> Page 20: Bottom. Morton [says] "swallowed ... etc." Too pat. Use instruments – flesh and metal. One blip on screen, both flesh & metal. "Do you suppose it could have swallowed the bell ... etc."
>
> Page 30: Alexa's line: "come after us on foot." Don't use this "on foot" business. Bottom of page: don't show this depressed bit [from the two inside the diving bell].
>
> Page 31: We can't have [Chief] Curley because we don't want comedy at all. ...
>
> Page 36: "Clam up..." Don't use. "All right, let's go for a walk." No....

Page 42: Nelson (near bottom): "Odds favor the house". No on the analogy. Too flip....

Page 48: When a whale dies, it sinks to bottom. They don't come up at all. "Quick study". No – too cute. "Time for lunch." Out. [10]

Irwin Allen turned in his own notes on January 30, telling his staff:

Speeches between Alexa and Nelson could be cut and checked for repetitions. Two people in such a situation might talk a little about their past lives and hopes for the future....

What are Curley, Kowalski and Patterson and other seaman doing in Mess Hall at a time like this, especially playing chess, reading, letter writing, etc. No one would be writing letters at a time like this!...

Morton's line – "You sure you want to go through with this" becomes a bad comedy line....

I think Crane should be the first to enter the mouth of the whale instead of Curley, as the whole thing is his idea and the other two are quite scared....

Too many times Alexa asks, "What if there is no rescue party?" ...

Nelson's reference to lunch seems out of place, and unpleasant....

The character of Alexa is very one-sided – She is sarcastic and nasty and domineering and often boring. We never really understand what has made her this way. She is also a coward, so we can't even respect her. In the rescue scene, she doesn't get a chance to redeem herself or apologize for her behavior. Since she is the guest member of the cast, she should either be the villain or turn out O.K. [11]

It was clear that something more had to be made of the character of Alexa. Allen had suggested she should be a villain, and this provoked discussions about a

Russian agent. It was also important to explain how she entered the story … perhaps as a survivor of a sunken Russian ship? And it was suggested that Alexa, the woman, be changed to Antrobus, a man. In fact, a draft of the script was written which effected this change. All this talk, and rewriting, prompted another memo from Allen. He told his staff:

> I feel it would be wrong to overload an already exciting show with proposed Russian woman and sunken ship (This could be premise for another script). The original idea of using a woman is ideal provided she is not another fanatical scientist [like Viveca Lindfors in Season One's "Hail to the Chief"]. If you make the mission a vitally important one and the presence of the whales migrating at this time or in these particular waters unusual, you can then have an ideal situation of a man and a woman thrown together in an almost hopeless predicament. In which case, they could react more like human beings, thus cutting out a lot of unpleasant repetition of sarcastic remarks. When two people are faced with death, they can become very important to each other in a surprisingly short time….
>
> Page 24, Scene 97 – "Stomach would crush whatever is inside." This is too ambiguous – we know the sphere has been swallowed; what we don't know is if it is still intact and if Nelson and whoever finally goes with him is alive. This is reason for not killing the whale….
>
> Page 28, Scene 115: Nelson's first logical move upon awaking should be to attempt to arouse Antrobus (or girl). This failing, he would then check gauges and meters, then return once again to other occupant….
>
> Page 29, Scene 123: Since Antrobus (or girl) knew the impending danger, why would he accuse Nelson of mishap? Why doesn't he ask normal questions, such as: "Why is it so dark outside?" etc.; see his camera and remark he hopes the film is all right. Any serious damage from collision? To these statements, Nelson's silence would cause the truth to dawn on him. The above applies to Scene 124. We should avoid petty childishness on either part. [12]

Another draft was written. Antrobus was out and Alexa was back in. She was no longer a Russian spy, and was an underwater photographer (from Russia). She and Nelson were in the bell to reach an automated lab deep under the ocean.

Also by this time, Henry Kulky had died of a heart attack and Curley was removed from the script.

On May 19, Mary Garbutt, from ABC's Continuity Acceptance Department, wrote:

> Standard caution on the screams of fear or pain, the "trickle of blood". Also caution that the harpoon hits are "clean"… and not accompanied by "gashes" or spurts of blood, etc.…
>
> Please use your special care in seeing that, in creating the illusion of the whale interior, the sets, etc., do not convey an overly-strong visceral effect (Heavily veined suction cups or tentacles for ex.). This can only be approved on color film. [13]

More changes were made. Then, Shimon Wincelberg read a William Welch reworking of the teleplay. He decided to stand up for his original work and sent a memo to Allen on June 17:

> Dear I.A. – I bow to no one in my profound respect for Bill's dialogue. But on scripts which bear my name, I tend to be partial to my own, and get a little restive at seeing myself rewritten purely for the sake of rewriting. Since we are still over-length, I've also restored some dialogue cuts. Mainly of bad jokes. – Yr. Obedient Srvt. S.W.
>
> PS: Please return my working copy after (I hope) having used it. [14]

By making the cuts, and without knowing it, Wincelberg had honored Adrian Samish's directive to Allen regarding keeping the serious tone of the series.

Meanwhile, Irwin Allen had a falling out with Wincelberg over the screen credit to be used on the pilot for *Lost in Space*. Wincelberg, not caring for the contributions to the script made by Allen, wanted his name replaced with his pseudonym S. Bar-David. Allen took offense and stopped offering work to Wincelberg after a second *Space* assignment, "Invaders from the 5th Dimension," and this *Voyage* script. (Wincelberg moved on to write for the first season of *Star Trek* in 1966, but, after being rewritten by Gene Roddenberry, opted to use the pseudonym of S. Bar-David for his two episodes.)

By the second season, Adrian Samish had exited, leaving Harve Bennett, who, as we know, wanted as little to do with Irwin Allen as possible. Lew Hunter was now serving as the network liaison to *Voyage*. This change, along with *Voyage*'s success, gave Allen more latitude in running his show the way he saw fit. One of the results was the addition of the comic character Riley, as well as the handling of the new Chief of the Seaview, who also brought elements of humor to the series.

Production:
(Filmed June 24 - July 6, 1965; 7 days)

Filming on the Fox lot at this time were the feature films *The Flight of the Phoenix*; the television movie *Stagecoach*; and TV series *Peyton Place, Daniel Boone, 12 O'Clock High, The Loner, The Long Hot Summer, The Legend of Jessie James*, and *Lost in Space*.

Sobey Martin returned to the series to direct. He had helmed seven episodes for the first season, most notably "Ghost of Moby Dick," "Mutiny" and "The Invaders." In all, Martin would direct 14 episodes of *Voyage*. Allen also put him to work on *Lost in Space*, beginning this season, for a total of 14 assignments, and *The Time Tunnel*, starting in 1966, with 14, and *Land of the Giants*, kicking off in 1968, with 21 directing jobs. Prior to working for Allen, Martin had been a busy TV director since the earliest days of the medium. In 1952 alone, he directed 21 half-hour episodes of the anthology series *The Unexplained*; eight episodes of *The Cisco Kid;* and 15 of the crime show *Boston Blackie*. In the mid-to-late 1950s, among other assignments, Martin helmed 11 installments of the espionage series *Passport to Danger,* and, of particular interest to Allen, 29 episodes of *The Silent Service*, an anthology show made up of "true stories" about the U.S. Navy submarine fleet. Martin seemed well prepared for multiple voyages to the bottom of the sea.

Gia Scala was the big guest star, with the big salary of $2,500 to go along with her billing. It was a good paycheck for a week's work on TV in 1965, but a giant step down from the reported $100,000 salary she was paid for appearing in 1961's *The Guns of Navarone*, which starred Gregory Peck, David Niven, and Anthony Quinn. Prior to that, while under contract to Universal, Scala co-starred opposite Glenn Ford in 1957's *Don't Go Near the Water*, Audie Murphy in 1958's *Ride a Crooked Trail*, and Cliff Robertson in 1959's *Battle of the Coral Sea*. But, after the death of her mother and the failure of her marriage, Scala became depressed and, in 1958, attempted suicide, jumping from London's Waterloo Bridge into the Thames River. A cab driver saw her jump and rescued her. Scala's career began a downward spiral, and she began accepting roles on television. Several years after filming this episode, in 1972, Scala was found dead in her Hollywood home from an

51

overdose of alcohol and sleeping pills. She was 38 then – 30 when cast to play Dr. Katya Markova – the name finally settled on for her character.

Richard Basehart got a second-season raise in pay, elevating him from $7,000 per episode to a flat fee of $8,000, perhaps the highest-paid series lead in television. In comparison, one year from now, William Shatner was making $5,000 per episode at *Star Trek*, plus 5% profit participation shares (should the series ever see profit).

David Hedison got a second-season pay increase, too, raising his per-segment flat fee from $2,500 to $2,750. Compare that to Leonard Nimoy's salary in 1966, for playing Mr. Spock, at $1,250 per episode.

Robert Dowdell got a raise, lifting him out of the not-so-spectacular pay scale of $500 per segment to that of $675.

Terry Becker started at scale – $100 per day, for a maximum of $500 per episode.

Del Monroe, for this episode, was guaranteed $650. [15]

Paul Zastupnevich, wardrobe designer for *Voyage* as well as its sister series *Lost in Space*, appears as Aleksei, who dies in the diving bell during the episode's teaser.

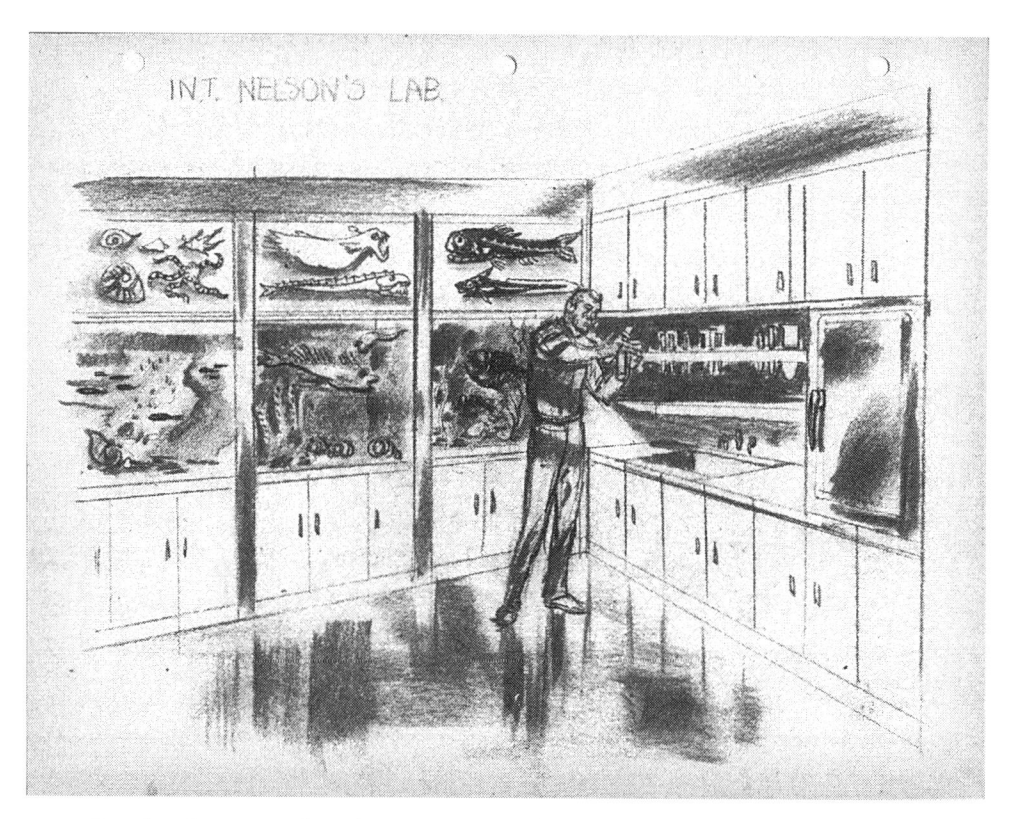

Production got a head start on Tuesday, June 24, 1965, at the backlot Moat, filming footage to be used in process plates for the "Ext. Nelson Institute Dock," a "Nondescript Navy Dock" and a "Nondescript Civilian Dock."

Six days later, on Monday, June 28, principal photography for "Jonah and the Whale" began on Stage 10, the new home of the Seaview, with a new set, "Int. Nelson's Lab," as well as "Int. Missile Room." The actors had a 6:30 a.m. make-up call, with the crew on set at 7:30. After a rehearsal for lights and camera, director Sobey Martin called "action" at 8:50 and continued filming until 7 p.m.

8201-40

8201-43

For the next three days, they filmed the Seaview sets built on Stage 10, taking their last shot on Thursday at 6:50 p.m.

Come Friday, Day 5 of the production, they began three days' work on their old home base, Stage B, now used as a secondary location and, on this day, as the inside of the whale, with and without diving bell. [16]

Regarding these sets, a joint 20th Century-Fox/ABC-TV

8201-120

54

press release, picked up by numerous U.S. newspapers in July 1965, reported:

> ... As executive producer of *Voyage to the Bottom of the Sea*, seen over ABC, Allen recently began production on the second season of his show in one of the most unusual, bizarre and complexing stage sets in the annals of film-making.
>
> The segment, "Jonah and the Whale," deals with extracting a Bathysphere (diving bell) containing Richard Basehart and Gia Scala from the stomach of a gigantic whale. For the sequence, the interiors of a whale's stomachs and giant esophagus were built on the studio stage.
>
> For three months prior to the start of construction, Allen and his art director William Creber, researched the project at nearby Marineland of the Pacific and other oceanographical laboratories. The pair viewed the X-rays of more than 200 whales, ranging in species from the friendly pilot to the giant Archeoceti. ... Whale's stomachs, Allen learned, contain huge air pockets that would allow a human being to breathe indefinitely ... [17]

Set Decorator Sven Wickman told Mark Phillips, "The actors on *Voyage* showed a keen interest in what we had created for every episode. It was an exciting, challenging show to work on as we created throbbing brains, futuristic alien gardens, and ghostly square riggers. I liked *Voyage*; it was prime family entertainment. I was also very fond of Irwin Allen. Years later, I dropped in to say 'hi' to him when he was with Warner Bros. in the late 1970s. He looked up and smiled. 'Sven! Have you come back to work for me?' He was a very loyal man and always appreciative of our work." [18]

Gia Scala had this comment about Wickman's "inside the whale" sets: "It was a horrible, frightening experience. It gave me goose pimples." [19]

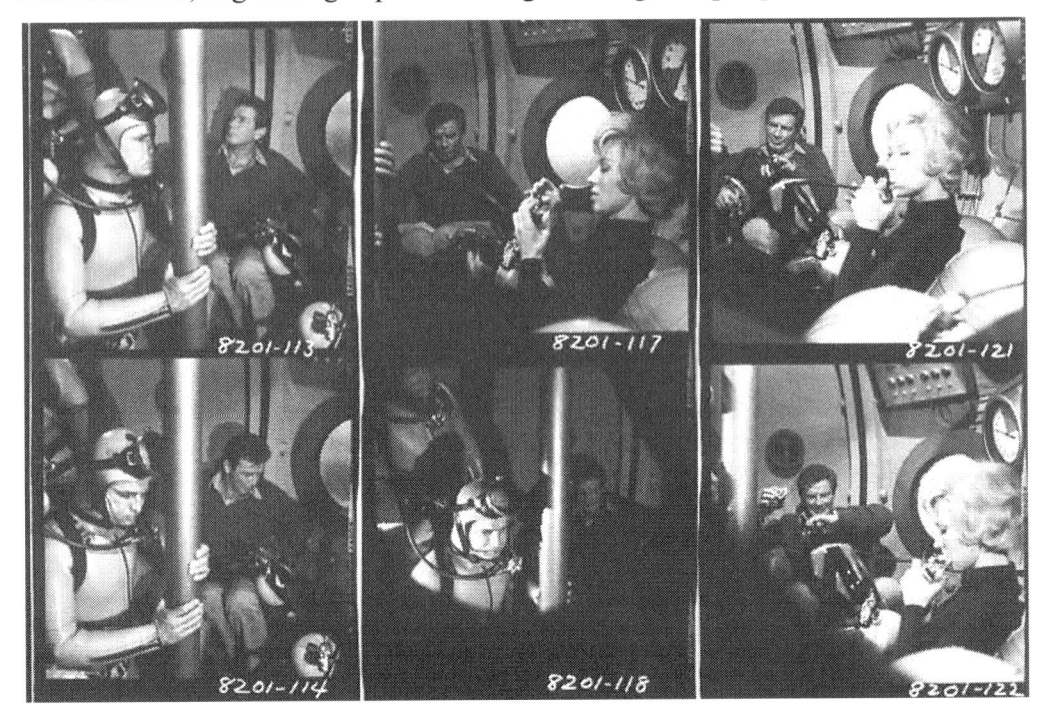

Richard Basehart's lighting double, Ray Didsbury, told Mark Phillips, "The whale interior was one of our best monsters, and I think that was because it was not made by Irwin Allen but rather taken from Fox's *Fantastic Voyage* movie. That film was about a sub being miniaturized and injected into the body of an important politician so that they could cure him. Allen, who was very good about using anything that wasn't nailed down, decided to use their sets for the whale's interior. Our production people may have made some changes, but, basically, it was the set from *Fantastic Voyage*." [20]

Even so, the set was seen first here. *Fantastic Voyage* didn't premiere until August 1966.

Allan Hunt added, "They never explained why it was so illuminated in the whale's stomach. It should have been pitch black!" [21]

The reason, of course, was to show off all the bright colors of *Voyage*'s new season.

Monday, July 5, was a holiday (since the Fourth of July had taken place on a Sunday). On this day, ABC repeated "The Indestructible Man."

The last two days of filming (Tuesday and Wednesday) included the diving team from the Seaview coming to the rescue. A photographer from *TV Guide* magazine was on hand to cover the colorful event.

Allan Hunt told Mark Phillips, "The three of us were in wetsuits and we were sloshing around inside this whale's stomach. We had diver's masks on so you couldn't see our faces, but it sure as hell was us. We spent two days in that whale. The stomach was made up of hundreds of red plastic bags, and there were strong forces of water spraying at us from all angles. We got knocked down a lot. The wetsuits

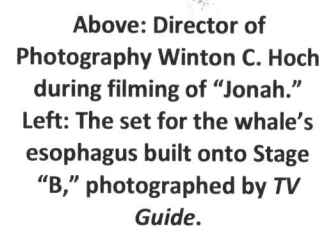

Above: Director of Photography Winton C. Hoch during filming of "Jonah." Left: The set for the whale's esophagus built onto Stage "B," photographed by *TV Guide*.

were also very hot; it was like being in a giant sauna. We were exhausted when we got out of there." [22]

Jerry Goldsmith was hired to write the score for this episode. His task included new theme music for the opening and closing credits. This music was meant to replace the Paul Sawtell-composed opening and closing theme for the second season, but the reaction to Goldsmith's theme was mostly negative, prompting Allen to switch back to Sawtell's theme with the next episode aired.

The budget had been set at $149,559. The final cost was $199,115. Miniature work alone (filmed in the "Green Tank") cost $1,445. And this didn't include the water. The tank, located on the backlot, was 20 feet deep and held 50,000 gallons of water. [23]

The Moat was even thirstier. It held 145,000 gallons and was used on average three times a week, and had to be drained after each use in order to enable clear photography. A total of 18,580,000 gallons of water were used annually, at a cost of $24,750. [24]

Release / Reaction:

(ABC premiere airdate: 9/19/65; network repeat broadcast: 4/17/66)

Shimon Wincelberg said, "The casting and direction were superb, and Irwin ingeniously made use of a set that had been built as a human interior for *Fantastic Voyage*." [25]

In the days before "Jonah and the Whale" aired on ABC, several iconic 1960s series were launched. *Lost in Space* premiered on CBS on Wednesday, September 15. Two nights later, the same network unveiled *The Wild, Wild West* and *Hogan's Heroes*. On Saturday night, NBC brought out the first of its new series, with *Get Smart* and *I Dream of Jeannie*. In the week to come, ABC debuted *The F.B.I.*, *F Troop*, *Gidget*, *The Big Valley*, and *Honey West*. CBS premiered *Green Acres*. NBC introduced *Run for Your Life*, *My Mother the Car*, *I Spy*, and *The Dean Martin Show*. The movie more people in America were seeing over the weekend than any other was *Once a Thief*, starring Alain Delon, Ann-Margret, and Jack Palance. The top-selling record album in America was *Help!* by the Beatles. And its title track was the song getting the most airplay on U.S. radio stations.

Sunday, September 19: *Voyage to the Bottom of the Sea* kicked off its second season. Joan Crosby, for her syndicated column "TV Scout," said:

> *Voyage to the Bottom of the Sea* returns to a new day, in color, with "Jonah and the Whale," a dandy piece of far-out, escapist entertainment. The special effects men and set decorators are the real heroes of this show, much of which takes place in the belly of a huge whale which has swallowed a diving bell containing Richard Basehart and Gia Scala. It's up to David Hedison to lead a rescue team into the mouth of the whale, a feat he accomplishes with the

help of a harpoon containing anesthesia. Fortunately, snoozing whales sleep with their mouths open, which makes the rescue watery but possible. ... [26]

Steven H. Scheuer, for rival syndicated column, "TV Key," said:

The kids will be delighted with this opening adventure. Admiral Nelson (Richard Basehart) and a lady scientist (Gia Scala) are trapped in a diving bell lodged in the stomach of a giant whale. The rescue party, led by Captain Crane (David Hedison), has to enter the whale's stomach and, thanks to some very good special effects, the sequence is as fascinating as it is incredible. [27]

Two days later, *Daily Variety* reviewed the episode, with critic "Daku" saying that the series "looks stronger than ever." He added:

... They opened with a suspenseful, tension-filled story by Shimon Wincelberg, in which a mammoth whale swallows a sea lab [sic] with its two occupants. Whether you call it a whale of a tale, or a tale of a whale, you're right either way. With much of the action taking place within the huge fish, a good deal of the credit goes to special effects, who recreated the interior of the whale realistically and strikingly. It's an auspicious start for another *Voyage*... Basehart and David Hedison register in their stet [continuing] lead roles and Miss Scala lends beauty as well as good thesping to her guest stint. Bob Dowdell is fine in a supporting role. Sobey Martin's directing keeps the tempo humming. [28]

Daku mistakenly credited Allen's effects team for the sets cribbed from the as-yet unreleased *Fantastic Voyage*, but this is understandable.

Tom McIntyre, writing for North Carolina's *Gaston Gazette*, said:

In the season opener Nelson and a Russian oceanographer, that week's girl, were descending into the depths of the sea in a diving bell when a migrating whale swallowed it. There they were trapped inside a diving bell inside the whale. Crane and a couple of aides don wetsuits and swim into the whale's gullet and tromp about on his intestines while being sprayed with gastric fluid. If you think that was bad you should have seen it in color.

Voyage is a brainchild of Irwin Allen and thus far has gone beyond *The Twilight Zone* and *The Outer Limits* in scope. Future episodes will feature more of the absurd, you can be sure of that, because the themes of this show are bound only by the extent of the writer's imagination and 20th Century-Fox studio technicians' craftsmanship. [29]

With such a high concept used to launch *Voyage*'s second season, how could it not hit? A.C. Nielsen pronounced *Voyage* the winner against its competition on CBS and NBC. [30]

A.C. Nielsen 30-City Survey (time period winner in boldface):

(7 – 7:30 p.m.)	Rating:	Share:
ABC: *Voyage to the Bottom of the Sea*	**19.9**	**34.4%**
CBS: *Lassie*	14.8	30.1%
NBC: *Decision*	10.4	21.2%

(7:30 – 8 p.m.)		
ABC: *Voyage to the Bottom of the Sea*	**18.4**	**35.1%**
CBS: *My Favorite Martian*	15.4	29.4%
NBC: *Walt Disney's Wonderful World...*	12.5	23.9%

4.2

"... And Five of Us Are Left" (Episode 34)

(Prod. #8202; first aired Sunday, October 3, 1965)
Written by Robert Vincent Wright
Directed by Harry Harris
Produced by Irwin Allen and William Welch; Story Editor: Sidney Marshall
Guest Star Philip Pine
Also Starring Robert Doyle and Teru Shimada

From the *Voyage* show files (Irwin Allen papers collection):

The Seaview sets out to investigate a message from survivors of a submarine thought to have been sunk in World War II. They find four sailors and a Japanese P.O.W. who have been trapped in an underwater tunnel for twenty-eight years. Nelson reaches them by flying sub but the Japanese officer, unable to face the loss of the war, sabotages the rescue vessel, leaving them all trapped again and now faced with an impending volcanic eruption.[1]

1965 production art depicting the "flying fish." (Courtesy Synthesis Entertainment)

Assessment:

This was the first episode to feature the Flying Sub (although we'd see it sooner, in "Time Bomb," the third episode filmed for the new season but the second to air). And we had the original *Voyage* theme music back, for both the opening and closing title sequences (after missing entirely from "Jonah and the Whale" and only half present in "Time Bomb").

A "first" with this episode: the "collision screen" protecting the glass on the observation deck's nose.

"… And Five of Us Are Left" is an enjoyable 51 minutes. Forget the amazing coincidence that the World War II sub captain's son just happens to be aboard Seaview and is therefore available to join Admiral Nelson on this mission. Or that the entire plot is set in motion by a note in a glass bottle fished out of the sea. Otherwise it's a taut story with plenty of conflict, including an element missing from most Irwin Allen productions, namely "Man Against *Himself*," in the son who struggles with decades of unresolved anger toward his father. This conflict is also demonstrated by the Japanese officer who betrays his friends in an effort to fight a war long since over, then regrets his actions. A third example appears in the heartfelt moment when one of the original survivors forgives the officer. When an audience is provoked to empathy this way, then the story has proven its worthiness.

Robert Vincent Wright, who wrote this episode, said, "Generally, people-oriented stories weren't Irwin's cup of tea. He shied away from them, but he did like the script. It was one of the few *Voyage*s that dealt with people and a semblance of reality, as opposed to giant clams and aliens." [2]

Script:

Robert Vincent Wright's writers contract: April 12, 1965.
Wright's story treatment approved: May 6.
Wright's 1st-draft teleplay approved: June 2.
Wright's Final-draft teleplay approved: June 18.
Rev. Shooting Final teleplay (green paper): June 25.
2nd Rev. Shooting Final (pink paper): July 1.
Page revisions (blue paper): July 7.

Robert Vincent Wright was 46 when he wrote the first of four episodes of *Voyage* (followed by "Graveyard of Fear," "The Terrible Toys," and "Deadly Waters"). He had already written scripts for Westerns such as *Lawman*, *Laramie*, and *Temple Houston*, five (so far) for *Bonanza*, and seven for *Maverick*. He'd also written an episode of *77 Sunset Strip*.

Wright said he did not pursue *Voyage*, but *Voyage* pursued him. He added, "Of what I saw of it, I really didn't care for the first year." [3]

Despite his reservations, Wright accepted the invitation to meet with Irwin Allen and Sidney Marshall. Interviewed by Mark Phillips, Wright said, "Irwin didn't have a great sense of humor. He was a very introverted man, very hyper and tensed up all of the time. But he wasn't unlikable. He was totally absorbed in what he was doing. So, Sidney invited me in to a staff meeting. I went in, and there was this big table with 12 guys sitting there, and I sat down. Irwin strode in and sat down. He pointed his finger at the set designer and said, 'Go!', and the guy said something like, 'Well, Irwin, we're coming along pretty fine with the sets and we'll submit some drawings to you later.' Irwin pointed to the next guy; 'Go!', and the next guy gave his report, and so on. Finally, Irwin got to me. He pointed his finger and said, 'Go!', and I said, 'Gee, Irwin, I don't have to go; I went before I came in.' There was a deathly silence in the room; no one said a word. Then, Irwin chuckled a little, and then everybody laughed. Later, Sidney said, 'Bob, you came awfully close to getting your ass kicked out of there!'" [4]

David Hedison said, "Irwin was totally devoid of humor. *He was*. I mean, you couldn't tell him a joke. He was a funny man; you could do imitations of Irwin, but he didn't understand humor." [5]

Regarding the origin of this episode's story, Wright said, "I had read an account of a Japanese soldier who had come out of the Philippine jungles years after the war. I thought, 'There's an interesting story,' and my first draft had Seaview rescue this poor devil, a Japanese officer who tries to sabotage the sub because he thinks the war's still on. I decided there wasn't enough of a story in that, but that's how it started."

The poem quoted at the episode's close was written by Wright for this story. "Poetry is very easy for me," he said. "And I had one of the nicest compliments ever given to me in this business; the network called and wanted my absolute assurance that I hadn't stolen that poem. I hadn't; it was original. My first ending had the Admiral point to a big Japanese cruise ship as it goes by and say, 'Does that look like Japan has been beaten down?' I liked the ending with the poem better, and so did Sidney Marshall. It was a fun script to write." [6]

Production:
(Filmed July 8 – 15, 1965; 6 days)

Harry Harris was hired to direct. He had started in television as a film editor. One series Harris worked on was a Western called *The Texan*, where he edited 44 half-hour episodes. One day he decided to try his hand at writing one. The producer not only bought the script but assigned Harris to direct it. This led to assignments on Steve McQueen's Western, *Wanted: Dead or Alive*, followed by *Rawhide*, *Daniel Boone*, and 65 episodes of *Gunsmoke*. He said, "Then, my agent at the time was connected with Irwin, and he went to Irwin and said, 'I think you ought to try him because he's got an editing background...' Irwin interviewed me a couple times, and then he said he'd try me for one of the shows, which I did, and consequently I worked for him for years, on everything he did." [7]

This work included more episodes on *Voyage*, as well as *Lost in Space*, *The Time Tunnel*, *Land of the Giants*, and *Swiss Family Robinson*.

Harris was nervous about his first *Voyage*. He told interviewer Kevin Burns, "I watched his pilot. I saw what he was doing, and I also saw that his budget wasn't big enough to do it. So, I was scared to do the show, because it was so big – the submarine goes into a cave that is submerged under the earth. It was terrific, but we spent a fortune. We had [water] tanks where submarines were floated, and all of that. In those days [the second season], he had a little more money to spend on it than later times. But I looked at what he wanted, and I knew, from the editing experience, how to do the kind of effects and give him things he wanted. And I learned a lot of things from Irwin that I didn't know… like how to make a submarine scene where everybody goes one way and the submarine goes the other way. There were a lot of things on that show. There was a lot of blue screen, through the front of the submarine. They started out with process, I believe, then went to blue screen. And lots of special effects. All of his shows had that stuff in them. You know, you had to have whistles and bells and fireworks going off every three and a half seconds." [8]

Phillip Pine, playing Ryan, got top guest billing, and $1,250. He was 44. Among the hundreds of roles in television and films, he had taken two trips into *The Twilight Zone* ("The Incredible World of Horace Ford" and "The Four of Us Are Dying") and was top guest star in the 1963 episode of *The Outer Limits* ("The Hundred Days of the Dragon"). Pine would also be featured as the notorious Colonel Green in "The Savage Curtain," a 1969 episode of *Star Trek*.

Phillip Pine, three years after his *Voyage*, in *Star Trek*'s 1969 "The Savage Curtain."

Pine said of "… And Five of Us Are Left," "It was an extremely good script and the character of Ryan appealed to me. I liked his determination to survive and his faith that his government would one day rescue him. The scenes where his son confronts him were also well written." [9]

Robert Doyle, cast as son Werden, got second guest billing, and $1,000. He was 26, and had appeared in *Voyage* twice before (in smaller roles as different characters), as well as a frequent guest on other TV series, usually as a troubled youth, with multiple appearances on *The Fugitive, The F.B.I., 12 O'Clock High, Bonanza,* and *The Outer Limits.*

Teru Shimada played Nakamura, and was also paid $1,000, which equates to about $9,000 in 2020. He was 59, and had played the Japanese sub commander in 1958's *Run Silent, Run Deep.*

Kent Taylor got to lie around for a good portion of this episode, as the injured and

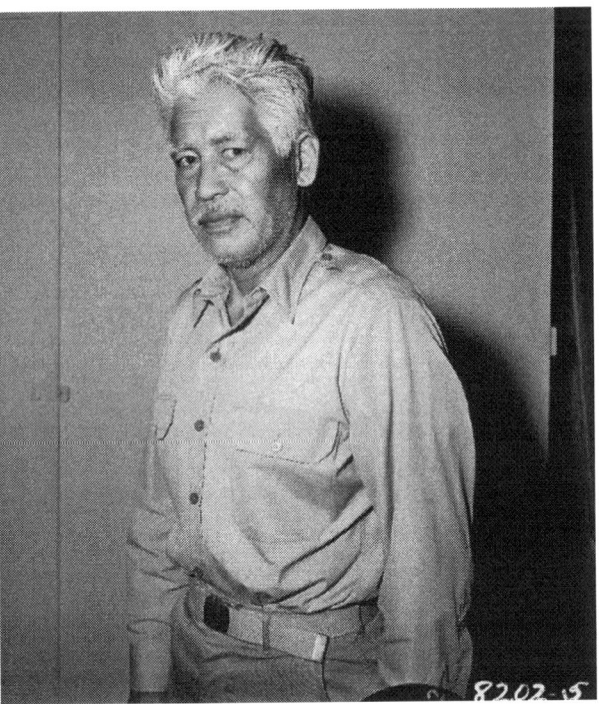

**Above: Teru Shimada.
Left: Kent Taylor (who played Johnson) in his heyday as a Hollywood leading man.**

dying Johnson. Taylor was a leading man in numerous "B"-films during the 1930s and '40s, before heading into TV, where he starred in two series – as the title character sleuth in 58 episodes of *Boston Blackie* (1951-53) and as Captain Jim Flagg, travelling West, in *The Rough Riders* (1958-59). He was 60.

James Anderson played Wilson, one of the "five of us are left." He was 43, although made to look older here, and had more than 150 screen appearances to his credit. Among them, he was in another group of five, as a nuclear war survivor, in the 1951 sci-fi *Five*; and shortly before *Voyage*, he gave a memorable characterization as a bigoted farmer in 1962's *To Kill a Mockingbird*. Irwin Allen put Anderson to work again in "Pirates of Deadman's Island," an episode of *The Time Tunnel*.

Françoise Ruggieri, 27 at this time, played Brenda, Captain Crane's date. A few weeks after appearing here, Irwin Allen cast Ruggieri as an alien settler in "The Sky Is Falling," on *Lost in Space*, then gave her a bigger role for a return trip to *Voyage*, for "The Machines Strike Back."

Lennie Hayton provided the score, his first of eight for *Voyage*. Hayton had impressive credentials – he shared in winning two Oscars (1949's *On the Town* and 1969's *Hello, Dolly!*), and was nominated for four others (including 1952's *Singin' in the Rain* and 1968's *Star!*). He also shared an Emmy nomination for a 1964 Lena Horne special.

Françoise Ruggieri, with Don Matheson and Eddie Rosson, in *Lost in Space*.

July 13: Françoise Ruggieri shares a cup of coffee, and a photo op, with David Hedison.

Filming began on Thursday, July 8, 1965, for the first of three days on Stage 10, utilizing the Seaview sets, as well as the Flying Sub (with process shots). Friday, the 9th, marked the very first day of filming in the Flying Sub. This episode also introduced the sleek leather flight jacket, worn here by Admiral Nelson.

Tuesday, July 13th, was the first of three days production on Stage "B," beginning with the sandy set for "Ext. Honolulu Beach," with Hedison and Françoise Ruggieri. She was paid $150.

The rest of the final three days of the production were spent on the sets for "Int. Lava Cave" and "Int. Tetra Sub."

Phillip Pine said, "I remember Teru Shimada was having difficulty pronouncing some words in the scenes where the depth charges are blasting us. Irwin Allen suddenly came down and he yelled at Teru and director Harry Harris, threatening to remove Teru from the scene. I finally had enough and told Mr. Allen off. I said that if he didn't leave the set right now, I was leaving. He left and Teru and Harry thanked me." [10]

Pine would never work for Irwin Allen again. Harry Harris did. He said, "There's a lot of stories about Irwin. He was an original. I called him an original. He was not an easy man to get along with… but I had a tremendous amount of respect for him because I came out of Columbia, as a mail boy, and Harry Cohn was the head of the studio. And then, at that period, there was L.B. Mayer, head of MGM, and Jack Warner [of Warner Bros.]. All the studios had the major guy that was in charge of the show. And when I got to know Irwin, Irwin was of that type. He was a showman. He ran his own ship. Fox didn't bother him; they left him alone because they didn't want to tangle with him. They gave him

Above: Becker and Doyle from the first day of filming. Below: First use of the Flying Sub in the series, and the flight jacket.

68

his way. And I respected what he did. I had difficult times with him; tons of difficult times, but so did everybody else, so it wasn't exclusive. But he liked me about as much as he liked anybody, because I never stopped working for him."[11]

Concerning the climactic earthquake, a press release sent to newspapers said:

> Special effects man Bobby Tait knows how to create a real, seismologic, Richter-scale rocking tremblor, and he comes up with one of his best on "... And Five of Us Are Left," in color on ABC's *Voyage to the Bottom of the Sea* (7-8 p.m. today).
>
> "It was shot in the C.B. de Mille manner with three cameras on giant booms. The results are amazing. I held on to my seat in a projection room when I saw the film," the quakemaker commented.
>
> "When that was shot, I was like a man with ball-bearing feet," Tait said," running about like a madman to see that everything was functioning properly. With cork, pyrocel and fuller's earth flying all over the place, it's pretty scary. Cork can be dangerous if it hits anyone at a bad angle."
>
> But the monumental earthquake was a smashing success. It was filmed in one take and cost about $15,000.[12]

After the earthquake, shots were taken inside Nakamura's Japanese mini-sub. And that was a wrap.

On this final day, they had begun filming at 7:30 a.m. in hopes of not running late, but the last shot wasn't completed until 9:30 p.m.

Ray Didsbury said, "Harry Harris was nicknamed 'Midnight Harry' because his work was slow. We got lots of overtime. He was liked in spite of – *or because of* – this. He was a nice man with a good sense of humor."[13]

The episode had been budgeted at $148,260, but ended up costing $189,839.34.

Release / Reaction:

(ABC premiere airdate: 10/3/65; network repeat broadcast: 4/24/66)

The week "... And Five of Us Are Left" first aired, *Mickey One*, starring Warren Beatty, was the most popular film in the movie houses across America.

"Yesterday," by the Beatles, was getting the most airplay on U.S. Top 40 radio stations. The Fab Four also had the top-selling album, with *Help!* Don Adams and Barbara Feldon, of *Get Smart*, had the cover of *TV Guide*. Irwin Allen's other show, *Lost in Space*, aired its fourth episode, "There Were Giants in the Earth," where the outer space castaways met a gigantic Cyclops. David Hedison was borrowed from the *Voyage* set by the Fox publicity men to take pictures with this iconic *Lost in Space* monster.

DAVID MEETS GOLIATH -- Substituting a pair of man-sized fists for the proverbial slingshot, actor David Hedison of ABC-TV's Sunday night "Voyage to the Bottom of the Sea" series meets up with a Cyclopean giant from CBS-TV's Wednesday night offering, "Lost In Space." Unlike his Biblical counterpart, the giant ends up with a draw. Reason? Irwin Allen, who produces both shows, isn't about to let any harm befall either actor.

Steven H. Scheuer previewed "… And Five of Us Are Left" for his syndicated "TV Key" column:

> Strictly for the youthful fans of this adventure series. It's a farfetched tale about the Seaview's rescue mission of a group

of World War II survivors who were trapped in an underground volcanic cave for more than 25 years! [14]

Joan Crosby, in her rival "TV Scout" column, in newspapers all across America, said:

> *Voyage to the Bottom of the Sea* is concerned with volcanoes -- those of nature and those of humans. The Seaview is on a mission to rescue five survivors, including one Japanese, who have survived for 20 years after their sub was sunk during World War II. They are in an underwater cave, with the mountain over their heads rumbling, and one of the rescuers also rumbling, for a reason which does have a bit of dramatic impact. [15]

Trade magazine *Variety* reviewed this episode on October 6. "Bill" wrote:

> It could be ... that ABC's pitchmen are showing sponsors demographics which claim *Voyage* is being viewed by some of Nielsen's vet infantilists. Show caught Sunday night (2) had the sub's captain under the palms clutching a sexy blonde to his mighty chest (he was called to duty in mid-clinch). This kind of action might convince some of Madison Ave's untouched that the stanza has adult appeal. But it also could be dangerous. Any theatre man will tell you that when Roy [Rogers] tries to kiss Dale during the Saturday matinee, the popcorn stand is struck by an avalanche of prepuberties. Ditto action in *Voyage* could touch off a dial stampede to *Lassie*.
>
> Anyhow, Blondie was dispensed with posthaste as the crew set out to rescue five "poor devils" trapped in an underwater cave since WW II, 28 years in the terms of the show's 1973 [sic] setting. They were eventually surfaced in a cumbersome script which had all the crude exposition and cliché action gambits tots have enjoyed suffering since *The Perils of Pauline*.
>
> Richard Basehart, as the sub commander, has the lightweight role thoroughly in hand, and makes skillful use of the script's rare intelligent moments. The closing scene between Basehart and Japanese actor Teru Shimada was a soaring

moment as these things go. Special effects are excellent, and no doubt as vital to *Voyage* as those four-legged props are to the oaters. [16]

Tom McIntyre, writing for the *Gaston Gazette*, in North Carolina, said:

> The thing that bugs this reviewer is how fully the actors seem to believe the material they perform when they can't quite make the viewer believe it. It's amazing how easily they pass off a message in a bottle found floating in the sea from a handful of men trapped in an underwater cave for 28 years. Oh, yeah. That was one of the themes. An American sub was carrying a Japanese prisoner when sunk at the close of World War II. Then in 1975 a bottle was found floating in the sea by some fishermen. The glass was analyzed and discovered to have been manufactured in the 1940s. Admr. Nelson and a young technician were sent to locate the underwater cave. They did, but the Japanese lieutenant, who was still alive, sabotaged the flying sub. He didn't want to live under American rule. He thought his country had been enslaved. He didn't know Japan had grown rich copying American know-how and selling it a little cheaper. The young technician turned out to be the son of the man in charge of the underwater cave. He hated his father because he had not returned to his mother after the war. They threw in an erupting volcano for good measure in that one too. [17]

Bob Shiels wrote in Canada's *Calgary Herald*:

> ... *Voyage* started out looking like a blockbuster, deteriorated rapidly, dropped out of sight, and now seems to be back, at least on a temporary basis.
>
> I still vividly remember the first show in the series. It had everything from atomic submarine to atomic bombs and it was a rouser from start to finish. ...
>
> By current standards, [the latest episode] of *Voyage* was almost interesting. We had an erupting volcano, a flying submarine, and a Second World War submarine crew trapped in an underwater cave – where they had remained for 28 years!

> A lot of other adventure [series] are similarly ridiculous. *Voyage*, however, has never acquired the knack of being able to laugh at itself. [18]

A.C. Nielsen 30-City survey from October 3, 1965 (time period winner in boldface)[19]:

(7 – 7:30 p.m.)	Rating:	Share:
ABC: *Voyage to the Bottom of the Sea*	**17.9**	**34.0%**
CBS: *Lassie*	19.4	33.9%
NBC: *America*	8.8	16.7%

(7:30 – 8 p.m.)		
ABC: *Voyage to the Bottom of the Sea*	**21.0**	**37.7%**
CBS: *My Favorite Martian*	18.1	32.5
NBC: *Walt Disney's Wonderful World of Color*	10.7	19.2%

Robert Vincent Wright said, "They did a beautiful job of casting the old Japanese man. Generally, all the actors did a fine job. Harry Harris directed that and he was a young guy at the time. He was the best director *Voyage* ever had." [20]

Harry Harris said, "That was an interesting show. But [Irwin] spent a lot of money on it. And the special effects department got an Emmy for it. That was probably the best show I ever had done for him, but that's when he was spending some money. We started cutting back, and they didn't have the time or money to do anything." [21]

4.3

"Time Bomb" (Episode 35)

(Prod. #8203; first aired Sunday, September 26, 1965)
Written by William Read Woodfield and Allan Balter
Directed by Sobey Martin
Produced by Irwin Allen and Frank La Tourette; Story Editor: Sidney Marshall
Guest Star Ina Balin; Co-Starring Susan Flannery

VOYAGE TO THE BOTTOM OF THE SEA - YEAR 2

TIME BOMB ... Katie (Susan Flannery) and Cmdr. Crane (David Hedison) hold Litchka (Ina Balin) at gunpoint in a tense moment from the "Time Bomb" episode of 20th Century-Fox Television's VOYAGE TO THE BOTTOM OF THE SEA series, seen this (day) at (time) on (channel). #8203/84

From the *Voyage* show files (Irwin Allen papers collection):

Red Chinese agents, determined to create a conflict between Russia and the U.S., inject Admiral Nelson with cesium, an explosive chemical when brought into contact with radioactivity. Nelson, unaware that he is now a potential human bomb, embarks on an undercover inspection tour of Russia's nuclear reactor. Crane, learning of the plot, accompanies a female undercover agent, with orders to stop Nelson, even if they must kill him. [1]

Assessment:

"A cold-war story that misses the mark," commented renowned *Voyage* fan and historian – and guest critic for this book series – Mark Phillips. "Ina Balin's Litchka is dull and the other villains are stereotypical. The few action scenes are routine, making this a tedious adventure." [2]

"Writer William Read Woodfield finally blows it," was fellow *Voyage* fan-historian and guest critic Mike Bailey's take. "That is probably being unfair, in that, after story sessions with Irwin and the production team, the writers were obviously coached on the new, lighter direction the shows were to take in this new season. Just the same, not a particularly good script. Nelson's shallow romance with the spy Litchka is gratuitous and lends a smarmy gloss to the story." [3]

As noted, humor was very present – with both Basehart and Hedison playing their roles a bit lighter than in most of the first season, and even daring to smile, made easier perhaps in the company of beautiful women. We even see Admiral Nelson, in a very atypical moment, give his Russian-based U.S. agent a smooch. It's strange that after that kiss, clearly meant to imply more, the picture dissolves to Nelson sleeping downstairs on the couch, and Litchka emerging from her upstairs chambers. Well, so much for trying to put a little James Bond-type sexiness into a TV show during the "family hour."

The episode is overworked with so many tricks that it out-tricks itself. Vice Admiral Johnson, like a pale imitation of 007's Q, explains secret gadgets to Nelson, then "Kate" does the same with Crane. None are very clever or even well realized. We are also given a midget pretending to be a boy, shooting Nelson with an air-hypo; the Seaview's close call with killer Soviet destroyers; a jet-boat race and crash; an insincere moment of jeopardy as Crane and Nelson nearly shoot each other; Nelson and Crane donning disguises; an underwater fight; an above-water fight; a ticking clock concerning the walking human timebomb (Nelson); and numerous other shenanigans. It's a game of watch-the-bouncing-ball, as the audience gets bounced more than once right out of the story.

More clutter: We are provided with a far-more technically jargoned-up introduction to the Flying Sub than in "… And Five of Us Are Left." The reason: Although "Five" was filmed first, "Time Bomb" was intended to precede it in the broadcast order. Captain Crane and Chip Morgan don flight jackets this time out, along with Admiral Nelson. They all look spiffy. And the flirtation between Crane and Tiffany Loveland, eh, "Kate," is played up, to serve as the start of something big … which would never be.

It was all too much, with too little time and insincere handling to make most of it work.

One may even wonder why Admiral Nelson, a famous former military man and heralded scientist, would be chosen for an undercover assignment such as portrayed in this story. Suddenly, we are to accept that this brilliant scientist and inventor is also skilled in parachuting, speedboat racing, foreign languages and mannerisms, stealth swimming missions, hand-to-hand combat, and also astute at handling espionage gadgets galore. Didn't Military Intelligence have any agents of their own in the region?

One thing that *Voyage* couldn't be faulted for was how the police and military men in the Soviet city speak English rather than their own language. This is how it was on American TV in the 1960s, and for quite awhile after. The networks weren't about to ask their audiences to read subtitles.

And while the emphasis on spy gadgets plays as a joke today, keep in mind that *Get Smart* and *The Wild, Wild West*, two series that played spy gizmos for all they were worth, along with *I Spy* and *Amos Burke – Secret Agent*, were just now going on the air. Up until now, we had only seen this sort of stuff from 007, *Danger Man*, and one year's worth of *The Man from U.N.C.L.E.* It had not yet been overplayed, although this episode pushed the gimmicks to the limit.

Script:

William Read Woodfield's and Allan Balter's writers contract for "Return of Billy Bones": May 12, 1965.
Woodfield's and Balter's final-draft teleplay approved: June 21.
Rev. Shooting Final teleplay: July 12.
2nd Rev. Shooting Final (on green paper): July 14.
Page revisions (purple paper): July 15.
Page revisions (yellow paper): July 16.
Page revisions (blue paper): July 22.

This was the second of eight *Voyage* scripts **Allan Balter** wrote with **William Read Woodfield** … and the first to carry his name. For "The Saboteur," his first collaboration with Woodfield, Balter used the pseudonym George Reed. He was an associate producer on *Voyage* at that time; now he was focusing entirely on writing.

Woodfield said, "I found it very lonely to sit there and write scripts for the first year. I knew Allan wanted to write, so I said, 'Hey, why don't we write 'em together?' Allan said he would love to, and Irwin said, 'Over my dead body!

Allan's an associate producer, Billy; you're a writer.' I said, 'We're gonna do 'em together or I walk and we'll write for someone else.'" [4]

For the next several years they were a team, writing for *Voyage* and Allen's other series from this time, *Lost in Space* and *The Time Tunnel*. They quit Allen to take the reins at *Mission: Impossible*, as writer/producers, where their scripts brought them three Emmy nominations and one Writers Guild Award nomination. They also collaborated, as writer/producers, on the 1971 sci-fi TV movie *Earth II*. Prior to his work with Woodfield, Balter was indeed an associate producer, first for Jack Lord's early 1960s TV series *Stoney Burke*, then for *Voyage*. As a writer, he had written two episodes for *The Outer Limits*. Woodfield had been writing for *Sea Hunt*, and co-wrote the 1960 low-budget horror film, *The Hypnotic Eye*. After ending their partnership, Balter stayed close to the sci-fi genre, as a writer/producer on 1977's *The Man with the Power*, and the short-lived 1983/84 supernatural series, *The Powers of Matthew Star*. He also served as a producer on *The Six Million Dollar Man*. Woodfield, meanwhile, wrote multiple scripts for TV's *Shaft* (which was produced by Balter) and *Columbo*.

"Time Bomb" was not Balter's and Woodfield's best moment, but we'll nonetheless take a moment to trace its development.

Mary Garbutt, of ABC Continuity Acceptance Department, wrote to Irwin Allen and staff on July 8:

> Per discussions with Mr. La Tourette ... The instigator of the plot will not be Red China or any other actual nation, but a fictitious organization made up of different nationalities which can include Orientals.
>
> Pg 1: Delete Peking Square, May Day celebration, Red China super (Please be sure to keep date 1977);
>
> Pg 2: Substitute for "included our country" in Li Tung's line;
>
> Pg 3: Delete "our great ally" in Li Tung's line;
>
> Pgs 66 & 67: Substitute for "Chinese" and "Red Chinese" in Nelson's lines. [5]

ABC wanted a time jump from the first season's date of 1973 to 1977 with this script. The network preferred the political intrigue stories depicted as far in the future as possible. Allen chose 1974 instead, which was superimposed on screen at the start of the episode. The network also preferred there be no reference to China. In fact, ABC didn't like any references to real foreign governments or even specific government agencies within the United States. The Soviet Union got a pass this time, as well as a city somewhere along the Black Sea, since the U.S.S.R. was not being depicted as the story's "heavies."

Garbutt's memo continued:

> Pg 12: Eliminate CHIEF on the brass plate on Vice Admiral's desk;
>
> Pg 13: Of course, there must be clearance for any paintings or art objects used;
>
> g 31, 36: Manhattan Galleries, *Picture World Magazine* must be fictitious names;
>
> Pg 32-34: Note to wardrobe: For this sequence Litchka must be dressed in something other than a negligee – "something day rather than night" type; Caution here and earlier that the soldiers' ribbing is light and good-natured and not on the sex innuendo side. Standard caution on the embraces, particularly the closing one on Pg 34;
>
> Pgs 37, 57, 58: Mind bottle, photographic equipment not identifiable as to actual trade/brand names;
>
> Pgs 37, 57, 58: Special caution in shots of Tiffany: Her distraction of the guards must be done lightly and not suggestively; of course, no over-exposure of leg or CU-ing of "special portions of her anatomy". Here and throughout, please do not CU [Close Up] on judo chops;
>
> Pg 50-51: Re: sighting effect on tele-photo camera gun: Do not duplicate crosshairs of actual telescopic rifle. Please create some <u>special</u> sighting effect (for ex: circle within a circle or some such) which would be particular to Crane's special gun; Substitute for "God's sake" in Nelson's line. [6]

Concerning the crosshairs of the telescopic rifle, since the assassination of President John F. Kennedy, ABC broadcast standards had been adamant that such visuals would not be shown on their network.

As for the sexiness written into the episode, it is likely that this was a "test case" to see how the audience would respond. But Richard Basehart and David Hedison had been pushing for more action of this type for awhile. Hedison told Erskine Johnson for a syndicated newspaper story in March of 1965, "I'm frustrated. I keep mentioning the lack of pretty young things in the plot and the producer keeps promising a story with an Embassy party where I could wear a dinner jacket, a blonde in one hand and a martini in the other. But I'm still waiting." [7]

Days later, Army Archerd reported in his *Daily Variety* column:

> Irwin Allen's adding sex appeal to next season's *Voyage to the Bottom of the Sea* – a femme member of the all-male Seaview sun cred; her name's "Tiffany Loveland." [8]

At the time this episode was filming, Hedison was profiled in an article for *The Los Angeles Times*. He said, "Everything I hoped for on the series will develop. ... Next year, there will be less of the submarine and we'll be on land more. There will be more girls, thank heaven, and we'll be seen more in civilian clothes." [9]

Richard Basehart told Dan Lewis of Hackensack, New Jersey's *The Record*, "We're going to have gals around this year! I won't have to shake hands with an octopus all the time this season." [10]

In the episode, when Vice Admiral Johnson introduces Nelson to his pretty Eastern European contact, Nelson smiles, "You know, this assignment is starting to look better." Basehart could have just as easily said, "You know, this season is starting to look better."

Production:
(Filmed July 16 – 23; 6 days)

This was **Sobey Martin**'s ninth directing assignment on *Voyage*, and the second of the new season (following "Jonah and the Whale").

Ina Balin, 27 when cast as Litchka, was paid $2,500. This was top guest-star rate at *Voyage*, and Balin had the status to ask for it. She had been the female lead on Broadway in 1957's *Compulsion*; she'd won the Theatre World Award for her performance in the Broadway play *A Majority of One* in 1969; and was now under contract at 20th Century-Fox, winning a Golden Globe Award as "Most Promising Newcomer – Female." She was nominated for another Golden Globe for her supporting role in the 1960 Paul Newman film, *From the Terrace*. Balin had the lead female role (billed under John Wayne and Stuart Whitman) in 1961's *The Comancheros*, and was cast opposite Jerry Lewis in 1964's *The Patsy*. The same year, she had the lead in *Act of Reprisal*, then fourth billing in the 1965 epic, *The Greatest Story Ever Told*.

Susan Flannery was paid $750, and billed as "co-star." This was her third appearance on *Voyage* (following Season One's "Hail to the Chief" and, more prominently, "The Traitor"). Here she plays Katie, Nelson's strong-willed secretary, who helps defuse the "time bomb." As noted by Mark Phillips, Flannery

Ina Balin (above) and Susan Flannery (below left) in promotional pictures taken during the production.

almost became a *Voyage* semi-regular. Writer William Read Woodfield said, "She was originally named Tiffany Loveland and she was supposed to be a James Bond-type girlfriend for David Hedison. Irwin hired some [other] girl he thought was attractive, but she was not in any way a Bond-type girlfriend. She made one appearance and was out." [11]

Without network approval to be a recurring character in the series, the name of Flannery's character was changed from Tiffany Loveland to "Katie." Allan would later cast Flannery in a *The Time Tunnel*, and in 1974's *The Towering Inferno*.

Regarding the lack of actresses on the series, Del Monroe told a convention audience, "We met so few women…. We thought [it was because] they required a hairdresser. That was the rumor – they required special attention and that cost more money." [12]

Allan Hunt, speaking to the same crowd, added, "They did try one episode; the girl came in and they thought of introducing her as a semi-regular – Susan Flannery…. I remember they tried that just to balance out the show…. It didn't work. Nobody liked her, I guess; you know, upstairs at ABC or something." [13]

William Read Woodfield mentioned that Irwin Allen did select someone after Susan Flannery to play Tiffany Loveland – someone Allen "thought was attractive, but she was not in any way a Bond-type girlfriend." Perhaps he was referring to Ina Balin. A 20th Century-Fox press release, issued in mid-August, announced:

> Ina Balin, who just completed a guest starring role in an episode of *Voyage to the Bottom of the Sea*, playing a Sino-Russian secret agent opposite the series star, Richard Basehart, has been informed by producer Irwin Allen that her part will be continued through an additional five episodes. [14]

You may also recognize **Richard Loo**, as the top Chinese (although never called "Chinese") man in the Teaser. Loo worked close to 200 times in TV and film. He should have; his wife was head of the Bessie Loo Talent Agency, which specialized in the casting of Asian-Americans.

Frank Delfino, who played the agent who pretends to be a little boy, worked often too, including being seen more than once on *Lost in Space*. For a while, he was also Billy Mumy's stand-in.

John Zaremba played Vice Admiral Johnson. The 56-year-old actor would make over 180 screen appearances in his lengthy career. He co-starred in 69 episodes of the 1953-56 Red-scare series *I Led 3 Lives*, as FBI Special Agent Jerry Dressler, and had a recurring role on *Ben Casey* in the early 1960s, as Dr.

Harold Jensen. After taking this *Voyage*, Irwin Allen cast Zaremba as a regular in *The Time Tunnel*, where he was seen 30 times as Dr. Raymond Swain.

Leith Stevens provided the score. He wrote the music for dozens of films in the 1940s and '50s, including some sci-fi classics – 1950's *Destination Moon*, 1951's *When Worlds Collide*, 1953's *The War of the Worlds*, and 1956's *World Without End* – as well as the Marlon Brando cult fave, 1953's *The Wild Ones*. Stevens got busy in television in the 1960s, scoring numerous episodes for *Mr. Novak*, *Burke's Law*, and *Daniel Boone*, among other series, and worked often for Irwin Allen. He would score eight more episodes of *Voyage*, as well as one *Lost in Space*, two for *The Time Tunnel*, and six for *Land of the Giants*.

Above: John Zaremba in *The Time Tunnel*. Below: July 23, 1965, director Sobey Martin (foreground) and the camera crew prepare to film the speedboat sequence.

As the second episode aired, "Time Bomb" gave the viewing audience one last taste of Jerry Goldsmith's somber alternate title music, but only on the end credits. The front title sequence was back to the original theme, with the much more effective Paul Sawtell score. Next week, the rest of *Voyage* would be back, and back on track.

Filming began on Friday, July 16,

1965, at *Voyage*'s home base at Fox, Stage 10. They filmed on the Flying Sub, in Nelson's cabin, and also on a temporary set – "Int. Johnson's Office." They also went outdoors to film around the studio's New Administration Building, which passed for the "Naval Intelligence Building."

On Monday, the company was filming at the Pico Blvd. gate to 20th Century-Fox, which passed for "Ext. Complex Gate" in the script, then onto Stage 10 for the Seaview Control Room, and a couple of temporary fly-them-in-and-fly-them-out sets: "Int. Washington Gallery" and "Int. Neutral Packing." With all the moving around, Sobey Martin found himself shooting until 8:30 p.m.

On Tuesday, the temporary sets on Stage 10 were now gone, and replaced by another temporary set – "Int. Li Tung's House," as well as one of the standing sets – "Int. Observation Nose and Control Room."

Wednesday, July 21, the company took over Fox Stage 15 for filming on the "Int. Litchka's Studio & Foyer" set.

Thursday, July 22, they filmed at the Moat on the backlot for "Ext. Dock and Car."

July 23 was the sixth day of filming, and the producers were determined it would be the last.

Above: Flannery, Balin, and Hedison in the spectator's bleachers. Below: Richard Basehart piloting a powerboat in the backlot Moat.

83

They began at the Moat, for "Ext. Dock / Hydro / Jet Pit Area / Sea / Palisades." All that, and then a company move to the "French Street" which provided for "Ext. Litchka Apt. & Street" and "Ext. Deserted Village." It was Friday, and that meant a late-night shoot with the last scene being filmed at 10:45 p.m.

During this time, a sixth day of production was handled by the second unit, with the various underwater shots, all filmed with stunt divers in the "Green Tank." [15]

The budget had been set at $151,229 by Allen's people. William Self, head of production at Fox, slashed it to $140,491. Despite the projections, the final cost: $180,283. [16]

Release / Reaction:
(ABC premiere airdate: 9/26/65; network repeat broadcast: 9/4/66)

Above and below: Scenes shot on Day 5, alongside the Moat, for "Ext. Dock & Car."

Richard Basehart was making publicity rounds in mid-September from one city to the next,

84

promoting the new season of *Voyage*. Ruth Thompson, for the November 13, 1965 edition of Pennsylvania's *The Gettysburg Times*, wrote:

> Even as rugged a chap as the fair-haired, square-jawed Basehart gets bushed coping with the demands of an hour-long show made considerably more demanding because of the plot-complicating gadgetry projected a decade into the future.... But a variety of roles he's definitely not missing. Not at present anyway. He's really loving his full-time science-fiction television whirl. ...

Basehart told Thompson, "The move to color was right. So, what if it takes a little longer to light and is a little hotter working. Ours *is* a color show if ever there was one. Our special effects really warrant it. Did you know that our cameraman, Winton Hoch, won three movie Oscars? And our special effects man won an Emmy?"

Basehart was also happy about the addition of the Flying Sub. "Now we get ashore more. It's no longer a matter of the cast going into a state of shock at the sight of a woman. Take the episode with Ina Balin. Mmm. Very good in the kissing department." [17]

That kiss was the first for Admiral Nelson. Alas, Basehart would learn, it would not be a recurring bit of action.

The week that "Time Bomb" premiered on ABC-TV, an event happened in the Philippines that seemed like an Irwin Allen disaster movie – Taal Volcano exploded, leaving approximately 200 people dead or missing. Meanwhile, a film called *How to Murder Your Wife*, a comedy starring Jack Lemmon, was No. 1 in the movie houses across America. The soundtrack album to *Help!*, by the Beatles, was in the middle of a nine-week stay at the top of the *Billboard* chart. The song getting the most airplay on Top 40 radio stations was "Hang on Sloopy," by the McCoys. And *Lost in Space* aired "Island in the Sky," its third episode on CBS, in which the Jupiter 2 crash-lands on a strange world.

With so many spy shows flooding the airwaves, and one series changing from a cop show to a spy show (*Burke's Law* to *Amos Burke – Secret Agent*), the critic for "TV Key" said:

> All of the adventure series are jumping on the Band-wagon these days, and this week it's Admiral Nelson's (Richard Basehart) turn to do some special agenting. He embarks on a mission to the U.S.S.R., unaware that he's been injected with an explosive set to trigger World War III. The gimmicks and

improbable chase sequence at the end are geared for the kids, and they'll probably enjoy all of it. [18]

Joan Crosby, of "TV Scout," must have had a childlike attitude. She raved:

Voyage to the Bottom of the Sea is a wet *Man from U.N.C.L.E.* and it's great fun. Ina Balin is a double agent who nearly does in Richard Basehart. He is injected, painlessly, with a dose of an unstable chemical element which will make him a living bomb if he ever gets near a nuclear reactor. It's up to Miss Balin to lure him to a Russian reactor, which she does. But we still have David Hedison, and a beautiful secretary, and lots of great gimmicks, to save Basehart, the day, and the world. [19]

Andy Stephen, looking at TV for Victoria, British Columbia's *Times Colonist*, commented:

Voyage to the Bottom of the Sea has gone wild this season. The first episode had star Richard Basehart and a lovely femme swallowed by a whale. It was hard to swallow and, I'm sure, the interior whale shots must have been appetizing in color. The second show was just as hard to put down. Basehart was turned into a human time bomb by a lovely femme. Man, this show is way, way out this fall. [20]

According to the A.C. Nielsen, *Voyage* was a strong second in its time period during the first half hour, and nosed out the competition during the second.

A.C. Nielsen 30-City survey from September 26, 1965 (the time period winner in boldface)[21]:

(7 – 7:30 p.m.)	Rating:	Share:
ABC: *Voyage to the Bottom of the Sea*	15.6	30.4%
CBS: *Lassie*	**16.1**	**31.3%**
NBC: *Bell Telephone Hour*	11.7	22.8%

(7:30 – 8 p.m.)	Rating:	Share:
ABC: *Voyage to the Bottom of the Sea*	**17.2**	**30.2%**
CBS: *My Favorite Martian*	17.0	29.8%
NBC: *Walt Disney's Wonderful World of Color*	14.7	25.8%

4.4

"Escape from Venice" (Episode 36)
(Prod. #8204; first aired Sunday, October 17, 1965)
Written by Charles Bennett
Directed by Alex March
Produced by Irwin Allen and William Welch; Story Editor: Sidney Marshall
Co-Starring Renzo Cesana, Vincent Gardenia, Delphi Lawrence

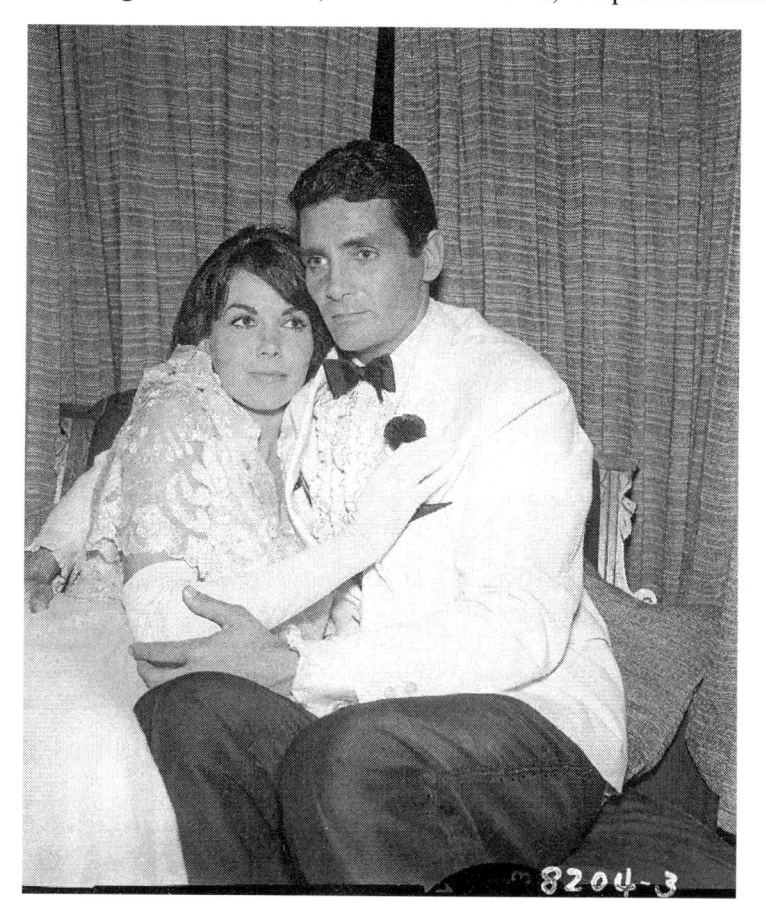

From the *Voyage* show files (Irwin Allen papers collection):

> When Crane is sent to Venice to obtain the deterrent to the ultimate weapon of an enemy power, he becomes trapped and hunted by both the police and the enemy. He is the only man in the world who possesses the sonic key to the secret information but, wounded and helpless, he has no chance to escape until Nelson effects his rescue.[1]

Assessment:

This spy caper might have worked better during *Voyage*'s first season, in the dark shadows of moody black and white. In bright, eye-popping primary hues, it comes off like a run-of-the-mill *Man from U.N.C.L.E.* emulation. Not bad; not great; certainly enjoyable.

Resident guest critic Mark Phillips said, "This episode was cut from *The Man from U.N.C.L.E.* mold (a schoolteacher helping the submariners, beautiful women everywhere, colorful villains, exciting chases). And it works. Although it's a backlot chase through Venice, the music and stock footage give it an added dimension. Renzo Cesana is so strange that his repellent charm is almost fascinating as nasty Count Staglione. Danica D'Hondt, as Lola Hale, is terrific, and it's too bad she didn't return for future shows." [2]

Co-guest critic Mike Bailey commented, "As Mark says, this episode feels more than slightly like *The Man from U.N.C.L.E.* show which caused ABC to move *Voyage* from its Monday time slot. This episode's a bit on the light side, complicated as all get-out and fun to watch. The budget, rather than being spent on effects, goes for back-lot location shooting and set dressing to excellent effect." [3]

We too found things to like. The idea of trying to escape from a city surrounded by water is intriguing. Terry Becker, as usual, is a delight, and Allan Hunt's Seaman Riley is finally given the chance to shine. The fight above and underwater between a wounded Captain Crane and a Venice policeman more bent on killing than arresting is well staged (pity poor David Hedison for spending hours submerged in the studio backlot Moat, with water that has been described as "foul"); and the fight in the pottery shop, with rack after rack of breakables, is also well played.

You may recall David Hedison's complaint that "the producer keeps promising a story with an Embassy party where I could wear a dinner jacket, a blonde in one hand and a martini in the other. But I'm still waiting." [4] Well, Crane finally gets to wear that dinner jacket – into the canals of Venice, spending a good portion of the episode in those wretched waters. Meanwhile, Richard Basehart got to keep his dinner jacket dry, has a blonde at his side, and gets comfortable in a casino with a bourbon and water. Could it really be true that Irwin Allen didn't have a sense of humor?

"Escape from Venice" makes an entertaining escape for viewers.

Script:

Charles Bennett's writers contract: May 5, 1965.
Bennett's story treatment approved on May 21.
Bennett's final-draft teleplay approved on June 18.
Rev. Shooting Final teleplay (gold paper): July 20.
Page revisions (pink): July 21.
Page revisions (green paper): July 22.
Page revisions (yellow paper): July 26.
Page revisions (beige paper): July 27.

Famed screenwriter **Charles Bennett**, who had written many of Irwin Allen's movies, including 1961's *Voyage to the Bottom of the Sea*, returned to the series after having written the late Season One entry, "Secret of the Loch." Bennett, now 65, had been nominated for an Academy Award for his screenplay for the 1940 Alfred Hitchcock film, *Foreign Correspondent*. He had also written other Hitchcock

Alfred Hitchcock and writer Charles Bennett in the 1930s.

classics: *Blackmail*, *The 39 Steps*, and both the 1934 and 1956 versions of *The Man Who Knew Too Much*, and others. Yet at this point, Bennett appeared limited to finding work with Irwin Allen's television shows. He finished his career with five more assignments on *Voyage* and one for *Land of the Giants*. And he grumbled all the way to the bank.

Mary Garbutt, from ABC's Continuity Acceptance Department, wrote to Allen and his staff on July 8, 1965:

> Standard caution on the "effects" of the blade dart, blood stains, and "marks of the furious battle." ... Pleace be sure that the Italian spoken is acceptable…. Hotel Danolo, the newspaper masthead and gossip column must be fictitious…. Your usual care in seeing that the cries of the pain, the arm pressures are not "over-done." [5]

Production:
(Filmed July 26 through August 2, 1965; 6 days)

Alex March was hired to direct. He was 44, and had directed the 1962 TV movie version of *The Paradine Case*, which starred Richard Basehart. Also for television, March directed episodes of the gritty police drama *Naked City*, as well as other hour-long episodics filmed in New York, including *The Doctors and the Nurses*; *The Defenders*; George C. Scott series *East Side/West Side*; and for the precursor for *Law and Order*, a series called *Arrest and Trial*. Moving to Hollywood, March directed episodes of *Ben Casey*, and then came to 20th Century-Fox with assignments on *The Long Hot Summer*. This was his first of two *Voyage* episodes for March.

Renzo Cesana, playing Count Ferdie Staglione, received $900. A more gifted actor in a lead guest star role would have commanded $2,500 in 1965. This is not to say that Cesana wasn't known. At 57, he had worn many hats – actor, screenwriter, author, songwriter, radio show creator, and advertising man. As an actor, Cesana starred in his own TV series during 1953 and '54, called *The Continental*. That was also the name of his character, who would welcome

Above: Renzo Cesana as "The Continental," circa 1952. Left: Christopher Walken impersonating Cesana on *Saturday Night Live*.

the camera (representing a desirable female visitor) into his plush apartment, light her cigarette, offer her champagne, and charm her with his continental ways. (Christopher Walken routinely parodied *The Continental* on *Saturday Night Live*.)

Vincent Gardenia played the mercenary contact Bellini. He was a highly respected character actor halfway into a career of well over 100 screen appearances. Besides winning OBIE and Tony awards for his work on stage, Gardenia won an Emmy in 1990, for *Age-Old Friends*, and was nominated twice for Oscars, for 1973's *Bang the Drum Slowly* and 1987's *Moonstruck*, as Cher's father. He may be best remembered, however, for a recurring role on *All in the Family,* as Archie Bunker's neighbor, Frank Lorenzo. He was paid $325 for one day's work on this *Voyage*.

Above: Vincent Gardenia with David Hedison.
Bottom: Delphi Lawrence in her leading lady of the B-pictures period.

Delphi Lawrence was 33 when cast as Julietta. She was big for a short while in small films, co-starring in 1955's *Murder on Approval*, 1957's *Strangers' Meeting*, and 1958's *Blind Spot*. Lawrence was also in the cast of 1958's *Son of Robin Hood*, which starred a young Al (David) Hedison. And she did a whole lot of TV in England. Lawrence received $500 for four days. In the early versions of the script, and even in the shooting schedule, Juliana was named Loveland.

Rachel Romen played Alicia, the female agent killed in the Teaser. They needed someone who could carry a tune and kiss, and since she played "Singing Nympho" in the 1961 exploitation film, *Shock Corridor*, Romen got the job. She had the lead in another exploitative offering, as the title character in 1965's *The Desert Raven*. She was also the title character in 1966's *Girl from Tobacco Row*.

Danica D'Hondt played Lola Hale, seen on the "video phone." She had been up for the Tiffany Loveland part – in the shooting schedule, the set we see her on is named "Int. Loveland's Office." In the hours before filming began, D'Hondt's character got a name change to Lola. D'Hondt had co-starred in an exploitation film of her own – 1961's *Living Venus*.

About Tiffany Loveland, David Hedison told Joan Crosby, of the syndicated "TV Scout" column, "The producer said he would know the girl the minute she walked into his office, and every actress in town has tested for the part. But so far no Tiffany." [6]

With what Irwin Allen saved on the cast, he made up for in production value and music.

Nelson Riddle provided the score. Riddle had been nominated for 13 Grammy, Emmy, and Academy Awards, winning two. His movies included *Oceans 11*, *Robin and the 7 Hoods*, *Paint Your Wagon*, *Can-Can*, *Li'l Abner*, *The Great Gatsby*, and *Lolita*. Some of the TV themes he did not get nominations for, but perhaps should have, included *The Untouchables*, *Naked City,* and *Route 66*.

Allan Hunt said, "That episode was the direct result of Richard Basehart's campaign to get us off the sub. That was one of his favorite wishes, and the episode was gratefully accepted by the cast." [7]

Filming began Monday, July 26, 1965 on Stage 10 for "Int. Observation Nose" (with "bubble tank"), "Int. Radio Shack," "Int. Nelson's Room + Balcony" (a hotel room) and "Int. Loveland's Office" (for "TV Burn In").

Day 2: The work on Tuesday was split between Stage 10 and the "French Street" on the Fox lot. On Stage 10, they finished with Nelson's Hotel room and balcony. The outdoor set served for "Ext. Alleyway + Venice Street." They filmed until 9:10 at night.

Day 3: Wednesday saw the company back on Stage 10 for additional temporary sets, with "Int. Staglione's Headquarters" and "Int. Casino."

Day 4: Thursday. The company was on Fox Stage 2, filming "Ext. Venice Street," "Ext. Glass Store, "Ext. Venice Alley" and "Int. Antique Shop."

Day 5: Friday. And since it was a Friday, everyone knew they would be filming late ... until 10:40 p.m., in fact. It started on Stage 10, for pickup shots needed in Nelson's Hotel Room & Balcony, as well as more pickups in the Int. Casino set, then outdoors to film around the Moat, both in daylight and after dark, for "Ext. Canal & Gondola Landing."

Day 6: Monday, August 2. The backlot Moat also provided for "Ext. Sidewalk Café," "Int. Gondola (Under Canopy)" and "Ext. Gondola Landing." In order to keep from going into a seventh day of production, director Alex March filmed until 9:12 p.m. [8]

A budget of $145,391 was approved by William Self. Due to the late-night filming, it ended up costing $173,277. [9]

Release / Reaction:
(ABC premiere airing: 10/17/65. Network repeat broadcast: 8/21/66)

The Cincinnati Kid, starring Steve McQueen, was the biggest film in movie houses. "Yesterday," by the Beatles, was still the song getting the most airplay on radio stations across America. And *Help!*, also by the Beatles, remained the fastest-selling album. Red Skelton had the top-rated CBS variety show, and the cover of America's top-selling magazine, *TV Guide*. Irwin Allen's second series, *Lost in Space*, aired its sixth episode, "Welcome Stranger," in which the Robinsons are visited by a lost space traveler from Earth, played by Warren Oates. A.C. Nielsen pronounced the series a hit, easily winning its time slot.

"TV Scout," syndicated around the country, said:

> *Voyage to the Bottom of the Sea* doesn't have much plot, but it hides that small detail under a superabundance of gimmicks, men talking into all kinds of communicating gadgets, and lots of people falling into Venice's canals. For it is here that David Hedison gets the snatch of melody that will unscramble a valuable computer tape, is framed for murder, and has to be rescued by Richard Basehart, who spends a lot of time at a gaming table. [10]

There were little to no science-fiction elements to this episode, which may have had a negative effect on the ratings. *Voyage* was a strong second place during its first half hour, but when *My Favorite Martian* and *Walt Disney* hit the air, *Voyage*'s predominantly young and male audience jumped ship.

A.C. Nielsen 30-City survey from October 17, 1965 (time period winner in boldface)[11]:

(7 – 7:30 p.m.)	Rating:	Share:
ABC: *Voyage to the Bottom of the Sea*	13.6	29.1%
CBS: Lassie	**17.3**	**37.0%**
NBC: Special	8.1	17.3%

(7:30 – 8 p.m.)	Rating:	Share:
ABC: *Voyage to the Bottom of the Sea*	12.8	22.4%
CBS: My Favorite Martian	**19.3**	**33.8%**
NBC: *Walt Disney's Wonderful World of Color*	18.7	32.7%

After this unexpected plunge in the ratings, associate producer Frank La Tourette wrote to Irwin Allen and staff:

> "ESCAPE FROM VENICE" was an excellent show ... with a ruinous rating. This bears out the conviction held by Adrian Samish [of ABC] that our shows must stick to the sea and stories relating directly to it. [12]

94

4.5

"The Cyborg" (Episode 37)
(Prod. #8205; first aired Sunday, October 10, 1965)
Written by William Read Woodfield and Allan Balter
Directed by Leo Penn
Produced by Irwin Allen and Frank La Tourette; Story Editor: Sidney Marshall
Special Guest Star Victor Buono; Co-Starring Brooke Bundy

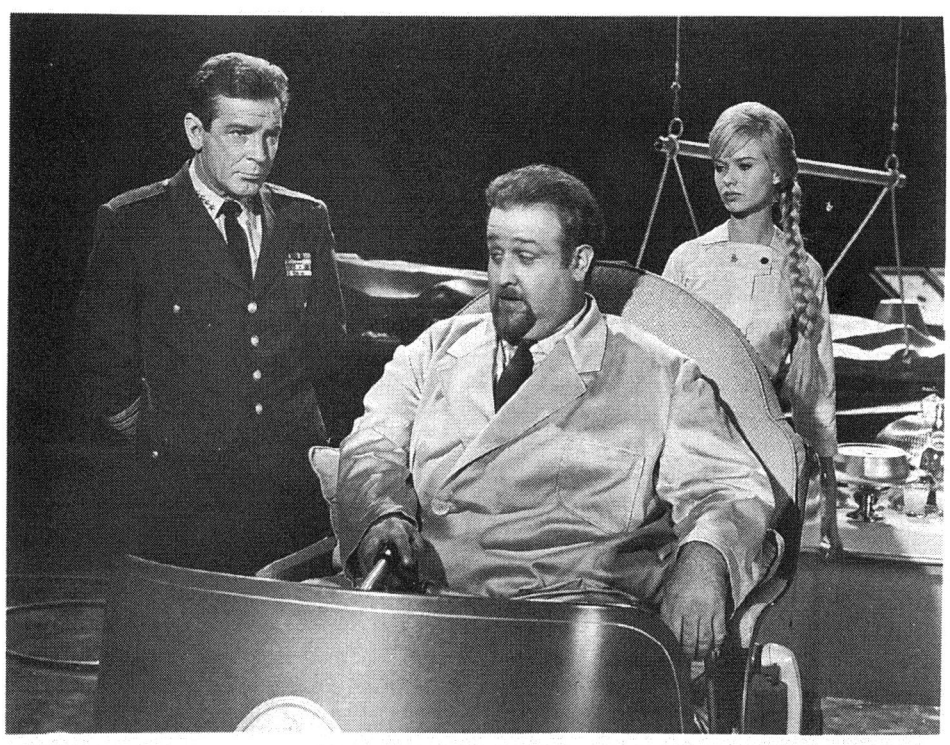

THE CYBORG ... Adm. Nelson (Richard Basehart) evaluates Tabor Ulrich's (Victor Buono) argument as Gundi (Brooke Bundy) looks on in "The Cyborg" episode of 20th Century-Fox Television's VOYAGE TO THE BOTTOM OF THE SEA series, seen this (day) at (time) on (channel). #8205/34

From the *Voyage* show files (Irwin Allen papers collection):

> A brilliant scientist has built a super computer which can equip a cybernetic organism with all human learning. On an inspection visit to the Nelson lab, Nelson is forced to feed his knowledge to the computer's memory bank. A cyborg, identical to Nelson both physically and mentally, is then sent back to the Seaview and deludes the crew into believing that World War III has already started. He attempts to convince

Crane to retaliate with Seaview missiles which, in the resultant crises, would enable the scientist to take over the world. [1]

Assessment:

A full year before *Star Trek* presented an evil android duplicate of the star ("What Are Little Girls Made Of?", October 20, 1966), a mad scientist makes a copy of Nelson. Does that earn a little respect? Not for some.

"*Voyage* gets really stupid for the first time," criticized resident guest critic Mike Bailey. "Many fans like these kinds of episodes for their wacky goofiness. My apologies – I felt (and still feel) that they were a waste of the show's potential. By now, we were all aware of what the cast, crew and writers were capable of – a lot! Although certainly not *Voyage* at its worst, it was this kind of pabulum that eventually killed the show. Despite Nelson's tacked-on comments about humanity, this episode is really the first *Voyage* that had nothing to do with making comment on the human condition, but rather existed solely for the purpose of providing over-the-top calisthenics for young eyeballs. Accepting *Voyage*'s new direction as a Sunday night kids show, writer William Read Woodfield had decided to take the money and run." [2]

We respectfully disagree. We consider "The Cyborg" a triumph. Victor Buono was delightfully icky. And Richard Basehart certainly earned his paycheck. His performance during the torture scenes alone is stunning, even somewhat disturbing for a show aired in the family hour on an ofttimes skittish TV network. But don't let these standout moments cause you to overlook the less flamboyant ones. Brooke Bundy is fetching; her underplayed characterization intriguing and, in the end, deeply moving. The clever Morse Code sequence at the climax is beautifully realized, by director and performer. Or, we should say, performers – David Hedison's reactions are priceless. And it's even more effective due to director Leo Penn's filming upwards through the transparent tabletop.

Penn delivers the goods throughout. He coaxed flawless portrayals from the entire cast. Nancy Hsueh's transformation from a tearfully emotional "Trish" Sweetly to expressionless vapid android is eerily effective. And watch for the tense reactions on the sweaty faces of the Seaview crew during the missile launch countdown – just one more moment that works flawlessly.

Alexander Courage's score is inspired; technical aspects are top-rate, from the manufacturing of the cyborg (dig that shaving cream coming alive from the wind of a fan!) to the split-screen process, to the quick cutting and rat-a-tat-tat gunplay that heighten the realistic shootout on the Seaview. And what about the shot to the head that brings it to a stunning end?! When was the last time you saw anyone take a bullet in the forehead in a 1965 TV program?

We get all these delights and a classic death scene for the villain, as his electrified body stiffens and, in frozen horror, mimics the sparking cut-out behind him.

The artists and technicians who came together for "The Cyborg" accomplished all of this, on a TV schedule and budget, and while programmed to service the network's family hour on the Sabbath. Remarkable!

Script:

William Read Woodfield's and Allan Balter's writers contract: June 22, 1965.
Woodfield's and Balter's story treatment approved on July 12.
2nd Rev. Shooting Final teleplay (on yellow paper): July 28.
Page revisions (on blue paper): August 2.

William Read Woodfield and Allan Balter were back at their typewriters.

Mary Garbutt, of ABC Continuity Acceptance Department, had a long list of concerns and grievances over the script. She wrote to Irwin Allen and his staff on July 21, 1965:

> Pgs 1 & 2: Of course, Falkonmatt Laboratory, International Bionics, Tabot Ulrich must be Fictitious names.
>
> Pg 2: Caution on the "skintight" outfit.

> Pg 2, 12, 13, etc.: Your usual care in seeing that the Cyborg figures, completed or in the process of being developed, do not tend towards the unpleasant or gruesome. For ex: the dermo-plasm indicated rather by blocks than a gelatinous substance; the muscular and nervous system indicated by wires rather than exposed muscle tissue and capillaries, etc. Can only be approved on color film. …
>
> Pg 19: Eliminate the "searing pain" induced by the machine so that Nelson's unconsciousness results not from pain but from his inner fight to stop the process of "the rape of his mind." [3]

And what an "inner fight" Richard Basehart presents. If his screams don't convey "searing pain," nothing will. Bully for Woodfield and Balter for describing it as "the rape of his mind" in the script, and bully to Basehart for interpreting it so compellingly.

Mary Garbutt continued:

> Pg 35A: Just before the simulated attack, please repeat the date 1976. Perhaps on this page: "Our 1976 Zurich Peace Conference, etc".
>
> Pg 42, Sc 97: The knife going into the Cyborg's head must be off camera. Per discussion with Mr. La Tourette: Pgs 45 thru 50: The whole Conelrad section, accompanying dialogue, beeps, etc., will be deleted, as this sequence will only tend to confuse and alarm viewers and/or listeners. …
>
> Pg 50: WJBT must be fictitious radio call letters; Please sub. for "Those dirty…" or complete the line.
>
> Pg 52 (voiceover filter): Delete: "This is the President of the United States"; "Dozens of our great cities are in flames and millions of lives have been lost"; "I call on you to avenge your country's dead and dying". [4]

Per ABC's request, the voice was not identified as belonging to "the President" in the aired episode. And the lines were made less descriptive and gruesome. But you will note that the words are nonetheless spoken with a Texas accent. Granted, this was supposed to be 1976 … but the episode was made in 1965, when LBJ, with a heavy heart, occupied the White House.

The censor's notes continued:

> Pg 55: Substitute for "The President..." in Crane's line.
>
> Pg 61-62: Please be sure that the Morse Code does not include SOS or other actual distress signal but reads as indicated "Abort firing" etc.
>
> Pg 63: Standard caution on blood [and] man hit by bullets. Please have automatic weapon "futuristic".

The gun was not futuristic. As noted earlier, it was a shot to the head. One final note, but Basehart saved the moment anyway.

> Pg 65: Of course, as indicated, Ulrich's death must be off camera. Also caution on Nelson's reaction – he must not shudder in horror. [5]

Production:
(Filmed August 3 – 12, 1965; 7 and ¾ days)

Director **Leo Penn** was paid $3,000. An actor turned TV director, Penn had directed 19 episodes of *Ben Casey* and nine for *Dr. Kildare*. He did well with hospital settings. But his one assignment on *Voyage*, as well as one for *Lost in Space* at this time ("There Were Giants in the Earth"), fell behind schedule. Penn was a good director, but hardly fast enough for Irwin Allen's needs. He also had trouble with his one and only *Star Trek* assignment ("The Enemy Within," filmed one year after this). Science fiction, with attendant effects, just

Leo Penn.

took too long for Penn. Less flashy productions were more his style, and Penn went on to have a successful career doing anything but sci-fi. Among many others, he helmed 19 episodes of *Marcus Welby, M.D.* and 27 episodes of *Matlock*. He did well as a father, too. His sons are award-winning actor Chris Penn, 1980s popular recording artist and soundtrack composer Michael Penn, and Sean Penn, the Oscar-winning actor and director.

Of his latest script with Allan Balter, William Read Woodfield said, "That was one of our best shows. I had read a book called *The Cyborg*, about cybernetic organisms. It was very early in the game for that kind of subject. We put a story together and Orson Welles ran through our minds as the lead, but we figured we couldn't get him, so that led to Victor Buono." [6]

Victor Buono, 27, was paid $2,500 to play Ulrich. He had been nominated for an Oscar in 1963 for his supporting role in *Whatever Happened to Baby Jane?*, and was becoming a big draw on television, usually as maniacal characters. He'd soon have recurring roles on *The Wild, Wild West* (as evil magician Count Manzeppi) and *Batman* (as the villainous King Tut).

Above: Robert Conrad with Victor Buono, in one of Buono's four turns on *The Wild, Wild West*. Right: Brooke Bundy.

Brooke Bundy received $750 for the role of Gundi. She was 20 and only in her third year of a screen acting career that would span three decades with more than 100 notable appearances, including stopovers on many iconic series from this period and beyond, such as *Route 66*, *The Man from U.N.C.L.E.*, *Gunsmoke*, *Bonanza*, *Dragnet 1967*, *Mission: Impossible*, and *The Mod Squad*.

The character of Loveland had been written into this script, but changed to "Tish Sweetly" and played by **Nancy Hsueh**. The lovely Hsueh had been making the rounds with guest spots on series such as *My Three Sons*, *Maverick*, and *The Man from U.N.C.L.E.*, with roles soon to come on *I Spy* and *The Wild, Wild West*. She would play the top female role in the 1968 cult film, *Targets*.

Alexander Courage provided the score. He had already scored two episodes of *Voyage* during its first season ("The Fear Makers" and "The Price of Doom"), with three more to go after this. One year from now, Courage would

Nancy Hsueh.

begin work on *Lost in Space*, scoring seven episodes for its second and third season, as well as working for *Star Trek*. He'd already put music to the two *Trek* pilot films (1964 and '65), and would score several episodes for the series. Also in Courage's future: an Emmy, plus two other Emmy nominations, and two Academy Award nominations (for *The Pleasure Seekers* and *Dr. Doolittle*).

Filming began on Tuesday, August 3, 1965 for the first of three days on Stage 10. On the first day, while filming in the Control Room and the Observation Nose, they also filmed color shots of the stars for the new opening title sequence. On the third day (Thursday), besides working on the Seaview sets, they filmed on two temporary sets – "Int. Ante Room (Konserthuset Hall)" and "Int. Tish Sweetly's Office."

The next five days were spent on Stage B, filming the remainder of the various new sets needed, with four-and-a-half of those days spent in the black void set identified in the shooting schedule as "Int. Konserthuset Hall." The blackout curtains in the background helped add to the surrealism. [7]

Richard Basehart gives a wallop of a performance in these scenes, and Victor Buono pushes back wonderfully as one of his patented diabolical foils. Both actors were insightful, and they spark off each other, elevating their scenes together to stimulating heights. Brooke Bundy, in a sense, is the "straight man" between these two dynamic personalities. Her serene contribution is an essential ingredient to this recipe of success.

On the final day of production (the eighth day of filming), after beginning on Stage B with "Int. Falkonmatt Lab," the company moved back to Stage 10 for the "Int. Flying Sub" set. The last shot was completed at 4:30 in the afternoon, bringing this production to seven and three-quarters days.[8]

Of course, this played havoc with the budget, which had been set at $144,738. When all was said and done, it reached $184,953. That translated to over $1.5 million in 2020.[9]

With this *Voyage* and his one *Lost in Space* both going into overtime, Penn was not invited for a return visit. It was our loss.

Release / Reaction:
(ABC premiere airdate: 10/10/65; network repeat broadcast: 3/27/66)

Anne Francis, as *Honey West*, TV's first female private eye, had the cover of *TV Guide*. Inside the issue was a striking color story on the filming of

Above: Inspired lighting "gags" enhanced this stylistic episode. Below: Richard Basehart in make-up, being transformed into an android.

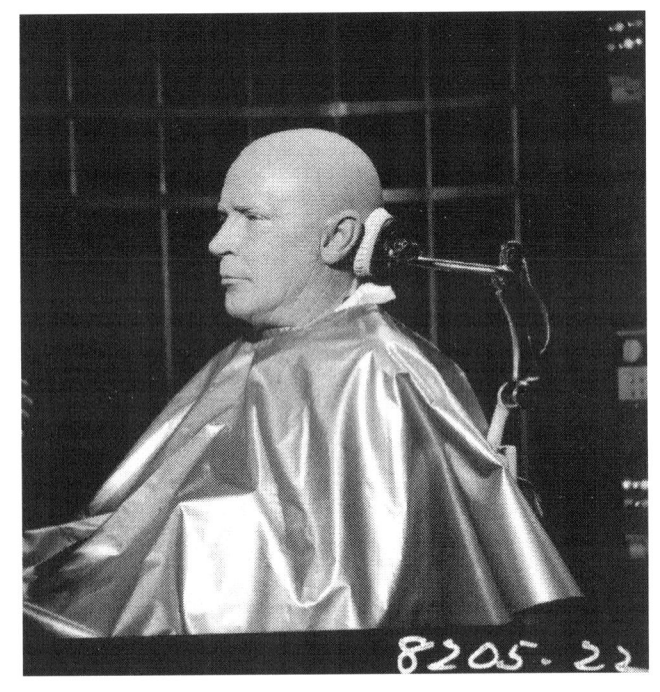

"Jonah and the Whale." David Hedison and two other Seaview divers, in wetsuits

and full scuba gear, were shown walking down the esophagus and into the belly of a giant whale.

Basehart, Buono, and Bundy rehearse, "blocking the shot" for the lighting crew, on Stage "B."

The week before "The Cyborg" first aired, Victor Buono was featured in a syndicated newspaper article called "Will Success – or Wide Screen – Spoil Vic Buono?" Its insensitive focus was the actor's weight. The unnamed writer said:

> Home viewers seldom have more than a 20-inch screen and that can fill up pretty easily when Buono hoves into camera range. He squashes the scales at 350 pounds worth every

time he weighs himself. But he's not worried at all. "Why, I'm positively thin," he said on the set where they were filming the Oct. 10 episode of *Voyage to the Bottom of the Sea*. "I used to weigh 412. My weight is distressing only to my tailor and the wardrobe people." [10]

Richard Basehart was the subject of a syndicated feature article the week "The Cyborg" aired. The unidentified writer said:

> No matter how wild or crazy the scripts of *Voyage to the Bottom of the Sea* get, Richard Basehart will take them seriously. [11]

Basehart told the interviewer, "Look, I hope to be acting a long time after the series goes off the air. I can't afford to take any episode lightly and fluff my way through. The script may stink but I don't want to." [12]

The writer revealed:

> Actually, Basehart, who is often considered one of the country's most distinguished actors, enjoys the "wild" episodes of his ABC-TV series more than he does the ones that are supposedly "sane and serious." He is delighted that this year he and co-star David Hedison (a good pal on and off the *Voyage* set at 20th Century-Fox) are being involved in cases with man-eating whales and submarines that also fly. They break the monotony. [13]

"Oh, once in a while we'd tear into Irwin Allen and threaten to leave the show, but we aren't really serious," Basehart said. "The worst show I've done on the series can't compare to any of the bad films I've done…. All I want to do is live my life with dignity – and that's what I'm doing now." [14]

"TV Scout," in newspapers across America, previewed this episode:

> World War III is averted by about three seconds on *Voyage to the Bottom of the Sea*. Seems gluttonous, mad scientist Victor Buono has created a Cyborg (Cybernetic Organism replica of Richard Basehart) which he sends aboard the Seaview to start the war. Things look bad for the crew of the Seaview when they receive, through computers in the glutton's lab, word that the war has started. But the real

Basehart, a prisoner of Buono's, makes magnificently imaginative use of Morse Code to save the day. [15]

Rival syndicated preview column "TV Key" said:

> The kids should eat this one up. It's a combination science-fiction adventure and horror story about a mad, obese scientist (Victor Buono), who rules an army of "cyborgs" (robot-like creatures who can be constructed to look like a duplicate of any human being), and devises an intricate plan to destroy all the major powers in the world. [16]

Richard Basehart named this episode as one of his favorites, from an acting perspective. He explained, "I won't say I have been happy with all the episodes we've done, but I will say I have been delighted with a few. Anytime I get a script which challenges my abilities as an actor, I get a tremendous lift and I play it to the hilt." [17]

According to A.C. Nielsen, *Voyage* ranked at No. 22 this week out of 107 network series, and was a strong second in its time period. Evidently cyborgs, like giant whales and monsters, translated to higher ratings.

A.C. Nielsen 30-city survey from October 10, 1965[18]:

(7 – 7:30 p.m.)	Rating:	Share:
ABC: *Voyage to the Bottom of the Sea*	17.8	33.1%
CBS: *Lassie*	**20.3**	**37.7**
NBC: *Bell Telephone Hour*	9.9	18.4%

(7:30 – 8 p.m.)	Rating:	Share:
ABC: *Voyage to the Bottom of the Sea*	17.9	31.3%
CBS: *My Favorite Martian*	**20.0**	**35.0%**
NBC: *Walt Disney's Wonderful World of Color*	12.6	22.1%

4.6

"The Deadliest Game" (Episode 38)

(Prod. #8206; first aired Sunday, October 31, 1965)
Written by Rik Vollaerts
Directed by Sobey Martin
Produced by Irwin Allen and William Welch; Story Editor: Sidney Marshall
Guest Star Lloyd Bochner; Co-Starring Audrey Dalton, Robert Cornthwaite,
and Robert F. Simon

From the *Voyage* show files (Irwin Allen papers collection):

The President of the U.S. tests a new, impenetrable shelter at the bottom of the sea and suddenly finds himself trapped and completely cut off. A retired five-star general, who helped Nelson construct the site, immediately blames the enemy and intends to launch an attack. The sabotage is actually the General's plan to provide himself with an excuse to strike the first blow at the enemy, and ultimately take over the country. [1]

Assessment:

Shades of *Dr. Strangelove (or How I Learned to Stop Worrying and Love the Bomb)*, with an obsessed General trying to start World War III. The idea of having the President of the United States trapped in the underwater facility intended to keep him safe was a good high-concept premise. Too bad the idea is wasted.

The plot in the generically-titled "The Deadliest Game" is by the numbers and the characterizations are shallow. Everything is on the surface with the maniacal General Hobson (Lloyd Bochner), his cohorts, General Michaels (Robert Cornthwaite) and Dr. Parrish (Audrey Dalton), and even, for the most part, the President (Robert F. Simon). They state the obvious and wear their one-dimensional personalities on their sleeves.

Something may have been made of Dalton's character – there is a hint of sinister intent in her – but, due to various script cuts during rewriting, the potential is never realized. As for the President, we must wonder how a man so undynamic got elected in the first place. He blindly trusts, even when it is clear to any five-year-old watching that he should not. Then, in a half-hearted effort to allow him to seem wise, he tells Crane, "Does any man ever know another?" A President should make a better effort than that to know the people he trusts!

The worst characterization is that of the chief villain. Gen. Hobson is a nothing character portrayed in a bland manner, wrapped up in a military uniform. Any writer, in his sleep, should have been able to do more with a top military man going rogue. Putting a gun in his hand is hardly a

Lloyd Bochner in Season One's "The Fear-Makers," with a bad-guy character you could almost root for, because of hie determination.

characterization. Despite the obvious mediocrity of the character as written, we expected better from guest star Lloyd Bochner. Compare this performance with the one Bochner delivered in Season One's "The Fear-Makers." The characters are similar – both trusted officials who are up to no good. But, in "The Fear-Makers," Bochner presents a multi-dimensional character, with emotional impact. Here, he seems to be phoning it in.

Mark Phillips said, "A lesson in how to disarm a great guest cast. The usually excellent Lloyd Bochner is wasted as General Hobson, and he is limited to standing around and issuing sinister threats with a phony mustache pasted on his face. Meanwhile, the great Audrey Dalton combines beauty and sensuous evil with a promising performance but she's cut off before she can have much fun. … Otherwise, an incredibly dreary and boring episode, one of the real snoozers of Year Two. Even the chase scenes look like they're out of the Republic serials, and scenes in an undersea reactor room seem to go on forever. The episode ends with a whimper, not a bang. One interesting note: this is the only *Voyage* episode, to my recollection, that actually mentions a contemporary, real-life person (Gen. Douglas MacArthur) and the events surrounding MacArthur's controversial firing by Eisenhower." [2]

Mike Bailey added, "To paraphrase a famous line in *King Kong*, 'It wasn't the airplanes that killed the episode, it was writer Rik Vollaerts and director Sobey Martin.'" [3]

Script:

Rik Vollaerts' writers contract: June 28, 1965.
Vollaerts' story treatment approved: July 12.
Vollaerts' Final Draft teleplay approved: August 5.
Rev. Shooting Final teleplay (beige paper): August 6.
Page revisions (blue paper): August 8.
Page revisions (pink paper): August 11.

Hendrik "Rik" Vollaerts had written for *Science Fiction Theatre*, a low-budget half-hour anthology, in 1955 and '56. He and *Star Trek*'s creator, Gene Roddenberry, separately, wrote for *Harbor Command*, a half-hour Ziv series about the Coast Guard (1957-59). That association got Vollaerts a *Star Trek* script assignment in 1968. In between, he wrote multiple scripts for Ziv cheapies like *M Squad* and *Highway Patrol*, and other series of the day such as *Whirlybirds* and *Lassie*. He even wrote a *My Favorite Martian*, before embarking on a pair of Season One *Voyage*s. Three more would follow during Seasons Two and Three.

Irwin Allen sent in his notes after reading Vollaerts' first-draft teleplay, and there were many – five pages, including:

P. 5: Hobson has asked "What can it be?" Nelson's answer is strange. He says they both know the answer. This is not true. Nelson's answer should be – "I don't know, but I hope it's nothing more serious than a failure in their radio contact." ...

P. 8: There is a point which should have been made by Nelson.
(1) Once contact with Deep Center was cut off, no one knows whether the President or anyone inside the Center is still alive.
(2) When Nelson contacts the Center over the cable, he should ask first for Crane and find out if the President is alright.
(3) Shouldn't there be some specific code used in making this contact?
(4) Shouldn't the President state that he will fire missiles only if it becomes evident that an attack is in progress and ask to be kept informed of any change in the alert system? ...

P. 14: Michaels says: "You must issue the order!" President should answer: "Gentlemen, <u>when</u> and <u>if</u> Intelligence pinpoints the country responsible for this attack, I assure you we will retaliate. But not until then!" ...

P. 20: Crane's reasoning about explosives would destroy the shuttle sub is not a good enough reason not trying them. It should be that the amount of explosives necessary to blast the outer door would most certainly cause the whole Center to collapse.

Somewhere in ACT I or the end of ACT I, a red light should have warned that the reactor was building up. This would lend some action to an otherwise action-less first Act, as Crane and one of his men would have to investigate and discover the build-up. Possible attempt to shut it off, resulting in some exciting action, should occur.

P. 22: It would be better if Crane doesn't address the man as "Mr. Secretary" as this might be objectionable [to ABC], intimating that the Secretary of State is mentally unstable.

> P. 25: Before Nelson contacts the Center, he should ask for the reactor build-up figures from the computer. The answer he gets should be such that the build-up is unstable and irregular – meaning that he cannot say for sure just when it will reach critical mass. You need this extra frightening element to add suspense to story.
>
> Pg 27: ... Instead of hearing a high-pitched whine, show the sub going crazy – lights lighting, sirens blowing, etc. Then Nelson saying, "Full battle evasion tactics!" (If the beam caused trouble at Deep Center, it is bound to do great damage to the Sub. No "ifs" about it.) ...
>
> P. 40: Bottom of the page: Why does Nelson allow Hobson to see the little black box? He wouldn't tell him everything as he suspects him already....
>
> ACT III needs an exciting ending. Perhaps Nelson and his men attempt to overpower Parrish and Act ends without our knowing if Nelson is dead or alive.
>
> ACT IV: P. 51: In this conference the President should finally tell all present about the atomic reactor. It should be a question of which will happen first – the oxygen running out in one hour, or the reactor reaching critical mass within minutes. Suspense! Suspense! Suspense!...
>
> General notes: Riley, Sharkey and Kowalski should be given some lines. They don't say a word <u>ever</u>. Action has been suggested in notes, instead of just reporting on what's going on. There is too much repetition of patriotic talk. [4]

Ironically, the character of Lydia Parrish was more developed in earlier drafts of the script, including a death scene. By the time the script was filmed, the character was a mere abbreviation.

Production:
(Filmed August 12 – 20, 1965; 6 days)

Sobey Martin was hired to direct. William Read Woodfield, whose office was next to Irwin Allen's, said, "Irwin either got very young directors, who were up-and-coming and good, or he got very old ones who shot *Voyage* fast. Sobey Martin would line everybody up in a row of five and, when they had a speech, they would lean forward and Sobey would get the shot in one take." [5]

Martin, who was certainly capable of good work, evidenced by his direction in superior episodes such as Season One's "Mutiny" and "The Invaders," and the series' two whale tales (to date), "The Ghost of Moby Dick" and "Jonah and the Whale," was snoozing through this assignment.

Lloyd Bochner was paid $2,500 for his second *Voyage*. Between the late 1940s and early 2000s, Bochner was never idle, making more than 200 screen appearances. Prior to *Voyage*, he had been a regular on Rod Taylor's 1960-61 series *Hong Kong*, and *The Richard Boone Show* (1963-64). Along with "The Fear-Makers," check out Bochner's portrayal of Zachariah Skull in the 1966 *Wild, Wild West* episode, "The Night of the Puppeteer"; his villainous characterization in 1967's *Point Blank*, where he beats Lee Marvin to a pulp; and his trip into *The Twilight Zone*, with the classic, "To Serve Man." Even though we don't see evidence of it here, Bochner had the acting chops.

Lloyd Bochner with Rod Taylor, in the TV series *Hong Kong*. (1960, 20th Century-Fox Television)

Audrey Dalton played Lydia Parrish. She was 31 and paid $200 a day with a two-day guarantee. She began her work in films with third billing in 1952's *My Cousin Rachel*, behind Olivia de Havilland and Richard Burton. Not a bad start. The curious *The Girls of Pleasure Island*, from 1953, followed, and Dalton was prominently featured in *Titanic*, from the same year. Next came the 1954 Bob Hope comedy *Casanova's Big Night*. She had top female honors (and second billing) in several movies, including 1954's *Drum Beat*, starring Alan Ladd, and 1957's *The Monster That Challenged the World*. Dalton was given the lead in 1959's *This Other Eden*.

Robert Cornthwaite was 43 when he played Gen. Reed Michaels, his second role on *Voyage* (following "Turn Back the Clock"). He was an actor on stage as well as screen, both big and small, with over a hundred appearances at this point, and another hundred plus to come, along with an Emmy nomination for the 1990s series *Picket Fences*. One of his most memorable performances was in 1951's *The Thing (from Another World)*, as Dr. Carrington, the

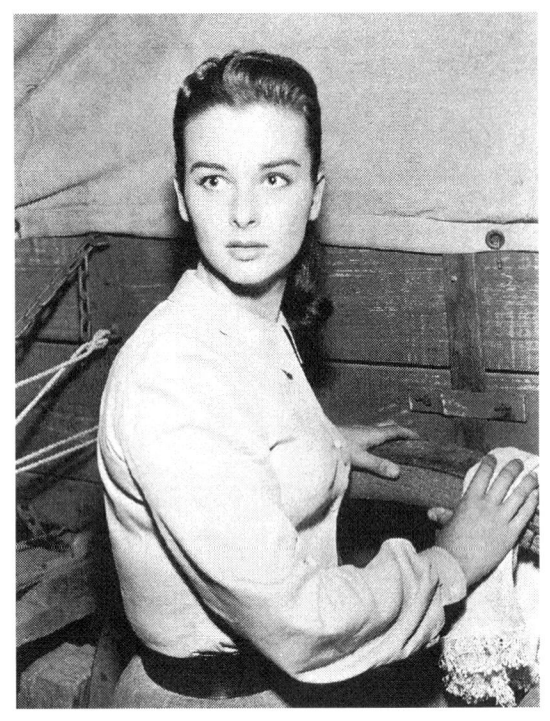

Above: Audrey Dalton in a 1959 episode of Wagon Train. Left: Robert Cornthwaite.

shortsighted scientist who tried to make friends with the murderous carrot (James Arness) from outer space. For this *Voyage*, Cornthwaite was paid $250 per day with a guarantee of two days.

Robert F. Simon was 56 when he played the President. He'd had a recurring role in the 1962-63 Nick Adams series *Saints and Sinners*. Simon often played military officers, judges and politicians. He played a General in the 1963 *Outer Limits* episode, "The Zanti Misfits," and would soon be a regular, as a U.S. Cavalry General, in 1967's *Custer* TV series, then another Army General in several episodes of *M*A*S*H*. For playing in "The Deadliest Game," Simon was paid $600 per day with a guarantee of two days.

The Control Room of the Seaview was manned by crewmen who rarely had lines of dialogue, but were familiar background faces and therefore added

112

continuity. Allan Hunt explained to a convention audience, "Phil was my stand-in, and Ray Didsbury was Richard's. A tall guy, Scott MacFadden, was David's stand-in. They would always be on the set anyway. Stand-ins are used constantly because there is a painstakingly slow process of lighting the set for every shot.

Robert F. Simon.

Once the director sets out how it is going to go, there is a 10-to-15-minute wait while the lighting is made appropriate. The actors usually go to their dressing rooms to conk out, or work on their lines, or something. If you stand under the lights it taxes all your energy, so that is why their stand-ins are there. In *Voyage*, those stand-ins were actual characters who would be in the background anyway, because they were already on salary and it didn't matter if they were tired, just as long as the stars on the show weren't." [6]

Ray Didsbury said, "It's the stand-in's job to observe the actor he is covering during rehearsal…. The nature of my job was to watch Richard when he was acting and then, when they called second team and he'd retired to his dressing room, I would go through his motions for the lighting." [7]

Day 1, Thursday, August 12, 1965: Filming took place on Stage 10, for the Seaview's "Int. Control Room," then outside the Old Writers Building on the Fox lot for exterior shooting.

Day 2, Friday: More filming in the Control Room, then a move to Stage 2 for an indoor street setting, "Ext. Weymouth Street (Nite)."

Day 3, Monday: Back to Stage 10 for additional filming in the "Control Room," plus utilizing sections of the Seaview to create the "Int. Ultrasonic Furnace" set.

Day 4, Tuesday: More filming on the standing "Control Room" set, and "Int. Nelson's Cabin," then onto a temporary set, "Int. Hotel Room," with Basehart, Terry Becker, Del Monroe, and Lloyd Bochner.

Day 5, Wednesday: Stage 2 was utilized, for a modified set, "Ext. Weymouth Street & Bookshop (Nite)," and a new one: "Int. Campus Bookstore

(Nite)," where Dr. Lydia Parrish gets the jump on Nelson and Kowalski with her ray-zapping gun.

Completed FX in the scene filmed the fifth day of production, "Int. Campus Bookstore."

Days 6 and 7, Thursday and Friday, August 19 and 20: Two days filming on Stage B, which provided the "Int. Deep Center – War Room" set. In the final hours of August 20th, the Casino set from "Escape from Venice" was flown in for pickup shots needed to complete that episode. [8]

The episode was budgeted at $140,491 but ended up costing $165,896. So far, every Season Two episode had exceeded its studio-approved budget. [9]

Release / Reaction:

(ABC premiere airdate: 10/31/65; network repeat broadcast: 5/29/66)

Steve McQueen's *The Cincinnati Kid* finished its third week as the top movie in America. *Help!*, by the Beatles, was now in its ninth week as the best-selling album in stores across the United States. The Rolling Stones had the song getting the most radio play on Top 40 stations – "Get Off of My Cloud." John Astin and Carolyn Jones, of *The Addams Family*, had the eye-popping cover of

TV Guide. And *Lost in Space* had its eighth CBS broadcast with the eerie "Invaders from the Fifth Dimension."

It was October 31, 1965 – Halloween, and *Voyage*'s key audience, the kiddies, would be out trick-or-treating instead of watching TV. That may be why tonight's episode had a bit more adult appeal.

The Indianapolis Star said:

> It's junior fail-safe time, damp version. The President is visiting the impregnable nuclear shelter under the sea when things begin going haywire atomically. There's a hot-headed general who screams attack "you know who!" Cooler heads prevail and much of the show involves the frantic search for a saboteur and the desperate attempt to deactivate a nuclear device. [10]

ABC wouldn't allow the script to specify who the "you know who" was. But anyone watching TV in 1965 and old enough to tie their own shoes knew it was the Soviet Union.

"TV Key," syndicated to newspapers, said:

> A tense adventure which should keep the children interested. Adm. Nelson and his crew are dealing with high stakes as they attempt to rescue the president of the United States and other dignitaries from an underwater bomb shelter, earmarked for destruction by enemy factions. [11]

"TV Scout," another syndicated review column, said:

> The President of the U.S. and Commander Crane (David Hedison) are among those trapped in the Deep Center (the one invulnerable bomb shelter) on *Voyage to the Bottom of the Sea*. Seems the nuclear reactor is building to a critical mass because of a high intensity electronic beam. It's up to Admiral Nelson (Richard Basehart) to locate the beam, and determine if it's the work of a traitor or the enemy. Once again, the world is saved from destruction by scant seconds. [12]

According to A.C. Nielsen, *Voyage* failed to pull in a 30 share. Worse, it came in third during the second half-hour. Irwin Allen and ABC both were taking note.

Nielsen ratings report from October 31, 1965 (winner in boldface) [13]:

(7 – 7:30 p.m.)	Rating:	Peak Share:
ABC: *Voyage to the Bottom of the Sea*	15.3	27.2%
CBS: *Lassie*	**22.8**	**40.5**
NBC: Special	9.3	16.5%

(7:30 – 8 p.m.)	Rating:	Peak Share:
ABC: *Voyage to the Bottom of the Sea*	15.6	25.4%
CBS: *My Favorite Martian*	17.6	28.7%
NBC: *Walt Disney's Wonderful World of Color*	**20.8**	**33.9%**

4.7

"The Left-Handed Man" (Episode 39)

(Prod. #8207; first aired Sunday, October 24, 1965)
Written by William Welch
Directed by Jerry Hopper
Produced by Irwin Allen and Frank La Tourette; Story Editor: Sidney Marshall
Guest Star Cyril Delevanti
Co-Starring Regis Toomey, Barbara Bouchet, Charles Dierkop, Judy Lang

From the *Voyage* show files (Irwin Allen papers collection):

A two-time winner of the Nobel Peace Prize is nominated as Secretary of Defense. On the eve of his confirmation by the Senate, Nelson receives information which leads him to believe the man may be a traitor but lacks sufficient evidence to prove it. Eventually he learns that the so-called great man is actually a pawn of a multi-millionaire whose ultimate aim is to obtain our top secret weapons and thus control the world. [1]

The man who warns Nelson about Noah Penfield, the Secretary of State nominee, is soon felled by the title character, an assassin who's working for the wealthy and influential Noah Grafton. This operative has a fake left hand that can be removed to expose a gun that fires poison darts, ergo his moniker. The next day, Penfield's daughter Tippy (a stewardess) arrives at the institute to warn Nelson he must intervene against her father. While the elder Penfield is aboard Seaview for an inspection tour, Tippy shows Nelson a reel of film proving the connection between Grafton (a known communist and crook) and her father. [2]

Assessment:

The title character is a sloppy assassin. He only succeeds in two out of five attempted kills with that tricky built-in gun he sports instead of a hand.
- Agent Cabrillo, in the Teaser: scratch.
- Nelson and Tippy Penfield: double miss.
- Nelson's secretary, Angie: miss.
- The guard on the Seaview: scratch.
- Nelson, in the series climax: miss – hitting his boss instead… just like the henchman in "Escape from Venice."

Although the idea of an assassin with a hand consisting of a poisoned-dart-shooting-gun starts out as an intriguing concept, in practice this character would have been more successful with a silenced pistol. Or throwing a rock.

Or maybe he should have used a Sixfinger. You may recall that Sixfinger was a toy weapon for aspiring kid spies. The 1965 offering from Topper Toys was a fake index finger which, according to the label, shot a cap bomb, a secret bullet, a message missile, or a fragmentation bomb. Come to think of it, maybe writer William Welch was inspired by a Sixfinger TV commercial!

Barbara Bouchet's role seems similarly unthought-through. A former model, she was new at the acting game, and it shows. It didn't help that her character who, as scripted and directed, is all over the place. Do you really get a sense that Tippy Penfield is worried about the welfare of her country when she first contacts Nelson, or truly worried about her father after her efforts to block his appointment are exposed? But let's not quibble; she's a lovely sight and, despite the missed potential for drama, adds a playfulness to the proceedings.

"Playful" and "fun" are perhaps two words to describe this episode. Mark Phillips summed it up as a "slightly above-average suspense story with an exciting conclusion," adding, "Barbara Bouchet makes for a fun heroine and Cyril Delevanti is perfect as the evil businessman. Many highlights, including a fantastic showcasing of the flying sub's abilities (great special effects)."

On the negative side, Phillips noted, "The story would have been a little better if Penfield's character had been developed a bit more." [3]

Regarding the showcasing of the Flying Sub's abilities, the sequence in which Crane takes Penfield for a thrilling air-show-ride wasn't in the episode just to dazzle the kids or pad the time. These scenes help establish Penfield as a highly likably character … who happens to have an interest in the Flying Sub. In the very next scene, Tippy Penfield tells Nelson that her father is a danger to the nation. After the previous ingratiating scene with Penfield, the viewing audience would naturally be suspicious of Tippy's intentions, and this is good storytelling, even if the delivery is mostly ineffective.

The villain behind the other villains is billionaire Noah Grafton. He tells Nelson that it is sweetly ironic that he (Grafton) is the most hated man in America, yet he "created" Penfield, one of the most loved. In the poignant finale, with both having perished, Penfield makes the front page of the newspaper … while Grafton's obituary is pushed to a small column on Page 3. Sweetly ironic indeed.

"The Left-Handed Man" is entertaining, and makes its point – "high crime doesn't pay" – in a fun fashion. (Not that many viewers were likely to become billionaires or Cabinet members.)

Script:
William Welch's writers contract: April 7, 1965.

Welch's final-draft teleplay approved on August 10.
Rev. Shooting Final teleplay (green paper): August 19.

After spending the entire first season polishing scripts, and having taken screen credit on a pair of teleplays which required substantial rewriting, **William Welch** delivered the first of many scripts credited solely to him. At the time, Richard Basehart said, "I would stack *Voyage to the Bottom of the Sea* writers up with those of any show. Science fiction is the toughest prose to write and Irwin Allen is the dean of science fiction. He surrounds himself with fine, able script writers. For example, during WWII, President Harry S. Truman personally selected William Welch to compose his speech announcing the Japanese surrender. I figure if one of our writers is good enough for the President of the United States, he's good enough for me." [4]

Now, the writer who had written for Harry Truman turned in his second-draft script, and awaited feedback.

August 10, 1965: Irwin Allen gave notes:

> P. 12: Insert word "known" – last line of Nelson's first speech, to read "no known antidote."
>
> P. 33: Have left-handed man remain behind curtain as long as possible until he is ready to aim at Angie. Take out the use of the sunglasses. This is too obvious and tends to dispel the suspense. A shot of the man preparing his lethal weapon behind the curtain should be shown. FIRST: In order to show that Nelson was intended to be the target for the poison dart, show the man on a ledge or something attempting to find an open window into Nelson's office – as no window is open, he moves to Angie's window and gains entry.
>
> P. 21, Sc. 61: At the end of this scene it would be logical for Nelson to express worry over the fact that the murderer now knows for certain that Tippy is involved in trying to stop her father from getting his appointment. It should be realized that now she is in danger and must be given protection. Tippy's reaction should be that she doesn't think they would harm her because of her father, but, on second thought, it wouldn't be a bad idea to have someone around she can trust….

P. 60, Sc. 157: Crane should say "we're setting down as close to the house as we can without being noticed," etc., etc. This scene should include some suggestion of a planned way in which Crane hopes to discover if Nelson is indeed being held by Grafton. The plan should not be stated, merely a line such as: <u>Crane</u>: "Now here's how we'll handle this...", <u>fade out scene</u>. The reason for the above suggestion is because Crane's entry on P. 61, Sc. 163 makes him look like some sort of idiot walking right into a touchy situation such as this. The audience will then realize that his entrance was part of the plan, giving the other 3 men time to place themselves advantageously.

P. 61, Sc. 163: It should be remembered that Grafton has never met Crane, therefore wouldn't he either ask him who he is or, if he thinks he can guess who Crane is, shouldn't he say something like: "Correct me if I'm wrong, but I believe our visitor is a close friend of yours, Admiral Nelson?" Then Grafton should give an order to the guard who opened the door for Crane to search the outside to see if Crane is alone. In this scene, Crane should obviously be stalling for time, so that no matter what he says, whether it makes sense or not, Grafton should cut him off with a nod to the one-armed man to proceed. [5]

ABC had its usual concerns. Among her requests on August 13, Dorothy Brown, Director of the network's Department of Standards & Practices, said:

[B]e sure George W. Penfield resembles in no way any prominent individual in today's roster of potential secretaries [of the U.S.].... Be sure the deadly drug is very fictitious.... Please be sure there is no real airline insignia on the uniform worn by Tippy.... Do not fire the missile into the camera.... Scenes of the flight: delete the cries of the dying; the distorted faces; and distorted bodies. This can only be fully approved when on film. [6]

Production:
(Filmed August 23 – 30, 1965; 6 days)

Jerry Hopper was hired to direct. He was 58 and had worked as an assistant film editor at Paramount Pictures. With that background, Hopper became an economic director. He had also been a World War II combat photographer who was awarded a Purple Heart after being wounded during the landing at Leyte, a province in the Philippines. Hopper's first feature-length film assignment as a director was 1952's *The Atomic City*, starring Gene Barry. He also directed the 1953 western *Pony Express*, starring Charlton Heston, and 1956's *The Sharkfighters*, starring Victor Mature. Hopper was well-liked in television and worked often on *Bachelor Father*, *Wagon Train* and *The Fugitive*, with more than a dozen assignments on each. He also had multiple directing jobs on series as diverse as *Gunsmoke*, *The Addams Family*, *Burke's Law*, *Perry Mason*, and *Gilligan's Island*. Now Hopper was stepping into the fantasy worlds of Irwin Allen, for the first of 15 episodes of *Voyage*, as well as one trip into *The Time Tunnel*. His salary was $3,000, the most Allen ever paid for a TV director.

Jerry Hopper with Gloria Grahame during filming of 1954's *Naked Alibi*.

Barbara Bouchet was paid $850 for five days work, playing Tippy Penfield. She was 23 and a former beauty-contest winner. Bouchet broke into show business

122

as a model in TV commercials. She was also a one-time girlfriend of James Darren, who would soon co-star in *The Time Tunnel*. Bouchet took a ride on *Star Trek* in 1968 ("By Any Other Name"), then was the female lead in the 1969 film *Stoney*, and again in 1970 for *Red Hot Shot*.

Cyril Delevanti was 67 when he got the top "guest star" billing – as this episode's evil mastermind – but was only needed for one day to play Noah Grafton (with a pay rate of $400). Delevanti was a well-regarded character actor, with over a hundred screen appearances dating back to 1931. He received a golden Globe nomination for 1964's *The Night of the Iguana*. His work in TV included four trips into *The Twilight Zone*.

Cyril Delevanti in *The Twilight Zone*.

Regis Toomey received second billing of the guest cast, playing George Penfield. He was paid $750 for three days in front of the camera. Toomey was a leading man in the 1930s, and an often-employed character actor in the 1940s and beyond. He finished his career with almost 300 screen appearances, including having recurring roles on several series, starting with *The Mickey Rooney Show* (1954-55). He was adept at playing cops, and did so on a regular basis as Lt. Manny Waldo on *Four Star Playhouse* (1952-56), then Lt. McGough on *Richard Diamond, Private Detective* (1957-58), and Det. Les Hart in 64 episodes of *Burke's Law* (1963-

Regis Toomey in 1931's *Touchdown*.

123

65). Toomey worked for Irwin Allen before, playing Dr. Jamieson in 1961's big-screen *Voyage to the Bottom of the Sea*, and would return for a 1967 tumble into *The Time Tunnel*.

Charles Dierkop was 28 when he played the Left-Handed Man. He was a Fox contract player. In 1969, he was Flat Nose Curry in *Butch Cassidy and the Sundance Kid*, but is perhaps best known for playing Detective Pete Royster in 91 episodes of the 1970s series *Police Woman*. Irwin Allen would bring Dierkop back for an episode of *Land of the Giants*. Unrecognizable under fright make-up, he would also play the "Mutant" on *Lost in Space*, in "One of Our Dogs Is Missing."

Judy Lang, 25, played Nelson's secretary, Angie. She had a ten-year screen career in which she

Charles Dierkop in a 1967 *Star Trek*.

played a recurring character on *Dr. Kildare* in 1965, and appeared in other series, such as *Honey West*, *Get Smart*, *Bewitched*, *The Virginian*, and *The Wild, Wild West*.

Michael Barrier was cast as Cabrillo, the agent seen in the Teaser, and the first victim of the Left-Handed Man. He had been making the rounds on network TV series, such as *Gunsmoke*, *My Favorite Martian*, and *Combat!* He was prominently featured in three episodes of *Star Trek* as Lt. DeSalle, taking command of the Enterprise in one – 1967's "Catspaw."

Production began on Monday, August 23, 1965 for the first of two days on Stage 10, for

Michael Barrier as Chief DeSalle.

the Seaview sets – "Int. Seaview Corridor," "Int. Observation Nose + Radio

Shack," as well as the Flying Sub, both process and "straight." Also scheduled were "Int. Nelson's Cabin" and "Int. Crane's Cabin." It was a lot to do in two days and when it was clear that overtime would be needed, "Int. Crane's Cabin" was stricken from the schedule. In its place, a line of dialogue in which Crane is told to go to Nelson's cabin to receive a communication. "Are you sure the Admiral asked me to take the call in his cabin?" Crane asks, and is given a mumbo-jumbo reason as to why that is the best place to have the conversation. Problem solved.

David Hedison and Barbara Bouchet take time out from the filming to pose for promotional pictures.

Day 2, Tuesday: The process shots needed for "Int. Observation Nose" were filmed. These were the shots that looked toward the observation windows. Additional sequences in the "Control Room" were filmed, as well as a temporary set: "Int. Lesher's Office." They also needed to do some retakes in the ship's corridors.

Day 3, Wednesday, was spent on Fox Stage 15, for the interior of the Grafton Mansion. This included the climactic fight, in which Chip Morton was actually given some action outside of the Seaview. They filmed to 8:10 p.m.

Day 4 saw the company working on Stage 16, for the interior of the jet (mock-up), then moving outdoors to the construction area where portions of the backlot were being razed for a new Los Angeles high-rise office complex to be called Century City. It was here that they filmed the "Ext. Airport & Airplane" shots, then moved onto Stage 2 for the interior of the Travel Agency and "Int. Jet (mock-up)."

The plane that you see Nelson, Kowalski, and the handcuffed Left-Handed Man enter was stored on the backlot for use in numerous TV episodes and films.

Also filmed on this day were the chase sequences involving the Left-Handed Man on the Fox lot, utilizing a second-unit shooting Day-for-Night. This technique was a widely used cost-saving measure. It was eclipsed by cheaper, faster film, then digital effects which could make the switch on demand.

Days 5 and 6, Friday, August 27, and Monday, August 30, the fifth and sixth days of production, were spent on Stage B, filming the "Int. Nelson Inner & Outer Office" sequences. The latest they worked on any of the six days was Friday – the day cast and crew had grown used to working late – when the camera ran until 10:55 p.m. [7]

The budget approved for this episode by William Self was $140,491. He was dreaming. It cost $156,108. [8]

Release / Reaction:
(ABC premiere airdate: 10/24/65; network repeat broadcast: 7/10/66)

The week that "The Left-Handed Man" first aired on ABC, the Gateway Arch was completed in St. Louis, Missouri; Pope Paul VI proclaimed that Jews were not collectively guilty of the crucifixion of Jesus; the Beatles were given their MBE awards (Members of the Most Honorable Order of the British Empire) at Buckingham Palace by Queen Elizabeth II; and Chuck Connors, of *Branded*, had the cover of *TV Guide*. Meanwhile, Irwin Allen's other series, *Lost in Space*, aired the whimsical "My Friend, Mr. Nobody."

The photos sent out to promote "The Left-Handed Man" didn't feature the title character. Pictures of Bouchet in a bikini were much more likely to see print. One shot of her and Hedison was captioned: "David

The assassin may have been left-handed, but David Hedison put both hands to good use, around lovely Barbara Bouchet.

Hedison as Captain Lee Crane helps Barbara Bouchet with her diving gear in a scene from 'The Left-Handed Man' on *Voyage to the Bottom of the Sea* at 7 o'clock tonight…" [9]

"TV Key," syndicated to newspapers across the land, said:

> More death-defying derring-do this week, which should please the young adventure fan. Admiral Nelson and company are up to their necks in political intrigues, would-be assassins, and split-second escapes, that keep the show on the move. [10]

TV critic Dwight Newton shared his opinion in *The San Francisco Examiner*:

> If there is a way to reduce TV programming to the level of comic book culture without going to jail, I daresay 20th Century-Fox Films will find it. … [11]

After giving mention to *Lost in Space*, *Daniel Boone*, and the upcoming *Batman*, Newton turned his attention to the series at hand:

> Oh, yes, and then there is *Voyage to the Bottom of the Sea*, a 20th Century-Fox waterworks which I saw again last night. The series used to be all wet. Last night it was aridly dry. …
>
> Down yonder in New Mexico there lived an extraordinarily wealthy extremist who spread propaganda and garnered military secrets in behalf of an unnamed country behind the Iron Curtain. His most valued stooge was a wishy-washy nincompoop whom the President of the United States had been bamboozled into appointing as the next Secretary of Defense, if you can imagine. The scheme failed because the nincompoop's glorious daughter (beauty Barbara Bouchet from the Bay Area) went to Admiral Nelson.
>
> Nelson volunteered to save the United States from disaster but about all he did was (a) get beaten up by a left-handed maniac, and (b) fall stupidly into a trap whereby he was captured and flown to the extremist's New Mexico hideout. Nelson would have been killed had not Comdr. Crane, our No.

2 hero, used something that looked like a flying dishpan to get there in time to kill the bad guys first.

The story was a fraud. So were 20th Century-Fox publicity photos of Barbara Bouchet in a bikini with diving gear, purportedly from the show, which some papers published as an inducement for viewing. Ha! From start to stop, curvy Barbara was attired in a primly trim airline stewardess outfit.

As for *Bottom of the Sea* adventures, the submarine barely got its nose salty. [13]

Well, at least newspaper readers got to enjoy Bouchet's assets.

"Left-Handed Man" was another espionage episode with a gimmick and a girl. *Voyage* began the hour a strong second-place contender, but as soon as the kids saw they weren't likely to see any truly fantastic sci-fi elements, they tuned out, submerging the show to third place.

A.C. Nielsen 30-city survey from Oct. 24, 1965 (winner in boldface)[14]:

(7 – 7:30 p.m.)	Rating:	Peak Share:
ABC: *Voyage to the Bottom of the Sea*	15.0	30.0%
CBS: *Lassie*	**16.3**	**32.6%**
NBC: *Bell Telephone Hour*	11.2	22.4%

(7 – 7:30 p.m.)	Rating:	Peak Share:
ABC: *Voyage to the Bottom of the Sea*	15.4	26.1%
CBS: *My Favorite Martian*	**18.5**	**31.3**
NBC: *Walt Disney's Wonderful World of Color*	17.2	29.1%

4.8

"The Death Ship" (Episode 40)
(Prod. #8210; first aired Sunday, February 20, 1966)
Written by Michael Lynn and George Reed
(William Read Woodfield and Allan Balter)
Directed by Abner Biberman
Produced by Irwin Allen, Frank La Tourette and William Welch
Story Editor: Sidney Marshall
Guest Star David Sheiner
Co-Starring Lew Gallo, Elizabeth Perry, Harry Davis, June Vincent

"VOYAGE TO THE BOTTOM OF THE SEA"

The production numbering goes a bit askew beginning with this episode. The previous episode filmed, "The Left-Handed Man" (Production No. 8207), completed shooting on August 30, 1965. Scheduled next was the lost *Voyage* script, "The Man from London" (Prod. No. 8208), written by Albert Aley, who had written two episodes for *The Man from U.N.C.L.E.* and a whole bunch of sci-fi with *Tom Corbett, Space Cadet*. It was a spy story, and featured the character Tiffany Loveland. Unable to find the right actress for the role, Irwin Allen put the script on hold and asked that Prod. No. 8209, "The Silent Saboteurs," be advanced in the shooting schedule. But this story required two key players – one male and one female – who had to be young, attractive, physically fit, proficient at acting, and, most importantly, Asian. The players desired weren't immediately available, so Prod. No. 8210 was pulled forward. It needed a bigger guest cast, but their particulars were less specific.

And, thus, the eighth episode filmed carries Production Number 8210. (We just didn't want you to think that we had skipped anything ... or lost track.)

From the *Voyage* show files (Irwin Allen papers collection):

> Nelson and Crane and eight scientists take the Seaview out without a crew to test new automation gear. A foreign power decides to take advantage of the situation to employ Seaview's missiles against an international meeting aboard a peace ship. One of their agents is among the civilians aboard the Seaview. In his attempt to take over the ship, he murders the others one by one, seemingly even Admiral Nelson, until apparently only Crane and a young girl remain alive. [1]

Assessment:

Mark Phillips raved, "This episode starts off with a bang and goes on to redo *Ten Little Indians*, and does a pretty good job." [2]

Mike Bailey said, "The episode is dark – *literally*. Seaview's reactor is put out of commission early in the game and emergency lighting is the rule – relatively gritty stuff for Year Two. Bodies turn up with great regularity and there is substance to the mystery, and danger in the way the story's characters interact. Elizabeth Perry is absolutely wonderful in this episode and could co-pilot my submarine any day." [3]

We like the episode, and Elizabeth Perry, too.

Recycled footage (of an enemy sub firing torpedoes, and crewmen scrambling to battle stations) is put to good use in the Teaser. Both were harvested from the 1961 *Voyage* movie. They had been recycled before, for Season One, but this was the first time seen on TV in color. Granted, the uniforms in the stock footage are out-of-step with the spiffier Season Two outfits, but who's to say that some of the seamen on the lower decks still don't dress this way?

Due to the squeamishness of the ABC-TV censors, care had to be taken to not let any of the dead bodies be seen "in a gruesome manner." One was supposed to have been hanged. That went out of an early draft at the insistence of the network. There was also a mandate to dilute the death by drowning (sorry). What was finally approved must leave one asking: Was that fellow actually drowned in a fish tank?! With no sign of a struggle? You see, struggles were out too – they might imply the dead person didn't go easily. As scripted in the climactic

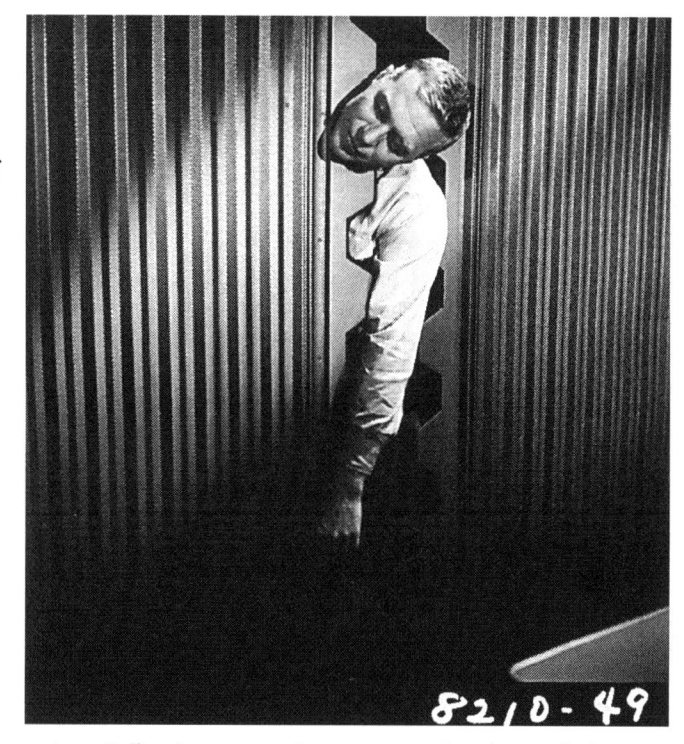

Lew Gallo, demonstrating a new use for the crash doors – a murder ABC allowed to be seen on camera in the episode. It was macabre but not overly gruesome. A few of the other corpses would either be shown in a less ghastly manner, or kept off camera entirely.

Act Four, Captain Crane was supposed to track down Tracy Stewart with gun drawn, and take aim at her head, threatening to shoot. And the look on his face was supposed to make her, and the viewing audience, believe he might actually pull the trigger. ABC scrapped that idea, making the final line in the episode, in which Stewart tells Crane she thought he was going to kill her, and his reply – "I almost did" – lose much of its impact.

With rules like these in place to keep television of this era "safe," you can see that the challenge for writers, director, and cast to inject jeopardy and terror into any "TV play" was immense. But "Death Ship" has its share of chills, nonetheless.

Script:

William Read Woodfield's and Allan Balter's writers contract: July 29, 1965. Woodfield's and Balter's story treatment, "One by One," approved on August 17.

Woodfield's and Balter's 1ˢᵗ-draft teleplay approved on August 26.
Woodfield's and Balter's 2ⁿᵈ-draft teleplay approved on September 1.
3ʳᵈ Rev. Shooting Final teleplay by Sidney Marshall (beige pages): August 31.
Page revisions by William Welch (blue pages): August 31.
Page revisions by Welch (pink pages): September 1.
New scenes written by Welch and Marshall (gold paper): January 26, 1966.

The script **William Read Woodfield** and **Allan Balter** wrote was called "One by One." The title was only changed after they had fulfilled their contract.

This was one of the few episodes to contain notes in the *Voyage* show files from Irwin Allen, associate producer Frank La Tourette, *and* story editor William Welch, providing a fair look at the communication between the three on the development of one the series' scripts. The exchange of memos took place on August 24. Frank La Tourette wrote:

> The Teaser is teasing but I don't quite understand the reason for it and its <u>relation</u> to the rest of the story. I would like to see it set up a bit better why the regular crew is missing from the test runs and why the eight people involved are aboard with Nelson and Crane. The Peace Ship also should be set up better. [4]

William Welch wrote:

> The Teaser needs work. If the sabotage is supposed to be an elaborate plot, it stretches credibility. The Oriental heavies apparently sabotage the sub in order to give their agent a chance to build in some specific equipment which will ensure a shakedown cruise with only a handful of people aboard. But the plot depends on a number of coincidences, not the least of which is that the rebuilding will be done and the trial held at the precise time the Peace Ship is in mid-Pacific. [5]

La Tourette said:

> On Page 18, it is a little unrealistic that someone would still be taunting somebody else with service with Germany during World War II. In 1975, that war won't even be the memory it is now. [6]

Irwin Allen wrote:

> P. 17, Sc. 29: The directions given after Nelson motions for Crane to come into the Engine Room are confusing and incomplete. If there is a chance that Rourke is still alive, why does Nelson cover his body with a tarp and why do they stand around for almost a page of dialogue in which Klaus is put in the position of defending himself when it hasn't been established as yet that Rourke was actually murdered?
>
> P. 18, Sc. 29: The Klaus discussion seems premature. This scene should not take place until after it has been determined that Rourke was murdered.
>
> P. 19, Sc. 30: In this scene, the fact that Rourke's death was no accident should be established. Rourke should have been dead right from the beginning. [7]

La Tourette noted:

> Also on Page 18, it is most obvious that Rourke is dead. Yet on Page 19, in the sickbay, Nelson asks: "Is there any hope?" [8]

Welch warned:

> It is wrong to draw the attention of the audience to the fact in advance that someone already presumed dead could be the murderer. [9]

Allen said:

> P. 20, Sc. 33: Chandler's statement that "someone in this room is a murderer" doesn't coincide with what he says in Sc. 34, P. 21. He now says the killer may be hiding on the ship. Act 2, dialogue should be a continuation of Sc. 33. It would appear that all the remaining members came running into the nose from all areas of the ship because they all heard the shot. That is an impossibility unless it is established that all of them were assembled in the control room.

> P. 22, Sc. 34: This is the first time anyone has mentioned attempting to use the radio. The fact that it doesn't work should have been brought out in Scene 28, P. 16, when someone should have tried to radio for help. Tracy was supposed to handle all communications on this mission. [10]

La Tourette advised:

> In view of the nature of this story, I think it would be most wise to stay completely away from the bodies once the different characters are found dead. There should be no morgue – or one that we can see, at least – and absolutely no time should be spent with the bodies after they are discovered.... In line with not seeing any of the bodies after their first discovery, some dialogue too should be eliminated, such as Templeton's remark on Page 33: "He said it made his flesh crawl to be in the same room with two dead men."
>
> I think the Templeton death needs cleaning up. He is drinking the coffee for about three pages, yet Ava says the poison is fast-acting – so fast, in fact, that one cannot taste it, which later doesn't make sense.
>
> On Page 25, there should be an intercom in the blower room that is dead. It is inconceivable that the magnificent new submarine would be lacking in any kind of equipment. [11]

Allen had issues with the Blower Room scene as well:

> In previous scripts, every compartment had a duct for the air revitalization outlet. How is it that this room (The Blower Room) doesn't have one anymore? Wouldn't it be better to have Nelson or Crane discover that this outlet has been effectively blocked? They should also find that the intercom system in this room has been rendered useless. [12]

La Tourette observed:

> The exchange between Nelson and Stroller could really be a dramatic and interesting scene if built up a little better. [13]

Allen recommended:

> P. 43, Sc. 76: Stroller – 1st speech – should read that, "Everyone knows that the Peace Conference will probably fail." Stroller – 2nd speech – the use of "they" should be clarified. Would be better as, "as long as there are countries which keep trying to enslave the world." [14]

La Tourette suggested:

> On Page 61, Crane should forget the gun in the climactic moment with Tracy. He raises the gun and then stands there with egg on his face while she turns, bolts, and runs out of the control room. Crane chases her to her room, forces his way into the room, then again stands there with his gun raised until the sound of the hatch slamming wipes the egg from his face. As written, this scene could not possibly be filmed without comedy overtones. [15]

Allen questioned:

> P. 64, Scene 133: In this scene, shouldn't Nelson try to find out why Chandler was interested in stopping the Peace talks and who he was working for, *if* he was working alone? This last fact is never discussed. [16]

Equally disappointed in the climax, La Tourette said:

> In the climactic scene between Nelson and Chandler, the "why" of Chandler's plan to take over the Seaview and sabotage the peace conference – this could be a wild scene in which the fanatic really exposes himself. [17]

Allen concluded:

> Crane and Tracy should have something to say in the Tag about the bad moments they had when it looked as if Crane was going to kill her. [18]

Welch closed with an eye toward expenses:

As it is now, Kowalski is used in the script and Riley is not. This is right [for the purposes of the story] except for the fact that we now have run out of shows in which we can drop Riley and therefore we have to pay for him whether he appears or not. [19]

La Tourette closed with:

There are some lines of dialogue that should be changed. Otherwise, probably handled writing-wise and direction-wise, this could make a good show. [20]

Dorothy Brown of ABC's Department of Standards & Practices had a thing or two to say on August 24th too:

Since this story is based on the *"Ten Little Indians"* style of murder-suspense, the progressive elimination of the members of the Seaview shakedown cruise is shock enough. There must be particular [care taken] in seeing that the bodies in death are in no way grotesque and that "horror" reactions of surviving members are not overdone.

Pg 19, 20 – Gun never pointed directly into camera.

Pg 30, Scs 67, 61 – Body must not convey "hideous watery death". Scream to minimum.

Pg 35 – Again, caution on scream.

Pg 39, Sc 72 – Since it is not necessary to story, delete shots, here and elsewhere, which create morgue effect. No panning on master shot of sheet-covered bodies.

Pg 40, Sc 75; Pg 48, 49 – Caution on blood, etc., in indicating wounded shoulder.

Pg 54, Sc 98 – SUBSTITUTE for the hanging.

Pg 58, Sc 103 – Delete directions which indicate we see Nelson with the current surging through his body – We can see him just before contact and as he falls; no more than quick shot of hand in contact, with camera covering only the sparks as quickly as possible – or something to this effect.

Pg 62, Sc 114 – Bring "hatch slamming" in sooner as Crane <u>begins</u> to raise gun – eliminating "gun to her head" and remainder of scene. [21]

ABC also had its usual trademark and brand-name concerns:

Pgs 2, 41 – Cigarette packs not identifiable as to actual trade/brand names.

Pgs 7, 36 – Name of shipbuilder co. must be fictitious. Please be sure that the name and product indicating the deadly poison is completely fictitious. [22]

And, of course, there were always those pesky words that the network, for some odd reason, found offensive:

Pg 29 – Delete direction "slightly dirty" in Stroller's line and delete Ava's "disgusting" line. [23]

One day later, after seeing a revised draft, an unidentified ABC exec advised:

Be sure bodies throughout are not grotesque. Use taste in shooting. ... Keep the reactions of the characters away from too much horror. ... Be sure the "deadly poison" is fictitious. ... Be very careful in the way we handle showing the bodies. ... With Crane's bloody shoulder, remember the show is in color, and keep it toned down. ... Eliminate the morgue scene. ... The death of Ava is too gruesome.... Crane's scene with Tracy on Page 62 has Crane cornering the girl, raising the gun, cocking the hammer and all but shooting her. Have the interruption come at the point that he raises the gun. ... This adds up to a rather grim hour, and we should avoid doing too many shows of this type. [24]

Production:
(Filmed August 31 thru September 7, 1965, plus pickup day; 6 days total)

Abner Biberman, 56, was hired to direct. He began as an actor in the 1930s and often played heavies throughout the 1940s before turning to directing with 1950s B-films, then into TV. He often directed for the Mike Connors' detective series, *Tightrope*, as well as *Ben Casey*, *Mr. Novak*, *77 Sunset Strip*, and *The Fugitive*. He also helmed an episode of *The Outer Limits* and four segments of *The Twilight Zone*. One of those was "The Dummy," with Cliff Robertson. This *Voyage* would be his only time working for Irwin Allen. The director found it easier going with long stints at *Ironside* and *Hawaii Five-0*.

David Sheiner played Chandler, and was given top guest pay and $1,250 for four days work. He had last been seen on *Voyage* in "The Exile" during Season One. He was 37.

Lew Gallo was cast as Stroller. He was 37, and had just finished playing Major Joseph Cobb in 14 episodes of *12 O'Clock High*. Irwin Allen would bring Gallo back for a second *Voyage* ("Deadly Waters") and two episodes of *The Time Tunnel* and one *Lost in Space*.

Elizabeth Perry played Tracy Stewart. She was 31 and the daughter-in-law of this episode's director, Abner Biberman. Perry had co-starred in "The Brain of Colonel Barham," an episode of *The Outer Limits*, as well as turning up on *Bonanza* and *Gunsmoke*. At this time in 1965, she had the lead in a daytime soap on NBC called *Morning Star*.

June Vincent played Ava. At 44, she had been a Hollywood B-film leading lady in the 1940s, beginning with a little trifle in 1944 called *Sing a Jingle*. She played opposite the likes of Dan Duryea in 1946's *Black Angel*,

Above: Actor / Director Abner Biberman, in the 1940s.
Lower right: Elizabeth Perry and Edward Mallory in the 1965 NBC soap opera *Morning Star*, for which she had the lead.

and, in 1948, opposite Kirby Grant in *Song of Idaho* and Chester Morris in *Trapped by Boston Blackie*, and with Wallace Ford in 1949's *Shed No Tears*. If you haven't heard of these leading men again, then you get the point.

The other victims were **Harry Davis**, as Templeton; **Ivan Triesault**, as Klaus; **Herb Voland**, as Carter; and **Ed Connelly**, as Rourke. They all worked regularly in films and TV as character actors.

Filming began on Tuesday, August 31, 1965 for five days on Stage 5, for what was supposed to be a six-day production. On this day, they covered scenes in the Flying Sub, "Falkonmatt's Lab," the Missile Room, the Crew Quarters, and a stairway on the sub.

June Vincent when a star of B-films in the 1940s.

Day 2 had the company in the Control Room and "Int. Projection Room."

Day 3 continued in the Control Room, as well as the Observation Nose, then on to the Engine Room and various corridors.

Day 4, on Friday, with work continuing in the Control Room / Observation Nose, they filmed until 7:40 p.m.

Monday was Labor Day. For Day 5, on Tuesday, they worked on more sections of corridor, then on to "Tracy's Cabin." And then Irwin Allen stopped the production. [25]

139

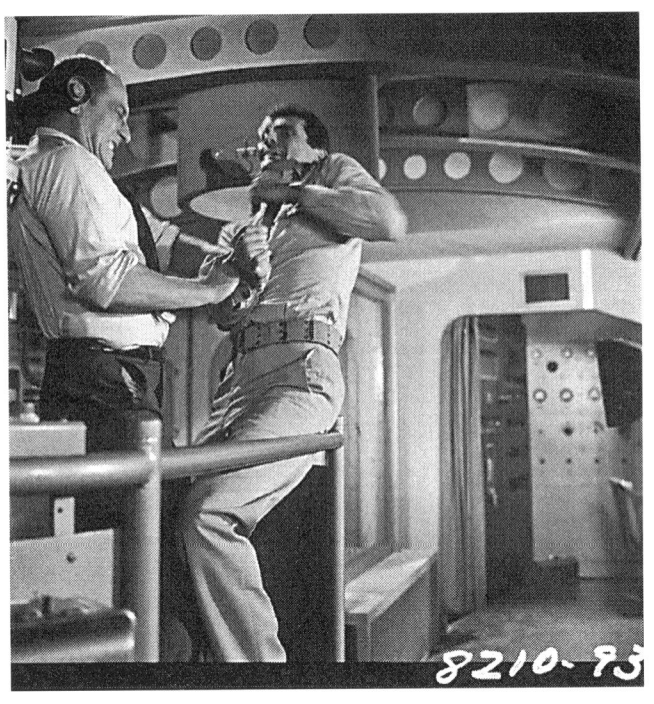

William Read Woodfield said, "The schmuck director, Abner Biberman, was running late, and Irwin said, 'I'm pulling the plug on Biberman and I don't have time to film the ending where it's all explained. Write another ending to show that an invisible monster has been killing the scientists.' We said, 'We're not going to do that.' Irwin said, 'I'm ordering you to do it!' We said, 'Screw you! No dice!' 'Then, I'll get Bill Welch to do it.' 'Fine,' we said, 'but take our names off it.' Irwin said, 'You'll be sorry; this show will win an Emmy!' I said, 'We'll take our chances. You'll be back to shoot our original ending.' And Irwin stormed out of the office. That sort of tore our relationship with Irwin. He did go back and shoot the original ending." [26]

Allan Hunt said, "Mr. Allen was very curt – a man of few words. He had a way of just telling you to do something in 'verbal shorthand' and, at first, I thought he was terribly rude and he didn't like me at all. But, the more I saw of him, I realized that was just the way he was. It was the way he was with his wife and everybody on the set, whether he was happy with you or unhappy. It was just his manner. He had a 'double-parked' way of life, as in double-parked; in a hurry. I always had the impression talking to him that … he needed to get out of there quickly." [27]

Elizabeth Perry said, "I remember that I loved being swept up in the fantasy of the show. The story was based on *Ten Little Indians*. I played a computer programmer and designer and I had no idea what that was! Here I was, this highly skilled technician, and I was running around in 3-inch heels. My father-in-law, Abner Biberman, directed this episode, but production was cut off because it ran so far overtime. This caused some dissension between Mr. Biberman and Irwin Allen. Several weeks later, I was called back to finish the show." [28]

On January 26, Allen had William Welch and Sidney Marshall write a couple of new scenes to be filmed (resulting in an extra day of production, filmed much later). This resulted in Woodfield and Balter taking their names off the episode, using the pseudonyms Michael Lynn and George Reed in the screen credits.

The sixth day of production would be saved for a later date and, as Elizabeth Perry noted, another director.

The final cost was $187,962. [29]

David Hedison received a few female admirers on the set during production of this episode. (Courtesy Synthesis Entertainment)

Release / Reaction:
(ABC premiere airdate: 2/20/66; network repeat broadcast: 5/08/66)

By the time "The Death Ship" was finally completed and aired, it was five-and-a-half months since the episode had begun filming. *The Silencers*, with Dean Martin as Matt Helm, and also featuring Stella Stevens and Victor Buono, was knocking them dead as the top film in the movie houses. *Whipped Cream & Other Delights*, by Herb Alpert's Tijuana Brass, was the best-selling record album in America. And Nancy Sinatra's "These Boots Are Made for Walking" was getting the most play on the radio.

The entertainment critic for North Carolina's *The Gaston Gazette* called "The Death Ship" a "first class murder mystery."

"TV Scout," in hundreds of newspapers coast to coast, said:

> *Voyage to the Bottom of the Sea* is a wet *Ten Little Indians*, as it borrows, killing by killing, from the Agatha Christie classic. Fans who are familiar with the mystery will be able to solve this one, since the same gimmick is used, and when you know the gimmick, it's easy to spot the killer. However, if familiarity doesn't breed contempt, you'll enjoy seeing Richard Basehart and David Hedison along with eight specialists on a shakedown cruise aboard the Seaview after it has been sabotaged. Soon, people start getting bumped off – even Basehart apparently, and the only ones left are Hedison and Elizabeth Perry. [30]

Jumping ahead in time to the air date of "The Death Ship," *Voyage* had been on a winning streak in the ratings. This non-sci-fi entry benefited by the increased popularity.

A.C. Nielsen 30-city survey from Feb. 20, 1966 (winner in boldface)[31]:

7 – 7:30 p.m.	Rating:	Peak Share:
ABC: *Voyage to the Bottom of the Sea*	**19.0**	**35.0%**
CBS: *Lassie*	17.1	31.5%
NBC: Actuality special	9.4	17.3%

7:30 – 8 p.m.	Rating:	Peak Share:
ABC: *Voyage to the Bottom of the Sea*	**18.8**	**32.3%**
CBS: *My Favorite Martian*	16.0	27.5%
NBC: *Walt Disney's Wonderful World...*	17.4	29.9%

4.9

"The Silent Saboteurs" (Episode 41)
(Prod. #8209; first aired Sunday, November 21, 1965)
Written by Max Ehrlich and Sidney Marshall
Directed by Sobey Martin
Produced by Irwin Allen and Frank La Tourette; Story Editor: Sidney Marshall
Guest Star Pilar Seurat
Co-Starring George Takei and Bert Freed

After Script # 8 was cancelled, and Script # 10 was pulled forward to be the eighth episode filmed, things got back on track, with Script #9 becoming Production #9.

From the *Voyage* show files (Irwin Allen papers collection):

> Our first returning space probe from Venus has all its information bled off by a mysterious electronic force and is then destroyed. Crane and two Seaview crewmen take the flying sub to the Asian jungle where, with the aid of a few resistance fighters (one of whom is a traitor), they must find and destroy the secret scientific complex responsible for the sabotage before the return of the second space probe.[1]

Assessment:

A real treat. And they didn't even bring Admiral Nelson along for the ride.

The mystery is well-played. Who is Major Lee Cheng – Pilar Seurat or George Takei? They'll keep you guessing long into the plot. Seurat and Takei are masterful. And Hedison never disappoints as Crane plays the odds with these two, and comes up with a winning hand.

The underwater shots of the Flying Sub traveling upriver are better than what anyone should expect, or even hope for, from a 1965 TV program. The jungle set is stuffed with greens and murky soil, and even water – an impressive undertaking considering the horrendously low budget the *Voyage* company had to work with.

Speaking of the "FS," for the first time in the series it is more than a seaplane, used for brief interior flying shots with one or two camera angles. We really get a feel for its innards this time around, and just how that belly hatch works (from inside and out).

Terry Becker and Del Monroe contribute nicely, as they enjoy a change of costumes and scenery.

The heavies are serviceable and meet a fitting end. And the underground complex, outside the control room, crawl space and all, are gritty and real, with effective action throughout.

What's not to like? Well, the interior space capsule sequences are pretty drab, and the model for the space capsule is, well, rather unimpressive.

Mark Phillips, to our surprise, called this inspired confection of 1960s pop-culture-sci-fi-entertainment "a standard story enhanced by a believable heroine (Pilar Seurat) and George Takei." At least he liked Pilar and George. However, he felt "the episode never really takes off" and that "the jungle setting is grimy and the bad guys are totally one-dimensional." [2]

We hoped Mike Bailey would see things our way, especially when he began, saying, "Big budget on Flying Sub effects sequences and fabulous jungle sets." But then he objected, "Big budget blown! Blown by lame script and even lamer direction from Sobey Martin. Endless scenes of Crane and others walking stultifyingly slowly through dark jungle. Music by Lennie Hayton that noodles inanely, compounds the torpidity of this outing. Takei and Seurat are good, but nothing other than rewriting and reshooting could have perked this snoozer up. On the other hand, the jungle sets and the Flying Sub sure look good." [3]

Good grief. Well … *we* liked it.

Script:

Max Ehrlich's writers contract: April 6, 1965.
Ehrlich's story treatment, "The Rescue," approved on April 22.
Ehrlich's 1st-draft teleplay approved on May 11.
Ehrlich's 2nd-draft teleplay approved on July 7.
Sidney Marshall's rewrite, Rev. Shooting Final, received on September 3.
Marshall's script polish, 2nd Rev. Shooting Final (gold paper): September 9.
William Welch's script polish (on blue paper): September 9.

Screenwriter **Max Ehrlich** was 55. He began as a newspaper writer, and then hit the airwaves where he was immensely successful at writing radio drama in the 1940s and early '50s, including scripts for hit series such as *The Big Story* and *The Shadow*. He also wrote for print, with *The Big Eye*, a popular science-fiction novel published in 1949, and followed with 13 more books, including the sci-fi mystery *The Reincarnation of Peter Proud*. On television, in the sci-fi genre, he provided several scripts for *Tales of Tomorrow*, including an adaption of Jules Verne's *20,000 Leagues Under the Sea*.

Ehrlich thought it would be fun to write a *Voyage to the Bottom of the Sea*. But once was enough. And his script was substantially rewritten. He would not work for Irwin Allen again, and switched to a different sci-fi series. Trekkers may know his name – Ehrlich wrote the 1967 *Star Trek* episode "The Apple." That too was substantially rewritten, but at least he kept his "written by" credit. Here, with "The Silent Saboteurs," Ehrlich had to share credit with one of his rewriters.

Sidney Marshall was the rewriter given co-teleplay credit – his first on the series. Of course, he had been doing a great deal of writing prior to this on *Voyage*; he was the Season Two Story Editor, having replaced William Welch. Welch, as you know, moved up to alternating associate producer, where he also had a hand in rewriting scripts.

Marshall had been a writer/producer in TV, on staff for the 1956 series *The Count of Monte Cristo*, then *The New Adventures of Charlie Chan* in 1957. This was followed by *Behind Closed Doors* (1958-59), *The Untouchables* (1959-60) and *Outlaws* (1961). He had also written scripts of his own for some of these series. And he worked as a freelancer on numerous other series, including *M Squad*, *Trackdown*, and *Mr. Novak*. All this, and he was only 54.

Mary Garbutt, of ABC's Department of Standards & Practices, expressed her concerns on August 23, which included:

> All names identifying the space mission must be fictitious –
> and not come close to actual scientists on our space program.

… Of course, clearance for capsule-space footage used. … Please establish future date [from the mid-1970s], audio, video, or both, before Pg. 5. Repeat in middle portion of show, if possible. … If any sighting effect is used here, be sure it does not duplicate cross-hairs of actual telescopic rifle. As usual, no firing directly into camera. … Standard caution on dead guerrillas, the guards shoot-out, Kowalski's reaction to jet of white smoke, and caution on his shoulder gun shot wound. … The muzzle may be close to Crane's head but must not be pressed against it. … Substitute for "Mayday" in Sharkey's and Kowalski's lines. Also, your usual care in seeing, in this and other scenes, that Morse type signals sent out are not duplication of any actual distress signals like the SOS, Mayday, etc.… This episode must not be scheduled on date which is just prior to or during progress of one of our actual space probes. Also, this story must be open for re-evaluation and approval in the event of "any unusual developments" in our actual space flights prior to air-date. [4]

Whew!

William Welch handled the final script polishing, which was designed to give Richard Basehart a break from shooting, with only a part-day's work to be plugged into the story, via video conference from his Nelson Institute office with Chip Morton on the Seaview.

Irwin Allen found much of the additions by Welch to be illogical, out of character, and downright silly. On September 4, he wrote to his staff:

P. 23 – Sc. 75: Nelson's answer 2nd speech, doesn't make sense. The fact is Lee [Crane] was probably walking into a trap, and Lee or no Lee the mission must be completed. Therefore, this speech should be revised to bring out the possibility that Lee may have eluded the trap and may still be able to complete mission. If they don't hear from him in a certain length of time, instructions should be given for someone else to follow through.

P. 24: The same applies to Nelson's last speech in answer to Morton's, "If he's still alive," etc. – Nelson answers, "He has to find it." Nelson sounds a little crazy.

> P. 27 - Sc. 80: Since Crane gives orders to Sharkey and then immediately cuts off communication, this can be used as an excuse for Sharkey not delivering the message he received from Morton regarding the foul-up in the underground. However, Sharkey should try to tell Crane but find he's been cut off. He should also mention that Major Cheng is waiting, but, of course, too late.
>
> P. 26 – Sc. 77: Crane's original plan was to meet Cheng and proceed to investigate and destroy the source of trouble. Since he changes his plan and is returning to the F.S., he should remark on this or give some excuse to Cheng as he is obviously suspicious of him. [5]

As Allen's notes continued, he came to the second "Major Cheng" – the part to be played by Pilar Seurat. While both characters claimed to be Major Cheng, only one was referred in the script by this name – the George Takei character. The Pilar Seurat character was identified as "Moana."

> P. 29: Moana last speech – How did she know there were more space capsules to be destroyed? We assume she knows of Arcturus 4 because she has just heard the message between Seaview and F.S., but she is using this as a reason for her prior behavior. She needs not say why she is there at all unless she is asked what her interest in it is. Her answer should be that she has a personal reason for wanting to help them. There is a point which should be brought out at this time. The underground should not be primarily interested in what happens to American space capsules so much as they should be working towards the destruction of anything and everyone who is involved with the oppressions of their country.
>
> P. 30 – Crane's reason [in who he choses to believe] should be that Cheng has not come up with a better plan. That is why he is going along with Moana's story of a safe house. Cheng answer should be that he and his band of guerrillas hoped to be able to overcome the fortifications but, now that their force is so small, he doesn't think it can be done.

P. 47 – Sc. 123: Cheng states that his superiors want Crane alive to question him. What about? This statement is also in contradiction to what Lago says in his last speech on P. 37. He is upset because his agent has not eliminated the guerillas who landed on their shores. [6]

Production:
(Filmed September 10 – 17, 1965; 6 days)

Sobey Martin sat – and, according to many, took some catnaps – in the director's chair. This was his twelfth episode.

Pilar Seurat was given top guest star billing and paid $1,200 to play Moana. She was 27 and often a guest player in television shows that called for Asian or Polynesian types, such as *Hawaiian Eye*, *Hong Kong*, *The Islanders*, *Adventures in Paradise*, and *I Spy*.

George Takei made $850 for four days work, playing the man impersonating the real – and really dead – Major Cheng. He was 29 and, this very year, made his first appearance as Lt. Sulu for the second *Star Trek* pilot, "Where No Man Has Gone Before."

Phil Posner, 36, played Stevens, the agent who puts the mission into motion. He had a brief role in this episode, and a short career working in TV in the 1960s.

Alexander D'Arcy, 56, played Lago, the officer in the bunker who activates the self-destruct mechanism. His face may ring a bell; he worked often in films during the 1940s and '50s, usually third or fourth billed, and was a frequent guest player on television throughout the 1960s. D'Arcy pocketed $300 for a single day's work.

Bert Freed, 45, played Halden, the bad guy in charge. He was a much-in-demand character actor in films and on TV, with close to 200 screen appearances spanning a 40-year career. He had been a regular on the 1966 series *Shane* (David Carradine played the title character). Freed was

Bert Freed and Alexander D'Arcy.

paid $400 for one day, working alongside Alexander D'Arcy.

Lennie Hayton, who composed the score for "… And Five of Us Are Left," was credited for the music heard in this episode.

Production began on Friday, September 10, 1965, on the *Voyage* home port of Stage 10, for "Int. Control Room + Nose," and two temporary sets: "Int. Washington D.C. Office" and "Int. Capsule (Space) #1 & #2." This was the only day Richard Basehart and the three bit-players playing astronauts were needed.

Days 2 and 3, Monday and Tuesday, September 13 and 14, were needed to film all the scenes (both flying and submerged) in the Flying Sub. The location remained Stage 10, with Pilar Seurat and George Takei joining David Hedison, Terry Becker, and Del Monroe.

Day 4, Wednesday. Stage "B," which contained a water tank, was turned into a shoreline (not to be confused with "river bank"), a lush jungle, and a jungle clearing. Hedison, Monroe, Seurat, and Takei were in the thick of it, with more than 11 hours of filming.

Day 5, Thursday: While Stage "B" underwent a conversion by the set-builders and decorators, the production company worked on Stage 17, housing "Int. Holden Complex Control Room," "Int. Main Corridor" outside the complex, "Int. Underground Complex Corridor," and "Int. Power Duct." This was the one day that Bert Freed and Alex D'Arcy worked … when their characters were blown to kingdom come. Considering all the gunplay and explosions, quite a bit of action was covered in 12 hours, with Sobey Martin finally calling a wrap at 8:30 p.m.

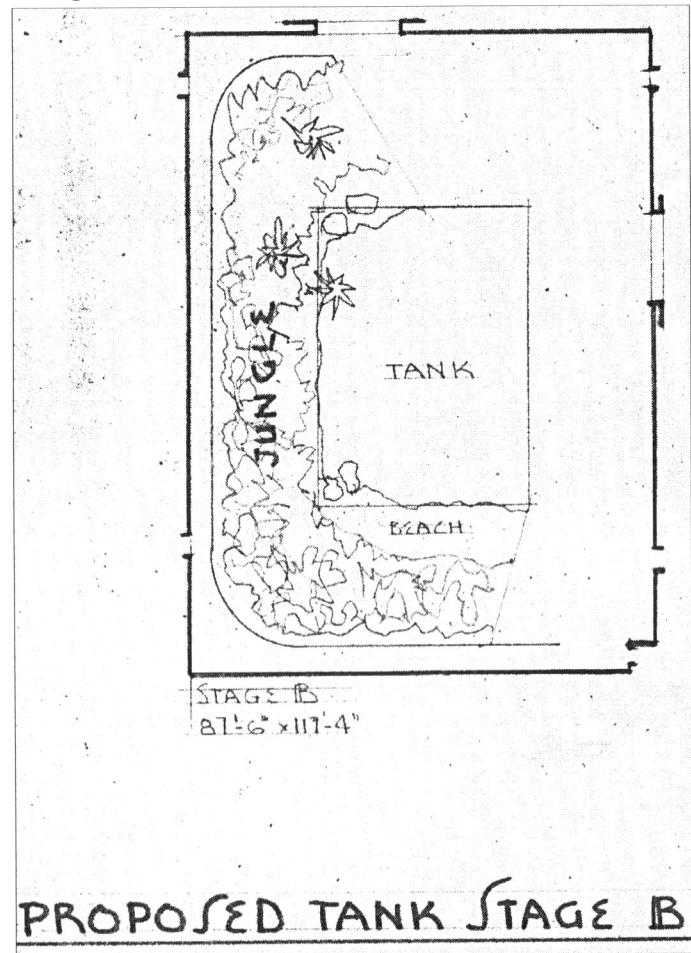

Day 6: The company returned to Stage "B" on Friday, which had been made over the day before to now contain "Ext. Jungle River Bank / Clearing / Nature Hut." Martin wrapped the episode at 7:25 p.m. [7]

The estimated budget was $142,263. William Self's office pushed it down to $140,491. The final cost of the episode was $168,210. [8]

Release / Reaction:
(Only ABC broadcast: 11/21/65)

King Rat was king in the movie houses. The World War II POW drama starred George Segal. "I Hear A Symphony," by the Supremes, was the hottest song on the radio. The best-selling record album in stores was *Whipped Cream & Other Delights* by Herb Alpert and the Tijuana Brass. Efrem Zimbalist, Jr., of *The F.B.I.*, had the cover of *TV Guide*. And *Lost in Space* had one of its best episodes: "Wish Upon a Star," in which Dr. Smith discovers a wishing machine.

"TV Scout," syndicated to newspapers across the U.S. of A., said:

> The Seaview plays a minor role in *Voyage to the Bottom of the Sea* as David Hedison goes ashore in jungle country belonging to "them" to make contact with an agent who will lead Hedison to "their" plant which is destroying U.S. spaceships returning from Venus. When the time for the rendezvous comes, two people claim to be the contact. One (Pilar Suerat) is prettier than the other, but it doesn't mean her motives are noble. Or does it? [9]

According to A.C. Nielsen, *Voyage* ranked No. 24 this week out of 107 network series. The ratings for its first half-hour helped, placing second. But, with no strange creatures in sight at the halfway point, it slipped into third position.

A.C. Nielsen 30-city survey from November 21, 1965:[10]

(7 – 7:30 p.m.)	Rating:	Share:
ABC: *Voyage to the Bottom of the Sea*	17.5	29.0%
CBS: *Lassie*	**21.8**	**36.1%**
NBC: *Bell Telephone Hour*	12.5	20.7%

(7:30 – 8 p.m.)	Rating:	Share:
ABC: *Voyage to the Bottom of the Sea*	17.2	27.0%
CBS: *My Favorite Martian*	17.6	27.6%
NBC: *Walt Disney*	**23.0**	**35.1%**

4.10

"Leviathan" (Episode 42)

(Prod. #8211; first aired Sunday, November 7, 1965)
Written by William Welch
Directed by Harry Harris
Produced by Irwin Allen and William Welch; Story Editor: Sidney Marshall
Guest Star Karen Steele, with Liam Sullivan as Dr. Anthony Sterling

REVERSE ENGINES, GIANT DEAD AHEAD -- Captain Lee Crane (David Hedison) and lovely distaff scientist, Cara Sloane (Karen Steele) are shocked beyond belief to see a man-giant approaching the submarine Seaview bent on destroying it. The action takes place in producer Irwin Allen's exciting series, "Voyage to the Bottom of the Sea." The segment, "Leviathan," airs in color Sunday, Nov. 7 at 7 p.m. over ABC-TV.

    If you have a sharp eye, you will note that from this point forward, the episode numbers (in the order they were filmed) are one decimal lower than the Production Number (the order they were *planned* for filming). This is because, as covered earlier, one of the scripts – "The Man from London" – was pulled from the schedule. (More about that "lost episode" when we get to "Return of the Phantom.") We now return you to this week's episode …

From the *Voyage* show files (Irwin Allen papers collection):

A scientist in an experimental undersea lab has located a fissure in the Earth's mantle from which exudes an exotic chemical which creates abnormal monstrous growth in living cells. The Seaview, sent to investigate, encounters a number of enormous sea creatures which endanger it en route. They then face the most monstrous creature of all, the scientist himself, who has grown to immense propositions. [1]

Assessment:

Painting by David Holderbaum. (Courtesy David Holderbaum; color rendition at iann.net)

"Leviathan" is an important chapter in the history of *Voyage to the Bottom of the Sea*. Without episodes like this one, the series would not have survived its second season. The ratings were falling, impacted by a difficult time slot against tough "family hour" competition. Parents were steering their kids toward *Lassie* and *My Favorite Martian* on CBS, or *Walt Disney's Wonderful World of Color* on NBC ... until high-concept episodes like this one became the topic of discussion on playgrounds across America, and kids wanted to see what they had been missing.

This episode had something for everyone – thrills and a giant for the kids, Karen Steele for the dads, David Hedison for the gals, Richard Basehart for the

153

sophisticates, and drug references for the teens. And all of it hung together in a story that, for the most part, competently connected the dots.

It was the first time on *Voyage* we saw a giant man (or manlike creature) engage in hand-to-sub combat with the Seaview – a spectacular effect for 1965 … which remains spectacular even today. No CGI here, baby! No cheating. This was actor Liam Sullivan (in close angles, with a stuntman in the wider shots) taking on the medium-sized Seaview model, wrestling it to the death in the "Green Tank." TV doesn't get more action-packed than this.

Mark Phillips said, "This episode begins with true horror, as a luckless diver frantically tries to out-swim a giant fish before being chomped to death in its jaws. From there, we follow the Seaview's perilous journey to an undersea lab. Some of the giant menaces are questionable, including stock footage of a manta ray and a studio-made octopus that looks too sluggish to be dangerous, but the schools of giant fish surrounding Seaview are extraordinary and Sterling's battle with Seaview is superbly filmed. A very good script, and well-acted by everyone." [2]

"A darn good show," Mike Bailey concurred. "Not only is the luckless diver seen chomped to death by a giant fish, as Mark points out above, but we see this happen from the perspective of inside the fish's gullet. Truly terrifying! The effects of Seaview steaming along amidst the giant fish were accomplished by shooting the four-foot model among the denizens of Marineland of the Pacific. The script rings true, and there is an appropriate sense of tragedy about the tale. … My only beef is with the goofy looking "wax teeth" stuck in the giant Sterling's mouth to make him look 'scary.' Oh well." [3]

The fangs can be explained – different parts of the body grow at different degrees – but how did his clothes grow? Perhaps the better question is *why*? Because ABC Broadcast Standards and Practices required it. And don't think too hard about the mass hallucination. It was a clever idea, that Cara (Karen Steele) would want to get the crew to see the impossible, to prepare them for the not-so-impossible that awaited them at the fissure to the Earth's core. But the idea concerned Irwin Allen, which he expressed in one of his memos while the script was being developed. Allen suggested that one crewmember would need to describe what he was seeing in order for the others to then believe they saw the same thing. It was a good point. So, the writers had Riley talk about seeing a giant sea monster. But what the crew sees – a giant squid – doesn't match what Riley described. And, in many of the moments of mass hallucination to follow, no one else describes what they see, to inspire the others to see the same sight. Shouldn't someone have exclaimed, "Gosh, look at the size of that jellyfish!" before others saw a giant jellyfish?

A missed moment of drama and horror, comes when the giant Dr. Sterling tumbles onto the undersea lab where the loving Cara is waiting to stand by her man. She literally gets crushed by love! But shouldn't we have had a quick camera cut to Cara's reaction to her big lover boy fixing to crash down on top of her? Gruesome? Perhaps. Dramatic? Absolutely. Alas, ABC censors would have none of it. Something like that might scare the kids. Worse, it would undoubtedly have their moms writing angry letters to the network.

Even without this ghoulish inclusion, we at least have Nelson's poignant remark at the end of the show, about what killed Cara in the end – and that love is more powerful than any gas … or hallucinogenic.

One other thing to note: This was the first *Voyage* aired to have the new, spruced-up opening title sequence, with the sonar sound effects and animated rings, followed by the Flying Sub sailing by. If you're watching the episodes in the order presented in this book – the order in which they were filmed – you've already seen that, in "Death Ship" (aired after the title sequence change), but this was the first time those of us watching in 1965 saw it. And it was an attention grabber.

"Leviathan" is a big man, a big problem, and a big episode.

Script:

William Welch's writers contract: August 20, 1965.
Welch's 2nd-draft teleplay approved on August 25.
Shooting Final teleplay (pale green paper): August 27.
Page revisions (blue paper): September 2.
Page revisions (dark green paper): September 17.
Page revisions (yellow paper): September 16.

William Welch wrote the script – his fifth for the series, in addition to all the rewriting he did during Season One.

A well-read man, Welch knew all about Leviathan, a creature from Jewish belief, with the form of a large sea serpent. Leviathan is referenced in the Hebrew Bible, as well as in the Old Testament books of Job, Psalms, Isaiah, and Amos. The Babylonian Talmud, *Baba Bathra*, described the enormous size of the Leviathan as follows:

> Once we went in a ship and saw a fish which put his head out of the water. He had horns upon which was written: "I am one of the meanest creatures that inhabit the sea. I am three

hundred miles in length, and [you will] enter this day into the jaws of the Leviathan."

With this as inspiration, Welch began to weave his tale.

Robert Hamner told Mark Phillips, "Most of the writers were good guys. Billy Woodfield was half crazy, but I liked him. Arthur Weiss was a nice man – a little quiet and a little strange but a good guy. Peter Germano was a Western writer; we worked on a *Cheyenne* together. Sid Marshall was a nice man, but not very creative. Bill Welch was sensational, but overworked and he was terrified of Irwin. [Director] Harry Harris was another nice guy and also terrified of Irwin. Guys like Bill Welch, Al Gail and Tony Wilson were under Irwin's thumb. Irwin was very difficult to work for, so that cut down on the talent pool a great deal. It's all psychological. Before *Voyage*, Irwin made a couple of features and they were made in last-minute panic situations. They became big hits and, in Irwin's subconscious, he thought, 'That's the way to have a hit! Get everybody into a panic.' And often Irwin would create a crisis at the last minute. That went with the territory with Irwin, but many people didn't want to work with him." [4]

Allen read Welch's script, then gave comments on August 25, saying, in part:

> P. 4, Sc. 16: Nelson should say that unless Cara can give him more information as to why Sterling wants him to help him, he can't take the Seaview away from its duties....

> P. 5, Sc. 18, Girl's voice states that Sterling is calling via Telstar. Why does Nelson say, "I thought he was in the South Pacific?" The fact that he uses Telstar should make that obvious. ...

> Cara's scene is really unnecessary as she doesn't give any reason for it other than Sterling needs help. Her presence on board Seaview later could be explained another way. Once Nelson agrees to go, Sterling could request Nelson to allow his assistant Cara Sloane, who is at present in California getting new supplies for the lab, to return with Nelson. While the phone conversation is in progress, Cara can arrive and arouse Nelson's suspicions by tensely asking Sterling if he's sure he feels alright. [5]

It was later determined that Cara's scene with Nelson was necessary. It established that she had been away from Sterling for a period of time … enough time for him to go through a pretty dramatic change.

Allen continued:

> The fact that sonar cuts out even though the squid and coelentera are still seen doesn't make sense as later in the script we are told that some of the encounters were actually true. If these were the true ones, sonar shouldn't cut out. If, however, these were hallucinations, then in each case the monster should be sighted first by one person who would report what he sees, thereby implanting in everyone's mind the type of monster it appears to be….
>
> It is never explained how it is that Sterling became exposed to the dangerous elements of the fissure. Therefore, we must assume the air inside the underwater lab is contaminated. If this is so, why would Sterling allow anyone, especially Cara, to come into that atmosphere? … When Nelson and Cara meet Sterling, they should have to talk to him through a glass enclosed room. This would ensure the fact that they will not to be affected by the gas. [6]

This concern was eliminated when it was decided that Sterling was exposed to the "strange emission" when outside the lab. The air within was safe to breathe.

More from Allen:

> Nelson should show more of an interest in the scientific side of the problem. How does he hope to remedy Sterling's giantistis [sic] if he doesn't know exactly what caused it?
>
> P. 52, Sc. 154: From here on the events are not convincing:
> 1) How does Nelson know Sterling is gone anywhere?
> 2) The idea of Sterling swimming all the way to the Seaview without any oxygen mask is doubly unbelievable.
> 3) Sc. 168: What does Cara mean that if the flying sub remains attached to the airlock it will endanger her more.

> 4) Some other less gruesome method of getting rid of Sterling should be found. Having Crane order the Seaview to fire on him is objectionable. [7]

Evidently electrocution was considered more civilized than a torpedo attack. As for Sterling's breathing under water, giving him air tanks wasn't about to solve the problem. Better that they hope the audience would think giant lungs could enable him to hold his breath for a really, really long time.

ABC's Department of Standards & Practices found a few items objectionable, as well:

> Please be sure that the "gaping jaws" do not bear down full on camera.... Special caution on shots of various "sea monsters" and Sterling in gargantuan proportions. His roar of pain [must be kept] to a minimum. As usual, this can only be fully approved on color film. ... Standard caution on Nelson being knocked unconscious; the slap. [8]

Production:
(Filmed September 20 – 28, 1965; 7 days)

Harry Harris was assigned to direct after making an impression on Irwin Allen, and all others, with his handling of "… And Five of Us Are Left."

Karen Steele was 34 when cast as Cara. A former model and cover girl, she was prominently featured in 1955's Academy award-winning Best Picture *Marty*, then had the female lead in numerous B-pictures, such as 1956's *The Sharkfighters* (with Victor Mature), 1957's *Bailout at 43,000* (with John Payne) and 1959's *Ride Lonesome* (with

One year in the future: Karen Steele seduces Captain Kirk in *Star Trek* … and lives to tell about it.

Liam Sullivan as the LSD guru who engages in a 30-minute battle of the wits with Joe Friday in a tripped-out 1968 *Dragnet*. (Universal Television)

Randolph Scott). She also had the top female spot in the 1960s mob-pic *The Rise and Fall of Legs Diamond*. A year from now, she would be cast as Eve, one of "Mudd's Women," on *Star Trek*.

Liam Sullivan played Dr. Anthony Sterling, both big and small. He was 42, and had appeared in two episodes of *The Twilight Zone*, including a memorable role in "The Silence," as a braggart who has his vocal chords removed so that he can win a bet that he can go a year without speaking. Irwin Allen would bring Sullivan back later in the year for "His Majesty Smith," an episode of *Lost in Space*. In 1968, Jack Webb cast Sullivan as a drug-promoting guru in the *Dragnet* episode "The Big Prophet." This intended anti-drug tale features a back-and-forth debate that lasts nearly the entire episode. Sullivan's breezy enthusiasm as the prophet is not to be missed. And, for "Plato's Stepchildren," a 1968 episode of *Star Trek*, Sullivan played the leader of a group of elitists who wield psychokinetic powers.

Speaking of *Star Trek*, **Alexander Courage**, who wrote that series theme and scored several of its episodes, provided the score for "Leviathan." If you've watched both shows, you may note that Courage borrowed from himself, and

Voyage, for one of his *Trek*s – "The Man Trap." He also borrowed from – or was inspired by – Bernard Herrmann's score for 1961's *Mysterious Island*. It all works swimmingly.

Filming began on Monday, September 20, 1965, for the first of six-and-a-half days on Stage 10 for all the Seaview sets, as well as the undersea lab set. We get a tour of the Seaview in this near "bottle show," including "Int. Crew's Mess," "Int. Seaview Corridor & Staircase," "Int. Observation Nose + Control Room," "Int. Seaview Lab," and, on the same stage, "Int. Flying Sub."

We learn why, when on the Flying Sub, one should wear one of those nifty flight jackets. Nelson tells Cara that each contains a built-in life jacket. In other words, buckle up.

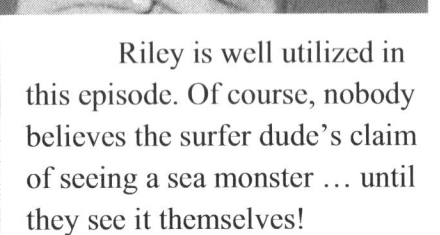

Riley is well utilized in this episode. Of course, nobody believes the surfer dude's claim of seeing a sea monster … until they see it themselves!

The poker game scene between Riley, Kowalski, and Sharkey is delightful. And Sharkey seems to feel the same way about women on his sub as Irwin Allen felt about them on his show. Sharkey says, "Listen, buster, I dig a pretty chick just like the next guy, but on a ship they are *nowhere*. Special attention; special quarters; special detail for all hands! Err, forget it!"

Stage "B" was needed for only half a day, for the interior of Nelson's stateside office, and "Int. Underwater Lab." Stage "B," you will recall, was the one that contained the water tank. The Underwater Lab, built above the tank, allowed divers to enter and exit through the floor portal.

David Hedison's performances, set against an array of sea serpents, monsters, giants, and spaced-out aliens, was always sincere, and just what the show needed.

Second Unit footage was taken without sound of Robert Dowdell at the backlot Moat, as well as the studio's Transportation Area, the Transportation Building, and the Old Writer's Building. And the Second Unit handled all the underwater action photographed in the "Green Tank." This constituted more than a day's filming, added to the seven days in which the main unit filmed. Four of those days went into overtime, wrapping at 7:20, 7:30, 7:30 again, and 8:55 p.m., respectively. [9]

Allan Hunt told interviewer Mark Phillips. "When I first read the script, I thought, 'This is a wonderful SF idea.' The big surprise is when Sullivan's character grows so tall that he can actually stand on the ocean floor and his head clears the surface. When he peers into the Seaview's windows, all you see are these big eyes and a nose. Well, it just killed me when they added fangs. They even used the same teeth from a *Lost in Space* monster! That was Irwin again. He couldn't leave those things alone. The way it was originally written, where Sullivan becomes the Amazing Colossal Man, was so good, but they went for the fangs, and I think they even had him growling." [10]

Growling underwater, that is. The *Lost in Space* episode filming at this time in which the fangs were first used was "One of Our Dogs Is Missing."

Regarding the stunts filmed in the Green Tank, including sequences with a non-stuntman – Liam Sullivan said, "The tank was 12 feet deep, and Harry Harris directed from behind a glass window. After the third take, I was supposed to jump up and catch one of the wires stretched over the tank. I missed the wire and fell back into the tank, totally out of breath. Two divers plunged into the tank and pulled me to the surface. It was a close call; I nearly drowned! Three weeks later, Irwin Allen looked at the footage and decided my make-up wasn't scary enough. So, we

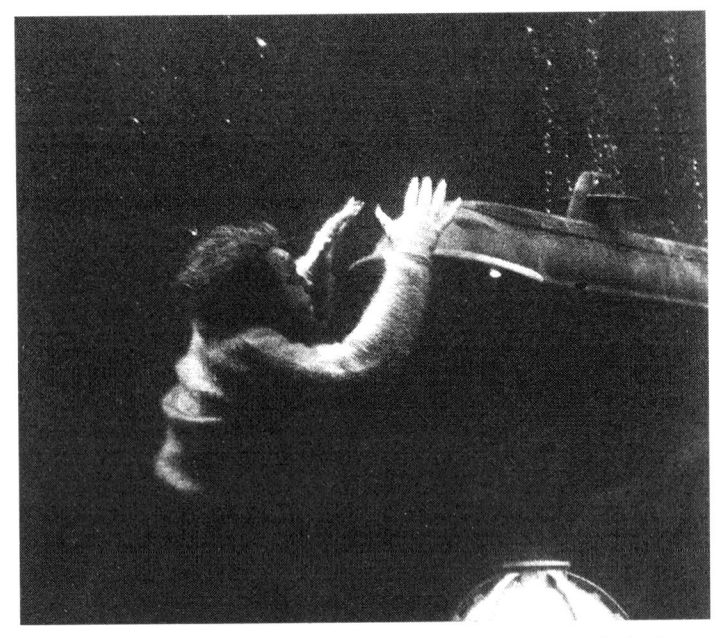

These murky still shots were taken in the Green Tank during the fight between two giants – Sterling and Seaview. While Liam Sullivan got plenty wet during the filming, a stuntman clearly handled these more difficult sequences.
(Courtesy Synthesis Entertainment)

did the whole damn thing over! Yech!"[11]

That's was when the fangs were added.

In an interview with Kevin Burns, director Harry Harris said of Allen, "He would have liked to have directed everything he ever did. But he had to have directors, so he hated the directors. But he hired them."[12]

The dilemma for Allen, in running two or more series at once, each with 26 to 30 episodes per season, was how to maintain control when he was forced to rely on the services, and the artistic whims, of other directors. Harris said, "When Irwin produces a show, he has a still man standing with him all the time, taking pictures of every shot he wants to make – hundreds of still shots! And he has a sketch artist, standing next to him, with him saying, 'See, I want to make this shot right here,' and the sketch artist draws it right there. Now, they go and they sketch it, then they go in this huge room and they put all these sketches on the wall. I'd get [memos as long as] books – *you'd get a whole book of how it's going to be shot*. They don't work all the time, but it's a guide. When you do it, you have that guide to go by. So, if you see it in there and it doesn't work, you've got to go to him and say, 'Irwin, this isn't going to work. It doesn't work because of so-and-so, and so-and-so.' Well, we had a hard time talking him out of it, but if it doesn't work, he won't do it, or if it's going to cost him some extra money, he won't do it. But you have to talk him out of things if he's got them on that sketch pad, and he *wants* it to work. ...

"I didn't agree with him, but he was paying the tab, so I did most of the things he wanted me to do. And I resisted him a lot of times, and we got into some biggies... And there was a side of him that I probably don't know too well. His wife probably knows. I think he was a softy underneath. And I sort of sensed it and I felt that he genuinely liked me, even though he had this crusty, rough attitude at times. I knew he liked me because he was always calling me back; always wanting me to do things for him. So, it was satisfying to work for him. It wasn't fun; at times it was awful, but it was okay." [13]

A budget of $142,689 was approved by William Self. The final cost was $163,037. [14]

Release / Reaction:
(ABC premiere airdate: 11/7/65; network repeat broadcast: 8/14/66)

This was the week the long-running soap opera *Days of Our Lives* premiered on TV; Ferdinand Marcos was elected the tenth President of the Philippines; and the big Northeast Blackout of 1965 occurred, plunging several states and parts of Canada into darkness, lasting for 13 hours. The film doing the best business in movie houses – that had electricity, that is – was *The*

Agony and the Ecstasy, starring Charlton Heston as Michelangelo, and Rex Harrison as Pope Julius II. The soundtrack albums *The Sound of Music*, with Julie Andrews, and *Help!*, by The Beatles, were the best-selling record albums in the U.S. The song getting the most play on the radio wasn't by Andrews or the Beatles, but the Rolling Stones, with "Get Off of My Cloud." June Lockhart and Guy Williams, floating about in their spacesuits from *Lost in Space*, had the cover of *TV Guide*. On that series this week, Dr. Smith ate untested fruit and grew to giant proportions. Two giants in one week on Irwin Allen's two shows! Do you think this gave him the idea for *Land of the Giants*?

During the week "Leviathan" aired, a curious filler piece appeared in the November 7th edition of the *Syracuse Post Standard*. The article was led with the headline: "Sexy Feet?" It said:

> Actor David Hedison, currently co-starring in producer Irwin Allen's *Voyage to the Bottom of the Sea* series, continues to receive more fan mail at the studio than any other actor. "And strangely," said David, "a tremendous amount of it is from little old ladies who ask for my sock size, wanting to knit me some argyles. I must have sexy-looking feet." [15]

Hedison admitted to us that one of those letters about his feet was from a man, determined to know his shoe size!

"TV Scout," syndicated in a newspaper near you, said of this episode:

> Science fiction fans should have a fine time watching *Voyage to the Bottom of the Sea*. The story builds slowly to a great climax that is a triumph for the special effects department. Karen Steele is the guest, a scientist who urges David Hedison and Richard Basehart to a Deep Sea lab where a scientist has discovered a fissure on the ocean's floor that leads to the Earth's core. But on the trip to the lab, the entire crew begins experiencing mass hallucinations (after she has done something to the ship's salt) involving gigantic sea creatures. [16]

And then they meet a giant who is not a mere hallucination.

"TV Key," in many newspapers that didn't carry "TV Scout," said:

> A show the children will not want to miss. The Seaview has seen combat with all types of underwater enemies, but they are up against a rather unique adversary in this outing – a gigantic human deep sea diver. The technical aspects of the production are the show's real stars this week. [17]

Entertainment columnist Tom McIntyre, writing in North Carolina's *Gaston Gazette*, had this to say:

> If you're looking for way-out entertainment, WSOC-TV's *Voyage to the Bottom of the Sea* should fill the bill. This hour-long journey into the realm of science-fiction usually comes up with some far-fetched themes ranging from the hero being swallowed by a whale to a gigantic man attacking the submarine Seaview. Most of the time the episodes bog down with technical gobbledygook which the actors rattle off just like they know what they're talking about. But once you get past all that, the show really disintegrates into overly long mute action. We will have to admit that when the show is good, it is good. However, when it is bad, it's terrible. Somehow there just doesn't seem to be a happy medium. [18]

On this night, despite *Voyage* offering a story that was a bit more fantastic, the ratings remained the same, with the series placing second during its first half-hour, then slipping into third place for its second, failing to grab a 30 share, the all-important renewal threshold.

A.C. Nielsen 30-city survey from November 7, 1965:[19]

(7 – 7:30 p.m.)	Rating:	Peak Share:
ABC: *Voyage to the Bottom of the Sea*	16.0	27.5%
CBS: *Lassie*	**21.7**	**37.5%**
NBC: *Bell Telephone Hour*	15.0	25.9%

(7:30 – 8 p.m.)	Rating:	Peak Share:
ABC: *Voyage to the Bottom of the Sea*	15.5	26.1%
CBS: *My Favorite Martian*	16.1	27.1%
NBC: *Walt Disney's Wonderful World of Color*	**21.8**	**36.7%**

When repeated in August 1966, "Leviathan" won its time period.

4.11

"The Peacemaker" (Episode 43)

(Prod. #8212; first aired Sunday, November 14, 1965)
Written by William Read Woodfield and Allan Balter
Directed by Sobey Martin
Produced by Irwin Allen and Frank La Tourette
Story Editor: Sidney Marshall
Guest Star John Cassavetes
Co-Starring Whit Bissell, Irene Tsu and Dale Ishimoto

From the *Voyage* show files (Irwin Allen papers collection):

A fanatical pacifist who defected to an enemy power and built them a deadly underwater weapon, discovers he has been deluded by their propaganda and that they intend to wage war with their ultimate weapon. He escapes and contacts the U.S. Crane rescues him and brings him and the weapon aboard the Seaview. Now obsessed with saving the world, he threatens to set off the weapon and annihilate most of the world, unless the heads of government capitulate to him and disarm. Nelson is now faced with disarming the bomb or destroying the scientist without touching off the greatest holocaust in man's history. [1]

Assessment:

We jump ahead to 1978 ... the date displayed at the start of this episode. ABC-TV was determined that stories with obvious present-day relevance be pushed as far in the fictional future as possible.

At the outset of Act I, the recycled iconic sequence of the Seaview shooting up from icy waters, first seen in the 1961 motion picture and sampled during Season One (in black and white), is utilized to good effect. This was the first time the footage was seen on television in color, and it made a dramatic moment. What follows, depending on one's personal tastes, may generate mixed reactions.

Mark Phillips said, "The very idea that someone like John Cassavetes (an acclaimed director/writer/actor) would appear on an adventure series like *Voyage* still boggles the mind. The dynamic Cassavetes towers over the pedestrian material and it's a shame that the worthy idea of the episode (global disarmament) wasn't developed better." [2]

Mike Bailey said, "It was unconscionable to bring in talent like John Cassavetes, with all of the implied power and potential to play off Basehart and Hedison, and then to simply throw it away on an insipid script directed by one of *Voyage*'s lamest house directors (Sobey Martin)." [3]

Sometimes the biggest fans can be the harshest critics. We, on the other hand, enjoyed this episode. Is it one of the best? Hardly. Is it entertaining? We think so. Does it have purpose? Absolutely.

We'll begin with the entertainment value. The Teaser is an attention grabber. Sure, those bodies in white lab coats riddled by machine-gun bullets should be bloodied ... but not during ABC's family hour during the 1960s. So, we'll have to take it for what it is – a bloodless artifact from a bygone era. Act I is greatly enhanced by excellent color stock footage from a 20th Century-Fox motion picture, showing the streets, the bay, the junks, and masses of people in Hong King. Captain Crane has a dirty undercover assignment as a legless beggar, reminiscent of Lon Chaney's similar look in the 1920 film *The Penalty*. You hadn't seen such a grim ruse on *Voyage*, nor would you see it again. The story moves quickly and has plenty of twists and turns, and thrills. Cassavetes is powerful, and Irene Tsu is stunning. What's not to like?

As the story progresses, we lose Ms. Tsu, in a sorrowful scene, beautifully played by Tsu and her two leading men. The opposite reactions from these men say much of their inner souls. Cassavetes' character, Everett Lang, though subtly remorseful, seems to shrug it off, thinking more about his own skin … or his own secret agenda. Captain Crane, with yet another perfect portrayal from David Hedison, is deeply grieved and reluctant to leave the girl. It's quite poignant.

Once on the Seaview, the crew's disdain for Everett Lang is immediate and clear. With the exception perhaps of Sharkey's determination to wring Lang's neck, and one justifiable flareup by Nelson, all are underplayed. The looks from Hedison are classic! Even Allan Hunt's disdain as Riley is right on the money.

The climactic scene – that showdown in the Missile Room with Lang threatening to detonate the bomb – may drag a bit, but it delivers the theme of the story. Peace should *not* be obtained by any means, at any price. We've all seen egocentric lunatics like Lang, either in our own lives, or in the news. They threaten the world with their blind ambition, determined that they know best, and whatever they do in the name of their cause is justified. Like many self-appointed leaders, they lack the moral compass and the empathy to do what's right. Everett Lang is one. And who better to play him than John Cassavetes, who had both the smarts and the looks to bring such a charismatic yet smug overachiever to life.

We never know if Everett Lang would have followed through with his threat and pressed the button, because his hand was forced by Nelson and Crane. Was he bluffing; did the button only get pushed as a result of the struggle? Or was this demented genius warped enough to actually blow himself and half the world to smithereens, just to make a point? We're left wondering.

Script:
Woodfield's and Balter's story title: "The Man Who Stole the World."
Woodfield's and Balter's teleplay retitled "The Peacemaker."
Revised Shooting Final teleplay: September 20, 1965.
3rd Rev. Shooting Final teleplay (yellow paper): September 23.
Page revisions (blue paper): September 30.

How interested was writer William Read Woodfield in the topic of nuclear warfare? He told interviewer Mark Phillips, "Very interested. I had read Herman Kahn and Henry Kissinger on thermonuclear war, and when I worked with Stanley Kubrick on *Spartacus* [as a still photographer], we talked a great deal about it. He went on to do something good with it [*Dr. Strangelove*] and I [played] around with it on *Voyage*." [4]

After reading Woodfield's and Balter's script, Frank La Tourette wrote to Irwin Allen:

> I think this will make a very good show. I have one main objection. ... We meet the lead character on Page 9. We meet him again briefly on Page 22. But he doesn't really come alive until the third and fourth Acts. This results in my opinion, in two shows. Or at least the story stops for a long time to allow Nelson and Crane to fool around inside China.
>
> Would it be possible to build up Lang a little more in the earlier part of the show? Perhaps, instead of Connors talking about Lang wanting to get out, a scene or two could be inserted showing a shattered Lang approaching Connors' man in China, asking to get out but <u>only on the Seaview</u> and indicating his obsession with peace and the necessity of his trying a new and bold plan. This would allow you to cut down on some of the rather dull stuff in China with Nelson and Crane, set up a great hooker with the audience as to what Lang has in mind, and make more palatable the attempt to get him out of China and Crane back to the Seaview. It would also allow perhaps for a little more action with Lang's making contact with Connors' man from which a bit of conflict could arise and in which Lang could be more revealed as a character with an objective. This is merely a suggestion. [5]

The suggestion was accepted.

ABC's Mary Garbutt, of the network's Department of Standards & Practices, wrote to Allen and his staff on September 21, saying in part:

> Please be sure that the following names are completely fictitious and not close to names of men in comparable positions or professions: DAVID ANDERSON, Sec'y of Defense; ADMIRAL WILLIAM CONNORS, Chief of Naval Intelligence; EVERETT LANG, nuclear physicist.
>
> Pg 8: Please "super" or establish future date here or earlier. Substitute for "Good Lord".
>
> Pg 10: These guns must not be automatic weapons and we must not see the bullets hit. Please be sure that the deaths are in no way grotesque. Can only be approved on film.

Pg 13: The fight as written is too violent and graphic: Delete direction "pummeling his head against the floor". Sc. 21: We can see Lang moving with the loop, [but] delete shot of loop around man's neck and delete Sc 22. Sc. 23: Delete direction that the man "smiles". Again, final approval on film.

Pg 19 & 20: Caution that beggar's make-up and guttural sounds are not over-done.

Pg 25, etc.: Please be sure that all dialogue in the Oriental language is acceptable.... To bring the armament-disarmament discussion into a fair balance, strengthen the argument that measures for the security of all nations must be provided before disarmament:

Pg 37: Bring in mention of world Disarmament Congress – Perhaps in Anderson's answering Lang's "holocaust" speech. Delete Anderson's "hero no matter what" speech.

Pg 48: Have Nelson refute Lang's "snail's pace" idea with need of safety measures for all nations to disarm so that security not endangered. ... [6]

Production:
(Filmed September 29 – October 6, 1965; 6 days)

Sobey Martin was brought in to direct. Between *Voyage* and *Lost in Space*, he was working full time now for Irwin Allen.

John Cassavetes played Everett Lang. He was 36 and took roles such as this to finance his own directorial efforts. His first known screen role was an uncredited bit part in Richard Basehart's 1951 film *Fourteen Hours*. By the mid-1950s, Cassavetes was gainfully employed as a guest player, mostly on prestigious television anthology dramas from the period. During the 1959-60 TV season, he starred in his own series, *Johnny Staccato*, as a jazz musician whose day job was working as a private eye. The year before agreeing to appear on *Voyage*,

John Cassavetes, actor extraordinaire. But what he really wanted to do was direct.

Cassavetes co-starred with Lee Marvin and Angie Dickinson in *The Killers*. He would leave the small screen behind shortly after this *Voyage* for co-starring roles in major films, such as 1967's *The Dirty Dozen*, for which he received an Oscar nomination, and 1968's *Rosemary's Baby*. Cassavetes would also become an acclaimed writer and director of art films, gaining attention and award nominations for his 1959 film *Shadows*, and 1968's *Faces*. He received an Oscar nomination for his 1974 film, *A Woman Under the Influence*, which he both wrote and directed.

Casting Director Joe D'Agosta said, "I brought John on. I had met him earlier; we never hung out together, but we maintained a connection. He would call me to help find work for his friends, who were working for him in the movies that he was making, *probably for nothing*. John would do an acting job, and then he would put all of his money into the production or post-production of a movie that he wanted to make. And I would be invited to his house to watch him film, and to his garage to watch him edit. And he would call me periodically and say so-and-so needs a job. And that was my relationship with him.

"On one of these phone calls, John says, 'Joe, I need some more money for my editing. If you've got anything, let me know.' I said, '*You're* going to do television?' He said, 'I need the money.' So, I walked over and said, 'Irwin, do we have a part for John Cassavetes?' And he said, 'Yeah!' And so, we hired him. I think we gave him 'double top' bill. I'm not sure about that, but I think that figure of $5,000 instead of $2,500, which was certainly the top." [7]

Cassavetes took the job on *Voyage* to help finance *Faces*. And while D'Agosta wanted to get him "double top" pay, Irwin Allen held the line at the "standard top" guest star rate of $2,500.

Whit Bissell played Connors. He was 55 and one year away from being cast as a regular in *The Time Tunnel*, as Lt. Gen. Heywood Kirk. Bissell had been a well-respected and often employed character actor in Hollywood since 1940, with over 300 film and TV appearances.

Irene Tsu was 21 when cast as Su Yin and fairly new in an acting career that would have her visit series such as *My Favorite Martian*, *I Spy*, *The Man from U.N.C.L.E.*, and *Hawaii Five-O*.

Dale Ishimoto was 42 when hired to play the Premier. Like many Asian-American actors in Hollywood, his bread and butter were series such as *Hawaiian Eye*, *McHale's Navy*, *I Spy*, and *Hawaii Five-O*.

Filming began Wednesday, September 29 on Stage B for Nelson's office, both interior and outer; Nelson's "war room"; "Int. Washington office"; and the "Ext. Seaview Con Tower," shot against a blue screen.

Day 2, on Thursday, was the first of three-and-a-half days spent on Stage 10, for the Seaview sets. They filmed on the sets for "Int. Nelson's Cabin," "Int. Control Room," and "Int. Observation Nose."

Day 3, Friday: Work continued on Stage 10 for "Int. Flying Sub," "Int. corridor & Missile Room," before the company moved outdoors to film on "Ext. Main Street" and "Ext. Another Street." The company filmed until 9:15 p.m.

Day 4, Monday: A full day was spent on Stage 10 and the Missile Room set.

Day 5, Tuesday: Still on Stage 10, more work in the Missile Room, for "Disarm bomb sequence," then a company move to Stage 16 for "Int. Boarded Up Ship" and "Int. Junk Cabin." [8]

Interviewed for this book, Allan Hunt said, "There was a scene between me and Terry Becker, when John Cassavetes was the guest, and they found out that the show was under and they needed to kill time. So, they wrote a quick scene between Terry Becker and me, so Terry and I got a chance to do something more character oriented. And Terry always said, 'That's the best scene I ever did,' because he got to be the Chief, as he saw the Chief. So, it was so good for us to be able to do that scene. But that episode was pretty tense; it was very nicely written." [9]

John Cassavetes didn't completely agree with the "nicely written" description. Joe D'Agosta said, "I walked over to the set to say 'hello,' and John [Cassavetes] said to me, 'I have no idea what I'm saying, Joe. I'm just spewing the words out.' Because there was a lot of technical dialogue." [10]

Allan Hunt said, "Cassavetes really openly *hated* being there. It was nothing personal against the other actors, but when we had lunch with him in the commissary, he would say, 'Come on! Are you kidding with this stuff? Do you guys do this *every week*?' He wasn't acting superior to us; he just had his sights set elsewhere, and he didn't care much for what we were doing. He was mainly there to raise money for one of his films. As I recall, the episode was pretty lame, about a maniac who had his finger on the bomb." [11]

Day 6, Wednesday, October 6: Work began at the backlot Moat for "Ext. Wharf," then "Ext. Sea." At midday, the company moved back onto Stage 16 for additional filming on the "Int. Junk Cabin" set, then a new set, "Int. Chougi Laboratory." Director Sobey Martin called for a wrap at 6:45 p.m. [12]

A budget of $144,474 had been approved by William Self. To save money, the music score was "tracked" with excerpts from past scores from different composers – and, as noted, John Cassavetes was held at $2,500. Regardless, the final cost was $158,636. [13]

Release / Reaction:

(ABC premiere airdate: 11/14/65; network repeat broadcast: 6/12/66)

Ironically, on the night that an episode of *Voyage* with the title "The Peacemaker" first aired on ABC, America fought its first major battle in Vietnam, with the U.S. Army and Marines against the People's Army of [North] Vietnam. When the Battle of Ia Drang was over, 250 U.S. troops were dead, and hundreds of others wounded. The estimates of Viet Cong killed went as high as 1,000.

Stateside, the war film *King Rat* was selling the most seats in movie houses. "I Hear a Symphony," by the Supremes, and "1-2-3," by Len Barry, were the songs playing the most on the radio. Joey Heatherton had the cover of *TV Guide*. *Lost in Space* was doing better than *Voyage* in the ratings. The episode this week was called "The Sky Is Falling," in which the Robinsons encounter an alien family trying to colonize the same planet they are marooned upon. *Voyage*, meanwhile, was trying an episode with less science fiction.

"TV Scout" said:

> John Cassavetes gives a good performance on *Voyage to the Bottom of the Sea* as a scientist who has helped the enemy develop a proton bomb. After they have attempted to kill him, he wants to come back home. The story has too many elements: rescue, recovery of the bomb, and the scientist's attempt to control the world by threatening to detonate the bomb. Some elements, however, are properly suspenseful. [14]

Not even John Cassavetes could bring them out. According to A.C. Nielsen, *Voyage* ranked at No. 72 this week out of 107 network series, a very bad showing. As seemed to be the norm of late, it ranked second in its first half-hour, although weaker than usual; then dropped – and did so like a lead balloon this week – to third at the halfway mark. A mid-season renewal was looking shaky.

A.C. Nielsen 30-city survey from November 14, 1965:[15]

(7 – 7:30 p.m.)	Rating:	Share:
ABC: *Voyage to the Bottom of the Sea*	14.7	25.4
CBS: *Lassie*	**24.5**	**42.4**
NBC: Actuality Special	11.6	20.1

(7:30 – 8 p.m.):		
ABC: *Voyage to the Bottom of the Sea*	14.8	23.4%
CBS: *My Favorite Martian*	**22.9**	**36.2%**
NBC: *Disney's Wonderful World…*	21.6	34.1%

4.12

"The Monster from Outer Space" (Episode 44)
(Prod. #8213; first aired Sunday, December 19, 1965)
Written by William Read Woodfield and Allan Balter
Directed by James Clark (with Sobey Martin and Harry Harris, uncredited)
Produced by Irwin Allen, Frank La Tourette and William Welch
Story Editor: Sidney Marshall

From the *Voyage* show files (Irwin Allen papers collection):

> The space probe returns with a strange form of life clinging to its surface. When Captain Crane attempts to retrieve the capsule, the alien life attached to it grows gigantic and deadly and has to be burned. Although Nelson takes every precaution to exterminate it, it reappears and slowly overtakes the Seaview crew. Each man it envelopes becomes slave to it until only Nelson and Chief Sharkey are left. [1]

Assessment:

"Houston, we have a problem. A monster from outer space is clinging to the returning space capsule ... and, worse, we've suffered a budget cut! Look what they've done to Houston Space Center, er, 'Space Central' – only one video monitor and technician! And the only ship in the area of the planned splashdown isn't the usual aircraft-carrier battle group, but a sub!"

ABC insisted the date "1978" be established at the top of the story. Gemini 6 was returning to Earth for a planned splashdown the same week this episode first aired, and, as hokey as the Teaser is, the network didn't want viewers to think that they were actually seeing our space capsule return ... with a monster clinging to it!

Beyond the cheesy Teaser ...

"Yes, this is a monster-on-the-loose episode," warned Mike Bailey. "But it's mounted in high fashion (there's a budget) and it's *not* dull. There is a reason it's not dull. It was directed by James B. Clark, who had, for years, cut his teeth editing films for top directors such as Howard Hawks, Leo McCarey, Samuel Fuller, Joseph L Mankiewicz, and John Ford. There is movement o-plenty, and seldom a slack moment throughout. Although the premise of the episode is suspect and a foreshadow of what would become standard fare in Year Three, the execution is not. There is no man in a rubber suit; there is no Dick Tufeld doing "You will obey!" monster dialogue; there *is* a kind of peek-a-boo, now you see it, now you don't nature to the creature's comings and goings that I still find fascinating and somewhat reminiscent of the 'bear' in the *Outer Limits* episode 'It Crawled Out of the Woodwork.' As far as the creature goes, there was no computer animation back then. Short of full cell animation or stop-motion photography, inflating and deflating balloons was probably the only way to represent the creature. The underwater shots are fairly believable. ... I think that, if taken alone, this show is not as execrable as it has been pigeonholed. In fact, I kind of like it. Go figure." [2]

Mark Phillips, however felt it was "the low point of Year Two." He added, "Although this 'alien-on-the-loose' story has more subtext than later alien stories, it's still a very unpleasant and limited story, with a giant balloon playing the alien. Only Wayne Heffley, as Doc, looks convincingly possessed (with his blank smile and glazed eyes)." [3]

We find ourselves in agreement with Mike Bailey. It's a monster tale, and an okay one at that. Sure, the fully inflated creature doesn't register more than a 1 (out of 10) on the fright meter, but there is a wonderful creep factor seeing that thing inflate out of a pinprick in a pipe, and then deflate just as eerily back into its hiding hole. Also, it's nice seeing Robert Dowdell (as Chip Morton) have something to do, and act a bit menacing. Wayne Heffley is quite convincing, as Mark noted, and David Hedison continues to impress. The element of remorse that the writers – but especially Hedison – inject into Crane when under the influence of the creature, is actually touching. And lines like Crane saying to Morton, "I hope they don't fight it like I did," are skin-crawlers.

Wayne Heffley, David Hedison, and Robert Dowdell, with a refreshingly subtle variation on the man-possessed-by-alien-creature premise.

Curious how Morton shares none of Crane's regret. "What difference does it make?" is his response. With such a lack of empathy, he may never make captain.

We'd see many man-under-the-influence-of-alien-creature scenarios later in the series, but, for this formative outing in that realm, the gimmick works pretty well, as Hedison plays Crane as more than a one-dimension-processed man.

The scenes shot in the Green Tank are topnotch – man, with underwater torches, against monster. The decontamination sequence is also well staged. This level of precaution adds a bit of realism to an otherwise just-for-the-fun-of-it fantasy.

As this is written in 2020, some might feel that the unity promised by the Monster is a good idea. As the possessed Crane tells Nelson, "Eventually, everyone in the world will be one giant organism." Such pabulum was also offered by the pods in *Invasion of the Body Snatchers*, you'll remember. The problem is, individuals were created with a messy thing called free will. The challenge, in this episode as in the dangerous real world of the present, is to use our autonomy to benefit others, not ourselves.

The actions of Nelson, Crane, and, yes, even Chief Sharkey, remind us that our individualism, our personal passions, and our inner sense of right are true measures of a person. Intentionally or not, "The Monster from Outer Space" demonstrates this truth.

Script:

Woodfield's and Balter's writers contract: February 13, 1965.
Woodfield's and Balter's story treatment and 1st-draft teleplay for "The Migrants" approved: October 1.
2nd Rev. Shooting Final teleplay (pink paper): October 4.
Page revisions (blue paper): October 5.
Page revisions (green paper): October 6.
Page revisions (gold paper): November 8.

"The Monster from Outer Space" was a **Woodfield/Balter** collaboration. Before the Allen-esque title change, the story began as "The Migrants."

Dorothy Brown, Director of ABC's Department of Standards & Continuity, wrote to Irwin Allen and his staff on October 4:

> Pg 1: Substitute for stock shots of the Houston Space Center to eliminate this mixing of fact and fiction. Please make nondescript and/or fictitious and establish future date.
>
> Pgs 1-5: It is not clear that this is an instruments-only technical probe capsule and unmanned. This must be completely clear before Pg 5.
>
> Pg 21: As written, this space monster seems unpleasantly "oozy and slimy" – Please be sure that this is not the case on color film. Isn't it possible for "hostile other world creatures" to sometimes look perhaps even "beautiful"? Also, particular caution in seeing that the sequences, in which the creature "takes over" the men, are not a painful ordeal for the men and consequently horrifying to watch....
>
> Pgs 47 thru 55: These machine guns (make futuristic) may be used against the creature but not against the men: Sc 120: Delete Nelson and Sharkey shooting into the men – They can use a smoke bomb to disperse or else must be able to bolt out the door by using "bullet splatters" for cover without hitting the men. Pg 127: Sharkey must over-come sailor in

some other way than shooting him in the legs with machine gun!

Pg 52: Delete "For God's sake" in Crane's line.

Pg 56, Sc 135: Your usual care in seeing that barrel of machine gun is not pointed into camera.

Pg 63: The death cry of creature must be something other than human and not of the blood-curdling variety. Standard citation on this whole sequence. [4]

Production:
(Filmed October 7 – 14, 1965; 6 days, plus November 10 & 11, for 2 days)

This single episode was actually directed by three different men: James Clark, Sobey Martin, and Harry Harris.

Wayne Heffley was the only guest player in this episode. Heffley made a couple of hundred screen appearances from 1952 through 2006. He had a recurring role on *Highway Patrol* in the 1950s as Officer Dennis, and was a regular on the daytime soap *Days of Our Lives* in the new millennium. In between, you name it, he did it – *Sky King*; *Alfred Hitchcock Presents*; *The Twilight Zone*; *The Fugitive*; *The Andy Griffith Show*; *Bonanza*; *The Wild, Wild West*; *Gomer Pyle*; *The Invaders*; *Mod Squad*; *Mannix*; *Kung Fu*; *Kojak*. And he did three more Season Two *Voyage*s, too, as "Doc."

Wayne Heffley with Robert Dowdell.

Filming began on Thursday, October 7, 1965. **Sobey Martin** had been hired to direct; he made it through the first day before falling ill. They filmed on Stage 10, in the Missile Room set.

Allan Hunt, quoted in *Science Fiction Television Series*, said, "The story was about this big walking blob. This was done in the days before satire. We were encouraged to play it as real as possible. If the story was ridiculous – and it was – it was up to us to make it work. To play it absolutely straight was the key." [5]

Day 2: Friday, October 8. **James B. Clark** stepped in to replace Martin. Clark was 57 and under contract to 20th Century-Fox. Irwin Allen didn't mind giving Clark a try – he had directed a circus movie, 1961's *The Big Show* (Allen had one of his own – 1959's *The Big Circus*). Clark specialized in movies about children and animals, including 1961's *Misty*, about a horse; 1964's *Island of the Dolphins*, about a little girl abandoned on an island and protected by a wild dog; and 1963's *Flipper*, which was spun off into a TV series about the titular dolphin. For television, Clark had been directing for other Fox shows, such as *Adventures in Paradise* and *The Legend of Jesse James*. He would soon be directing for the studio's *Batman* series.

Director James B. Clark.

On this second day, they continued filming in the Missile Room. The following week, for an additional three-and-a-half days, Clark stayed on Stage 10, filming more Seaview sets. Halfway through the sixth day of production, the company moved to Stage B to film the "Int. Space Center."

After watching the rough edit of the episode, Irwin Allen felt the show needed something more. William Welch and Sidney Marshall whipped up some additional scenes and Harry Harris was given the task of directing them, on Wednesday and Thursday, November 10 and 11. Harris used various Seaview sets, and, seen for the first time in this episode, sequences in the Flying Sub and "Int. Air Duct." [6]

The budget was set at $140,491, with a final cost was $170,495. Most episodes had been going as much as $20,000 over budget; this one topped it by $30k. [7]

Release / Reaction:
(ABC premiere airdate: 12/19/65; network repeat broadcast: 5/1/66)

A Patch of Blue, starring Sidney Poitier, was the top-grossing film in the United States this week. *Whipped Cream & Other Delights* by Herb Alpert and the Tijuana Brass was still the fastest selling album in America, for its fifth out of six weeks at the top. It had the hit single "A Taste of Honey," but the real draw was that album cover! And Jim Nabors, of *Gomer Pyle,*

No, we didn't get mixed up. This *was* production No. 8213. But they were a day or two late shooting the promotional pictures. The capsule had already been taken off the set, so these were likely shot in storage. You will also note that Allan Hunt is not in Season Two's jumpsuit attire. That must have been in storage too.

U.S.M.C., had the cover of the bestselling magazine in all of the U.S.A. – *TV Guide*.
With the shift underway to more monster-

themed episodes, people were tuning in again, *en masse*. You may have heard of some of those people. Mike Bailey said, "*Voyage* has had its share of famous fans. In her autobiography, Melissa Gilbert (Laura on TV's *Little House on the Prairie*) recalled that Richard Basehart was one of her favorite guest stars on *Little House* because he had been starred as Admiral Nelson on one of her favorite shows – *Voyage*. In an interview before his death, John Lennon recalled some of his favorite TV shows, one was the then-current *Dallas*, another was *Voyage*. Mel Gibson referred to *Voyage* fondly on Arsenio Hall's TV show, and novelist Jacqueline Susann loved *Voyage* and posed for photos with the cast on the set. And when film star Victor Mature visited the *Voyage* set in 1965, Irwin Allen put him to work for a day and cast him in an unbilled cameo as a radio officer in the background." [8]

Then came the ratings. *Voyage* was moving up.

William Read Woodfield said, "Curiously, the episodes I wrote always did better in the Nielsen ratings than the average episode. I kept pointing this out to Irwin and he would say, 'But how can that be, Billy?' I said, 'The way they're written up in *TV Guide*, they sound more interesting.' The best thing about writing for *Voyage* was that you would write a script and a week later, it was being shot. You could see what worked and what didn't. It was a great way to learn your craft." [9]

Associated Press entertainment correspondent Cynthia Lowry watched two events from space over the weekend – the splashdown of Gemini 6 and "The Monster from Outer Space." She then wrote:

> Television's really exciting show the past weekend was the second of its two-part drama on the recovery of the record-breaking astronauts, complete with happy ending. The Saturday morning live coverage from the carrier Wasp was as expert and satisfying as it had been two days before. It would have been even more thrilling if we had been able to see the astronauts as they actually emerged from the capsule, but their eagerness to get out as soon as possible was easy to understand.
>
> Viewers eventually will become accustomed to front-row seats on history as it happens. But right now, when it is new and stimulating, the effect is to make television's usual action-adventure series seem even more contrived and trite than usual. Thus, it was a long, long dive from Saturday morning's return of the space travelers to Sunday night's

> *Voyage to the Bottom of the Sea.* The latter seemed like a comedy-satire.
>
> The colorful special effects of the ABC series are marvelous, particularly the scenes inside that very convincing submarine of the future. But the story lines often leave something to be desired. [10]

For the jaded, the episode's title said all they needed to know. Joan Crosby of "TV Scout" and Steven H. Scheuer of "TV Key" didn't even bother to take a look. But many in front of their TV sets on the evening of December 19, 1965, did. Author Marc Cushman was ten at the time, with three older sisters. They controlled the family TV set, and had drifted away from *Voyage* for the escapism of *My Favorite Martian*. And that meant he had drifted away, too. But word of mouth at school, from those who had seen the preview, said this episode might be a bit more fun than many of the recent outings. And so, ABC-TV got the family's business that night. They weren't the only infrequent *Voyage* watchers to tune in. A.C. Nielsen pronounced "The Monster from Outer Space" to be a strong second place for its first half hour. While the numbers slipped a little during the second half, the series still had second place honors.

A.C. Nielsen 30-city survey from December 19, 1965:[11]

(7:30 – 8 p.m.)	Rating:	Share:
ABC: *Voyage to the Bottom of the Sea*	17.3	31.2%
CBS: *Lassie*	**17.8**	**32.1%**
NBC: *Bell Telephone Hour*	15.2	27.4%

8 – 8:30 p.m.		
ABC: *Voyage to the Bottom of the Sea*	17.2	29.6%
CBS: *My Favorite Martian*	14.0	24.1%
NBC: *Disney's Wonderful World of Color*	**22.7**	**39.1%**

4.13

"The X Factor" (Episode 45)
(Prod. #8214; first aired Sunday, December 5, 1965)
Written by William Welch
Directed by Leonard Horn
Produced by Irwin Allen and Frank La Tourette; Story Editor: Sidney Marshall
Guest Star John McGiver; Co-Starring Jan Merlin

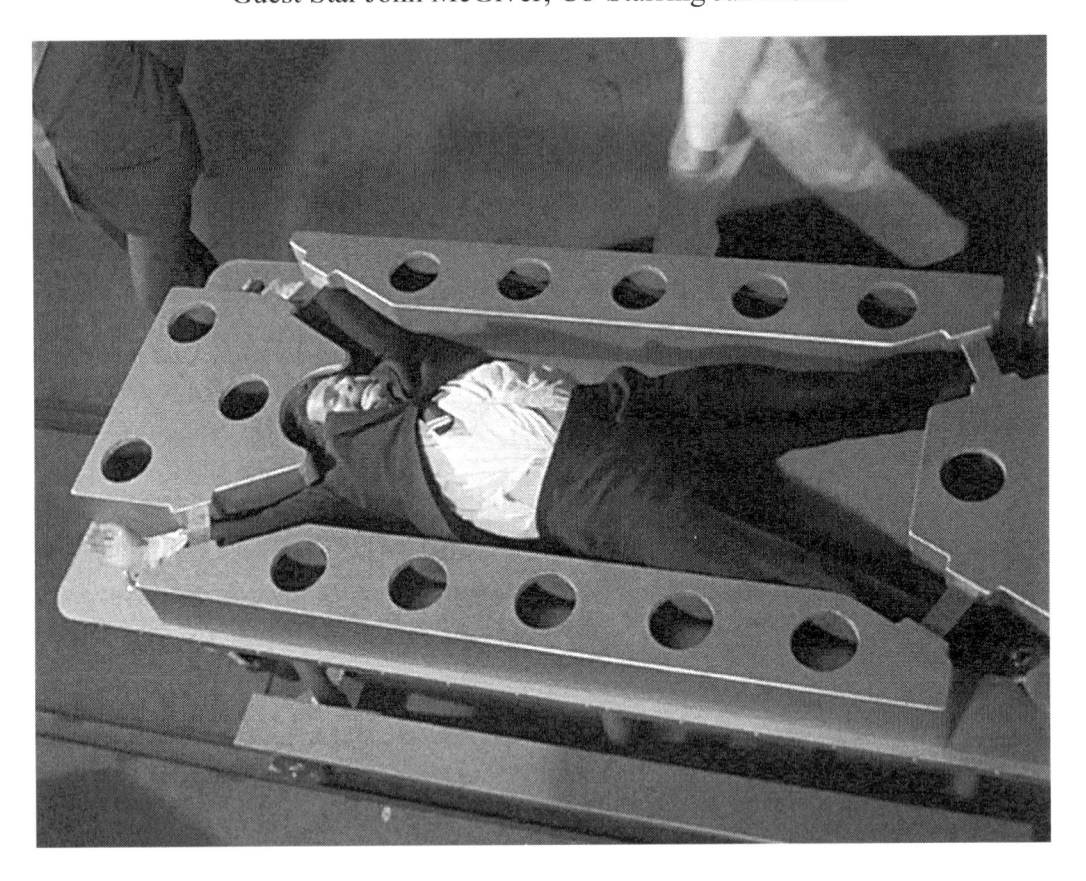

From the *Voyage* show files (Irwin Allen papers collection):

A toy manufacturer, whose company is a cover for espionage operations, kidnaps an important scientist and transforms him into a wax-like immobile doll. Before he can be smuggled out of the country, Admiral Nelson discovers his whereabouts and goes to rescue him. He is also kidnapped and is about to suffer the same fate... [1]

Assessment:

This episode is a window to 1965 … despite the date of 1978 which opens the show. We get a tour of the 20th Century-Fox studio grounds, work areas, and what was once a large portion of the backlot, with the towers of the still-in-construction high rises of Century City looking down on all the action. Rows and rows of parked mid-Sixties (and earlier) cars of studio workers and construction crew are also part of the show, as cast members run between and around them. We are even taken underground into the catacombs of the studio's power plant and waterworks. For us, it's a fascinating dive into the past. Oh, yes, there is a melodrama going on, too, about spies smuggling wax-covered scientists out of the country via a toy factory. This may distract you from the now-vintage milieu.

"Crazed toy manufacturers make for boring villains," complained Mark Phillips. "Still, their desperately antic efforts to kill Admiral Nelson are so comic-strip in nature that it provides some brief fun. William Hudson, who was killed off as Captain Phillips in the pilot, returns here so that he can die in a 'stock footage' death. Hudson gives a likable but fascinatingly stilted performance." [2]

Mike Bailey remembered, "On first viewing during its original network run, I felt the whole thing was overly contrived, as were many of Season Two's spy shows, and that *Voyage* was trying to copy *The Man from U.N.C.L.E.*, but without the tongue-in-cheek wit. The blatant use (or re-use might be a better way to put it) of the X-marks-the-spot car-chase scene with Bill Hudson was kind of a shock, even back then." [3]

Different viewpoints for different people. We rather enjoyed John McGiver's character, Alexander Corby – a delightfully devious, eccentric, and macabre fellow. It was a part Victor Buono could have sunk his teeth into, or Michael Dunn, but McGiver does fine. He swaps his familiar snooty schtick for something more sinister. Jan Merlin, playing Corby's No. 1 henchman, isn't as threatening here as he was in Season One's "No Way Out," but that was a high benchmark hard to beat. He is nonetheless sinister, sadistic, and lethal. And we didn't find Bill Hudson "stilted" at all. As military brass, he struck us as relatively relaxed and natural, and, taking into account that all of his scenes were filmed in a single day (with the exception of the recycled stock footage), his performance can hardly be faulted.

Granted, as pointed out by Mike Bailey, several minutes of action footage was lifted from the pilot film, but it was well integrated into this story. It was also the first time these sequences aired in color. The reason for the recycling was that the series was way overbudget, and in danger of being cancelled. Irwin Allen was under pressure to keep costs down for these final episodes in the initial Season Two order of 16. So bully for Allen, writer William Welch, and director Leonard Horn for seamlessly weaving the appropriated footage into this outing, and making it count, with a bang.

We admit that the underground chase, while visually (and historically) interesting, does little for the story. Crane and the boys, after all, pop up through the same manhole they went down several minutes earlier, with nothing to show for it. But sometimes, the best part of an excursion is the sights seen along the way. This jaunt into the subterranean chambers of 20th Century-Fox from that bygone era is fascinating.

One last guilty pleasure: Alexander Colby's office, with toys all around, gives a nod to Irwin Allen's office. What a kick that must have been for designer Paul Zastupnevich, and set decorators Norman Rockett and Walter M. Scott, to whip up this set.

Bottom line, the episode is a bit clumsy, and it *does* show evidence of padding and compromise – but if you can overlook these transgressions, maybe you can sit back and enjoy the ride. We feel there's plenty to appreciate.

Script:

William Welch's writers contract: October 4, 1965.
Welch's 2nd-draft teleplay approved on October 12.
Rev. Shooting Final teleplay (beige paper): October 14.
Page revisions (blue paper): October 14.

This was the sixth of 34 scripts to be written for *Voyage* by **William Welch**, in addition to the 31 scripts he polished while serving in Season One as the Script Editor. During this period, Irwin Allen would also get Welch to write four episodes for *Lost in Space* and eight for *The Time Tunnel*. It's a staggering output, with Welch writing more scripts for Allen than any other. Eventually, all the overwork would take a toll (more about that later).

Concerning the latest Welch script, Mary Garbutt of ABC's Department of Standards & Practices was keeping an eye out for what she considered excessive violence. In her October 14 memo, she told Allen and his staff:

> Pg 1, Sc 5: This is too graphic, please telescope [film it from a distance]: As the man comes up from back seat and we see the rope coming over driver's [head and neck]; cut away to Liscomb or guard gate; eliminate our hearing the choking or seeing the rope tightening and body being pulled back over

the seat; Please do not come back to scene until the point [where] the guard has been placed in [the] back seat and "new driver" is taking place at wheel and putting on helmet.

Pg 2, Sc 8: Eliminate or keep off camera the stuffing of the body in the trunk of car; Sc 10: Also caution that the subduing of Liscomb is done quickly with no unnecessary brutal handling by the two men....

Pg 6: Please delete Liscomb's scream here. In later "dolly sequence" no screams are indicated – Please do not add any....

Pg 43, Sc 127: Please be sure that driver is not attacked by all <u>three</u> men at once. [4]

Production:
(Filmed October 15 – 25, 1965; 7 days)

This was **Leonard Horn**'s seventh of nine directing assignments for *Voyage*.

John McGiver was 51 when he played Alexander Corby, and was paid $1,850 to do it. McGiver was the star of his own sitcom the season before, *Many Happy Returns*, which co-starred Mark Goddard (now on *Lost in Space*). He was also a regular on the short-lived 1967 sci-fi comedy series, *Mr. Terrific*, and put to work again on a regular basis on 1971-72's *The Jimmy Stewart Show*. Fact is, John McGiver was all over the dial, and on the big screen, too, throughout the 1960s, with a dip into the two decades on either side. Did he go into *The Twilight Zone*? Twice. *The Man from U.N.C.L.E.*? Sure. *The Wild, Wild West*? You bet. *I Dream of Jeannie*? But of course.

Gilligan's Island? You better believe it. We grew up watching this guy. But this was his only turn on an Irwin Allen show.

Jan Merlin was paid $1,000 for playing Henderson. This was the second of three appearances on *Voyage* for Merlin, who was last seen, served to perfection, in "No Way Out," and would return for "Death from the Past."

William Hudson was 46, and tossed $250 for one day's work playing Capt. Shire. Hudson, as mentioned, died the same death in the *Voyage* pilot episode, "Eleven Days to Zero." But the actor's real claim to fame was playing opposite a really big gal, in 1958's *Attack of the 50-ft. Woman*.'

Leith Stevens got the credit for the music – his third of nine *Voyage*s.

Filming began on Friday, October 15, 1965, for the first of two days on Stage 10. In this first session, they filmed on the "Int. Observation Nose / Control Room" double set, as well as some sequences in the Flying Sub.

Day 2, Monday. All of the scenes involving William Hudson were covered, including "Int. Shire's Office," "Int. Nelson's Cabin," and "Int Flying Sub." It came to more than 10 pages from the script, and Hudson had to sing hard for his $250 supper. Don't feel too bad for him – those 250 bucks equate to a little more than $2,000 in 2020, and they came with residuals for five repeats as well. Also, the new scenes, combined with the footage of Hudson lifted from "Eleven Hours to Zero," got him special "guest star" billing in the front of the show, always a boost to a TV actor's career.

With so much on his plate for a single day, Leonard Horn rushed the Flying-Sub-Out-of-Control scenes, and it shows. At times the actors aren't even in synch concerning which way they are to lean, as the FS rolls and dives. No time for more rehearsals or retakes, for, as they say in the business, "We're on the wrong set; we're moving on!" After wrapping all the scenes involving Hudson, Horn was also able to shoot an additional scene without the actor on the "Int. Corridor + Missile Room" set. He had his last shot in the can by 6:25 p.m.

Day 3, Tuesday. The company was outdoors in the studio's nursery area (for "Ext. Road Phone," "Ext Street" and "Ext. Greenhouse"), then off to the studio's Tram Area near the Olympic Blvd. gate (for "Ext. Wall" and "Ext. Nelson Institute"). Helping to speed things up, these scenes were filmed without sound. The heavy traffic we see on Pico Blvd. in the background would have made sound recording impossible anyway. The few lines of dialogue were looped in afterwards.

The company then filmed "Ext. Toy Building & Sign" around the Century City Area, where office towers were being built out of what used to be a large portion of the studio's back lot.

Day 4, Wednesday. A return to the Fox Nursery Area, this time dressed to pass for "Ext. Conversion Tank."

Day 5, Thursday. The morning was spent in the Nursery Area, continuing to film the "Ext. Conversion Tank," then onto Stage B for "Int. Kaber's Office." They were unable to finish all the sequences needed on this set, and Stage B was not available the following day. This meant they would need to dissemble the office set, move it to another stage, and rebuild and decorate it there. That's show business, folks.

Day 6, Friday. The morning was spent on Stage 5, finishing the scenes in Kaber's Office. The company then moved out onto the Fox lot – or, actually, under it – for "Int. Power Plant at Fan Ventilation Room" and "Int. Underground Passageway."

When asked about the catacombs, Allan Hunt said, "I remember being told that it was a kind of WWII thing; an underground safety thing, in case we were ever attacked." [5]

With water and power generators, plus room for studio employees underground, 20th Century-Fox Studios was intended to a be safe place during the war years.

Day 7, Monday, October 25. The Second Unit filmed outdoors this day with David Hedison, Terry Becker, and Allan Hunt, finishing up their running-around sequences, while the main unit began work on the next episode, "The Machines Strike Back." The final shots needed in the underground passages were taken, without sound recording, then the group moved onto "Ext. Hillside." They wrapped at 12:30 p.m., allowing the actors to join the main unit for work on the next episode. [6]

During the filming of this episode (Production No. 8214), the set photographer collected portrait shots of supporting cast members Robert Dowdell and Terry Becker.

A budget of $140,491 was approved by the front office. The final cost was $154,082. [7]

190

Release / Reaction:
(ABC premiere airdate: 12/5/65; network repeat broadcast: 4/24/66)

This was the week *A Charlie Brown Christmas* first aired on CBS. The movie that everyone seemed to be flocking to was Disney's *That Darn Cat*, whose human stars were Hayley Mills and Dean Jones. It was No. 1 in the movie houses. "Turn, Turn, Turn," by the Byrds, was getting the most radio play. The top record album in America was still *Whipped Cream & Other Delights* by Herb Alpert and the Tijuana Brass. Barbra Streisand was in second place with her second album – *My Name Is Barbra, Two*. On *Lost in Space* this week, the Robinsons found a dog inside a space capsule. By the end of the episode, they had apparently lost the dog offscreen … because we never saw it again.

Syndicated "TV Key" previewed "The X Factor":

> A rousing adventure which should keep the youngsters riveted to the set. The plot has Admiral Nelson and his company of nautical detectives hot on the trail of a group of espionage agents whose headquarters is, of all places, a toy factory. [8]

No monsters this week, but there was a mad toy manufacturer whose machine turned his enemies into freeze-dried giant toys. Almost as good. Lord Nielsen proclaimed *Voyage* second in its time period (both half hours). But Irwin Allen knew all too well that the less-than-30-percent audience share could drop the ax on the show at any time.

A.C. Nielsen 30-city survey from December 5, 1965:[9]

(7 – 7:30 p.m.)	Rating:	Share:
ABC: *Voyage to the Bottom of the Sea*	16.5	28.5%
CBS: *Lassie*	**18.8**	**32.5%**
NBC: *Bell Telephone Hour*	16.2	28.0%

(7:30 – 8 p.m.):		
ABC: *Voyage to the Bottom of the Sea*	16.7	26.4%
CBS: *My Favorite Martian*	16.0	25.3%
NBC: *Disney's Wonderful World* …	**25.1**	**39.7%**

4.14

"The Machines Strike Back" (Episode 46)
(Prod. #8215; first aired Sunday, December 12, 1965)
Written by John and Ward Hawkins
Directed by Nathan Juran
Produced by Irwin Allen and William Welch; Story Editor: Sidney Marshall
Guest Star Roger C. Carmel; Co-Starring Françoise Ruggieri

From the *Voyage* show files (Irwin Allen papers collection):

A drone submarine refuses to obey commands and aims its missiles at New York City. Admiral Nelson enlists the aid of an Admiral of an allied nation who helped design the drones in order to discover the cause of the failure. The admiral is actually a revolutionary who is reprogramming the drones to bomb U.S. cities in order to seize power in his own country.[1]

Assessment:

The date that opens the episode says 1976 … instead of 1978, as the last couple of episodes stated. It was a case of one hand not knowing what the other was doing, resulting in the dates not always being consistent.

The episode was made in 1965, a worrisome time regarding nuclear armaments. Polaris subs, armed with nuclear missiles, patrolled the seas; B-47 bombers carried their deadly weapons overhead; drones were being used more and more by the military; and debates over the uneasy balance of terror being waged by the U.S. and its nuclear adversary, the U.S.S.R., raged on. "The Machines Strike Back" was topical in 1965, its setting of 1976, and today too.

History aside, "The Machines Strike Back" is a thrilling hour that should satisfy any fan of the series. First-rate episodes such as this could even attract new fans.

Mike Bailey said, "This story is driven by its special effects, which are, for the most part. outrageously good, and integrated in such a way that they augment the story rather than just being the story. That's a very good thing. Actually allowing a nuke to land in upstate New York and flatten acres of forest was not the kind of thing *Voyage* often did. It sets the stakes for the episode right out of the gate. … One of Season Two's more enjoyable actioners." [2]

Mark Phillips commented, "A very entertaining episode, with the usually campy Roger C. Carmel reeling himself in with a good performance. The special-effects budget goes into over-drive with many interesting shots of Seaview pursing a deadly, yellow submarine." [3]

Roger C. Carmel said, "I was in the right place at the right time. The 1960s was an over-the-top decade, and I could certainly play over-the-top." [4]

Script:

John and Ward Hawkinses' writers contract: August 25, 1965.
1st-draft teleplay approved October 5.
Rev. Shooting Final: October 19.
2nd Rev. Shooting final teleplay (green paper): October 22.
Page revisions (pink paper): October 26.
Page revisions (yellow paper): October 26.
Page revisions (gold paper): November 10.

Fellow *Voyage* writer Robert Vincent Wright said of John and Ward Hawkins, "John and I served as story editors on *Bonanza*. John and Ward came from Portland, Oregon, where they wrote as a team for several years. They were well known for writing pulp SF. They later wrote for *The Saturday Evening Post* and other magazines." [5]

Brothers **John and Ward Hawkins** had written numerous episodes each for *Rawhide*, *The Virginian,* and *Bonanza* before coming to *Voyage* for this, their first of four assignments.

After reading the Hawkinses' script, Irwin Allen told his staff:

> P. 7: There should be a stock shot of NEW YORK city immediately preceding Scene 23 and 24. This would help to build tension.
>
> P. 9, Sc. 28: The diving bell has just been brought aboard, therefore Nelson should give immediate orders for Seaview to begin tracking the rogue drone, even before he speaks to Crane. When Crane asks "what happened to the drone," Nelson's answer should be more specific and talkiness could be cut down on by combining the dialogue in Scenes 28 and 28A....
>
> P. 10 thru P. 15: Can some of this talk be cut or condensed. The same ground seems to be covered by Kimberly, Johnson and Halder. It might help to show a shot or two of the drone in between the dialogue scenes.
>
> P. 22, Sc. 48: If it is too expensive to show actual blowing up of the drone and men, or you wish to avoid an unpleasant shot like this, shouldn't there at least be a shot of the aftermath of the explosion showing debris either ext. or on the monitor in the control room. The reeling of the sub has been used so often in past episodes that it no longer has much excitement visually. It should, however, be left in....
>
> P. 60-A: The fourth act curtain should end on the explosion of the East Command station and also show the effects of the explosion on the Flying Sub, leaving us [to] wonder if Nelson and Crane were successful in getting away. Otherwise, the story is over and the audience may lose interest. [6]

It is interesting that among Allen's concerns, he commented on the rock-and-rolling of the Seaview being overused. Despite this, it would continue to be included in many episodes to come over the next two-and-a-half years. It was a way to inject excitement into the show without raising the costs.

Production:
(Filmed October 25 - November 2, 1965; 7 days)

Nathan Juran was hired to direct. He was 58. This was his first assignment on *Voyage*. Juran started as an art director, and won an Academy Award in 1942 for *How Green Was My Valley*. As a director, he was nominated for a Hugo Award (sci-fi's answer to the Oscar) for 1958's *The 7th Voyage of Sinbad*. Other science fiction "classics" from Juran: 1957's *The Brain from Planet Arous*, 1958's *The Attack of the 50-Foot Woman*, and 1964's *First Men in the Moon*. He had directed sci-fi for television as well, with four episodes each of 1959's *World of Giants* and 1960's *Men into Space*. A movie that no doubt appealed to Irwin Allen was Juran's 1961 adventure film, *Flight of the Lost Balloon*. Allen did his own balloon movie a couple years later. Juran was a feather in Irwin Allen's cap, he was brought back for two more episodes of *Voyage* before switching over to *Lost in Space* (for 13 episodes), *The Time Tunnel* (with five) and *Land of the Giants* (also with five).

Less impressed with Juran was Ray Didsbury, who wore many hats at *Voyage*, but was credited as a "production assistant." He said, "Nathan Juran was a fussy old lady, always changing his mind." [7]

Roger C. Carmel was 32 when he played Admiral Halden, and received $1,750. Carmel had been successfully making the rounds on television, gaining more attention with nearly each appearance, including multiple turns on *Naked City*, *The Man from U.N.C.L.E.*, and *I Spy*. In the coming two years he would play his best-known character, Harry Mudd, in two *Star Trek* episodes (with a third to follow in 1973 on *Star Trek: The Animated Series*).

Françoise Ruggieri made her second appearance on the series. We had last seen her, briefly, in "… And Five of Us Are Left." Now she had a more prominent role, as Captain Verna Trober. And how about *Voyage to the Bottom of the Sea* for portraying a woman as a Captain! Even *Star Trek* at this time, preparing to shoot its second pilot film, had to drop its "No. 1" character (played by Majel Barrett) over complains from that network – at least according to Gene Roddenberry – that the time wasn't right for a woman in a command position on television. Ruggieri was 27.

John Gallaudet, 63, played Admiral Johnson. Gallaudet was all over the dial, with over 200 screen appearances. Among those, he played a judge in 20 episodes of *Perry Mason*.

Bert Remsen played Senator Kimberly, representing the concerns of many viewers who lost sleep over the escalating arms race. Remsen had been acting in front of the camera since 1952, and worked often. Through the end of the 1990 he'd racked up over 200 screen appearances.

Filming began on Monday, October 25, 1965, for seven straight days on Stage 10. Besides the Seaview sets, which included "Int. Diving Bell" (all filmed during the first five days of production), they also had one new set – or complex – "Int. East Command." This was filmed on the sixth and seventh days of production. The many sets within the grander set included "Store Room," "Transmitter Room," "Int. Drone," "Int. Cabin," and "Int. Valve Room."

Arch Whiting (Sparks) with Basehart in this episode.

Interviewed for *Seaview: A 50th Anniversary Tribute* by William E. Anchors and Frederick Barr, David Hedison said, "The only time I got burned was the episode with Roger C. Carmel – 'The Machines Strike Back.' The lighter/welder they gave me licked back and burned my fingers. If you watch the episode, you will see I have bandages on my fingers covering the burns and, later on, healed scabs over the burns." [8]

A lion's share of the credit for the episode's success must go to the special effects department. That wonderful yellow submarine ("drone") is as cute as a bug, and it comes with a nasty sting too. Perhaps 10% of this episode was shot in the Green Tank. [9]

The budget approved by 20th Century Fox was $140,491. As with every single episode this season, the final cost was higher: $166,486. [10]

Release / Reaction:
(ABC premiere airdate: 12/12/65; network repeat broadcast: 6/5/66)

Larry Storch, Forrest Tucker, Melody Patterson, and Ken Barry, of *F Troop*, had the cover of *TV Guide*. Popular record albums this week included *Highway 61 Revisited*, by Bob Dylan; *The Beach Boys' Party*; *December's Children*, by the Rolling Stones; *Look at Us*, by Sonny & Cher; and *Help!*, by the Beatles.

Speaking of the Fab Four, they got a kick out of *Voyage*. John Lennon named it as one of his favorite programs, and the group was known on one occasion to delay a press conference in America so they could stay in their hotel room to watch *Voyage*, in color (the show was only seen in black-and-white in the 1960s in England). One must wonder if they saw this episode, about a yellow drone sub. Their single "Yellow Submarine" was released in August 1966, eight months after this episode first aired, and two months after it repeated. Countering speculation that the lyric was either drug induced or referenced, Paul McCartney called it "a children's song." Well, many called *Voyage* a "children's show." Regardless, both song and TV show were a trip. The appearance of two pop-culture yellow subs: coincidence or conspiracy? We report – you decide.

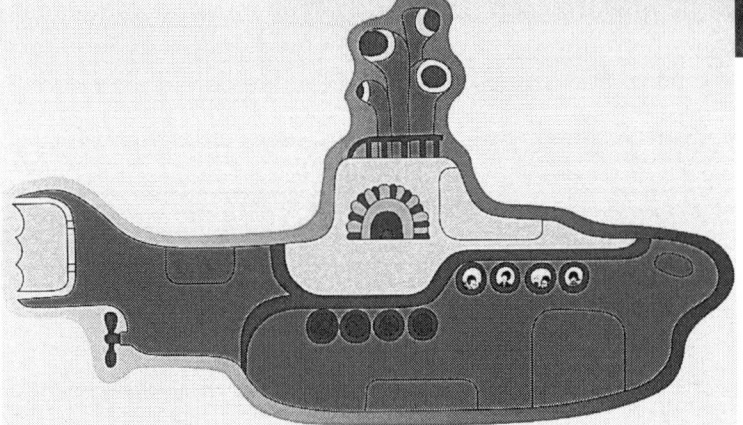

The week this episode first aired, Richard Basehart was featured in an article by Harold Stern and syndicated by TV Time Service, appearing in various newspapers. Stern was gunning for Basehart, like nearly all others who interviewed him since he was cast in *Voyage*. The title of the article made it clear: "Basehart Doing TV Series Basically for Money." Stern wrote:

> All I really persisted in wanting to find out was why a truly distinguished actor, like Richard Basehart, had succumbed to the blandishments of TV by agreeing to star in what is essentially an adventure series for children, *Voyage to the Bottom of the Sea*, on ABC-TV.[11]

Basehart defended himself and his series. "The basic drive was financial. The money is good. And I thought it might be fun. And, as the show progressed, I developed some strong personal relationships.... I stayed away from TV series in the past, but I'm happy to be doing this show. It's a pleasure to come to work in the morning." (We note that interviewer Stern did not reveal if his column was written "basically for money.")

It must have seemed to Basehart that whenever he met with the press – one of his obligations as star of the series – he was ambushed. Still, he met the challenge with dignity. He told Harold Stern, "I admit that last year there were times when I'd say, 'Oh, no, not again!' But this year we've got human beings in the series. And we've got color. We had budget problems last year; we couldn't get out and swing; we were confined to the submarine. This year we're getting around. That was the original intent of the series, but we were stymied by budget and time. Last year we wound up our last show six days before air date. It became not the best way to get it done, but the quickest."

Basehart added, "Maybe the series was corny when it started, but now we've got babes – *good looking* babes. Even our monsters are good looking."

More seriously: "Last year we weren't doing the series we wanted to do; we intended to do. But when you get handed your script the day before shooting, there's no time to exercise script control. And walking out of a series doesn't solve anything. So, it's a matter of fighting, moment by moment, for script values. Sometimes little things can only come up during the actual shooting. I think this year, we've got a head start. We've got a few good scripts."

Basehart reflected, then said, "Actually, we're still living from hand to mouth as far as scripts are concerned. We're never ahead. We can't read, analyze and correct a script; there's no time. We have to correct as we shoot and sometimes that's impossible. Even, ideally, it's impossible to get 33 scripts in a year's time that are worth doing on a series.… As an actor, you only know what you'd like to do; what you'd like to see done. As an actor, you roll with the punch. What we've achieved is compromise among Irwin Allen, 20th Century-Fox, ABC, and myself. If we get the kind of show we want to do, in return, we have to do a show with monsters for those who want that.… I'm not ashamed of what I've done. I defy you to name an actor who could have done it better." [12]

"TV Scout" hadn't bothered to preview the last few episodes. Now Joan Crosby's review column was back:

> *Voyage to the Bottom of the Sea* displays a nice sense of humor with the title "The Machines Strike Back." There's nothing funny about the script, however, as drone submarines with deadly missiles suddenly begin going rogue and aiming their weapons at the U.S. Since Richard Basehart has been instrumental in the design of these subs, he finds himself on the spot. So, he calls in old friend Roger C. Carmel,

who also helped design the subs. But the old friend, from one of those unnamed countries, has his own master plan. [13]

"TV Key," running in newspapers across America, said:

> Another fast-paced, action-packed adventure for the youngsters. Adm. Nelson and his gallant crew have a dangerous task tonight – they have to locate and destroy what they assume to be faulty, remote-controlled, subterranean craft armed with nuclear missiles. [14]

The ratings were picking up, slightly. *Voyage* finished second during both its half-hours. According to A.C. Nielsen, the series ranked No. 21 this week out of 107 network series.

A.C. Nielsen 30-city survey from December 12, 1965:[15]

(7 – 7:30 p.m.)	Rating:	Peak Share:
ABC: *Voyage to the Bottom of the Sea*	17.4	29.7%
CBS: *Lassie*	**21.8**	**37.3%**
NBC: Hallmark special	9.4	16.1%

(7:30 – 8 p.m.)	Rating:	Peak Share:
ABC: *Voyage to the Bottom of the Sea*	16.7	26.9
CBS: *My Favorite Martian*	16.5	26.6%
NBC: *Walt Disney's Wonderful World of Color*	**20.6**	**33.2%**

4.15

"Killers of the Deep" (Episode 47)
(Prod. #8216; first aired Sunday, January 2, 1966)
Written by William Read Woodfield and Allan Balter
Directed by Harry Harris
Produced by Irwin Allen, Frank La Tourette, and William Welch
Story Editor: Sidney Marshall
Guest Star Michael Ansara; Co-Starring Patrick Wayne

From the *Voyage* show files (Irwin Allen papers collection):

> While searching in the flying sub for a missile stolen from an underwater silo, Nelson and Crane spot a submarine which opens fire on them. Nelson is rescued but Crane is picked up by the enemy submarine. Its Captain, with Crane as his prisoner, and Nelson aboard a destroyer, then engage in a deadly duel to destroy each other. [1]

Assessment:

You can call this *Voyage to the Bottom of the Sea* meets *The Enemy Below*. Not that the stories are that similar, but because a good chunk of the 1957 20th Century Fox war film, which starred Robert Mitchum, Curd Jürgens and David Hedison, can be seen in "Killers of the Deep." All of the color sequences depicting the stalking of and battle between a U.S. destroyer and an enemy submarine (both World War II vintage) came from the film. And that allowed *Voyage* to present a rousing, even spectacular (by TV standards), episode, and almost stay on budget. It may be a bit of larceny, but it was inspired larceny. And a must-see episode.

Before he was Captain of the Seaview, David Hedison was Executive Officer, under Robert Mitchum, searching for *The Enemy Below*. (1957, 20th Century-Fox)

Mark Phillips said, "Crane's escape from the enemy sub is told in harrowing footage skillfully blended from *The Enemy Below*, a film which featured special effects by *Voyage* master L.B. Abbot and makeup by *Voyage* master Ben Nye – a perfect match of stock footage to story." [2]

Mike Bailey said, "It was a particular thrill in Season Two to encounter an episode of *Voyage* which returned to Season One's level of dead-serious, gritty intensity. There were no outrageous schemes or villains to be found and the episode plays realistically once you get past the premise of stealing nuclear weapons with a basically obsolete World War II sub. William Read Woodfield turned in a tight script and the reliable Harry Harris directed this episode with punch. Great music culled from the *Voyage* library. The entire episode is loaded with fine L.B. Abbott miniature photography." [3]

If you have seen *The Enemy Below*, you'll admire the way footage from that film was integrated into this new story. A job very well done, in all aspects. "Killers of the Deep" is one of the best-looking episodes made for the series, and an exciting tale.

Script:

William Read Woodfield's and Allan Balter's writers contract: October 2, 1965.
Woodfield's and Balter's 1st-draft teleplay approved on October 9.
2nd Rev. Shooting Final (gold paper): October 19.
Page revisions (blue paper): October 29.
Page revisions (pink pages): November 1.

Regarding the supporting cast, **William Read Woodfield** told interviewer Mark Phillips, "We had to write them a certain amount of lines and hopefully it wasn't too stupid. The first chief [Henry Kulky] was a bulldog-looking guy; the second Chief [Terry Becker] was a better actor. He was always asking us to give Chief Sharkey more depth. We would say, 'Look, we've only got a limited amount of depth and the stars get it, so leave us alone."[4]

Director Harry Harris said, "On *Voyage to the Bottom of the Sea*, we would have many meetings – concept meetings – and they would go on and on and on, right up to the day before you filmed. And Irwin had two writers there named Woodfield and Balter, and they sat in a room down from his office. They were good writers… but these two guys were really clowns – they were fun, funny guys, and they even made Irwin laugh! So, we had a final meeting with them that afternoon [before the start of filming on 'Killers of the Deep']. They were going to make some changes in the script and I was going to take the script home and start shooting the next morning. But they went in their office and they locked the door, and nobody was allowed to go into that office except Irwin. I waited and waited and waited, and it got to be about six-thirty and I'm sitting there, and Irwin comes walking down the hall. He said, 'Why aren't you home? You've got to film tomorrow.' I said, 'Irwin, I don't have a script yet.' He said, 'You don't have the script?!' I said. 'No.' He said, 'Well, we gave them a lot of changes.' I said, 'Well, I'm just waiting for them.' He said, 'Come with me.' So, he goes to his desk and he gets the key, then we walk down the hall and he listens at the door. It's got a glass on the door, and you hear these typewriters going like a hundred miles an hour. So, he turns to me and he says, "Now, don't make any noise; I don't want to disturb them,' then he puts the key in the lock and we push our way in. Here's what I saw: Woodfield is like about a 275 pound man – he's real heavy – and he's got his jacket off, and Balter, who's a short little guy, has a stethoscope and he's listening to Woodfield's heart. And they've got a tape recorder on and it's [playing the] clicking of the typewriters. Irwin said, 'What are you doing?! Where is the script?!' 'Well, it's not quite out yet.' He said, 'Get to work! We've got a director waiting for a script! We've got to have it right away!' 'Yes, Irwin.' So, they put the stethoscope down, and then, in another half hour, the pages come out. I go down to my room, and I'm putting them in the [master] script and I'm looking over all the stuff that they did. And then I came out, and, at the top of the stairs, Irwin's standing there holding two briefcases. Woodfield has put his coat back on, and Balter is listening to Irwin's heart!" [5]

Such was a typical day in the mad, mad world of Irwin Allen Productions.

Production:
(Filmed November 3 – 10, 1965; 6 days)

Harry Harris occupied the director's chair.

Michael Ansara made his second of two appearances on *Voyage* (following the first-season episode "Hot Line") – *three* appearances if you include 1961's *Voyage to the Bottom of the Sea*, the motion picture. This time, he played renegade Captain Tomas Ruiz.

Ansara had been the star of two TV series – *Broken Arrow* (1956-58), as Cochise, television's first American Indian protagonist, and *Law of the Plainsman* (1959-60), as Deputy Marshall Sam Buckhart. Irwin Allen would also have Ansara guest star in an episode of *Lost in Space*, a pair of *Time Tunnels*, and one *Land of the Giants*. Ansara worked well in Westerns and sci-fis. Concerning the latter, he was top guest star in "Soldier," a 1964 episode of *The Outer Limits*, and as Kang, a Klingon Commander, in "Day of the Dove," a 1968 episode of *Star Trek*. He

Michael Ansara, from *Broken Arrow* (1956-58).

appeared three times on *I Dream of Jeanie*. (No surprise – he was married to Barbara Eden.) Ansara was 43.

Patrick Wayne was 26. He was the son of John Wayne, and had worked with his dad in *The Searchers*, *The Alamo*, *The Comancheros*, and *McLintock!*, among other films. In 1958, he won a Golden Globe award as Most Promising Newcomer.

James Frawley (29) played Manolo, the grimy executive officer to Captain Ruiz. This was his third *Voyage*, having appeared in Season One's "The Price of Doom" and "The Exile." He'd also appeared as a

Above: John Wayne and son, from *The Searchers*.
Right: James Frawley, beginning his transformation from actor to director, with The Monkees in 1966.

prominent character in the two-part 1964 episode "The Inheritors," on *The Outer Limits*. He was seen more than once on *Dr. Kildare*, *The Man from U.N.C.L.E.*, *McHale's Navy*, and *The Monkees*. Then he moved to directing, starting with 28 episodes of the before-mentioned *Monkees* show, plus a bunch of episodes for *That Girl*, *Columbo*, *Cagney & Lacy*, and *Judging Amy*, among other series. He also served as executive producer on the latter.

Bruce Mars played the Bosun's Mate. If he looks familiar, maybe you saw him on *Star Trek*, as a rascal named Finnegan in the 1966 episode "Shore Leave." Mars would return to *Voyage* to play a guard in the 1968 episode, "The

Abominable Snowman." He also turned up in an episode of *The Time Tunnel*, playing George Armstrong Custer's brother, Tom.

Filming began on Wednesday, November 3, 1965, on Stage B for the first of two days spent on the "Int. Ruiz Sub Control Room" set. The executive officer (James Frawley) says, "This is an old submarine." The set is wonderfully grimy for *Voyage*, a series which usually presented clean-looking interiors.

Above: Bruce Mars, from a 1967 episode of *Star Trek*, and (below) with Richard Basehart.

Friday, the third day of production, began on Stage B for "Int. Destroyer Passageway." After soaking Richard Basehart, the company moved to Stage 10 for "Int. Seaview Control Room / Radio Shack" and "Int. Ruiz Sub Store Room."

Day 4, Monday: The company began on Stage 10 for the interior of the Flying Sub, then moved to Stage B for "Ext. Destroyer Bridge / Int. Destroyer." There was a method to what seemed to be the madness of TV production, as the company moved from Stage B to 10 and then back to B. Old sets had to be removed and new ones constructed, and this could only be done while the camera crew was elsewhere … or at night.

Day 5, Tuesday: Cast and crew spent the day on Stage B on the sets for "Ext. & Int. Destroyer Bridge & Sonar Room," "Ext. Sub Hatch," and "Ext. Surface of Sea." Because this was November, with a chill in the air, the latter scenes, with Richard Basehart, were not filmed in the Moat, but in the much warmer (and cleaner) water tank inside of Stage B.

Day 6, Wednesday: The company continued filming the "Ext. Surface of Sea" sequences, this time with David Hedison in the drink, then back into the Ruiz Sub, for Hedison to crawl around within "Int. Air Duct." Director Harris wrapped at 3:50 in the afternoon, bringing this episode in under the six-day schedule, at five and three-quarters days. The final cost was $141,966. [6]

Release / Reaction:
(ABC premiere airdate: 1/2/66; network repeat broadcast: 4/10/66)

This week a new law took effect, requiring cigarette manufacturers to include the understated (but bitterly debated) warning "Caution: Cigarette smoking may be hazardous to your health." On the day that "Killers of the Deep" premiered on ABC, the Green Bay Packers, with Coach Vince Lombardi and quarterback Bart Starr, beat the Cleveland Browns for the NFL championship game. Also at the top, in their respective fields: *Dr. Zhivago* was No. 1 in the movie houses; *Bonanza* was the No. 1 show on TV; *Whipped Cream & Other Delights*, by Herb Alpert and the Tijuana Brass, was the No. 1 album in stores; and "The Sounds of Silence," by Simon & Garfunkel, was the No. 1 song on the radio.

Of "Killers of the Deep," writer William Read Woodfield said, "They did a beautiful, *beautiful* job of integrating stock footage from *The Enemy Below* into that show. To have duplicated some of those battle scenes would have cost a million dollars." [7]

Syndicated "TV Scout" said:

> Don't worry about the plot of *Voyage to the Bottom of the Sea*. Just sit back and enjoy some excellent special effects and a tense duel between a submarine and a destroyer. The sub is not the Seaview, however. It is a renegade sub, commanded by Michael Ansara, and David Hedison is a prisoner on board. And the destroyer it is fighting is commanded by Richard Basehart, after a tragedy has put him in charge. [8]

With no featured monsters, "Killers of the Deep" wasn't able to push the show above second position in the ratings at its peak, and third spot at its worse. [9]

A.C. Nielsen 30-city survey from January 2, 1966:

(7 – 7:30 p.m.)	Rating:	Share:
ABC: *Voyage to the Bottom of the Sea*	18.2	28.6%
CBS: *Lassie*	**20.6**	**32.4%**
NBC: *Bell Telephone Hour*	14.1	22.2%

(7:30 – 8 p.m.):		
ABC: *Voyage to the Bottom of the Sea*	17.9	27.4%
CBS: *My Favorite Martian*	**21.7**	**33.2%**
NBC: *Walt Disney's Wonderful World…*	18.5	28.3%

Two days after "Killers of the Deep" aired, Charles Aukerman wrote in Ohio's *Medina County Gazette*:

> Contrary to the opinions often expressed in the *Gazette* office by Television Editor Betty Marsh, *Voyage to the Bottom of the Sea* isn't really a bad science-fiction program. In fact, considering the drivel that the industry usually attempts to pass off as science-fiction, it's pretty good. …
>
> The acting is professional and competent, especially that of the two leads, David Hedison and Richard Basehart, which cannot be said about the acting in *Lost in Space*, the other prime-time science-fiction entry this season. …

The script-writing has been good, basically, but the Seaview fights an overwhelming number of deep-sea battles with huge sea monsters. In part, this is due to the limitations placed on the writers by the specified setting. But it is also possible that this is a lazy writer's method of appearing to work. Write in four or five minutes of battle each week with a giant squid, etc., and save that much writing time. The pay is the same, anyhow.

Jules Verne thought of the idea first, and used it several times in epic *20,000 Leagues Under the Sea.* Imitation is the sincerest form of flattery. In fact, the whole Irwin Allen-created series is basically a steal from Verne, from the comparison of the Nautilus and Seaview, to the weapons used by the voyagers. But, if it's a steal, it's not a bad one....[10]

What do you know – a media critic presenting both sides of a debate!

4.16

"Terror on Dinosaur Island" (Episode 48)

(Prod. #8217; first aired Sunday, December 26, 1965)
Written by William Welch
Directed by Leonard Horn
Produced by Irwin Allen, Frank La Tourette, and William Welch
Story Editor: Sidney Marshall
Co-Starring Paul Carr

From the *Voyage* show files (Irwin Allen papers collection):

A volcanic explosion forces Admiral Nelson and Chief Sharkey to ditch the flying sub and land on a newly-emerged island. With Sharkey injured, they become trapped there by gigantic prehistoric monsters. Crane and three Seaview crew members form a search party in spite of their knowledge that the island is due to be destroyed momentarily.[1]

Assessment:

In this yarn, Irwin Allen recycled footage from his 1966 film *The Lost World*. But don't let that keep you from enjoying "Terror on Dinosaur Island."

Writer Mark Phillips said, "This episode always gets unfairly rapped as lifting reels from Allen's movie, *The Lost World*, but, actually, stock footage is very limited from that film. There *is* exciting stock footage from some previous episodes [of *Voyage*], but there's also a lot of expensive new footage – the Flying Sub soaring over an island cliff, a dinosaur's attack on Seaview, and some absolutely breath-taking shots of the Seaview literally beached on the island – outstanding miniature work! All in all, a fun adventure, with lots of action." [2]

"Forget logic," Mike Bailey said. "This story works on the level of 'seeing is believing.' And you definitely see: a) An island rise from the ocean; b) Seaview beached on said island; c) dinosaurs, erupting volcano; d) The island explode – and much more. … In the midst of all the carnage, there is a story with human motivation and dimension." [3]

We insist on a smidgen of logic. How in the world – even a *Lost World* – could dinosaurs exist on an island which had just popped up out of the sea? Nelson speculates that the trees and other foliage exists because the island had not been submerged for long – but could these giant lizards breathe underwater? Crane sums it up nicely in the finale: "I know it's pretty hard to swallow."

Lack of dinosaur aqualungs aside, it's a fantastic and entertaining romp. And, as noted by Mike Bailey, injected with personal conflict. At the center is Paul Carr, returning to *Voyage*, not as the unhinged Seaman Clark we'd seen him play a few times in Season One but as the unhinged Seaman Benson. Crane has blood on his hands, in Benson's mind, anyway, for letting Seaman Grady die earlier in the story. It was a hard decision for Crane; but a harder thing to accept for Benson. You see, Benson has blood on his hands too – his actions inadvertently contributed to Grady's death. And now Benson plans on washing the guilt away by killing Crane.

Mike Bailey said of Carr: "He turns in a killer performance (so to speak) and bows out of *Voyage* in style … except for the ghostly cameos in later seasons via stock footage." [4]

Dinosaurs, human treachery, and vengeance too! This is not merely Man Against Nature (gone wild), but Man Against Man, with a dash of Man Against Himself tossed in for good measure. And it all works.

"Terror on Dinosaur Island" offers even more. This episode served as a major stepping stone in the relationship between Admiral Nelson and Chief Starkey – and prompted a friendship between Richard Basehart and Terry Becker.

Script:
William Welch's writers contract: October 27, 1965.
Welch's 2nd (final) draft approved on November 2.
Rev. Shooting Final teleplay (yellow paper): November 8.
Page revisions (blue paper inserts): November 9.
Page revisions (pink paper inserts): November 15.

With this, **William Welch** turned in his seventh original script for *Voyage*.

We learned more about Chief Sharkey in this episode. Terry Becker said, "William Welch, one of our writers, loved the character and gave the Chief a first name – Francis. The Admiral used to tweak the Chief about that." [5]

ABC's Department of Standards & Practices wasn't very bothered by this one, since it was pure fantasy. Mary Garbutt requested:

> Stock dinosaur-sequences can only be approved on film. Your usual care in seeing that the dinosaur-creatures are not "too terrifying" for a family audience with following particular cautions: Pg 27, Sc 70: Please be sure that this closing shot is not one of dinosaur seeming to move through camera frame; Pg 49, Sc. 159: Caution on Crane's reaction: It can be grim but please eliminate "revulsion" direction.
>
> Pg 12, Sc 23: Standard caution on this shot of water engulfing the men. [6]

And then they were off to the races … the dinosaur races, that is.

Production:
(Filmed November 12 – 22, 1965; 6 ½ days)

Leonard Horn returned to direct. This was his eighth assignment, with one more to go.

Paul Carr was back, this time as Benson. The 31-year-old had previously appeared in five episodes during *Voyage*'s first season, as Seaman Casey Clark, often on the brink of mental collapse. Loony or not, he always *meant* well, and stayed loyal. This time out, Carr's character crosses the line … which is why he was given a different name. Carr went straight from here to the second pilot film for *Star Trek*, "Where No Man Has Gone Before," as Lt. Lee Kelso. There were few series from the 1960s, '70s, and '80s in which Carr didn't appear at least once. He ended his career with close to 200 screen credits. He was paid $1,250 for up to six days of filming in "Terror on Dinosaur Island."

Paul Trinka finally returned to the series as Patterson. He had appeared in 17 first-season episodes, and was listed in many of the early draft scripts already shot for the second year. A film commitment – 1965's *Faster, Pussycat! Kill! Kill!* – caused him to miss several episodes. Trinka would make it back for three more Season Two *Voyage*s, then stay close to the show for its third and fourth seasons. He was 33.

"Paul was always on the show," Allen Hunt told us. "Sometimes he didn't have lines, but there were three or four of the crew guys who were representative

213

of Richard, David, Bob, Del, and me when the set was lit. They were always crewmembers on the show in the background, and, between shots, would double for the person they most resembled for lighting adjustments." [7]

Better utilized in this episode was Terry Becker. He told interviewer Mark Phillips, "When I joined the show, my hair was just thinning, and Irwin wanted me to wear a toupee. He said the chief might get involved with women. I said, 'Hey, that's an interesting idea. A woman falls in love with a bald guy and he scores!' But all of those ideas got cut out. We ended up making love to giant lizards." [8]

Filming began on Friday, November 12, 1965, for the first of two days on Stage 10, with the Seaview sets, as well as the Flying Sub. If they were working past 9 p.m., it had to be Friday! This was certainly a hell of a way to begin a production, with Leonard Horn taking his first shot at 7:45 in the morning and completing his last at 8:50 p.m. With make-up time (both in and out), and crew time (preparing *and* wrapping the set), it had turned into a 13-hour day … plus travel to and from the studio.

A second day was spent on Stage 10, including a scene in which David Hedison and Paul Carr were treated to a public shower. When the liquid refreshment ran out the two, dried and given fresh costumes (plus a robe for Hedison), entertained a group of female guests with a tour of the stage.

Day 3, Tuesday: Horn and the Company moved to Fox Stage 6 for two days for filming on sets identified as "Ext. Rock Area #1," "Ext Rugged Terrain Area #2" and "Ext. Rock Cave Area #3." No TV series cooked up steamy jungle sets like *Voyage*. Thick with greens and steam, and, in this outing, mounds of dirt and rock clusters. Few motion pictures did better.

Terry Becker told interviewer William Anchors, Jr. about an incident when he and Richard Basehart were asked to ad-lib a few minutes of extra dialogue. He recalled, "It was 'Terror on Dinosaur Island,' and it was that thing with my telephone book, and I don't know, we kind of came up with an idea…. They said they were two minutes short and it wound up that the director had to say, 'Whoa, that's enough. Cut! Cut!' We could have gone for another fifteen or twenty minutes…"

Becker credited this moment of improv for creating a bond between him and Basehart. He said, "[U]p until that point, Richard and I had an initial meeting at the photography session before the shooting started, and I admired his work… and I went up to him… and I said, 'I admire your work very much.' And he looked at me and said, 'Yeah, okay. So what? Thank you.' And he walked away. So, then, I yelled after him and said, 'Fuck you, too!' So, we never really did talk until we got into the 'Dinosaur Island' thing.' And when we got finished, he looked at me and said, 'I'm going up to Irwin right now and tell him we need two seasons together – *at least two seasons*, for sure. I like you a lot.' And that was it. And from that time on we hung out" [9]

Thursday and Friday, Days 5 and 6, found the company on Stage B, filming on the sets "Ext. Clearing Area A," "Ext. Falling Rock Area B," "Ext. Peak Area C & D" and "Ext. Rugged Terrain Area E." Late in the day on Friday, they moved back to Stage 10 to film in the Observation Nose of the Seaview, using process shots. Knowing all too well that Horn was not going to finish, cast and crew were released at 6:55 p.m. and the production was held over for part of a seventh day, delaying the start of "Deadly Creature Below!"

Monday, November 22. The camera rolled from 8:05 to 11 a.m. as Leonard Horn took the last of his shots in the Seaview Control Room and Observation Nose ("straight" shots not requiring process), and into one of the sub's corridor areas for pickup shots. After that, director Sobey Martin was given the company to begin his episode.

The final cost was $162,358. [10]

Release / Reaction:
(ABC premiere airdate: 12/26/65; network repeat broadcast: 4/2/66)

Thunderball, the fourth James Bond movie, starring Sean Connery, was packing them in at the movie houses. The two songs receiving the most radio play

VOYAGE TO THE BOTTOM OF THE SEA - YEAR 2
TERROR ON DINOSAUR ISLAND ... Adm. Nelson (Richard Basehart) struggles with the controls of the Flying Sub in an exciting scene from the "Terror on Dinosaur Island" episode of 20th Century-Fox Television's VOYAGE TO THE BOTTOM OF THE SEA series, seen this (day) at (time) on (channel). #8217/36

across America were "Over and Over" by the Dave Clark Five and "The Sounds of Silence" by Simon and Garfunkel. Herb Alpert and the Tijuana Brass still had the top-selling album with *Whipped Cream & Other Delights*. And the fourth, with *Going Places*.

And then there was "Terror on Dinosaur Island." ABC's Lew Hunter had fought a losing battle to keep this episode off the schedule for December 26. He said, "Irwin and I were having a dispute over playing one of the episodes around Christmas time or not. He wanted to play a good episode that night and I, representing ABC, wanted to play one that was not good, or do a rerun. We were sitting on a couch, and, after the conflict went on for a while, he leaned over and he tapped me on the knee and said, 'Kid, I can have you pumping gas in two weeks.' Now, I don't consider myself a comedian, but I looked at Irwin and I said, 'My only response, Irwin, is Regular or Ethyl?' And that got me off the hook. He went and got a bagel and some cream cheese, and we had a cup of coffee, and that was it. But there was no talking him out of what he wanted to do." [11]

"TV Scout" said:

> The special effects department can take a bow for "Terror on Dinosaur Island" on *Voyage to the Bottom of the Sea*. Richard Basehart and Terry Becker are marooned on an island inhabited by all the major species of dinosaurs. But, look, here comes David Hedison leading a rescue crew (after the Seaview has to be beached for repairs), while fighting off crewman Paul Carr, who has decided to kill Hedison for his own reasons. [12]

A.C. Nielsen 30-city survey from December 26, 1965 [13]:

	Rating:	Share:
(7:30 – 8 p.m.)		
ABC: *Voyage to the Bottom of the Sea*	12.6	26.4%
CBS: *Lassie*	**18.6**	**38.9%**
NBC: AFL game (football)	8.7	18.2%
(8 – 8:30 p.m.):		
ABC: *Voyage to the Bottom of the Sea*	14.4	28.7%
CBS: *My Favorite Martian*	**18.2**	**36.3%**
NBC: *Walt Disney's Wonderful World…*	11.6	23.1%

Lew Hunter had been right, and Frank La Tourette wrote to Irwin Allen:

> Christmas is a disaster for us. It is strongly urged that we try for a preemption next Christmas. [14]

5

Season 2 / ABC's Back Order of 10

ABC-TV *had* to pick up ten more episodes, keeping *Voyage* on for a full second season. After all, it had entered the pop-culture pantheon by being lampooned by *MAD* magazine's "usual gang of idiots"!

The send-up appeared in the March 1966 issue of *MAD*, on newsstands in January. With spot-on caricatures by Mort Drucker and script by Dick DeBartolo, the title – "The Attack of the 1000 Foot Glop" – sounds like an alternate title for Season Two's The Monster from Outer Space."

David Hedison pretends to read *MAD* magazine's send-up of *Voyage* … one issue early! (The *Voyage* spoof appeared in *MAD* #101.)

Promotional pictures were taken on the Control Room set during the making of "Deadly Creature Below" – the first of the back 10 to film – of David Hedison as he pretended to read the parody. This required some acting from Hedison, since the lampoon wasn't yet in print. He mugged with issue #100 instead.

By midseason 1966, there would be another factor in story development: Television was crawling with spies – too many spies. The espionage tales of *Voyage* and *The Man from U.N.C.L.E.* had been joined by *I Spy*, *Secret Agent*, *The Avengers*, *Amos Burke – Secret Agent*, and, just for laughs, *Get Smart*. But there was more – a hybrid part-Western, part-sci-fi, part-spy show called *The Wild, Wild West*. Later in the fall, *Mission: Impossible* would add to the clutter. But, with *The Outer Limits* now out of production, the only TV series spinning tall tales of monsters were *Voyage* and, new to TV, *Lost in Space*. Irwin Allen would be one among many if he continued with the first season's and early second season's bent for undercover and espionage storylines, but he could have a monopoly on creature features. This called for a change at *Voyage to the Bottom of the Sea*.

For that matter, the ratings had not been good, with the series often failing to secure a 30% or higher audience share, but the more fantastic episodes fared better.

From *Variety*, on December 8, 1965, Murray Horowitz reported:

> For ABC, Sunday nights next season may very well be without *Voyage to the Bottom of the Sea* and *FBI*. The web and Warner Bros. are fighting hard to retain *The FBI* series for another season; deal will depend whether Ford [Motor Co.] comes back next season. *Voyage* is in doubt.[1]

By the middle of Season Two, the writing was on the submarine walls. Deep-six the spies; release the monsters!

220

5.1

"Deadly Creature Below!" (Episode 49)
(Prod. #8218; first aired Sunday, January 9, 1966)
Written by William Read Woodfield and Allan Balter
Directed by Sobey Martin
Produced by Irwin Allen, Frank La Tourette, and William Welch
Story Editor: Sidney Marshall
Guest Star Nehemiah Persoff; Co-Starring Paul Comi

Artwork by David Holderbaum (Courtesy the author and iann.net)

From the *Voyage* show files (Irwin Allen papers collection):

> While the Seaview is on a mission to plant a new missile guidance destruct device off the Grand Bahamas, they rescue two convicts who have escaped from the nearby penal colony. When it becomes clear to the men that Nelson intends to return them, they attempt to escape, in spite of a monster that is lurking on the ocean floor. [1]

Assessment:

Mike Bailey bemoaned, "In comparison to Season One's 'The Condemned,' the infamous Deadly Creature of the title headlines a pointless exercise rather than a riveting story with a point." [2]

Mark Phillips noted, "Like many Year Two segments, this episode juggles two stories at once – desperate convicts who terrorize Seaview, and a two-headed jellyfish that is simply defending its turf." [3]

Each of the two primary stories leave much to be desired. The two criminals are not fleshed out to any realistic degree, and it suspends belief that these two simpletons could deceive Admiral Nelson, allowing them to roam free into sensitive areas of the ship where they can observe operations and then throw monkey wrenches into the works. Kowalski is suspicious, and tells Sharkey, but this suspicion is never voiced to any of the officers. That just makes Sharkey look dumb, too. Crane doesn't like the cons being in the missile room, but Nelson doesn't see a problem in it. Security on the Seaview has never been more relaxed, especially considering the "McGuffin" at play (the guidance-system prototype). We are never shown Dobbs and Hawkins to be much more beyond one-dimensional criminal stereotypes, yet look at all the trouble they cause.

The deadly creature below is equally underdeveloped. What is it; why is it; how is it? And why, in the entire expansive ocean, do our heroes and the two desperate felons repeatedly fall into its clutches? This giant thing seems to be merely tossed into the story to generate jeopardy and excitement. But how much honest jeopardy and true excitement can it contribute when its menace is as undeveloped as the criminals' characters? All we get from Nelson is, "I've never seen anything like it."

Despite these criticisms, this episode is somehow entertaining. A great deal of the credit goes to the underwater effects, with the monster and the miniatures of the Seaview and the Flying Sub. It's more than a good-looking episode; the accelerated pacing makes it feel like a speedy plot. And there is an amusing ingredient concerning Dobbs and Hawkins – at times they bicker like an old married couple who have spent too much time in one another's company.

Hawkins, while wrapping his leg wound, appeals to Dobbs, "Listen, if this was you, I'd try to help ya. *I would!*" The cynical Dobbs retorts, "Sure you'd help. What would you do?" "I-I'd try to find a doc," Hawkins insists. "What would you do; pick up the phone and call sickbay?" Dobbs scoffs. "Forget it!" Then, mocking Hawkins's painful grunts, Dobbs adds, "Ah – ah - ah. You make me sick."

When creeping toward the hatch leading to the Flying Sub, Hawkins pauses to aim at the back of an unknowing Nelson, whispering, "That creep Admiral's the one that shot me in the leg. This'll even the score." Dobbs pushes the gun away, harshly whispering, "Are you crazy? You shoot him and they'll lock this thing so tight, we'll never get away."

When the escape attempt in the FS goes awry, and the FS is grabbed by the monster, Hawkins panics and makes a run for the hatch. "I'm getting out of here before that thing crushes us like an eggshell!" "No, you're not!" Dobbs yells, chasing after Hawkins. "You open that thing and we're done for!" But Hawkins reaches for the hatch anyway. Dobbs clobbers Hawkins, with a not too sincere, "Sorry, pal."

And, later, he shoots him, terminating the partnership. Quite a love-hate relationship!

If we are willing to switch off our brains, the seemingly disjointed pieces, with illogical but colorful characters and monster, combine into 51 minutes of better-than-passable escapism. Set your expectations to medium-low, and enjoy the cruise.

Script:

Woodfield's and Balter's writers contract for "Escape": October 28, 1965.
2nd Rev. Shooting Final teleplay (pink paper): November 18.
Page revisions (on blue paper inserts): November 22.
Page revisions (on yellow paper inserts): November 30.
Page revisions (on beige paper inserts): December 13.
Page revisions (on gold paper inserts): December 14.

Irwin Allen was doing a good job as series continuity man, reading the first-draft teleplay by **Woodfield** and **Balter**, and then writing to his staff:

> P. 23, Sc. 63: One of the crew was gunned down by Hawkins. Now that Hawkins and Dobbs no longer are armed, some of the other crew members should go to him to see if he is alive and Sharkey should give orders for them to remove his body. He seems to have been forgotten by everyone....
>
> There is a discrepancy throughout the script in regards to the depth of the trench in which the action takes place. It is established in Scenes 16 and 37 that the bottom depth is approximately 5440 feet. But in Sc. 23, the bell is reported

at 9000' with 1100' from bottom, and Sc. 118 has the Seaview at 9280' and dropping. It then is reported at 4800' and dropping in Scene 132. Sc. 99: Crane says that the bottom is 500' below Seaview's crush depth. This can't be correct if the original depth of the ocean is maintained at approximately 5440'. The Bell went down this far and in other episodes the Seaview has descended much farther. [4]

"Escape" was the original title. After Woodfield and Balter fulfilled their assignment, Irwin Allen had the title changed to the less generic "Deadly Creature Below!" Although, considering the series, even that new title was a bit generic.

ABC was more concerned with the violence than the title. Mary Garbutt of Standards & Practices wrote to Allen's staff on November 5, saying:

> Pgs 1-3: Noted that machine gun to be used in penal colony sequence, but under condition, as presently indicated, that no one is hit.
>
> Pg 1, Sc 6: Change this POV [Point of View] – Delete machine gun firing into camera.
>
> Pg 2, Sc 11: Please be sure that all we see is the blinding flash and that there is no accompanying human cry….
>
> Pg 3, Sc 13: Again, tracer bullets firing away and not into camera.
>
> Pg 5, etc.: Your usual care in seeing that the "creature" is not on the "too frightening" side for family viewing. Also caution on its "cry". Can only be approved on film.
>
> Pg 18, Sc 49: Substitute for machine gun here and in later sequence, Pg 56, Sc 20 in particular.
>
> Pg 21, Sc 59: Particular care that "writing" is not over-done – caution on blood.
>
> Pg 27 & 28: The whole of Sc 68 to be modified to eliminate the physical pain-sadistic nature of the scene.

> Pgs 30-33: Even in mock agony, please be sure the screams are not overdone.
>
> Pg 33, Sc 73; Pg 34, Sc 76; Pg 56, Sc 145: Standard caution on these men being knocked out; Do not CU [Close Up] on the blows.
>
> Pg 35, Sc 83-84; Pg 37, Sc 87: Please be sure the [rifle] "sighting" is not at Nelson's head – Of course, no "crosshairs".
>
> Pg 41: Delete "My God" in Hawkin's line…. [and] "I'll blow your guts out".
>
> Pg 58: Substitute for "tear your insides out". [5]

Of course the producers and writers knew they wouldn't be able to leave lines like "My God," "I'll blow your guts out" and "tear your insides out" in the episode. Some over-the-top lines, and some of the graphic descriptions of violence, were intentionally put in to give the censors something to nitpick over, to distract attention from other elements that were more essential to the story. This was a typical practice in the motion-picture industry as well, with early cuts of films stuffed with objectionable material in the hopes that censors would take out some but leave others behind.

November 15, 1965. After reading the next draft of the script, Mary Garbutt found less to object to:

> Pg 1, Sc 4: The guard in foreground can shout into camera but his gun must be below camera frame.
>
> Pgs 25 thru 26: There is far too much blood indicated to be acceptable on color film (For ex.: Delete "pool of blood," Sc C-67). Please cut down and, of course, no CU [Close Up] of wounded leg. Also lose at least one of the "bleeding" references in Hawkins lines.
>
> Pg 27, Sc 68: The implication that the doctor is working on Hawkins' leg without a local anesthetic is not acceptable. Modify. He can be scared but not crying out in agony. Of course, any shots of doctor working on leg must be covered or out of camera frame. [6]

With ABC's blessing, the episode was sent to production.

Production:

(Filmed November 22 – December 2, 1965; 7 days)

Sobey Martin – no one's favorite director – except maybe Irwin Allen – was again hired to guide the episode.

Nehemiah Persoff played Dobbs, and was given top guest-star pay of $2,500. He was 46, and would amass 200 appearances in films and television. TV series from the 1950s and '60s that bought him back more than once as a featured guest star included *Playhouse 90*, *The Untouchables*, *Naked City*, *Alfred Hitchcock Presents*, *Mission: Impossible*, *I Spy*, *Burke's Law*, *The Mod Squad*, and *The Wild, Wild West*. Irwin Allen put Persoff into an episode of *Land of the Giants*.

Paul Comi was tapped to play Hawkins, with a fee of $1,000. Comi took his voyage to the bottom of the sea one year before going on a star trek. He told this author, "The submarine show and the spaceship show had one thing in common, and that was that the producers took those programs very serious. *Voyage to the Bottom of the Sea* shouldn't have. *Star Trek*, maybe. I can tell you that [Gene] Roddenberry was really a lovely man; he was fantastic, but I had no idea what *Star Trek* was all about. But it was easy to find the drama in the material and play off the other actors. The submarine show was a different story. I remember Nehemiah Persoff and I were laughing a lot over that script. It was pretty absurd, the things we had to do and say. And the director didn't have any idea what we were laughing about." [7]

Filming began on Monday, November 22, 1965, for the first of four days on Stage 10, with focus on the Seaview sets, including Int. Diving Bell and Int. Flying Sub.

On Monday, the fifth day of production, the company moved to Stage B where sets had been prepared for "Ext. Yard," "Ext. Jungle," "Ext. River Bank" and "Ext. Open Sea."

For Tuesday, Day 6, they were back on Stage 10 for more work on the Flying Sub set, then into the Observation Nose for process shots.

Wednesday, December 1, no work was done on *Voyage*. Instead, the *Voyage* production crew helped out its sister series, *Lost in Space*, shooting several scenes for "Attack of the Monster Plants," trying to get that series back on schedule and enable it to make its delivery date to CBS.

After this episode aired, a nationally syndicated "TV Mail" column received a letters asking where viewers could find the schematics of the Seaview seen here. [8]

Thursday, December 2, was the seventh and final day of work on "Deadly Creature Below!" with the company spending the entire day on Stage 10 and the Control Room set. They wrapped at 7:03 p.m.

The final cost was $187,965. [9]

227

Release / Reaction:
(ABC premiere airing: 1/9/66; network repeat broadcast: 6/26/66)

Agent of H.A.R.M., a science-fiction spy thriller, was tops at the movie houses. The No. 1 selling album in the U.S. was *Rubber Soul*, by the Beatles. They also had the top-selling single, with "We Can Work It Out" b/w "Day Tripper." During the week, the Who were performing on ABC's *Shindig*. In three days, America would meet *Batman*.

"TV Scout" previewed "Deadly Creature Below":

> Oh, the problems for the men of the Seaview on *Voyage to the Bottom of the Sea*. One is the "Deadly Creature Below," a lovely, two-headed, red-eyed monster so ably turned out by the special effects department. The other two are Nehemiah Persoff and Paul Comi, a pair of dangerous criminals picked up by the Seaview. [10]

Forget about the "two-headed, red-eyed monster." The real threat to the Seaview on the night of the broadcast lived in Emerald City.

A.C. Nielsen ratings report, Jan. 9, 1966:[11]

(7 – 7:30 p.m.)	Rating:	Share:
ABC: *Voyage to the Bottom of the Sea*	15.8	26.5%
CBS: Movie special: *The Wizard of Oz*	**30.4**	**51.4%**
NBC: Actuality Special	8.5	14.3%
7:30 – 8 p.m.		
ABC: *Voyage to the Bottom of the Sea*	16.1	25.7%
CBS: Movie special: *The Wizard of Oz*	**29.8**	**47.6%**
NBC: *Walt Disney's Wonderful World…*	11.8	18.8%

According to Nielsen, *Voyage* ranked No. 33 this week out of 107 network series.

ABC didn't consider second place so bad, when up against *The Wizard of Oz*, and especially in light of out-pulling Walt Disney. In the days after "Deadly Creature Below" aired, the network announced that *Voyage* was on its draft schedule for the Fall. This meant ABC would be looking for sponsor commitments. Renewal, which seems unlikely just weeks before, was now a fair possibility. [12]

5.2

"The Phantom Strikes" (Episode 50)
(Prod. #8219; first aired Sunday, January 16, 1966)
Written by William Welch
Directed by Sutton Roley
Produced by Irwin Allen, Frank La Tourette, and William Welch
Story Editor: Sidney Marshall
Guest Star Alfred Ryder

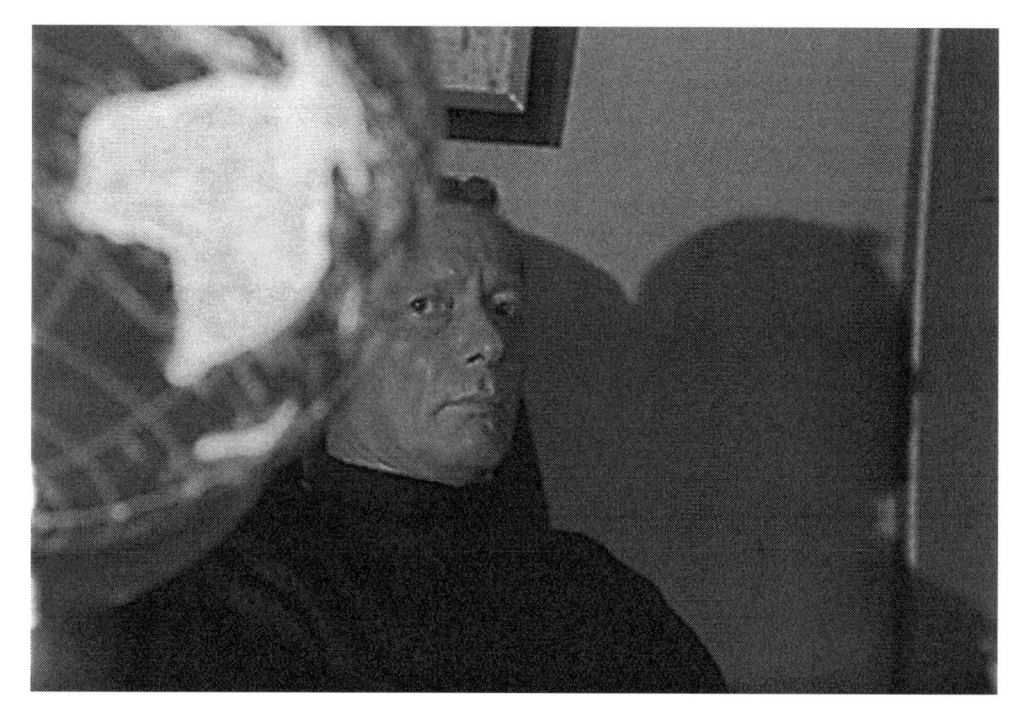

From the *Voyage* show files (Irwin Allen papers collection):

After sighting a sunken derelict, a World War I submarine which abruptly vanished, Nelson rescues a German Captain adrift in the ocean. He claims that his vessel was sunk by the strange sub. The mystery increases when Captain Krueger eludes his guards, tampers with the Seaview's equipment, and manages to escape from the brig. He then confronts Nelson and demands Crane's life because he wishes to use Crane's body to restore his own youth. Nelson is powerless to control him, and unable to discover whether he is faced with a lunatic, a dangerous criminal, or a phantom. [1]

Assessment:

A classic spin on the tale of "The Flying Dutchman." Alfred Ryder shines as WWI German U-boat commander, Captain Krueger, a restless spirit with an agenda. First-time *Voyage* director Sutton Roley took care to instill William Welch's script with appropriate tingles to the spine. And he was given an excellent performance from Alfred Ryder to bring the ghostly Krueger to life.

Mike Bailey said, "Among fans of the show, 'The Phantom Strikes' is one of *Voyage*'s most popular episodes – and for good reason. It is filled with rich performances by regulars Richard Basehart and David Hedison, who always rose to the occasion of a decent script. Then there is the fine acting of guest Alfred Ryder, as the ghostly Gerhardt Krueger, World War I captain of the German U-444. Plus there is just a ton of unique special effects involving Krueger's derelict U-444, and some great eerie shots of Seaview plying a becalmed, fog-bound night sea." [2]

From the story's conclusion:

Krueger: "What kind of torpedo did you shoot at the U-Boat?" *Crane*: "It wasn't a torpedo. It was a metal seeking missile." *Krueger*: "And the fog – it provided no cover?" *Crane*: "Our infra-red searchlights saw right through it." *Krueger*: "Gentlemen, I must ask your forgiveness. I am beginning to realize I have made a mistake … I know now that I am behind the times. Too far behind. It was so much simpler. Everything was so much simpler. So, gentlemen, I apologize – and I leave you to your modern world with all its bewildering hardware." After a thoughtful pause, Krueger asks, "I wonder where it will take you?"

Script:

William Welch's writers contract, "The Ghost Ship": November 17, 1965.
Welch's 1st-draft teleplay approved on November 21.
Welch's 2nd (final) draft teleplay approved on November 24.
Sidney Marshall's script polish, Shooting Final teleplay: November 24.
Welch's script polish, 2nd Rev. Shooting Final teleplay (on paper): December 3.
Welch's page revisions (on pink page inserts): December 3.
Welch's page revisions (on yellow paper inserts): December 13.

Writer **William Welch** was a firm believer in ghosts. He wrote a 1975 book called *Talks with the Dead*. He said, "My earliest recollection of psychic experience occurred when I was about two. Although this is pretty young to remember anything, the incident was apparently startling enough to have produced an indelible impression. I was being given a bath one evening when I happened to look down the hall through the open door behind me. There I saw several liver-colored figures of indefinite and changing shape. Somehow, I could make out enough of their features to sense that they were laughing at me or mocking me. The experience terrified me, and it was quite a long time before my mother could quiet me down. Not much of an experience, perhaps, but one which made, as I have indicated, a lasting impression. I can still see those figures in the hall as clearly as I must have seen them then. I recall now that during my childhood I often thought back to that occurrence with great interest and something approaching awe. I suppose the seeds of my desire to know more about psychic matters were planted on that one occasion." [3]

The story Welch wrote for *Voyage* in November 1965 was called "The Ghost Ship." He sped through the writing process with customary rapidity. Within days of pitching his story to Irwin Allen and Frank LaTourette, he had a contract (dated November 17) and handed in a short treatment that same day. Days later, by November 21, he had delivered a first-draft teleplay.

Allen gave the script a quick read, along with drafts of other scripts for both *Voyage* and *Lost in Space*, then came back with some notes for Welch. He began with a general thought regarding the Teaser:

> THERE IS SOME UNNECESSARY repetition in the requests for readings from different instruments. These tend to slow down the action and lessen the excitement. The ending of the teaser should be revised so that the real excitement comes from the fact that the sub is heading straight at the Seaview on a collision course.
>
> P. 2, Sc. 4: Patterson – since the sub is at present motionless in the water, the word "bearing" may be incorrect in this instance. He should say, "Metal contact, (zero-two-zero relative?), range, one thousand yards." Perhaps he should add that the contact is stationary, otherwise the chief would have to inform Crane immediately to avoid a possible collision.
>
> Why does Kowalski report "Definite metal contact"? The fathometer is supposed to give readings on <u>depth</u>.

P. 6, Sc. 12: Cut Nelson's speech which doesn't make much sense as the sub is moving on a definite line, not floundering as it might due to a strong current. After Crane speech (which could be given to Nelson), Crane should say "Activate force field!" Someone would try to do so, but would report it inoperative. Last scene of teaser should be a shot of the sub seen through the nose window, as all present watch in terror....

Act I: Should pick up on the continuation of the Teaser last shot and just as it seems that the sub is about to ram the Seaview, all lights and instruments should go out for a split second. Then the red emergency lights should come on and Scene 16 dialogue should be revised to include some astonished remarks about the fact that the sub can no longer be seen through the window. The reports on the various instruments would then follow as written in script.

P. 19, Sc. 39: Kowalski should have some definite weird experience to relate to the other men. It should be something which Sharkey is able to explain in his own inimitable way. Since it is brought out later that someone tampered with the navigational system during the night, perhaps it could have something to do with Kowalksi's having seen Mann [later renamed Krueger] suddenly standing at the end of the corridor when he knew he couldn't possibly be there at all. But just to make sure, Kowalski looks into Mann's cabin, only to find him asleep in his bunk....

P. 27, Sc. 53: How can Nelson continue to speak of the sub as being a derelict, and a wreck, when it obviously is moving about in the water as though someone or something was directing it? Sonar and the hydrophone should report no contact in the same manner as they do the first time the sub disappeared. The question Nelson and Crane should be asking is how to account for the strange reactions from the instruments. The idea of the sub being operated by remote control is logical, but this should bring up the question of who is controlling it and why?

Up to this point in the script it is the sub which has given everyone the best reason to be upset and on edge. It has

> never actually been proven that Mann was responsible for the sabotage. It could have been one of the crew for any number of reasons but this point has never even been brought up. Kowalski's scene with Mann (P. 30) doesn't point up anything unusual in Mann's manner. Something should happen which would really shake up Kowalski so that he would have a good reason for another discussion with his crew mates. The men never discuss the phantom sub. They should....
>
> P. 35, Sc. 65: Crane's first speech: He should tell the Admiral that the man guarding the brig swears he didn't know Mann was out of it. He was so shook-up he had to be taken to sick bay.
>
> P. 36, Sc. 65: Nelson's 2nd speech: Should add, "I'm not sure it will work." This would help establish the fact that Nelson is beginning to sense that Mann is a ghost.
>
> P. 57, Sc. 113: Why isn't the sub a ghost ship if Mann is a ghost? Wouldn't it be more frightening if the torpedoes went right through the sub, if it suddenly disappeared before their eyes. A Ghost ship is believable but a ship that has substance and can be blown up is a real ship and this couldn't be real....[4]

Then Allen made a suggestion which would influence many episodes to come, pushing *Voyage* more toward fantasy rather than science fiction. He wrote:

> Since Mann is a ghost, all sorts of strange things could happen to the crew and the Seaview which would never have to be explained later. He could cause things to disappear right before their eyes like whole instrument panels, the control room, etc., and all because [he] is angry at not being taken to his island. This kind of thing would be enough to make the crew want to get out and swim for land rather than stay on the "crazy" sub. The men would be reporting to sickbay in droves. Nelson, Crane, Sharkey would have their hands full trying to keep the men from mutiny. Some of them would refuse to even stand guard over Mann....[5]

Now Bill Welch had Allen's permission – even encouragement – to throw logic, and even believability, out the porthole and inject any idea he liked into the script. Given free rein, Welch followed his narrative impulses down several shady alleys. This ghost wouldn't just pop in and out, but he would make all kinds of other things pop in and out of existence, too. In spiritualistic terms, this kind of occurrence is called an "apportation."

Another suggestion from Allen affected the ending. He told Welch:

> P. 58, Sc. 116: Mann should be given another reason for leaving the Seaview other than it being a too modern ship with futuristic technology which was too much for him. He threatens to destroy the Seaview. He could do it easily without his old sub if he really wanted to. There is nothing futuristic about torpedoing a sub. Shouldn't he say that he can't bring himself to destroy them even though they have tried to destroy him. So, therefore, he has decided to leave them.[6]

This change was also made. Its inclusion contributed to a somewhat poignant ending.

Welch took Allen's notes and with remarkable speed had a second-draft script sitting on everyone's desks only a few days later, on November 24. After Story Editor Sidney Marshall's review, the script was reformatted as a shooting script. It went to the Mimeo Department next, with copies distributed to all department heads for their budget breakdowns and feedback, as well as going to the network for coverage. The script then went back to Welch to make changes based on notes from Irwin Allen and ABC.

Allan Hunt said, "This was the kind of episode Richard had asked for – a story dealing with the men and the psychology of being on a submarine."[7]

Production:
(Filmed December 3 – 14, 1965; 7 ½ days)

Sutton Roley was 43 when he directed the first of three episodes of *Voyage*. Allen would also have him direct four episodes of *Lost in Space*. Roley got his start as a television director working for Ziv Productions' low-budget half-hour shows, such as *Highway Patrol* and *Harbor Command*. In 1959 he graduated to Desilu's half-hour Western, *U.S. Marshal*, then stepped up to the hour-long

Western, with *Wagon Train* and *Rawhide*. He got into World War II reenactments with *Twelve O'Clock High* and *Combat!*, directing 15 episodes for the latter.

Alfred Ryder was 49 when paid $2,000 to play the Phantom. Ryder was a busy stage actor and director. He worked often during the Golden Age of Television on anthology series, such as *The Philco-Goodyear Television Playhouse* (with seven episodes) and *Robert Montgomery Presents* (with four). They liked him at *Ben Casey*, where he also did four episodes, and *Naked City*, where he was seen in three. Ryder had worked with David Hedison before, in the latter's series, *Five Fingers*. Now he was beginning a period in his career that would take the serious actor into the worlds of sci-fi and fantasy, with guest spots on *Voyage*, *The Outer Limits*, *One Step Beyond*, *Star Trek*, and *The Invaders*.

Production began on Friday, December 3, 1965 for the first of eight days on Stage 10. First up, filming on the Control Room and Observation Nose, with the "Bubble Tanks."

This effect was often added as a process shot, utilizing a blue screen. Sutton Roley wanted real bubbles, more satisfying to the eye, but also audible to the ear.

Only the standard Seaview sets would be needed for this production, making it a "bottle show." Despite this, director Roley took seven-and-a-half days to finish.

Allan Hunt told a convention audience, "I think Alfred and Richard knew each other from the old days. They had a great kind of reunion on the set. Alfred looked to Richard, in a sort of 'If you do it, I'll do it' way, to be on the show. There were a couple guest stars like that – John Cassavetes was on a show, I

235

remember, and Victor Buono, Roger C. Carmel, and John McGiver – actors who had stature. I think Irwin's vision was always starting with Richard Basehart. Richard lent a certain authority and authenticity to all the zany proceedings. When you do that, it lends credibility."[8]

This was director Roley's first time experiencing what the regular cast and production crew referred to as the "Rock and Roll," as the Seaview is jolted and rocked from side to side. Interviewed by Mark Phillips, Roley told a now-familiar story this way: "The prop man would sit with a tin can and hammer, and when he hit the tin can, the actors would fake their falls. It bothered the actors to do it this way. Richard Basehart was particularly embarrassed by the tin can, but it worked."

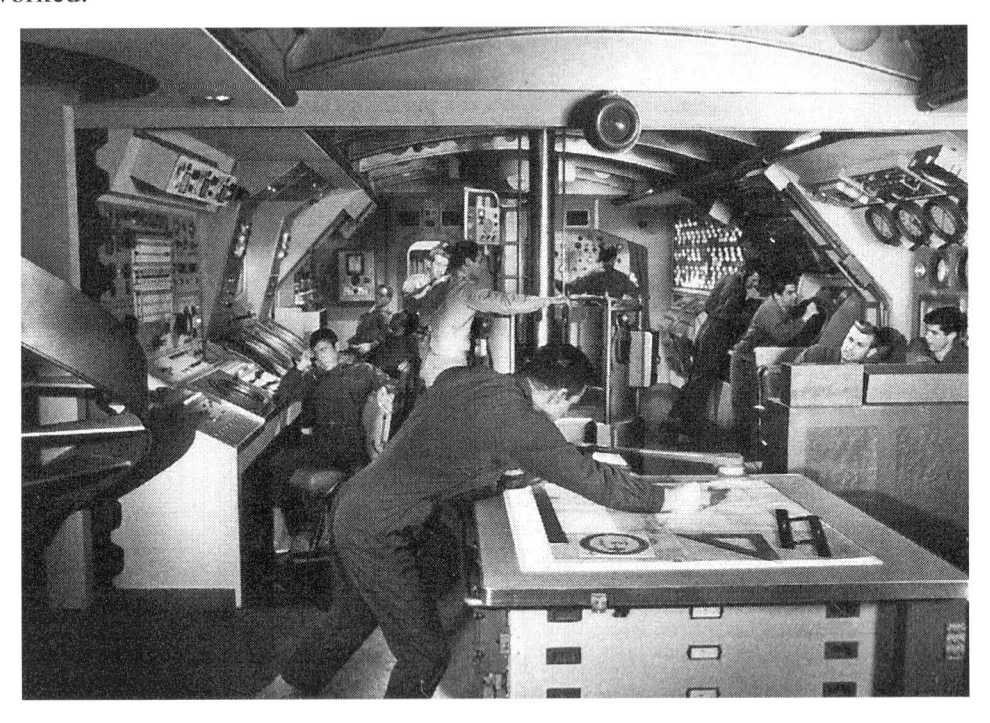

Roley had his own problems working within the confining rules of the Irwin Allen TV factory. He said, "Irwin had a very cut-and-dry approach. He was a great believer in storyboarding. He had his artists draw every shot of the script beforehand. I can't work that way. Whenever you surprised Irwin by doing something different, he could be quite a shouter."

But, among the stable of recurring directors on Irwin Allen's television series, Roley was the maverick. He said, "The sub's control room was built like a real submarine, totally enclosed. I asked the grip, 'Does this sub come apart?' He said the whole side did. So, I said, 'Rip the whole thing off!', and it was unbolted. This way I could shoot over the computers and give the scene some visual leeway. We set it up and the cameraman shook his head. 'You're gonna get blurred images,' he said. I replied, 'Is that right? Well, this is the way we're gonna do it.' So, the cameraman called up Irwin, and I was called to the phone. 'What are you doing down there?' Irwin yelled. 'You've got everybody upset.' I said, 'It's gonna work, Irwin. And I think you're gonna like it.' As we shot it, I had everybody against me, except for Richard Basehart and David Hedison. After the shot was completed, Basehart said, 'I knew we were okay, Sutton, as soon as I saw half of that goddamned submarine set taken away. I'm tired of being stuck in here. It gives me claustrophobia.'

"We wrapped the scene at 2:30 that afternoon, which was unheard of. In the dailies the next day, everyone was watching as my shot came up. When the scene was over, Irwin suddenly tapped me on the shoulder. 'It really did work, didn't it?'" [9]

Hunt told interviewer Mark Phillips, "Alfred [Ryder] was pleasant to be around, but, when those cameras rolled, that face, which would break into a smile and be so cherubic off-screen, became a vital look of ghostly consternation. It really gave all of us the creeps. He was very effective in that show, and it was so successful that they made a sequel." [10]

The final cost was $180,328. [11]

Release / Reaction:
(ABC premiere airdate: 1/16/66; network repeat broadcast: 7/31/66)

Our Man Flint, a spy spoof starring James Coburn, was making more money than any other film in the movie houses. "We Can Work It Out," by the Beatles, and "The Sounds of Silence," by Simon and Garfunkel, kept taking turns as the song getting the most radio play, and selling the most 45 rpm records. The top album honors went to the Beatles for *Rubber Soul*, even though "We Can Work It Out" was nowhere to be found on the LP. Robert Culp and Bill Cosby of *I Spy* had the cover of *TV Guide*. But that show didn't start until 10 p.m. The younger crowd was more likely to be watching *Voyage to the Bottom of the Sea*.

Alfred Ryder received attention for his performance on *Voyage* in a syndicated article from the week "The Phantom Strikes" first aired. Published in the January 16, 1966 edition of the *Pasadena Independent Star-News*, the article said in part:

> New York-born Alfred Ryder unlimbers his Teutonic accent for his guest-starring role of the phantom captain of a sunken World War I U-boat in the colorcast of *Voyage to the Bottom of the Sea*. Sunday the accent isn't any problem for him. He's

played Frenchmen, Germans, Italians, Russians and Englishmen. "Very few New Yorkers, though," he pointed out. "Luckily I have a good ear for dialects, although I've never made a study of them... My face isn't that of an all-American boy, so a facility with dialects comes in handy."

The well-known character actor created a sinister picture as he sat in the shadows of the submarine corridor between takes, his craggy features accented by the black garb he wears in the drama titled "The Phantom." [12]

Ryder told his interviewer, "This is an unusual character and script, and only the fourth time I have played someone involved in the bizarre or supernatural. The first was on Roald Dahl's live TV series, *Way Out*. In it I played an actor appearing in *The Hunchback of Notre Dame* who couldn't remove the grotesque Quasimodo makeup. The other two were in the *One Step Beyond* TV series. In one I was a man who couldn't be hung – the rope kept breaking; the other was the story of a man who changed into a mountain lion.

"I definitely would recommend lots of stage experience before attempting anything in movies or on television. It's extremely difficult to sustain a characterization through the many short scenes peculiar to film work. We don't always shoot scenes in sequence, either. With a stage background, an actor becomes increasingly flexible, and can adapt to new situations quite rapidly. Why, I learned to walk through walls in just two days here on *Voyage*!" [13]

"TV Key" previewed the episode for newspapers across America:

A mixture of fantasy and science fiction which should appeal to the youngsters. The Seaview is pursued by a phantom ship, sunk during the first World War. When they pick up a survivor who seems to be everywhere at once, things get mighty complicated. A suspenseful hour that will keep the kids on the edge of the sofa. [14]

According to A.C. Nielsen, quite a few kids were perched on sofa edges – probably some parents too. [15]

Nielsen ratings report from January 16, 1966:

(7 – 7:30 p.m.)	Rating:	Share:
ABC: *Voyage to the Bottom of the Sea*	**22.2**	**36.5%**
CBS: *Lassie*	16.7	27.4%
NBC: *Bell Telephone Hour*	14.8	24.3%

7:30 – 8 p.m.
ABC: *Voyage to the Bottom of the Sea*	**22.4**	**36.4%**
CBS: *My Favorite Martian*	12.4	20.2%
NBC: *Walt Disney's Wonderful World...*	19.5	31.7%

Del Monroe said, "Our ratings [had] dropped terribly. We were sure that we were going to be cancelled. And then we did an episode with Alfred Ryder. Our ratings shot up astronomically. In fact, it was so successful that when Alfred returned [for the sequel 'Return of the Phantom'], he told us that people were coming up and congratulating him on the streets of New York. He was a classically trained actor, and he told us, 'People were throwing accolades in my face about *Voyage*, which was flattering, but it was also a little irritating because I've never received acclaim like that for all the great things I've done!'

"That episode's success led Irwin to think this was the direction to take the series. And he was right, because, otherwise, we would have been cancelled." [16]

Terry Becker said to a convention audience in England, "I also heard the story that we weren't doing well. Even in the beginning of the second year we had no monsters with the first two or three shows, but then there was an episode with Al Ryder, called 'The Phantom.' He came on board and, for whatever reason, that show's ratings went through the roof. ... and Irwin said, 'Ah, I've got it!', and he sat down at a sewing machine and started sewing monsters." [17]

Allan Hunt, speaking to the same crowd of fans, added, "I just remember hearing often that when there was a monster, the ratings were better, much to Richard's dismay. He always wanted episodes about the man, you know, his inner conflicts and all that sort of stuff ... and political uprisings... I guess because it was originally on Sunday nights at 7 p.m., it was a 'family hour' show [aimed at] kids. Every time there was a monster the ratings seemed to be good, so that was the end of the game." [18]

Sutton Roley said, "The point was to scare people, and ['The Phantom Strikes'] did. It worked very well. Irwin Allen loved it, and they asked me to do a sequel." [19]

5.3

"The Sky's on Fire" (Episode 51)
(Prod. #8220; first aired Sunday, January 23, 1966)
Written by William Welch, from a screenplay by Irwin Allen and Charles Bennett
Directed by Gerald Mayer
Produced by Irwin Allen, Frank La Tourette, and William Welch
Story Editor: Sidney Marshall
Guest Star David J. Stewart
Co-Starring Robert H. Harris and Frank Marth

From the *Voyage* show files (Irwin Allen papers collection):

A meteor shower ignites a radiation belt over the Southern Hemisphere, causing the sky to turn to flame and threatening the world with fiery destruction. The United States sends a committee of three to assist Nelson in containing the fire which is spreading rapidly. The experts cannot decide, however, on whether to follow Nelson's drastic advice on how to avert annihilation. Two of its members are killed aboard the Seaview and now Nelson is faced with an enemy bitterly opposed to his strategy and determined to stop him.
[1]

Assessment:

Irwin Allen's original idea for the 1961 *Voyage* movie is given a new adaptation by William Welch, making a first-rate episode. This isn't just a re-tooled script; it's a whole new take on the premise. Both the film and this episode start from the same foundation – a radiation belt circling the Earth has ignited, making it appear that the sky has caught on fire. Admiral Nelson is sure the way to douse the flame is with a nuclear blast, pushing the ring of fire into space where lack of oxygen will snuff it out. But it must be done quickly, at a specific time and from a precise trajectory point. Other scientists have a conflicting opinion – to let the phenomenon just burn itself out, gambling that it will not cook everything in the Southern hemisphere in the meantime. Even if it does, those in the North may escape peril. It is calculated by these believers that the fire will burn out in several days. Nelson is equally adamant that waiting that long will result in the annihilation of life on Earth.

From this beginning, the *Voyage* movie and "The Sky's on Fire" take very different paths before world-saving conclusions. In many ways, this episode is a cleaner – certainly swifter – telling of the story. It also utilizes recurring cast members to good effect. Nelson is of course at the center of the tale, but William Welch wrote excellent parts for Crane, Morton, Sharkey, Kowalski, and Riley too. No one is given short shrift.

It's interesting to compare such different branchings from the same story root. Mike Bailey said, "It is interesting to compare the movie cast to the television cast in their handling of basically the same story. Basehart's Nelson is much more intense than Walter Pidgeon, who in some ways walked through the movie role. The same can be said of David Hedison's portrayal of Crane versus that of Robert Sterling. Just the same, a decent show. (Re)writer William Welch had a pretty good script from which to work." [2]

Script:

William Welch's writers contract: November 24, 1965.
Welch's 1st-draft teleplay approved on November 28.
Welch's 2nd (and final) draft teleplay approved on December 6.
Shooting Final (on pale green paper): December 7.
Page revisions (on blue paper inserts): December 14.
Page revisions (on pink paper inserts): December 27.

Quoted by Kevin Kelly in *The Boston Globe* on June 14, 1961, Irwin Allen said that the concept for his new *Voyage to the Bottom of the Sea* movie began with a dream. "I had a nightmare," he told Kelly. "Not last night; several months ago. I got up, wrote it down, and turned it into the story that's the basis of the film. You see, there are two belts of radiation surrounding the Earth which were discovered by a scientist named Dr. Van Allen, and I dreamed that one of the belts caught fire. I got to thinking what would happen to a space ship trapped in the blaze at the 300-mile level." [3]

William Welch's first stab at the teleplay based on Allen's original story was delivered only days after the assignment was given to him. Irwin Allen wrote:

> From Page 10, Scene 34 thru P. 32, Scene 87, there is too much talk and very little action. Neither the F.S. 1 [Flying Sub 1] or the Seaview are ever in any danger. ...
>
> Nelson's involvement should come from the fact that he contacts Washington to report the phenomena and finds out that the whole world is working on the problem because it is so wide spread. (Nelson at first couldn't know how far reaching the flaming belt was.) Nelson would request all available information from McHenry and would start his own scientific investigation resulting in the plan which he would then make known via T.V. McHenry would agree to pass on the info to the committee for study and, in the meantime, Nelson and the Seaview could be on their way to the coordinates as per his plan. On the way, Nelson would receive word that the appointed committee was going to join him for further study of it as not all of them agreed with his theory and therefore he could not be given a go-ahead at that time. This would cut down on the duplication of scenes involving a discussion of who is right. It would also make Weber's actions in passing out his rum drops more believable since it would have given him time to obtain them in case he needed them. As it is now, it seems as though he carries them with him at all times. [4]

With the next draft of the script, the "rum drops" were dropped in favor of a ring that can prick the skin and inject a drug.

Allen continued:

> It seems hard to believe that Washington couldn't find a way to reach the Seaview if they wanted to, even though it was on radio silence. And why was it on radio silence? Since the Seaview works so closely with Washington it is unlikely that they would not have some secret means of making contact at all times. [5]

A line of dialogue solved the concern. The ship had been under the South pole for days, therefore unable to receive radio communications.

More from Allen:

> Either the Seaview or the plane carrying the committee should encounter some difficulty en route, due to the raging holocaust. [6]

They now would. Extreme heat would cause circuits to burn out, resulting in Nelson diving the "FS" into the ocean to cool it off.

> Once Nelson is informed of Weber's plan, he should show some interest in it by requesting time to study it and, of course, find something in it with to disagree, or agree that it might work but that if it didn't it would be too late to put his plan into effect. This point was made in the picture [the feature-length *Voyage to the Bottom of the Sea*], and without it we are left with the fact that the important question is: which ego-maniac is going to get his way?'

> It should develop that the northern hemisphere is beginning to be affected by the fiery belt so that the situation becomes much more serious every minute.

> There is discrepancy in the script concerning the involvement of the rest of the world. At first, we are given to understand that in all likelihood the north will also be destroyed unless the belt stops or is stopped somehow. Then, at several points, Weber says that, at least [with] his way, only one half of the world will perish, if he is wrong. If this is retained, it will weaken the story because it lessens the need for Nelson's plan. [7]

ABC wasn't taking any chances on alarming its viewing audience. Mary Garbutt of Standards & Practices told Allen's people:

> Somewhere in the opening establish future date.
>
> Pg 10, 17: Please give the radiation belt a fictitious name and substitute for Van Allen.
>
> Pg 21, Sc 62: Modify Nelson's "nonsense" and "tangled in red tape" speeches. As written, Nelson seems to be setting himself as the law above the President and the UN. [8]

In other words, what had worked in the movie wasn't going to happen on ABC. Garbutt continued.

> Pg 34, Sc 94: Caution that the choking and coughing is not over-done.
>
> Pg 35-36: Standard caution on McHenry's body in death....
>
> Pg 48, Sc 21: Delete "let them be turned into cinders" in Kowalski's speech.
>
> Pg 50, Sc 126: Delete Carlson's cry of terror here – and, of course, we must not see Carlson at the point of explosion.
>
> Sc 63, Sc 176: We must not see the bodies hit by the explosion – This must be covered [with alternate camera angles] in some way. [9]

Production:
(Filmed December 16 – 27, 1965; 7 ¼ days)

This was the first of four *Voyage* episodes for director **Gerald Mayer**. He was 46. After cutting his teeth in short subjects, Mayer directed his first feature with the 1950 film noir *Dial 1119*. After another B-film (1951's *Inside Straight*), Mayer got a shot at a pair of smaller A-pictures for 1952, with *The Sellout*, starring Walter Pidgeon, and *Holiday for Sinners*, staring Gig Young. More B-pictures followed, including 1958's *Diamond Safari*, which Mayer also produced.

Above: Director Gerald Mayer with actress Dorothy Dandridge during the making of 1953's *Bright Road*. Below/left: David J. Stewart. Below/right: Robert H. Harris.

He made the move to television and became a recurring director on numerous series, including *The Millionaire* (1956-58), where he also served as associate producer; Charles Bronson's crime-scene investigator series *Man with a Camera* (1958-59); Jack Warden's crime drama *The Asphalt Jungle* (1961); Ed Binns' crime drama *Brenner* (1959-64); and the prime-time medical soap opera, *The Doctors and the Nurses* (1963-65), among others. He also directed an episode of David Hedison's series, *Five Fingers*.

David J. Stewart was 50 when given top guest billing, and $1,750 for up to four days of filming. Stewart had gained attention as a New York stage actor before also trying his skills in films and TV. He had appeared in an episode of David Hedison's *Five Fingers,* as well as multiple episodes of the prestigious anthology series *Studio One* and *Playhouse 90*. Stewart also made repeated visits on other popular series, such as *Naked City*, *The Defenders*, and *The Doctors and the Nurses*. He did a *Man from U.N.C.L.E.* after this, as well as appearing in the movie *Who's Minding the Mint?* before dying at the age of 51 following a surgery.

Robert H. Harris got second billing, and $1,250 for up to four days in front of the camera. He was 54 and had played Jake Goldberg on the 1950s sitcom *The Goldbergs*. He was also the co-star of the short-lived late 1950s series, *The Court of Last Resort*. He had the lead in the 1958 horror film *How to Make a Monster*. Irwin Allen would bring Harris back for an episode of *Land of the Giants*.

Frank Marth was paid $750 for up to three days of filming. He was 43 and worked constantly in television, with multiple appearances on *The Honeymooners*, *The Phil Silvers Show*, *The Big Valley*, *Hogan's Heroes*, and countless other series.

Filming began on Thursday, December 16, 1965 for the first of eight days on Stage 10. Because of an early work cutoff time on two days of production (Christmas Eve, when they filmed until 1 p.m., and the final day of production, when director Gerald Mayer wrapped at 2:55 p.m.), the episode took a little more than the equivalent of seven days to film.

Ray Didsbury recalled, "One night, we were having our annual Christmas party. Someone booked a stripper to perform on the set. Irwin arrived late at the party and he walked in right during the middle of her act. He went ballistic. He screamed and he yelled that we were going to be busted and raided. He ordered the sound mixer to reconnect the studio's red light outside the stage. This meant for visitors to keep out, that the cameras were rolling. So, the light was activated, and stayed on until the party was over." [10]

This was Terry Becker's last second-season episode as Chief Sharkey. The actor left the show when Irwin Allen refused to increase his salary. Becker told writer William Anchors, Jr, "When I was hired by Irwin Allen, he said, 'You've got to work for minimum until you prove that you're worthwhile; that you're important to the show. You've got to prove that to me. You have to work your way in.' So, I said, 'Okay, sure. Why not?' And Sharkey and 'Dinosaur Island' started that relationship with Basehart which gave me the opportunity to work with him and for me to build the character out of those scenes – where I was, who I was, what I needed – and nobody explained anything about the role, especially Irwin, because I don't think Irwin knew. As a matter of fact, I'm going to tell you this: After the second season – my first season on the show… I went up and I spoke to Irwin and I said, 'You remember you said we'd renegotiate. I think I've proven that I'm worthwhile for the show.' And he said, 'Yeah, you are. So?' 'You said that we'd negotiate the contract.' He said, 'I never said that. I don't remember that.' And I said, 'I'm here to remind you.' Anyway, we went into a long kind of conversation, and I said, 'Well, I'm quitting the show,' and I started to walk out. And he called me back, [but] he wouldn't budge. He was going to give me a buck and a half. I mean, literally a dollar and a half for a raise, and I was getting [SAG] minimum. So, I said, 'I'm leaving.' So that last episode, I don't know if you remember it, I jump on the grenade and I save the ship. Well, that was supposed to be the death of Chief Sharkey." [11]

"The Sky's on Fire" was actually the twentieth of twenty-six episodes produced for the second season. Becker was getting paid better than scale … slightly. So far, he had only appeared in 18 episodes. Stock footage would be used to put Becker into a nineteenth second-season episode. What he could not know was the budget problems Allen was having, trying to make half a science-fiction movie each week on an approved budget of $140,500. Regardless, for Season Three, a deal was arranged to bring Becker back, with a raise in salary.

The final cost of "The Sky's on Fire," even with effects footage appropriated from the 1961 *Voyage* movie, was $187,530. [12]

Release / Reaction:
(ABC premiere airdate: 1/23/66; network repeat broadcast: 5/22/66)

The Ghost and Mr. Chicken, starring Don Knotts, and *Dr. Zhivago* were the top two films at the movie houses. *Up the Down Staircase*, by Bel Kaufman, *Hotel*, by Arthur Hailey, and *The Green Berets*, by Robin Moore, were on *The New York Times* Best Seller List. *Rubber Soul*, by the Beatles, was still selling more copies than any other record album in America. And the group's "We Can Work It Out" single was still tied with Simon & Garfunkel's "The Sounds of Silence" in getting the most radio play. David Janssen, star of *The Fugitive*, had the cover of *TV Guide*.

Irwin Allen's plan to lean *Voyage* away from espionage stories and push the science fiction was working. For the second week in a row, the series won its time slot for the entire hour.

A.C. Nielsen 30-city survey from January 23, 1966: [13]

(7 – 7:30 p.m.)	Rating:	Share:
ABC: *Voyage to the Bottom of the Sea*	**19.9**	**35.1%**
CBS: *Lassie*	18.3	32.3%
NBC: Actuality special	8.0	14.1%

(7:30 – 8 p.m.):		
ABC: *Voyage to the Bottom of the Sea*	**19.4**	**31.5%**
CBS: *My Favorite Martian*	14.8	24.1%
NBC: *Walt Disney's Wonderful World...*	17.5	28.5%

5.4

"Graveyard of Fear" (Episode 52)
(Prod. #8221; first aired Sunday, January 30, 1966)
Written by Robert Vincent Wright
Directed by Justus Addiss
Produced by Irwin Allen, Frank La Tourette, and William Welch
Story Editor: Sidney Marshall
Guest Star Robert Loggia

From the *Voyage* show files (Irwin Allen papers collection):

A Nobel scientist and his secretary are the sole survivors of an attack by a monstrous Portuguese man o' war on their research vessel. They persuade Nelson to return them in the Seaview to the sunken ship to retrieve their scientific discovery: a vita synthesis which restores youth. The sub is attacked by the monster and Crane decides to return home for repairs. In order to maintain the youth of his secretary, who has been the guinea pig in his experiments, the scientist first risks his own life, then traps Crane in the flying sub and threatens all the Seaview in his desperation to retrieve his discovery.[1]

Assessment:

A better title would have been "Graveyard of Sunken Ships" – more evocative, and descriptive of one of the plot devices seen in this episode. Regardless …

Mark Phillips said, "A perfect blend of *The Portrait of Dorian Gray* and giant jellyfish blues. Everything works here, including the jellyfish effects. The old-age makeup on Marian Moses is top-notch and Robert Loggia does well as the scientist driven by desperation. Exciting and dramatic, this is one of the all-time classic *Voyages*." [2]

"Yes, everything works," Mike Bailey agreed. "The story has power and a sense of desperation that lends the affair credibility once you get past the fountain-of-youth premise. The writing, although not brilliant, is certainly adequate. The acting is virtually flawless and the special effects are particularly good. The music cues, mostly taken from Jerry Goldsmith's soundtrack for 'Jonah and the Whale,' resonate perfectly. … I agree with Mark – this truly is a *Voyage* classic." [3]

We agree. There are multiple ticking clocks in this story – Karyl's accelerating aging pushes Dr. Ames to take greater risks with each passing minute; and he in turn pushes Nelson and Crane to risk their necks, and those of their crew, so that he can get retrieve the formula which will rejuvenate Karyl. The clock ticks equally loud for Crane, when trapped in the submerged Flying Sub, with a gas leak contaminating the air. All the while, the beast outside the ship is breathing down their necks. When Crane makes it back to the Seaview, the pressure is still on. "You have ten minutes," Ames tells him and Nelson, as the timer on the torpedo ticks away. You see, the rapidly aging Karyl will

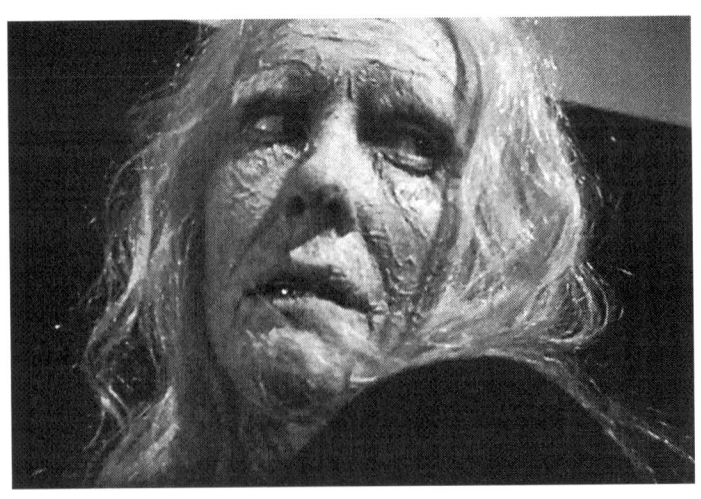

Marian Moses (as Karyl), well into the aging process … as the clock ticks.

be beyond the point of no return in that amount of time, and Ames is willing to kill everyone to stop this.

The characters are properly motivated, and the bad guy is not portrayed as merely one-dimensional – he is a man driven by love. We empathize with his plight, and the poignancy in his final statement at the end, and his reunion with Karyl. The moment is not overstated, as the episode fades to black. The point to the story is made in the final striking visual.

The effects in this episode cannot go without mention. *Voyage* had depicted a giant jellyfish before to great effect, in Season One's "Mutiny." We get a glimpse of that black-and-white footage here, tinted blue. But most of the footage is new, and quite spectacular, as we see the monster go after a diver, and the Flying Sub, and, last but not least, the Seaview.

Have no fear of "Graveyard of Fear." It is among the series' best.

Script:

Robert Vincent Wright's story treatment approved on November 4, 1965.
1st- and 2nd-draft teleplays approved on December 1.
Rev. Shooting Final teleplay (on blue paper): December 13.
Page revisions (purple paper inserts): December 17.
Page revisions (yellow paper inserts): December 20.
Page revisions (green paper inserts): December 27.

Robert Vincent Wright told interviewer Mark Phillips, "I got the idea from *The Picture of Dorian Gray*. I turned it into a woman's role and made up this chemical which would make her young again. I kicked that ending around with Sid [Marshall]. We discussed a happy ending, but it made for a much more dramatic conclusion. The makeup people did a beautiful job aging her."

Talking about *Voyage*'s Sid Marshall, Wright said, "[He] was the best story editor I've ever known. In story sessions, he was very business-like, asking, 'Is there entertainment value in the story? Is it something we've done before?' Or, if it was a good story, he might say, 'You're asking for a million dollars here!'"

Wright also got feedback from associate producer William Welch, when Welch wasn't busy writing his own scripts. Irwin Allen liked Welch's scripts and wanted more, and Welch didn't dare say "no." Wright said, "William Welch was a workaholic and he died of a heart attack that everybody felt was due to stress." [4]

Among the coverage notes received by ABC on December 9, Mary Garbutt wrote:

> Please modify Ames speech slightly so that he does not seem to imply that old people are useless people…. Caution on make-up in Karyl's aging process that it is not too unpleasant and grotesque. [5]

Irwin Allen didn't have anything to say about the aging process, or the character of Ames. From his notes, dated December 18, he said:

> Nelson's last speech: Since the monster has been changed from an electric eel to a type of gigantic jellyfish with electricity shooting from its tentacles, Nelson's opinion as to what it is must be more complete and sound as scientific as possible. His speech should read something like this: "An unknown species of the Physalia Coelenterate, more commonly known as the Portuguese Man-O-War, with the usual ability to produce electric shock waves." (And its unusual size should be remarked upon) …. In shot of monster, we should actually see electricity coming from its tentacles. [6]

Wright added, "The trick was to treat the absurd seriously and give it credibility. Irwin used to say, 'Look, let's not spend time explaining things we can't explain.'" [7]

Production:
(Filmed December 27, 1965 - January 5, 1966; 7 days spread over 8)

This was **Justus Addiss**'s first of 16 directing assignments on *Voyage*. He also directed two episodes of *Lost in Space*. Addiss was 49 and had worked as a dialogue coach on several movies in the 1950s before stepping up to directing for anthology series such as *Schlitz Playhouse*, *Studio 57*, and *Alfred Hitchcock Presents*. He worked frequently on Westerns, with multiple assignments on *The Restless Gun* and *Rawhide*, and he directed three episodes of *The Twilight Zone*.

Ray Didsbury said, "One of my favorite directors was Justus Addiss. He was always prepared, and wasn't afraid to ask for help if he needed it. He was a sweet and sensitive person." [8]

Robert Loggia was 35, and paid $2,500 for up to six days' work to play Dr. Crandall Ames. He had starred as *Elfego Baca*, "The man who couldn't be killed," in 10 episodes of *Walt Disney Presents* from 1958 through 1960. One year after appearing in *Voyage*, Loggia would have his own series, *T.H.E. Cat*, as a former acrobat and cat burglar who becomes a bodyguard.

Marian Moses (aka Marian McCargo) was 33. Irwin Allen had spotted her when she was a guest player on a circus series he loved to watch, *The Greatest Show on Earth*. She had also appeared on *The Man from U.N.C.L.E.*, *Perry Mason*, and *Dr. Kildare*. She appeared with John Wayne and Rock Hudson in 1969's *The Undefeated*. Her salary here: $600 for three days.

Marian Moses in 1970's *The Undefeated* (above) and already into the aging process (left) in *Voyage*.

Allen was very taken with Moses in "Graveyard." He paid for a full-page ad in the *Hollywood Reporter*, with a picture of Moses in her old-age make-up, calling the Television

Academy members' attention to her performance, suggesting she be given a nomination for an Emmy award. However, this didn't happen.

Production began on Monday, December 27, 1965 for the first of eight days on Stage 10, filming on the various Seaview sets, as well as the Flying Sub. On Day 6 (Monday), they spent half a day on Stage B filming "Nelson Institute Dock of Research Ship." The eighth and final day of production was only half a day, with the last shot taken at 1 p.m., making this a seven-and-a-half-day production.

The final cost was $190,778, which was a whopping $50,000 over what 20th Century-Fox wanted to spend for each episode. [9]

Release / Reaction:
(premiere ABC airdate: 1/30/66; network repeat broadcast: 9/11/66)

This was the week that the first operational weather satellite (ESSA-1) was launched by the U.S. Meanwhile, the Soviet Union was racing the U.S. to the moon, and accomplished a soft landing on the lunar surface with Luna 9. It seemed Mother Russia was everywhere, for *Doctor Zhivago* was tops in the movie houses. "My Love" by Petula Clark was the song getting the most airplay, nudging out the Beatles' "We Can Work It Out." The Fab Four still had the best-selling album in the land, with *Rubber Soul*.

Syndicated "TV Scout" said:

> *Voyage to the Bottom of the Sea* has another formula show. Outside the ship there is a huge monster menacing them (this time it's a gigantic Portuguese man-of-war with enough electrical power to prevent a New York blackout), while inside, they must deal with the fanatic scientist (Robert Loggia) who will sacrifice anyone, including David Hedison, to

recover his "Vita Synthesis" from a wrecked ship. Despite its familiarity, the story is fun to watch. [10]

"TV Key" said:

> The Seaview's crew tussles with a giant undersea monster in the deep, and deals with a maniacal scientist aboard, in a rousing hour of action and suspense geared to the youngsters at home. [11]

Those youngsters at home tuned in by the millions and, for the third week in a row, *Voyage* won its time period.

A.C. Nielsen 30-city survey from January 30, 1966:[12]

(7 – 7:30 p.m.)	Rating:	Share:
ABC: *Voyage to the Bottom of the Sea*	**25.4**	**38.0%**
CBS: *Lassie*	22.7	34.0%
NBC: *Bell Telephone Hour*	11.6	17.4%
7:30 – 8 p.m.		
ABC: *Voyage to the Bottom of the Sea*	**25.9**	**36.5%**
CBS: *My Favorite Martian*	19.4	27.4%
NBC: *Walt Disney's Wonderful World of Color*	19.0	26.8%

Frank La Tourette, who was a UCLA professor as well as a member of the *Voyage* staff, sent a memo to Irwin Allen shortly after "Graveyard of Fear" had hit a home run in the Nielsen ratings. He told his boss:

> There is little correlation between monster and non-monster shows….
>
> There is little correlation between well-written, well-directed, well-produced shows and high ratings. The single exception in two seasons seems to be "Sky Is Falling' [from Season One] which had a peak rating without any other discernible factors influencing it…. [13]

La Tourette was more a numbers man than a creative writer/producer. He missed the fact that "The Sky Is Falling" was both nicely written and directed, and dealt with the Seaview's first encounter with a flying saucer.

His report continued:

> A comparison of the first two seasons leads to one unmistakable conclusion: *Voyage* did exceptionally well the first season until [*Man from*] *Uncle* came on opposite it. *Uncle* was – until *Batman* – the best promoted show in television.
>
> In the second season, *Voyage* did badly until an elaborate promotion campaign was instituted. Within four weeks of that time, ratings soared and have continued to climb. The obvious conclusion is that extensive promotion is the single greatest factor in building and maintaining a rating.
>
> A point of illustration: "Graveyard of Fear" currently has the highest rating among the episodes. It is very possible that a large part of that rating is attributable to the fact that the previous week's trailer showed the 200-year-old woman and created great curiosity and anticipation among the audience. [14]

Irwin Allen begged to differ with La Tourette. He believed the increase of popularity in the Second Season was absolutely attributable to more monster shows. With the fright make-up used, one could argue that a 200-year-old woman was a type of monster.

In a syndicated newspaper article called "TV Group Rates Kiddie Programs," out this week in 1966, entertainment correspondent Jay Fredericks reported that the National Association for Better Radio and Television (NAFBRAT) had issues with *Voyage to the Bottom of the Sea*. NAFBRAT said, "This series, strategically placed in the early evening to attract children, is far too tense and horror ridden for such an audience. The stories and situations are too ridiculous for anyone more mature." [15]

According to A.C. Nielsen, *Voyage* ranked No. 32 this week out of 107 network series. Luckily for Allen and millions of American children, the networks had more faith in Nielsen than NAFBRAT. [16]

5.5

"The Shape of Doom" (Episode 53)
(Prod. #8222; first aired Sunday, February 6, 1966)
Written by William Welch
Directed by Nathan Juran
Produced by Irwin Allen, Frank La Tourette, and William Welch
Story Editor: Sidney Marshall
Co-Starring Kevin Hagen

From the *Voyage* show files (Irwin Allen papers collection):

A scientist, experimenting with whales and in pursuit of a giant killer whale, has his ship demolished in restricted waters. Rescued by the Seaview crew who are about to blast a canal with a nuclear device, he begs them to let him save the whale. Nelson refuses, but the whale returns and swallows the bomb, threatening not only Seaview, but also the President, whose ship has come into range of the possible holocaust.[1]

Assessment:

Some fans of the series dismiss this episode for its extensive use of things seen before. Mike Bailey said, "Not only was tons of stock footage used, but it was used in almost the same editing configuration as it appears in Season Two's nifty opener, 'Jonah and the Whale.' Not only that, but extensive blocks of dialogue are lifted directly out of 'Jonah.' Not only that, but the basics of the story are so similar to 'Jonah' that one wonders how William Welch had the *?*%$#s* to put his name in the credits as writer. ... I don't hate this episode, but it's hard to deal with the creative collapse rampant throughout, not on the part of the actors, but on the part of the story editor, writer, and the producer (Irwin Allen on a particularly bad day)." [2]

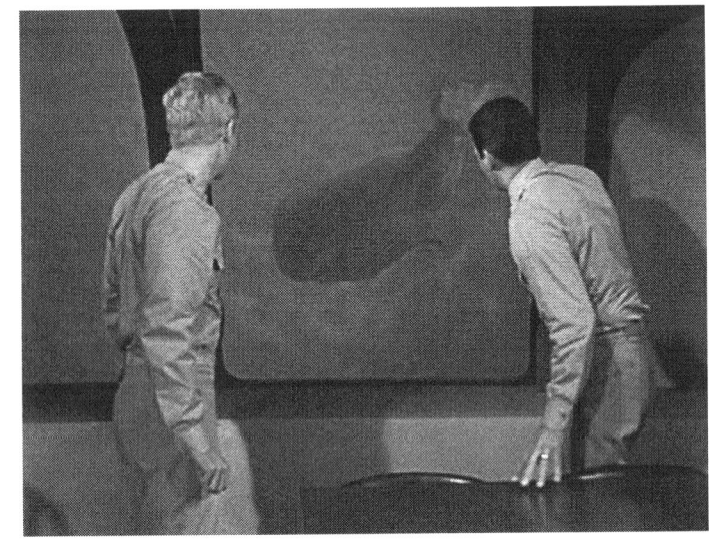

"Thar she blows!" Some fans felt they had seen it all before. But, for others, "The Shape of Doom" offered more than merely recycled footage.

Mark Phillips yawned, "Whenever the giant whale swims off screen, it turns into boresville. Lots of dialog and slowly-edited scenes that stretch this into a weary hour. The evil scientist is strictly one-note. This is a stock footage episode, with clips from previous whale shows, so it's astonishing that they actually took time to film an expensive new miniature, where the whale swallows a nuclear bomb." [3]

Well, we see it differently. The story, concerning a scientist injecting a whale with growth hormones, is an intriguing one. The mounting jeopardies include the whale swallowing a nuclear bomb, then swimming off in the direction of an aircraft carrier on which the President of the United States is a passenger. Tick, tick, tick ...

The scientist – named Holden – may refer to himself as a "mad scientist," but his agenda wasn't anything that real science hasn't experimented with – even in 1966. A little research will reveal that the FDA began allowing the meat industry to use steroids and other hormones since the 1950s. Holden is simply extending the idea. His problem is that his notes, samples, and equipment now languish in the belly of the giant beast he has been tampering with. Holder is willing to do nearly anything to get those crucial materials back, or, at the very least, new samples, before the whale gets away or perishes. He tells Nelson, "I have a time problem, too." Obsessed people are often so singularly focused that they can appear one-dimensional, as Holden does to some viewers. But it's a very dangerous dimension.

Captain Crane gives Holden a terrific set-up line when he tells Nelson, "Do you realize that whale's a swimming bomb?" A short time later, he tells the crew to brace for impact. Holden sardonically quips, "How do you brace for a nuclear bomb?"

Holden had warned Crane that the tranquilizer administered to the whale was too low a dose. He now calmly says, "I told you you'd just make him mad. My whale's a killer, gentlemen. And he's coming back."

Also at risk is the President of the United States on a nearby aircraft carrier. Holden says, "You see what a mad whale can do. I assure you a mad scientist can be far more destructive."

To this end, writer Welch and actor Kevin Hagen give Holden enough urgency, ego, and wit, to make his obsession very unsettling.

The stock footage – from "The Ghost of Moby Dick," from "Jonah and the Whale," from Jim Lamb's second-unit work off the Bahamas, from shots taken inside the Green Tank, and even from other episodes, such as "Submarine Sunk Here," is seamlessly tinted (or color corrected) to match and then cleverly woven together. Notice how, in new footage, one of the crewmen is dressed in a Season One uniform, in order to help usher in sequences from earlier episodes. And this uniform once and for all makes it clear that, on the Seaview at this time, the men in the lower decks, such as the engine room, wear the 1960s-era Naval attire.

It's a very impressive way to make an imitation-silk purse from leftovers. And, for anyone who hadn't seen the earlier episodes that selective shots were harvested from, it's one hell of a show. For some of us, it's one hell of a show anyway. But "The Shape of Doom" opened the door for more episodes of this type – a script designed to recycle. As a result, the future of *Voyage* would be taking a new course … downward.

Script:

William Welch's writers contract for "Denizen of Doom": December 21, 1965.
Welch's 2nd (and final) draft approved on December 24.
Rev. Shooting Final (still "Denizen of Doom," on yellow paper): December 31.

Page revisions (on blue paper inserts): January 4.
Page revisions (on green paper inserts): January 5.

The script was written in late December 1965, with the episode beginning production in the first week of the new year. At this time, it didn't look likely that *Voyage* would be picked up for a third season. The pressure was on Irwin Allen to find a way to improve the ratings *and* reduce spending. He was certain that monsters and spectacle were the answer to luring men and kids away from *Lassie*, *My Favorite Martian*, and Walt Disney. But monsters couldn't – or, at least, shouldn't – be featured every week, and spectacle doesn't come cheap ... unless the big-ticket items were available courtesy of stock footage.

The ever-reliable William Welch had his marching orders – fashion a story to string together footage from past episodes, and make it big; a whale of a tale.

By the time Irwin Allen read the script, called "Denizen of Doom" at this stage, he had already approved the story, so it's not surprising that he didn't comment on the similarities between this episode and "Jonah and the Whale" and "Ghost of Moby Dick." Instead, for his memo from January 4, he focused on:

> Pg. 9, Sc 30, Holden's last speech: Is this the proper place to try to establish Holden's intense interest in the whale. He sounds a little crazy asking if they have a harpoon. Why doesn't he ask how far they are from the nearest port? Crane and Morton both sound unduly rude in referring to Holden as "Him" and "He" right in front of him.
>
> Pg 9, Crane's 4th speech: Why doesn't he answer Holden's question about Nelson. Crane sounds snotty. He could just as easily say, "Yes," or "That's right," and then continue with his speech about answering questions.
>
> Pg 12, Sc. 31... Holden's last speech is very melodramatic. He makes the loss of his lab [sound] worse than the deaths of his crew.
>
> Pg 13, Sc 31... Holden's first speech means nothing – he should say something about how he would have thought Nelson, of all people, would have understood the importance of his experiments....

> Pg 17, Sc 37: Holden seems upset that they are thinking of killing his whale, but he himself shot a harpoon into it, which would most likely have killed it, and, later, on Pg 25, Holden again suggests putting a harpoon into it. [4]

ABC's biggest concern, according to a memo from the Department of Standards & Practices dated January 5, was:

> Pg 13, Sc 31: Please delete Nelson's business of making a circular motion at his temple to indicate that the man is considered to be mentally unbalanced. [5]

The network was always adamant that programming not demean what they believed to be a large segment of their audience.

Production:
(Filmed January 5 – 12, 1966; 6 days)

Nathan Juran, having made a favorable impression with his first *Voyage*, "The Machines Strike Back," returned as director.

Kevin Hagen was cast as Holden. He was 37 and had been gainfully employed in television since 1957, popping up more than once each on popular shows such as *The Rifleman*, *Thriller*, *The Untouchables*, *Wagon Train*, *Perry Mason*, and *The Man from U.N.C.L.E.* He was a regular on the 1958-59 western series *Yancy Derringer*. Irwin Allen took a liking to Hagen and brought him back for a *Lost in Space* ("His Majesty Smith"), then four episodes of *The Time Tunnel*. Hagen would appear in another *Voyage* ("Attack"), then was given a recurring role in nine episodes of *Land of the Giants*, as Inspector Dobbs Kobick. Hagen is best

Don Dubbins, Jeff Morrow, and Kevin Hagen, in 1960, as three astronauts who have landed in *The Twilight Zone*.

known for playing Dr. Hiram Baker in 113 episodes of *Little House on the Prairie*, plus three additional made-for-TV movies based on the series. His salary here: $1,269.

Production began Wednesday, January 5, 1966, at 2 p.m., for the first of six days on Stage 10. This episode only required Seaview sets, plus one – "Int. Whaler Wheelhouse," also built onto Stage 10 for the last day of filming.

Nathan Juran filmed this "bottle show" in five-and-a-half days. Wednesday the 12th was the final day of production, with Juran wrapping at 8:07 p.m. The studio approved budget: $140,491. The actual cost: $162,312.[6]

On the second-to-last day of production, word came down from ABC-TV that *Voyage* was on the first-draft network schedule for the Fall. No guarantees.

Release / Reaction:
(ABC premiere airdate: 2/6/66; network repeat broadcast: 7/17/66)

ABC's lack of concern over the use of previously-aired sequences in *Voyage* is demonstrated by the network's choice of one of those stock-footage scenes to promote the latest "new" episode.

The Rare Breed, a Western starring James Stewart, was out-grossing all other films playing in the movie houses. *Rubber Soul* was *still* the top-selling record album in America. And Petula Clark's "My Love" was getting more spins on the radio than any other 45. Barbara Eden and Larry Hagman, of *I Dream of Jeannie*, had the cover of *TV Guide*, America's top-selling magazine.

In a syndicated article out the week "The Shape of Doom" had its network premiere, Richard Basehart said, "We do tend to go heavy each week. But, again, it's the same old story. The script. For two years we've been pleading for a break from the mold. I personally would be delighted to play it light once in awhile."

There was precious little time to fight over the scripts, or find ways to make the ones coming down the chute better. Basehart said, "Understand, though, we're working against the clock and budget on each show…. [W]e'll have to do in six days what it should take a couple of months to do well to meet the air dates." [7]

"TV Scott" said of this week's offering:

> *Voyage to the Bottom of the Sea* proves it is possible to have a repeat without having a rerun. "The Shape of Doom" is merely an imitation of a show done earlier this year in which a whale swallowed a diving bell containing Richard Basehart. This time a whale swallows a nuclear device imperiling the President of the U.S. [8]

The ratings continued to impress. Nielsen's 30-city survey, February 6, 1966:[9]

(7 – 7:30 p.m.)	Rating:	Share:
ABC: *Voyage to the Bottom of the Sea*	**20.8**	**35.5%**
CBS: *Lassie*	18.4	31.4%
NBC: Actuality special	11.2	19.1%

(7:30 – 8 p.m.)		
ABC: *Voyage to the Bottom of the Sea*	**21.7**	**34.7%**
CBS: *My Favorite Martian*	13.8	22.0%
NBC: Danny Thomas special	20.7	33.1%

5.6

"Dead Men's Doubloons" (Episode 54)

(Prod. #8223; first aired Sunday, February 13, 1966)
Written by Sidney Marshall
Directed by Sutton Roley
Produced by Irwin Allen, Frank La Tourette, and William Welch
Story Editor: Sidney Marshall
Guest Star Albert Salmi

From the *Voyage* show files (Irwin Allen papers collection):

> Four hundred years after a sea pirate placed a curse on his sunken treasure ship, a multiple defense weapon unexpectedly explodes immediately after the discovery of a treasure coin near its site. An Allied Command observer aboard the Seaview, a dead ringer for the ancient pirate, has warned of such a curse. When he disappears aboard the mini-sub, the flying sub, sent to search for him, is almost destroyed by what appears to be an ancient pirate ship. Crane is captured by the same observer, now dressed as a pirate, who claims to be a reincarnation of his forebear.[1]

Assessment:

Irwin Allen and company splurged on this one – the most expensive episode of *Voyage*'s second season. So, was all the expense worth it?

Mark Phillips said, "Wonderful stock footage of pirates fighting, and a great fade-out on Albert Salmi for the teaser, promise some thrills, but the episode is neither supernatural nor a straight-forward tale of modern-day pirates (which could have made for a good dramatic story). Instead, it's over-the-top antics by Salmi and his crew, which compromises any danger." [2]

Arrr! The first half of the episode seems to work. Salmi is even low-key during this portion of the story; underplaying his role for once. But, as Mr. Phillips warned, things go south following the halfway mark. You'll be scratching your head – at least, we were. Was the 16th-century pirate ship, "La Reina Isabella," which fired on the Flying Sub, for real, or some form of facade? We never see Brent or modern-day crew (in yesteryear attire) on the ship; only on the island, in the cave, and in their underwater facility. And why exactly did Brent need to plant gold doubloons and do all this monkey business? He was a Naval officer, and on board the Seaview anyway. If his game was really about the inter-continental ballistic missiles, why all the pirate mumbo-jumbo? How did that get him closer to his goal of, dare we say, taking over the world? Very confusing nonsense.

Script:

Rev. Shooting Final teleplay (blue paper): January 7, 1966.
Page revisions (pink paper inserts): January 10.
Page revisions (green paper inserts): January 11.
Page revisions (yellow paper inserts): January 21.

This was **Sidney Marshall**'s second teleplay for *Voyage*, following his rewrite of "The Silent Saboteurs" earlier in the season. Of course, he had been rewriting many other *Voyage* scripts, as the series' story editor. "Dead Man's Doubloons," however, was his first original story.

This section will be short. We're not holding out on you; we could not locate any notes regarding the script, either from Allen, his staff, or the network. Maybe the episode *is* cursed. We wouldn't be surprised.

Production:

(Filmed January 13 – 21, 1966; 7 days)

This was **Sutton Roley**'s second of three *Voyage* directing assignments.
Albert Salmi, as Brent, was paid $2,500 for up to six days before the camera. He was 37 and had just played a space pirate for Irwin Allen in *Lost in Space*. With close to 200 film and TV roles in a career that spanned the 1950s,

'60s, '70s, and '80s, usually cast as outdoorsmen, thugs and bandits, Salmi received recognition in 1958 with a National Board of Review award as Best Supporting Actor for his work in two films, *The Bravados* and *The Brothers Karamazov*. The latter also featured Richard Basehart. Salmi stepped into *The Twilight Zone* three times. He had just finished a year of being a regular on *Daniel Boone* (as Yadkin).

Production began Thursday, January 13 on Stage 10 with the sequence needed from Admiral Howard's office (to be used as a "burn-in" on a TV screen), then the Control Room and Observation Nose, utilizing the "bubble tank." Director of Photography Winton Hoch was out sick, so he called a friend to stand in for him – cinematographer Paul Vogel, who took over the camera crew on this day and the next. Like Hoch, Vogel was an Oscar winner. He received his

At the same time as playing a pirate on *Voyage to the Bottom of the Sea*, Albert Salmi was doing likewise on Irwin Allen's *Lost in Space*.

for 1949's *Battleground*. He was nominated for a second Oscar for 1962's *The Wonderful World of the Brothers Grimm*.

On Friday, they filmed at the Moat on the backlot, for "Ext. Beach & Rocks" and "Ext. & Int. Cave."

On Monday, for the third day of filming, Sam Leavitt stepped in for Vogel, who had stepped in for Hoch, to lead the camera crew as cinematographer. He would remain for the rest of the production. He was also an Oscar-winning cinematographer, for 1958's *The Defiant Ones*. Leavitt was nominated the following year for *Anatomy of a Murder*, and again, in 1961, for *Exodus*. Irwin Allen was making sure *Voyage* had the best support possible, if not on the written page, at least with camera and lighting.

The company continued filming at the Moat location on this day, with the beach and rocks, and the cave, but also "Ext. Sea." In the mid-afternoon, they returned to Stage 10 for additional filming in the Control Room.

On Tuesday and Wednesday (Days 4 & 5), work continued on Stage 10 for additional Seaview sets, plus "Int. Brent's Cabin" and the Flying Sub.

Day 6: The company was on Stage B on Thursday, filming "Ext. Deck of Pirate Ship." Sutton Roley failed to finish on schedule, needing a seventh day of production, on Friday, January 21. Stage B provided for "Int. Brent's Complex," then a move back to Stage 10 allowed for filming in the Missile Room. Roley didn't complete his final shot until 8:07 p.m.

Roley, quoted in the book *Science Fiction Television Series*, said, "Richard Basehart was a consummate actor, and he just stuck his tongue in his cheek and played the thing. I'd catch him on occasion and say, 'Richard, you're doing a little number there.' He'd smile and say, 'Ah, you caught me again.'" [3]

Final cost was $209,286, a staggering $69,000 over budget, making this one of the series' most expensive episodes. [4]

Release / Reaction:

(ABC premiere airdate: 2/13/66; network repeat broadcast: 5/14/66)

Dr. Zhivago was back on top in the movie houses. The song getting the most radio play was "Lightnin' Strikes," by Lou Christie. The top-selling album in America was *Whipped Cream & Other Delights*, by Herb Alpert and the Tijuana Brass. And Ryan O'Neal and Barbara Parkins, of *Peyton Place*, had the cover of *TV Guide*.

Steven H. Scheuer of syndicated "TV Key" said:

> The children will eat this one up, what with underwater action sequences and a plot gimmick about pirates and buried treasure. Albert Salmi guest-stars as Capt. Brent, a sinister man who unfolds a wild plot that leaves Adm. Nelson and his crew baffled up until the exciting finale. [5]

Some of us remain baffled to this day!

Pirates seemed as appealing as monsters to those who were following the series in 1966. According to A.C. Nielsen, *Voyage* ranked at No. 40 this week out of 107 network series. And it won its time slot.

A.C. Nielsen 30-city survey from February 13, 1966: [6]

(7 – 7:30 p.m.)	Rating:	Share:
ABC: *Voyage to the Bottom of the Sea*	**20.6**	**33.7%**
CBS: *Lassie*	20.2	33.0%
NBC: *Bell Telephone Hour*	12.4	20.3%
7:30 – 8 p.m.		
ABC: *Voyage to the Bottom of the Sea*	**21.4**	**34.5%**
CBS: *My Favorite Martian*	15.7	25.3%
NBC: *Walt Disney's Wonderful World…*	18.3	29.5%

5.7

"The Monster's Web" (Episode 55)
(Prod. #8224; first aired Sunday, February 27, 1966)
Teleplay by Al Gail and Peter Packer; Story by Peter Packer
Directed by Justus Addiss
Produced by Irwin Allen, Frank La Tourette, and William Welch
Story Editor: Sidney Marshall
Guest Star: Mark Richmond

From the *Voyage* show files (Irwin Allen papers collection):

A Naval test submarine, skippered by a fanatical commander who has invented a super-fuel, is destroyed by a giant underwater web. The Commander is accused of reckless action, despite his defense that an underwater monster exists. When the Seaview goes to the scene in order to retrieve some of the potentially dangerous fuel cylinders, both the flying sub and the Seaview are attacked by a spider-like creature and in peril of destruction by the monster. [1]

Assessment:

There was a louder ticking clock behind the scenes than on camera with "The Monster's Web." Richard Basehart fell ill after the first day of filming, which was only one of two planned for the Flying Sub set. No one knew if he would be out for a day, or two, or for weeks. The production soldiered on, with the script rewritten daily to make excuses for the absence of the show's co-lead. Basehart's lighting double was photographed from the back, or in sickbay with a bandaged head and face, with the star's voice later looped in to give a semblance of life to the near-immobile character. The fact that they got it made, and on the air, with only days to spare, is miracle enough.

Mark Phillips said, "A grade-B adventure with a giant spider that struggles to look real (and occasionally succeeds – its attack on Seaview is eye-catching, thanks to brilliant lighting). Not a bad episode." [2]

"Okay, here's where I lose all credibility," Mike Bailey said. "I pretty much like this episode. If it's a monster outing, give me a struggling miniature over a man in a suit any day – no matter how stiff. As Mark admits, the spider effects are occasionally very effective, although on the other hand, sometimes NOT. … This episode is no work of art, but you gotta give the effects boys and the actors credit for trying – and it's loaded with action." [3]

One problem that cannot be excused by Basehart's absence is the blaring illogic of some key story points. It is never made clear what happened to the rest of the crew of the test sub. We are told that the crash resulted in deaths. How many? Clearly not all, because we later discover the executive officer, barely alive, on the sub. If the two top-ranking officers lived, and if Captain Gantt made it out of the ocean without a scratch or limp to show for his close call, then other men must have too. What *is* verbalized is that no one believes Gantt's story about the giant spider. This strains logic. If he saw it, didn't any other survivors see it?

While we're at it, *how* did Gantt escape? Did he quickly suit up in diving gear and swim to the surface, to be plucked from the sea by rescuers? If so, and if, by some incredible leap in logic, he did so alone, why didn't anyone investigate the downed sub and look for additional survivors? If they had, they certainly would have found some, for, as we see when Gantt and Riley board the ship, areas of the inside of the sub are still dry as a bone and have a breathable atmosphere.

The scene in which Gantt blows the hatch in order to get to Lt. Balter is also absurd. In a sunken sub, with a compromised hull, this nutjob is going to use his super-duper fuel to create an explosion?! And he does this before getting the four tanks of unstable fuel off the craft – the very reason they are risking their necks in the first place, to save "millions" of people from perishing from the gas the fuel can create?

And why does Gantt have Riley clumsily juggle all four fuel tanks in his arms after telling him that the slightest sudden move can set the fuel off? Shouldn't Riley have made several trips? He was just taking them around the corner. Well, we asked Allan Hunt about this. He said, "That kind of stuff happens very quickly. You realize on the spot that they need to either kill time or condense some movements to save time. And there's often a bit of improvisation that goes with that. We were looking for quick solutions to keep the urgency of what was going on, as Barry Coe (exec officer Balter) comes through that door, and he's close to passing out. That's the purpose of the scene and any logic concerning the other business sometimes gets sacrificed." [4]

As for that that giant spider, it was a shared prop, also used at this time for the *Lost in Space* episode "The Keeper, Part 2." This typical example of Allenesque scavenging is made more glaring by the consideration that these two episodes aired on competing networks only five weeks apart!

As you see, the problems with "Monster's Web" began before Richard Basehart dropped out.

Script:

Peter Packer's writers contract (for "Web of Destruction"): November 17, 1965.
Packer's story and 1st-draft teleplay approved on December 8.
Packer's 2nd (final) draft teleplay approved on January 7, 1967.
Al Gail's rewrite (4th-draft teleplay) turned in by January 16.
Al Gail's polish, Shooting Final teleplay: January 21.
3rd Rev. shooting Final (green paper): January 31.

Writer **Peter Packer** was 59. Despite being born in London, England, he loved Westerns and mostly wrote for that genre in a television career that began in 1955. Prior to that, he wrote novels, such as *White Crocus* and *Love Thieves*. Later, he wrote the screenplay to the 1956 Western *7th Calvary*. On TV, Packer had multiple script assignments for *Bonanza* and *The Big Valley*. He created *Man Without a Gun*, a half-hour Western series in the late 1950s. He produced *Law of the Plainsman*, another Western series (1959-60). In addition, Packer served as a producer on two other TV series: *My Friend Flicka* and *The 20th Century-Fox Hour*. Irwin Allen put Packer to work on *Lost in Space*, writing 25 scripts – more than anyone else. However, this was his only script for *Voyage*. And what a doozy it is.

Al Gail took over for Packer, with the third draft script and what followed.

They were filming a few weeks ahead of their air dates, so the upturn in the ratings was just becoming evident. Irwin Allen was certain that a giant spider (and its web) threatening the Seaview and the Flying Sub would get the kids to tune it, and bring many of their parents along for the ride. And he needed those audience numbers to stay high in hope for a third-season renewal. But Allen still wanted the story to make sense … somewhat. After reading the Fourth Draft script, he wrote to his associate producers and story editor:

> Pg. 4: There should be a scene showing the Giant Spider Web directly in the path of the approaching Sub right after Scene 10.
>
> Pg. 5: There should also be an exterior scene showing the Sub smashing into the Web. This should be inserted right after Gantt says, "We'll make it – We'll make it!" …
>
> Pg. 27-32: Spider seen in Scene 65 and not again until Sc. 76. This is too long a time. We should see him continuing to build his web.
>
> Pg. 33, Sc. 80: Change Riley hep talk to normal dialogue in this scene. Or add proper manner of address by Riley to Admiral.

Pg. 39, Sc. 109: Gantt 2nd speech should be, "You're the one who's cracking up!"

ACT III, Pg. 41, Sc. 112: ... When last seen the Seaview was at dead stop hovering in the water. Now it is coming the last 2 thousand yards at flank speed. We should have heard Crane give this order in Sc. 96, Pg. 37, and flank speed would be an unsafe speed. It should be coming dead slow.

Why aren't Crane and Morton still watching the FS-1 on the T.V. monitor? If they were, they would have seen the attempt to break loose of the web? ... [5]

What is remarkable, when considering these notes, is how no mention was made concerning the holes in the plot that you could sail a submarine through. Allen seemed to be overlooking various plot-holes and characterization oddities.

Production:
(Filmed January 24 through February 3, 1966;
7 days with Main Unit, 2 with 2nd Unit)

Justus Addiss was back in the director's chair.
In an undated memo, Frank La Tourette wrote to Irwin Allen:

Herewith for your approval, a tentative cast budget for "Web of Destruction." We could get by with a less expensive actor for Gantt, but I believe this script can use all the help it can get. For that reason, I suggest you allow us to go for a good actor. [6]

Everyone agreed the script could use help, so they went for a good actor.
Mark Richmond (pictured at the top of the chapter) played Gantt, and was paid $2,500, top guest-star dollar in 1966. Richmond was 38 and had starred in his own series, *Cain's Hundred* (1961-62). He had the lead in an episode of *The Twilight Zone*, in "The Fear," as a State Trooper who encounters a UFO. He also starred in two episodes of *The Outer Limits* ("The Borderland" and "The Probe"). Richmond would return to take another *Voyage* ("Secret of the Deep"). Irwin Allen would also bring him back to do a *Land of the Giants*.
Barry Coe played Balter. He was 22, and had won a Golden Globe Award in 1960 as "Most Promising Newcomer – Male" for his role in 1959's *A Private*

Affair. Coe was under contract with 20th Century-Fox and had costarred in the 1961-62 Fox series, *Follow the Sun*, with Gary Lockwood.

Production began on Monday, January 24, 1966 on Stage 10. Winton Hoch was still out sick, so Sam Leavitt filled in as Director of Photography. The company began with what was supposed to be two days of filming in the Flying Sub. Richard Basehart was present on this day, but no other.

Interviewed a short time later, Basehart said, "I was carried off the set to the hospital suffering with influenza. We've had an epidemic out here and I fell victim while working on that show. The bug kept me out of the next two shows also. My double was used as best as could be and I tape recorded my lines from my hospital bed. There was no way to explain my absence, so we worked around it." [7]

Barry Coe with Jayne Mansfield in 1962.

Day 2: Tuesday, January 25. With Basehart out, they changed the schedule and filmed on the "Int. Nuclear Sub" set.

Day 3: On Wednesday, work with the Main Unit was cancelled due to Basehart's illness, and the second unit filmed in the Green Tank, with Paul Stader directing. Stader also played one of the divers, along with Dick Dixon, Frank Grohan, and Peter Peterson. This footage would be combined with wider shots taken off the Bahamas by John Lamb.

Come Thursday, Basehart was still out, so the Main Unit stood down and the second unit did additional filming in the Green Tank.

By Friday, knowing Basehart would not be able to return, the Main Unit went back to work on Stage 10 with a revised script, eliminating Admiral Nelson from the scenes filming that day. They shot in the Control Room, Nelson's Lab (without Nelson!) and the Missile Room.

Allan Hunt said, "That was done late in the second year, and Richard got very sick during filming. He had been ill a couple of times before, but this really hit him hard, and it was difficult for him to recover. So, they moved up my part and had me doing all the things that Richard would have done. It was probably my biggest part on *Voyage*, but it was only because of Richard's illness." [8]

Actor Sean Morgan said, "When the giant spider grabs the sub, the control panels blew up. Some sparks landed on my ankle and burned a hole through my socks. I said, 'Geez, I'm glad I'm not doing this show every week.'" [9]

On Monday, January 31, more new pages of the script arrived, omitting Admiral Nelson from further sections of the story. The company proceeded with filming on Stage 10 in the Missile Room, as well as the ship's corridor. Pickup shots from a previous episode were also taken in the Observation Nose. Director Justus Addiss completed his last shot at 8:28 p.m.

On Tuesday and Wednesday, work again continued without Basehart, with the company now working on the Sick Bay set, as well as in the Observation Nose and Control Room, and then onto the Flying Sub. For the latter, they shot freshly revised script pages depicting Nelson (played by Basehart's lighting double) getting knocked out and tucked into a sleeping compartment, thereby allowing the rest of the action on this set to be filmed without the participation of Admiral Nelson.

Day 7: Thursday, February 3, was the final day of production, all spent on the Flying Sub set, finishing the scenes written for that set, now omitting Nelson.

Final cost was $158,594. This was $18,000 over budget, mostly attributable to difficulties caused by Basehart's sick spell. [10]

Release / Reaction:
(Only ABC-TV network broadcast: 2/27/66)

The week that "The Monster's Web" first aired (its one and only time on ABC), it was announced that American soldiers deployed in Vietnam had risen to 215,000. It was also reported that John Lennon had told a reporter that the Beatles were now bigger than Jesus Christ. Meanwhile, current album sales figures seemed to suggest that, for the time being, Herb Alpert and the Tijuana Brass were bigger than the Beatles! The group's *Going Places* was the top-selling album in America. Their *Whipped Cream & Other Delights* was in second place. The Beatles' *Rubber Soul* was No. 3. "These Boots Are Made for Walking" was the song getting the most action on the radio. *Harper*, a detective film starring Paul Newman, was No. 1 in the movie houses. Charles Briles, Linda Evans and Barbara Stanwyck, of *The Big Valley*, shared the cover of *TV Guide*.

"TV Scout" said:

> *Voyage to the Bottom of the Sea* has what is becoming its alternate week show: the-monster-of-the-deep-and-the-fanatic-scientist-plot. In "Web of Destruction," the monster is a gigantic spider which imprisons the flying sub in its web, and may be about to do the same to the Seaview. The scientist is Mark Richman, a man who can't believe he can ever make a mistake. He very nearly is right. [11]

Voyage continued to be a juggernaut in the ratings race, trampling the competition which had once threatened its cancellation.

A.C. Nielsen 30-city survey from February 27, 1966: [12]

(7 – 7:30 p.m.)	Rating:	Share:
ABC: *Voyage to the Bottom of the Sea*	**22.5**	**40.3%**
CBS: *Lassie*	16.6	29.7%
NBC: *Bell Telephone Hour*	8.7	15.6%

(7:30 – 8 p.m.):		
ABC: *Voyage to the Bottom of the Sea*	**23.7**	**37.9%**
CBS: *My Favorite Martian*	18.2	29.1%
NBC: *Walt Disney's Wonderful World...*	12.9	20.6%

According to Nielsen, *Voyage* ranked No. 33 this week out of 107 network series. Even though the quality of the series was dropping with episodes such as this, the ratings were better than ever. The parade of monsters – even cheesy ones – had returned *Voyage* to hit-show status.

Because Richard Basehart did not appear in this episode, it was not given a repeat broadcast on ABC.

5.8

"The Menfish" (Episode 56)

(Prod. #8225; first aired Sunday, March 6, 1966)
Written by William Read Woodfield and Allan Balter
Directed by Tom Gries
Produced by Irwin Allen, Frank La Tourette, and William Welch
Story Editor: Sidney Marshall
Guest Star Gary Merrill
Special Guest Star John Dehner; Co-Starring Victor Lundin

From the *Voyage* show files (Irwin Allen papers collection):

A scientist, working on transplantation of human genes on small fish, comes aboard the Seaview. A Naval Admiral, who had once jailed him for illegal experimentation on humans, is in charge in Nelson's absence and now under orders to assist the scientist. When the Admiral discovers that once again the experiments imperil human life, the scientist seizes him, makes him subservient to his will, and, although in conflict with Crane, who is increasingly suspicious of the whole experiment, proceeds with his plan. Utilizing a member of the

Seaview crew, the scientist creates a man-fish which, over-radiated, grows to immense proportions. [1]

Assessment:

A guilty pleasure, provided you have acquired a taste for the absurd. Not all fans have:

"The script reads like a bad comic book," Mike Bailey complained. "Actor John Dehner took this tripe and ran with it for the nearest goalpost, flattening everyone and everything who/that got in his way. It is painful to hear him ranting about 'my menfish' and how he will create a new super-race. Not that there isn't budget-o-plenty on screen – there is, and that's part of what hurts, that decent money was spent to create this silliness, which would have been more at home in *Voyage*'s third season." [2]

Mark Phillips concurred: "Any realism is quickly destroyed by John Dehner's campy mad scientist routine, which is better suited for the 1930s horror films. It's also unfortunate that such a good actor as Gary Merrill gets turned into an emotionally-flat slave so quickly. This episode is pretty standard and almost cartoonish, but the last 15 minutes showcases *Voyage*'s best monster vs. Seaview struggle. The giant monster scenes are absolutely spectacular and this thrilling payoff is worth waiting for." [3]

"Thrilling pay-off or not," Mike Bailey countered, "here's an episode that really deserves the deep-six." [4]

We now appoint ourselves counsel for the accused. As an actor, John Dehner is almost always worth watching. While this is not his best performance, Dehner nonetheless injects playful nuances into his acting that keeps him someone to watch. Besides the intelligence Dehner always conveys, there is a slyness to the near schizophrenic Borgman. One moment he is a calm, calculating, sociopath, nonchalantly lacking in any human decency or empathy to balance against his blind ambition; the next he is excited into a near-homicidal rage.

The relationship between Borgman and his slave, Hansjurg, is also curious. As written, and played by Victor Lundin, the submissive, mostly silent assistant slowly reveals himself as hating his master. We don't understand the control Borgman has over Hansjurg until after it is revealed just how the mad scientist also controls Admiral Parks. Neither are zombies; they understand everything that is happening and are aware of all they are made to do, but the pain Parks is subjected to, and the obvious pain Hansjurg suffered in the past, have conditioned both to do as told … or else. We think it's a more interesting approach than simply hypnotized henchmen.

Further, if you watch closely enough, you may see that Gary Merrill's take on Admiral Parks is not as emotionless and flat as has been suggested. The key is to watch his eyes, and, at one point, a wink of an eye. This is no flat-liner. And Parks certainly comes to the rescue in the end. You could expect nothing less of the Academy Award-winning actor.

The plot, highlighted by the dual battles in the climactic reel – Man-Against-Man *and* Man-Against-Nature – is invigorating. You want to wring Dr. Borgman's neck – and so does Hansjurg. The good news is that audience and Hansjurg alike are treated to just that in the first of two climaxes. The other finale, with the supersized Manfish wrestling the Seaview, is, as Mark Phillips noted, simply spectacular.

The Manfish itself is a delightful monster, in all its green-gilled glory, with a face only a mother could love. The scene in which it bursts through the hull to attack Captain Crane is worth the price of admission alone, but we also get an underwater brawl with three divers, and its to-the-death bout with Roy Jensen aboard ship, before the main event – the epic fight with the Seaview.

Yes, the standard "roar" of underwater creatures has gotten old by this point on *Voyage*, and one must wonder if this gilled creature is holding its breath during all the time it lies on a wet mattress aboard the Seaview. But, things like this aside, "The Menfish" is a hoot.

Script:
William Read Woodfield's and Allan Balter's writers contract: December 27, 1965.
Rev. Shooting Final teleplay (blue paper): February 1, 1966.
Page revisions (pink paper inserts): February 7.

William Read Woodfield told interviewer Mark Phillips, "Irwin came into our office holding a coat hanger with a monster suit on it. 'Can you guys write a story around this?' he asked. **Allan Balter** and I started laughing. 'How many suits have you got, Irwin?' we asked. 'Just this one.' 'Sure, we can write a show.' 'What's the title?' Irwin asked. 'The Menfish.' 'No, no. I've only got the one suit!' I said, 'Write down Menfish, Irwin.' So, he left the suit with us and we wrote a show. We got around the one suit by never having more than one Manfish in any given scene. We had some that grew into giants and some that remained little menfish in tanks. That was Frankenstein." [5]

Within weeks, the same monster suit, minus the gills, was featured in an episode of *Lost in Space* ("A Change of Space").

Allan Hunt said of Irwin Allen, "He was, shall we say, notoriously frugal. Next door to us was *Lost in Space* and later *The Time Tunnel*, and for a while he really was king of the airwaves. Well, we began to notice that our monster would end up on *Lost in Space* the following week. It might be disguised with a little more hair or have an added row of teeth, but it was the *same* monster." [6]

As for the decision to have one of the menfish turn into a giant, Woodfield explained, "They [monster-of-the-week shows] were easier to write and, judging from the ratings, the people seemed to like them. Irwin Allen was the self-proclaimed king of special FX. He wasn't going to do *Tea and Sympathy*. I mean, when a guy brings a monster suit and says, 'Write a show about it,' you're going to end up with some kind of a monster show." [7]

Allen didn't like the name "Menfish" and, for his notes, suggested another title – "Sea Demons." But "Menfish" stuck.

After reading the second-draft teleplay, Allen wrote to his staff:

> P. 16, Sc. 27: Nelson should bring out the fact that the scientific report, or the Navy Dept. report, made no mention of the need for humans in Borgman's experiments or he should ask how Borgman was able to get a clearance from the scientific committee for his project and just where does he intend to get his volunteers from? When Borgman answers these last two questions, then Nelson has a chance to say he's ordering the Seaview back to port. This would help build the reason for Borgman to pull the gun on him. As it is done now, it lacks impact and dissension...
>
> P. 39, Sc. 55: Nelson, 3rd speech: Nelson states that Borgman's ability to keep humans alive and well is pure theory and Borgman agrees with him. This was discussed earlier on P. 16 at which time Borgman said he had completed the cycle once, with Hansjurg as living proof. But what about the man they froze in the teaser? Did he die? Did he recover completely or in the same manner as Hansjurg?

P. 24, Sc. 124: What does Hansjurg mean, "The freezing hadn't affected the crew men yet?" They were supposed to remain frozen for 24 hours in order to give the pineal gland time to regenerate itself. (This, of course, is impossible). Did Hansjurg discover that it was the freezing which killed the others? [8]

Frank La Tourette wrote to Allen:

> I think this can make a good show. With that in mind, may I offer the following thoughts:
> 1. I find the pineal transplant gimmick distasteful and unnecessary. Would it not be possible for Borgman to have discovered a secret process by which a human being is first transformed into a small fish and then is irradiated into a big manfish. This, in my opinion, would be more effective from a dramatic standpoint and have more shock value.
> 2. If kept as it is at present, the teaser should indicate that the small fish in the tank can be irradiated into giant manfish. Otherwise, all the talk about the threat from this monster has no value from an audience standpoint. It is difficult to pose any jeopardy from a fish the size of a goldfish swimming around in a small tank.
> 3. I agree one hundred percent with Bill Welch that Borgman cannot have been guilty of murder, or at least found to be so by the commission headed by Nelson. Otherwise, it is unbelievable that he is still allowed to run around conducting the same experiment. In addition, it certainly makes Nelson look awfully stupid in allowing Borgman the use of the Seaview to conduct the same experiment.
> 4. I find also distasteful the manner in which Nelson is operated upon and made subject to the will of Borgman. If it is absolutely necessary that Nelson must lose control of his will, it should be done in a more clever way. But, again, is it absolutely necessary that Nelson lose control of his will?
> 5. The whole sequence in which Crane gets rid of the two new potential menfish might read good on paper but

visually and dramatically I think it will prove to be dreadfully dull.
6. As a whole, the show really doesn't build to a crashing climax, but it sort of dribbles to an end in bits and pieces. Borgman dies, Nelson (without explanation) somehow gets out from under control of Borgman, the manfish attacks the Seaview, is beaten off, and Hyransburg (or whatever the hell his name is) turns and becomes a good guy. It would be nice if all these elements could coalesce in some way into a crashing climax.
7. I think our esteemed writers have tried to be too logical in the development of this show. They also have packed too much into it. The manfish is a good gimmick, and I think more emphasis should be put on it – its discovery, its development, and the horror and danger that results.
9

ABC had a few thoughts, too, and shared them in a January 28, 1966 memo:

Pg 1, Sc 1: Your usual care in seeing that the "menfish" are not too unpleasant or horrifying for family viewing.

Pg 1, Sc 1: Please be sure that the man's face is in repose and not shocking in effect.

Page 1, Sc 2: Caution that there is no CUing [Close Ups] on back of skull as Borgman works or when the coring device is removed [in] Scs 1 & 2. Caution on man frozen in cylinder.

Pg 12: Again, no CUing of wires and electrodes being removed.

Pg 17: Of course, the hypo injection must be off camera or completely covered [with wider angles].

Pgs 17 & 23: Please substitute for "I can turn you into a hapless vegetable" and "He'll be a vegetable".

Pgs 29-32 & Pgs 53-54: Telescope [wide angle] these "throttling" scenes as much as possible and please no CUing of hands or victim's face. Caution on "cries".

> Pg 32, Sc 52: The idea that the electrical control unit inflicts excruciating pain is too much – Delete "pain cry". Note that when the device is used on Nelson no cry is indicated – Please do not add any. [10]

This was William Read Woodfield's and Allan Balter's last script for the series. Of his swan song for *Voyage*, Woodfield said, "*Voyage* was a special experience in that I learned something about my craft, no doubt about it. I also met my wife Lili there. She worked on the show, spotting the stock footage and changing the episode titles to monster shows…. Generally speaking, *Voyage* was not a very good show. Balter and I wrote some interesting shows, but when Al Gail was going to write a show, or Bill Welch, or Arthur Weiss, give me a break! Welch once said to me, 'I've finally written a *Voyage* that has absolutely no content whatsoever. It's about *nothing*.' And he was very proud of that. The most prestigious writer on *Voyage* was Charles Bennett. He's a nice man, but I don't think he wrote very interesting *Voyage*s. His stories were kind of literary. It wasn't his kind of show." [11]

David Hedison told interviewer William Anchors, Jr., "We had two really good writers the first season – Allan Balter and William Read Woodfield. We lost them to *Mission: Impossible* in 1966. I would have liked to have seen them write those tense thriller scripts for our show." [12]

Woodfield and Balter were expecting to move over to *Star Trek*, where they had pitched a story idea. Woodfield said, "We screened the pilot film and we thought it was pretty good. Then, we went upstairs [from the *Star Trek* office at Desilu, later Paramount] to see Joe Gantman, who was *Voyage*'s associate producer during the first year, and he needed writers for a new show called *Mission: Impossible*. We watched that and I said, 'I don't want to write for this; it's the worst piece of *blank* I've ever seen, next to *Voyage*.' Joe said, 'But have you got any ideas?' I said, 'Sure,' and so we ended up with two writing assignments the same morning!" [13]

The writing team never made it to *Star Trek*. They stayed on as writers, then producers, of *Mission*, instead, and won a couple of Emmy awards.

Production:
(Filmed February 4 – 11, 1966; 6 days)

Tom Gries was hired to direct for the standard fee of $3,000. He was 42, and had won an Emmy the year before for an episode of *East Side/West Side*, a drama starring George C. Scott. He had also directed multiple episodes for David

Janssen's first series, *Richard Diamond, Private Detective*, along with *Route 66*, *Stoney Burke* (which co-starred Robert Dowdell) and *Combat!* Gries was also a writer, and would soon create the series *Rat Patrol*. Gries had numerous Emmy nominations ahead of him (including *Helter Skelter*, the 1975 movie about Charles Manson), and another win (for the TV movie *The Glass House*). Only one year after this *Voyage*, Gries began directing films, including 1967's *Will Penny*, starring Charlton Heston, and the 1969 Western *100 Rifles*, starring Jim Brown, Burt Reynolds, and Raquel Welch. "The Menfish" was his only work for Irwin Allen.

Tom Gries (center) with Ben Gazzara and Lee Remick during the making of 1974's *QB VII*.

Gary Merrill was paid $2,500 (top guest-star rate for 1966) to replace Richard Basehart in this episode, playing Admiral Park. Basehart's condition was serious enough that Merrill's contract had a renewal provision allowing Irwin Allen to draft him into service for the remainder of the season.

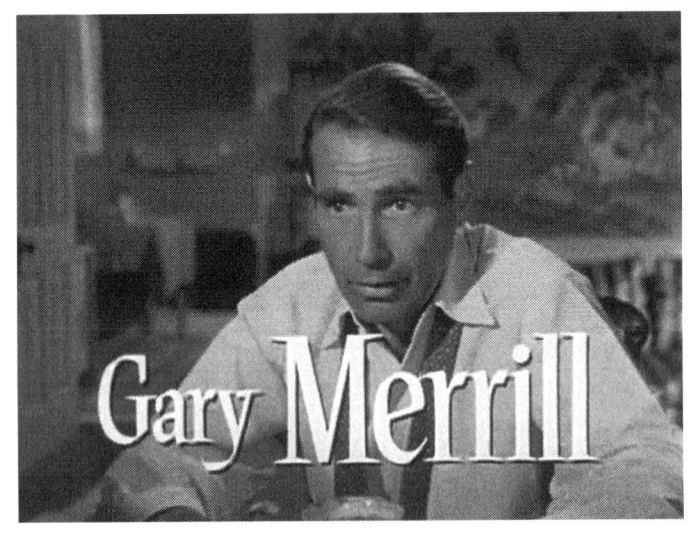

Allan Hunt said, "There was a time during the season that I was on the show when Richard got very sick. He was so sick that they thought they might have to replace him and Gary Merrill was the actor they brought in. Gary, as you know, was married to Bette Davis, and he had stature like Richard." [14]

John Dehner was 50, and was also paid $2,500. He played Borgman, the "mad scientist." Dehner had been a regular on two television series prior to this – *The Roaring 20s* (1960-62) and *The Baileys of Balboa* (1964-65). He would go on to be a regular on *The Doris Day Show* (1971-73), as well as *The New*

Temperatures Rising (1973-74); *Young Maverick* (1979-80); *Enos* (1980-81); and *Bare Essence* (1983). He had the lead as a rancher in a short-lived 1977 series, *Big Hawaii*. There was barely a series that Dehner didn't visit at least once in a career comprising nearly 300 appearances. He dropped in on *The Virginian* seven times; *Maverick* five times; and five each for *77 Sunset Strip* and *Rawhide*. The *Rifleman* had him four times, as did *Tales of Wells Fargo*; and he appeared three times each in *Wanted: Dead or Alive, Bronco, Hogan's Heroes, Judd for the Defense*, and *The Twilight Zone*. And we're only mentioning the series we think you'll remember. *Gunsmoke*, by the way, featured him in 12 episodes, usually as top guest star.

John Dehner, from this very year, as "The Steel Assassin," one of two turns on *The Wild, Wild West*.

Victor Lundin was 35 when paid $1,000 to play Hansjurg. He had just played "Friday" in 1964's sci-fi classic *Robinson Crusoe on Mars*. He would make a cheesy return, as the title character "The Lobster Man" in *Voyage*'s fourth season. Irwin Allen would also cast Lundin in an episode of *The Time Tunnel*.

Roy Jenson (39) played Johnson, the crewmember who wakes the slumbering Manfish to disastrous results. A stuntman who often doubled for Robert Mitchum, and an actor, Jensen filled his career with well over 200 screen appearances. You just can't forget his portrayal of Mulvihill in 1974's *Chinatown*; Trekkies know him well as Cloud William, in the 1968 *Star Trek*, "The Omega Glory"; and he was the first man beaten up by Caine (David Carradine), in the 1972 premiere of *Kung Fu*. Jensen, paid $750, is sprinkled about in various scenes over the course of six production days. And they didn't have to hire a stuntman to double for him in the fight with the Manfish!

Wayne Heffley (39) earned $750 for playing the Seaview's alternate Doctor one last time. The Seaview's regular Doc (Richard Bull) had not been available this season due to other commitments, so Heffley had three turns on the series (following "The Monster from Outer Space" and "Deadly Creature Below!").

Roy Jensen takes a *Star Trek* in 1968, as a savage on an apocalyptic world.

It was never easy putting a *Voyage to the Bottom of the Sea* episode into production. Everything had to be planned in great detail. Typical of this preproduction phase is Frank La Tourette's memo for this episode, saying, in part:

> Page 2, Sc. 1: For the freezing units, the plan is to use the glass capsules from *Lost in Space*. However, instead of releasing a fine spray of refrigerant into the capsules in which there will be men, the plan is to have the capsules optically glow and pulsate with varicolored lights which will be less dangerous as far as the actors are concerned and much more effective visually.
>
> Page 2, Sc. 3: The fish to be used throughout will be bull carp from 18 to 24 inches in size. They and the menfish into which they are transposed will always be seen in large aquarium-like tanks, and not the jars mentioned throughout the script. In the teaser, there will be one such tank. Later, in the missile room, there will be a second tank approximately the same size. The size of both tanks will be determined by Babe Lydecker [Howard Lydecker, special effects] so that he can properly manage the burn-ins of the menfish....
>
> Page 22, Sc. 31: Three divers will wear orange scuba gear. One diver will carry the manfish unit. The second will carry the irradiant unit. The third will carry and put into place an

aquarium-like tank, open at the top, in which the manfish will be dropped and irradiated.

Page 23, Sc. 32: What Crane and Hansjurg are seeing on the monitor will be a burn-in and should be indicated in a new Scene 34-A….

Page 36, Sc. 54: This requires another burn-in of the manfish swimming about in the water outside the observation nose and should be indicated in new scene 54-A. Same burn-in to be used for action in middle of page….

Page 46, Sc. 62: In order to get the effect through a bubble tank of water in the escape hatch, eliminate last words of scene – "as the water floods the escape hatch." Insert new scene 62-A: "EXT. ESCAPE HATCH – DAY. ANGLE ON NELSON as he sees water flood air lock and Crane goes up the ladder."

Page 47, Scene 64: To avoid having to bring the Seaview hatch into the green tank, eliminate "Crane emerges from the hatch" and sub "as Crane swims up from the o.s. hatch carrying menfish unit."

Page 47, Sc. 66: To eliminate a burn-in in this scene, add new scenes 66-A and 66-B to indicate straight production cuts of action involving Crane.

Page 48, Sc 69: To eliminate another burn-in, insert new Scene 69-A to indicate production cut as manfish suddenly convulses, stiffens, then straightens out and starts settling toward the bottom….

Page 51, Act 4: Because of the confinement of the green tank, it will be impossible for Babe Lydecker to supply enough film to satisfy all the indicated requirements of the manfish approaching the Seaview, which the monster does almost interminably….

Page 53, Sc 81: Hedison would like to have opportunity to get out of scuba gear before reporting to the control room. This could be done by having Nelson ordering him to get out of his gear on the double and then reporting to the control room.

> Page 53, Sc 85: Consensus seems to be that Borgman should die in a more dramatic way. The small irradiation unit really hasn't been placed too well audience-wise, and it seems to be too easy a way to get rid of the villain.
>
> Page 54, Sc. 87: Please eliminate monitor scenes and indicate straight production cuts for what the men in the control room are seeing – this to eliminate excessive burn-ins….
>
> Page 56, Sc 93: Babe Lydecker says he can get better visual action here if Crane's order reads: "All ahead flank" instead of "Back all engines emergency."
>
> Page 57, Sc. 100: Tommy Gries will shoot this so that action on the monitor is not visible, thus eliminating another burn-in.
>
> Page 59, Sc. 104: Eliminate references to "frames" snapping, breaking, falling into scenes. Everyone has agreed such action would be impossible on a submarine…. [15]

Next came the difficult task of designing the monsters. Interviewed by columnist Charles Witbeck for an April 1966 syndicated newspaper article, Paul Zastupnevich said, "These underwater sequences are tricky. You just can't put an actor into a fish costume and throw him into the water. You have to construct a costume so the actor is able to regulate his buoyancy; he must be able to get rid of the necessary weights around his body in a hurry. Secondly, he needs an air hose, because we can't shoot him with a bulky air tank on his back. If the actor used a tank, air bubbles would result and ruin the whole effect. At the moment, we'll probably have the actor work a minute under water and then come up for air." [16]

In a later interview with Kevin Burns, Paul Z. said, "Unfortunately, Irwin always got enamored with monsters, and disasters. It got to where budgets were so limited that he'd want a monster in and he'd say, 'We'll borrow what you did in *Lost in Space*. You've got to revamp it.' So, I would have to try to revamp it in time. And the main problem with doing the series, either one of them, is we never knew who was going to play a monster, or we never knew who the cast was until maybe two or three days before. So, the costume had to be what I call expandable. A lot of the costumes I did in those days were made out on wetsuits. The only problem with that was you'd put an actor in them, they'd lose about ten pounds after a week of shooting, because they would perspire so badly. And I was always so afraid that one of these days I was going to drown somebody because, they'd have difficulty wearing the outfits, especially the fishman underwater. They would have to go to the bottom and get a whiff of air out of the tank and then come back up do the scene, and go back and forth. It was very difficult." [17]

Production began Friday, February 4, 1966 for the first of six days on Stage 10. Other than the standard Seaview sets, they also filmed on the "Int. Surgical Lab (Limbo Set)" and the Flying Sub. Being a "bottle show," production moved along at flank speed, wrapping between 6:30 p.m. (at the earliest) and 8 p.m. (at the latest) during the six days.

David Hedison said, "I remember there was a great scene where I'm walking down a corridor and, as I turn the corner, Whammo! The manfish breaks through the wall and attacks me. Now that was a nice stunt!" [18]

Vic Lundin, interviewed by Mark Phillips and Frank Garcia, said, "John Dehner's character was an evil scientist who was like the father of my character, Hansjurg. At the end, I strangle him. There was a ten-second close-up of me with tears in my eyes. When Irwin Allen saw the rushes, he screamed at Tom Gries, 'What the hell do you think we're doing – *Playhouse 90*!?' It was too intense for him, and they cut it down to two seconds. Irwin wasn't a director who was sensitive to actors. He went for special effects." [19]

Final cost, with all those special effects, was $160,355. This was $20,000 over the target budget 20th Century-Fox was pushing for. [20]

Release / Reaction:

(ABC premiere airdate: 3/6/66; network repeat broadcast: 8/7/66)

Happening this week in 1966: North Vietnamese soldiers captured a U.S. Green Beret Camp at A Shau Valley. Ironically, the song getting the most airplay on the radio was "The Ballad of the Green Berets," by Staff Sgt. Barry Sadler.

Sadler also had the top-selling album in America. The top movie was *The Group*, about several female college students who talk about, and experience, free love, contraception, abortion, and lesbianism. Andy Warhol was hired to design this week's cover of *TV Guide* – and he chose Barbara Feldon of *Get Smart* as his subject. More pop culture going strange ... tonight's episode of *Voyage*:

Syndicated entertainment column "TV Scout" said:

> *Voyage to the Bottom of the Sea*, running out of fresh ideas, returns to the one about the mad scientist building a race of creatures with which he can rule the world. John Dehner is this chap, who takes fluid from the pineal glands of men, injects it into fish, irradiates the fish and turns them into controllable, large scaly creatures that look like men with bad skin. He even manages to insert something in the brain of Gary Merrill, the admiral of the night (Richard Basehart is "away," and he is lucky), so that Merrill, too, can be controlled. [21]

PARLEY—David Hedison as Capt. Crane, left, confers with Adm. Park, played by Gary Merrill, about a strange experiment of creating a fish with human characteristics. This will take place aboard the Seaview on "Voyage to the Bottom of the Sea" in color at 7 o'clock tonight on channels 2K, 3E, 5M, 7 and 13.

Another monster, another hit in the ratings. A.C. Nielsen 30-city survey from March 6, 1966: [22]

	Rating:	Share:
(7 – 7:30 p.m.)		
ABC: *Voyage to the Bottom of the Sea*	**18.6**	**34.4%**
CBS: *Lassie*	12.2	22.6%
NBC: Children's Theatre, "Stuart Little" (special)	13.9	25.7%
7:30 – 8 p.m.		
ABC: *Voyage to the Bottom of the Sea*	**20.5**	**34.3%**
CBS: *My Favorite Martian*	15.5	25.9%
NBC: *Walt Disney's Wonderful World...*	15.3	25.6%

5.9

"The Mechanical Man" (Episode 57)

(Prod. #8226; first aired Sunday, March 13, 1966)
Written by John and Ward Hawkins
Directed by Sobey Martin
Produced by Irwin Allen, Frank La Tourette and William Welch
Story Editor: Sidney Marshall
Guest Star James Darren; Special Guest Star Arthur O'Connell

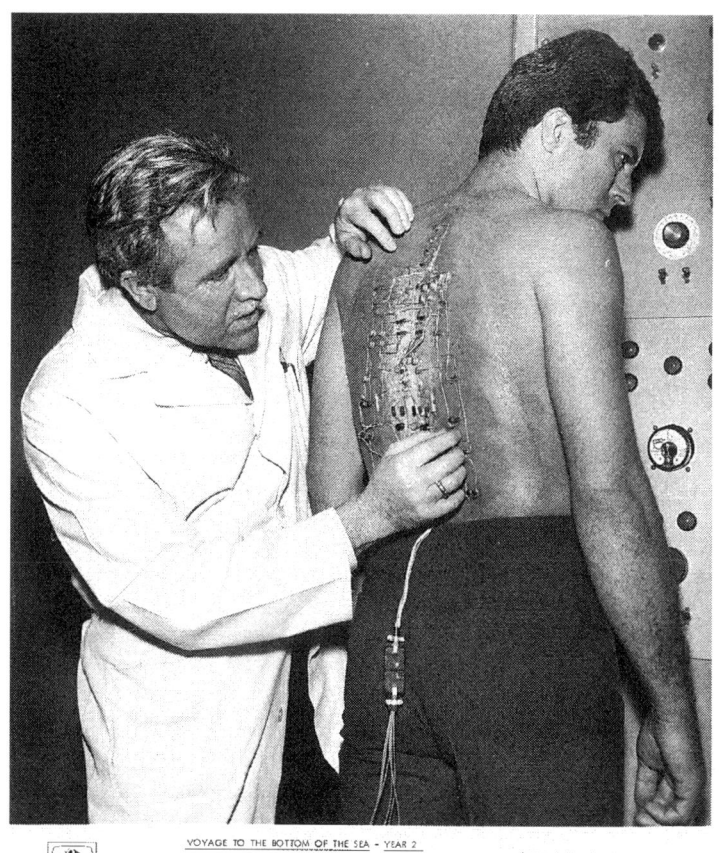

From the *Voyage* show files (Irwin Allen papers collection):

During an attempt to drill a Mohole [through Earth's crust], a scientist and his created Android have discovered a source of pure energy on which the Android feeds and which has enabled it to control his master. In order to insure a supply of this new element, the Android sabotages drilling safeguards, causing earthquakes and volcanic eruptions around the world. Crane tries to plug the Mohole but the android gets telepathic control of the head of the project and Crane is stopped. [1]

Assessment:

Despite numerous Seaview rock and rolls, and many explosions, the deliberate pacing of this episode is calmer; the performances set to light "purple" (less melodramatic), and the soundtrack a bit less bombastic. It's kind of refreshing. It could be argued that James Darren's performance is flat, but – he's an android! There is something wonderfully menacing about this gentle-speaking, tranquil-moving machine, making threats without the slightest inflection in his voice, and sending stun (and death) rays from his fingertips toward anything and anyone daring to inconvenience his plan. It's nothing personal; you just need to go to sleep … or die.

"The Mechanical Man" is a good-looking episode, filled with color and effects, cleanly produced and guided by well-oiled direction. That director – Sobey Martin – gets his knocks for not having an artistic signature, but, with this episode, he delivers the meat and potatoes on a warm plate.

Our guest resident commentators were not as kind. Mark Phillips found the episode to be made up of "a dull android, a dull scientist, and a dull story." [2] Mike Bailey said, "The themes herein could have made a tight and ecologically conscious story, but they lose steam and direction as the episode progresses. James Darren always seemed a bit stiff when not pushed by a good director, and Sobey Martin was not, in general, the one to push. Regardless, this production is vastly superior to the previous outing, the execrable 'The Menfish,' and is marginally satisfying. And hats-off to LB Abbott and Howard Lydecker – the miniature effects created for this outing are expansive, varied and finely executed." [3]

You've heard the opinions, good, bad, and indifferent. Now watch the episode, for the first time or see it again, and come to your own conclusion.

Script:
John Hawkins' and Ward Hawkins' story treatment approved on December 14, 1965.
Hawkinses' 1st-draft teleplay, "Final Warning," approved on January 4, 1966.
Hawkinses' 2nd (final) draft teleplay approved on January 31.
Rev. Shooting Final teleplay (pink paper): February 8.
Page revisions (blue paper inserts): February 14.
Page revisions (gold paper inserts): February 18.

John and Ward Hawkins returned for their second *Voyage* script assignment, following "The Machines Strike Back."

Story Editor Sidney Marshall sent a memo to his producer bosses on December 27, 1965, preparing them for what he felt was a problematic script.

> The Teaser should avoid explanatory technical talk about the installation. It would be better if Vernon were another scientist whom Omir had to do away with before Nelson and the senators came to visit the installation. As it is now, it is hard to believe that Nelson would take Peterkin and Spaulding to the Sensor Center via flying sub, without noticing that Verndon was not with them; and Verndon's reason for spying on Omir sounds contrived.
>
> A good deal of the scenes throughout the script are contrived and repetitious. The sequences of events are confusing, making it difficult to follow the action.
>
> Nelson comes off in an unfavorable light because he seems much less intelligent than Omir.
>
> Much of the dialogue is old fashioned, especially Omir and Kirt.
>
> Since Omir is so cold-blooded a murderer, it seems strange that he keeps Kirt alive or Nelson for that matter.
>
> There is a lot of visiting of the Sub by Omir to no apparent purpose.
>
> At the end of Act I, Omir and Kirt are riding out the tremor yet Act II opens with Omir being able to swim from the underwater lab through the turbulence to Seaview with apparent ease. This doesn't make sense. He then offers a very weak reason for the faulty reading which Nelson buys.
>
> There are numerous T.V. discussions about the impending tragedy and much confusion surrounding Nelson's plans to out-maneuver Omir. So much explanation gets boring.... [4]

Production:
(Filmed February 14 – 22, 1966; 7 days)

Sobey Martin was hired to direct, his fourteenth and final assignment on *Voyage*. The following year, Irwin Allen kept Martin busy on *The Time Tunnel*, directing 14 episodes in a single season, as well as one episode for *Lost in Space*. Several assignments on *Land of the Giants* followed.

James Darren was paid $2,500 to play Omir. He was 30 and became a teen idol when he co-starred in 1959's *Gidget*, as Moondoggie, opposite Sandra Dee; its sequel, 1961's *Gidget Goes Hawaiian* (with a different Gidget, now Deborah Walley); and 1963's *Gidget Goes to Rome* (now with Cindy Carol as the "Gidge"). In between, Darren co-starred in 1960's *All the Young Men*, billed under Alan Ladd and Sidney Poitier, then 1961's *The Guns of Navarone*, under Gregory Peck, David Niven, and Anthony Quinn, and 1962's *Diamond Head*, starring Charlton Heston. Darren could also sing, and was doing well in the pop-music charts, performing the theme to *Gidget*, as well as the Top 10 hits "Goodbye Cruel World" and "Her Royal Majesty." He had just co-starred in Irwin Allen's *The Time Tunnel* pilot.

Above: Sandra Dee and James Darren at the beach, in 1959's *Gidget*. Right: Arthur O'Connell never made it aboard Seaview, but he served on a sub under the command of Cary Grant, in 1959's *Operation Petticoat*.

Arthur O'Connell was 58 when cast to play Paul, and paid $2,500. He had been a stage actor, and a successful character actor in films and television since

294

1938, with nearly 150 screen appearances. On two occasions, he received nominations for Academy Awards: 1955's *Picnic* and 1959's *Anatomy of a Murder*. O'Connell became a series regular shortly after this, as young Monte Markham's son (!) in *The Second Hundred Years* (1967-68). Irwin Allen would hire O'Connell again, to play the elder Chaplain in 1972's *The Poseidon Adventure*.

James Darren and O'Connell entertain guests on the set of "The Mechanical Man."

Production began on Monday, February 14 for the first of three days on Stage 10, utilizing the standing Seaview sets, as well as "Int. U.N. Office."

Thursday, the fourth day of production, was the first of three to be spent on Stage B, for "Int. Drill Control Drone & Reactor Room," "Int. Drill Control Room" and "Ext. Under Sea" (utilizing the "Green Tank"). Meanwhile, a second unit team led by Director Bill Faralla and Cameraman Dale Deverman worked with Robert Dowdell, Del Monroe, and Seymour Cassel at the backlot Moat location, filming the "Int. Instrument Cave" sequence.

The final cost was $159,153.94, which was nearly $19,000 over the studio's target budget. [5]

Release / Reaction:
(ABC premiere airdate: 3/13/66; network repeat broadcast: 7/3/66)

The top film in movie houses was the Western *Johnny Reno*, starring Dana Andrews and Jane Russell. *The Ballad of the Green Berets* by Staff Sgt. Barry Sadler was the record album selling more copies than any other in America. It was also the most-played song on the radio, shutting out the Rolling Stones' "19th Nervous Breakdown."

James Darren was getting press over this episode, including a piece called "Heart Throb Turns Heavy" from many newspapers the day before "The Mechanical Man" aired. *The Hutchinson News* in Kansas carried it, saying:

> James Darren, the teenage heart throb of such films as *Gidget* and *Gidget Goes Hawaiian*, plays his first villain role in ABC-TV's *Voyage to the Bottom of the Sea*…. Having just completed a pilot film for Irwin Allen, creator of *Voyage*, Darren admitted that the producer interested him in playing the off-beat role. "Villains usually aren't my cup of tea," he said, and added with a grin, "especially mechanical ones." [6]

Darren said, "I'm having a lot of fun with this role, but I'm finding it frustrating, too. This man's not villainous in that he decides to do evil things. He's just a machine with a Hitler complex. When a radio transmits bad information, you can't blame the radio. The frightening part of this story is that the man is evil because he's only motivated by intelligence, not emotion. It's quite a shift from *Gidget* to gadget, but the results should be very interesting." [7]

"TV Scout" said:

> James Darren plays an android on *Voyage to the Bottom of the Sea*, a mechanical man who has taken power away from his creator (Arthur O'Connell), and is mining the Earth's core for a substance it has discovered which gives it pure energy. The Seaview is involved in the scientific expedition, but things get out of hand when the pressure from the drilling gets so high that volcanoes and earthquakes begin erupting all over the world. David Hedison decides to stop the drilling but this doesn't fit the android's plan, and he is a hard monster to stop. [8]

A.C. Nielsen 30-city survey for March 13, 1966: [9]

(7:30 – 8 p.m.)	Rating:	Share:
ABC: *Voyage to the Bottom of the Sea*	**20.0**	**37.4%**
CBS: *Lassie*	14.4	26.9%
NBC: *Bell Telephone Hour*	9.1	17.0%
8 – 8:30 p.m.		
ABC: *Voyage to the Bottom of the Sea*	**19.5**	**32.5%**
CBS: *My Favorite Martian*	13.8	23.0%
NBC: *Walt Disney's Wonderful World…*	18.0	30.0%

5.10

"The Return of the Phantom" (Episode 58)

(Prod. #8227; first aired Sunday, March 20, 1966)
Written by William Welch
Directed by Sutton Roley
Produced by Irwin Allen, Frank La Tourette, and William Welch
Story Editor: Sidney Marshall
Guest Star Alfred Ryder; Co-Starring Vitina Marcus

From the *Voyage* show files (Irwin Allen papers collection):

Captain Krueger (the phantom World War I U-boat Commander seen in 'The Phantom Strikes') is buried at sea. Nelson then encounters a beautiful phantom girl who tells him he must kill Crane. Krueger then reappears and Nelson, unable to resist his urging, shoots Crane. Krueger enters Crane's body and leaves for an island to find the woman he had loved. Mistaking his mortal granddaughter for his phantom wife, he abandons the severely wounded Crane when she spurns him. [1]

Assessment:

The story picks up right after the burial at sea of Captain Krueger from "The Phantom Strikes." Just pretend that the Tag scene of the original episode, in which Krueger appears before the Control Room crew and says farewell, never took place – maybe it was merely a part of Nelson's dream, which opens this chapter of the story. As structured, this could have been the concluding half of a two-part episode. It was handled that way for a specific reason – to be combined with the first episode, and marketed overseas as a feature film. This plan also allowed Irwin Allen to splurge a little on the budget, bring back the Seaview's primary doctor (Richard Bull), add a leading lady (Vitina Marcus) into the story, and make sure a good director (Sutton Roley) was at the helm, with one eye toward TV and the other focused on the big-screen. It all works, making one of the best episodes of Season Two. Robert Dowdell is certainly given one of his best parts in the series, with highly emotional interactions between Chip Morton and Captain Crane, and, particularly, Admiral Nelson. And David Hedison achieves an acting triumph.

"On the human level, Nelson's attempts to explain to Chip Morton what has happened to Crane is very well done," said Mark Phillips. "Sutton Roley was one of *Voyage*'s most imaginative directors and you can count on him to liven things up." [2]

Mike Bailey took the compliments to the next level: "Director Sutton Roley could take crabgrass and turn it into a stunningly verdant lawn. Since the script for 'Return' wasn't that bad to begin with, *Voyage*'s final outing for its second season turned out just fine. David Hedison cites this as one of his favorite *Voyage* episodes. It is certainly one of *my* favorite Year-Two episodes." [3]

Script:
William Welch's writers contract: February 9, 1966.
Rev. Shooting Final teleplay (pink pages): February 21.
Page revisions (blue insert paper): February 22.
Page revisions (green insert paper): February 22.

By this time, with the espionage stories performing badly in the ratings, and Irwin Allen and ABC never able to agree on an actress to play Tiffany Loveland, Albert Aley's script for "The Man from London" was permanently sent to the reject files. A new script was needed to serve as the twenty-sixth episode of Season Two; something more fantastic, in line with episodes that were doing so well in the ratings of late. There had also been talk at 20th Century-Fox about putting two episodes together and making a makeshift motion picture for overseas distribution, as Desilu had done with a two-part episode from *The Untouchables*, and MGM had done with several episodes from *The Man from U.N.C.L.E.* And then it occurred to Irwin Allen and **William Welch** that they already had the ideal property. "The Phantom Strikes," the highly successful episode from a few months earlier, was ripe for a sequel, which could become the second half to a movie. Even better: Welch was Allen's fastest writer, and could certainly write to order.

David Hedison said, "When I heard Irwin Allen was doing a 'Return of…,' I was overjoyed." [4]

Production:
(Filmed February 22 - March 4, 1966; 7 & ½ days filmed over a 9-day period)

Sutton Roley had never made a theatrical movie. But, for a TV director, he had style. And, since he had directed "The Phantom Strikes," it was only logical that he helm the sequel.

Alfred Ryder was paid $2,000 to reprise his role as Krueger. Ryder would continue his journeys into TV sci-fi, guest-starring in "The Man Trap," NBC's first broadcast episode of *Star Trek*, then appearing on *The Wild, Wild West*, which featured him as an outraged madman determined to end sea pollution.

Vitina Marcus was paid $1,000 for playing Lani … and the unnamed dancer who is almost strangled to death so that the ghost of Lani can possess her body. Marcus was 29, and had appeared as the Native Girl in Irwin Allen's *The Lost World*, which included David Hedison in the cast. Marcus and Hedison were teamed up for the first-season *Voyage* episode, "Turn Back the Clock," and now brought together for a third time.

Marcus was also close to Irwin Allen, and very aware how others reacted to him. "Irwin used to scare people," she said. "When he was talking to people, everybody seemed to be frightened to talk to him, because he talked so fast and he went from one thought to another, like lightning speed. It's just that he thought really fast, and that's what happened – people were trying to keep up with him and it was a strain on them. And he went in to everybody's department; nobody could escape him! He was in the makeup; the wardrobe; every department there was; he was in and out of them all. He didn't leave anyone alone! But Irwin didn't scare me at all. I think he treated women a little differently than men. I think he was more sensitive to women." [5]

Shortly after this, Allen cast Marcus in a pair of *Lost in Space* episodes ("Wild Adventure" and "The Girl from the Green Dimension"), as well as two trips into *The Time Tunnel* ("Chase Through Time" and "Attack of the Barbarians"). She also made a delicious appearance as "Girl" in *The Man from U.N.C.L.E.*'s "The My Friend the Gorilla Affair," considered by many fans the dumbest episode of all – featuring Solo doing the Frug (or was it the Watusi?) with Girl and her pet gorilla.

Irwin Allen didn't take kindly to Marcus appearing in *The Man from U.N.C.L.E.*, a series that had hurt *Voyage* during its first season. Marcus said, "Irwin was kind and understanding, and he was always there to help, but he had his other side – he expected extreme loyalty from everyone. He didn't like it when people worked for other producers and other shows. And he was especially always upset if I was working for someone else. And that wasn't good for me as an actress. I was afraid to do other work. One time I went in to *The Man from U.N.C.L.E.* to audition for a lady Tarzan type character, and I got the part. Irwin got so upset about that, he threatened to see that I'd never work again. I don't think he really meant it, but he was very possessive. He put me to work several times – a couple times on each of his shows – but I often wondered if that really hindered me, because I wasn't making the kind of income that I needed to make to support me and my daughter." [6]

Production began Tuesday, February 22, 1966, for the first of five-and-a-half days on Stage 10, covering all the Seaview sets. On this first day, they worked until 8:45 at night. Work resumed on the standing sets for Wednesday, Thursday, and Friday, with wrap on the last day not coming until 10:18 p.m. Monday, February 28, and part of Wednesday were also spent on the Seaview sets, finishing in the Control Room. Next came a company move to Stage B, for the sequences on the "Ext. & Int. Waterfront" set. And this day didn't end until 8:09 p.m.

On Wednesday, March 2, already the seventh day of filming, the company remained on Stage B for the "Ext. Island" set.

Day 8: Thursday began on Stage B, continuing work on the "Ext. Island" set, then a company move back to Stage 10 for sequences in the Flying Sub, as well as the Observation Nose and Missile Room, two locations that had not been covered when the company had been on Stage 10 earlier in the production.

On Friday, March 4, the Second Unit took over, with Irwin Allen directing and Bill Abbott running the camera crew. They were on Stage 10, filming the "Limbo set" with Alfred Ryder and Vitina Marcus. This had been planned for the Main Unit, but wasn't even started. While this was filmed, the regular cast and crew, including cinematographer Winton Hoch, began their summer hiatus. Allen finished with the second unit at 3:30 p.m. [7]

Talking about "The Return of the Phantom," David Hedison said, "I didn't think that Alfred's accent was all that good; I didn't believe it as a good German accent, but what I did was study the way that Alfred was doing it, and I thought I spoke exactly the way that he did." [8]

"David Hedison was a wonderful actor," Vitina Marcus said. "That was a rough scene, when he had to strangle me, and it could have gotten a little carried away. But he didn't hurt me at all. And, even when we weren't shooting, he was a perfect gentleman; always professional. It didn't matter how wild the stories were, he always gave it his all." [9]

Director Sutton Roley said, "The series was a comic strip. I mean that literally. The stories were way out, and reality was flown to the wind. Irwin was mainly enamored with the submarine and its Christmas lights. He tended to treat the actors like buffoons. I didn't like that attitude."

Roley said of this episode, "It wasn't as good [as "The Phantom Strikes Back], but it was okay." [10]

David Hedison said, "It was great fun working on 'The Phantom' with Sutton [Roley]." [11]

Release / Reaction:
(ABC premiere airdate: 3/20/66; network repeat broadcast: 8/26/66)

David McCallum and Robert Vaughn, of the popular *The Man from U.N.C.L.E.* series, had the cover of *TV Guide*. You could buy a copy for 15 cents. Gas cost 32 cents a gallon. The average price for a new home was $23,300. You could find the latest Beatles and Tijuana Brass albums on sale for $2.69 in a city near you. And ABC was about to introduce America to a pair of very cool spies – John Steed and Emma Peel, with the US premiere of *The Avengers*.

Tom McIntyre interviewed Richard Basehart from the set of "The Return of the Phantom" for an article published in the March 13, 1966 edition of North Carolina's *Gaston Gazette*. Basehart said, "We've had our troubles in trying to remember exactly what we did in that first part in order to set up the same mood in the show we're doing now. When it is finished and aired, both parts will be spliced together for release to movie theaters." [12]

McIntyre wrote:

> *Voyage to the Bottom of the Sea* is something unique on television today. Granted, it wallows deep in science-fiction, which thank God I'm not too so-called sophisticated to enjoy, and there is a certain amount of repetition, but any straight action-adventure series which is pitted against the slightly martyred *Walt Disney* and survives can't be all bad.
>
> Much to Basehart's dismay, *Voyage* is a stickler for tense action and performances. When it's good, it's very good, but when it's bad, it's very bad. Basehart laughed heartily at this and said, "I'm on your side. But it's strange, it seems some of the shows I consider not our best have been the ones to reach and build us an audience. We've had a number of good scripts in our two seasons. We've also had some not so good scripts. There are some fine writers out here, but, unfortunately, we don't have many of them." [13]

Basehart explained, "You see, the script is that all important item. Without it we're nothing. David and I pick over the scripts searching for something we can play unusually different from the one before. There are circumstances involved in television production which more or less force us more and more into the same channels each week. That's why the writing has to be unusually good." [14]

David Hedison said, "I was very proud of that show. I'd worked very hard on it to try to get his accent right, and to do all that interesting sort of stuff, you know, that actors love to sink their teeth into." [15]

Basehart and Hedison, for the most part, had been happy with the second season. There were some turkeys; perhaps to be expected in the days of cranking out 26 or more episodes a year. But the season contained a great variety of story types, and some strong acting moments for both of the stars, as well as various members of the supporting cast. "The Return of the Phantom" allowed both to end the season on a very high note. And, by now, it was confirmed that the series had been renewed by ABC-TV for a third season. Cast and crew could break for the spring, with renewed enthusiasm about what laid ahead.

"TV Scout" previewed the episode, saying:

> Thanks to some ingenious backtracking in the script, Kreuger (Alfred Ryder), the World War I ghost who appeared on *Voyage to the Bottom of the Sea* several weeks ago, returns

to haunt Richard Basehart into shooting David Hedison (The ghost wants to inhabit Hedison's body, remember?). And, by golly, Basehart does just that, leaving Hedison so weak it's a snap for the spirit to walk right in and make David well again. Hedison does a good acting job as nice Commander Crane, who isn't so nice when he is possessed. [16]

Rival television review column "TV Key" called it this way:

This adventure delves into the supernatural world and comes up with a tale about the ghost of a German sub commander who wants to inhabit Captain Crane's body so he can live again. Alfred Ryder, who plays the phantom commander, was seen in an earlier episode this season and returns to good advantage here. [17]

Maybe fans thought it was a rerun, because the ratings dipped a little. A.C. Nielsen 30-city survey from March 20, 1966: [18]

(7:30 – 8 p.m.)	Rating:	Share:
ABC: *Voyage to the Bottom of the Sea*	15.7	33.1%
CBS: *Lassie*	**17.7**	**37.3%**
NBC: Actuality special	6.4	13.5%
(8 – 8:30 p.m.):		
ABC: *Voyage to the Bottom of the Sea*	15.4	29.4%
CBS: *My Favorite Martian*	15.6	29.8%
NBC: *Walt Disney's Wonderful World…*	**15.7**	**30.0%**

6

Fall 1966 - Welcome to the Monster Mash

Alternate shot of promotional picture sent out during Season Two, connecting *Lost in Space* (the cyclops monster) and *Voyage*. Bring on the monsters!

It had been a slow, hard climb to the top of the ratings during *Voyage*'s second season. The series began in its Sunday evening time slot as the second- and sometimes third-place runner. Come midseason, it clawed its way to a firm second position, then, within weeks, it was beating the formidable competition of *Lassie* and *Walt Disney's Wonderful World of Color*, and had put *My Favorite Martian* to rest after a three-season run. The last time ABC had held its own during the early Sunday slot was with *Maverick*, which performed well on Sunday

305

evenings for four seasons, before dying on the ratings battlefield in 1961. What followed was a revolving door of series, none surviving more than a season. *Follow the Sun*, *The Jetsons*, and *The Travels of Jaimie McPheeters* all failed to take hold. And the once-mighty *Wagon Train* also expired after being moved to the Sunday battle line. But by 1966, *Voyage* had persevered, and then dominated. The ABC programmers were elated. There was no question that the series would remain on Sunday nights from 7 to 8 p.m. for its third season. By this time, Irwin Allen had begun to embrace his pre-prime-time niche. ABC's Lew Hunter said, "He loved the early Sunday time slot, because he knew he had a show that would appeal to kids. So 7 o'clock was much better than any other hour that he ever had." [1]

The competition on NBC would be unchanged. During the first half hour against *Voyage*, the network was sticking with the underperforming *Bell Telephone Hour*, from 6:30 to 7:30 p.m., alternating every other week with a series of "actuality specials." NBC had no realistic alternative; Bell Telephone owned the hour slot and wanted to stay on course, even though the ratings had been slipping. *Walt Disney's Wonderful World of Color*, then, would have to get by with the weak lead-in. On CBS,

The new competition on CBS – *It's About Time.*

Lassie would lead into a new sci-fi comedy series, *It's About Time*, following the adventures of two American astronauts who return to Earth to find that they have crossed a time barrier and are now in the stone age, dealing with harmless, lowbrow Fred Flintstone types.

The big change at *Voyage* for the third season was a push to reduce costs. The series had routinely exceeded the budget set by the studio during its first two years, with its second season being even costlier than the first due to salary raises and the switch to color film. Between *Voyage* and *Lost in Space*, and now with the addition of *The Time Tunnel,* 20th Century-Fox was experiencing heavy deficit financing. Fox made it clear to Irwin Allen that he must discover a way to reduce overall costs. One solution was to have the writers come up with more "bottle shows" – stories which could be staged entirely on the Stage 10 Seaview sets, saving the time of moving from one stage to another, going outdoors or constructing temporary sets. Further, these episodes would be planned as five-day productions (although few would achieve the

The Time Tunnel **makes three for Irwin Allen. Pictured: James Darren and Robert Colbert.**

goal). For the stories which required sets beyond the Seaview and the Flying Sub, writers were asked to try to limit their needs to the island set which was now built on Stage B, and its water tank, allowing for a small beach area. Other cost-cutting solutions included the hiring of fewer "name" guest stars, as well as fewer women (which Allen figured would save time and money when it came to wardrobe, make-up and hairdressing). The word also came down to hire fewer extras. The one thing there would be more of was stock footage. Sometimes entire sequences from previous episodes would be inserted into the new shows. Furthermore, they would recycle more monsters.

Voyage Assistant Story Editor Al Gail told interviewer Kevin Burns, "It was very difficult doing a series like *Voyage*. But, as you got into your second and third and fourth year, it got progressively easier, because you knew exactly where you were going. You knew what you needed. You knew how many pages you needed in a script. You knew what actors would fit where and when…. And, again, turning out a show each week was not easy, but we had very good people with us – story people, story editors, and directors. We didn't stop to think about how hard it was. We just plowed ahead. If you stopped to think, you were in trouble." ²

Irwin Allen not only had three one-hour series running simultaneously for the 1966-67 TV season, but more projects in the works. The only other producer to rival Allen was Quinn Martin, also with three concurrent series – *The Fugitive, 12 O'Clock High,* and *The F.B.I.* And the only other producer to attempt science fiction during this time, beginning Fall, 1966, was Gene Roddenberry, with *Star Trek* – and that one series put him in the hospital, suffering from exhaustion. The series' demands also put Roddenberry's associate producer, Robert Justman, in the hospital, as well as their photographic-effects man, Darrell Anderson. Making half a science-fiction movie every week was that great a strain. So far, Allen appeared to be meeting the challenge. In fact, thriving on it.

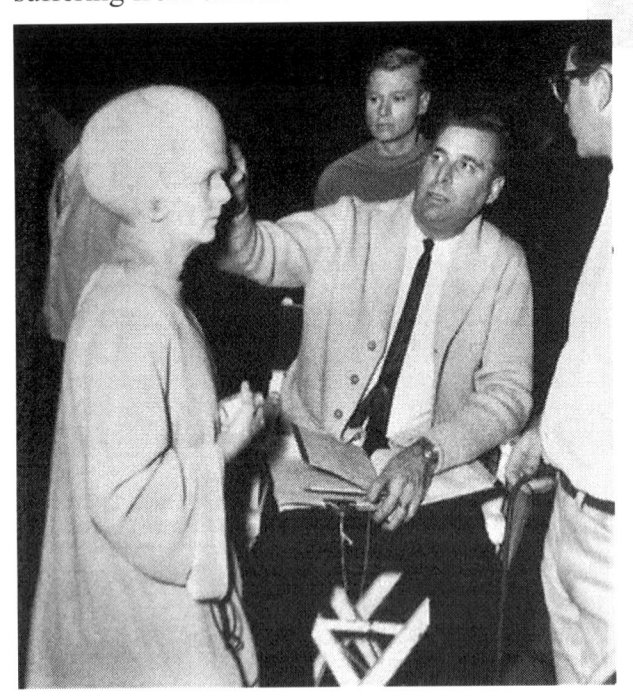

Irwin Allen's rivals: Quinn Martin (above), also boasting three series for the Fall of 1966, and Gene Roddenberry, the only other producer to dare science fiction, with *Star Trek*.

Al Gail said, "He'd go home every night with these big yellow pads and he'd come back the next morning and they'd be full of notes. So, he ate and slept motion pictures and television. He loved what he was doing, so he didn't resent it. There was no strain. A lot of others felt the strain, but there was no strain for him." ³

The downside of all this work was that Allen's focus and judgment were diffused in many directions. As for his support team, they were greatly limited in what they could contribute, by the very nature of Allen's personality and the internal structure of his show-business empire.

Case in point: Lew Hunter said, "Al Gail was a nice guy, but the only thing he brought to the table was to say, 'Yeah, that's right, Irwin,' or 'I think Irwin's idea is best.' But he was such a good guy that we didn't dislike him at all. We didn't respect him, but we didn't *dis*respect him."

Regarding Frank La Tourette, Hunter commented, "We would call him 'Frank Toadie' at the time. 'Toadie' was a phrase we used when we were thinking about the entourage that accompanied Irwin. Irwin would say something, and Frank would say, 'Yeah, you're right, Irwin.' He did whatever Irwin wanted. He was a lovely guy, and I enjoyed him at UCLA [where La Tourette was an administrator], but, at the network, we didn't have a lot of respect for him." [4]

La Tourette appeared to have had enough. He exited the employ of Irwin Allen as soon as *Voyage* wrapped its second season. His replacement was Bruce Fowler, Jr.

"Bruce Fowler was a very likable guy, too," Lew Hunter said. "All the people around Irwin were really good guys, but all of them were 'yes men,' or they didn't stick around. They all had their different ways of saying 'yes' – like 'Yes, Irwin' or 'Good idea, Irwin' or 'That makes sense to me, Irwin,' but the end results were the same. It was Irwin's own personality that drove people into the ground. He had to be in control of them. I mean, if people disagreed with Irwin, then, the next thing you knew, they weren't there. So, there was always a tension around the office that you sensed as you walked in the door. And that's how they got along with him; they gave him what he wanted. But that's kind of the way the major studios were at the time. "At Warner Brothers, Jack Warner had sycophants all around him. And you had Louie B. Mayer – he was the king of MGM. And you had Harry Cohn at Columbia, *who was a monster*. And Irwin had known Harry Cohn, so he was really following that particular lead. They all had the sycophants around them. They were all kind of little lords, and they thought of themselves as that. Why have people around who don't agree with you? And, of course, Hollywood is run on fear – the fear of losing your job. But most of these moguls had one person in their group who could really tell them what he thought, or could relay information from other people who were afraid to do it themselves. With Jack Warner, the only one he really respected was Hal Wallis, who was the head of the studio for about five or ten years. In Irwin's case, Bill Welch was one, Arthur Weiss [*Voyage* writer and *The Time Tunnel* story editor] was another." [5]

Irwin Allen was loyal to his people and made sure they had jobs for as long as they wanted them. Case in point, Allen presides over his team in the early 1970s ... all but one of whom had worked on *Voyage to the Bottom of the Sea* nearly a decade earlier. Left to right: Paul Zastupnevich (art designer, wardrobe, and general assistant); Stirling Silliphant (the new kid on the block; screenwriter); Al Gail (cousin and story editor); William Welch (story editor and associate producer); Bill Creber (art designer); and Sidney Marshall (story editor).

With success comes increased power. With two popular series on the air and a third preparing to launch, Allen was now a force to be reckoned with. ABC's influence over the series was little to none by this time. Of course, Allen's story editors would make concessions for Broadcast Standards (the censors), but Allen himself paid little attention to what program directors had to say. Lew Hunter admitted, "I gave notes on every episode, and sent them to Irwin, with copy to Harve Bennett, who was the West Coast Head of the TV Division at the time. But I don't remember those notes making much of an impression on Irwin. I know there were a few times I tried to manipulate him, and he would either accept my suggestions or not, but he didn't do it an awful lot. Let's say two or three times, total. I remember one time that Harve Bennett told me, 'You can't tell Irwin what to do, Lew, so don't lose too much sleep over it.' He said something else, without actually saying it, which, in a sense, was, 'You were put on this show because you're new to the department; Irwin's going to do the fucking show the way he wants to do it; and just ride the wave.' So, as far as the so-called notes I gave, I did it just to go through the motions – to show Harve that I was giving notes, and hope they might help, then try not to lose sleep over it."

Even with this more passive stance, the network executive was still too proactive for Allen's liking. Hunter recalled, "He banned me from the lot once because I had disagreed with him on the scheduling of something. I was carrying a message from ABC and Harve Bennett, and I suppose I was trying to show my balls so that Harve would not be pissed off with me. But, showing my balls got me banned. And I was told to go see Bill Self. So, I went into the office of Bill Self, who was the dearest man you could possibly imagine, and he took one look at me and said, 'Well, you've been banned from the lot, haven't you?' I said, 'I guess so, Bill.' He said, 'Let me tell you a story,' and he told me how a producer named Jerry Wald was banned from the lot by [20th Century-Fox head] Darryl Zanuck, who said, 'Jerry, you're off the lot! I'm pissed off at you! But we'll see you at the poker game on Sunday night.' There was that kind of 'on the edge' relationship between everybody in those days. So, I got back to ABC and Harve said, 'So, Irwin's got you kicked off the lot, huh?' And I said, 'Oh, God, yes.' And Harve was really congenial about the whole thing. He said, 'I'm going to go have a cup of coffee and a Danish with Bill Self and he'll figure out a way to get you back on.' And that's what happened. I think it was, like, 24 or 48 hours, and Bill said, 'Come on, Irwin, this is all bullshit.' We probably ended up caving on whatever it was I was trying to get done."

It was an ongoing battle, with ABC making most of the concessions. Hunter said, "In Irwin's mind, it was us against him. I never saw him get crazy with the suits from New York; he was always very congenial to them. He saved the adversarial act for those of us who were on the West Coast. He never said, 'It's my way or the highway,' but he would say, 'It's my way – *period*.' He was very, very strong. And I think that was one of the reasons I was on the show, because I was new to the programming department and they had figured, 'Oh hell, Irwin's going to do what he wants to do anyway, so let Hunter run that and get some experience. And, boy, did I get some experience!" [6]

***

Shortly after returning to work for the third season, David Hedison was profiled in *TV Guide* for its July 16, 1966 issue. The unattributed article was called "Torpedoed by Success," and suggested that the popularity of *Voyage* was bad for his credibility as a "serious" actor.

Hedison did as Richard Basehart often had when interacting with the press: He defended himself. "If you can make this believable, you have really accomplished something." [7]

Basehart was quoted in the article as saying, "*Richard III* was easier than this because the *lines* were there."[8]

But Hedison did have one beef. "I'm so damned sick of this uniform. I envy Robert Vaughn. As 'the Man' from U.N.C.L.E., he can go so many places and be with women and wear a tuxedo."[9]

In the August 3, 1966 issue of *Daily Variety*, Dave Kaufman wrote:

> Just about a year ago, word was being spread out of 20th Century-Fox TV that its *Voyage to the Bottom of the Sea* would have a new look, a James Bond flavor, with girls, girls, girls, including a regular with an unlikely name of Tiffany Loveland. Among those spreading the good tidings was producer Irwin Allen. But something happened, and instead of beauties, *Voyage* came up with monsters in many a seg. In the behind-the-scenes contest between beauty and the beast, the beast won. Recalling this background, David Hedison, who stars with Richard Basehart in the series, isn't too happy about it. Particularly since they plan to have a monster in every third show on the average, as the series goes into its third season.[10]

The reality was closer to a monster in every other episode. And, before the third season cleared, one in nearly every show. Allen figured that having a beast-of-the-week would be a good fit for his show's time slot. Plus, this would be counter-programming against the wholesome yet comparatively tame *Lassie* and *Disney*.

David Hedison told Kaufman, "We thought we should do well with girls and romance, but when we opened last season, the ratings were not good and we were in the danger area. It seemed, however, when we had a monster, the ratings would go up, and we finished last season with monsters. They never did cast Tiffany Loveland."

Monsters scared up the ratings; that was Allen's thinking, according to Hedison. Hedison's thinking, according to Hedison: "My own theory is that the audience just got used to our new time slot. My fan mail tells me they like the show, they like Basehart and me; they don't mention the monsters as a reason for their liking the series. I guess Irwin Allen and I get different fan mail, because he says his is for the monsters, that even a female monster helps the show. We haven't had a girl guesting yet, and we are on our sixth show for next season. I think it's wrong. I don't mean we should have girls stand around and look pretty, and who have nothing to do with the show, but that they should participate in the action. Women I've met on p.a.'s [public appearances] and elsewhere told me they like to see women in the show. Dick Basehart feels the same way. I would like to play a six-page romantic scene with a girl, but I know that it's wrong for this show…. Kids will turn it off if there's a long kissing scene. It's not their kind of action-adventure, but my own kind…. But it's wrong to have no women at all." [11]

Herman Rush, Irwin Allen's television agent, said, "There was research that was being conducted by Fox as well as ABC. And Irwin was a researcher, and he paid attention to it. When he saw there was a need for more monsters, he gave them more monsters. That was part of his reasoning as a producer. He took advantage of the research that was available in the early days of television. I think the reasoning behind the changes in the series was brought about by a combination of things – Irwin recognized the research and he thought that would be to the advantage of the show in order to garner a larger audience, so he was easily convinced to do so. But, also, you had Irwin's personal taste. Anything with science fiction appealed to him, and the monsters would fall into that category. And special effects would fall into that category. He loved special effects and he always sought them out to be larger in volume. The pictures were always bigger with Irwin. Now, eventually, he became known as 'The Master of Disaster,' because he always preferred that type of a production. You see, he did not like 'talking heads,' and did not really relish doing scenes that were just dramatic. He liked to have action going on. And, in those days of television, particularly with a young audience, that's what they wanted, too. These shows were fantasies; they were escapism. And that's what Irwin recognized." [12]

Season Three also brought a new set of casting decisions. Chief of the Seaview Terry Becker had tested well during the second season, but missed many episodes because he and Irwin Allen could not come to terms over salary (see "The Sky's on Fire" from Season Two). Becker, interviewed by William Anchors, Jr., said, "[T]he third season started and [Irwin] was working with this director whose name I can't remember right now, and they're looking for a replacement, and they had everybody in there – every actor, [including] Ernest Borgnine.... they had everybody [test] for Sharkey, and Irwin kept saying, 'No, that's not my chief. No, no, no.' So, the director had to prepare the show, and he said to Irwin, 'You want Terry Becker, *call* Terry Becker.' So, I got a call from his office and it said, 'Will you come in?' And I was like, 'I don't know if I want to go in because he was just insulting me.' But I did. I went in. He had this big office, a big desk, and he was like a mayor sitting on a high chair, and you sat on a low chair. All that kind of crap. And he said, 'Listen, now you know how it is to be without a job.' … But, anyway, we started to talk and the ballet began again. And I got up again and said, 'Nah, Irwin.' He was talking like pennies, and so I started to go. He was, like, 'Come back!' We must have done this five times. And, the last time, I said, 'Irwin, if you don't meet what I want – because I think it's reasonable – I'm going to get out of this fucking chair and I'm walking. I don't care what you do – you can cry; you can cuss; you can do whatever you want to do – but I'm going to walk. Now are you going to do what I asked you to do and give me what I deserve?' And he looked at me for a moment, and said, ''Well, wait a minute. If you do this for me… when you're on the set, would you tell me who's making trouble?' I said, 'What the hell are you talking about? You want me to go on the set to be your spy? Take your money and keep your part and…' 'No, no, no. Okay, okay, don't get up!' Because I was going to walk and keep walking. And we finally settled and he gave me what I wanted." [13]

David Hedison was happy that Becker was back for the third season, after missing several episodes from the later part of Season Two. He said that Chief Sharkey, played by Becker, would be "giving the script what it desperately needs – humor." Hedison added, "People ask me why I don't smile [in the show]. How can I, when I'm in a situation where the world is going to explode? But the show needs comic relief. Richard and I try to lighten certain scenes; not make them so

314

heavy and grim. The show would run seven years if it had these ingredients. It could be an underwater *Wagon Train*." [14]

But, as we know, *Wagon Train*, after having been the top-rated series on television, and enjoying a seven-year run, died a quick death when moved to Sundays at 7 p.m. On ABC. *Voyage* was now thriving.

Robert Dowdell was given a raise too. And that was likely thanks to David Hedison, who had been a supporter of Dowdell from the beginning. Allan Hunt shared, "David told this story about Bob Dowdell and Irwin Allen. Whenever Irwin Allen was choosing somebody for a role, he would look at film. One day, according to David, Irwin said, 'Come with me; I want to look at film on actors who are being considered for Chip Morton.' So, they went to the screening room, and Bob Dowdell was in an episode of *Stoney Burke*, and the film was of a scene that had been chosen to show Irwin that Bob was right for the part of Chip Morton. Well, the scene went up, and it was a very serious scene, and Bob's character had been hurt, and he's not expected to come through, and he's in someone's arms and saying, like the song, 'Tell Laura I love her.' David said, 'Ah, man, this guy's good.' And he kept glancing over at Irwin, who had a very passive expression – not good, not bad, just watching. Finally, when it was over, David turns to Irwin and says, 'Irwin, that was good.' And Irwin said, 'I don't like it.' And David said, 'Really? Why?' Irwin says, 'He doesn't have a sense of humor.'"

Hunt laughed, as did we. Allen was the one who supposedly had no sense of humor! Hunt continued, "I don't know how it went from there to get Bob the part; maybe David talked Irwin into it; maybe they changed the character to not have a sense of humor, because you know how things went with my casting. So, my guess is Chip Morton may have been meant to have more humor to the character, but they made him serious because that's how Bob came off to Irwin in that

315

clip. And that's how Bob was on set too. Whenever I worked with Bob, he was friendly; he was pleasant, but he was just quiet; he wasn't one of the boys." [15]

Hunt's character Riley would be missing from the Seaview for the new season. Hunt told interviewer Mark Phillips, "The height of the build-up of the Vietnam War was 1966, and I was classified 1-A with the draft. Because I wasn't in college or married, it made me very eligible. They were taking just about any case they could, and they weren't interested in hearing about my having a job that I didn't want to lose. When it became apparent that my being drafted was imminent, I told Irwin Allen that I was going to enlist voluntarily in the Marine Corps, which had a special two-year enlistment. This gave me a little more say about where I was going and what I would be doing. I didn't want to wait around for the Army to come and get me. …

"To finally get a role [like Riley] and then have to leave voluntarily – it was very tough. It drove me crazy to have to leave. They had already been renewed, and I was enlisting in the Marine Corps just as the third year was about to begin production. It was very hard not to be part of that. When you're young, it's even tougher because you think your world is going to end." [16]

The only thing going for Hunt was that he was well-liked – by Irwin Allen as well as the audience.

"I had an open offer from Mr. Allen to return to *Voyage*," Hunt said. "They deliberately didn't replace my character. It was always their hope – and certainly mine – that I would come back to *Voyage* in two years. The cast was very generous with their encouragement. Everyone was saying, 'We'll be right here waiting for you.' Richard Basehart was especially kind and sympathetic. He shook my hand, looked at me with mock sternness and said, 'Now you come back.'" [17]

Because Riley wasn't replaced, Paul Trinka's character Patterson would be far more visible in the episodes to come.

***

It was a busy time on the Fox lot. Four feature films were in production when *Voyage* began filming its third season. They included *Caprice*, starring Doris Day and Richard Harris; *Doctor Dolittle*, starring Rex Harrison; and *In Like Flint*, starring James Coburn. The fourth film, having returned from more than six months of location production in the Far East, and now spending an equal amount of time at the studio, was *The Sand Pebbles*, starring Steve McQueen and directed by Robert Wise. Also taking up space on the lot were the TV series *Peyton Place*, *Daniel Boone*, *12 O'Clock High*, *Felony Squad*, *The Tammy Grimes Show*, *The*

Monroes, and the three from Irwin Allen. Crowded out were *Batman* and *The Green Hornet*, both Fox series, which rented sounded stages at nearby Desilu/Culver, but would come home to the Fox lot to film exteriors.

Billy Mumy, in the center of it all while appearing in *Lost in Space* as Will Robinson, said, "You couldn't have asked for a cooler place to be every day…. I loved the *Green Hornet*, and I hung out with Bruce Lee. He taught me a few martial arts moves. So, there's Van [Williams], and there's Bruce Lee over there, and here's Burt Ward and Adam [West], and they look great. And

In the middle 1960s, working at 20th Century Fox was like vacationing at Disneyland. Pictured: Billy Mumy of *Lost in Space* and Burt Ward of *Batman*.

you had all the guys from *Voyage*, and their goofy monsters, literally sharing a candy machine with us between Stage 10 and 11. You have *Fantastic Voyage*, this movie where everybody is going inside corpuscles and arteries and stuff; you have *The Time Tunnel*; you have *Daniel Boone* going on; you have *Peyton Place*, and I could sit and go to lunch with Mia Farrow and Barbara Parkins and Ryan O'Neal. I used to go visit all the other sets when I had an extra half hour and could sneak away. And, honestly, when you're 12 years old and you're hanging out in between scenes and you're sitting in the Batmobile, or you're sitting in the Black Beauty [from the *Green Hornet*], you're thinking, 'This is pretty cool!'

"And from the eyes of Billy Mumy in the 1960s, you couldn't have asked for a cooler place to be every day. I loved being at Fox, and I loved the fact that there were so many colorful characters and fantasy shows going on simultaneously. It was great being in the middle of that." [18]

Now, with *Voyage*'s Season Three, bring on the monsters!

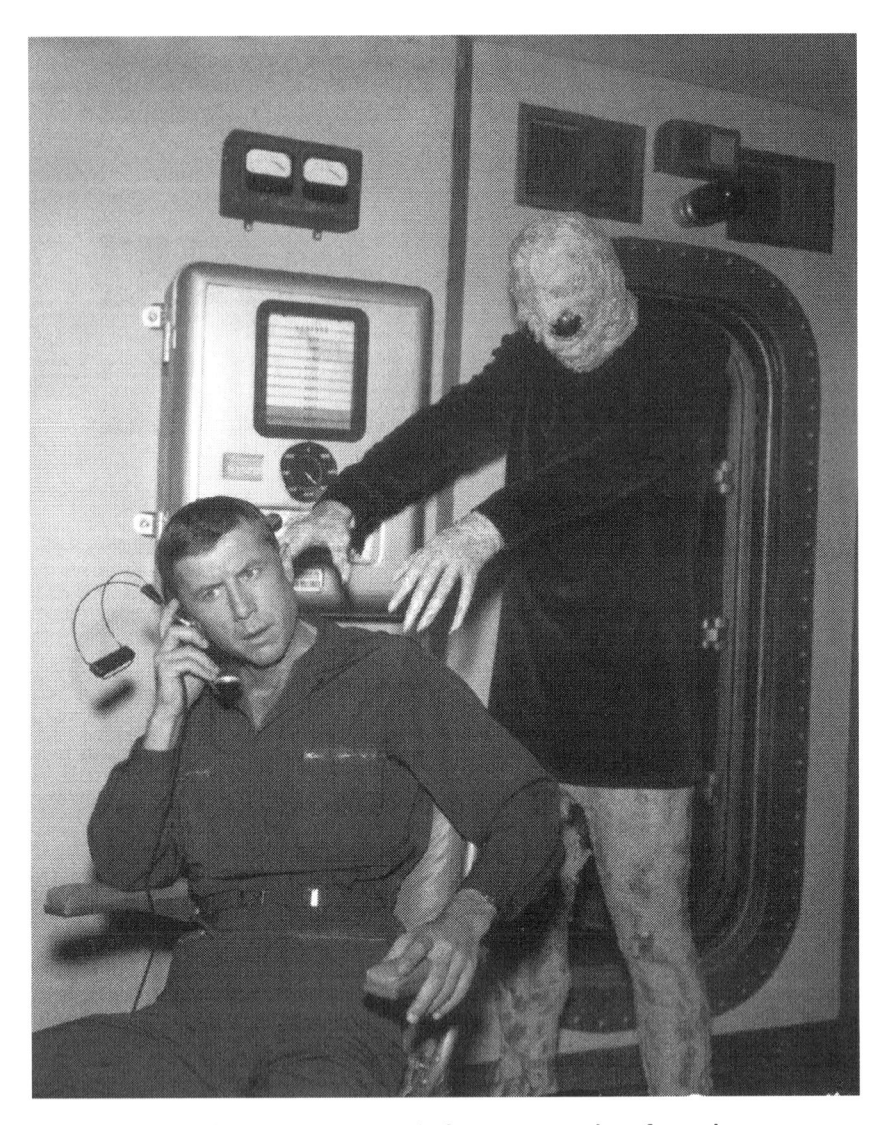

You wouldn't see it in an episode from *Voyage*, but, for a photo op, Dawson Palmer, in make-up from a *Lost in Space* episode, dropped by to menace Paul Trinka (Patterson), and signal *Voyage*'s new direction.

7

Season Three / ABC's Initial Firm Order of 16

SEAVIEW SETS SAIL FOR THIRD SEASON -- Producer Irwin Allen's fantastic atomic-powered submarine-of-the-future, Seaview, sets sail on a weekly cruise of adventure and derring-do in "Voyage to the Bottom of the Sea," for its third season, Sunday, Sept. 18 over ABC-TV in color. Actor Richard Basehart (Admiral Harriman Nelson) is shown astride the Seaview, while flying overhead is David Hedison (Captain Lee Crane) atop the ship's combination spaceship/submarine, the Flying Fish.

ABC was encouraged enough by Season Two's ratings upturn to pick *Voyage* up for a full season (26 episodes), with an option to increase that order to 29 … or cut it back to 16. The networks made the rules and could change the game in a New York minute, influenced by the ratings and commitments from sponsors. Bottom line: The creative staff at *Voyage* had to prepare 26 scripts, with an understanding that they might only get 16 of them produced and on the air.

As with all Irwin Allen shows, work resumed with a flurry. The race was on to develop stories and get treatments and script drafts into work. The budget was increased from an average price of $145,000 per episode to $160,000, not that anyone really expected to stay within that price rage.

This increase might make you think things got easier at *Voyage*. Not at all. Most of the second-season episodes had hit or exceeded the $160,000 mark, so the studio was merely being more realistic. Meanwhile, inflation was resulting in more dollars needed to accomplish what less could just a year earlier. And, by contractual stipulation, everyone got raises. Richard Basehart's and David Hedison's salaries alone went up by a thousand dollars each per episode. Irwin Allen, now busy overseeing two other series, and putting together presentations for more, was bound to be less attentive.

Al Gail said, "It was pretty much, after a while, like a well-oiled machine. We all knew what we had to do. We all knew we had to have scripts in on time. We couldn't miss an airdate. And you had the pressure of doing that. You were always behind, and it was a situation I understood that's still going on today; they're always behind on scripts. And then, once you get the script, then the stage [crew] will say, 'Hey, we're short here; come down, we need four pages; we need three minutes, or [it's] too long, and they'd say, 'Come down, we're running over another day; cut some of the script.' So, you had that pressure going on all the time. And, to illustrate the pressure involved in television, is that every story editor who worked on all of our shows, none of them are alive, unfortunately, except me. And they all died fairly young. It was just too much pressure. Sad, but that's television." [1]

7.1

"Monster from the Inferno" (Episode 59)

(Prod. No 9201; first aired on Sunday, September 18, 1966)
Written by Rik Vollaerts
Directed by Harry Harris
Produced by Irwin Allen and Bruce Fowler, Jr.; Story Editor: Sidney Marshall
Guest Star Arthur Hill
(Dick Tufeld provided the voice of "the brain")

From the *Voyage* show files (Irwin Allen papers collection):

Lindsay, a specialist in electronic energy, has been lent to the Seaview by the Navy to investigate the cause of a mass, 1000-mile blackout. While on an underwater reconnaissance, he discovers a brain-shaped rock which emits EEG waves strikingly similar to those of human cerebral tissue. The brain creature brings Lindsay under its influence and compels him to have it brought aboard the sub, where it takes over Crane also. Through him, it plans to use the Seaview as its body.[1]

Assessment:

Mark Phillips warned, "This episode has almost every story device that would later sink *Voyage* into repetition: arrogant aliens, possessed officers, nuclear reactor shenanigans, and the creation of last-minute devices to save the day ... and yet, this is one of my favorite third-year shows. The story line, a space-age *Donovan's Brain*, is freshly told, with a realistic looking monster.... Dick Tufeld is absolutely the right person to do the alien voice – threatening and petulant. Arthur Hill, an unlikely guest star for *Voyage* but an excellent actor, brings an authentic presence to the show as the ill-fated Lindsay. The rest of the cast, especially Richard Basehart, are unusually energized as they plunge through this action-packed story. Finally, a special note to composer Leith Stevens, who does a great score for this show, which is eerie and exciting." [2]

"An odd combination of budgetary upshots," Mike Bailey said. "Being a season premiere, Irwin Allen allotted an inordinate amount of money for the episode, in a year when *Voyage*'s budget had been cut [sic]. It enabled cool animated electrical effects, new underwater photography and a great monster brain. On the other hand, lights shining in people's faces, signaling their being taken over, was a cheap trick that ran rampant in later shows. All in all, 'Monster from the Inferno' looks good and is well directed, despite some really terrible dialogue of the 'we will destroy you if you do not serve us' variety attributed to the monster brain. At least Dick Tufeld's delivery is much more restrained than in some of the other voice-overs he provided for the series. The acting is top-notch and the music serves the episode well. Put simply, 'Monster from the Inferno' is not all that bad." [3]

Far be it from us to damn with such faint praise. We'll say it flat out: This episode has its silly, ineffective moments, which sabotage any chance of impressive thrills.

Regarding the "we will destroy you if you do not serve us" dialogue, it is excruciating. Here is a typical line from the episode: "Nothing can defeat us; no human can stop us from our ultimate destiny. I still have superior means at my command." Keep in mind, this is the "brain" talking to its slaves, who supposedly know all of this. And it talks, talks, talks this way throughout the episode. This is no superior thinker, though it might bore you into compliance.

Admiral Nelson is supposed to be the brainy type too, but watch as he pulls red-hot "rods" out of the nuclear reactor, without any form of shielding, or a protective environment suit, or even goggles! And Chief Sharkey is right next to him, equally underdressed for the party, pulling – and exposing himself to – those rods! (Maybe this inspired Mr. Spock to do the same in *Star Trek II*.)

We liked Dick Tufeld on *Lost in Space*. He helped make the Robot a unique character, and often carried the show when the writing didn't. Nevertheless, in this *Voyage*, we found his delivery as flat as the scripted lines.

As mentioned by Mike Bailey, each time the disembodied brain gives commands to those under its spell, a light is flashed in their face. This is so the viewing audience will know these individuals are being hyp-no-tized. One must wonder why director Harry Harris didn't show a lightbulb over the brain every time it got an idea.

Script:

Rik Vollaerts' 1ˢᵗ-Draft teleplay: April 18, 1966.
Vollaerts' 2ⁿᵈ-Draft teleplay: April 29.
Vollaerts' 3ʳᵈ-Draft teleplay: May 6, 1966.
Shooting Final teleplay (4ᵗʰ Draft): May 13.
Rev. Shooting Final teleplay (blue paper): May 23.
Page revisions (pink paper): May 26.
Page revisions (green paper): May 27.
Page revisions (yellow paper): June 14.
Page revisions (yellow paper): June 20.
Page revisions (beige paper): June 21.

Rik Vollaerts had contributed three scripts to the series before this (Season One's "The Amphibians" and "The Creature," and Season Two's "The Deadliest Game"), with two more assignments on the horizon.

After reading Vollaerts' first-draft script, Irwin Allen sent notes to his staff on April 21. As was customary with Allen's memos, he didn't talk about the story in general – its plot or theme – but, instead, focused on pacing and details concerning technical jargon and continuity.

> Page 9: Crane's last speech – find another way of saying "thing."

> Page 15 Seaview Lab: There should be a scene between Lindsay and the creature alone, before Nelson enters, in which the creature gives further instructions to Lindsay so that we will understand why Lindsay is disappointed at Nelson not touching it....

> Page 23: Nelson – first speech – he doesn't sound too bright.
>
> Page 24: Crane – last speech – sounds silly and unmanly. Nelson first speech – bad dialogue. Crane second speech – bad dialogue.
>
> Page 25: The author is confused about the control room layout. It is [now] on the same level as the observation nose and would be manned by a number of crew members....
>
> Page 27: A great deal of the dialogue seems childish and trite.
>
> Page 27 and 28: Lindsay asks too many unnecessary questions and the creature goes into too great detail to answer them.
>
> Page 28 and 29: Scene between Nelson and Kowalski – all of a sudden the brilliant scientist Nelson is fascinated by Kowalski's explanation of the brain's capabilities. This is absurd. So far, as of Page 28, the show has bogged down in a great deal of technical talk and it is hard to become involved with or interested in what is happening....
>
> From Page 30 on the script becomes very alive and interesting. [4]

Calvin Ward, of the ABC Department of Broadcasting and Practices, sent his notes on April 29.

> Caution that the texture and appearance of the brain, and the accompanying symphonic cacophony of sounds, is not too gruesome and frightening for "living-room" viewing, especially in the later scenes when it is enclosed in the tank, glowing and pulsating amid the bubbles, etc. The entire visual and audible effect of the brain throughout the script can be approved only on film.
>
> Page 7: Directions at the bottom of the page: It must not appear that Lindsay is being electrocuted. This caution

> applies throughout the script whenever the "brain effect" touches or acts upon any person.
>
> Page 22, Scene 36: Here, again, it must not appear that Morton is being electrocuted.
>
> Page 25: Crane's first line: delete "Hell." [5]

May 6: Two days after the third draft arrived, Allen fired off a memo to his staff, saying in part:

> The Teaser should be built up with action dialogue in order to make it at least 2 pages longer.
>
> Page 5, Scene 11: States that Lindsay lies unconsciously or dead on the ocean floor, but in Scene 13, Lindsay still floats lifelessly. Scene 13 should read that Lindsay's lifeless body slowly rises from the ocean floor and begins floating towards [the] the brain-like basalt rock.
>
> Act I is only 10 ½ pages long. It might be lengthened by enlarging Scene 27 or 29 as follows: Nelson's attitude towards Lindsay's behavior should become apparent. He should suggest to Lindsay that he needs rest and should leave the brain alone unless others are present. Lindsay would of course resent this vehemently and at first show his temper with Nelson, then, as though he had received a further message from the creature, his attitude should change noticeably to an over willingness to agree and be overly pleasant which half convinces Nelson that he will be his own self shortly.... [6]

May 15: After reading the fourth draft, Allen wrote:

> Why do Nelson and Sharkey don anti-radiation suits in order to burn their way into the lab when actually they should have had them on in the reactor room, as should all the others in that room. [7]

As the series progressed into its third season, Allen's order that the men in the reactor room wear anti-radiation suits was often ignored. Putting on protective gear would slow things down too much.

Production:
(Filmed June 20 – 28, 1966; 7 days)

Director **Harry Harris** had pleased Irwin Allen with his handling of three previous assignments (the second-season episodes "… And Five of Us Are Left," "Leviathan," and "Killers of the Deep"), as well as three episodes of *Lost in Space*, also during the 1965-66 TV season. Now he was given the honor of directing what everyone in the *Voyage* production offices knew would be the premiere episode of Season Three (first shot and the first to air).

As noted earlier, **Bruce Fowler Jr.** joined the series as associate producer, replacing Frank La Tourette and William Welch, who shared that post for Season Two. (Joseph Gantman and Allan Balter were at the controls for Season One.) Unlike the others, Fowler had no experience as a writer. This may be why the scripts for *Voyage* seemed a bit less fussed-over from this point forward – one less writer giving input. Fowler's job was specifically to serve as a "nuts and bolts" producer, to take the script written by others and realize the production. In that regard, he cannot be faulted – *Voyage* looked as good as ever.

Fowler had worked his way up in television, from assistant director (on series such as *Four Star Playhouse* and *Richard Diamond, Private Detective*), to production manager (*Law of the Plainsman, The Detectives, The Rifleman, Ensign O'Toole, The Lloyd Bridges Show*, and *Burke's Law*), to associate producer (*The Rogues, Honey West*, and, briefly, *The Wild, Wild West*). Fowler stayed at this post for the next two years, ensuring that *Voyage* retained the mark of a well-produced show. He would later be associate producer for *Land of the Giants*.

With a non-writer now in the associate-producer chair, the responsibility for keeping the scripts on track rested entirely with **Sidney Marshall**, remaining as story editor from Season Two, and, to a lesser degree, **Al Gail**, who had served as assistant story editor since the series' inception. The job of a story editor, besides working with the freelance writers to develop their stories and scripts, is to do the final rewriting after the freelancer has delivered an approved story outline (treatment) and two drafts of the teleplay. In most instances, with the story structure already worked out during the writing of the treatment and the "writer's drafts" of the script, this final phase of script polishing is intended to tidy up the dialogue, making sure the continuing characters speak and behave as they should, and address notes from the network regarding censorship and further notes from the production arm, usually to do with cost. And, of course, to address Irwin Allen's directives.

Concerning the look of the series, Winton C. Hoch had departed the series after two years' service to head up the camera and lighting crew for *The Time Tunnel*. The temporary cinematographer, for this episode and the next three to film, was **Carl E. Guthrie**. He had sat in for Hoch four previous times on the series, and proven his ability to maintain the look of the show, which had been set by Hoch.

Leith Stevens returned to *Voyage* to provide the music. The three-time Academy Award-nominated composer had scored some early Season Two episodes.

Arthur Hill was contracted for $2,500 for up to six days' work. He was 43 and, while having struggled as a younger performer, was now coming into his own as an in-demand character actor. He had fourth billing in Paul Newman's 1966 film *Harper*, and had been making the rounds as a guest player on popular series, such as *The Defenders*, *Slattery's People*, and *Mission: Impossible*. He would have his own series in the early 1970s with *Owen Marshall, Counselor at Law*.

Above: Lee Majors starred with Arthur Hiller in the early 1970s series *Owen Marshall, Counselor at Law*. Left: Richard Bull, from *Little House on the Prairie*.

Richard Bull returned as the Seaview's "Doc." He had played the part seven times in Season One, but only made it out for the final voyage of the second season. Now, Bull would be seen more regularly in the series, with 19 more turns in sickbay over the next two years.

As noted in the Assessment, **Dick Tufeld**, the voice of the Robot on *Lost in Space*, provided the voice of the brain.

William Self approved a budget of $162,576. Everyone knew it would cost more. The final numbers, however, were not present in the show files.

Filming began on Tuesday, June 21, 1966 for the first of seven days on Stage 10. Underwater footage (in the studio's Green Tank) was filmed by a second-unit team on July 8. A new shot depicted the Seaview hitting the ocean bottom nose first and scrapping along until it settles to a stop. We'd see it again in numerous episodes. [8]

This time, Morton gets an electrical zap in the circuitry room. The shocking effect would become fairly commonplace over the next two seasons to follow.

Director Harry Harris told interviewer Kevin Burns, "Richard did the show, and he bitched all the time about doing the show, but he did well on it and he was a pleasure to work with. I would read the script and I'd say, 'Wonder how he's going to play this scene, because it's kind of corny.' And I'd rehearse it and I'd listen to him and, by God, I believed every word he said. Richard Basehart made the whole thing come to life." [9]

From a 1966 interview by Dick Strout, David Hedison said, "[Richard] is such a marvelous actor. I think he's the best actor on television. And I don't think

I'm prejudiced. I've seen some of the shows he's done. I try to analyze it. I don't know what it is." [10]

When asked about the contemporaneous and continuing appeal of Irwin Allen's shows, director Harris said, "Because they kind of had a magic in them. He had a Disney in him. He had that monster running up and down the hall, and he knew how to get kids. I don't think *Voyage* was necessarily a kid's show, but it sure as hell appealed to kids, and *Lost in Space*, certainly, and *Giants*. And I think it was a mystery how you do these things. He did fantasy things. And it's kind of nice. It's escape. Even his stuff today is escape, from all the junk we watch to remind us of how crappy the world is. That's what we're seeing now, how horrible the world is today. And if you go look at his stuff, he wasn't sending any messages out. There were no drugs, there was no booze; it was just kind of fun. It was fun things to watch; scary things to watch. He never thought in terms of trying to get a message across to anybody – *never*. Just entertaining himself. Create for yourself, not for the audience. You create for yourself and present it to them. If they don't like your work, you're out. If they like your work, you're in. But you only do it for you. He was doing it for himself." [11]

Hedison said, "[Irwin's] got more enthusiasm than I've ever seen anyone have. He comes onto the set and he just reeks of enthusiasm, and he tells us about the stories coming up, and you just get excited along with him, because he does have some marvelous ideas, and he's so devoted to *Voyage* and all his other series." [12]

During a Twentieth Century-Fox interview conducted to promote the new season, Richard Basehart said, "When you start one of these things, you never know where you're going to go, and I'm amazed to find myself in this third year, and the ratings are holding up very well, and it looks like it may even go beyond that, for which there are rewards, as you well know."

Regarding working with David Hedison, Basehart stated, "It's a great joy to have someone you really like and enjoy working with. If there were antagonism there, or ill feeling, it would just be impossible to do the series. You just couldn't do it."

Of the sets, gadgets, and blinking lights, he declared, "Those flashing lights behind you can really kill you. We try to angle the shots so they don't absolutely take over. Give the actors a little bit of a chance…. There's some new things [this season] like a new escape hatch with real water in it so you can get *really* wet, and things like that."

When asked to comment on the imagination of Irwin Allen, Basehart chuckled, and then responded, "If it's an Irwin Allen production, it's way out." [13]

Release / Reaction:
(ABC premiere airdate: 9/18/66; network repeat broadcast: 6/18/67)

Who's Afraid of Virginia Woolf?, starring Elizabeth Taylor and Richard Burton, was selling more tickets at the movie houses than any other film. The Beatles' *Revolver* was the best-selling record album in the U.S. The top five songs on the radio were "Cherish," by the Association; "You Can't Hurry Love," by The Supremes; "Sunshine Superman," by Donovan; "Yellow Submarine," by the Beatles; and "Bus Stop," by the Hollies. And this was the week that *The Monkees* TV series premiered on NBC. They would soon be on the hit parade, too. Also new on TV: *It's About Time* (opposite *Voyage*), *Felony Squad, Iron Horse, Rat Patrol, The Girl from U.N.C.L.E., That Girl, The Green Hornet, Tarzan, Star Trek*, and *The Time Tunnel*.

Syndicated "TV Scout," in newspapers from coast to coast, said:

> *Voyage to the Bottom of the Sea* sails back for its third season, crew intact and Arthur Hill aboard as a guest. Hill is very good as an electronics expert who finds a huge brain which emits electronic waves and takes over his brain. Soon he is wandering like an automaton, taking the Creature's orders so the Creature can take over the Seaview and have creature comfort. Nothing new, but good special effects and some fun for fans of the genre. [14]

"TV Key," also syndicated to numerous newspapers, said:

> Sea monster epic about a massive brain in search of a body – namely, our hero's sub, the Seaview – kicks off the series' third season. The Monster's talking, pulsating brain, product of a clever special effects man, will intrigue the kids before exploding in the grand finale. Guest star Arthur Hill plays a second fiddle to the giant cranium. [15]

"Pit," writing for *Variety* on September 21, reviewed the season opener:

> Creator Irwin Allen's submarine fantasies have churned into a third network season, which leaves very little to say on the value medium. Allen's talents are probably better realized on the large screen bijou, but even on the mini-screen he manages to get an awful lot of production value passing in

review. And that's probably at least half of it, re, the click of *Voyage*.

> [*Voyage*] launched the new semester with a well-grooved sci-fi tale, about a brain-shaped super-intelligence that attempted to subjugate all hands aboard the Seaview sub. It made for some interesting moments, but generally was pretty mild stuff in the scarum league.
>
> *Voyage* has developed some comparatively good characterization, and its leads – Richard Basehart and David Hedison – are a pair of sympathetic types. Premiere seg guest-billed Arthur Hill in the rather flat role of a scientist "taken over" by the brain mass and made to do its bidding.... Direction by Harry Harris was workmanlike. Ditto the Rik Vollaerts teleplay. In the same Sunday top-of-the-schedule slot, *Voyage* looks to continue bon [strong]. [16]

"Daku," the critic for sister trade *Daily Variety*, supportive of *Voyage* in the past, had finally seen enough. For the trade's September 20 edition, he said:

> The brain-shaped mass with a superior intelligence mesmerizes men in obeying its commands, and takes over the submarine in *Voyage to the Bottom of the Sea*. That's the plot hook for the third season of what was once a unique sci-fi, futuristic series which had class and quality. Now that they've married the monster format-wise, it's a B-pictureish tv-version of the horde of monster pix turned out *en masse* years ago. Apparently, they are going all out for the juves by switching to monsters, but in so doing are apt to lose the oldsters (anyone over 15 in TV).
>
> Rik Vollaerts' script was an unbelievable, familiar piece of business about the "mass," ensconced in the sub, and with a power greater than man's, as the cliché goes.
>
> David Hedison and Richard Basehart did well with what little they had, but Michael Fox [sic: Dick Tufeld] – who wasn't seen – had the best part, because he was voice of the monster. Arthur Hill, Terry Becker, Bob Dowdell and Del Monroe offered okay support.

Trailer shows another monster "guester" next week. Last ABC-TV series to switch format entirely to weekly monsters was *The Outer Limits*, which didn't survive the change. Harry Harris' direction was so-so. [17]

A.C. Nielsen's overnight Trendex ratings ranked *Voyage* as a strong second place at 7 p.m., and part of a close three-way horse race from 7:30 to 8 p.m. [18]

Nielsen Trendex Rating Report, September 18, 1966.

(7 to 7:30 p.m.)	Rating:	Share:
ABC: *Voyage to the Bottom of the Sea*	11.0	31.8%
CBS: *Lassie*	**13.3**	**38.4%**
NBC: News	5.7	16.5%

(7:30 to 8 p.m.):	Rating:	Share:
ABC: *Voyage to the Bottom of the Sea*	13.2	30.9
CBS: *It's About Time*	**14.0**	**33.3**
NBC: *Walt Disney's Wonderful World...*	13.1	30.6

7.2
"Werewolf" (Episode 60)

(Prod. No. 9202; first aired on Sunday, September 25, 1966)
Written by Donn Mullalley
Directed by Justus Addiss
Produced by Irwin Allen and Bruce Fowler, Jr.; Story Editor Sidney Marshall
Guest Star Charles Aidman

From the *Voyage* show files (Irwin Allen papers collection):

> The Seaview is investigating a dangerous, radioactive volcano on a Pacific island, which, if allowed to blow, could cover the world with radio-active ash. Nelson believes the only way to prevent this is to implode the volcano inward with torpedoes. An advance party of two volcanologists, Witt and Hollis, are already on the island. They are attacked by what appears to be a wolf, but the radioactivity has changed it into a werewolf. Witt is killed, and Hollis is infected as the dying Witt's nails scratch his hand. After coming aboard the Seaview, Hollis changes into werewolf form and, in a struggle, infects Nelson before escaping back to the island. The only hope for Nelson is a vaccine made from Hollis' blood. Although the torpedoes are already set to go off, Crane follows Hollis to the island where he is attacked by the original werewolf.[1]

Assessment:

Doctor: "I'm sorry, Admiral, but I don't know how to cure a werewolf! Incantations and witches' broths were never my strong subject!"

A werewolf on *Voyage to the Bottom of the Sea*? Even for this show, the idea was way out. But several components work together to make this episode effective:

- Justus Addiss's direction includes slightly sped-up film when the werewolf leaps into action, and it actually looks good. It doesn't cheapen the effect by appearing that it was shot with an undercranked camera, but, instead, makes the actor in werewolf drag appear to be on amphetamines;
- The make-up is terrific (for a 1966 TV program);
- Richard Basehart and David Hedison lend their usual sincere approach, dignifying an otherwise silly escaped-monster tale;
- The characters of Chief Sharkey, Patterson, and "Doc" are used affectively to inject humor into the proceedings. Terry Becker (Sharkey) and Paul Trinka (Patterson) could have taken their "How long have you been serving aboard the Seaview" comedy routine on the road, and Richard Bull (Doc) is given many nuggets of witty dialogue. Case in point, when Admiral Nelson questions if all the fuss over some scratches on his hand is necessary, the Doc explains that it is, with a simple, "Major amputations always shake me up";
- The whole thing moves like a bat out of hell.

Mark Phillips was on the fence: "This episode is hurt by a lack of subtlety – the director does little to enhance or create suspense. The wolfman looks kind of cool at first but the more you see of it, the more it looks like a shaggy dog. The biggest detriment to the show is the one-dimensional Dr. Hollis. Charles Aidman is a good actor but he plays it with so little vulnerability that you don't get caught up in his tragedy. The sets are good, the action scenes play pretty well, and I like the scenes where Nelson is behind the cage, fighting off his own werewolf transformations, as Richard Bull (Doc) has a very worried look on his face. And if this had been an episode of *Star Trek: The Next Generation*, we would have had several long and boring scenes explaining how a wolf got trapped on a tropical island! *Voyage* offers no explanation, which is part of its charm."[2]

To Mark's point, Nelson shrugs off the potential hole in the plot with a mere, "Alright, so there's a wolf on the island; there's probably some explanation on how it got there." In an episode with this much madcap action, that's good enough for us.

Script:
Donn Mullally's story and 1st-draft teleplay approved on April 29, 1966.
Mullally's 2nd (final) draft approved May 25.
Shooting Final draft: May 11, 1966.
Fourth Rev. Shooting Final teleplay (green, yellow, and blue paper): June 28.
Page revisions (gold paper): July 6.
Page revisions (beige paper): July 8.

Donn Mullally had served as story editor on three series you probably never heard of – the crime drama *Boston Blackie* (1953), the comedy mystery *Mr. & Mrs. North* (1954), and the adventure drama *White Hunter* (1957-58). He also wrote numerous scripts for each, and was a regular contributor to many other series, such as the anthology *Your Favorite Story* (1954); the spirited comedy *Topper* (1954-55); the Western *Cisco Kid* (1953-56); the Red Scare drama *I Led 3 Lives* (1953-55); David Janssen's first series, *Richard Diamond, Private Detective* (1958-59); the Western *Laramie* (1959-61); the cop show *87th Precinct* (1961-62); and long-time TV hits like *Bonanza* (1964-66) and *The Virginian* (1962-67). Irwin Allen was happy to have Mullally, for this first of three *Voyage*s.

May 15, 1966: Irwin Allen's mind worked on a different level than most other sci-fi creator-producers. Someone like *Star Trek*'s Gene Roddenberry would worry that presenting a supernatural creature like a werewolf might diminish the credibility of his science-fiction drama. But Allen liked werewolves. He had put one in outer space the previous year, on *Lost in Space*, so why not in the middle of the Pacific, on *Voyage*? His notes for the script draft turned in on this date displayed no worries over the premise whatsoever, only over the details.

> P. 1: There should be an establishing shot of the Seaview – Ext. travelling underwater at top speed before we have an Int. shot. ...
>
> P. 23-A: Why is it necessary for Seaview to come to flank speed since it was laying just off the reef before the tidal wave? ...
>
> P. 28: Nelson – 1st speech: Says he'll be in the control room in five minutes and in the last speech on this page he says they'll be passing the sickbay on their way. This is a mistake as the

observation nose, in which they are at present, adjoins the control room. Perhaps this scene should take place in Nelson's lab or his cabin. In which case, the island could be viewed by means of T.V. monitor. [3]

In Allen's defense, he likely provided feedback concerning the actual story, the characters, and the theme, in his Method Meetings, when he and the staff gathered around the board table.

May 30: Mary Garbutt, of the ABC Department of Broadcast Standards and Practices, sent in her notes.

> The acceptability of this episode, on film, will depend very heavily on the wolf creature and the werewolf not being, by means of make-up, sounds or camera angles, too frightening for a family audience. Please, your special care on this.
>
> Please modify camera angles in following scenes where viewer, with children particularly in mind, is placed in the POV of the victim or possible victim:
>
> Pg 5, Sc 13; Pg 8, Sc B-30: the animal must not "spring through camera".
>
> Pg 20, Sc 77: Do not CU [Close Up] wolf baring fangs and snapping at camera.
>
> Pgs 7, 8, 15, 16, 39, 50, 51: Your usual care in seeing that the wounds, the men in death and dying, are in no way horrible or grotesque to view – Blood, etc. to a minimum.
>
> Pg 37, Sc 125: Standard caution on this fight – <u>No repeated</u> pounding of head against deck.
>
> Pg 38, Sc 130; Pg 39, Sc 131, etc: Here and generally, special caution on those wolf sounds – They must not be of a blood-curdling variety – Also, Kevin can shout but no scream. Sc 131: This TCU [Tight Close Up] of Hollis seems too frightening – modify or please be sure to have covering shot not in CU.
>
> Pg 61, Sc 201-205: Special care that this sequence is not brutal and shocking to view. Can only be approved on film. [4]

May 31: Lew Hunter, the only one at ABC concerned with the actual merits of the story, sent a letter to Sid Marshall, with cc to Irwin Allen and ABC's Harve Bennett.

> Dear Sid: Just finished reading the *Voyage* script by Donn Mullally, "Werewolf." It seems to me you're on the verge of another very good episode. Here are some thoughts I had after thinking about this show:
>
> 1. The script does not delve into Hollis's human reaction to his four changes into a werewolf. What goes on in his mind should be of enormous interest to the audience. I don't usually like stream of consciousness dialogue, but maybe this is a place it would work well. My main point is that I feel Hollis should be either totally aware of his situation, or totally unaware at a given point prior to his complete transformation. If we don't know the boundaries of his mental structure, we continually wonder, and this wonderment hampers the total impact of the episode.
> 2. I feel you should more clearly delineate the circumstances that cause Hollis to change into a werewolf. I assume it to be the rubbing of his hand but I'm not really sure. If we were more aware of the signs, you'd have the audience by the short hairs even more.
> 3. We're not given any clue throughout the script about the circumstances that cause Hollis to regain his normal body appearance. I assumed that a fresh kill was the reason, but in the first time on the island with Crane, he doesn't kill anyone but just changes into a normal Hollis for no reason. I think the audience will want their curiosity satisfied on this point.
> 4. Would it be right to make more of Nelson's change into a werewolf at the end? My thought is not to even see Nelson as a werewolf, but have the anti-serum shot at him in the restraining cage and we see only a hairy hand and hear a few groans. If we don't have the scene like this, I think our audience will feel cheated.
> 5. Since we are having four Hollis transformations in the show, I feel that we should not see a great deal of his

werewolf body in the first two instances. A little more of him should be viewed in the third occasion and full bore in the final change. I gathered by the directions in the script that this is what you have in mind. If my assumptions are right, I feel you are most correct in this building of the werewolf exposure.

6. For my money, you could do without the crewman with Witt at the beginning of the show. In most references to the poor dead Witt, the show character forgot about the poor dead crewman, Witt's companion, i.e., top of Page 11.
7. Page 37: Why does Hollis expose his wound to the live reactor? Apparently Hollis is trying to cure himself, but referring to my first point, I just don't know his posture as a rational human being at this stage as well as throughout the show.
8. Page 43: Would it be logical for Crane or Nelson to ask about Hollis's whereabouts at this point?
9. In the teaser, how about a line from Nelson or Crane that tells us that they are at the island investigating the potential danger in the volcanic disturbance? I think a factual statement would help lay any audience questions to rest here.
10. Last point: on Page 56. May I suggest "Frank Buck" or "Great Hunter" (no personal plug intended), instead of Mr. Daniel Boone. The thought of even subliminally pushing another network show makes my minority ABC stockholder's heart quiver.

I hope these thoughts are helpful to you because, if they can be put to rest, I think you've got another excellent show in the hopper. [5]

Hunter's suggestions that viewers get a glimpse into a character's thoughts thoughts were ignored.

Interviewed for this book, and regarding "Werewolf," Hunter said, "I do remember that I wanted to see him with more remorse over becoming a werewolf. But it was impossible for Irwin to get subtlety. He did not have an inkling of what that word was. He wanted to show the monster-of-the-week right up front. He felt that was one of the things that made him successful, as 'the master of disaster,' is that he wanted to show the danger right away. But that turned out to be a good episode, because it scared the shit out of most people." [6]

Production:
(Filmed June 29 through July 8, 1966; 7 days)

William Self approved a budget of $166,298.

Justus Addiss was given his third directing assignment on *Voyage*, following "Graveyard of Fear" and "The Monster's Web." He had 13 more.

This was **Charles Aidman**'s only time working for Irwin Allen, but the much-in-demand actor certainly made time for nearly every other producer in town. In a 40-year career with nearly two hundred screen appearances, Aidman was especially popular at *Have Gun – Will Travel*, *Gunsmoke*, *Wagon Train*, *Run for Your Life*, *The Bold Ones*, *Quincy, M.E.*, and *The Wild, Wild West*, in which he appeared three or more times in each. Aidman also took two trips into the original *The Twilight Zone*, and, later, in place of Rod Serling, he narrated the mid-1980's remake. He was 41 at the time of his only *Voyage*.

Charles Aidman in "And When the Sky Was Opened," a 1959 episode of *The Twilight Zone*.

Academy Award-winning composer **Lennie Hayton** provided the score, on the heels of four episodes from Season Two, including "… And Five of Us Are Left" and "The Phantom Strikes."

Days 1, 2 and 3: Filming began on Wednesday, June 29, 1966, for the first of three days on Stage 10, covering the Seaview sets.

Day 4: Monday was the July 4th holiday. Cast and crew returned to work on Tuesday for work on Stage B, for the jungle sets, then out onto the Moat on the backlot, for the beach and rocky areas, filming after dark until 10:55 p.m.

Actor George Robotham told interviewers Mark Phillips and Frank Garcia, "The guy who doubled for Charles Aidman's wolfman character turned out to be a real loony. He was a half-assed stuntman who wanted to be an actor.

The guy really believed he was a wolf. He got caught up in the tragedy of this poor guy trapped with a wolf's head. He was obsessed with establishing the wolfman's motivation." [7]

Maybe he'd read Lew Hunter's memos? As for the stuntman, well …

Robotham added, "I doubled for David Hedison in one scene, and I went up on a ledge with the werewolf guy. There's an earthquake, and we're both supposed to fall off the cliff. This guy was so busy acting like a wolf, he wouldn't fall off the ledge. I pretended to stumble and I shoved him off. Unfortunately, he landed on my landing pads. I had nowhere to fall. Luckily, I missed the rocks and landed safely." [8]

Day 5: Wednesday was again spent on Stage B for more simulated nighttime scenes in the jungle areas, and sequences filmed on and around the water tank which provided for the beach area. The company then moved out to the backlot Moat area to shoot on the cliffs, in real night, filming until 10:50 p.m.

Day 6: Thursday was spent on Stage B, finishing up the island filming.

Day 7: It took an unplanned seventh day of production to finish the episode. They were back on Stage 10, picking up interior Seaview sequences. Wrap time came at 7 p.m. [9]

With seven days of filming, you can be sure it exceeded that 166 grand which had been allocated.

Release / Reaction:

(ABC premiere airdate: 9/25/66; network repeat broadcast: 4/30/67)

Who's Afraid of Virginia Woolf? was the hottest ticket at the movie houses; "Cherish," by the Association, was the song America was cherishing the most; the Beatles had the top-selling album in the nation, with *Revolver*; Barbara Eden, of *I Dream of Jeannie*, had the cover to *TV Guide*.

For his syndicated "Show Beat" entertainment column, Dick Kleiner spoke with David Hedison, then reported:

> We are moving into the third year of ABC's *Voyage to the Bottom of the Sea*, which is perfectly all right with David Hedison. "I bought the suit and so I'll wear the jacket," is the way he puts it. He means that he agreed to do the show, so he'll ride with it as long as it goes. [10]

According to *Daily Variety* on September 29, four days after the airing of "Werewolf," Irwin Allen, with three series running concurrently (*Voyage, Lost in*

Space and *The Time Tunnel*) was already cooking up two more – "The Spirit" and "Journey to the Center of the Earth." His formula for success: monsters. He said, "Monsters give us our highest ratings."

Allen was hoping to get back into making movies, too. He said, "We'll have made 90 TV shows in seven months, and take 12 months for one feature film. But I'll use everything I learned, dollar-wise, from TV for the feature." [11]

It wasn't to be … at least, not until 1972's *The Poseidon Adventure*. The feature Allen had in mind in 1966 didn't happen, nor the two projected TV series, although he was able to get an animated version of *Journey to the Center of the Earth* on to ABC for its Saturday morning schedule. *The Time Tunnel* would fail to get a second season. But *Land of the Giants* was in Allen's immediate future.

Syndicated "TV Scout" sarcastically stated:

> It's another humdrum day for the men of the Seaview. All they have to contend with is a South Pacific island with a volcano threatening to erupt with radioactive ash, and the island "resident," a wolf, whose bite turns Charles Aidman into a werewolf. Ho, hum. [12]

October 9, 1966: TV critic Ken Murphy wrote,

> *Voyage* never deals with small-scale irritations. Their constant problems are cataclysmatic [sic]. For a recent example, we have a volcano. It looks like a kind of bush league volcano, but is it? No, for this lonely Vesuvius is threatening momentarily to blow up and spray radioactive ash all over the globe and vicinity, thus doing away with men, women, children and even television performers. Well, that isn't going to daunt our intrepid under-water warriors. All they have to do is induce the volcano to implode, thereby forcing it to choke on its own poison.
>
> If you don't regard that as of enough troubles for a little band of men, there is interwoven into the plot a werewolf. The scientists aboard the Seaview quickly diagnose blood from the cut of a rabies virus, but far more dismaying…. Some vaccine is needed….
>
> With the barest kind of a bow to Guy Endore's classic statement of the myth, our heroes are soon struggling through the vegetation of the volcano island looking for the

mad scientist – or a wolf. The setting resembles closely that of a Polynesian Room of any clip joint. They dispose of the werewolf, and get the vaccine to the admiral. He is acting mad, but that wouldn't generate much attention, except that he is getting hair on the back of his hands, alarming under the circumstances. He recovers in time to see the volcano implode and the world saved. [13]

A.C. Nielsen 30-Market Survey (September 25, 1966): [14]

(7 – 7:30 p.m.)	Rating:	Share:
ABC: *Voyage to the Bottom of the Sea*	**19.7**	**40.9%**
CBS: *Lassie*	16.1	33.1%
NBC: Bell Telephone	4.8	9.9%

(7:30 – 8 p.m.):		
ABC: *Voyage to the Bottom of the Sea*	**24.7**	**42.4%**
CBS: *It's About Time*	15.9	27.3%
NBC: *Walt Disney*	11.6	19.9%

Nielsen ranked all the prime-time shows, with a report in *Broadcasting* on October 17, 1966. The top-rated sci-fi series on any of the three networks was *Star Trek*, at No. 33 out of 92 prime-time shows. *Lost in Space* was No. 42. *Voyage to the Bottom of the Sea* was No. 64. *The Time Tunnel* was at No. 66. [15]

7.3

"Day of Evil" (Episode 61)

(Prod. No. 9203; first aired Sunday, October 23, 1966)
Written by William Welch
Directed by Jerry Hopper
Produced by Irwin Allen and Bruce Fowler, Jr.; Story Editor: Sidney Marshall

From the *Voyage* show files (Irwin Allen papers collection):

> Alien beings plan to cause a nuclear holocaust on Earth, after which they will take over the world themselves. To accomplish this, one of these beings assumes the form of Admiral Nelson, enters the Seaview and sabotages the nuclear power system. To save the crew, Crane shuts down the reactor, receiving a fatal dose of radiation while doing so. The Alien's power saves Crane's life, and it tries to bargain with Nelson to fire a nuclear missile in return into the massed Pacific Fleet with which they are about to rendezvous. Nelson's resistance is too strong so it tries to use Crane, taking on the appearance of both men to confuse them and the crew. [1]

Assessment:

The more you see it, and the more you know about it, the better "Day of Evil" gets.

Mark Phillips said, "As a kid, I was dismayed that the alien economically assumes the shape of Nelson or Crane ('What, no monster makeup!'). But the episode once again proves just how good the *Voyage* regulars were. There's an intense scene between Nelson and Crane that plays really well and you feel sorry for Patterson's impending doom." [2]

Mike Bailey revealed, "My original review started like this: 'A convoluted walkabout that in the end has no point other than to save budget.' Upon reviewing this episode, I've changed my opinion. Yes, it's a budged saver, but 'Day of Evil' is very well done. ... William Welch's script plays out remarkably intelligently, despite the fact that the aliens – typically – want all us humans dead. The acting is good. In fact, very good. It's interesting to see Nelson posed against himself as a laughing, sneering bastard who just wants to destroy the whole planet. Incidentally, the ship that crashes into the ocean at the beginning of the episode is Klaatu's vehicle from *The Day the Earth Stood Still*. Somehow, I can't help but think Klaatu might not have approved." [3]

The acting throughout is impressive. Basehart's interpretation of the alien may be his best performance in the series; the mad gleam in his eye, the sheer sinister joy he conveys. Watching Basehart (as the alien) and Basehart (as Nelson) act opposite himself is a delight. Kudos to Hedison, Terry Becker, Richard Bull, and Paul Trinka. The script gives each an excellent role to play, and no one disappoints.

Evil personified. Look deep into the eyes. An acting triumph for Basehart.

The story, as originally written, was not about aliens from another planet wanting to destroy mankind, but about the Devil wanting to use the Seaview to start World War III. The story behind the story, and why the Devil was changed to an extraterrestrial, follows.

Script:
Welch's story, 1ˢᵗ- and 2ⁿᵈ-draft teleplays approved April 7, 1966.
Shooting Final teleplay: April 29.
2ⁿᵈ Rev. Shooting Final teleplay (pink paper): June 10.
Page revisions (green paper): July 7.
Page revisions (yellow paper): July 12.

William Welch was no longer listed as an associate producer on the series, or as story editor. Irwin Allen wanted Welch to devote all his time to writing original teleplays. His latest was a story all were very excited about – the crew of the Seaview encounter a stranger who turns out to be the Devil. The Devil can take on the appearance of anyone, and does indeed appear to be Admiral Nelson and Captain Crane, using their likenesses to realize an agenda to start a nuclear war. It was a frightening concept which merged religious beliefs and the fears over the dangers of a nuclear doomsday that were so prevalent in the 1960s.

April 30, 1966: Irwin Allen approved William Welch's story treatment and 1ˢᵗ- and 2ⁿᵈ-draft teleplays in fast order, knowing that Welch was available for more rewriting, with the help of story editors Sidney Marshall and Al Gail. After reading what was in a sense the third draft of the script, Allen presented his notes to the staff. For a change, his comments had much to do with story structure, characterization, and theme.

> ... Page 21, Scene 41: It is not clear why Patterson acknowledges a greeting from the Doc [who is really the Devil]. Shouldn't we see the stranger materialize out of the fog so as to avoid confusing the audience....
>
> Page 57, Scene 140: It seems strange that the stranger should say that Nelson has become a dangerous maniac in as much as he is the one who wants the total destruction of mankind.
>
> The same weaknesses are present in this version as were in the last.
> 1. Neither Nelson or Crane could ever be persuaded, even under penalty of death, to push the button.
> 2. Stranger's speech #1 on Page 47 is the weak link as it states that the devil can only accomplish his ends

through the willful act of some individual. This must be changed so that what the devil says on Page 49, about having power over Nelson because of their bargain, is brought out sooner. Then more time can be spent on their battle of wills, which should be built up.

3. Crane must seal his bargain with the Devil before he is told what it is the Devil wants him to do, so that Crane's inability to resist will be due to the fact that the Devil now believes he has full control over Crane's will, as he did with Nelson. In Crane's case, the Devil feels surer of success because of Crane's weakened state due to the pain he has undergone (as stated on Page 61, Scene 150).

4. Page 57: The stranger interrupts his own mission just to have Nelson put in the brig. This action has nothing to do with the story. Surely the Devil is not afraid of Nelson. It is also not in keeping with his threats to Nelson that he would let Crane die before his eyes in great agony. What happened to this idea? In any case, these scenes in which the Devil gives orders for Nelson's arrest should precede his scenes with Crane on Pages 55, 56 and 57.

5. The tag is a big letdown. Just because Nelson succeeded in destroying one missile hardly seems reason enough for the Devil to give in. This is why the time element suggested in previous notes is so important. Both the Devil and Nelson must be aware that at a given time the Devil's powers will run out. This could also be the reason the Devil wants Nelson locked up and safely put out of the way. This tag should be a continuation of the result of the firing of the missile as well as the disappearance of the Devil. It should end with a request from Fail Safe headquarters for an explanation of the fired missile. Nelson and Crane would be recovering from their ordeal and attempting to convince themselves that what they went through didn't really happen when the call from headquarters comes over the speaker. The show should end on their amazed realization that it did indeed happen but just how are they ever going to explain it to the authorities. They'll just have to say there was a malfunction. [4]

Irwin Allen's *Voyage* was well on its way to going where no show had gone before. Not even Gene Roddenberry's *Star Trek*, which was now in production and would soon be breaking network taboos weekly on NBC, had succeeded in telling a story about the devil. And it's not because they didn't try. For now, it was looking as though Irwin Allen would chart this new territory alone.

June 2: The notes from ABC arrived. They were the standard concerns, all easily addressed. Mary Garbutt of Broadcast Standards and Practices asked of Allen and staff:

> Your Usual Care in seeing that the "burned marks" are not too graphic, and the processed Nelson and Crane are not "too angry" for family viewing – also caution on the accompanying cries…. In context with the Almighty, please modify "make a deal"…. Caution that Crane's spasms of pain and writhing are not "over-done". [5]

But, while Standards and Practices was focusing more on specific lines of dialogue and moments of physical action, other departments at the network were having conversations on a deeper level. Did ABC really want to have a program in which the Devil tries to start a nuclear war on Earth … during the family viewing hour of 7 to 8 p.m. … on the Sabbath?

At ABC, on June 8, Leonard Goldberg, Lew Hunter and Vice President in Charge of Programs Harve Bennett came to a decision, and then Bennett was elected to write to Irwin Allen. Bennett, who would later become a producer and even make a *Star Trek* movie with the premise of the Enterprise encountering God (or the Devil pretending to be God), wrote:

> Dear Irwin: We have read "Day of Evil" and I must confess to you I share the same deep concerns that I expressed to you after reading the springboard. While I applaud the ingeniousness of using The Devil, I feel strongly that the mystical and religious overtones of this character are far too atypical for the show. I know you would be the first to agree that *Voyage*, while it contains marvelous science fiction elements, should not be reminiscent of *One Step Beyond*, but this is, I believe, the effect of using The Devil character.
>
> I promised you I would read the material objectively in script form, and I believe I have done so. But in the interest of

keeping *Voyage* the wonderful and unique show that is it, may I urge you not to film this episode. ... [6]

Allen called Bennett the following morning. Later in the day, Bennett wrote again to Allen, saying:

> Thank you for the helpful and creative telephone conversation of today and for your confirming letter regarding "Day of Evil." The idea of changing the "Stranger" into a character who has originated from outer space rather than being the Devil incarnate does make, if you will pardon the pun, all the difference in the world. I believe that regular fans of *Voyage* will be much more ready to accept the magical powers of the character on this basis, and I think the story will tell itself with even greater interest. Thank you for the promptness of your response and your understanding of my concerns about this show. I look forward to the revised script with the character change. [7]

Lew Hunter said, "Irwin had fear, if only subtly, which was the fear of having his shows cancelled. And that's why he probably gave ABC, and me, too, a little bit more respect than we might have deserved, because he wanted us to be his advocates when we were in programming meetings." [8]

The network also requested that *Voyage* use a futuristic date – 1980, this time – since a nuclear holocaust was in the works. Better 1980 than 1966!

Regardless, the script, although not improved by the changes, still shines, and is brought to life by the fine cast. It is easy to see what was originally intended. Forget about the tagged-on stock footage in the Teaser of the flying saucer (which we had seen before, anyway – not just in *The Day the Earth Stood Still*, but in Season One's "The Sky Is Falling"). Forget the few line changes, when "the stranger" says he's from another planet, instead of identifying himself as the Devil; and the climax, in which the alien says he is being "recalled," instead of the Devil saying he is being "cast out" – and you will have a clear idea of what would have played out over the airwaves if ABC hadn't chickened out.

We may have TV series now with titles like *Lucifer*, but in 1966 this was television at its riskiest ... at 7 p.m., on the ABC-TV network.

Production:
(Filmed July 11 – 18, 1966; 6 days)

The budget, approved by William Self, was for $158,937.

Filming began Monday, July 11, 1966 for the first of six days on Stage 10. The "bottle shows" were the easy ones. Days 1 and 2 had the company covering the

Captain Crane (right) looks into the face of evil (above). A brilliant use of acting subtleties used by Hedison, in facial expression, body posture, and, especially, the eyes.

scenes written for the Control Room and Observation Nose. Day 3 was spent in the Admiral's Cabin. Day 4 brought the company into Corridors 1, 2 and 3, as well as Sick Bay. Day 5 was used to finish work in Sick Bay, then move on to the Corridor at the Reactor Room, then inside the Reactor Room. Day 6 took care of the scenes in the Missile Room.

The only complaint Irwin Allen had was that the work should have been done in five days, not six.

David Hedison had a complaint, too. "It [the show] started very well the first couple of years," Hedison said. "Then it went downhill, I think, in the third and fourth year. They made it more for kids. I think the saving grace was that some of the acting was so good and my relationship with Basehart was terrific. We had a great rapport." [9]

Stories such as this, which let the heroic leads play evil parts, also no doubt provided a welcome chance to stretch their acting muscles.

Release / Reaction:
(ABC premiere airdate: 10/23/66; network repeat broadcast: 5/7/67)

Promotional card with original artwork sent by Irwin Allen's office to newspapers and ABC affiliates across America. The tease read: "The destruction of the world by nuclear holocaust is threatened by an invader from outer space! Admiral Nelson and Captain Crane struggle desperately to combat the mysterious forces of the devilish invader who seeks to destroy the world through the possession of their minds and bodies!"

The threat in this episode, the start of a nuclear war, was a very real concern in October 1966 when "Day of Evil" first aired on ABC. In the fall of that year, President Lyndon Baines Johnson sent bombers north of the Demilitarized Zone in Vietnam. Soon China, the USSR, and America conducted rounds of nuclear tests, each seeking to intimidate one another. And the Devil was having a good day.

Meanwhile, on a lighter note, Elvis Presley's *Spinout* was the big moneymaker in the movie houses. The top three songs on the radio were "96 Tears" by Question Mark and the Mysterians, "Last Train to Clarksville" by the Monkees, and "Reach Out, I'll Be There" by the Four Tops. Top-selling album honors went to the Supremes, with *Supremes A' Go-Go,* and the Beatles, with *Revolver.*

The staff of "TV Scout" kept their opinions to themselves, merely writing:

> Wispy smoke from the Seaview's atomic reactor causes a lot of trouble on *Voyage to the Bottom of the Sea*. The smoke, it seems, can take the form of any man and chooses, in turn, to

look like evil versions of Richard Basehart and David Hedison. All because it is an alien being and wants to start an atomic war. Before this one is over, Hedison has made the supreme sacrifice to save his crew. [10]

Steven H. Scheuer's "TV Key" let this one pass without mention. A.C. Nielsen 30-Market ratings report for October 23, 1966: [11]

(7 – 7:30 P.M.)	Rating:	Share:
ABC: *Voyage to the Bottom of the Sea*	**20.9**	**39.9%**
CBS: *Lassie*	18.4	35.1%
NBC: *Bell Telephone Hour*	5.5	10.5%

(7:30 – 8 P.M.):		
ABC: *Voyage to the Bottom of the Sea*	**22.1**	**40.0%**
CBS: *It's About Time*	14.0	25.4%
NBC: *Walt Disney*	12.7	23.0%

Devil or angel … or alien, *Voyage* was still tops in the ratings, and with a 40 share!

7.4

"Night of Terror" (Episode 62)
(Prod. No. 9204; first aired on Sunday, October 9, 1966)
Written by Robert Bloomfield
Directed by Justus Addiss
Produced by Irwin Allen and Bruce Fowler, Jr.; Story Editor: Sidney Marshall
Guest Star Henry Jones

From the *Voyage* show files (Irwin Allen papers collection):

Nelson, Sharkey and Sprague, a mineralogist, are exploring underwater for new metals when a tidal wave detaches the diving bell they are in from the Seaview. The wave deposits the bell on an island where they are threatened by a gigantic lizard, descendant of the prehistoric dinosaurs, and a strange gas in the island's mists causes hallucinations. They finally manage to restore communications with the Seaview, and Crane and the flying sub leave to rescue them while the stranded men try to find a beach. Sprague, thinking he sees a pirate, follows him to an imaginary treasure and is entrapped in quicksand, endangering the lives of the others. [1]

Assessment:

This episode, whose working title was "The Real and the Unreal," plays like an acid trip. Its theme is how we determine what is real. Some people get paranoid when on drugs; some get violent; some get mellow; and some become downright giddy. We see all these reactions played out, including a somewhat light approach, something different for *Voyage*.

Mark Phillips said, "An early casting memo for this episode suggests Martin Sheen for the role as the geologist. He would have done better than Henry Jones' annoying Dr. Sprague, whose "Dr. Smith" antics wear thin after a while. Otherwise, the story is fairly interesting, mainly due to the remarkable special effects, including the tidal wave and the giant lizard destroying the diving bell and threatening Nelson on a beach. To put the old misinformation to rest, the lizard sequences are all new. There's not a stitch borrowed from Irwin Allen's *The Lost World*." [2]

From Mike Bailey: "Loaded with great L.B. Abbott lizard/dinosaur visuals, the effectiveness of this episode is dragged down by slow direction… In spite of the fact that the outing is titled 'Night of Terror," it is played lightly, almost like a comedy in many places – certainly in those scenes with Dr. Sprague and the ghostly pirate. The acting style of Henry Jones tends to put a smarmy kind of gloss on events which worked with his other *Voyage* character, Pem [in 1967's upcoming 'A Time to Die' and 1968's 'No Way Back'], but not here. In spite of all these negatives, it's worth watching for the great special effects, which as Mark points out, were all (with the exception of the tidal wave…) created for this episode." [3]

By the time you get to the end of this episode, you may agree with the Grateful Dead. "What a long, strange trip it's been."

Script:

Robert Bloomfield's writers contract: April 27, 1966.
Bloomfield's story & 1st-draft teleplay, "Spanish Gold," approved May 26.
Bloomfield's 2nd (and final) draft teleplay approved on June 15.
Shooting Final teleplay (now titled "The Real and the Unreal"): July 1.
2nd Rev. Shooting Final (on green paper): July 15.
Page revisions (on yellow paper): July 18.

Writer **Robert Bloomfield** recalled, "Fantasy and SF were never my genres, so how I came to write that is a mystery." [4]

Bloomfield felt more comfortable with mysteries, Westerns, and family fare. He'd had multiple script assignments on TV's *Lassie*, *Zorro*, *Perry Mason*, *Rawhide*, and *Daniel Boone*. He was also a playwright (*Portrait of Murder*), a novelist (*When Strangers Meet*) and a screenwriter (with 1961's B-film, *Fear No More*). "Night of Terror" (or "Spanish Gold," as it was originally called, then a further change to "The Real and the Unreal") would be the writer's only *Voyage* assignment, and his only time working for Irwin Allen.

In an early draft, instead of a giant lizard chasing Nelson and Chief Sharkey, the writer called for a crocodile. Script Editor Sidney Marshall wrote to Irwin Allen:

> I suggest we replace the crocodile with a live iguana. This eliminates the danger and difficulty of working with the larger animal and, at the same time, the iguana will give us a monster that is more unique and bizarre in appearance. [5]

ABC's Lew Hunter, reading the same script draft, had other concerns. He wrote to Sid Marshall on June 20, with cc to Irwin Allen and ABC exec Harve Bennett:

> I found the script to be very fascinating and loaded with exciting action. After reading it, many questions as to "why" things happened cropped up in my mind. I'm sure we agree that at the end of every *Voyage*, we, as an audience, should be privy to the knowledge of what the "monster" can do as well as why the "monster" exists. If we aren't aware of this information, we are consciously or sub-consciously bothered by the show's believability. So, with this in mind, I feel that these questions should be answered either completely, or more fully through dialogue or visuals.
> 1. Why is the crocodile real? We shouldn't have the audience for a second think that this creature is a hallucination. Perhaps, Nelson should give a more complete reason as to how the crocodile might have existed on the island when it was submerged below the sea.
> 2. I know the sword and the money are real, but the "mint condition" line threw me off track. It led me to believe that they had been planted by the pirate and it was doubly confusing when we see hallucinary [sic] treasures through Sprague's eyes. Perhaps, if they were extremely

rusty, we could better differentiate them from the hallucinations.
3. I'd like to see a line from Nelson that we as an audience can accept as fact regarding why the hallucinations appear and disappear at given moments within the character's mind.
4. Why isn't Crane affected by hallucinations?
5. Assuming that the swirling mist causes the hallucinations, why does Kowalski, inside the sealed "flying sub," get them....

... If we can get clarification on the first five points I raised, you should have another excellent episode. [6]

Irwin Allen, ever the literalist, tabulated "The Real and the Unreal":

Page 16, Scene 63: "Lee" is an hallucination of Nelson's mind.
Page 18, Scenes 72-73-74: Buccaneer is an hallucination of Sprague's' mind.
Page 29, Scene 110: Skeleton and sword are real.
Page 30, Scenes 111-112: Doubloon is real.
Page 31, Scene 116: Man creature – unreal.
Page 39 + 48: Chest + all jewels held out to Sprague are unreal.
Page 44: Mountain peak seen by Kowalski is unreal; so is one seen by Crane, P. 49.
Page 52: Mantra Ray – is real. [7]

The Mantra Ray, however, did not survive further rewriting.

Mary Garbutt, of ABC's Broadcast Standards and Practices, in two separate memos, wrote:

Pg 14, Sc A-56: In this added scene, no cuts, of course, of diver being actually attacked by shark – the man must be "swimming free." ...

Your usual care in seeing that the crocodile and the creature are not visually, or through sounds and camera angles, too frightening for family viewing. Special caution Pg 31, Sc 117 – As described, it seems too much. Can only be approved on film.

Pg 15, Sc 60: Of course, blood to a minimum here.

Pg 28, Sc 110: Please no CU [Close Up] of the skeleton. ...

Pg 31, Sc 117: Repeated caution that this creature is not too frightening for family viewing. ...

Pgs 40, 41, etc.: Standard caution on this quicksand sequence. Noted that Sprague does not "go in" much deeper than the waist. [8]

Did they cool the action down enough to properly address Mary Garbutt's concerns, and clear things up enough to satisfy those of Lew Hunter? Watch the episode and see what you think.

Production:
(Filmed July 19 – 26, 1966; 6 days)

This was **Justus Addiss'** fourth of 16 directing assignments with *Voyage*.

Henry Jones was paid $2,500 to play Sprague. He was 53 and had appeared in dozens of popular plays on Broadway between 1931 and 1960. During those years, he often worked in TV anthology series, with five turns on *Studio One*, eleven on *Kraft Theatre*, four on *Robert Montgomery Presents*, and five episodes of *Alfred Hitchcock Presents*. He was a regular on the 1963-64 series *Channing*, as the dean of the fictional Channing College which served as the series setting. The was Jones' first of three appearances on *Voyage* (continuing with two turns as Mr. Pem, as noted earlier). Irwin Allen would also cast him as Jeremiah Smith, kin to Dr. Zachary Smith, in "The Curse of Cousin Smith" on *Lost in Space*.

William Self set the budget at $161,528.

Filming began on Tuesday, July 19, 1966 for the first of five days on Stage B where they had prepared sets for "Int. & Ext. Diving Bell," "Ext. Jungle," "Ext. Quick Sand Area," "Ext. Rocky Cove & Cave" and "Ext. Boulders & Rocky Beach."

What helps the shenanigans on the island work is the chemistry and playful interplay between Richard Basehart and Terry Becker. The two actors had struck gold when asked to improvise for a few minutes during the filming of Season Two's "Terror on Dinosaur Island," to pad an episode which was timing out short. That padding became the best part of the show. So, Basehart and Becker were invited to inject a bit of their routine into this outing – which again featured a jungle setting and a giant, prowling lizard. We feel that the scenes between Nelson and Sharkey are highlights of the episode.

On Tuesday, July 26, the sixth day of production, the company worked on Stage 10 for the Seaview's Control Room and the interior of the Flying Sub. As with nearly every day of filming on *Voyage*, Irwin Allen was never far away. [9]

David Hedison remembered Allen's frequent visits to the set … and a brand of cologne that was new on the market beginning in 1966. He said, "I'll tell you, I think of Aramis, the cologne, because he [Allen] used to come on the set of *Voyage to the Bottom of the Sea*, and I always knew he was there because I smelled Aramis! And I cannot stand that smell to this day. It terrifies me. And that's what I think of Irwin." [10]

357

Release / Reaction:
(ABC premiere airdate: 10/9/66; network repeat broadcast: 4/9/67)

Valley of the Dolls, by Jacqueline Susann, was at the top of *The New York Times* Best Seller list. The top-grossing movie across America was *The Bible: In the Beginning*, directed by John Huston. *Revolver*, by the Beatles, was still the best-selling album. And "Reach Out, I'll Be There," by the Four Tops, was again the song getting the most radio play. The median family income was $7,000 per year. Richard Basehart, on the other hand, was getting $9,000 per episode during *Voyage*'s third season. The average price of a house in America was $14,200. In Los Angeles, it was closer to $23,000.

Neither the syndicated "TV Scout" nor "TV Key" bothered to review this episode. Nor did *Variety* or the other trades. Regardless, it won its time slot.

Nielsen 30-Market ratings report for October 9, 1966: [11]

(7 – 7:30 p.m.)	Rating:	Share:
ABC: *Voyage to the Bottom of the Sea*	**17.3**	**34.9%**
CBS: *Lassie*	15.5	31.3%
NBC: AFL Football Game	6.8	13.7%
(7:30 – 8 p.m.):		
ABC: *Voyage to the Bottom of the Sea*	**17.2**	**32.4%**
CBS: *It's About Time*	14.4	27.1%
NBC: *Walt Disney*	12.7	23.9%

7.5

"The Day the World Ended" (Episode 63)

(Prod. No. 9205; first aired on Sunday, October 2, 1966)
Written by William Welch
Directed by Jerry Hopper
Produced by Irwin Allen and Bruce Fowler, Jr.; Story Editor: Sidney Marshall
Guest Star Skip Homeier

From the *Voyage* show files (Irwin Allen papers collection):

> Strange things happen shortly after Senator Laird comes aboard the Seaview on an inspection tour. All forms of ocean life vanish. The Seaview cannot get radio contact with any other ship or sub. Nelson, Sharkey and Laird take off in the flying sub and find Washington and New York deserted cities. No living person can be seen. Aboard the Seaview, Crane decides the trouble must be caused by the X-4, a new invention of Nelson's that can locate every nuclear sub in the world. After giving orders to dismantle it, Crane finds that Patterson does not seem aware of all these strange happenings, and he was the only member of the crew who did not shake hands with Laird. [1]

Assessment:

This was *Voyage*'s second "hallucination" episode in the third season (following the generically titled "Night of Terror"). They had also used this gimmick in the second season, for "Leviathan." In that story, the character played by Karen Steele spiked the salt so that, when they were given a mental suggestion, the crew would think big – as in very big fish. Irwin Allen and his creative staff were recycling again, but the intriguingly titled "The Day the Earth Ended" outclasses the rest.

Senator William Dennis has the power that most politicians wish they had – and some certainly attempt, via the media – namely, the ability to carry out mass hypnotism. A shake of the hand, a moment of eye contact, then a mental suggestion planted into the mind of his target, and Dennis has his victims seeing anything he wishes. The flaw in the plan is that he cannot control a person's actions; how they react to what they think they see is their own choice. And, when Dennis is not near those who have been afflicted by his hallucinogenic suggestions, their imaginations stray. This is why both Crane and Morton think they see San Francisco through the periscope. Dennis isn't there to suggest something different.

At the end of the day, a man like Dennis can win your vote, but can he maintain control? This top-notch episode answers that question, with a bang.

"My favorite year-three episode," Mark Phillips enthused. "An intriguing mystery buoyed by the perfect casting of Skip Homeier as the Senator. The special effects are also first-rate, including the flying sub soaring through the sky, skimming and landing on the ocean surface, and a spectacular shot of it flying over a couple of buildings. Exciting and involving, this is a genuine third season classic." [2]

Mike Bailey said, "In spite of an ending that could have been much better explained, this is one of the eeriest of all of *Voyage*'s 110 outings and stands out as a classic. Events pile one on top of another until it feels as if you're cut off from the rest of the world. Indeed, as far as civilization goes, there apparently *is* no rest of the world. The location shooting and fabulous footage of the Flying Sub are edited into the show at an exciting pace. Del Monroe turns in a standout performance as Kowalski, tortured by the knowledge he has almost killed Patterson. Writing makes the difference. Tight direction, editing and great overall production values make this proof, once again, that *Voyage* always had the talent on board." [3]

Script:

William Welch's story and 1st-draft teleplay approved on June 15, 1966.
Welch's 2nd (final) draft teleplay approved by Irwin Allen on June 21.
Shooting Final teleplay: July 12.
Rev. Shooting Final teleplay (on blue paper): July 25.
Page revisions (on pink paper): July 26.
Page revisions (on yellow paper): July 27.
Page revisions (on gold paper): July 28.

William Welch didn't have all the twists and turns of his story worked out when he sold Irwin Allen on the idea of "The Day the World Ended." It only took two paragraphs:

> Suddenly and without warning, every living thing in the world seems to have vanished. There are no fish in the sea, no birds in the air. Animals and people alike have disappeared from the face of the Earth. In the once-teeming cities, streets and buildings are eerily deserted. All the world appears to have become one enormous "Marie Celeste" [the abandoned mystery ship]. In homes, food still cooks on unattended stoves; coffee perks cheerily in automatic percolators; cars stand empty on the streets, their motors idling; escalators run dutifully and electric signs flash their messages -- but there is no life. Only Seaview and its crew appear to remain in an otherwise deserted, lifeless world. This is the beginning of the most bafflingly weird situation the men of Seaview have ever faced in a story of breathless suspense and nameless terror. [4]

By the time the catalyst behind all the strangeness was concocted, and a script prepared, ABC reacted with its standard lists of concerns, at the top of which was a need for care to be taken so that the viewing audience wouldn't think the world had really become a series of ghost towns. Mary Garbutt, of the network's Department of Broadcast Standards and Practices, said:

> Pgs 1-7: Please establish future date wherever possible in the teaser.
>
> Pg 1: Please be sure that Senator William Laird is completely fictitious and not close, by name or representation, to any actual senator.

Pgs 7; 45-46; 52: Your usual care in seeing that these sequences with various "creatures" are not too frightening for family viewing. Can only be approved on film.... [5]

Production:
(Filmed July 27 through August 3, 1966; 6 days)

This was **Jerry Hopper**'s third of 15 *Voyage* directing assignment.

Producer **Bruce Fowler, Jr.** had some casting suggestions for the guest-starring role of Senator Laird, soon renamed Senator Dennis. In a July 19 memo to Irwin Allen, among the names mentioned were Eli Wallach, Jack Warden, Mark Richman, Martin Landau, and Michael Connors. Allen had someone else in mind.

Skip Homeier was 36 when paid $1,650 for six days' work. He had begun his career at 14 as "Skippy" Homeier. His first film role had him cast as a callous German youth, in 1944's *Tomorrow the World* (pictured here).

Homeier also had a successful career as a TV guest player. He visited hundreds of series, appearing frequently on *Studio One*, *The Virginian*, *Alfred Hitchcock Presents*, and *Combat!* He was given his own NBC series in 1960, as *Dan Raven*, a cop whose beat was the streets of Hollywood. Homeier also showed up on *The Outer Limits*, with *Star Trek*'s James Doohan, in the episode "Expanding Human." Speaking of *Trek*, Homeier appeared in two episodes: 1968's "Patterns of Force" and 1968's "The Way to Eden." He had appeared in *Voyage* once before, in "The Amphibians," and would return for "Attack!"

Robert J. Bronner was the new cinematographer, beginning here and staying for the remainder of the series. He was 58, and had been the Director of Photography on Elvis Presley's 1957 film *Jailhouse Rock*, along with many other pop culture hits, such as 1959's *The Mating Game*, starring Debbie Reynolds and

Tony Randall; 1960's *Please Don't Eat the Daisies*, starring Doris Day and David Niven; 1961's *Gidget Goes Hawaiian*, starring James Darren and Deborah Walley; 1964's *7 Faces of Dr. Lao*, starring Tony Randall, with Barbara Eden. Irwin Allen always hired the best technical people.

Production began on Wednesday, July 27, 1966, for the first of four days on Stage 10, filming the Seaview sets and the Flying Sub.

On Tuesday, the fifth day of the production, the company spent the morning hours outdoors on Fox's New York Street, for filming "Ext. N.Y. Street," "Ext. Washington Street" and "Ext. Theatre + Lobby." By midafternoon, they moved back onto Stage 10 where a new set had been prepared – "Int. Theatre Lobby."

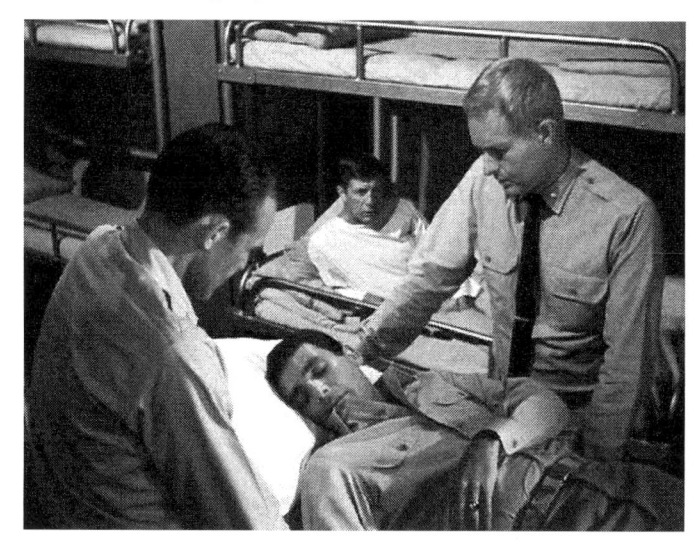

Wednesday, August 3, was the sixth and final day of production, with the company remaining on Stage 10 for additional filming on board the Seaview, including Sickbay, Int. Crane's Cabin, and "Int. Corridor A & B."

The budget approved by William Self was $158,896. [6]

Release / Reaction:
(ABC premiere airdate: 10/2/66; network repeat broadcast: 5/28/67)

The week that "The Day the World Ended" first aired was also the week that LSD (lysergic acid diethylamide) was declared illegal in the state of California. Meanwhile, the drug-influenced Beatles album *Revolver* was the best-selling LP in America. John Lennon admitted he was tripping on acid when he wrote the album's closing track, "Tomorrow Never Knows." The Association's "Cherish" was the big song on the radio. *The Bible: In the Beginning* was still the biggest film in the movie houses.

Syndicated "TV Scout" said of this episode:

> Series has its best episode of the season in "The Day the World Ended." Fans of both science-fiction and this series will be able to figure out the gimmick without too much trouble,

but watching the show is still fun. All kinds of terrible things happen aboard the Seaview, right after Skip Homeier, a visiting senator, comes aboard. Monsters appear, fish disappear, radio communications are non-existent, and the periscope shows the San Francisco skyline, even though the sub is apparently in the Atlantic off the Norfolk coast. [7]

A.C. Nielsen 30-Market ratings report for October 2, 1966: [8]

(7 – 7:30 p.m.)	Rating:	Share:
ABC: *Voyage to the Bottom of the Sea*	**17.7**	**37.9%**
CBS: *Lassie*	11.1	25.3%
NBC: Actuality Special	8.7	18.6%
(7:30 – 8 p.m.):		
ABC: *Voyage to the Bottom of the Sea*	**18.0**	**32.7%**
CBS: *It's About Time*	11.2	20.2%
NBC: *Walt Disney*	16.6	30.2%

Following the broadcast, Bill Summers wrote in his column for Florida's *Orlando Evening Star*:

> For pure escapism, Sunday's *Voyage to the Bottom of the Sea* was all you could want. Skip Homeier guest starred as Sen. Dennis, an evil master of mass hypnosis.
>
> The monster in this episode was a writhing thing with an angry appearance, probably resembling Pittsburgh Pirate manager Harry Walker after Saturday's doubleheader loss to San Francisco Giants. [9]

Bob Shields wrote in Canada's *Calgary Herald*:

> *Voyage to the Bottom of the Sea* came up with an episode this week that was almost as entertaining as the first show in the series. The only objection would be that it was a long wait. [10]

7.6

"The Terrible Toys" (Episode 64)
(Prod No. 9206; first aired Sunday, October 16, 1966)
Written by Robert Vincent Wright
Directed by Justus Addiss
Produced by Irwin Allen and Bruce Fowler, Jr.; Story Editor: Sidney Marshall
Guest Star Paul Fix

Watch your step – you may crush these tiny terrors and end the episode prematurely.

From the *Voyage* show files (Irwin Allen papers collection):

> An U.F.O. crashes into the ocean for lack of fuel. It needs the titanium in the hull of the Seaview to supply getaway power and to obtain it, the aliens aboard seize a sailor, Burke, whose boat they wrecked. In his possessions are some wind-up toys, bought for trading purposes. They program these toys to destroy the Seaview. Burke, brought aboard the sub, is too afraid of the aliens to reveal the secret. The U.F.O. holds the sub by a magnetic beam so that it cannot escape while the toys go about their mission. [1]

Assessment:

This episode is proof that high concept and lowbrow can coexist. Kids may have loved it; adults, probably not.

Mark Phillips noted, "This is the first episode where the weekly menace is way over the top – malevolent department store toys. Holy retail sale! ... It's a very juvenile and noisy episode and the tug-of-war between Seaviewers and toys gets tiring." [2]

The pacing drags a bit; the toys are hardly menacing. Surprisingly, the episode is not as terrible as the terrible toys. It's certainly diverting. The moments involving Admiral Nelson inside the alien ship, meeting the alien spokesman (Francis X. Bushman, decked out like a kindly Jehovah), are intriguing. And the underwater work with miniatures, animated tractor beams, and divers, keep the story afloat ... although one lengthy sequence involving divers was blatantly lifted from Season Two's "Monster's Web" – including one extra diver!

The idea of dangerous playthings was in the air. The previous year, in 1965, both *Get Smart* ("Our Man in Toyland") and *The Man from U.N.C.L.E.* ("The Deadly Toys Affair") featured weaponized toys. So sit back, remove the batteries from the kids' toy tanks, and you may be pleasantly surprised.

Script:

Wright's story and 1st-draft teleplay approved on May 25, 1966.
Wright's 2nd (and final) draft teleplay approved on June 3.
Shooting Final teleplay: July 22.
2nd Rev. Shooting Final teleplay (on pink paper): August 1.
Page revisions (on green paper): August 2.
Page revisions (on gold paper): August 4.

This was **Robert Vincent Wright**'s third of four *Voyage* script assignments. For Season Two, he had written "… And Five of Us Are Left" and "Graveyard of Fear."

"I think Irwin was intrigued by 'Toys' because of the seeming innocence of toys turning into villains," Wright speculated. "Toys were so benign as compared to giant jellyfish and other menacing creatures." [3]

The story premise, as explained in an internal production document, said:

> Several Seaview crewmen, on liberty in a foreign port, find some unusual little toy figures in an out-of-the-way bazaar. They buy the toys to bring home as souvenirs. Once aboard, and with Seaview homeward bound, several inexplicable events take place which all but destroy the sub. Almost too late it is discovered that the quaint "toys" are actually miniature humanoid devices with the power to multiply and destroy. Their ultimate goal is to seize the sub, land in the United States, multiply geometrically and devastate the country. [4]

Once Wright began writing, the first thing to go was the "out-of-the-way bazaar." A set like that, staffed by costumed extras, would exceed the episode's budget. For his story treatment, Wright wrote:

> The Seaview's radar picks up a strange object careening at incredible speed over the Indian Ocean. Suddenly this object wavers, disappears into the sea. The Seaview is jolted by a tremendous shock wave. Cruising to investigate, the sub finds a few pieces of floating wreckage and an unconscious survivor laying on a hatch. The man is taken aboard, put into sick bay. Nelson opens a burlap bag found with the man. It contains three brightly-painted, strange tin wind-up toys. One of them is a soldier with rifle; one is a fireman with axe, and the third is a drummer boy. [5]

This was an affordable opening. Next, the idea of Admiral Nelson's encounter with the alien spokesman onboard the spaceship was introduced into the script.

Production:
(Filmed August 4 – 11; 6 days)

This was **Justus Addiss'** fifth directing assignment on *Voyage*.

Paul Fix was paid $1,500 for up to five days' work. At 65, he had close to 300 credits in television and films, including the recurring role of Marshal Micah Torrance, the third cast member on TV's popular *The Rifleman*. One year earlier, he had played the ship's doctor on the U.S.S. Enterprise for the second *Star Trek* pilot film, "Where No Man Has Gone Before."

Francis X. Bushman, playing "Old Man," was paid $250 for one day before the camera. Bushman was a famous screen idol during the 1920s. His career declined during the start of the talkies, in part because his butler had accidentally insulted a movie mogul during a Hollywood party. Bushman died from injuries suffered in a fall only three weeks after filming this episode.

Robert Vincent Wright said of Bushman, "He hadn't worked in years and I was glad he got even this minor part."

As for the toys, Wright said, "My wife and I went shopping for them. We visited a toy store and we found the robot. It was walking around by itself and he looked so friendly, but, boy, in the episode, add that music and be became ominous as hell. He had to be revamped a bit by the prop department. They gave him a little chest door that opened up and shot a beam at you. Once we picked out the toys, we gave a list to the prop people and they went out and bought them." [6]

**Above: Paul Fix took a *Star Trek* prior to his *Voyage to the Bottom of the Sea*.
Below: Francis X. Bushman in his silent-movie days.**

The budget was set at $161,120 by William Self.

Production began on August 4, 1966 for the first of six days on Stage 10, including all Seaview sets, plus the Flying Sub, plus "Int. Alien Disc."

Two additional days of production, on August 29 and 30, were conducted by the second unit team, directed by Paul Stader. They filmed on the Seaview sets, with those terrible toys, but no other cast members, shooting close-ups of the toys moving about. This work was done while the Seaview sets were not otherwise needed – during the wee hours of the night. On both days, Stader began at 7:30 p.m. and didn't finish until after 4 in the morning. [7]

Release / Reaction:
(ABC premiere airdate: 10/16/66; network repeat broadcast: 4/2/67)

Promotional card sent out to newspapers and ABC affiliates. Its text: *"Voyage to the Bottom of the Sea presents one of the most diabolical plots in the history of the universe! Alien creatures turn innocent children's toys into monstrous, deadly weapons that threaten to destroy the fabulous nuclear submarine Seaview! Richard Basehart and David Hedison star in an hour of spectacular entertainment for the whole family!"*

The day that "The Terrible Toys" was first broadcast across America, Joan Baez and 123 other anti-draft protestors were arrested in Oakland, California. *Hawaii*, starring Julie Andrews, Max von Sydow, and Richard Harris, was the top-grossing movie in the country. The Beatles' *Revolver* and the Supremes' *A'*

369

Go-Go were the top two albums in the land. The Four Tops, with "Reach Out, I'll Be There," were getting the most radio play. And Peter Deuel and Judy Carne, of *Love on a Rooftop*, had the cover of *TV Guide*.

ABC was pleased with "The Terrible Toys." The network's Lew Hunter said, "We had that wonderful show about the toys that activated themselves and went on a rampage of the ship. We went along with the change to 'monster of the week.' We certainly didn't discourage it. I guess I was pretty much involved and encouraging the monster of the week, too, and the toys that went crazy on the submarine, and the things invading the submarine. I think Irwin was going to do it anyway, but I was saying, 'Go, go, go! Keep it going. That's wonderful.'" [8]

Joan Crosby, in her syndicated "TV Scout" column, seemed to be saying, "No, no, no!"

> There's a kind of macabre version of Santa Claus on *Voyage to the Bottom of the Sea* in a script that sounds as if a father had taken revenge for having to buy his youngsters too many windup, destructive toys last Christmas. A bag of toys is brought aboard the Seaview; a drummer, a knight, an executioner, a parrot, and so on. And they plan to take over the ship with acts of sabotage. Also present, the late Francis X. Bushman as a sort of Grand Guignol Santa. Ugh! [9]

In the report covering the week that "The Terrible Toys" aired, a 30-City survey by A.C. Nielsen ranked the Top 15 prime-time network shows as follows: 1) *Bonanza*; 2) Jim Nabors variety special; 3) Friday Night Movie; 4) Sunday Night Movie; 5) Tuesday Night Movie; 6) *The Jackie Gleason Show*; 7) *The Lucy Show*; 8) *Felony Squad*; 9) *Rat Patrol*; 10) *The FBI*; 11) *The Andy Williams Show*; 12) *I Spy*; 13) *Peyton Place* (Monday); 14) ***Voyage to the Bottom of the Sea***; 15) *Occasional Wife*. [10]

As for how *Voyage* did in its time slot, a Nielsen 30-Market ratings report for October 16, 1966 ranked the shows as follows:

(7 – 7:30 p.m.)	Rating:	Share:
ABC: *Voyage to the Bottom of the Sea*	**22.7**	**42.6%**
CBS: *Lassie*	14.8	27.8%
NBC: *Bell Telephone Hour*	7.8	14.6%
(7:30 – 8 p.m.):		
ABC: *Voyage to the Bottom of the Sea*	**23.3**	**42.7%**
CBS: *It's About Time*	11.6	21.2%
NBC: *Walt Disney*	13.6	24.9%

7.7

"Deadly Waters" (Episode 65)
(Prod No. 9207; first aired Sunday, October 30, 1966)
Written by Robert Vincent Wright
Directed by Gerald Mayer
Produced by Irwin Allen and Bruce Fowler, Jr.; Story Editor: Sidney Marshall
Guest Star Don Gordon

From the *Voyage* show files (Irwin Allen papers collection):

The Seaview rescues a trapped Navy diver from a wrecked atomic sub. He is Stan Kowalski, brother of one of the crew. Before they can get away, torpedoes from the wrecked sub, activated by water seepage, fire and hit the Seaview. Badly damaged, it now lies on the bottom, unable to move, with only two hours air supply left. All efforts to escape prove unsuccessful. The last faint possibility is to [inflate] Stan's pressure suit and have someone try to make it to the surface to get help. Stan, who has panicked, refuses to go, but, when he sees Nelson preparing to make the trip and realizes the Admiral, whose hands are badly burned, will never make it, he takes Nelson's place.[1]

Assessment:

It was a surprisingly personal story for *Voyage*, in this case zeroing in on Kowalski. The tale brought something else we didn't see much on the series: "Man Against Himself," as brother Stan struggles with his own fears, and then, despite them, becomes a hero. It's a nice change of pace.

But, as an Irwin Allen production, the prime directive to the writer and director was "action, action, action," and this tale is jammed full. A little less action, as one of the critics who reviewed this episode when it first aired commented, might have made an even stronger story.

Mark Phillips said, "Another 'Seaview sinks to the bottom' story, but this suspenseful tale of survival works on several levels, including good characterizations. Don Gordon is excellent as Stan Kowalski and brings intensity to the role." [2]

Mike Bailey commented, "The story is riveting and loaded with substance; there is tension in the dialogue. Kowalski is made more real by his reaction to his brother's uncharacteristic cowardice. Nelson displays the kind of moral clarity so prevalent in the black and white shows. My goodness, the darned episode works remarkably well, with motivation, rectitude and logic pushing the doings." [3]

"Deadly Waters" rides high in the water as one of *Voyage*'s best.

Script:

Robert Vincent Wright's 1ˢᵗ-Draft teleplay: June 15, 1966.
Wright's 2ⁿᵈ (and final) draft teleplay: July 15.
Rev. Shooting Final teleplay (blue paper): August 9.
2ⁿᵈ Rev. Shooting Final teleplay (pink paper): August 11.
Page revisions (blue paper): August 19.

This was the last script written for *Voyage* by **Robert Vincent Wright**, following "... And Five of Us are Left," "Graveyard of Fear," and "The Terrible Toys." Robert Vincent Wright told Mark Phillips, "It was a good show. Stan Kowalski wasn't a bad guy; he was a man traumatized by a near-death experience and it affected his nerve." [4]

Wright's 22-page undated treatment began:

> Under flank speed, the Seaview races to the scene of the sinking of an atomic sub. A Navy diver has succeeded in rescuing the crew but has been hopelessly trapped himself

when the hulk had suddenly shifted. Not only has he a limited supply of air in his special, self-contained suit, but the deadly torpedoes aboard the sunken craft have malfunctioned, and their firing timers are running. An additional note of urgency is added when it is revealed that the trapped diver is Sam Kowalski, the older brother of the Seaview's Kowalski.

Arriving at the scene, Crane and Nelson can see that the sunken craft is teetering on the edge of a narrow ledge above a deep abyss. The Seaview is forced to settle on the same ledge to enable Crane and Kowalski to don scuba gear needed for the rescue attempt. Crane and Kowalski find Sam unconscious, his leg trapped under wreckage. With great difficulty, Sam [later changed to Stan] is freed, but the return to the Seaview is slow, for Crane and Kowalski must support Sam's cumbersome diving suit between them.

As he steps out of the escape hatch into the missile room on the Seaview, Crane jerks off the scuba mask, gives orders for immediate emergency departure. The renegade torpedoes fire themselves from the sunken craft. The Seaview takes desperate evasive action, enough to avoid a direct hit, but one torpedo hits the ledge near them, and the powerful warhead detonates in a blinding explosion. **END OF TEASER**.[5]

After reading Wright's 1st-draft teleplay (dated June 15, 1966), Irwin Allen wrote:

> Mention of the flying sub is questionable. The release doors for the FS-1 are on the bottom of the sub and the sub is lying on the bottom. How would they release the FS-1? This note concerns Scene 54 as well. This note is vital to the whole story and therefore the solution lies in having the Seaview settle on a ledge with its foreword part hanging free until the sub is sent out and retrieved.[6]

The series was on tilt too, according to Wright. "It was running out of life. It was a pretty tight cocoon as opposed to what I could write for *Bonanza*. I enjoy writing dialogue interplay between characters, and there wasn't much opportunity for that on *Voyage*. There was a sameness to the series. Generally, the dialogue was simplistic and you were restricted to the sub. There always had to be an enemy – a weird enemy, generally – and storylines became harder and harder to come by. You can only be attacked by so many denizens of the deep…. Once, Irwin asked me if I had something new. I said, 'Sure. How about an episode where the Seaview is attacked by a giant anchovy? There is a terrible battle but the Seaview finally kills it.' 'What happens then?', Irwin asked. 'Well, the crew makes the biggest Caesar salad known to man!' 'Very funny!' Irwin snapped."[7]

Production:
(Filmed August 12 – 19, 1966; 6 days)

The was **Gerald Mayer**'s second of four *Voyage* directing assignments (following Season Two's "The Sky's on Fire").

Associate producer **Bruce Fowler, Jr.** suggested five actors to play Stan Kowalski: Lyle Bettger, Charles Bronson, Dane Clark, John Ireland, and Richard Devon. Irwin Allen had someone else in mind.

Don Gordon was paid $2,500 to play brother Stan Kowalski. He was 39 and had been a co-star on the 1960-61 series *The Blue Angels*, about Navy pilots. He made two trips into *The Twilight Zone* (including the lead in "The Self-Improvement of Salvadore Ross," about a man who can trade physical characteristics with others), and two journeys into *The Outer Limits* (including the lead in the excellent "The Invisibles"). Gordon had been nominated for an Emmy in 1963 for a guest spot on *The Defenders*. Among numerous TV jobs, Gordon appeared in two episodes of *Wanted: Dead or Alive*, and became a good friend with that series' star, Steve McQueen. As a result, Gordon was given memorable roles in three McQueen movies – *Bullitt*, *Papillon*, and *The Towering Inferno*. The latter was produced by Irwin Allen.

Don Gordon in the frightening "The Invisibles," a 1963 episode of *The Outer Limits*.

William Self approved a budget of $161,461.

Production began on August 12, 1966 for the first of six days on Stage 10. Along with the Seaview sets, and the Flying Sub, they made room for "Int. Navy Rescue Ship (Wall)" and "Int. Salvage (Diving Bell)."

Interviewed for a newspaper filler story during the week this episode aired, Richard Basehart tried to explain why actors were unusual people. "An actor, by the very nature of his trade, is a purveyor of make-believe. He plays not one part, but *many* parts, and he plays them so that they may be understood by his audience. Most people are protective of their emotions; actors are just the opposite. They are in the business of emotion. It is their job to share with an audience what that audience will not, perhaps, share with each other – the deepest secrets of their character. What people seem to forget is that we actors can also be human. And in being human we conflict within ourselves with all the drives that make us actors. It's a constant battle." [8]

Release / Reaction:
(ABC premiere airdate: 10/30/66; network repeat broadcast: 7/2/67)

DEADLY WATERS

IRWIN ALLEN'S VOYAGE TO THE BOTTOM OF THE SEA

IN COLOR · SUNDAY · OCTOBER 30 · ON abc

Promotional card sent by Irwin Allen's office to newspapers and ABC affiliates across America. The copy reads: "*Voyage to the Bottom of the Sea* presents an hour of spellbinding suspense! Torpedoes from a wrecked submarine fire at the fabulous nuclear submarine Seaview, damaging her badly! With only two hours of air left, all efforts to escape the death trap are unsuccessful! Admiral Nelson, Captain Crane and the men of the Seaview are doomed to die!"

This is the week that Lunar Orbiter 1 became the first U.S. spacecraft to circle the Moon. After over 500 orbits, and beaming more than 200 photos back to Earth, it was directed into a crash landing. The Jerry Lewis outer-space comedy, *Way... Way Out*, was the big hit in the movie houses. The soundtrack to *Dr. Zhivago*, the Monkees' self-titled debut album, and The Supremes' *A' Go-Go* were the long-playing records selling best in stores. The Monkees were also getting the most play on the radio, with "Last Train to Clarksville." Van Williams and Bruce Lee, of 20th Century-Fox's *The Green Hornet*, had the cover of *TV Guide*.

"TV Scout," from a platform of hundreds of newspapers, said:

> No monsters on *Voyage to the Bottom of the Sea* and that's a huge relief. If this show had resisted the urge to pile on problems, it would have been an excellent study of a man facing what he thinks is his own cowardice. As it is, there are some good moments, provided by Don Gordon, as the apparently yellow brother of crew member Kowalski (Del

Monroe). But, among other problems: the ship is dead on the ocean floor, the air is running out, the hull is in danger of being crushed, and radiation from a sunken sub nearby is reaching the critical point. [9]

"TV Key," syndicated to numerous newspapers, said:

This underwater adventure series gets around to one of the standard submarine plots, and it's a good one crammed with tension-building suspense. The Seaview suffers a great setback while on a rescue mission, and the sub's crew feels doomed. Naturally, Admiral Nelson and Captain Crane, with an assist from a frightened diver, employ some last-minute life-saving tactics. [10]

A.C. Nielsen 30-Market ratings report for October 30, 1966: [11]

(7 – 7:30 p.m.)	Rating:	Share:
ABC: *Voyage to the Bottom of the Sea*	**20.9**	**37.4%**
CBS: *Lassie*	18.6	33.3%
NBC: Campaign - Candidates	5.5	9.8%

(7:30 – 8 p.m.):		
ABC: *Voyage to the Bottom of the Sea*	**23.4**	**39.8%**
CBS: *It's About Time*	13.2	22.4%
NBC: *Walt Disney*	12.5	21.3%

7.8

"Thing from Inner Space" (Episode 66)
(Prod. No. 9208; first aired on Sunday, November 6, 1966)
Written by William Welch
Directed by Alex March
Produced by Irwin Allen and Bruce Fowler, Jr.; Story Editor: Sidney Marshall
Guest Star Hugh Marlowe

From the *Voyage* show files (Irwin Allen papers collection):

Commentator Bainbridge Wells persuades Nelson to go with him to a tropical island to help bring back a sea monster which had killed his camera crew on a previous expedition. Crewman Patterson, whose father was one of these men, is bent on revenge. When they reach the island, Patterson endangers the expedition by disobeying orders in order to salvage a roll of film from the sea, while the Seaview is attacked by one of the monsters. They manage to capture another specimen ashore, immobilize it with tranquilizers, and drag it aboard. Patterson, meanwhile, has developed the film which proves Wells was responsible for the death of his father. During a struggle between Wells and Patterson for possession of the film, they set off an ultrasonic device which arouses the monster. [1]

Assessment:

"One of Year Three's best shows," voted Mark Phillips. "This 'black lagoon' redo is exciting, with Hugh Marlowe giving a likeably earnest performance as Dr. Wells. However, it's the monster that makes the show. It looks convincingly menacing, especially when it peers through the Seaview's observation windows." [2]

"It's not badly written," enthused Mike Bailey, "it's excellently directed by Alex March, and the music cues (mostly by Jerry Goldsmith from 'Jonah and the Whale') drive this episode straight forward." [3]

This isn't just another monster tale – it's bigger and meaner. The monster (played by Dawson Palmer) is an eye-catcher – both at seven feet, battling camera crews on land and divers in the water; and as the super-sized 200-foot version, wrestling with the mammoth Seaview.

You've got to love Crane's line to Nelson: "You mean to tell me they come in two sizes?!"

We'd seen an aquatic behemoth doing battle with the Seaview model in the Green Tank – in "Leviathan," "The Menfish," and "Deadly Creature Below." But somehow this "Thing from Inner Space" brings a new thrill to the gimmick.

Terry Becker again delights, providing much-appreciated comic relief in appropriate moments. And anytime they gave the talented Paul Trinka more to do – be it comedy with Becker, as seen here, or heavy-hearted pathos, also seen here – the result was a resounding jackpot.

Script:

William Welch's writers contract: July 20, 1966.
Welch's story treatment: June 29.
Welch's 1st- and 2nd-Draft teleplays approved by Irwin Allen on July 27.
Welch's script polish (revised 2nd draft teleplay): August 1.
Shooting Final teleplay (pale green paper): August 11.
Rev. Shooting Final teleplay (blue paper): August 17.
Page revisions (pink paper): August 17.
Page revisions (green paper): August 19.
Page revisions (yellow paper): August 29.
Page revisions (gold paper): September 1.
Page revisions (beige paper): October 3.
Page revisions (blue paper): October 6.

For his story treatment, **William Welch** wrote:

On a small island in the Pacific some eight hundred miles west of Chile, a group of motion picture technicians has set up a camera and sound boom on the beach. Facing the camera lens is a lean, sun-bronzed man of middle age who carries himself with an air of complete self-assurance.

"This is Bainbridge Wells," he says into the boom mike as the camera rolls, "bringing you another episode in my continuing series 'Science on the Move.' I am speaking to you now from the shoreline of tiny Murro Atoll in the South Pacific where, for years, there have been persistent stories of a fire-spouting sea monster. The so-called respectable scientists have scoffed at these reports, as they always do whenever their own neatly ordered little worlds are threatened, and so I have decided to make a personal, on-the-spot investigation in order to bring you the real truth."

As the man is speaking in his easy, urbane manner, there is a sudden broiling eruption just off-shore and the hideous head of a weirdly formed beast appears. Fire seems to come from its gaping jaws as it wades ashore, heading directly for the terrified camera crew. Roaring, lashing out with its powerful

> reptilian tail and spouting flames, the horrifying, nightmarish creature attacks. Only Wells himself escapes, managing to conceal himself in the thick underbrush at the edge of the beach where he watches in helpless horror while the crew and its equipment are demolished. And yet, in spite of his paralyzing fright, he manages somehow to snap a quick picture of the marauder. [4]

It wasn't *Playhouse 90*, as Irwin Allen would readily admit. But it was the kind of (literal) scenery chewing that he and ABC wanted. And no one could feed scripts to the hungry television production machine faster than Bill Welch.

Irwin Allen read Welch's first draft script, then wrote:

> Script is approximately 8 pages too long.... Quite a lot is made of Miller's [renamed Patterson] attempts to prove that Wells caused his father's death, but no one but Miller and Wells ever discover the truth. The fact should come to Nelson's attention somehow.... Miller is taken to sick bay presumably in Scene 152, Page 63, but nothing more is heard about him... End of story leaves the problem of the monsters and their scientific benefit to man hanging in the air. Actually, Seaview has not accomplished anything except finding the truth of their existence. [5]

Calvin Ward, of ABC's Department of Broadcast Standards and Practices, warned:

> Caution that the appearance and actions of the Creature is not too hideous and frightening for "living-room" viewing. Particular caution on Close-ups and those shots in which the Creature is coming directly at and appears to overpower the camera. Can be approved only on film. [6]

It had become apparent that monsters were more likely to be accepted by the censors than stories about political intrigue, nuclear doomsday, or supernatural threats. For the overworked creative staff, it only made sense to stick with what worked. Research conducted by Allen and the network – and as indicated by the Nielsen ratings – backed up this conclusion.

ABC's Lew Hunter said, "We didn't challenge Irwin because the ratings were of such that we figured, 'Well, the audience likes what he's doing.'" [7]

Production:
(Filmed August 22 – 29, 1966; 6 days)

A budget of $158,930 was approved by William Self. Well … it was something to shoot for.

Alex Marsh was paid $3,000 to direct. This was his second of two *Voyage* episodes (following Season Two's "Escape from Venice"). He would continue working in television through the mid-1980s.

Hugh Marlowe was paid $1,750 to play Bainbridge Wells. He was 55 and had been a radio announcer and stage performer. He also had an extensive résumé in film and television. Marlowe had played mystery-writer/private detective Ellery Queen on television in 1952's *The Adventures of Ellery Queen*, which was rechristened as *Mystery Is My Business* in 1954, with Marlowe still in the role. Other big-ticket items included *The Day the Earth Stood Still* and *Earth vs the Flying Saucers*. Marlowe was also featured well in the then-recent film *Seven Days in May*.

Above: Hugh Marlowe. Left: Dawson Palmer in costume as *Lost in Space*'s cyclops.

Dawson Palmer (29) played the Thing. The former basketball-player-turned-stuntman played lots of "things" for Irwin Allen, particularly on *Lost in Space*. And he even got to play a role in which he was not encased in a rubber monster suit, for that series 1966 episode "The Space Croppers."

Production began on Monday, August 22, 1966 for the first of six days on Stage 10. We'd seen monster stories on *Voyage* before, but this episode presented something new for the series, as far as we know – a Black crewman! Across town, *Star Trek* was filming its first season, with an interracial cast. But none of those episodes had been aired yet. Regardless, *Voyage* would have some catching up to do in adding a bit of color to its cast, and to the crew of the Seaview. This represented one small step for mankind. (If we missed any instances of interracial casting of the submarine's crew prior to this, then this will be "one *more* small step for mankind.")

In the afternoon on the sixth day, the company moved to Stage B for the "Ext. Murro Beach Atoll" set.

On September 9 and 12, Paul Stader directed underwater footage with the second unit camera crew in the 20th Century-Fox Green Tank. He also picked up shots for "The Terrible Toys."

Harry Harris was paid $297.68 for directing two days of pickup shots on October 4 and 7. [8]

Release / Reaction:
(ABC premiere broadcast: 11/6/66; network repeat broadcast: 5/14/67)

The Professionals, starring Burt Lancaster and Lee Marvin, was the top film in the movie houses. "Last Train to Clarksville," by the Monkees, and "Poor Side of Town," by Johnny Rivers, were the two songs getting the most airplay on the radio. The Monkees were also selling the most records in America, with their self-titled debut album. Robert Vaughn and David McCallum of *The Man from U.N.C.L.E.* had the cover of *TV Guide*. It cost 15 cents. You could buy the *Voyage to the Bottom of the Sea* board game, from Milton Bradley, for only 77 cents at toy and department stores everywhere! Better – Al's Value Center in Denver had Aurora's plastic model kit of the Seaview discounted to only $1.88 from its list price of $2.37!

"TV Key" previewed "Thing from Inner Space," saying:

> Lively entry with plenty of stress on action. There's a sea monster in this one, a captured creature that wreaks havoc on the sub and its crew, and the climactic scenes should delight young series fans. [9]

If one monster could win a time slot; two could bring in a 40 share. A.C. Nielsen 30-Market ratings survey for November 6, 1966: [10]

(7 – 7:30 p.m.)	Rating:	Share:
ABC: *Voyage to the Bottom of the Sea*	**24.2**	**40.9%**
CBS: *Lassie*	16.5	27.9%
NBC: AFL Football Game	11.1	18.8%

(7:30 – 8 p.m.):		
ABC: *Voyage to the Bottom of the Sea*	**23.2**	**37.6%**
CBS: *It's About Time*	11.1	18.0%
NBC: *Walt Disney*	20.5	33.2%

384

7.9

"The Death Watch" (Episode 67)

(Prod. No. 9210; first aired on Sunday, November 13, 1966)
Written by William Welch
Directed by Leonard Horn
Produced by Irwin Allen and Bruce Fowler, Jr.; Story Editor: Sidney Marshall

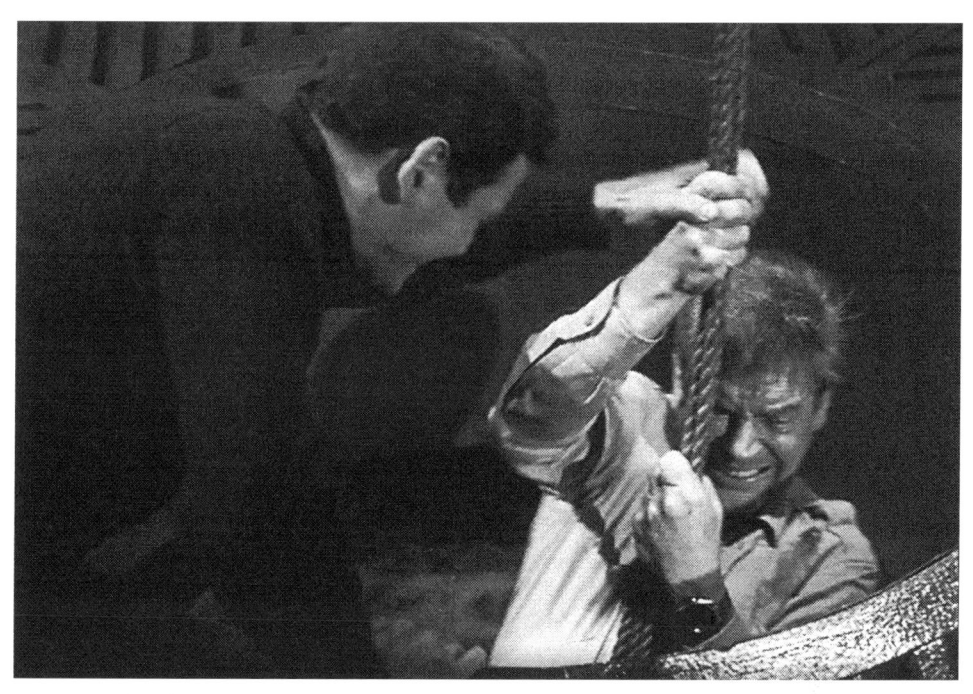

David Hedison and Richard Basehart performed most of their own stunts in the intense climactic fight sequence.

From the *Voyage* show files (Irwin Allen papers collection):

> Nelson, coming aboard the Seaview, finds it eerily deserted except for Sharkey. The rest of the crew and all weapons are ashore, purportedly in accordance with his own orders, which he can't remember having given. He then finds that Crane has come aboard in order to kill him. Sharkey, torn between his loyalties to both, does his best to keep them apart. Continual bleeps from a tape recorder seem to have a marked effect on both men, and a girl's voice coming over the intercom informs them both of the other's presence. [1]

Assessment:

Mark Phillips said, "You almost have to admire the audacious nerve of this episode. Nelson and Crane run around the empty ship, ostensibly to kill each other, but the real point is to kill time and keep the production budget low. On that level, it's annoying. Yet Leonard Horn was a superb director who establishes some measure of nightmarish tension and it's kind of fun to see Nelson emerging from his hypnotic fog and trying to reason with Crane (Hedison excels here – a scary, obsessed, unreasoning visage of murderous fury). The episode definitely has its moments." [2]

Those "moments" build on one another as this taut drama works its way toward an intense finale.

The recipe for this tasty treat is simple – a three-character play; enacted on the enclosed set of the Seaview; with an accelerating life-or-death conflict between the players; and an audience kept in the dark regarding the catalyst until the final reveal.

A three-man show can hardly go wrong when the performers are David Hedison, Richard Basehart, and Terry Becker.

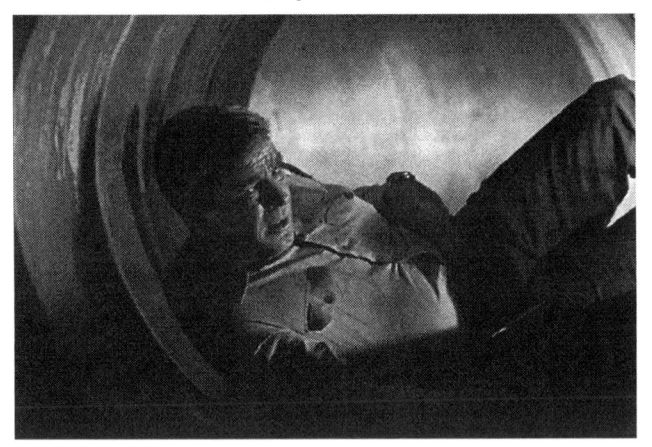

386

Mix; shake, don't stir; until the contents are ready to explode. We'd seen *Voyage* mix up this formula for drama before, but it still has plenty of punch.

Script:
William Welch's writers contract: August 18, 1966.
Welch's story, 1ˢᵗ- draft and 2ⁿᵈ-draft teleplays, and Shooting Final teleplay all approved by ABC on August 25.
Rev. Shooting Final teleplay (blue paper): August 26.
Page revisions (pink paper): August 29.
Page revisions (green paper): September 1.

After Irwin Allen read Welch's script, he wrote across the cover, "Must be shot in five days." It was a "bottle show," and that made a shorter production period a possibility. Allen wanted all further rewrites to be designed with an eye toward making a five-day filming period a reality. Allen also authorized the use of two cameras simultaneously to film dialogue and action sequences, which would help speed the production along. Keeping the filming period down to five days would make up for other episodes which had exceeded the budgets set by 20ᵗʰ Century-Fox.

Voyage made episodes like this possible due to its confining environment (you can't easily get off a submarine!) and its brilliant cast. When you have two exceptional actors like Richard Basehart and David Hedison, it is only reasonable for the creative staff to look for opportunities to put the characters they play at one another's throats. Conflict is the fuel that drives drama, and, with these two, the makers of a TV series have a pair of trump cards just waiting to be played. Granted, it became an overused ploy on *Voyage*, but the temptation to play the hand just one more time – until you get caught cheating – is understandable.

Production:
(Filmed August 30 through September 6, 1966; 5 days)

Enlivening the concept was a talented director. While working almost exclusively in television, with only two feature films (1968's *Rogue's Gallery* and 1972's *Corky*), **Leonard Horn** excelled in his craft, directing episodes of many cream-of-the-crop dramas, such as *The Outer Limits*, *The Fugitive*, and *Alfred Hitchcock Presents*. He worked well with actors and brough a visual intensity to his assignments.

Sue England was the only guest performer featured, and only her voice was needed. She was heard twice in *Lost in Space,* most notably as a deadly cool robot, in 1967's "Deadliest of the Species." Academy Award-winner **Lennie Hayton** provided the music, only the third episode from Season Three so far to include an original score.

The budget, for five days, utilizing two cameras, and with no onscreen guest stars, was set at the bargain basement price of $137,630.

Production began on Tuesday, August 30, 1966, for the first of five days on Stage 10 utilizing standing sets only – the first of many episodes designed this way to save money and time. Story Editor Al Gail said, "Budgets are always a struggle, as you will find out. No matter what you do, somehow, it's hard to do it on the time schedule the studio gives you, because the budget department is looking at one thing and the creators are looking at something else entirely differently." [3]

Only one stock shot was used to set the story into motion – that of Captain Crane, dressed in black, lurking about the dock at the Nelson Institute and sneaking aboard Seaview. This was lifted from the 1963 pilot film.

Terry Becker told writer William Anchors, Jr. that "Death Watch" was a gratifying assignment. He said, "I think, for me, it was such a pleasant departure because it wasn't so much the creatures, but it was the three of us, and so that it was a relationship thing and [in this story] I was being used to abuse them…. I loved every minute of it and I think we did a good job on that show – Hedison, Basehart and myself." [4]

A highlight of the production is the climactic fight between Nelson and Crane. Basehart and Hedison perform most of the action, stunt doubles used only for some wider shots. The two actors got quite a workout, and gave their all.

Release / Reaction:
(Only ABC broadcast: 11/13/66)

From the promotional card sent to ABC affiliates and newspapers across America: *"Voyage to the Bottom of the Sea* presents an hour of spine-tingling, spellbinding suspense! Admiral Nelson boards the fabulous nuclear submarine Seaview to find it eerily deserted, with the crew and all weapons ashore, purportedly in accordance with his own orders – orders he doesn't remember giving! Nelson suddenly discovers he is being stalked by a killer – his junior officer, Captain Lee Crane!"

The drama *Madame X*, starring Lana Turner and John Forsythe, was doing the best business in the movie houses. "You Keep Me Hangin' On," by the Supremes, and Johnny Rivers' "Poor Side of Town" were the two hottest songs on the radio. The Monkees, with their first album, were No. 1 in stores. It would stay that way for the remainder of the year. Marlo Thomas, *That Girl*, had the cover of *TV Guide*.

"TV Scout" previewed "Death Watch":

> There are just three actors and one woman's voice on *Voyage to the Bottom of the Sea* in "Death Watch," an absorbing episode. Seems Richard Basehart and David Hedison are aboard the Seaview, along with seemingly bewildered Terry Becker, and Basehart and Hedison are stalking each other with murder in mind. That woman's voice, which announces conditions aboard the ship and informs the "crew" that the ship is putting out to sea, obviously has something to do with this, but what? And what are those "beeps" which keep

making our heroes strong in their purpose? A bit more imagination at the end would have helped, but it's still a good episode. [5]

"Daku," the TV critic for *Daily Variety*, reviewed "Death Watch," saying, in part:

> Terry Becker, who usually has a secondary stet [recurring] role in *Voyage*, was elevated to a co-star niche with Richard Basehart and David Hedison in this episode, and he performed with a high degree of competence. It was a three-man show, no other characters in it, an unusual, albeit far-fetched chapter in this sci-fi series. … William Welch tale has Hedison as captain of the sub stalking Basehart, its admiral, trying to kill him. Becker is the man in the middle, trying to prevent it. For almost the entire running time, the viewer is in a quandary as to what this is all about. When it's passed off as an experiment as to how man reacts in life-and-death struggle for existence, with only Becker in on it, it adds up to pure hokum. However, acting by Becker, Basehart and Hedison was uniformly good, as was Leonard Horn's direction. [6]

A.C. Nielsen 30-Market ratings report for November 13, 1966: [7]

(7 – 7:30 p.m.)	Rating:	Share:
ABC: *Voyage to the Bottom of the Sea*	**16.7**	**30.6%**
CBS: *Lassie*	**16.7**	**30.6%**
NBC: Actuality Special	7.0	12.8%
(7:30 – 8 p.m.):		
ABC: *Voyage to the Bottom of the Sea*	**17.4**	**29.3%**
CBS: *It's About Time*	14.3	24.1%
NBC: *Walt Disney*	15.2	25.6%

Due to the dip in the Nielsens, "Death Watch" was not given a repeat airing by ABC.

7.10

"Deadly Invasion" (Episode 68)

(Prod. No. 9209; first aired on Sunday, November 20, 1966)
Written by John and Ward Hawkins
Directed by Nathan Juran
Produced by Irwin Allen and Bruce Fowler, Jr.; Story Editor: Sidney Marshall
Guest Star Warren Stevens

From the *Voyage* show files (Irwin Allen papers collection):

> The Seaview is penetrated by shell-like objects which turn out to be miniature spaceships. The shells appear to be impenetrable, but the occupants, who are of an electronic nature, escape in the form of either an anesthetizing gas or electrical energy. Nelson surmises that their objective is to take possession of Sato Six, the underwater reserve atomic base, since, once in command there, they could control the world. [1]

Assessment:

We kept hearing from the fans that the third season of *Voyage to the Bottom of the Sea* wasn't very good – too many juvenile monster shows. But, so far, we've enjoyed most of the previous nine episodes. We vaguely remember some of them from our youth; others are being seen for the first time. And what fun we have been having!

"Deadly Invasion," while generic in title and running a bit out of steam toward the end, is effectively eerie and consistently entertaining. We watched with great curiosity as Admiral Nelson and Captain Crane tried to discover the mystery of the bullet-shaped cylinders which had penetrated the hull of the Seaview. What would they find inside those things? Warren Stevens, who takes on the appearance of Sam Garrity, a WWII colleague of Admiral Nelson's, is equally intriguing. There is a calmness to him, an outward serenity, but what is this alien in disguise up to? We liked those rock-faced alien soldiers too; always silent, strangely quiet, and very deadly.

Two examples of the effectiveness of underplayed danger – Warren Stevens, calmly diabolical; and (below) his silent but deadly henchmen.

Mark Phillips said, "This show contained one of the scariest scenes I had ever seen on television as a kid – where crewman Peters hears footsteps clanking around a corner behind him and out of the shadows walk two monsters, immune to gunfire. Not only do they kill him, but they don't leave a mark on his body. Even thinking about the scene gives me goose bumps. Of course, not as scary today but thanks for the memory! … The fact that the alien assumes the form of Nelson's long-dead friend Sam Garrity is creepsville and the energy bubbles surrounding Nelson and Sharkey are also a neat idea." [2]

Neat ideas abound. And some not-so-neat ones. We were bothered that an underwater nuclear base would be left unguarded. A secret code is the only precaution taken to safeguard it? Things like this interrupt one's willing suspension of belief. And then, there's that ending. While not necessarily bad, it is bound to disappoint after the effectiveness of all that came before. These gripes aside, "Deadly Invasion" makes enjoyable escapism.

Script:

John Hawkins' and Ward Hawkins' writers contract: April 7, 1966.
Hawkins' story treatment, "The Invaders," approved by Irwin Allen on April 7.
Hawkins' 1st-Draft teleplay: May 4.
Hawkins' 2nd-Draft teleplay: May 12.
Shooting final teleplay: August 19.
Rev. Shooting Final (on pink paper): September 7.

"Deadly Invasion" began under a different title – "The Invaders." Among notes from Irwin Allen:

> Title must be changed (ABC has a new series by the same title).... Script is now 5 to 6 pages too long. ACTS 1 and 2 are each 20 pages long. They must be cut by at least 4 pages each. ACT 3 is only 7 ½ pages in length – too short. Dialogue needs polishing throughout....
>
> Page 3: Crane – 1st speech – should read "Captain to control room – etc." Actually, he's only a few steps from the control room and would probably not have to use the mike. ... Full shot – Nelson and Crane. Voice (over) with damage control report is too soon and not asked for as usual. How would they know the extent of damage so soon? In any event, damage control should address itself to Captain Crane. ... Would it be possible to show objects striking the sub as it is starting its steep dive? ...
>
> Page 4: Sharkey: What does he mean by "Automatic hull repair?" This would seem to imply that some mechanism automatically seals punctures without the help of the crew members....
>
> Sharkey: Change "We were hit, Captain." This is obvious.

Page 5: Crane's and Nelson's first speeches need rewriting. Crane would probably think that the object was part of the sub, torn loose by the meteor impact. Nelson would know that it is not part of the sub and would be confused by the fact that so small an object could pierce the hull. (1) How do they know it is not an artillery shell? (2) Why isn't there a flow of water in the control room due to the object's penetration?...

Page 14: Crane and Nelson exchange of dialogue is too repetitious: [re] P. 5: Crane "But what is it?" Nelson: "I don't know..."; P. 7: Crane: "But how?" Nelson: "I don't know."; P. 14: Crane: "What was that?" Nelson: "I don't know." ...

Page 14, Scene 45: Nelson: "It's a space ship!" Mightn't this line get a laugh as the cylinder is so small. It would read better as "It's a miniature space ship." ...

Page 16: It seems too much of a coincidence for Nelson to have a photograph of Garrity on display.

Page 24: From Crane's second speech: "Why did it happen to us?" through Page 27 – The dialogue is bad. There is too much recapping of past events, and too many unexplained holes in the story. Why is Nelson going to see if the cylinders have already reached Sato 6?...

Page 40: The radar operator says he has New York harbor on the scope. It is not possible to use radar for this purpose. Both the harbor and the octopus and any other definitive pictures should appear on the T.V. screen, not the radar scope....

The point that Nelson and the others have undergone a similar situation involving hallucinations once before should be more clearly brought out or the audience will be confused by their lack of concern over these events.[3]

Allen's final comment, about the crew having experienced hallucinations before was a curious nod to continuity. Rarely did anyone on Seaview refer to past adventures, and the sea creatures, monsters and aliens they had encountered; nor did Nelson or Crane ever speak of past brain-washings or possessions which had turned them against one another. The slate – and the characters' recollections – were wiped clean after each episode. Suddenly, Allen was taking notice. Unfortunately, Bruce Fowler, Sidney Marshall and Al Gail chose to ignore this note. Addressing it might have made the series better … but it would surely have made their jobs harder.

Mary Garbutt, of ABC, had her usual concerns:

> Your usual care in seeing that these fights are not unnecessarily prolonged. … Caution that we don't see the fingers biting into Nelson's throat. Nelson's facial contortions should not be overly grotesque. … Please be sure that there are no close-ups of hands around the throat – Nelson can convey "effort" but, of course, nothing such as "bulging eyes" or choking, gurgling sounds. … Throughout the script the scenes where people are killed, stunned, etc., by the "electrical" effects can be approved only on film. Particular caution on scenes 210 & 212, we should not get the impression that we are electrocuting a human being.

Ms. Garbutt also spotted the word "god" in one of Captain Crane's lines. She told Irwin Allen: "If this is not a typo for 'good,' please substitute." [4]

Production:
(Filmed September 7 – 14, 1966; 6 days)

William Self approved a budget of $168,710.

Associate Producer **Bruce Fowler, Jr.** suggested eight possible actors for the role of Garrity: Carroll O'Connor, James Gregory, Harold J. Stone, Lyle Bettger, Eric Fleming, Pat McVey, Don Ameche, and Richard Devon. Most would have commanded the top guest-star salary of $2,500. Allen wanted to pay less.

Warren Stevens earned $1,250 for playing Sam Garrity. This was Stevens' second of three appearances on *Voyage* (following "The Saboteur" and, yet to come, "Cave of the Dead"). Stevens had a reputation among casting directors as a guest star willing to lower his price in exchange for promises of future work. And that kept him exceedingly busy, with hundreds of screen appearances spanning six decades. Among them was his starring turn alongside Philip Carey in the 1956-57 series, *Tales of the 77th Bengal Lancers*, and 422 episodes of the soap, *Return to Peyton Place*, from 1972 through 1974. Stevens

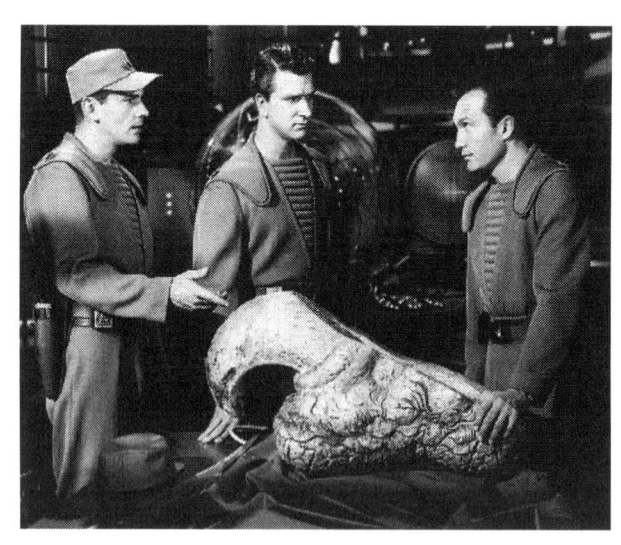

Above: Jack Kelly, Leslie Nielsen, and Warren Stevens in the 1956 sci-fi classic, *Forbidden Planet*. Below: Marco López in the 1970's series *Emergency!*

was no stranger to science fiction and fantasy, having co-starred in the 1956 film *Forbidden Planet*, taken trips into *Science Fiction Theatre*, *Men into Space*, *The Twilight Zone*, *The Outer Limits*, *The Time Tunnel*, *Star Trek*, *Wonder Woman*, and a pair of *Land of the Giants*.

This was the second of 20 episodes to feature **Marco López** as an unnamed crewmember (he first appeared in Season Two's "The Phantom Strikes"). He said, "Irwin Allen was like a mini-mentor of mine. He was very good to me and he was very loyal. Many people were afraid of him because they didn't know how he would react. I found that if you had something important to say to him, you said it and he listened. But if it was trivial, then don't bother the man!" [5]

Another mini-mentor of López's was Jack Webb, who cast the actor in 14 episodes of *Dragnet* as various characters; then in a dozen episodes of *Adam-12*, as the recurring character of Officer Sanchez; then 123 episodes of *Emergency!*, as a character who had the same name as the actor – Fireman Marco Lopez.

Production began on Wednesday, September 7, 1966 on Stage 10 for the Control Room and Observation Nose set.

Days 2 and 3, Thursday and Friday, were spent on Fox Stage 19, for "Int. Sato Entry and Corridor" and "Int. Sato Control."

On Days 4, 5 and 6 (Monday, Tuesday and Wednesday), the company was back on Stage 10 for additional Seaview sets, as well as the Flying Sub and "Int. Haines' Office."

396

They got it done in six days, but only by running up some overtime. On Day 5, they filmed until 8:33 p.m.; then, on Day 6, didn't wrap until 8:17.[6]

Release / Reaction:
(ABC premiere airdate: 11/20/66; network repeat broadcast: 6/4/67)

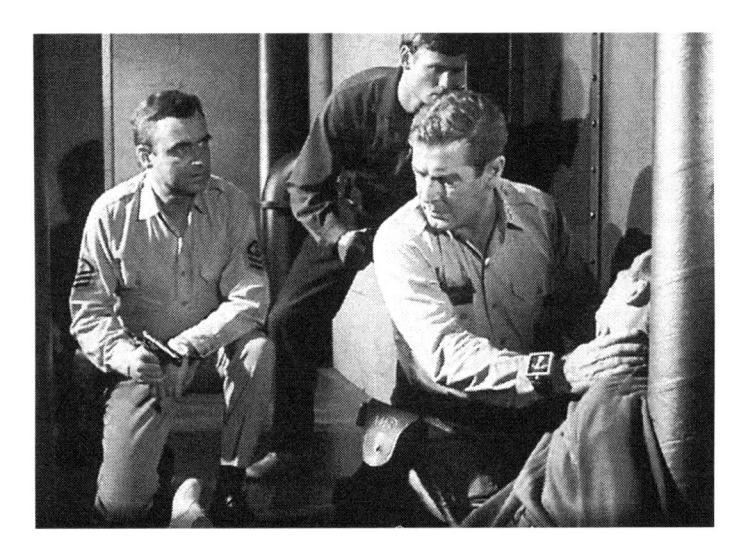

Promotional copy: "When the fabulous nuclear submarine Seaview is penetrated by miniature alien spaceships, Admiral Nelson and Captain Crane are trapped into a life and death struggle against the unknown assailants, whose plan is to take command of the Sato Six underwater atomic base! And then the world! A fantastic and way-out hour of adventure for the entire family!"

This was the week that an eerie blanket of smog engulfed New York City and, according to many sources, killed up to 400 people through a combination of respiratory failure and heart attacks. It was the smoggiest day in the city's history – a tragic occurrence that would have seemed at home in a horror movie … or an episode of *Voyage to the Bottom of the Sea* – except that it was a dreadful reality. The highest-grossing movie across America was *Penelope*, a sexy comedy starring Natalie Wood, with Peter Falk, Jonathan Winters, and Dick Shawn. "You Keep Me Hangin' On," by the Supremes, was the song getting the most spins on radio-station turntables. Of course, *The Monkees* was the top-selling album in stores. Bob Crane and Robert Clary of *Hogan's Heroes* had the cover of *TV Guide*.

Syndicated "TV Scout" said:

> Some more creatures from outer space, desperately in need of electrical energy, invade the Seaview on *Voyage to the Bottom of the Sea*. They arrive in miniature spaceships, and are seen as either an admiral under whom Richard Basehart once served, or as faceless beings. They are hard to stop, as they head for SATO Six, a huge reserve underwater atomic base, but a broken watch crystal provides the clue to their demise.[7]

"TV Key" raved:

> Fast-moving episode begins in high gear and keeps the gimmicky pyrotechnics pretty much on the upbeat. The good ship Seaview, imperiled by an infiltration of mysterious metallic objects which seem to be attracted to the electrical system, puts Admiral Nelson, Captain Crane and the entire crew in grave danger. Plenty of action and pseudo-scientific jargon for the fans.[8]

Nielsen 30-Market ratings report for November 20, 1966:[9]

(7 – 7:30 p.m.)	Rating:	Share:
ABC: *Voyage to the Bottom of the Sea*	**21.2**	**38.0%**
CBS: *Lassie*	16.1	28.9%
NBC: *Bell Telephone Hour*	6.6	11.8%

(7:30 – 8 p.m.):		
ABC: *Voyage to the Bottom of the Sea*	**20.3**	**35.1%**
CBS: *It's About Time*	10.4	18.0%
NBC: *Walt Disney's Wonderful World...*	16.7	28.8%

7.11

"The Lost Bomb" (Episode 69)

(Prod. No. 9211; first aired on Sunday, December 11, 1966)
Written by Oliver Crawford
Directed by Gerald Mayer
Produced by Irwin Allen and Bruce Fowler, Jr.; Story Editor: Sidney Marshall
Guest Stars John Lupton and Gerald Mohr

From *TV Guide*, December 10, 1966 issue.

> The Seaview engages in a deadly race against time and an unidentified submarine. The crews of both vessels are trying to recover an activated superbomb that has sunk to the ocean floor. [1]

Onboard the Seaview is bomb expert "Doc" Bradley, a childhood friend of Chief Sharkey's. Bradley's assignment is to help pick up and deliver a superbomb to an underwater installation. But they soon detect another sub (the Vulcan) in the area, just as it launches a missile which destroys the delivery plane. The bomb plunges into the sea but doesn't detonate. It is quickly recovered by the Seaview.

Attacked by the renegade sub, the Seaview's sonar is knocked out, as are its torpedo and missile-firing system. While frantic efforts are made to repair the damaged systems, Captain Crane and Kowalski take the Flying Sub in an effort to decoy the Vulcan. The effort fails as they are shot down and taken prisoner by Commander Vadim and Captain Zane on the Vulcan.

The reunion of two old friends gives a personal element to this Man-Against-Man/Bomb/Sub tale.

What follows is a ticking-clock scenario, as the superbomb, now aboard Seaview, continues its deadly countdown. Bradley's and Nelson's efforts to deactivate it are hampered by mistrust of Bradley (there is a spy aboard ship, who is homing the enemy sub Vulcan in for a kill) and the violent rocking of the ship as it comes under fire.

Assessment:

"The Lost Bomb" harks back to the more realistic dramas of the first season, with jeopardy stacked upon jeopardy, and believable reactions and interactions from the characters. This taut story also benefits from new optical effects and exciting action sequences. We see the Seaview's spectacular nosedive into rock formations and the sandy bottom of the sea. The original effects sequence had been filmed from different angles by multiple cameras, and, while included in a few previous episodes, it is presented here more fully, featuring fresh perspectives. We even get a new chase (no stock footage this time out), as the Vulcan closely pursues the Seaview, with both subs seen in the same shot.

"The Lost Bomb" boasts a small but impressive guest cast, featuring John Lupton as Dr. Bradley and Gerald Mohr as the skipper of the enemy vessel. With their sharp performances, countered by those of the regular *Voyage* cast, we are treated to a gripping Man Against Man tale instead of the more common Man Against Monster melodrama.

The action scenes are well staged and passionately performed. Note that when Kowalski belts the enemy guard, something goes flying from the point of impact and spins on the floor in the background. Was this part of a ring, a watch, or even a tooth? Whichever, you can feel the impact! The struggle over the live hand grenade is equally intense. And Sharkey belts his old friend after learning of his questionably loyalties. It's an emotionally charged reaction, and the icing on the cake is how Admiral Nelson does nothing to stop it.

And we find out Chief Sharkey's full name – Francis Ethelbert Sharkey – with Nelson's amusing reaction, and the embarrassed counter-reaction from Sharkey.

Mark Phillips was high on "The Lost Bomb," saying, "An exciting episode, which benefits from new optical effects and good action sequences. One of the more realistic Year Three episodes." [2]

Mike Bailey called it "pretty darn good." [3]

Script:

Oliver Crawford's writers contract: April 14, 1966.
Crawford's story treatment approved by Irwin Allen on May 13.
Crawford's 1st draft teleplay: May 24.
Crawford's 2nd draft teleplay: June 10.
Shooting Final teleplay: August 30.
2nd Rev. Shooting Final teleplay (on pink paper): September 13.
Added scene written on October 26.

This was screenwriter **Oliver Crawford**'s only script for *Voyage*. The formerly blacklisted writer, a victim of the 1950s Red Scare, had written regularly for various series, providing scripts for the kiddie show *Terry and the Pirates*, the anthology series *Climax!*, and *Ben Casey*. He'd also written for *The Fugitive*, *The Wild, Wild West*, and *The Outer Limits*. Crawford wrote (or co-wrote) three episodes of *Star Trek*. Irwin Allen bought another of Crawford's scripts for *Land of the Giants*. The writer was 55.

Crawford told interviewer Mark Phillips, "Whether I was writing about people in outer space or underwater, the key to a script's success was how you dealt with the people and their relationships to each other. The special effects on *Voyage* were very good and they enhanced the story. The series was made for entertainment and succeeded as such."[4]

Notes from Irwin Allen on various script drafts reveal the development of the story. Dr. Bradley was originally named Klausner; it was Patterson who was teamed up with Klausner to recover the bomb, not Chief Sharkey; and Sharkey, not Kowalski, was paired with Captain Crane as prisoners on the Vulcan.

> … It has never been explained why the bomb is being transferred to the Seaview in the first place. …
>
> Page 3 and 5: Check possibility of Hydrophone being able to pick up above surface explosion.
>
> 800 Ft. – Depth. Can you use scuba gear at this depth? Yes, but only if you make reference to special "anti-compression oxygen."
>
> Page 2 – 11: There's no mention of the unidentified sub. Nelson should have given orders to Sonar to trace its position and also the picket ship should have been alerted to intercept it. …
>
> Page 11: Crane – first speech – He cannot report "Dead stop and holding trim" to the Admiral in the same speech as he gives orders to control. It shouldn't really be necessary to report back to Nelson as it would be obvious they are dead in the water. …
>
> Page 16: Crane orders missiles fired. Shouldn't he be sighting the enemy sub through the periscope or does he have some other means by which he determines the correct location of the sub? …
>
> P. 23: Klausner calls Patterson "Pat" throughout the script. This seems too personal a relationship between a scientist and a crew member. …
>
> Page 52: It seems strange that with less than 18 minutes to go, Nelson would stop working on the bomb to make a speech about an enemy agent. …

P. 59: Thirty seconds seems to be too little time to allow Crane and the Chief to fight off their attackers and make their getaway in the FS-1. It should be at least 1 or 2 minutes.[5]

Since Allen didn't like the unmotivated chumminess between Klausner and Patterson, a plot beat was inserted stating that Klausner and Sharkey were childhood friends. This prompted a name change from Klausner to the less ethnic-sounding Bradley.

Production:
(Filmed September 15-22, 1966; 6 days)

This was director **Gerald Mayer**'s third of four *Voyage* assignments. The budget was set at $163,464.

John Lupton was paid $1,150 of that budget to play Dr. Bradley. He was 38 and had co-starred with Michael Ansara in *Broken Arrow* from 1956 through 1958. He was a regular on a soap opera *Never Too Young* at the time of

Above: John Lupton, from TV's *Broken Arrow*. Left: Gerald Mohr in the 1966 *Lost in Space* episode "A Visit to Hades."

this *Voyage*. Irwin Allen would also cast Lupton in "The Alamo" segment of *The Time Tunnel* from this same year.

Gerald Mohr earned $800 for two days of filming, playing Vadim. He had been a member of Orson Welles' Mercury Theatre of the Stage.

Mohr was also a CBS Radio staff announcer. Soon he was a radio star, playing the lead in several series, most notably *The Adventures of Philip Marlowe*, from 1948 through 1951. He was named Best Male Actor on Radio by *Radio and Television Life* in 1949. On the screen, he was the resident villain, Slick Latimer, in the 1941 serial *Jungle Girl*, and this led to many other villainous roles. He played the good guy, albeit a dark take, in 1946's *The Notorious Lone Wolf*, and then was tapped for two sequels in 1947. On television, he starred in the 1954-55 series *Foreign Intrigue*. Irwin Allen would cast Mohr in a standout *Lost in Space* episode from this time ("A Visit to Hades"). That, and this *Voyage*, were two of Mohr's last roles. He was in Sweden filming a TV pilot in 1968 when he died of a heart attack at age 54.

George Keymas, 40, played Zane, first officer of the Vulcan. He was a frequent player in TV and films, with close to two hundred appearances, including a previous role on *Voyage*, as Igor in Season One's "The Buccaneer." Irwin Allen would bring him back for an episode of *The Time Tunnel*. Keymas payrate was $250 per day, for two days.

Alexander Courage, working for *Star Trek* at this time (including composing the main title theme), provided the score – his fifth of six for *Voyage*.

Production began on Thursday, September 15 for the first of six days on Stage 10. Besides the standing Seaview sets and the Flying Sub, they also dressed sets to pass for "Int. Vulcan Brig," "Int. Vulcan Corridor" and "Int. Vulcan Control Room."

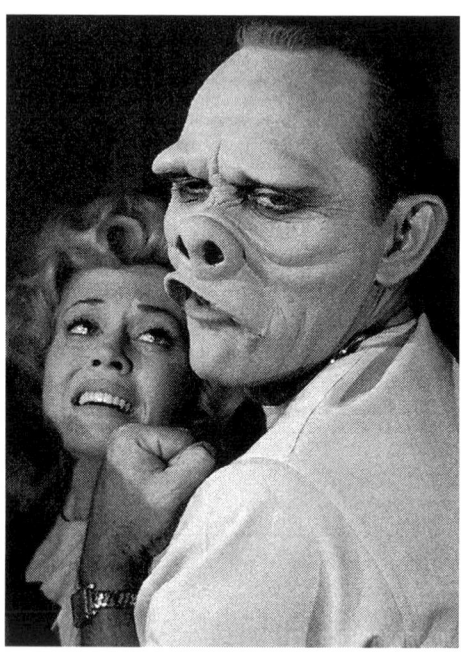

George Keymas played many villains on TV, and also this oddity, in a 1960 episode of *The Twilight Zone*.

Director Gerald Mayer, quoted in *Science Fiction Television*, said, "Richard Basehart was a marvelous actor. He was absolutely wasted in the series. … He was obviously unhappy with the show because he could deliver the character of the admiral in his sleep. … One couldn't feel sorry for him because he was making a barrel of money." [6]

Mario López, in this episode as an unnamed crew member, told interviewer Mark Phillips, "[T]he cast was fun to work with. David Hedison was terrific. He would always joke and laugh with us. Richard Basehart was absolutely the best. The show wasn't his cup of tea but he had signed the contract.

He was such a refined actor and here he was in an adventure series playing the Admiral. You never saw a bad side of him on the set. Never. He did his work and he was wonderful." [7]

The Green Tank underwater shots were taken on October 12, with Paul Stader directing.

Gerald Mayer also shot a new scene which was written after the first edit of the episode was viewed. This took place on October 27, from 1 to 7 p.m. [8]

Release / Reaction:
(Only ABC broadcast: 12/11/66)

This was the week the U.S. Air Force first started bombing Hanoi, North Vietnam. James Arness, *Gunsmoke*'s Matt Dillon, had the cover of *TV Guide*, America's No. 1 magazine; *The Bible: In the Beginning* was still No. 1 in movie houses; "Winchester Cathedral," by the New Vaudeville Band, was No. 1 on the radio; *The Monkees* was the No. 1 album in record stores; *The Secret of Santa Vittoria*, by Robert Crichton, was No. 1 on the *New York Times* Best Seller list; and Twister, from Milton Bradley, was the hottest "toy" for Christmas.

Days before the broadcast of "The Lost Bomb," a press release promoting the episode and focusing on guest-star Gerald Mohr playing a "heavy" was issued by 20th Century-Fox.

> Gerald Mohr is "heavy" with a light touch. Mohr guest-stars with Richard Basehart and David Hedison on "The Lost Bomb" episode of producer Irwin Allen's *Voyage to the Bottom of the Sea* series from 20th Century-Fox Television, which will be seen tonight in color on ABC-TV. A "heavy" in television and motion pictures is the villain of the piece. The man people always love to hate. Mohr is one of the best. [9]

The suave actor explained, "The best heavies, however, are those actors who play the part with a little humor, a little love of life thrown in. You've got to look like you enjoy the job. When you break a hero's arm, smile. When you throw sand in his face, chuckle a little. When you push the old lady down the stairs, wave goodbye as she goes. Audiences are happiest when they can watch a man who loves his work." [10]

Syndicated "TV Key" saw "The Lost Bomb" this way:

> The series turns away from the supernatural plots it's been using lately and reverts to a good old-fashioned adventure yarn. Adm. Nelson and the stalwart crew of the Seaview have to locate and deactivate a bomb capable of destroying an entire hemisphere. To add to the danger and the complications, an enemy sub is tracking the Seaview. [11]

Only a portion of the A.C. Nielsen report from December 11, 1966 was located during our research, providing the ratings for the first half-hour: [12]

(7 – 7:30 p.m.)	Peak Share:
ABC: *Voyage to the Bottom of the Sea*	22%
CBS: "*A Charlie Brown Christmas*" (special)	**57%**
NBC: *Walt Disney's Wonderful World of Color*	40%

Sadly, this above-average *Voyage* episode was pitted against the premiere of "A Charlie Brown Christmas," and got clobbered in the ratings. Irwin Allen and ABC zigged when they should have zagged. They assumed "The Lost Bomb" underperformed because it didn't feature a monster, so it was not given a second network airing.

7.12

"The Brand of the Beast" (Episode 70)

(Prod. No. 9213; first aired on Sunday, December 18, 1966)
Written by William Welch
Directed by Justus Addiss
Produced by Irwin Allen and Bruce Fowler, Jr.; Story Editor: Sidney Marshall

The production numbering goes a bit askew here. This is catalogued as Production No. 9213. It was intended to be the thirteenth episode made for the third season. It was actually the twelfth made. "The Plant People," the episode filmed after this, was catalogue number of 9212. It was supposed to shoot first but had to be pushed back a week, with "The Brand of the Beast" pulled forward, in order to accommodate needed guest performers.

From *TV Guide*, December 17, 1966 issue:

> The Seaview becomes a den of terror when a virus again transforms Admiral Nelson into a werewolf. The virus, no longer vulnerable to vaccine, threatens to turn the entire crew into a pack of monsters.[1]

Assessment:

This was *Voyage to the Bottom of the Sea*'s second sequel (following the success of "The Phantom Strikes" and "The Phantom Returns"). This time, the source material was "Werewolf," and the results merely serviceable. But the episode isn't completely devoid of merits. If you wanted more after "Werewolf," or felt cheated that Admiral Nelson was infected with the mutated rabies virus but didn't transform into a man-beast, your wishes are hereby granted. Further, this story provides a handful of highly effective sequences. One – actually a series of scenes – presents Chief Sharkey's dilemma over having to countermand Captain Crane's order, to keep his word to Admiral Nelson. This includes the payoff – the confrontation between a stern Crane and an evasive Sharkey, before the guilty eyes of Nelson. Another plus is the depiction of Nelson's final resolve to make the ultimate sacrifice in order to protect the crew.

On the liability side of the ledger, we again have a nose-dive crash of the Seaview prompted by a bull in a china shop – in this case, the werewolf in the circuitry room. We'd see it before – instigated by various saboteurs and monsters – and we'd see it again, too often. By the time you get to the end of the fourth season, you'll no doubt agree that this circuitry room, both the heart and the Achilles heel of the Seaview, should *always* have a guard on the door, or, better still, a door of reinforced steel, with quadruple locks!

Flare-up in the circuitry room! It was becoming a recurring event on *Voyage*.

And, for heaven's sake, strap those circuitry racks into place!

Back to the plus side: Mike Bailey said, "The acting is terrific. Basehart may have hated this stuff, but he made it work, as did everyone else." [2]

On the fence, Mark Phillips wrote, "This is another example where a great cast really works for its pay (Chief Sharkey caught between the orders of Nelson and Crane; the bewildered Doctor grappling with the Admiral's condition; Crane's confusion, etc.). Story wise, the episode is frustrating for its many lapses in logic and the werewolf makeup is more comical than frightening. There's even a weird scene where Chip Morton's character suddenly appears for a cameo. It's another budget saver, but it's the dedicated cast who really saves this one." [3]

Enjoy the acting and set your brain to cruise control for the rest of what they could have called "Where wolf? There wolf! Again!"

Script:

William Welch's writers contract: September 13, 1966.
Welch's story idea, "The Mark of the Beast," undated.
Shooting Final teleplay, "The Brand of the Beast," (on pale green paper): September 19.
Page revisions (on blue paper): September 21.
Page revisions (on pink paper): September 22.
A new scene was written on November 2.

Irwin Allen and his creative staff felt they had something special with "Werewolf," the second episode made for the new season. Despite the wild premise, the cast seemed to enjoy it too. And the episode did contain the springboard for a sequel: Admiral Nelson's being infected. So, before the audience's reaction could be gauged, Allen asked **William Welch** to write a sequel to the Donn Mullally-written original.

Welch's story treatment entitled "The Mark of the Beast" was only two pages long:

> An accident to Seaview's nuclear power plant threatens an important mission. Only Nelson can effect the emergency repairs. In the course of making the repairs, he has to expose one hand to an excessive radiation dose. Once the mission is resumed, Nelson is startled to find a change taking place in the exposed hand ... nails elongating, hair appearing, etc. He realizes, from a past adventure, that he is not rid of the strange virus which once had threatened to transform him into a werewolf. Anticipating what is about to happen, he swears Chief Sharkey to secrecy and has him lock him up until a specific time. The Chief obeys in spite of counter orders from Crane.
>
> Nelson makes the transformation into a monstrous creature and then tries to get out, first by force and then by guile. But Sharkey, obeying orders against all odds, keeps the Admiral confined until the attack is over.
>
> Crane, angry over Sharkey's apparent insubordination, has the Chief locked in the brig, destined for court martial when

the mission is over. Nelson, without explanation, countermands the orders. Then, unexpectedly, another attack comes as he changes into the monstrous form; free to roam the ship. A chase begins throughout the sub to kill this horrific creature before it kills the crew or destroys the ship. And only Sharkey, knowing secretly it is the Admiral, is able to prevent Nelson's murder. Yet eventually Sharkey himself is nearly killed by the creature. [4]

And there you have it – a chase aboard the Seaview, with a monster!

The most interesting aspect of the story involved the relationship between Nelson and Sharkey, first established in the Welch-penned "Terror on Dinosaur Island." Welch's werewolf-sequel synopsis explained, "When Nelson reverts to his own form, he believes he actually has killed the Chief." This prompted Nelson's next action – one of self-punishment and ultimate sacrifice:

> To save the sub and the rest of the crew, he has himself launched in the diving bell, then severs the cable. The bell sinks to terrific depths and comes to rest on the bottom. There, under the crushing pressure, awaiting death, he discovers a chemical change in his blood. The enormous pressure has killed the viral infection and made him normal ... except that he is trapped and doomed. ...
>
> The Chief – not knowing of Nelson's cure – confesses what has happened to Crane. Nelson, knowing himself to be incurable and wishing to save the lives of his crew, has deliberately marooned himself on the bottom to await death. Crane is unwilling to accept this and persists in risking everything to save the Admiral.... [5]

This framing of the story is emotionally charged on a personal level for Nelson, Sharkey, and Crane. But then ABC got involved.

Mary Garbutt, of the network's Department of Broadcast Standards and Practices, told Allen and his staff:

> As written, this episode seems acceptable. Your special care [required] in seeing that the werewolf sequences are not directed beyond what is indicated in the script and the video and audio effects are not too frightening for young viewers; Can only be approved on film.... Note in particular that the

werewolf does not attack the men beyond shoving them aside and tearing the shirt. Caution that the viewers are kept, as written, in the POV of the objects attacked or the men involved, with no added shots of the werewolf lunging at or snarling into camera. Also caution that his sounds are not too "blood-curdling" for family viewing. [6]

These days, things fly at the camera all the time, but not in 1966, in the "family hour," on the ABC Television Network.

The biggest change ABC wanted involved Nelson's self-exile in the diving bell at the bottom of the sea. The network wanted this to be understated, and kept brief, in an effort not to endorse suicide. In pruning back this section of the story, and eliminating a self-tortured Sharkey's admission to Crane that he knows what Nelson's goal is, the climax was watered down (sorry). What would have been a poignant ending was transformed into something that felt rushed and underdeveloped.

Production:
(Filmed September 23 – 30, 1966; 6 days;
plus pickup shot on November 3)

The budget was set at $155,500. There was no guest star in this episode, to keep costs down.

Mark Phillips cited Jerry Catron as the stuntman in the werewolf costume. However, the Daily Production Reports identify **Frank Graham** as the creature. He worked on five of the seven days needed to film this episode (six initial production days plus one extra day scheduled later). Paul Stader was hired to do a stunt for one day, and Ron Stein, who worked two days – each doubling for other cast members.

Production began on Friday, September 23, 1966, for the first of six days on Stage 10, with the Seaview sets, plus diving bell. Only one day required overtime, with Addiss filming until 7:30 p.m.

Because a chunk of the story's guts were removed at the network's insistence, the rough edit for this episode came in short. Two new scenes were then written to make up for the loss, which Justus Addiss directed on Thursday, November 3, also on Stage 10. The first was a page of dialogue between Richard Basehart and Terry Becker, padding the scene in Nelson's cabin in which he reveals his condition to Sharkey and asks the latter to keep the secret. These inserts, at the start of the conversation between the two, had Nelson hide his hairy hand behind his back. This doesn't seem to accomplish anything, since Nelson ends up showing the hand to Sharkey anyway. But the stall added a minute of screen time. And that's what they were after.

The second one-minute add was worse, a page-and-a-half of meaningless banter. The sequence was shot in the Missile Room, with David Hedison and Robert Dowdell, accounting for Chip Morton's only appearance in "Brand of the Beast." Crane and Morton say nothing that we haven't already heard, or could anticipate without it being verbalized – an unneeded recap ... taking the place of a passage of what would have been emotionally gripping drama. [7]

Release / Reaction:
(Only ABC broadcast: 12/18/66)

On the day "Brand of the Beast" aired on ABC, the USSR performed a nuclear test at Eastern Kazakh/Semipalatinsk. The population of the United States was 195 million, with 500,000 of them serving in Vietnam. *The Monkees* was still top album in the U.S.; "Winchester Cathedral" by the New Vaudeville Band was still top single, with Donovan's "Mellow Yellow" breathing down its neck; *A Man for All Seasons* was top film; *Bonanza* was top TV show. *Voyage* would be up against the debut of *How the Grinch Stole Christmas* on CBS this night, and *TV Guide* gave *Grinch* a Close-Up listing as well as a color feature article.

Despite the competition, both "TV Scout" and "TV Key" singled "The Brand of the Beast" out as one of the evening's "Best Bets."

"TV Scout" said:

> *Voyage to the Bottom of the Sea* has a follow-up to a recent segment in which the scratch of a werewolf turned Richard Basehart into a snarling beast. Now, when he is forced to expose his scratched right hand to a dose of radiation to repair a problem in the Seaview's reactor pile, the symptoms

recur. Basehart gives a good performance, especially as he realizes that he must make the supreme sacrifice. But the solution to the problem is a hasty wrap-up that doesn't quite close the doors on future episodes on the same subject. [8]

"TV Key" commented:

Series fans, who recall an episode titled "Werewolf," will be intrigued by the tale tonight. Admiral Nelson (Richard Basehart) suffers a relapse of a virus infection which turns him into a raging werewolf. The kids will be engrossed in this combination horror-sea adventure. [9]

A.C. Nielsen 30-Market ratings report for December 18, 1966: [10]

7 – 7:30 P.M.:	Rating:	Share:
ABC: *Voyage to the Bottom of the Sea*	9.3	17.7%
CBS: *How the Grinch Stole Christmas*	**25.0**	**47.5 %**
NBC: *Bell Telephone Hour*	11.4	21.7%

7:30 – 8 P.M.:		
ABC: *Voyage to the Bottom of the Sea*	12.9	22.2%
CBS: *It's About Time*	15.7	27.1%
NBC: *Walt Disney's Wonderful World…*	**23.6**	**40.7%**

As with "The Lost Bomb," *Voyage*'s ratings were down due to scheduling opposite a must-see holiday family special. Irwin Allen and ABC wondered if a second dose of the werewolf theme in the same broadcast season might also to be to blame for a lack of interest on the part of the audience, so "The Brand of the Beast" was not given a network repeat airing.

7.13

"The Plant Man" (Episode 71)

(Prod. No. 9212; first aired on Sunday, December 4, 1966)
Written by Donn Mullally
Directed by Harry Harris
Produced by Irwin Allen and Bruce Fowler, Jr.; Story Editor: Sidney Marshall
Guest Star William Smithers

From *татTV Guide*, December 3, 1966 issue:

> Nelson must defeat an ingenious adversary who has learned to control vegetable growth. The power-mad scientist is planning to create a conquering army of plant creatures.[1]

The power-mad scientist also has a twin brother, and the two are telepathically connected. They have developed a new form of plant life, supposedly to help with the world's food supply. But Ben, the ambitious and dominant one, forms a diabolical plan to use these plant creatures as an army.

As Seaview approaches, with Ben on board, he orders brother John, at a sea lab on the ocean floor, to complete the experiment. Unable to resist his brother's will, John uses a massive dose of radiation to create a giant plant monster. As the Flying Sub, with Nelson and Ben aboard, approaches the sea lab, the creature attacks. Nelson sends out a distress call and Seaview speeds to the rescue.

Assessment:

With a name like "The Plant Man," it's got to be bad. Right?

There are moments of subtle camp in this episode which prompt a few laughs. On the other end of the spectrum is a look at sibling dominance and poetic justice in how to remedy such a situation. There are also some excellent effects, including a new shot of the Seaview, with collision doors closed, propelled at ramming speed into the plant-thing's gut. Then, there is the rest of the episode.

"Shootout at the Greenhouse Corral" – one way to try to kill plant men. Hope those are water pistols loaded with herbicide!

Mark Phillips said, "Sadly, the episode can't be taken seriously – the plant men run around like Tasmanian Devils, and was someone putting us on with that wild west shootout at the end, as our heroes stand side by side blasting away at the plant men?" [2]

Mike Bailey noted, "Surprisingly good undersea effects of the giant plant, the undersea lab, and flying sub, all wasted on an idiotic story. There is no explanation as to why Ben is so evil and no justification for his thinking an army of giant underwater plant men would do him any good. … Once again, the cast, including guest William Smithers, does an amazing job of giving straight dramatic treatment to laughable material; it is too bad the writing didn't match their talent." [3]

These walking refugees from a pumpkin patch may not be as scary as James Arness's "walking carrot" in *The Thing (from Another World)*, but this tale is still a rollicking diversion.

Script:
Donn Mullally's writers contract: May 2, 1966.
Mullally's 1ˢᵗ-Draft teleplay: June 7.
Mullally's 2ⁿᵈ (and final) draft teleplay: July 18.
2ⁿᵈ Rev. Shooting Final teleplay (on pink paper): October 3.

This was **Donn Mullally**'s second of three *Voyage* scripts (following "Werewolf," and with "Destroy Seaview" yet to come). His one-page story springboard read:

> A Hydroponics Station experimenting in artificial radiation as a growth factor in underwater plant life explodes and is destroyed because of a stubborn, willful act on the part of one of its engineers, who dies in the catastrophe.
>
> Aboard the Seaview, which is supervising the experimentation, is another such engineer, a brother of the dead man, who blames negligence and a seeking-after-fame on the part of Nelson for his brother's death.
>
> As the diving bell descends to investigate, it is attacked by a Plant Man, a creature obviously brought to life by the radioactive lighting used in the experiment. The creature wrecks the diving bell, comes aboard the Seaview when the bell is brought aboard, and almost succeeds in destroying the submarine and its crew. Its actions are aided and abetted by the dead man's brother, who is seeking his personal revenge on Nelson.
>
> Not until the creature is driven off the submarine and is hunted down and destroyed ashore on a nearby island is this potentially catastrophic danger to the world obliterated. [4]

Irwin Allen and Sidney Marshall tossed out the revenge theme, keeping only the idea of two brothers – with the names of Wilson and Minor Trueblood – and their powerful man-plant. Allen, in fact, seemed singularly focused on the idea of the Rock 'Em Sock 'Em plant, and just how mighty such a creature could be. After reading the first draft script, Allen responded:

> Page 7, Scene 28: Wouldn't water pour into the Sea-lab (or at least seep into it) if the leafy thorn tipped appendage was able to gain entry through a supposedly water tight hatch. This needs explaining.
>
> Since the Plant Man has such fantastic strength, it certainly seems that it would be able to rip apart the hatch.
>
> This note applies as well to Scene 138, Page 40 in which Crane and all but one of his diving companions enters the lab and finds it dry. [5]

… and, of course, important dialogue changes, along the lines of:

> Page 42; Scene 147: Sharkey – change "the old man…" to "The Skipper."
>
> Page 45; Scene 154: Sharkey – What does he mean by "If Kowalski can hold his face right?"
>
> Page 61; Scene 206: Crane – Last speech – "Because I'm the Captain" sounds too cocky. … [6]

We could think of more important things to fuss over with this script, but the strain of overseeing three series was taking a toll on the workaholic Irwin Allen. He had to rely on staff members to find the faults in scripts, including the production problems created by a writer's overactive imagination.

A key member of that staff had become Production Coordinator **Les Warner**, who sent his comments to Allen, with cc to Sidney Marshall, Bruce Fowler, and numerous production heads, on June 27. He wrote, in part:

> INT. SEA LAB – Scene 5: The airlock in this set is a very expensive item. As to concept, I am thinking of a similar underwater set in *Voyage*'s "City Beneath the Sea" which necessitated a water-proof tank built into a stage floor pit out of which underwater cast doubles emerged with practical

scuba gear. This expense was justified then because it was a key set, but it is not justified in this story…. SOLUTION: Couldn't we assume the airlock is immediately o.s. [off screen] around a corner?...

EXT. AND INT. SEA LAB – Scenes 14, 30, 34, 77: The Sea Lab should not be bowled over on its side: … shooting the Interior this way would create impossible Set and Cost Problems…. This would also mean another Miniature setup…. It would "open a can of beans" as to how our people later enter and exit the Sea Lab through the airlock, which must be full of water and couldn't be if the Lab is on its side. NOTE: Suggest the explosion and percussion violently rocks the Sea Lab and damages it enough to destroy communication, power, etc., but it is not knocked off its foundation….

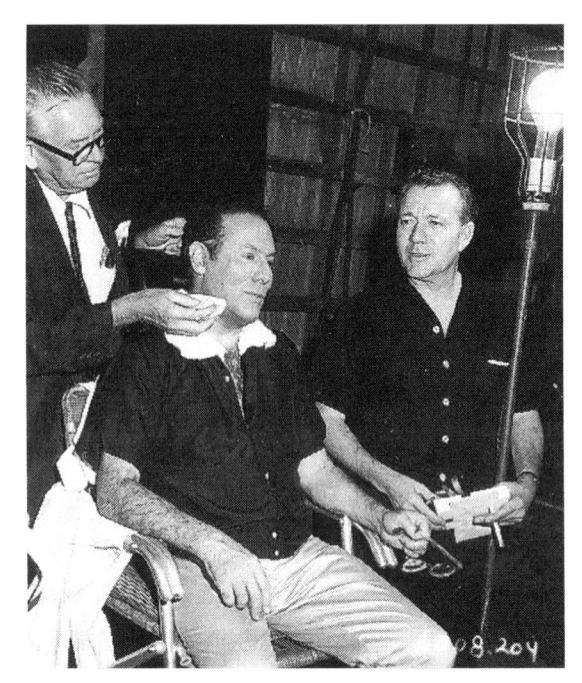

Les Warner's script notes became key on Irwin Allen's shows from this period. Warner (at right) is pictured on the set of the 1961 Voyage *movie, with make-up artist Ben Nye prepping Allen for promotional pictures.*

INT. FLYING SUB – Scene 39: DELETE the Plant Man's "thorns" penetrating into the ship. Incidentally, the FS1 would leak like a sieve if this happened….

EXT. UNDERSEA – Scene 85: We shouldn't see Wilson's dead body as men carry it. It should be wrapped up.

NOTE: Due to the writer's unfamiliarity with the Seaview, the following discrepancies will have to be corrected: … Scene 101: The Seaview does not have this Interior Airlock. The divers would have to come out of the Escape Hatch into the Missile Room. But they can't because the Plant Man is supposed to be there at this time…. SOLUTION: Couldn't we cover Scenes 98 through 101 with a PA announcement to Crane in Control Room that divers have returned with the black box – and we assume they boarded sub some other way?...

SCENE 155: If the Plant Man is so huge that he can rock and destroy the Flying Sub and practically fill a Seaview corridor, how can he crawl all over in the Interior Air Duct system?...

PHOTO EFFECTS: A RED FLAG here, considering the amount of underwater Miniature work and effects that are indicated – involving: A) Underwater Hydroponics Station with Sealab and Cultivation Area; B) Wrecking of above station (EXPLOSION); C) Rock bombardment of the Sealab; D) Flying Sub undersea search for Hydroponic Station; E) Three Laser beam animations; F) Two BURN-INS on Monitor screens; G) Process Plates of some of the above....

2ND UNIT – GREEN TANK: There is an exorbitant cost problem with the amount of 2nd Unit work now indicated and the nature of the shots required – involving the following:
A) Undersea growing frames and divers;
B) Ext. Sea Lab airlock entrance and divers;
C) Swim-throughs of various groups of divers;
D) Plant Man and wrecked frames;
E) Plant Man on rocky elevation;
F) Plant Man chases divers;
G) Plant Man fights Nelson;
H) Plant Man wrecks Flying Sub.
NOTE: It would be impossible, cost and time wise, to shoot the scenes now indicated for above item #H alone. A large, full-detailed miniature of the Flying Sub would have to be built in size ratio to the Plant Man. Also, this diver would have to work without scuba gear which creates a critical hazard considering the costume he'll have to wear. I earnestly recommend that all Plant Man underwater shots be reduced to a bare minimum and that his Flying Sub sequence be confined to one exterior section at which he somehow sabotages the machine; otherwise, we can never shoot this.
7

Remember – this kind of production scrutiny was required for *every* *Voyage* script, far in advance of coming before the camera.

The next day, Associate Producer Bruce Fowler turned in his notes to Sidney Marshall, with cc to Irwin Allen and Al Gail.

> The general idea of this script is an excellent one for the *Voyage* series. However, I feel that this version has one drawback. That is, a very stilted approach to the dialogue in the first part of the script, which, in turn, affects the actions and reactions of our characters. So much attempt to use colloquialisms detracts from the speeches and the story line, i.e., on Page 20, when Crane answers Nelson, with regard to driving off the monster with a blow torch, he uses the following expression: "I don't think it appreciated our little cookout." This is but one example of several of the same type that appear in this script. So, that, overall, I believe that the weakness in the present script is the dialogue, and we need to make it sound more like our people, and to lose its present cuteness. The action is well paced, and the monster is a good one.
>
> Page 12 – Scene 39, INT. FLYING SUB: Nelson's attitude towards the menace of the Plant Man attacking the sub seems too blasé – even for a "detached scientific attitude." I feel this scene and others in the early part of the script call for a more direct response from Nelson, rather than the seemingly flip one now there.
>
> Page 44 – Scene 127: Nelson's statement that Minor is the real menace is too abrupt and premature at this point – it is a complete reversal of his attitude, without any lay-in for it in the scene. I also feel that the character of MINOR TRUEBLOOD is still not clear to the author. He keeps changing him from good to bad – without any real indication as to which way the character has gone – except for a short scene in the Missile Room, when he has him express a grin in Scene 118, which is supposed to indicate that he is playing a double role. A clearer indication of his true nature should be shown.
>
> Then the Plant Man physically keeps changing in size all the time. He goes from rather small in the beginning to

tremendous when the electric curtain hits him in Scene 53, to a normal size for the rest of the picture. This would also present a difficult problem, production-wise. ... [8]

Fowler had put his finger on the problem with the story at this stage. The character of Minor Trueblood (besides urgently needing a name change) seemed bipolar. One minute, he was a fairly good guy; the next, a power-mad nut. The solution: change the brothers names to John Wilson and Ben Wilson, toss in the twin-brother-psychic-link angle, and, presto – one good brother under the mental control of a bad brother. Next, show the good brother eating a vegetable in the Teaser, establishing his motivation – to grow bigger plants to feed a bigger population of the world. Then establish that the bad brother, always a bully, decides that these giant plants, if controlled, could be used to bring great power. Dare he say, he could rule the world?!

Perhaps due to all the rewriting, they forgot to give the audience insight into the bad brother's thinking processes.

Production:
(Filmed October 3 – 10, 1966; 6 days)

Harry Harris was back in the director's chair and not surprised to see another script with another monster ... and another script lacking in emotional depth for the lead actors. He agreed with Paul Zastupnevich, who said that Allen seemed afraid of emotion, or at least, afraid to show it on the screen. Harris said, "Maybe [Paul's] right. Irwin didn't want to touch on those. We never had any of that in there.... Maybe on some of the movies he made, but not in his television stuff; there was never anything between the people. Never. None that I can recall. It was always man against the elements, man against the monsters, or the little people against the giants. You know, it was always pitting one against the other. I believe Paul made a good statement in that respect, because I never had any experience [in an Irwin Allen show] with any kind of love affairs on the screen or any couples getting together. Maybe man and wife holding hands, hugging, something like that, but no more than that."

The increase in monsters and bottle shows was due to lack of money. Harris said, "It went into 'Lettuce Man' and the 'Monster in the Closet,' and all that stuff, because [Irwin] had to cut his budget. They went to color, and they had to cut the budgets back because the shows were very expensive. The special effects were expensive, and there were a lot of effects in his shows, and miniatures. So, the more costly it became, the more they made him cut it back." [9]

This was the thirteenth episode filmed in the third season (despite a production number indicating that it had been planned to be the twelfth), and there had not been a single woman featured in any of them.

Terry Becker said, "Frankly, none of us were happy with the emphasis on monsters. We got tired of doing that. It got really boring. That wasn't the show we wanted to do but it was cheaper to have us battle a guy in a monster suit than take us out on location." [10]

After much cutting, and with a monster in the cast, William Self set the budget at $158,598.

Bruce Fowler suggested seven possible actors to play the dual roles of John and Ben Wilson. They were Keith Andes, William Talman, Richard Carlson, Mark Richman, Mike Connors, Jack Kelly, or Martin Landau. As often happened, Fowler's suggestions were ignored in favor of someone a mite less expensive.

William Smithers was paid $1,650 to play John *and* Ben Wilson. He was 39 and played hundreds of roles on TV and in the movies between 1952 and 1994. Among his list of credits, 50 turns on *Dallas*, as Jeremy Wendell.

Production began on Monday, October 3, 1966

Bad William Smithers (above); good Smithers (right); Irwin Allen got two Smithers for the price of one.

for the first of six days on Stage 10 for the Flying Sub set, the Seaview sets, as well as "Int. Reactor Room," and "Int. Sealab & Store Rooms."

Second-unit filming took place in the Green Tank on October 26, 27 and 28, with Paul Stader directing. The stunt divers were Mark Waters, Pete Peterson,

John Lamb, Peter Dixon, and Stader. Michael Donavan was the stunt diver inside the monster outfit. [11]

Mario López, in this episode as an unnamed crewman, said, "I watched the show when it originally ran and I was always impressed by how it looked. Irwin was a genius with special effects. The explosions, the aliens, the monsters, they all looked good." [12]

Donn Mullally told interviewer Mark Phillips, "I liked what they did with my scripts. They weren't monumental in my writing career, but I enjoyed writing them. They had a hell of an art department. When I described the plant man, they came back with a storyboard picture that was perfect. The cast was fine. They didn't have to do anything special, just frown." [13]

They did far more than "just frown."

Release / Reaction:
(ABC premiere airdate: 12/4/66; network repeat broadcast: 4/16/67)

This was the week that the U.S. and the U.S.S.R. signed a treaty to prohibit nuclear weapons in outer space. "Good Vibrations," by the Beach Boys, and "Mellow Yellow," by Donovan, were competing for the most airplay on radio stations. Larry Casey, Chris George, and Justin Tarr of *The Rat Patrol* had the cover of *TV Guide*.

As for "The Plant Man," "TV Key Previews" said:

> For the kids. This week's adventure is a weirdie, complete with giant plant mutations, a mad scientist and his good twin brother, and the brave, hard-fighting crew of the Seaview. Admiral Nelson really has his hands full when he and his crew have to combat atomic-fed plant life capable of destroying all mankind. [14]

"TV Scout" said:

> *Voyage to the Bottom of the Sea* gurgles spryly with an interesting mystery: "The Plant Man." William Smithers plays a devious sort who controls his twin (a role he also plays) as easily as he does some underwater vegetables. There is a lot of science-fiction chatter about the powers of telepathy and "monsters" with minds of their own. [15]

A.C. Nielsen 30-Market ratings report for December 4, 1966: [16]

7 – 7:30 P.M.:	Rating:	Share:
ABC: *Voyage to the Bottom of the Sea*	**19.3**	**36.0%**
CBS: *Lassie*	17.0	31.7%
NBC: *Bell Telephone Hour*	6.8	12.7%

7:30 – 8 P.M.:	Rating:	Share:
ABC: *Voyage to the Bottom of the Sea*	**20.0**	**35.2%**
CBS: *It's About Time*	11.4	20.1%
NBC: *Walt Disney*	17.5	30.8%

Say what you will about "The Plant Man," he pulled in a 36 audience share for *Voyage*. That was all ABC needed to see. Evidently vegetables *are* good for you!

7.14

"The Creature" (Episode 72)

(Prod. No. 9214; first aired on Sunday, January 1, 1967)
Written by John and Ward Hawkins
Directed by Justus Addiss
Produced by Irwin Allen and Bruce Fowler, Jr.; Story Editor: Sidney Marshall
Guest Star Lyle Bettger

From the *Voyage* show files (Irwin Allen papers collection):

> The Seaview, on a mission to recover a life form released in the sea by its creator, Dr. King, locates it by instruments. Crane and Kowalski go out to verify the instruments' finding, and Crane is overcome by the Creature. Rescued by Kowalski, and back on board the Seaview, Crane finds he is now controlled by the Creature, as is King, and they are both forced to betray others into the Creature's power. [1]

Assessment:

A generic title like "The Creature" may have you think the episode is less-than-inspired. Still, we found many things to like.

Guest "star" Lyle Bettger, as Dr. King, is effective. Man, how this guy's eyes lock onto those of the people he wants to control! That gaze sells the concept, along with the usual excellent acting from the regular players – David Hedison and Richard Bull in particular, when under Dr. King's spell. They somehow project a sense of remorse as they go about their dastardly deeds. The physical confrontation between King, Crane, and "Doc," as the latter realizes what is happening and resists the creature, is intense.

The scene involving the death of Captain Crane is gripping. Okay, we know that he will somehow be brought back to life – status quo must rule, after all – but the shocked silence conveyed by the cast has impact.

The creature too is startling. It registers high in creep factor, with a swampy, leafy texture, gaping square mouth, and high-pitched cries. The concept involving its rapid growth, doubling in size every few hours, and its violent disposition, makes it a believable threat. It's "walking" toward the Pacific Coast of America. Projections estimate it will be "almost the size of a city" by the time it reaches its destination, with an electrical potential to destroy a metropolis six times the size of San Francisco. It should be destroyed long before then, right? But, while underplayed, Nelson is conflicted. His gut says "snuff it out," but during the first half of the story he is hard-pressed to come up with arguments to support his emotional inclination.

The relationship between King and the creature – then its control over King, Crane, and Doc – is interesting. The "thing" may have profound influence over these men, but they still maintain their memories, a trace of independent thinking, and a level of compassion. They're not walking zombies. Dr. King expresses both awe and fear during the mission to collect samples from the giant creature. Crane and "Doc" exchange looks of apprehension as the mission progresses, all under the curious gaze of Morton. There are other subtleties – blink and you'll miss them – such as, after the creature has been shot in the gut by two tranquilizer missiles, Captain Crane puts a hand over his own stomach. We like how Chip Morton is an intelligent observer. He watches Crane and the Doc, suspicious about what may be going on; then, without a word spoken, or his hand being revealed, Morton shows up to prevent the capture of Nelson and Sharkey. And how about an uneasy Kowalski, on guard duty, being stared down by several men in the brig, their unrelenting gaze beckoning him closer to the cell to be contaminated by their touch.

In other ways, the episode disappoints. The creative staff once again utilized the Seaview-taking-a-nose-dive sequence, which we just saw in the previous episode ... and at least three others before that!

"The Creature" has its detractors. Mike Bailey, said, "There is really no point to this episode. By this time in *Voyage*'s devolution, all moral discussion had flown, leaving this outing with only the bones of a monster story with no flesh on it. Given that – at least it features new effects and a creature which is something other than an anthropomorphic-looking man in a rubber suit. ... Although the issue of the creature's right to life and Dr. King's responsibility for its creation were virtually ignored by the script, Basehart snuck moral judgment into Nelson's reaction to Dr. King. ... However, the disregard for human life displayed by everyone, including Crane and Nelson, is unconscionable." [2]

Mark Phillips *wanted* to like it. "Almost every *Voyage* episode had a great teaser and the one here is no exception, as Crane is engulfed by a giant monster. Seaview's tangles with the creature are also impressive, as is that peculiar and creaky 'whine' the monster makes. ... And yet, this has to be the most repulsive episode the series ever produced, and it ranks in the bottom five. Possessed crewmen are mercilessly killed, Crane and officers are transformed into disgusting seaweed-slime people and Bettger is supposed to play a really repelling villain and he succeeds, perhaps too well." [3]

In our view, it's not merely a monster story. The acting chops shown by the reluctantly overcome crew provide something worthwhile.

Script:

John and Ward Hawkins' writers' contract: May 5, 1966.
The Hawkinses' story treatment approved by Irwin Allen on June 15.
The Hawkinses' 2nd draft teleplay: August 1,
Shooting Final teleplay: August 30.
Rev. Shooting Final teleplay (on blue paper): October 7.
Page revisions (on pink paper): October 10.
Page revisions (on green paper): October 12.
Page revisions (on yellow paper): October 18.

This was the last of four scripts **John and Ward Hawkins** wrote for *Voyage*, on the heels of "The Machines Strike Back," "The Mechanical Man," and "Deadly Invasion." Next stop for the brothers: several assignments at *Bonanza*, continuing a longtime association there, and then several for *Little House on the Prairie*.

Production Coordinator Les Warner sent his notes to Irwin Allen after reading the second-draft teleplay by the Hawkinses. Again, Warner's memo illustrates the many challenges involved in making what was essentially half a science-fiction movie in six days, on a 1966 TV-series budget. He said, in part:

... Scenes 202, 213: Would suggest deleting these references to sparks (from the welding-cutting machine on the other side) coming through "door edges":
A. To begin with, these are not "doors" but thick watertight hatches that sparks could not leak through.
B. The required effect would necessitate Animation, which is not affordable in this production....

Scenes 211, 220: "Doors (hatches) glowing under an electrical attack:" These are not story points (added suspense only) and the added cost is not warranted. DELETE....

PHOTO EFFECTS: A RED FLAG!... BURN-INS: A total of 7 for scenes 5, 12, 18, 24, 29, 82, 116. NOTE: I have arbitrarily deleted many, many more of these in the Master script as the cost would have been exorbitant! All burn-ins are in the Nose TV screen and we can still be in trouble here if the Director and Assistant do not hold these down to the barest minimum as now indicated in the Master method....

ANIMATION: A total of 3 Creature's bolts of electricity for scenes 23, 41, 135. NOTE: You will note in the Master script I have arbitrarily changed the reference of "webs of bolts shooting out from the Creature" to one essential bolt in each scene....

MECHANCIAL EFFECTS: A RED FLAG! There are an alarming (and prohibitive) number of scenes in which are indicated burning circuits, shorting panels, flames, sparks and smoke.... NOTE: Because of story points, none of these could be deleted without script revision; which should be done. And a BIG ALERT here that all references retained in the script must be carefully screened and moderated or the overall Effects cost for this production will be intolerable!

STORY NOTE: It is amazing to me how, with all the continued burning and shorting of panels and circuits in the sub and FS1, they can go on functioning whenever the story conveniently requires same....

2ND UNIT – GREEN TANK: An Alert! ... There is a total of 22 scenes (with no doubt additional shots to cover)...

considering the several required re-dress areas and the amount of work, this could be at least 2, if not 3, days' work....

THE CREATURE: In scenes 11 and 16 it is described as "huge, shapeless, amoeba-like, lighted by pulsing inner glow". Yet King, when he metamorphosizes into a similar creature, walks around inside the Seaview. The logic is contradictory and must be straightened out – and the script changed to conform. Remember that sample tissues are taken from the giant creature and featured in scenes in the Lab....

SUMMARY: This is a good, exciting story but reflects an overall costly production, and particular retrenchment must be made in: PHOTO EFFECTS, MECHANICAL EFFECTS, MECHANICAL PROPS, 2ND UNIT [Green Tank sequences]. [4]

After reading the next draft of the script, another hefty memo came from a worried Les Warner. He wrote, in part:

Scenes 90, 92 and throughout: The "Creature marks" on the cast: This is an excellent idea to eliminate the original 25 "glows of light" on foreheads, but I feel it must be even more simplified to cut down the set-wait during production. This should be something that is prefabbed in the Makeup Department and can then be applied and removed on the set with minimum waiting time. I realize this is a matter of concept, but I feel that all references to King's marks being "much more extensive" be deleted as this will surely create a problem on the set....

Scenes 215: King is "destroyed" by the electrodes; The creature tissue sample was "burned to a crisp", but surely not King?! Stage direction should be clearly indicated; possibly a flash of light (set effect) and smoke, then his crumpled body as the smoke clears?...

MECHANICAL EFFECTS: My RED FLAG is still waving! The original references to "burning circuits, shorting panels and flames" in the all too many instances that I objected to have all been changed to "sparks and smoke", which actually mean the same thing; therefore, I can only suggest (because of story points) that these be controlled at meetings and on the set…. [5]

Burning circuits, shorting panels, flames – as well as sparks and smoke – didn't come cheap. As Irwin Allen was fond of saying, "Time is money," and such effects always took a great deal of time. Les Warner's reports were always helpful in saving both. But Warner, dividing his time between three series, was not always available to cover every script. Sometimes others, less familiar with all the aspects of each series, would step in and try to rough out a budget.

Recalling one such situation, Al Gail said, "Talk about something strange – on a submarine, Sparks is the operator of the wireless. Now, in the script, they said 'Sparks is in the control room.' So, the budgeting department budgeted for fire, and sparks, and everything else. So, the budget came in and they went about five thousand dollars over budget. We said, 'Oh, that can't be.' And we sat down with the budget department and they said, 'Look, you've got sparks in the control room.' I said, 'That's the name of the operator!' They said, 'Oh.' So, that's the type of thing you'd run into. Nothing vital but it'd kill you on the budget." [6]

Production:
(Filmed October 11 – 18, 1966; 6 days)

Director **Justus Addis** was now on his seventh *Voyage* episode, with nine more to go. Not even halfway there and already running out of steam … or juice.

Lyle Bettger played Dr. King. He was 51 and had a prolific career on the stage before transitioning into A-list movies during the first half of the 1950s, usually as third-billed and the "heavy." He is perhaps best known for playing Klaus, the mean-spirited elephant trainer in the 1952 circus movie *The Greatest Show on Earth*. In the later part of the decade, Bettger landed the lead in two TV series: *The Court of Last Resort* (1957-58) and *Grand Jury* (1959-60). Guest roles on television followed.

Lyle Bettger as attorney Sam Larsen in TV's *The Court of Last Resort*.

Mark Phillips recalled, "As a kid, I was always aware that the adults around me considered many of *Voyage*'s guest stars to be of less than stellar marquee value, so I was astonished when my Aunt raced out of the room… and announced in a surprised voice to the other adults that Lyle Bettger was doing a *Voyage*! I had no idea who Bettger was, but I was pleased to see such looks of astonishment on everyone's faces that a 'name' star was doing *Voyage*." [7]

Production began on Tuesday, October 11, for the first of six days on Stage 10.

Paul Strader was the director for three days of second-unit work in the Green Tank, on November 17, 18 and 21, featuring Strader and Mike Donovan.

Release / Reaction:
(ABC premiere airdate: 1/1/67; network repeat broadcast: 7/9/67)

From the ad copy: "While on an important mission to recover a mysterious life form released in the sea, the fabulous nuclear submarine Seaview encounters 'The Creature'! Captain Crane, after a deadly attack by the monster, is suddenly possessed by it, as is the Creature's creator, Dr. King! Both King and Crane are forced to betray other members of the Seaview's crew into the Creature's control, while Admiral Nelson fights desperately against time to save the Seaview and his crew!"

It was New Year's Day when "The Creature" first aired on ABC. Earlier in the day, the Green Bay Packers defeated the Dallas Cowboys in the NFL championship game. Also on this Sunday, the Kansas City Chiefs beat the Buffalo Bills in the AFL championship game. The Packers and the Chiefs would face off on January 15 for the first Super Bowl. *Voyage* would be airing "The Creature" that night. Yes, another monster.

Ray Didsbury, Richard Basehart's lighting double, said, "There was sorrow by everyone when we began doing stories about monsters. I, like everyone else, felt Irwin was really missing the boat by cheapening the show with these very inexpensive, rubber-suited monsters. Richard and David, in particular, felt that we had the premise of a submarine and a flying sub that could go anywhere in the world, and yet we were doing the same show, week after week, with interiors only, and no production value." [8]

In the news, Beach Boy Carl Wilson was indicted for draft evasion. The top movie in America was *The Sand Pebbles*, starring Steve McQueen. "I'm a Believer," by the Monkees, was getting more radio play than any other song. You would have to come up with 60 cents to buy the single, because "I'm a Believer" wasn't on *The Monkees* album, which was still the top seller at the stores. The LP would cost you about five bucks.

"TV Scout" skipped previewing "The Creature," until it repeated on ABC in July. At that time, Joan Crosby said:

> David Hedison is in for another of his horrible misadventures with science-fiction transformations on *Voyage to the Bottom of the Sea*. You may remember this as the one with that huge, undulating mass or blob of newly created sea life which gets out of the control of the scientist who made him, or it. Hedison, as Captain Crane, swims off to investigate the blob and becomes one himself. [9]

"TV Week," with "You Are the Critic," invited its readers to review the series. It published one on *Voyage*, appearing in the December 25, 1966 edition of the Galveston *Daily Review*. The letter said:

> Way back – about a year or so ago – when this series was in its infancy, I enjoyed tuning in each week for the tales of the men of the Seaview, and every now and then an occasional tale about a power-mad monster. I would sit and sneer at the monster's attempts to take over the Seaview (and the world). I knew full well that it was never any match for Admiral Nelson and company. I didn't even mind them sneaking in yardage from the movie *Lost World*, in faithful observation of

"national cut-your-production-cost week." But this year, every time I tune in, I see a monster. And not only that, but a couple of weeks ago my astute powers of observation caught them using a monster they had used *last* year! (Have they cut your budget again, Special Effects?) The thing that really gets me, though, is that all the monsters make the same noise. A sort of irritating roar.

Of course, there's always the brave, heroic, intelligent Captain Crane; and brave, heroic, intelligent Admiral Nelson, bravely, heroically and intelligently (?) trying to make something of their lines....

However, you'll notice I'm still watching the show, though I'm not sure how much longer I can hang on. I guess I'm just waiting for a "happening" — a slight improvement would do for a start. Hey, Fellas, how about a monster that meows?? Oh well... (Karen P. Durpham, Los Angeles) [10]

A.C. Nielsen 30-Market ratings report for January 1, 1967: [11]

	Rating:	Share:
7 – 7:30 P.M.:		
ABC: *Voyage to the Bottom of the Sea*	19.1	34.6%
CBS: Lassie	**20.1**	**36.4%**
NBC: *Bell Telephone Hour*	8.5	15.4%
7:30 – 8 P.M.:		
ABC: *Voyage to the Bottom of the Sea*	**19.1**	**33.7%**
CBS: *It's About Time*	13.9	24.6%
NBC: *Walt Disney*	17.7	31.3%

7.15

"The Haunted Submarine" (Episode 73)

(Prod. No. 9215; first aired on Sunday, November 27, 1966)
Written by William Welch
Directed by Harry Harris
Produced by Irwin Allen and Bruce Fowler, Jr.; Story Editor: Sidney Marshall

From the *Voyage* show files (Irwin Allen papers collection):

Time stands still for the Seaview when the Admiral's 19th century ancestor, Captain Nelson, comes to persuade him to join the Captain aboard his square rigger. Despite the offer of immortality, Admiral Nelson refuses the invitation, only to learn the Captain considers it an order! With one hour in which to choose between the Captain's offer and the death of the Seaview and all aboard her, Nelson must think fast. [1]

Assessment:

Voyage's episodes were becoming more fantastic; some episodes were downright silly, some were redundant, some didn't completely come off. But most, from the latter part of the second season right to this point of the third, were high-concept, adrenaline-fueled, high times in front of the old TV set. "The Haunted Submarine" is nothing less. Sure, it borrows from "The Phantom Strikes." And, certainly, there are places where the low budget shows, and recycled shots are blatantly injected to save dollars. But how much fun is it seeing Richard Basehart opposite Richard Basehart, one with a jolly Irish brogue? And how clever are those frozen crew shots, as a bewildered Admiral Nelson wanders amongst mannequin-like crewmembers, doing their best – and succeeding pretty darn well – to hold their breaths and not blink? Director Harry Harris even dared to shoot master shots only, tracking along with Basehart with the camera on dolly tracks, from one group of statue-like men to the next, for minutes at a time. No one except Basehart could move for these long takes. And they didn't!

You will recall that in "The Phantom Strikes," and its sequel, "The Return of the Phantom," that the ghost of Captain Krueger pressured Nelson to kill Crane. Writer William Welch takes the idea one step further here, with the ghost of Captain Nelson pressuring Admiral Nelson to kill *himself*.

The Ghost: "I'm offering you immortality."
Admiral Nelson: "How? By killing me?"
The Ghost: "Well… there would be certain formalities involved. But think of the rewards, lad!"

There is much more to savor. The scene in which Chief Sharkey takes a cigarette break with Admiral Nelson ushers in one of the story's themes – to trust your gut. Sharkey's advice to Nelson: Sometimes we know the right answer without even thinking about it. We *feel* it. The other theme has to do with penitence. "Captain" Nelson was a slave trader, and now he is a slave of his past.

The creative staff was certainly giving Robert Dowdell better roles. The part for Chip Morton in "The Creature" was a step up. In this episode, the scenes between Morton and Chief Sharkey are a delight. And so are the ones between Nelson and Sharkey. Mike Bailey noted: "This budget-cutter is primarily known for the admittedly very entertaining bit with Nelson, Sharkey, and the fire extinguisher. Sharkey has absolutely no clue as to how he became foam-covered, but Nelson certainly does, having been the culprit, and his struggles to contain his amusement are a delight. It's history that Basehart and Becker got along famously, and the relationship shines through in this scene." [2]

We are not blind to the blemishes in this episode. Act IV drags a bit; the ending seems to be missing a proper summation; and, believe it or not, they use the Seaview-nose-diving-into-the-ocean's-bottom yet again. Is this the fifth time? Or the sixth? We've lost track.

So, it ain't perfect. In fact, Mark Phillips felt the episode lacked imagination. Well, that all depends. We think William Welch used great imagination in coming up with something that could be shot under the average budget, and in only five days. Considered in that context, "The Haunted Submarine" lifts *our* spirits.

Script:
William Welch's writers contract: October 7, 1966.
Shooting Final teleplay (on pale green paper): October 14.

Page revisions (blue paper): October 18.
Page revisions (pink paper): October 19.
Page revisions (yellow paper): October 21.
Page revisions (green paper): October 21.
Page revisions (gold paper): October 25.

William Welch had struck gold with "The Phantom Strikes" and "The Return of the Phantom," so was encouraged to spin another ghostly tale for *Voyage*. Fascinated by ghosts and other things that go thump in the night, Welch was all too happy to comply.

Fellow *Voyage* writer Robert Vincent Wright told interviewer Mark Phillips, "William Welch was very interested in the occult. He told me that if a high-quality tape recorder is left running in an empty room, it will record spirits of the dead. He seriously believed it. I listened to the tapes, and there were bits and pieces of spoken words on them!" [3]

Welch, you may recall, wrote a book in which he told all about his *Talks with the Dead*.

Welch's story springboard for "The Haunted Submarine" read:

> "Seaview" has been plagued by a series of minor but annoying disturbances which have upset the crew. All efforts to track them down and explain them are fruitless. While the matter is under investigation, radar picks up a blip from the surface which is obviously a ship. But efforts to contact the vessel by radio are unsuccessful, so Crane orders Seaview to surface for visual signaling. On the surface, he is surprised to see an old-fashioned square rigger. Then he is astonished when the ship unleashes a broadside volley, nearly wrecking the sub. A crash dive takes them out of range and Crane is tempted to blow the attacker out of the water. But, before resorting to that, he radios for information about any ship which answers the description of the unidentified vessel. Replies by radio indicate there is no ship anywhere in the world at this late date which answers that description. Nelson, in his cabin, is so notified. He tells Crane he will come to the Control Room to confer with him about their next step. But when he arrives there, he finds Crane and every officer and man in the area frozen into silent immobility. It is as though each of them has been carved out of stone. Baffled and incredulous, Nelson starts through the ship trying to find someone – anyone – who is not similarly affected. He is

unsuccessful. And during his trip he encounters further evidence of strange noises ... even distant ghostly laughter!

Finally, Nelson makes his way back to his own cabin only to see the outlines of a ghostly figure in the shadows. The intruder wears the uniform of a 19th Century sea captain. As Nelson stares, the man steps into a shaft of light and there, to his utter astonishment, he finds himself looking at a 19th century image of ... himself. The sea captain proves to be an ancestor of Nelson's ... a family legend of a man who had earned great riches plying his sailing vessel on voyages to the China Coast where he engaged on the tea trade. The ghostly intruder has come to see his great, great grandson because he knows he has salt water in his veins. He wants Nelson to join him and sail with him on the Seven Seas, offering him a unique sort of immortality. Nelson refuses and a conflict builds between two men which threatens to destroy the sub, the crew, and Nelson himself.

And, finally, Nelson discovers that the old captain had earned his fortune, not in the trade but as a slaver! This is his penance ... to roam the seas until he can persuade one of his descendents to take his place. Now, his secret discovered, the old slave trader is defeated and leaves in sorrow. Instantly, the crew comes to life again, acting as though no time had elapsed and nothing had happened to any of them. Nelson, seeing the blip has disappeared from the radar, decides to keep the secret of the ancestor to himself. [4]

Irwin Allen felt he could count on Welch to flesh out the story in script form and come up with an entertaining tale. He likewise counted on Welch to write a script that could be filmed as a bottle show in five days, and to finish two drafts of that script in short order – usually in less than a week. And this is exactly what Welch delivered.

Production:
(Filmed October 19 – 25; 5 days)

Harry Harris returned to direct his fifth out of twelve episodes for *Voyage*. Harris' direction of "Haunted Submarine" is inspired. The camera tracking Basehart as Nelson enters the Control Room – revealing the frozen crew – is only one example of the "Harris touch."

William Self approved a budget of $146,151.

Production began on Wednesday, October 19, 1966 for the first of five days on Stage 10 for this "bottle show." [5]

Ray Didsbury said, "I believe Richard did the series for money. I think he felt the series was beneath him as an actor. If he didn't, he *should have*, because he

Richard Basehart receives visitors to the set during the filming of "The Haunted Submarine."

was a great actor. I recall only one episode that really interested him. He played a dual role [as the Admiral and the ghost of an ancestor]. He had to create this character to play off Admiral Nelson, and he liked the demands that put on him as an actor." [6]

Interviewed at this time by Dick Strout, Basehart said, "I played Nelson, of course, the admiral of the submarine, and an ancestor of his, who died in 1822, who returns. He's an Irishman, and says, 'Ah, lad, I've got some important information for you.' …. And all of those things took place between Nelson, the admiral, and the sea captain… and that becomes very confusing and very difficult because you jump back and forth, you know, between the two parts…. [But] playing the dual character was very interesting and a lot of fun." [7]

Release / Reaction:
(ABC premiere airdate: 11/27/66; network repeat broadcast: 6/11/67)

The song getting the most play on the radio was *still* "Winchester Cathedral," by the New Vaudeville Band. Now you know why some baby boomers were sick of it. The best-selling album was *still The Monkees*. The songs, such as "I Wanna Be Free," "Saturday's Child," "Last Train to Clarkesville," and "Tomorrow's Going to Be a Brand New Day," were also being heard on *The Monkees* TV series. The biggest film in the movie houses was *still The Bible: In the Beginning*. The TV show more people were tuning in than any other was *still Bonanza*. At least the cover of *TV Guide* had something new – Ron Ely, TV's *Tarzan*, wearing nothing but a loincloth … and a smile.

The ad copy reads: "Time stands still for Admiral Nelson when the ghost of his 19th Century ancestor, Captain Shaemas [sic] O'Hara Nelson, visits him aboard the fabulous nuclear submarine Seaview! Captain Nelson orders the Admiral to join him in the past aboard his square rigger ghost ship, with an attractive offer of immortality dangled as bait! If the Admiral refuses, the Seaview and its crew will be destroyed! Richard Basehart stars in an exciting dual role as both Admiral Nelson and his ancestor, Captain Nelson, with David Hedison co-starring as Captain Lee Crane, in 'THE HAUNTED SUBMARINE' episode of VOYAGE TO THE BOTTOM OF THE SEA."

"TV Scout" previewed "The Haunted Submarine" in newspapers across America:

> Series has a silly rehash of familiar material that is notable only because it gives Richard Basehart a chance to play two roles. Besides Admiral Nelson, he is seen as one of his antecedents, the 19th century captain of a square rigger. The ancient ship attacks the Seaview, and the captain threatens

to destroy the sleek sub if Nelson doesn't join him on the square rigger. [8]

A.C. Nielsen 30-Market ratings report for November 27, 1966: [9]

7 – 7:30 P.M.:	Rating:	Share:
ABC: *Voyage to the Bottom of the Sea*	**20.3**	**35.5%**
CBS: *Lassie*	17.0	29.7%
NBC: AFL Football Game	11.1	19.4%
7:30 – 8 P.M.:		
ABC: *Voyage to the Bottom of the Sea*	**20.6**	**34.2%**
CBS: *It's About Time*	15.0	24.9%
NBC: *Walt Disney*	15.3	25.4%

Would an Irish ghost lure in *Voyage*'s young audience as well as a monster? Aye, laddie. "The Haunted Submarine," providing a double dose of Nelsons, beat the AFL's championship game in the ratings!

7.16

"Death from the Past" (Episode 74)

(Prod. No. 9216; first aired on Sunday, January 8, 1967)
Teleplay by Sidney Marshall and Charles Bennett. Story by Charles Bennett.
Directed by Justus Addiss
Produced by Irwin Allen and Bruce Fowler, Jr.; Story Editor: Sidney Marshall
Guest Stars John Van Dreelen and Jan Merlin

From the *Voyage* show files (Irwin Allen papers collection):

Thirty years after the defeat of Hitler's Germany, a fanatical Nazi General attempts to wreak havoc upon a peaceful, unsuspecting world. Awakening from suspended animation in his secret laboratory at the bottom of the North Sea, the German General attempts to use the powerful nuclear missiles of the Seaview to realize Der Fuhrer's mad dream of world conquest or destruction. [1]

Assessment:

"Death from the Past" takes the theme of Season One's "The Last Battle" (with the same guest star, John Van Dreelen) and amps it up through the device of time travel, accomplished by suspended animation. The latest treatment of a recycled theme has all the usual conflicts, jeopardies, action, and special effects expected in *Voyage to the Bottom of the Sea*. They are delivered with competence and gusto. But this does not ensure that all fans will be impressed.

Mike Bailey said, "This episode has nothing to recommend it. Boring. No social comment (it's hard to do a story about Nazis and not have some implied moral point or subtext – sorry, nothing here). Van Dreelen is bored and Jan Merlin is wasted. Compare this effort to Season One's 'The Last Battle' (which also stared John Van Dreelen as a Nazi) and you get the difference between night and day. 'The Last Battle' attempted to do much more than just fill 53 minutes of air time. Then again, this episode must have at least one thing to recommend it – no rubber suited monsters." [2]

Mark Phillips said, "This could have been a contender but its storyline is so unimaginative and by-the-book that it's extremely boring. It's also annoying that the Nazi duo don't show any real surprise or interest in the fact that they've awakened in 1980. They simply want to rule the world. Talk about one-dimensional." [3]

Responding to Mr. Phillip's disappointment in how the Nazis react to waking up 35 years after they were overcome by the gas, we feel their behavior is appropriate. They do not believe they have been sleeping for more than three decades. Why should they? They haven't aged. Granted, their surroundings have, with metal showing traces of rust, and the Seaview is certainly beyond anything they could have imagined in 1945, but these men believe they are being tricked. As far as they know, despite what they are told by the "enemy," the war could still be raging. Their side had been losing, and they were under orders, as that "last hope for the Third Reich," to launch the missiles. They are obsessively focused on fulfilling their mission, as any good Nazi would be. We don't find Admiral Baron Von Neuberg to be one-dimensional at all. A surprising, but believable, element in the characterization of this loyal Nazi is when he becomes despondent, believing that he has failed. Von Neuberg laments, "It's all over. The war is lost." As the underwater facility fills with water (off camera), Admiral Nelson declares that they have to get out while there is still time. "Get out of here – why?" Von Neuberg shouts. "There's nothing left for me here [on Earth]. The last hope for the Third Reich – gone in a puff of smoke."

Regarding Mr. Bailey's assertation that there is no point to this story, we counter by proposing an alternate title for the episode: "The Lost Cause." As in any good war movie, the audience is shown the results of a blind devotion to duty; the tragedy of war; the waste in time, materials, property, and life. Science fiction can examine such a theme in ways contemporary stories cannot. Von Neuberg's sudden aging at the end of the story illustrates this point with stunning impact.

One moment, he is in his late-40s, with the memory of war fresh in his mind; the next moment, he is in his mid-80s, dead or dying, his world-wrecking cause having failed long ago. Von Neuberg's dreams, his ambitions, his sense of duty, are rendered pointless by time. That's the very *point* of the story.

We'll give Admiral Nelson the last word, which should please our resident critics: "I think it's time we stopped fighting World War II."

Script:
Charles Bennett's First Draft teleplay: June 14, 1966
Sidney Marshall's Rev. 1ˢᵗ-Draft teleplay: October 14.
Rev. Shooting final teleplay (blue paper) October 25.
Page revisions (pink paper): October 27.

Charles Bennett wrote the story treatment and first-draft teleplay. The story wasn't well-liked; Bennett was released from the assignment, and the tale was set aside until four months later, when *Voyage* began running low on scripts. At that point, Production Coordinator Les Warner was asked to provide suggestions for what could be done with the material. His five-page memo to Irwin Allen and Sidney Marshall read, in part:

> Scene 20: Int. German Sealab: A) If everyone suddenly "went to sleep" while at duty posts, who turned the lights out? Wouldn't it be even more awesome (and logical) to have the lights on in this seaweed-covered installation when we enter? Also, this "switch" they turn on doesn't read like a master control so why wouldn't lights have to be turned on in the rest of the area in this installation as we enter them? B) The above also goes for the air purifier – who turned it off? And how could they have lived for 33 years without air? They weren't in "suspended animation" because in Sc. 24 we are told they're alive ... asleep ... breathing....

> Scenes 79, 108, 110" The German Installation Missile Chamber: These are P.O.V.'s only – with no cast action in the set. Although the writer indicates we should use our Seaview Missile Room and disguise it with lighting (?); I don't think it would be possible and, after all, is this set really necessary? Better not to see it [at] all than to be caught in a gross deceit!

Scene 85: A "type of television screen" in the 1943 German installation? Research might prove this possible, but I question it.

Scene 95: A) If the Seaview Armory was "blown" (and it would have all been blown if a bomb were detonated in it): It is hard to believe that the Seaview, with its futuristic atomic explosives, wouldn't have been practically disintegrated. B) And I'm sure that we can't afford a wrecked Armory Corridor for Sc. 96....

Scene 111: If the German Sealab missiles failed to function "after thirty odd years of rotting", how come the lighting system, air purifier – all undersea autonomous power – is still functioning?...

Scenes 155-161: The exploding hand grenade in the control Room: A) Where did Ober get the grenade? B) It "shatters the door and the immediate wall area". The flying shrapnel and the concussion would do a lot more damage than that and, obviously, we can't afford any of this visual damage effect. C) Von Neuberg and his S.S. men are in the middle of the explosion and are felled. If the set is "shattered", these guys must be a ghastly sight. And what about our Seaview crew? Although the boat is on the bottom, some would have had to be at duty posts and they are now asleep (or were before this explosion).... [4]

Next, Sidney Marshall wrote a Revised 1st-Draft teleplay, dated October 14. Warner sent his comments three days later to Irwin Allen, with cc to Marshall.

With the exception of Item #5, all items from #1 through #15 in my original Analysis were complied with. However, the following new items are presented from this rewrite: ...

Scene 3: ... Regardless of the "effect" now indicated of the Lab being "wracked" by the depth charges, the audience is going to be confused as to what this is and where it is. Shouldn't we get these points across through dialogue in this scene?... Unless this has already been resolved, I still wave a flag at the cost to provide "fantastic scientific equipment" (circa 1945) for this Lab....

> Scene 41: Immediately after Von Neuberg "awakens" in a strange place: Don't you think his attitude is too casual (no reaction) regardless of the script direction on the bottom on Page 12 – which, incidentally, belies the ensuing dialogue and action on the next page? ...
>
> Scene 45: Is it contrived that a detailed schematic diagram of the Seaview should happen to be on the wall of the Sick Bay – and with all the details as per Von Neuberg's 7th and 10th speeches?
>
> Scene 75: I still maintain that the 1980 Seaview Missile Room cannot be disguised enough to look like a 1945 German "missile room." ...
>
> Scene 92-99: The planting of the third person in the Neuberg Lab who could be Hitler: A) Who or what revived him from the 1945 exposure to the gas? And how was he exposed to it in the first place? If not, then he is now 85 years old and would hardly resemble the Hitler of 1945. B) This must be Hitler because Von Neuberg addresses him over the intercom mike as "Mein Fuhrer" in Scene 92, and again in Scenes 100 and 102. C) Whether Hitler or someone else, why didn't Von Neuberg contact him immediately at the first of many opportunities? ... [5]

As you will see by watching the episode, the idea of a guest appearance by Hitler was tossed out.

Warner continued:

> Scene 131: A) Von Neuberg is dead on the floor and now in his middle eighties. What did he die of – old age? B) Froelich suddenly disappears from the script. He'd still have to be here in the Missile Room. Is he dead also – and from what? Wouldn't he also be an old man now? He must be conjecturing between Nelson and Crane in Scene 133 as to what might have happened in 1945?
>
> Scene 133: Nelson's last speech: Isn't this pretty far-fetched about "shadows playing weird tricks"? There is no doubt in

any of our minds, including Nelson's, that, with all the action now indicated in the script, <u>someone</u> was in there. [6]

It was plain to Warner that writer Sidney Marshall still had plenty to address.

Production:
(Filmed October 26 through November 3, 1966; 6 and ¼ days)

Justus Addiss was hired to direct at the pay rate of $3,000 for one week of preparation and up to seven days of production.

John Van Dreelen played Admiral Van Neuberg, at a pay rate of $2,500. We last saw him in the first-season episode "The Last Battle." And you've seen him in just about *everything* that was shot in the 1960s, and quite a bit more from the 1950s, '70s, and '80s. Here is just a sampling of TV series on which he made multiple appearances: *Hawaiian Eye* (five episodes); *77 Sunset Strip* (seven); *12 O'Clock High* (six); *The F.B.I.* (five); and *It Takes a Thief* (three). He did two each for *The Man from U..N.C.L.E.*; *The Six Million Dollar Man*; and *The Wild, Wild West*.

Jan Merlin played Brandon, and was paid $1,500. This was his third and final *Voyage*, having appeared to better results in the Season One episode, "No Way Out," followed by the second-season entry, "The X Factor." He

Above: John Van Dreelen, in his first *Voyage*, 1965's "The Last Battle." Below: Jan Merlin in his first, 1964's "No Way Out."

also did a *Time Tunnel*. Merlin had been a regular on *Tom Corbett, Space Cadet* (1950-55) and *The Rough Riders* (1958-59).

Richard Bull, still working as a guest performer, was paid $750 for three days before the camera.

Paul Trinka, as Patterson, was paid $525 for his three days.

Leith Stevens, now on his fifth *Voyage*, provided the score.

Filming began Wednesday, October 26 for the first of seven days on Stage 10, although only six-and-a-quarter days of that time would be spent on "Death from the Past." The "Int. Neuberg Lab" set was built on the home-base stage, allowing time to be saved, especially during the first day of filming as they alternated between working on that set and the "Int. Control Room."

On Thursday, Addiss was only able to film his episode until 1:06 p.m., at which point he had to turn the camera unit over to director Gerald Mayer who needed to shoot an added scene for "Time Bomb" from 1:48 to 7 p.m.

Addiss had the company back on Friday, for more work in the Neuberg Lab, then on to the missile room and sick bay.

Addiss continued filming "Death from the Past" on Monday, Tuesday, and Wednesday. On Thursday, the seventh day of filming, he wrapped "Death" at 4:12 p.m., then shot an added scene for "Brand of the Beast." [7]

Interviewed at the time of the filming of this episode by Dick Strout, Richard Basehart said, "The fan mail that I get is pretty well split between the 13, 14-year-olds, and older people, in their 40s and 50s…. And one thing interesting that Irwin told me the other day, they made some kind of a survey and, actually, even though this [series] is reputedly sort of a kiddie show, 80 percent of our audience are adults.... You see, we have a variety; we get some crazy monsters now and then, which are... you'd say, strictly for the kids, but we also have enough realistic type of shows that there's something for the adults to get their teeth into." [8]

"Death from the Past" certainly doesn't seem "realistic." But, at this time, cryonics was getting a great deal of attention in the press, with the possibilities of freezing a person and reviving him later. Also, the use of Nazis as villains would certainly appeal to older viewers who had lived through the World War II years ... only twenty years earlier.

Release / Reaction:
(ABC premiere airdate: 1/8/67; network repeat broadcast: 7/16/67)

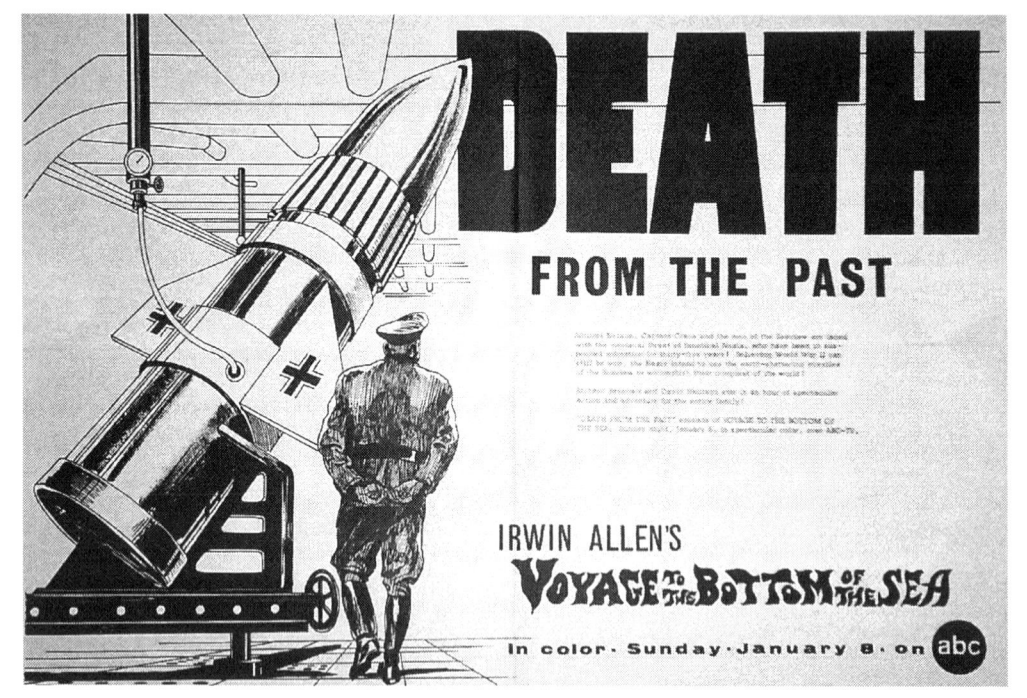

The ad copy read: "Admiral Nelson, Captain Crane and the men of the Seaview are faced with the maniacal threat of fanatical Nazis, who have been in suspended animation for thirty-five years! Believing World War II can still be won, the Nazis intend to use the earth-shattering missiles of the Seaview to accomplish their conquest of the world!"

Dragnet returned to NBC, now in color, and with an episode dealing with the LSD problem. It was quite a trip. Steve McQueen and *The Sand Pebbles* were the hot ticket at the movie houses. "I'm a Believer," written by Neil Diamond and sung by the Monkees, was still the song to beat on the radio. "Snoopy vs. the Red Baron," by the Royal Guardsmen, was trying to replace it, but stuck at No. 2. It was the same old story in the record and department stores – that first Monkees album was still the big seller. *S.R.O.* [Standing Room Only], the new one by Herb Albert and the Tijuana Brass, was right behind it in second position. Ben Gazzara, of *Run for Your Life*, had the cover of *TV Guide*.

Syndicated "TV Scout" passed this one over when it first aired. Who'd imagine an episode such as this would be given a network repeat? Allen did. And so did ABC. "TV Scout" paid attention the second time out:

> A pair of Nazis who have lived in a state of suspended animation since 1944 and still are trying to conquer the world for the glory of the Third Reich, give *Voyage to the Bottom of the Sea* one of its best adventures of the past season. John Van Dreelen and Jan Merlin are the chaps who are alternately captives and captors of Richard Basehart and/or David Hedison. The Nazis, who have a deadly nerve gas, are determined to launch missiles – theirs or the Seaview's – to destroy London, Paris, Moscow and Washington. [9]

A.C. Nielsen 30-Market ratings report for January 8, 1967: [10]

7 – 7:30 P.M.:	Rating:	Share:
ABC: *Voyage to the Bottom of the Sea*	**20.0**	**35.8%**
CBS: *Lassie*	18.3	32.7%
NBC: Actuality Special	8.1	14.5%

7:30 – 8 P.M.:		
ABC: *Voyage to the Bottom of the Sea*	**19.6**	**34.6%**
CBS: *It's About Time*	13.6	24.0%
NBC: *Walt Disney*	10.3	25.4%

8

Season Three / ABC's Back Order of 10

The order had been for 26 episodes, with a network cut-back option to 16. It didn't take long for ABC to pick up its option for what was known in 1966 as "The Back 10." The first few episodes of *Voyage* which aired in the Fall of 1966 easily won their time period. That was all it took.

At this point in the TV season – in any television series – cast and crew started feeling the strain. The average season, 26 to 29 episodes – an initial 16 followed by a back order of 10 to 13 – was exhausting. The creative staff was usually flying on empty by the final stretch. This situation was compounded at Irwin Allen Productions, since there were currently *three* series in production. And further ones were being developed.

And there was little money. Season Two had gone severely overbudget, with every episode exceeding its allotted money. The studio was adamant that this could not happen during the third year. If the early episodes exceeded their budgets, slashes would be made to those that remained.

Allen chose to spend more money on the initial order of 16, feeling that, if he had to tighten the belt, better to do so later in the season, after securing a back order for more episodes. They had made use of stock footage in the past, and even entire scenes from previous episodes had been used on occasion. Now, those practices would be stepped up. William Welch was the writer Allen trusted to devise new stories threaded together from the hides of past ones.

Besides finding ways to make *Voyage* for less, there was a mandate for more monster tales. These stories had brought in the best ratings during the second season, and continued so in the third. Besides, a stuntman in a rubber suit roaming the corridors of the Seaview was far less expensive than outdoor shooting with guest stars, extras, new sets … or, God forbid, female guest players, with their special needs for costuming, make-up, and hairdressing, and private dressing rooms and bathrooms.

Prepare yourself! (We dare not suggest you hold your breath.)

Behind the scenes of a forthcoming Season Three monster fest, "Doomsday Island." Allen with Lars the Amphibian and episode director Jerry Hopper.

8.1

"The Heat Monster" (Episode 75)

(Prod. No. 9217; first aired on Sunday, January 15, 1967)
Written by Charles Bennett
Directed by Gerald Mayer
Produced by Irwin Allen and Bruce Fowler, Jr.; Story Editor: Sidney Marshall
Guest Star Alfred Ryder

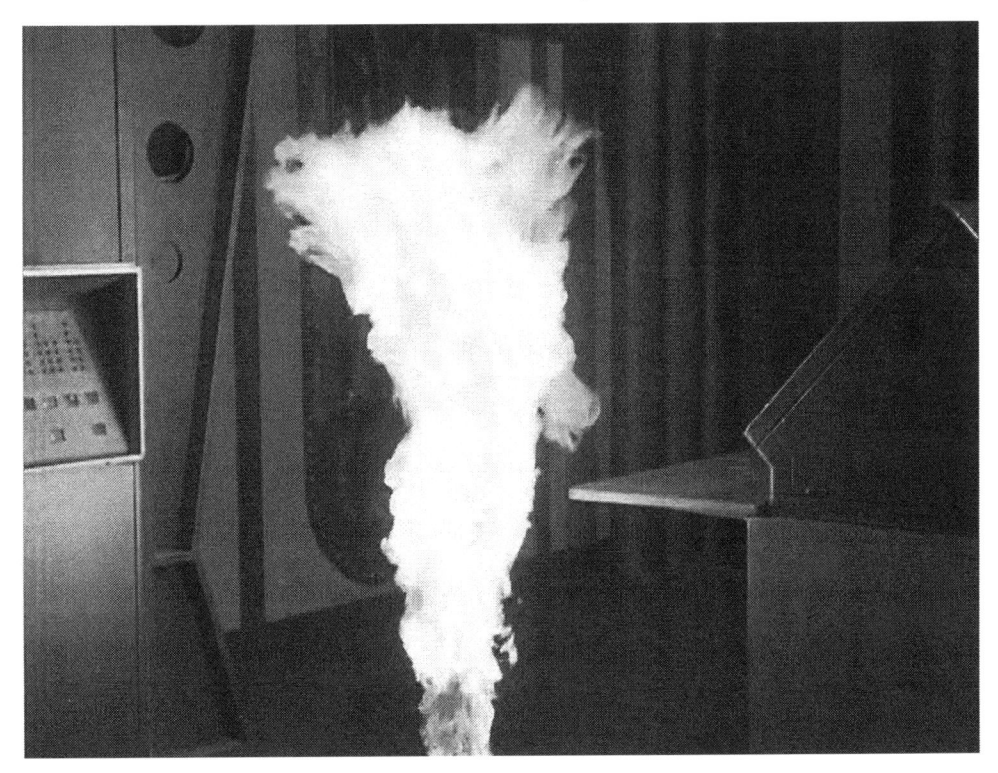

The titular sprite embarks on its quest to give the Seaview crew a hotfoot.

From the *Voyage* show files (Irwin Allen papers collection):

Dr. Bergstrom, a communication expert working in an Arctic Ice Station, is probing deep space with a powerful Laser beam. An invisible "Heat Monster" comes to Earth along the Laser beam pathway, manifesting itself in the shape of a searing, undulating flame. It uses its blistering heat against the Seaview and attempts to melt the ice in order to free other alien creatures who have been entombed in the frozen ice.[1]

Assessment:

"Okay, here comes…," warned Mike Bailey. "Terrible writing in this one, which is a pity, because the staging, sets, stock shots, and effects were right on the money. … Alfred Ryder was much better as Gerhardt Krueger because his dialogue in the Phantom episodes was better written, and the character's motivation was so much more believable. … At least the monster wasn't another man-in-a-rubber-suit." [2]

"This has an exciting teaser, as the heat monster broils the ice station," Mark Phillips said. "But, despite the able presence of Alfred Ryder, this heads straight for the deep freeze. There are some good comic bits of dialogue from the monster, especially its chilling last gasp of, "Cold...soooo cooold." [3]

That last gasp, actually, is delightfully camp. "The Heat Monster" is not without its merits.

First, for a money-saver (which the series needed to do every few episodes), the creative staff found a fair balance – the stinginess didn't spoil *all* the fun. They came up with a monster which wouldn't cost much – it's a flame. And the further idea that this alien can enlist Dr. Bergstrom (Alfred Ryder) to serve its needs by turning him invisible – another money-saver! Only one new set was needed – Artic Listening Station X2-5 (before and after the fire monster's touch). It's okay. And stock shots from the 1961 *Voyage* movie are sprinkled throughout, with some being seen on TV in color for the first time.

The heroes here are the special-effects crew. Flames are well-managed, with one of the scenes particularly intense, as Kowalski and Patterson try to escape the Heat Monster, barely making it out of the compartment with smoking jumpsuits. The smoking footprints left in the hallway by the monster, while illogical, are nonetheless pretty nifty. And the recurring cast bring their usual professionalism to their roles, even without particularly inspired material.

On the minus side are the three guest players – Alfred Ryder, Don Knight, and, as the voice of the Heat Monster, Jim Mills. As Mike Bailey noted, Ryder is not up to snuff. Mediocre dialogue or not, he doesn't have a lock on the character. We saw what he could do with the Phantom, and what we get here is the polar opposite. He seems lost.

And Jim Mills merely delivers your standard "I command you" alien voice – bombastic, narrow in inflection, and soaked in melodrama.

Regardless, "The Heat Monster" isn't really that bad. It moves along at a good clip, it amuses, and it has moments that actually impress. It's just that – as Mike Bailey said of "Death from the Past" – this story lacks purpose. There's no lesson; nothing to think about for even a minute once the episode fades down; therefore, no lasting impressions. It's non-offensive yet forgettable. This heat monster is merely lukewarm.

Script:

Charles Bennett's writers contract: June 3, 1966.
Bennett's story treatment, "The Hinges of Hell," September 10.
Bennett's 1st-draft teleplay approved by Irwin Allen on October 13.
Bennett's 2nd-draft teleplay, now "Heat Monster," approved by Allen on Nov. 4.
Shooting Final teleplay: October 27.
2nd Rev. Shooting Final (pink paper): November 4.
Page revisions (green paper): November 4.
Page revisions (yellow paper): December 7.

Is the writer of this trifling tale really the same **Charles Bennett** who had written such successful movies as *The 39 Steps*, *The Man Who Knew Too Much* and *Foreign Correspondent* (all directed by Alfred Hitchcock)? Sadly, yes. More to the point, this was also the same Charles Bennett who had co-written such not-so-classic movies as *The Story of Mankind* and *Five Weeks in a Balloon* for Irwin Allen. Bennett's writing prowess was apparently greatly impacted by who employed him.

Bennett delivered a 14-page story treatment on September 10, more than three months after being given the assignment. The title he chose was "Hell's Hinges are Hot." Many treatments often open with a "logline" – also known as a "one-liner" or "a "pitch line" – a single sentence which exemplifies the story. Bennett's "one-liner" at the top of his treatment said volumes:

> ONE LINER – representing the new construction in relation to the use of existing STOCK FOOTAGE. [4]

Throughout Bennett's treatment, he wrote asides to the producers, such as:

> TEASER – STOCK SHOTS SHOW THE ICE FIELD (This shot exists, taken from a moving airplane) …. SEAVIEW – already far north – moves in. There is good STOCK used in the pilot… SEAVIEW moving under the ice pack. Then she BREAKS SURFACE in the Arctic. Crane and Kowalski move out from the sub… now up there on the ice… (STOCK EXISTS). We use STOCK SHOTS of the "Snow Cat" … leaving the sub, going away. These shots are good and do not identify our characters. The "Snow Cat" reaches a point on the ice pack

(Good existing STOCK)... then we DISSOLVE TO: THE QUONSET HUT – EXTERIOR. This shot will show the heavily damaged front door to the hut, with some ice and snow in foreground. NOT A BIG SET. ...

There are good STOCK SHOTS of officers on the SEAVIEW bridge. One of Nelson, Crane and Kowalski which could be used before the "Cat" goes out onto the ice; another of Nelson, Chip and Kowalski, which we can use if we need it in TELEPLAY. ... [5]

Bennett seemed to relish the challenge of framing a new story containing as much stock footage as possible. But his enthusiasm eventually waned. From the final page, he wrote:

THE TAG

We see SEAVIEW breaking surface again amid the ice. (STOCK EXISTS.)

We see Nelson, Crane and Chip on the bridge. (STOCK.)

We see a SHOT across the ice. (This could be the "Snow Cat" – I don't know. I can find what we need if I look at the pilot again.)

IN A CLOSE SHOT OF NELSON AND CRANE, supposedly on the bridge, Nelson states that all is well. Nothing is left out there. The cold of the Arctic has defeated any further danger. Everything's back to square one and normal.

THAT'S IT [6]

Bennett's creative flame blew out along with the Heat Monster. But he had fulfilled his assignment, and was promptly sent to script.

After having a look at the first-draft script, Associate Producer Bruce Fowler wrote to Story Editor Sidney Marshall, with cc to Irwin Allen and Al Gail:

I like this script. It contains the elements of action and excitement, and has a new type of heavy. It seems to be well plotted and moves along at a good pace. [7]

On the other hand, Fowler wrote,

> One of my objections is to the character of Dr. Bergstrom. He is almost believable, as we establish him and his dedication to science in the hut, but, on the sub, he seems unreasonable to me, unless we can give him an even stronger motivation. As a suggestion, if we have him sustain an injury that temporarily deranges him in the explosion, perhaps that could be an explanation for his actions. [8]

They never did come up with anything to help motivate Bergstrom or account for his about-face.

Fowler continued:

> I am puzzled as to why our intrepid crew remain aboard the Seaview, with all its heat and torment, and do not either open the hatches and get the cold Arctic air inside, or go outside themselves and cool off. There has to be some explanation of this – maybe to the effect the hatches are sealed by the heat – then we have to explain how Crane and the bomb leave. In any case, some thought should be given to this. [9]

This note was never addressed either. And Fowler was right – it's a plot point that begs explanation.

> But certainly the dialogue must be cleaned up in spots – as for instance, where Crane says to the Admiral: "Good thinking, Admiral!"
>
> The technical problems in the picture are not overpowering, and the effects are interesting – the cost of them being the determining factor here. I like seeing the tracks of the monster smoking but do not believe seeing Bergstrom's frozen footprints on Page 52, Scene 159…. [10]

They kept the monster's smoking footprints and dropped those of Bergstrom. (And we appreciate it.)

More from Fowler:

> On Page 58, Sc. 176, where Bergstrom tells Nelson to use something cold to stop the monster, and Nelson thinks of Freezall – that sounds like something from *Batman*. Why not use our LOX, or liquid oxygen containers, which we have used, and which are certainly more of a scientific nature than Freezall….
>
> On Page 49, Sc. 134 – Where the invisible figure of Bergstrom hits the snow – we can't show blood here, can we?...
>
> The problem of the new sets, i.e. INT. BERGSTROM'S HUT and EXT. of the same, do present somewhat of a cost problem above that we normally have. But they are of such importance to the story, and add so much to the picture, that I feel strongly that we should retain them.
>
> The other set – EXT. OF THE BRIDGE – should be only an establishing stock shot, and the dialogue transferred to an existing set.
>
> On correcting these minor problems, I know that this will be a fine script for our show. [11]

Production Coordinator Les Warner weighed in after reading the next draft:

> Scene 13: Where does this fire come from when the Quonset hut door blows open? The hut is certainly metal, and there's nothing outside but snow and ice. This is a tricky, costly effect and I think the door blowing open should be deleted. What kind of exterior backing are we planning if the whole door aperture is exposed?
>
> Scene 14: We could delete the "blast of fire" and just have the papers explode into flame – presumably from the intense heat. Otherwise we would have to have a terrific blast of fire to justify its reaching across from the open door….
>
> Scene 103: If THE VOICE knows our men are heading for the Quonset Hut, he must also know <u>why</u> they are going, so why

doesn't he instruct Bergstrom to kill them <u>before</u> they blow up the listening station?

<u>Scene 119</u>: The four ice blocks glowing red in the Hut: If these "entities" came down on the Laser Beam and they hate the cold so much, how come they are nicely packaged in individual "ice blocks"?

<u>Scene 120</u>: The Laser Beam: These new entities have "come in over the Laser Beam". Does this mean the Beam is still on? And that it was still on when Crane and Sharkey rescued Bergstrom in Sc, 28? And what about the horrible sound that accompanied Bergstrom's turning it on in Scs. 4-6?...

<u>Scenes 152, 153, 162</u>: How could cold kill these entities when they survive and pulsate inside blocks of ice?...

<u>Scenes 203-205 (Tag)</u>: ... Why would the Seaview make that hazardous return trip back under the ice just to confirm that the Quonset Hut was blown up? Would there be any doubt in their minds after all that Seaview "panic" with the explosion and all those Stock shots of the undersea ice avalanche? ... This SEAVIEW BRIDGE set will be costly to renovate, and time consuming to move it in and shoot it, and it will need a backing and wet-down. The other two scenes on this Bridge (Scs. 24, 27) could very well be changed to the Control Room.... The Tag could be played in the Nose as they are once again on their original mission. [12]

We'd seen the Flying Bridge often in Season One, and on occasion in Season Two. But it was too large to be kept as a standing set. When needed, it had to be brought in, and other sets had to be moved to make room. With the budget restrictions of Season Three, the Flying Bridge had become cost-prohibitive.

Production:
(Filmed November 4 – 11, 1966; 6 days)
(Added scene filmed December 9, 1966)

Gerald Mayer was back in the director's chair. This was his last of four episodes for *Voyage*. He would work for Irwin Allen again in 1976, with three episodes of *Swiss Family Robinson*.

The budget was set at $164,173.

Alfred Ryder was paid $2,000 to play Dr. Bergstrom. That's $500 less than he received when he played the Phantom, for the initial episode and its sequel. But then again, Dr, Bergstrom was no Phantom.

Don Knight got $700 for three days on set, playing Sven Larson. He had just done a *Time Tunnel*. Irwin Allen would also hire him for a couple *Swiss Family Robinson*s in the 1970s. Knight had a reputation for being reliable, so worked a fair amount, with close to 100 screen appearances. Few of his roles were notable, but fans of fantastic TV might recall him as a semi-regular on *The Immortal* (1970-71), in 12 episodes as "Fletcher," and in *Manimal* (1983), in seven segments as "Chase's Father."

Production began on Friday, November 4, 1966, for the first of six days on Stage 10, utilizing the Seaview sets, plus a new one – "Int. Quonset Hut."

Gerald Mayer said, "There was a lot of concern over whether the flame creature looked convincing on camera. At the time, I didn't think it did but we did the best we could." [13]

Harry Harris stepped in to direct a pair of new scenes written after the rough edit had been viewed. These pickup scenes were filmed on Friday, December 9, on Stage 10, using the "Int. Engine Room" and "Int. Locker Room" sets.

Interviewed on the set at around this time by Dick Strout, a somewhat weary Richard Basehart said, "I'm in every episode, of course, and the weekends are all that is left to me. And I'm pretty much working on the new script over the weekends. So, I don't get away; I don't have anything like the freedom I used to have, in doing pictures, or the stage, or whatever, where I'd be having maybe a couple of months in between. But the compensations in terms of actually working [regularly] are tremendous. I'm a much better actor today, because I did this series, than I was when I started." [14]

Release / Reaction:

(ABC premiere airdate: 1/15/67; network repeat broadcast: 5/21/67)

Steve McQueen ruled the movie houses with *The Sand Pebbles*. The Monkees and the Tijuana Brass still had a lock on the best-selling albums in record stores, but there was a new top song on the radio – "Kind of a Drag," by The Buckinghams. Art Carney, in his *Honeymooners* getup, had the cover of *TV Guide*.

The first Super Bowl, between the American Football League champs, the Kansas City Chiefs, and the National Football League top team, the Green Bay Packers, was carried on both CBS and NBC from 4 to 7:30 p.m. Why two networks for one game? NBC had the contract to carry AFL; CBS held the rights to NFL competitions. If King Solomon had been around, he may have cut the game in half (with one network carrying the first half; the other the second). As it went, each network was hoping football fans would prefer its commentators. CBS, as you'll see when we get to the ratings, won by a yard.

Previewing the alternate choice to football, "TV Scout," in the *Kokomo Tribune*, from Kokomo, Indiana, said:

> Better keep your room temperature low while watching *Voyage to the Bottom of the Sea*. It's about "The Heat Monster," a perambulating flame who appears in a rush of wind and speaks to scientist Alfred Ryder, who doesn't want the "being" destroyed. [15]

The double network football coverage meant that *Voyage* was the logical choice of non-sports fans. And firebugs. On the gridiron, the Packers carried the game. But *Voyage* won by default with non-sports nuts.

A.C. Nielsen 30-Market ratings report for January 15, 1967: [16]

7 – 7:30 P.M.:	Rating:	Share:
ABC: *Voyage to the Bottom of the Sea*	**19.4**	**33.8%**
CBS: Super Bowl I	13.8	24.0%
NBC: Super Bowl I	12.3	21.4%
7:30 – 8 P.M.:		
ABC: *Voyage to the Bottom of the Sea*	**19.8**	**33.9%**
CBS: *Lassie*	10.9	18.7%
NBC: *Walt Disney's Wonderful World of Color*	16.0	24.4%

Yes, "The Heat Monster" smoked the competition. But was it only a flash in the pan?

8.2

"The Fossil Men" (Episode 76)

(Prod. No. 9218, first aired on Sunday, January 22, 1967)
Written by James Whiton
Directed by Justus Addiss
Produced by Irwin Allen and Bruce Fowler, Jr.; Story Editor: Sidney Marshall
Guest Star Brendan Dillon

The Fossil Men get sedimental with Admiral Nelson.

From the *Voyage* show files (Irwin Allen papers collection):

> As a result of a great cataclysm ages ago, human life had taken a subterranean detour along the path of evolution to evolve as Rock People in an underwater grotto. In modern times, an English submarine captain survives the wreck of his ship to find himself among these fossil men. He physically becomes one of them and awakens in them a desire to return and conquer the Earth, using the Seaview as their safe passage to the upper world. [1]

Assessment:

Pure escapist fun! The Fossil Men costumes are eye candy, the grotto and cave/lava-pit sets are alluring, and the language adapted by this rock creatures – the clicking of the digits – is eerie and clever. From a writing perspective, it was effective to have Kowalski be the one to kill Richards (the Seaview crewman who has transformed into a Fossil creature), since a friendship between the two had been alluded to.

Here's a surprise – you can find a theme in this monster tale, too. It's a simple one – no matter our outward differences, we should respect each other as equals. The Fossil Men display the worst traits of humankind – arrogance, blind ambition, lack of empathy – even as they proclaim their superiority. And Admiral Nelson gets to make things clear.

Be warned, there are some unexplained story points. We see the final phase of Richards' transformation, but how did it happen so quickly, even in those times he wasn't with the Fossil Men?

There are also a few leaps in logic. Why does Captain Crane have Richards locked in the circuitry room, where he can easily do the most harm to the Seaview? Wouldn't it have been better to get him to a less sensitive area of the ship? And, once they witness Richards easily break through the metal walls of the circuitry room, why do they lock him up in a storage room just like it? Wouldn't he break through those walls just as easily? For that matter, why doesn't he?

The key to enjoying "The Fossil Men" – and there is much to enjoy – is to not ask the questions.

Mark Phillips said, "This is a fun episode, with lumbering rock men costumes that look great. Some scenes are definitely played for laughs, especially when Nelson and Sharkey converse with Capt. Jacob Wren in the grotto. A silly adventure but lots of fun." [2]

Mike Bailey agreed, "Yes, silly," but also saw the negative ramifications of too many stories of this type. "It's not that the writers didn't have ideas; it was more that, in general, the producers didn't want more complex stories. When non-fans remember *Voyage*, they remember Seasons Three and Four and the monster-of-the-week shows, which is why *Voyage* never became a franchise. Too bad; it had as much, if not more, potential than *Star Trek* (IMO). It certainly had a brilliant cast that could deliver real drama in addition to the action, if only they'd been served more completely developed scripts." [3]

All disclaimers aside, you'll be hard-pressed not to get a kick out of this one.

Script:

James Whiton's 2nd (and final) draft teleplay approved on October 12, 1966.
Rev. Shooting Final teleplay (on blue paper): November 11.
Page revisions (on pink paper): November 11.
Page revisions (on yellow paper): December 13.
Page revisions (on beige paper): December 14.

James N. Whiton only worked once for Irwin Allen, writing this episode. During the same year, he wrote one script for *The Man from U.N.C.L.E.* Four years later, he co-wrote the screenplay for the Vincent Price chiller *The Abominable Dr. Phibes*. The trades reported that Whiton was co-writing the sequel, 1972's *Dr. Phibes Rises Again*, but his name did not appear as one of the screenwriters. Another movie, 1982's *Murder by Phone*, gave him a "story by" credit shared with three other writers. The Hollywood trades reported that Whiton was involved as a writer on two other film projects, neither realized: "The Ballad of the Black Lance," in 1968, and "Barracuda 2000 A.D.," in 1971. Beyond this, his career appears to have been short-lived. Perhaps "The Fossil Men" was hard to live down.

Regarding his brief association with *Voyage*, Whiton said, "I pitched three spy stories to the producers and they shot them all down. They said they were no longer interested in spy material and that they wanted monsters. As I stood outside the studio, I saw rocks in a nearby park and wondered what would happen if they suddenly came alive? I jotted down the idea for a story on the back of an envelope and when I pitched it to the *Voyage* people over the phone the next day, I got the script assignment." [4]

ABC Standards and Practices had their usual concerns:

> Your usual care in seeing that rock-like humanoids (or their death explosion...) are not too grotesque or frightening for family viewing. Also usual care (Scs 28, 78, 207, etc.) that audience, as indicated in script, is given POV and monsters do not move "thru camera".... Caution that "twitching" and "moaning" not over-done... Standard caution that fights are not unnecessarily brutal or prolonged. No CU [Close Up] of blows with oar/crowbar. [5]

Production:

(Filmed November 14 – 21, 1966, plus added scene shot on December 16, 1966;
6 and ½ days)

So, who was the poor actor who spent days under that Fossil Man getup? It was Brendan Dillon, showing his face in 1968's *The Killing of Sister George*.

Justus Addiss was brought in to direct the rocks ... and everything else; his ninth assignment on the series.

There were no guest stars in this episode, even though the opening credits would imply otherwise, listing **Brendan Dillon** as "Guest Star." Dillon was 48 and made approximately a hundred appearances in films and on television, starting in 1955. He was paid $850 for four days in front of the camera in this *Voyage*, playing Captain Wren, the leader of the Fossil Men. Beneath all that rubber, we only see his right eye. The character's voice was supplied by **Bart La Rue**, who did a lot of voice-over work for all of Irwin Allen's 1960s TV series, and for *Star Trek* (he voiced the Guardian of Forever in the classic *Trek*, "The City on the Edge of Forever," among other episodes).

Jerry Catron (34) played Seaman Richards. The good-looking actor-stuntman spent most of his five days before the camera in a rubber Fossil Man suit. He had played a Buccaneer in the 1966 *Voyage* episode "Night of Terror," and would return for two more outings ("Destroy Seaview" and "Terror," both in 1967). He'd play an

Jerry Catron, as a doomed Seaview crewman.

android in a 1967 episode of *The Time Tunnel*, and a really big sentry in a 1968 episode of *Land of the Giants*. Catron had small roles in three episodes of *Star Trek*.

On November 8, Bruce Fowler sent Irwin Allen a note, explaining why there would be no big names, allowing the "Fossil Men" to carry the show. He said:

> I wish to call your attention to several things with regard to the attached Cast Budget on "Fossil Men". First – this breakdown is based upon a script before Sid had completed his re-write and will therefore be subject to almost certain change. Second – the amount of money in this budget is caused by the amount of stunts as shown here – 17 – which cuts down the amount we could spend for other cast, and of course brings up the total figure so high. [6]

In his estimated budget, Fowler had put aside $1,000 for the part of Capt. Jacob Wren. And $2,400 for stunt performers. As he predicted, the amount of money for guest actors would dwindle.

Filming began on Monday, November 14, 1966 for the first of two days on Stage 10, filming in the Control Room, Observation Nose, Nelson's Cabin, and Sickbay.

The third day of production was spent on Stage B for the "Ext. Beach & Lake," "Ext. Outcropping Rock" and "Int. Grotto."

Terry Becker told an audience at a convention in England, "Richard and I read the dialogue and we thought, 'Oh … okay.' And we had an agreement between us that any time we had something to do, if it were possible to make a 'No' sound like a 'Yes' and a 'Yes' sound like a 'No,' we'd do it just to give ourselves some kind of interest in life, besides dealing with monsters. So, we read the dialogue just as it was written, but the attitude – the approach – was a little funny. I get out of the boat and Richard was pulling up the rowboat, or whatever it was, and I look up and the monster there is a rock. So, I see it, and it's moving. So I say, 'Admiral…' Richard says, 'Yeah?' and I say 'The rock…' He says, 'Yeah, what about the rock?' I say, 'It's moving.' Richards replies, 'Oh, come on, Chief.' 'No, the rock, it's moving.' So, he turns around and takes a look and says, 'Yep.' Well, we did that and the next day Irwin sees the dailies with the ABC people and everybody is breaking up as they think it is funny, and Irwin's just absolutely livid. He comes charging in on the set, asking, 'Where is he [Basehart]?! Where is he?!' I'm standing with Richard, and when he heard Irwin yell, Richard turns himself around and now I'm face-to-face with Irwin Allen, and he says, 'What are you doing to my show?' I said, 'I don't know.' And Allen said, 'It's not a comedy. You're making it a comedy!' Basehart is making faces at me (mimicking Irwin) and I found it hard to keep a straight face. I thought I was going to be fired right there. Irwin is saying, 'This is a serious show.' I don't know what to do. I said, 'I'm not doing it,' [then] pointing at Richard, 'He's doing it!' Irwin just stopped and said, 'Don't do it again.'" [7]

Thursday, the fourth day of filming, was split between Stages B and 10. The latter location was used for the Flying Sub set.

The final two days were spent on Stage 10, for sequences in the Seaview's corridors, the Missile Room and the Circuitry Room.

Justus Addiss filmed an added scene nearly two months later, on Friday, December 16, on the Missile Room set. [8]

Release / Reaction:

(ABC premiere airdate: 1/22/67; network repeat broadcast: 7/30/67)

This was the week that a fire in the Apollo 1 Command Module killed astronauts Virgil "Gus" Grissom, Edward White, and Roger Chaffee during a launch rehearsal. Top gun at the movie houses was the spaghetti Western *A Fistful of Dollars*, starring Clint Eastwood. After six months of near seclusion while writing and recording *Sgt. Pepper's Lonely Hearts Club Band*, the Beatles were back with a new look and sound, and they had the No. 1 song on the radio, "Penny Lane." "Strawberry Fields Forever," the psychedelic flip side, was also in the Top Ten. Diana Rigg and Patrick Macnee, of *The Avengers*, had the cover of *TV Guide*. And how we loved Mrs. Peel.

Voyage was airing Saturday nights in Jamaica on JBC-TV (Jamaican Broadcasting Company). The day that "The Fossil Men" first aired, the Kingston *Daily Gleaner* said, in part:

> Continuing in the coming weeks is a contingent of grotesque characters, some of the most fiendish, ghoulish and evil-looking monstrosities ever to enchant television viewers of

all ages who love spine-tingling excitement in their television fare – all this, and more is to be found on JBC TV's *Voyage to the Bottom of the Sea*, showing every Saturday at 8 p.m. [9]

Irwin Allen was quoted, "Since time immemorial, people have been fascinated by monsters, evil spirits, and demons, and today monsters have really carved a place for themselves in our society. People love to be frightened when they know it's only make-believe. Take, for example, the all-time box office champions in motion pictures -- monsters-prone epics like *King Kong, Frankenstein, Dr. Jekyll and Mr. Hyde* and many others." [10]

The article continued:

As the foremost authority on science-fiction-fact in the entertainment industry today, Allen is so far ahead of his time that he has been consulted by the U.S. Military on various space projects, and in *Voyage to the Bottom of the Sea*, [he] has certainly produced many of the most breath-taking and startling special effects ever committed to film. [11]

Syndicated "TV Scout," in the January 21, 1967 edition of the *Edwardsville Intelligencer*, out of Illinois, said:

Rock men in a grotto beneath the sea cause the wreck-of-the-week. With their leader, Capt. Wren, they plan to take over the world (so what else is new?). They wouldn't mind turning Adm. Nelson (Richard Basehart) into one of them, either, a little chore that begins with immersion in a fire pit. [12]

While *Voyage* continued to win at least part of its time slot, the numbers were on their way down. For many, the parade of monsters was starting to get old.

A.C. Nielsen 30-Market ratings report for January 22, 1967: [13]

7 – 7:30 P.M.:	Rating:	Share:
ABC: *Voyage to the Bottom of the Sea*	18.2	31.8%
CBS: Lassie	**19.4**	**33.9%**
NBC: Actuality special	10.5	18.3%
7:30 – 8 P.M.:		
ABC: *Voyage to the Bottom of the Sea*	**19.1**	**32.4%**
CBS: *It's About Time*	16.4	27.8%
NBC: *Walt Disney's Wonderful World of Color*	16.0	27.1%

8.3

"The Mermaid" (Episode 77)

(Prod. No 9219; first aired on Sunday, January 29, 1967)
Written by William Welch
Directed by Jerry Hopper
Produced by Irwin Allen and Bruce Fowler, Jr.; Story Editor: Sidney Marshall
Guest Star Diane Webber

Captain Crane and the mermaid (Diane Webber) strike a blow for interspecies romance.

From the *Voyage* show files (Irwin Allen papers collection):

> Admiral Nelson believes the Captain is losing his mind when he reports the sighting of a ... Mermaid. The Captain, determined to prove his sanity, searches for the beautiful creature of the sea, finds her, then brings her aboard the

Seaview. A Merman, seeking his mate, almost wrecks the giant craft in his efforts to free her. Before returning her to the sea, Crane pleads for her help in locating a secret undersea installation that could threaten the peace of the world. [1]

Assessment:

This is the ninetieth episode, deep into the third season, and the first this season to include a female cast member. It might be worth watching "The Mermaid" for that reason, but be warned that very nearly everything else has been seen before.

This was the first of several William Welch-written episodes that were specifically designed to connect pieces from past *Voyage*s and other stock sources. Welch sat through screenings of the 1962 low-budget underwater adventure film *The Mermaids of Tiburon*, with special attention paid to scenes involving lovely Diane Webber, as a mermaid being pursued in the ocean by a male diver (who bore a resemblance to David Hedison). He then watched a few past episodes of *Voyage* (1965's "The Peacemaker," 1966's "The Menfish," and any of half a dozen to feature the now-redundant sequence of the Seaview taking a nosedive into a rock formation and then doing a belly-flop on the ocean bottom). The fun in watching this episode, besides getting an eyeful of Miss Webber, is to see how Welch did it. But that kind of fun can only take you so far.

"A real disappointment," Mark Phillips sighed. "The first half of the segment really works, creating a fragile, almost mythical adventure as Crane pursues the mermaid, but, as soon as the amphibious monster makes its appearance at the halfway point, the creative atmosphere is totally destroyed and the beautiful mermaid's participation is reduced to a cameo. Even the monster scenes are clumsily choreographed…. A lost opportunity to have done something special." [2]

Mike Bailey mourned, "A pity to have thrown Diane Webber's wonderful mermaid into the trash bin. Delightful for the first half; much of the last half is hard to take. The damn monster bellows and bludgeons his way senselessly through much of the episode. Then he bellows some more. In the end, after the bomb is disarmed, the mermaid is forgotten, having had no real relevance to the story other than to eat up stock footage from *The Mermaids of Tiburon*, which by the way, was directed by *Voyage*'s chief underwater photographer, John Lamb. This was one of *Voyage*'s most frustrating failures for me because it had such potential and was so viciously savaged by writer William Welch." [3]

So – is "The Mermaid" a great catch, or all wet? Webber's fetching outfit tips the scales for us.

Script:

William Welch's writers contract: October 31, 1966.
Welch's story, 1st- and 2nd-draft teleplays approved by Irwin Allen in Nov. 3.
Shooting Final teleplay: November 3.
2nd Rev. Shooting Final teleplay (pink paper): November 18
Page revisions (green paper): November 18.
Page revision (yellow paper): November 22.
Page revision (gold paper): December 30.

When asked why ABC allowed the series to be cheapened this way, network production manager Lew Hunter told this author, "We *weren't* doing quality television. That was something we all kind of hung our heads a little bit about. But we were serving popcorn. And Irwin would be the first person to tell you, 'I'm serving popcorn; you can get the caviar from Gene Roddenberry.'" [4]

Roddenberry, we expect you know, created and produced *Star Trek*.

For this episode, Mary Garbutt, of ABC's Department of Broadcast Standards and Practices, wrote:

> Standard caution that monster is not too grotesque or frightening for family viewing. Special care, please, that these fights are not brutal and unnecessarily prolonged; telescope [shoot from wide angles] as much as possible. [5]

Mike Meads, from the same department, added:

> I'm not sure just what the well-dressed mermaids are wearing these days, but please be sure that whatever it is, that it does provide adequate cover for the human parts of the anatomy. [6]

It is curious that, of the two network censors, the woman focused on the violence, and the man kept an eye on propriety. But no one seemed to care that much of what was going to be seen in this episode had been paid for by the network before.

Production:
(Filmed November 22 – 29, 1966; 5 days)
(Added scenes filmed January 5, 1967)

Jerry Hopper directed. This was his fourth of 15 episodes for *Voyage*. Hopper, who had once had a promising career (directing over a dozen films before making the move into television), was now a slave to the steady work and corresponding paycheck of the episodic-TV factory.

The episode budget was set at $156,579. This didn't allow for much to play with when hiring the two guest players.

Diane Webber was 34 when cast as the mermaid. She was born Marguerite Empey and went by that name when she posed as Playmate of the Month in the May 1955 and February 1956 issues of *Playboy* magazine. Empey/Webber stood 5'2" and had measurements of 39C-23-37. An avowed nudist, Webber appeared on the covers of many publications that endorsed the "naturalist" lifestyle, and she was a popular pin-up girl of the 1950s and 1960s. You can see her in (and often on the covers) of such men's magazines as *Frolic*, *Escapade*, *Tiger*, *Modern Sunbathing*, *Mermaid*, *Fling*, *American Nudist*, and *Esquire*. She was also featured on the covers of the LPs *Sea of Dreams* by Nelson Riddle and *Jewels of the Sea* by Les Baxter. In films, Webber portrayed "The Mermaid Queen" in the 1962 risqué cheapie, *Mermaids of Tiburon*, but her work in front of the moving camera was otherwise sporadic. And, for this reason, Irwin Allen was able to get away with paying Webber only $250 per day, for two days. She made a total of $500. In 2020, this translates to less than $4,000. Not a bad deal for Allen, considering Webber brought her own mermaid outfit.

Production began on Tuesday, November 22, 1966, for the first of three days on Stage 10, with Int. Control Room / Int. Observation Nose. They also filmed on this set during part of Wednesday, the 23rd, before moving to Int. Missile Room to get shots with the regular cast only.

Thursday, the 24th, was Thanksgiving and the stages were dark. The company returned to work on Friday, filming on "Int. Seaview Corridor (Lab door; Circuitry room door)," "Int. Circuitry Room," and "Int. Pressure Hatch." The latter was the location of the fight between Nelson and the merman creature (played by stuntman Ron Stein), then another fight, waged between the creature and Chief Sharkey and two of his crewmen (stuntmen Frank Graham and Bob O'Neal).

On Monday the 28th, they continued filming the fights in the Missile Room, then onto something more pleasurable – a short scene between Hedison and Diane Webber, with her splashing into the pressure hatch. Promotional stills of the two were also shot. The company then moved outdoors by the Moat for "Ext. Beach and cliffs" sets, with Hedison and Webber. In order to match footage from *The Mermaids of Tiburon*, Hedison wore only swim trunks, a scuba tank, and facemask. Now you know why Captain Crane requests that Chief Sharkey put these specific items into the rubber raft. The last shot taken was on the Moat, showing Crane sharing his dinghy with the mermaid.

The fifth and final day of principal photography was spent in the Corridors, the Laboratory, and the Admiral's Cabin. Along with Basehart, Hedison, Becker, Dowdell, and a few stuntmen/extras, was Diane Webber. All she had to do for her second day of work was lie around.

You may recognize the footage from past episodes, woven into "The Mermaid." The man-fish creature, first seen in Season Two's "The Menfish," is featured in several stock scenes, including the fight with a crewman in red jumpsuit (stuntman Roy Jensen), the crash through the wall, and the ensuing fight with Captain Crane. The underwater fight between this creature and three Seaview divers in red wetsuits was also from "The Menfish." The sequence in which Crane and Kowalski, in wetsuits, dismantle the bomb, was taken from "The Peacemaker." The Seaview crash-dive was becoming way too familiar by now. And the sequences in which Crane follows the Mermaid underwater, and she gets chummy with a shark, were lifted from *The Mermaids of Tiburon* ... with the exception of close-ups of Hedison, shot in the Green Tank.

Weeks later, when the first edit for this episode came in short, half of a sixth day of production was scheduled (for Thursday, January 5, 1967) to film added scenes in the Missile Room and a section of corridor. Hopper was again in the director's chair. The new script pages were merely meant to pad. [7]

Release / Reaction:
(ABC premiere airdate: 1/29/67; network repeat broadcast: 8/6/67)

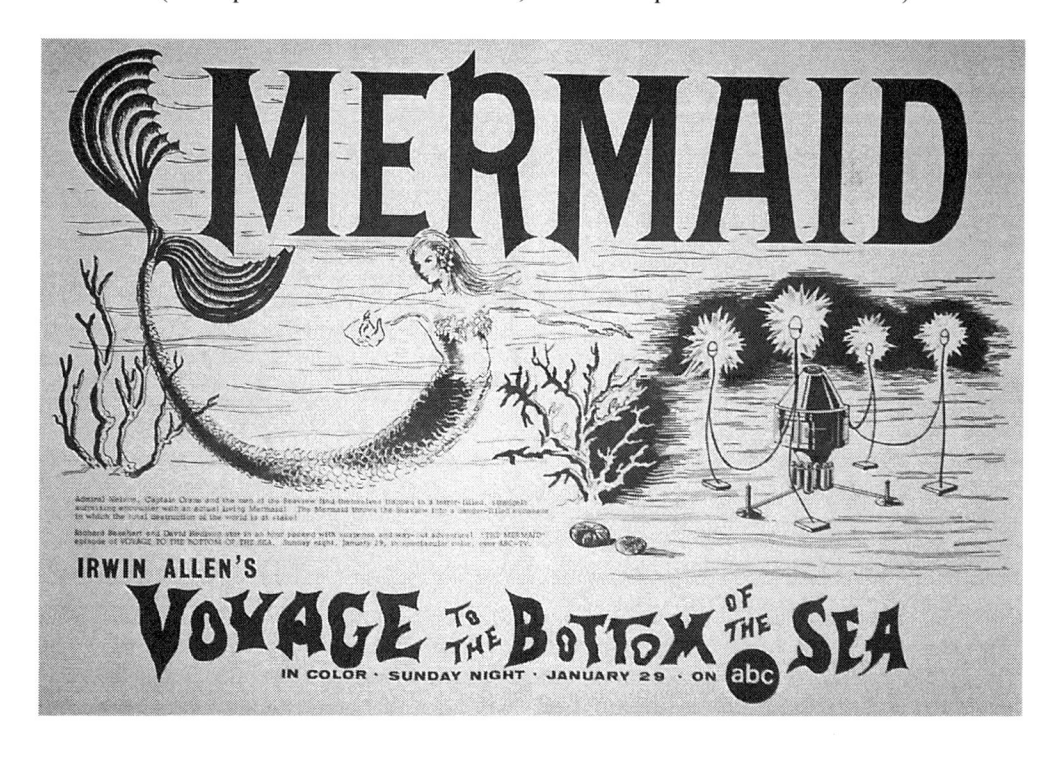

Mickey Dolenz, Michael Nesmith, Peter Tork, and Davy Jones, of the Monkees, had the cover of *TV Guide*. They also had the No. 1 song on U.S. radio, with "I'm a Believer," and the top-selling album in the nation, with *More of the Monkees*. At No. 2 in the L.P. charts, was their first album, *The Monkees*, still holding strong.

Diane Webber was on tour with a nightclub act when this episode first aired on ABC-TV. During the week of its broadcast, she was appearing in Bakersfield, California at the Hi Life Club. An article about her in the January 20, 1967 edition of the *Bakersfield Californian* tied the 1962 film *The Mermaid* to her appearance in *Voyage*, and mentioned her latest film appearance in Ann-Margret's *The Swinger*.

> Miss Webber is one of America's highest paid and most popular glamour models. Her picture has adorned numerous magazine and album covers. According to *Variety*, Hollywood's leading trade publication, she is one of Hollywood's 10 most beautiful women. [8]

"TV Scout" had this to say about the episode:

> "The Mermaid," on *Voyage to the Bottom of the Sea*, is good science-fiction fun. While on a mission to take a seal census, Capt. Crane (David Hedison) sees a mermaid. He becomes so obsessed with proving this is what he saw that he leaves the ship without permission to follow her. And that's how he becomes involved with a monster who thinks the girl-fish is his. [9]

A.C. Nielsen 30-Market ratings report for January 29, 1967: [10]

7 – 7:30 p.m.:	Rating:	Share:
ABC: *Voyage to the Bottom of the Sea*	**21.8**	**37.4%**
CBS: *Lassie*	18.4	31.6%
NBC: *Bell Telephone Hour*	10.1	17.3%
7:30 – 8 p.m.:		
ABC: *Voyage to the Bottom of the Sea*	**22.8**	**38.6%**
CBS: *It's About Time*	14.5	24.6%
NBC: *Walt Disney's Wonderful World…*	14.1	23.9%

The excellent ratings this night implied that plenty of American fathers and big brothers tuned in to ogle the mermaid. Maybe more lovely guest stars were in order? Irwin Allen demurred. He felt that those who tuned in did so to see the mer*man* monster, which had been featured in the "coming next week" trailer one week earlier.

8.4

"The Mummy" (Episode 78)

(Prod. No. 9220; first aired on Sunday, February 5, 1967)
Written by William Welch
Directed by Harry Harris
Produced by Irwin Allen and Bruce Fowler, Jr.; Story Editor: Sidney Marshall

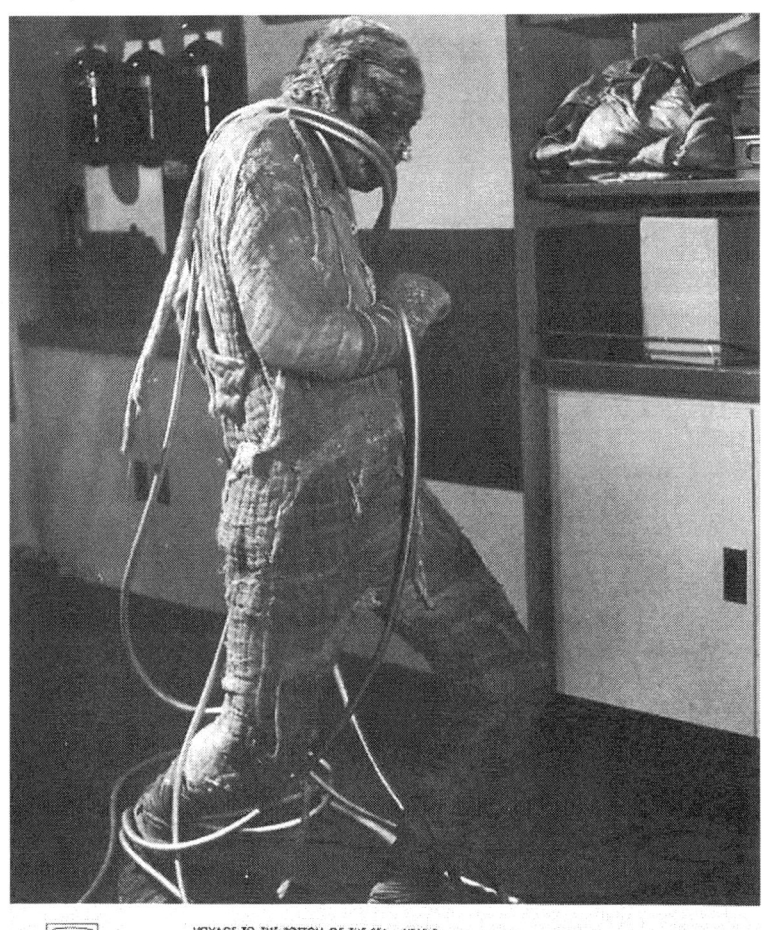

From the *Voyage* show files (Irwin Allen papers collection):

> A three-thousand-year-old Mummy – secretly being returned to its native land by the Seaview – comes back to life. Possessing supernatural powers, it controls the minds of men and turns them into instruments of destruction. [1]

Assessment:

"A mummy?" Chief Sharkey said, responding to Kowalski. "Big deal. How long has it been dead?"

"Well, like, uh, 2000 years," answered Kowalski.

"Okay, then, it's *real* dead," retorted Sharkey. "It can't do us any harm."

What did fans think? Mark Phillips wasn't impressed. "Another budget saver with a seedy-looking mummy who has all the charisma of an Egyptian sand flea. It's such a lumbering, dehydrated entity that its brief romp through the Seaview's corridors produces neither chills or suspense." [2]

Mike Bailey felt the less seen of the titular monster the better. "The Mummy is on screen very little, which is why some of this episode works fairly well. A budget saver? Yes. But (have I mentioned this before?) it's amazing what great music cues (Bernard Herrmann) can do to lift a tepidly written, bare-bones genre story from the muck. Style distracts from a lack of intelligible content." [3]

Herrmann's music cues were part of the Fox library, harvested primarily from *The Egyptian* (1954), with some cues from *The Day the Earth Stood Still* (1951). With this excellent (though tracked) music, and the darker lighting (nighttime on the Seaview), and less crewmembers up and about, the episode does project an eerie vibe. An effective lighting trick occurs when Sharkey, on patrol in the corridors, sees a shadow cast by something around the corner. It appears to be the mummy, until the shadow transforms into that of Captain Crane (who is possessed by the creature). And while one of our resident critics found the monster-of-the-week to be lacking, we liked its cavalier demeanor. Note that after strangling the crewman in the Flying Sub, the mummy tosses him aside like yesterday's trash.

We'll even forgive the creative staff for implementing the somewhat-tired-possession-ploy. With a top-notch regular cast like this, and that Herrmann score complemented by the moody lighting, the chill factor is high.

Speaking of recycling, the old sabotage-the-circuitry-room, making-the-Seaview-rock-and-roll-and-spark, then nose-into-the-bottom-of-the-ocean trick is yet again worked in to the show. It's the seventh, eight, maybe even ninth time this season! At least this time they had a guard on the door to the circuitry room, for what good it did.

No explanation is given for the mummy's meanderings. What brought it to life? What is its agenda (other than kill some, and possess the rest)? William Welch took the easy way out, at the end of the story, in having Admiral Nelson shrug the whole affair off by saying, "I think there are some things that are better left unexplained."

Script:
William Welch's writers contract: November 23, 1966.
Shooting Final teleplay (pale green paper): November 21.
Page revisions (blue paper): November 28.
Page revisions (pink paper): November 29.
Page revisions (yellow paper): December 6.
Page revisions (gold paper): January 3.

William Welch did have something timely to say with this script. In the past, *Voyage* had often commented on the Cold War paranoia from the 1960s. Now, a nod was given to tensions in the Middle East.

When this script was being written, the Middle East was plagued by war – with Israel on one side and Egypt, Syria and Jordan on the other. Numerous armed conflicts erupted in 1966, cumulating in June 1967 with the bloody Six-Day War. The political tensions mentioned in this episode were very real, and the war Admiral Nelson was hoping to avoid had become a reality by the time "The Mummy" repeated on ABC.

Mary Garbutt of ABC's Department of Broadcast Standards and Practices voiced her usual concerns, with a memo dated November 28, 1966:

> Pgs 16, 18, 31, 35, etc.: Your usual care in seeing that "the monster" is not too grotesque or frightening for family viewing. Standard caution, in the closing of acts that mummy does not seem to move through camera frame.
>
> Pg 46, Sc 130: Please substitute something other than fire extinguisher for the weapon. Usual caution that fight is not unnecessarily brutal or prolonged.
>
> Pg 47: Of course, hypo injection off-camera or covered [with reverse camera angles]. [4]

The network understood the viewing audience didn't want to see needles. And they remained convinced that children would be too frightened if a monster – in this case, a mummy – appeared to be coming through their TV screens to get 'em. But what about the fire extinguisher? How could using that as a weapon possibly cause concern at ABC? The answer was simple: The network didn't want kids to get the idea that a blast in the face from a fire extinguisher could be fun.

Production:
(Filmed Nov. 30 – Dec. 6, 1966)
(Added scene filmed on January 5, 1967; 5 ½ days)

It was a cheap one, which is exactly what Irwin Allen knew he could count on William Welch to write. The budget was set at a measly $148,544, which was $17,941 *under* the targeted Season Three per-episode goal. These savings would compensate for other episodes that had exceeded the amount 20th Century-Fox had mandated.

Director **Harry Harris**, who had played it straight and directed hundreds of TV Westerns before stepping into the fantasy worlds of Irwin Allen, said of Allen: "He loved all of those kinds of things that he did. To Irwin, to do straight things, okay, he would do it, but he wasn't that crazy about doing it. He wanted always to have the skeleton in the closet. He always wanted to plant the monster somewhere, and then let the show go on, and the audience knowing it's lurking out there. He had a knack for thinking these things up; thinking of what he wanted to do, and then he always had the showmanship ability to go out and get people with names – people that he wanted to do these things with. One incident when I was doing *Voyage to the Bottom of the Sea*... I heard a few of the crew guys saying one day, 'Boy is he lucky to have Richard Basehart.' And I was standing right there. I said, 'No, he's not lucky enough to have Richard Basehart, he's *smart enough* to have Richard Basehart. He always got the right people to do the show. So, he had that knack, too." [5]

So, who was under all the Mummy's wrappings? A fellow named **Darryl Scott McFadden**. The stuntman turned up in numerous *Voyage*s, usually as aliens, monsters, robots, amphibians, and sometimes even crewmen. And, of course, he did stunts.

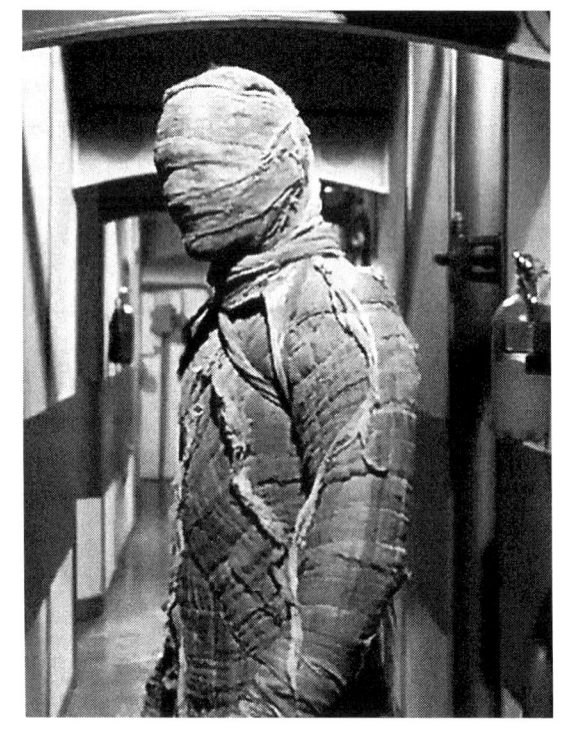

Production of this "bottle show" began on Wednesday, November 30, for the first of five days on Stage 10, utilizing only the standing Seaview sets and that of the Flying Sub. Each day went like clockwork, with wrap times falling between 6:10 and 7 p.m., except for the last day of filming. On Tuesday, December 6, they worked until 8:15 p.m.

Like many of the five-day "bottle show" productions, this one came in a few minutes short, and a partial sixth day was scheduled to shoot an additional scene. This took place on January 5, 1967, with Jerry Hopper now directing. [6]

Release / Reaction:
(ABC premiere airdate: 2/5/67; network repeat broadcast: 8/13/67)

The two hottest tickets at movie houses across America were *A Fistful of Dollars*, starring Clint Eastwood, and *Hotel*, starring Rod Taylor. The top-selling album in the stores continued to be *More of The Monkees*. It would stay at the top for 18 consecutive weeks. In second place: you guessed it, the Monkees' debut album, which had been No. 1 for 13 consecutive weeks. Top song on the radio was still "I'm a Believer." The night "The Mummy" first aired on ABC was also the night that, at a later hour, the controversial *Smothers Brothers Comedy Hour* premiered on CBS.

It was another high-concept story on *Voyage*, and various newspapers across the country printed the press release. One was the December 10, 1966 edition of the *Bakersfield Californian*. The Fox PR people told us:

> How do you play a 2,000-year-old mummy? That was the problem facing Darryl McFadden in "The Mummy" segment of Irwin Allen's production of *Voyage to the Bottom of the Sea*. "You play it like Lon Chaney," quipped Darryl.
>
> All wrapped up in his work for the episode, Darryl talked about the difficulties involved in playing an embalmed citizen from Egypt's ancient history. "It's hot under these bandages and about the most frightening thing I can do is drag a foot like Chaney did. And my strength is enormous. It's funny to think that a 2,000-year-old stiff can be so strong. I give those submarine guys a pretty rough time." [7]

"TV Scout," in a newspaper near you, said:

> It's Mummy's Day on *Voyage to the Bottom of the Sea* as the Seaview transports some national treasure, but has trouble keeping track of a mummy that keeps rising from its

moorings and prowling the ship. It's Basic Science-Fiction Plot 2A, but kids should get a kick out of the creature. [8]

A.C. Nielsen 30-Market ratings report for February 5, 1967: [9]

7 – 7:30 p.m.:	Rating:	Share:
ABC: *Voyage to the Bottom of the Sea*	**20.3**	**37.7%**
CBS: *Lassie*	14.9	27.6%
NBC: Actuality special	8.3	15.4%
7:30 – 8 p.m.:		
ABC: *Voyage to the Bottom of the Sea*	**22.2**	**37.6%**
CBS: *It's About Time*	12.6	21.4%
NBC: *Walt Disney's Wonderful World…*	13.5	22.9%

Despite good ratings, *Voyage* commanded less per advertising minute than its competition. ABC had set the price for $37,500 per minute on *Voyage*, while CBS was getting $45,000 per minute on *Lassie*, and NBC was getting, $51,600 per minute of commercial time on *Walt Disney*. There were two reasons: 1) ABC had fewer affiliates than NBC or CBS; 2) Dog-food companies were willing to pay premium rates for time on *Lassie*, while *Disney*'s audience, according to Madison Avenue, was a more loyal crowd, willing to stay in their seats and pay attention to the commercials. *Voyage*'s audience was a bit fickle, more prone to switch channels during commercial breaks, run to the refrigerator, or excitedly run around the room, reenacting chase scenes with monsters, or, as ABC feared, blasting one another with fire extinguishers.

8.5

"Shadowman" (Episode 79)

(Prod. No. 9221; first aired on Sunday, February 12, 1967)
Written by Rik Vollaerts
Directed by Justus Addiss
Produced by Irwin Allen and Bruce Fowler, Jr.; Story Editor: Sidney Marshall

From the *Voyage* show files (Irwin Allen papers collection):

> The Seaview rams a strange craft that came to Earth from outer space and is, in effect, swallowed up. Then follows an unequal life and death struggle against an adversary who is impervious to attack by any conventional weapons, an implacable enemy who can evade detection by any of the five human senses. Although he is powerless to kill humans, he does have the ability to take over the minds of crewmen and force them to carry out his deadly purpose. [1]

Assessment:

You heard right. Another alien, impervious to attack by any conventional weapons, takes over the minds of Seaview crewmembers. Could the creative minds behind *Voyage to the Bottom of the Sea* offer a fresh approach to another story of this type?

Mark Phillips didn't think they made it work. He commented, "Alas, just a guy in a black sheet moving his arms around and talking like a villain from vaudeville. The only fun here is listening to The Shadowman, whose raspy delivery of dialogue is incredibly campy." [2]

Mike Bailey was similarly disappointed. "There is NO budget visible in this episode. When laser guns fire, no beam is seen, just a flash of light and a puff of smoke to indicate the gun fired. No external shots of the alien craft. No external shots of Seaview inside the giant ship. Nothing. In fact, the only miniature shot in the entire episode is a several-seconds-long establishing stock shot of the submarine." [3]

While the lack of external shots of the Seaview were prompted by budget concerns (eliminating the need to show the sub approaching an alien spacecraft, or shots of the Seaview in a black void), it can be argued that this was a valid way of presenting the story. Admiral Nelson and Captain Crane are in the dark, literally, with only blackness outside the observation-nose windows. Limiting this perspective to only what they see, the audience is equally blind. And this is effective.

Also somewhat effective is the alien – or a shadow of the alien. While the presentation of the entity was again determined by lack of money, at least it is played down for a change, as a soft-spoken, lurking presence. And the final shot in the episode, showing a shadow etched onto the bulkhead of the ship like an atomic sunburn, makes a surprising impact. Sometimes less money can result in a more effective means of telling a story.

Sadly, not much else is satisfying.

The idea of Seaview on maneuvers with only a skeleton crew never comes off as anything but a budget-saver … and a means of making it easier for the alien to dominate the playing field, with Crane, Sharkey, Morton, and Kowalski all under its spell, with Nelson, at the end, left on his own. Writer Rik Vollaerts made no effort to properly set up or justify these contrivances; he merely tossed them in because they served the writer's need.

As noted above, it's yet another story involving possession of crew members by an alien entity (good Lord, they just did this in the previous episode!). Even the excellent cast seems to be going through the motions, with trite lines such as "I'm going to kill you, Admiral." This makes a 50-minute episode feel *so much longer.* It certainly loses energy before the final curtain.

What might have saved this story was a purpose – a theme or statement to distinguish it from the previous episodes that had used the same story devices.

Writer Vollaerts did actually provide one, if you dig deeply enough. The Shadowman tells Nelson that his kind are from the star galaxy we know as Centauri. An Earth probe will be launched shortly, with the help of Seaview, with Centauri as its destination. And that bothers these aliens.

"Why are you afraid?" Nelson asks. "Our probe was intended as a friendly act," says the admiral whose sub carries a full complement of nuclear missiles.

"We do not believe you," the shadow says. "Our ships have observed your Earth for many centuries now. We have seen your manmade disasters; your careless destruction; your wars. We want none of these to infect our peaceful civilization."

"Peaceful?" Nelson scoffs. "Well, your actions so far haven't been what I'd call peaceful. You've already sabotaged three attempts to launch the probe."

"We act only in self-defense," says the shadow, whose plan is to get the men on the Seaview to kill each another! At least the "peaceful" aliens intend to go home eventually, with no threats made of destroying the rest of the Earth.

While awkwardly handled by Vollaerts, the door was opened a crack for a comment on man's inherent violence, which had provoked a similar violent reaction from a race that considered itself peaceful. *Star Trek* would have handled it that way. But after figuring out how to destroy the alien, Nelson gives the go-ahead to launch the probe, as if none of this had ever happened. And if the Shadowmen complain, we now know how to kill them.

Mike Bailey noted, "Lip service is given to the concept that the shadow people want to prevent Earth from contaminating Alpha Centauri with violence. But that's all it is – lip service that rings hollow. In many ways, this is latter-year *Voyage* at its worst. Bottom line – another Rik Vollaerts penned Third-Season stinker." [4]

Don't you imagine that many parents, encountering these shadows with the power to cloud men's minds, half expected them to sound like Orson Welles? After all, Welles famously played *The Shadow* on radio in the late 1930s.

We'll give the last word to Admiral Nelson. When Captain Crane, finally free of the Shadowman's mind control, wakes from his fog, he asks Nelson what happened. The answer: "A long, long nightmare." Do yourself a favor and pass this nightmare by.

Script:

Rik Vollaerts' writers contract for "The Shadow People": September 23, 1966.
Vollaerts' story treatment approved by Irwin Allen on September 28.
Vollaerts' 1st-Draft teleplay: October 4.
Vollaerts' 2nd (and final) draft teleplay, now "The Shadowman": November 9.

Rev. Shooting Final teleplay (blue paper): December 5.

At first, **Rik Vollaerts** called his story "The Shadow People." As he developed the first-draft teleplay it became "Attack of the Shadowmen." Then, with his second draft, and from that point forward, it was "The Shadowman." One Shadowman would certainly be cheaper than several.

Production Coordinator Les Warner read Vollaerts' first-draft teleplay … and then reacted.

<u>Scene 2</u>: Crane's last speech to Kowalski, "Take over here": Would a Seaman take over the con unless in dire emergency? Besides, Kowalski doesn't do anything but stand there and talk with Crane in Scene 4.

<u>Scenes 3, 27</u>: The sonar screen "images": Sidney Marshall advises there will be no images or blips actually seen. They will just be talked about.

<u>Scenes 8, 9</u>: How do we get this effect of the sub standing on its nose from inside the Control Room?! Even by tilting the camera, what would be happening to our people?...

<u>Scene 28</u>: Shouldn't we delete the reference to the Sonar screen exploding (imploding) and just use the other effects as indicated?...

<u>Scenes 143-146</u>: The "monster": Sidney Marshall advises that the monster will no doubt be deleted from the script.

<u>Scene 145</u>: If it is not deleted, would Nelson and Crane just walk away and leave this fantastic monster still lying there on the deck?...

<u>NOTE</u>: The minimal cast cost may justify a suggestion to ADD one more: The sub Doctor for the Sick Bay hypodermic scenes. It does not now seem logical that Nelson doesn't play these scenes with the Staff Doctor, who certainly should be aboard, instead of doing all this by himself….

<u>PHOTO EFFECTS</u>: … All references to the Shadow men, their materialization thru walls, their moving shadows, etc., as I

understand it was determined at the Method Meeting today to explore the possibility of getting all these effects completely on the set without the use of Photo Effects.

MECHANICAL EFFECTS: A RED FLAG!: Not only could we never afford the innumerable references to fires and explosions in the sub (time-consuming, and damage to our permanent props) but there is always the logic that they could never get this sub to function again in the time indicated. ...

COMMENTS:
A. I started indicating in the Master script the various sets that should have the Emergency Red Lighting effect but got confused and gave up. This should be worked out and specifically indicated in the script for Breakdown and Shooting.
B. Nelson has the most amazing acumen throughout this script, re: the Shadow men and what is in the blackness outside. His observations, no matter how fantastic, are right on the nose! [5]

After reading Vollaerts' rewrite, Warner sent out another memo:

Scene 144-A, 146: The Monster is still in although Sidney Marshall felt at the time of my original Analysis that this would be written out. As described, not only could this be an expensive item (for just these two scenes) but I feel that, story-wise, showing anything in physical form is contrary to the concept we now have of the Shadow People.

Scene 145: NOT complied with, and I still feel that Nelson and Crane would not just walk away and leave this fantastic monster still lying there alive on the deck. It does not now dematerialize until _after_ they have gone....

Scenes 110 D-G: The grenade booby trap explosion of the console: If Nelson were "knocked across the room to the opposite wall", it is hard to believe that a minute later he gets up with "a few cuts on his face" and leaves the room.

Scene 131: The Reactor console was reduced to a "shambles" by the grenade explosion, but now it is functioning perfectly….

Scene 134: Nelson's first speech in the Missile Room. I don't believe he would tell Kowalski to "lock the door". Wouldn't it be "dog the hatch", or something like that?

NEW COMMENT: What with the small cast (6), minimal sets, and NO atmosphere, this might well have been an easy schedule, low budget picture but for the Shadow Men concept and the Mechanical Effects panics, explosions…. The Major problems are still:
A. Shadow Men concept
B. Mechanical Effects. [6]

Irwin Allen took a couple weeks before sending in his notes, in part:

Page 18, Scene 35: No reason is given for Crane's cease fire. Therefore it would be better if we ended Act I on the scenes in which Nelson is avoiding being hit by Crane. Preferably at a point when Nelson is unable to take further cover and stands exposed, gun in hand, facing Crane. Act II should then pick up the action at this point but the Shadowman would appear in time to stop the match and gesture to Crane to follow him, saying that the time for him to kill has not yet come. This would explain why Nelson doesn't inform the others, over the intercom, to be on the lookout for Crane and the Shadowman. [7]

A more appropriate comment might have pointed out that the audience might be sick of seeing the Seaview crew under mind control. Had they yet tried tinfoil hats?

Allen seemed numb to repetition of such gimmicks, *ad nauseam*. His notes, unlike those from staff members like Les Warner, were becoming less insightful. Instead of addressing major story problems, Allen now focused on nuances, such as:

Page 32, Scene 83: Once again the question arises as to why Kowalski did not warn Nelson about Morton as soon as he revived. So, it would be better if Kowalski was just coming around when Nelson calls to him for help. This would change some of the dialogue between Nelson and Kowalski to suit the occasion. [8]

Allen concentrated on minor plot contrivances rather than being concerned with telling compelling and sensible stories. And sadly, with the restrictive budget, Les Warner's notes were likewise more about saving money and less about exciting the viewers.

Production:
(Filmed December 7 – 15, 1966; 6 ½ days)
(New scene filmed January 13, 1967)

Justus Addiss was on his tenth of 16 directing assignments at *Voyage*.

Good news for the accountants: A guest star would not be required to fill the Shadowman's shoes. Only a voice, provided by **Jim Mills**. You last heard him as the "The Heat Monster."

Production began on Wednesday, December 7, 1966, for the first of seven days on Stage 10, with all the standing Seaview sets, and some new features, including "Int. Missile Flight Control" and "Int. Work Shop." It did not take seven full days to film the episode. On the third day of production, Friday, December 9, a quarter of the day was spent filming an added scene for Production 9217, "The Heat Monster." On the final day of filming, they finished one-quarter day early, at 3:10 p.m. This, then, was a six-and-a-half-day production … if that were all there was to it. But after reviewing the rough edit, it was determined additional scenes were needed. Justus Addiss returned to direct them on Friday, January 13, from 8 a.m. until 3:30 p.m. [9]

Release / Reaction:
(ABC premiere airdate: 2/12/67; network repeat broadcast: 6/25/67)

Steven Hill, Barbara Bain, and Martin Landau of *Mission: Impossible* had the cover of *TV Guide*. *The Fox*, starring Sandy Dennis, was No. 1 in the movie houses. "Kind of a Drag" by the Buckinghams was No. 1 on the radio. *More of the Monkees* was No. 1 in record and department stores. *Bonanza* was No. 1 on TV. *Voyage to the Bottom of the Sea* had "The Shadowman." Would it be No. 1 in its time slot? The ratings report follows.

"TV Scout," in the Madison *Capital Times*, Wisconsin, among other newspapers, saw the writing on the wall:

> It's getting so that the only way you can tell the episodes of *Voyage to the Bottom of the Sea* apart is by the Monster-of-the-Week. Tonight it's the Shadowman who comes aboard the Seaview (which is on a delicate six-man mission), and proceeds to take over the minds of half the crew. If it sounds familiar to you, it should, like so many other *Voyage* plots. [10]

The competition on CBS was the classic film *The Wizard of Oz*. With a wicked witch, a tin man, a cowardly lions, a talking scarecrow, and flying monkeys, who would be watching "The Shadowman"?

A.C. Nielsen 30-Market ratings report for February 12, 1967: [11]

7 – 7:30 p.m.:	Rating:	Share:
ABC: *Voyage to the Bottom of the Sea*	13.6	24.5%
CBS: *Lassie*	**25.5**	**45.9%**
NBC: *Bell Telephone Hour*	9.0	16.2%
7:30 – 8 p.m.:		
ABC: *Voyage to the Bottom of the Sea*	15.3	25.7%
CBS: *It's About Time*	**27.3**	**45.8%**
NBC: *Walt Disney's Wonderful World…*	10.4	17.4%

In the days after "The Shadowman" first aired, a letter was published in the TV section "Mail Bag" of the February 18, 1967 edition of the *Hutchinson News*, in Hutchinson, Kansas:

> I'd like to know why whoever is responsible has gone to such lengths to destroy what began as, and is yet basically, a good program. The program is *Voyage to the Bottom of the Sea*. It began as a sort of *U.N.C.L.E.* program based in a futuristic type submarine. Now they have stories with subjects such as shadowman, fishmen, mummies, pirates who walk through walls, etc. – Unidentified writer. [12]

8.6

"No Escape from Death" (Episode 80)

(Prod. No. 9222; first aired on Sunday, February 19, 1967)
Written by William Welch
Directed by Harry Harris
Produced by Irwin Allen and Bruce Fowler, Jr.; Story Editor: Sidney Marshall

Considering the amount of stock footage, a better title may have been "No Escape from the Vault." Pictured: Paul Carr from Season One, is *still* crawling around the Seaview's vents in Season Three!

From the Irwin Allen Private Papers Collection:

> Searching the waters for a strange Sealab, the Seaview runs afoul of its guardian submarine, and both plunge to the bottom. Because the air pumps have been put out of commission, Crane takes out a diving party to tap the air supply in the Sealab, but they are engulfed by one of the most horrifying creatures they have ever encountered. Only quick thinking by Admiral Nelson and Chief Sharkey saves not only the diving party but Seaview and her entire crew from the incredible fate. [1]

For Irwin Allen, there was nothing wrong in giving away the ending of a story in a synopsis, at least in respect to one of our heroes saving the day. Of course, we knew that the stars of the series would not perish – there would be another episode next week. The secret story point was *how* they would triumph. You'd have to tune in to find out about that.

Assessment:

Mark Phillips reported sadly, "My vote as the worst episode of *Voyage* ever, a tired story stitched with clips from past shows. Virtually unwatchable." [2]

Mike Bailey said, "Interesting. I actually found this episode refreshing in an odd roundabout way. Because it bodily lifts action sequences from previous bigger budgeted, better directed episodes, the inserted footage makes the show feel snappier than it might otherwise. On the other hand, any *Voyage* junkie can recognize the footage for what it is and therefore, as Mark points out, it doesn't go down well. … 'No Escape from Death' pretends to be a new adventure. But it's not new at all, having been stitched together from hauntingly familiar footage, especially in the case of Paul Carr's reappearance for the first time since either Season One (as Clark) or Season Two (as the deceased Benson), depending on how you look at things. To anyone who knew what was going on, a cheap and demeaning trick (with extensive use of protracted sequences from 'Submarine Sunk Here,' 'Hail to the Chief,' 'Jonah and the Whale,' and 'Graveyard of Fear')." [3]

"No Escape from Death" certainly doesn't rise to the level of the other sunken-submarine tales spun on *Voyage*, but it is still a tension-filled drama, with mounting jeopardies and overlapping dangers, sincerely acted, and effectively directed. Kudos to Harry Harris for shooting much of this episode on a severe tilt. To accomplish this, the camera was askew; the cast had to pretend the sets were also on a slant, as they leaned into walls – no easy task when walking along a corridor or trying to shore up a wall, or put a fire out.

The stock sequences, for the most part, are seamlessly inserted through efficient editing and the use of blue and red tinting (allowing the black-and-white footage of the first season to blend in with the color photography of the third). Sure, we can complain that the stock footage is here in the first place, but Irwin Allen and his staff had little choice; they'd used up nearly all of the Season Three budget.

As for the acting, this recurring cast never gave short shrift to anything. Whatever was asked of them by the script and the director, they excelled. It's hard

Above: Mr. Morton watches one of the stock footage scenes along with the TV audience – one of many clever techniques used to use the recycled scenes.
Below: The camera, on tilt, catches Sharkey and his men shoring up a bulkhead, while Captain Crane makes his way toward them, bracing himself against the wall.

not to get sucked into the drama when the characters on the screen convey their dilemmas with such sincerity and urgency.

As for the writing: William Welch's assignment, as with the recent script for "The Mermaid," was to devise a story which could pull together stock-footage sequences from previous episodes. Also, as with "Mermaid," this would be no mere flashback episode; the story had to be "new," despite its luggage from the past. Some have dismissed Welch for not being clever or original. We defend Welch because we know that it is far easier for a TV writer to make everything up than to fashion a new story out of existing – and previously unrelated – scraps. Welch had proven his creativity time and again in the past; now he was being called on to demonstrate his talents another way – assembling a working engine out of used parts. We think he did okay.

Script:
William Welch's writers contract: November 23, 1966.

*Welch's treatment, plus 1st- and 2nd-draft scripts approved by Irwin Allen on Dec. 6.
Shooting Final teleplay (pale Green): December 9.
Rev. Shooting Final teleplay (blue paper): December 14.*

Many may feel that writer **William Welch** took the Seaview to new depths as he implemented Irwin Allen's dictate to cannibalize earlier episodes. Welch was, in a sense, playing with Tinkertoys – recombining pre-fabricated pieces to offer something new. The idea of a sentry sub ramming the Seaview to keep it from discovering the Sealab, and the creature created there, was a new idea for the series. As was Nelson's desperate plan to expel the three divers from the giant man o' war, by pumping air into it … when the Seaview had little air to spare. Welch certainly had his moments.

Most of the script, however, is a rehash of things done better before. Note that his contract was dated November 23, 1966. This was right after a meeting with Irwin Allen and Sidney Marshall, in which they concocted this salvage-job tale. Within two weeks, Welch had turned in a treatment, followed by both 1st- and 2nd-draft teleplays.

Production:
(Filmed December 16 – 23, 1966; 5 & ½ days)

Harry Harris directed the new scenes, carefully crafted to seamlessly lead into and out of the designated stock footage.

Filming began on Friday, December 16, 1966 for the first of six days on Stage 10, for this bottle show which only required the standing Seaview sets and series regulars (including one who hadn't been a regular for a while, now back through the use of stock shots). It was supposed to be a five-day production, but Harris fell behind, requiring the morning of a sixth day for the last of the Control Room sequences, as well as a section of the ship's corridor. He finished at 11:20 a.m. on Friday, December 23. [4]

Harris said, "There was always something hitting the submarine. So, when the submarine got hit, or was on the bottom, it would always go one way and the people would go the other way. So, they moved the camera, tipped this way, and all the people had to go that way. And you had a tin can – a five gallon can, and, when you hit the can, the camera went one way and the people went the other, and all the props went with the people. By the end of the season, this can that I had would look like a piece of mangled metal! At the wrap party, [Irwin] had it sprayed in gold and he had the hammer welded to the top of the can, and gave it to me as a trophy." [5]

Release / Reaction:
(ABC premiere airdate: 2/19/67; network repeat broadcast: 8/20/67)

The Vietnam War continued to escalate, as 25,000 U.S. and South Vietnamese troops launched "Operation Junction City" against the Viet Cong. It was the largest U.S. airborne assault since World War II. Back at home, *Hurry Sundown*, starring Michael Caine, Jane Fonda, and Faye Dunaway, was the top-grossing film in the movie houses. "Kind of a Drag" was still the song heard most on the radio, and *More of the Monkees* was king at the record stores. Dean Martin and a handful of his Golddiggers had the cover of *TV Guide*.

"TV Scout" previewed "No Escape from Death," and there was no escaping critic Joan Crosby's dismissive tone:

> *Voyage to the Bottom of the Sea* waddles along with a tale which provides little new interest to the series. It's a soggy episode concerning the plight of the Seaview after it is rammed by another submarine. Best scenes involve a huge Portuguese Man o' War, with a healthy appetite, which swallows a diving party on its way to get aid at an underwater laboratory. It's enough to keep you on a fish-free diet for a lifetime. [6]

A.C. Nielsen ratings report from February 19, 1967: [7]

7 – 7:30 p.m.:	Rating:	Share:
ABC: *Voyage to the Bottom of the Sea*	16.1	no data
CBS: *Lassie*	**18.5**	**no data**
NBC: News Special: *Battle Asia*	10.6	no data
7:30 – 8 p.m.:		
ABC: *Voyage to the Bottom of the Sea*	17.7	29.3%
CBS: *It's About Time*	14.9	25.9%
NBC: *Walt Disney's Wonderful World…*	**21.9**	**36.9%**

Now *Voyage* was second in its time slot, and sinking faster than the Seaview heading for the bottom.

8.7

"Doomsday Island" (Episode 81)

(Prod. No. 9223; first aired on Sunday, February 26, 1967)
Written by Peter Germano
Directed by Jerry Hopper
Produced by Irwin Allen and Bruce Fowler, Jr.; Story Editor: Sidney Marshall
With Jock Gaynor (Scorpion leader)

Be honest. Doesn't this amphibian look like one of the Teletubbies?

From the *Voyage* show files (Irwin Allen papers collection):

> Among routine specimens taken aboard the Seaview from the ocean bottom is a weird and enormous "egg." From then on, it takes all the skill and courage of Admiral Nelson, Captain Crane and their crew to prevent the invasion of Earth by a race of strange and awesome Amphibians from deepest space. [1]

Assessment:

The story presented yet another alien race bent on taking over the world. To accomplish this, they project illusions. No one was possessed this time around, merely subjected to a freeze-control, and attempts to intimidate and confuse.

The episode has its moments, such as when a frozen Crane and Kowalski are seated in a partial mockup of the Flying Sub interior build by the aliens, with this image projected to the Seaview in an effort to disguise an approaching missile. Another winning moment has Chip Morton, believing it is the real FS1, is reluctant to fire on it. Then, believing Crane and Kowalski have been killed, he erupts in anger toward Nelson. It's nice stuff, but hardly makes up for all the rest.

Mark Phillips said, "A ridiculous episode propped up by some really great special effects. ... "This whole episode is the closest *Voyage* came to being a live-action cartoon, with its grunting red amphibians and mind-numbing action. Lars, the alien leader, was definitely spoiled as a baby amphibian because his malevolent monologues are interrupted by his childish, silly temper tantrums. Fun in a silly sense but if you begin to reflect on how far the series had fallen since the early days, this will bring a bitter tear to the eye." [2]

Mike Bailey reflected, "Episodes like this were the reason I had to get a television set of my own at the tender age of sixteen – so I could hole up in my bedroom and watch this kind of tripe without having to be seen in public and explain myself. My family was then under the impression that, although not their cup of tea, *Voyage* was still a pretty good show. And, indeed, it still was a pretty good show on a hit and miss basis. But *Voyage to the Bottom of the Sea* had become a series which, while when it was good, could still be very, very good (Year Three's 'Day the World Ended' and Year Four's 'Man of Many Faces,' for example), but when bad, could stink to high heaven (as with 'Doomsday Island'). This being said, the budget was back in this episode, with new Flying Sub footage, tons of animated ray-gun blasts, and that nifty matte-shot of all those eggs on the beach. Damn thing views nicely with the sound down, except for the idiotic looking aliens." [3]

We recommend you follow Mike Bailey's lead: Watch this one when alone, or with someone who won't think less of you for indulging in such a guilty pleasure.

Script:

Peter Germano's writers contract: June 3, 1966.
Germano's story treatment: June 7.
Germano's 1ˢᵗ-draft teleplay: June 14.
Germano's 2ⁿᵈ (and final) draft teleplay approved by Irwin Allen on August 4.
Shooting Final teleplay (pale green paper): December 15.
Page revisions (blue paper): December 21.
Page revisions (pink paper): January 3.

This was 53-year-old **Peter Germano**'s first assignment on *Voyage*. Therefore its development was heavily supervised. Germano had worked as a war correspondent during World War II and written articles documenting the action seen by the Marines. Later he became an author, writing short stories and novels, mostly Westerns, although he also dabbled in science fiction. Germano's background in television was also with Westerns, including multiple script assignments for *The Rebel*, *Maverick*, *Tales of Wells Fargo*, *Cheyenne*, and *Iron Horse*. The Western he worked the most for was *Wagon Train*, with 11 scripts. Germano was given his one and only *Voyage* assignment after selling one of his stories to *The Time Tunnel* ("End of the World," with teleplay by William Welch).

Of Germano's first-draft script, Irwin Allen had only three notes. The first had to do with modifying one line of dialogue for Crane. The second pointed out misnumbered pages ("There are 2 pages marked 19 and 2 marked 30 – They are duplicates except for certain slight differences. Which pages are correct?"). Only the third item was of consequence, and was something Les Warner also commented on, to far greater and more effective detail. Regarding a scene where Crane and Kowalski, having journeyed to an island only to be captured by amphibian creatures and held in a lab where they believe they see the Flying Sub (which is only an illusion), Allen said:

> Page 44: Crane and Kowalski are let out of the cage on the pretext that they are to return to the Seaview. They are then taken to the Grotto. Why? We next see them alive on Page 51 – back in the Lab. In what way was their presence in the Grotto necessary to Lars' plan of sending out the imaginary flying sub? [4]

Fortunately, Allen's staff members were more attentive. Associate Producer Bruce Fowler said:

> For a first draft, I think that Germano has caught the flavor and excitement of the VOYAGE series very well. The characters are well drawn, and our people speak in a familiar manner. [5]

Regarding suggested changes, Fowler wrote:

> There are too many new people in the crew whom we have not met before, speaking lines, and, perhaps, some of these

can be consolidated and the rest given to familiar people. There are some production problems – as in any first draft – such as the number of burn-ins, the amount of amphibians, both under water and on the surface – but nothing of a nature that cannot be licked. [6]

Of a more constructive nature, he added:

Page 28 -- Scene 86: Since we do not have a shot of the Flying Sub on a beach, why don't we transpose this scene to:
A. FLYING SUB ANCHORED ON WATER, and/or
B. Crane and Kowalski coming onto beach on a rubber raft. We can handle either of these.

Pages 28-29 – Scenes 88 thru 94: Where did the Starfish come from, and why? A rewrite to use the hidden menace of the amphibians would be better and more exciting….

Page 40 – Scene 118: How does the amphibian get out of the Seaquarium. Would it not be more effective if we have him break through the glass wall and into the lab on scene?

Page 46 – Scene 125: I think the author got a little mixed up here technically. Shouldn't we fire a torpedo instead of a missile? I see in Scene 129, Page 28, that we now do this. This still needs straightening out, however. [7]

Production Coordinator Les Warner turned in the most detailed and helpful notes. It was a seven-page memo, with Warner saying, in part:

INT. MISSILE ROOM -- Scenes 2-17:
A. It is highly illogical that only Crane and two Seamen are handling the involved and very important operation of hauling in the netted egg by winch. Realize this was necessary story-wise, at this writing, but suggest: (1) Crane is supervising a full complement of personnel necessary for this operation, with Sharkey in charge. (2) After the egg is revealed, Crane must leave for Control Room to check coordinates (with Morton) for Nelson. He orders Sharkey to clear Missile Room and place it under security – which Sharkey does, putting the brothers on

guard. (3) DELETE Bill's going for his camera (which is rather contrived) and have the Monster first K.O. Bill before going after Stanley. Then later Bill can still blame himself for not being on the alert while on guard.

B. <u>Scene 10</u>: Kowalski would not personally deliver the message that Nelson, on the radio, wants to talk with Crane. Morton, though, would do this. Then Crane could say to pipe Nelson through. Nelson could then ask for a coordinates check. Crane would mention the "egg" emergency, and couldn't Morton do this. Nelson would say this isn't a routine check, but to secure Missile Room until he gets back. NOTE: This would put Kowalski in the Flying Sub with Nelson and Morton back in the Control Room (where he <u>would</u> be in command if Crane is down in the Missile Room).

C. <u>Scene 12</u>: If you agree with the above Item B, then change the "egg" dialogue here with Crane on radio to Nelson, and introduce a hint of the urgency of the Seaview's original mission — which will build additional suspense along with the "egg" business.

D. <u>Scene 17</u>: For security reasons, Nelson would know the background of every man on his boat. He may have to be <u>reminded</u> here, but he would certainly have known there were <u>brothers</u> aboard!...

<u>INT. CONTROL ROOM AND NOSE</u> – Scenes 40-52, 81, 95, 104, 110:

A. It would probably be impossible (or at least too costly) to show a P.O.V. of the island through the sub's nose while surfaced. Also, script calls for varying degrees of size of the island, as sub approaches.

B. Story-wise, this also seems illogical. Why, if all stations are on alert (Scene 41), would they surface this close to a hostile island? Wouldn't they use their periscope, through which we would see the island? Also, this depth would be more logical from which to use their sub-terrestrial scanner. NOTE: Using the periscope would eliminate five BURN-INS at the Nose Window....

<u>INT. FLYING SUB</u> – Scene 88: Through window as FS1 skims down over water and grates to a stop on sandy island beach. This is indicated as a BURN-IN and I must go along with this

with hope we'll find STOCK FILM, which I sincerely doubt. If not, and to avoid an expensive Miniature, I suggest we cheat this with a reverse on Crane telling Nelson on radio that they are going in, then simulate landing with CAMERA and cast movements.

EXT. BEACH – Scenes 89-94: Sequence with the two giant starfish: RED FLAG! This short sequence in the middle of an act (NOT an act ending) is prohibitively expensive and time consuming:
A. Two mechanical starfish miniatures which would have to be built.
B. Two miniature sets: toward jungle and toward ocean with water.
C. New live sets to match – for cost.
D. Split screens.

STORY: Why do the two amphibians go to all the trouble of "disguising" themselves as starfish when they are already prepared to surprise-trap our men in a steel net – which they do? This is an obvious dragged in suspense bit that is not necessary to the situation. SOLUTION: DELETE the entire starfish business and develop the amphibians and steel net business for added suspense….

INT. UNDERGROUND ALIEN LABORATORY:
A. Scenes 110-B: "… control panel … intricate looking machinery and other paraphernalia…" Can we assume these way-out, highly-advanced aliens (amphibians) have humanoid-type equipment rather than the futuristic, stylized type we usually use? Realize Crane later uses one of their "thick power cables" (which happens to be conveniently running along the floor right in the middle of the set – Scene 123), but couldn't we use another gimmick?
B. Scene 110-B and on: Is the monkey in the case, and its later business, really necessary? Added cost and time consuming. Also, it will tend to be conflictingly numerous in scenes that should all build with drama and suspense.
C. Scene 110-B: Lars' last speech, also Scene 112: If he has been here "hundreds of years" waiting for his eggs to hatch, how come a young, ostrich-sized egg grows to full

maturity and releases a full-grown amphibian in less than one day on the sub? ...

D. Scenes 110-B, 111: This business of Lars inoculating the embryo inside an egg. Any importance of this business? Story (is there?) cannot possibly justify the expense of specially manufactured props, photographic effects and set time consumed. SOLUTION: DELETE or extremely modify.

INT. SEAVIEW LAB AND CORRIDOR – Scenes 115-117: Scene 116: The giant egg, in the Seaquarium, cracks open and a full-grown amphibian comes out. The problem of sealing a man into a six-foot break-away egg, getting it into a glass tank of commensurate size, and keeping it there under water until we can get the shot on film, is practically impossible. SOLLUTION: DELETE this scene and use 115 as is, as the egg is beginning to crack – and 118 as is, as the amphibian is already out of the broken shell but still in the tank.

INT. UNDERGROUND LAB – Scene 124: Robinson destroying the illusionary Flying Sub: We later learn this was an illusion. I know the writer wants us to believe Crane and Kowalski are really in it, but isn't the business in 124 carrying it too far? The business of taking them out of the locked cage and starting them toward the grotto where the FS1 really is when we later learn they never were put in it? This is really deceitful writing – which the audience will later resent. SOLUTION: Would we not get the desired effect by using Lars' line, "How would you like to return to the Seaview, Captain?" and then end scene on Crane's amazed but wary reaction and Lars' sly chuckle? This would be misleading, but still honest writing. [8]

Production:

(Filmed December 27, 1966 through January 4, 1967; 6 days)

Jerry Hopper was back in the director's chair. This was his fifth of 15 *Voyages*.

Jock Gaynor played Lars, the alien leader. He was 32 and had been a regular in the 1960 series *The Outlaws*. He was also a regular on the 1963 series

The Doctors ... as a doctor. Gaynor would return to *Voyage*, as a human being, in "Man of Many Faces."

Production began on Tuesday, December 27, 1966, for the first of five days on Stage 10. The first four days were spent on the standing Seaview sets. The fifth day, Tuesday, involved the Flying Sub set and the "Int. Complex with Flying Sub" and "Int. Reactor Room." The sixth day of production, Wednesday, January 4, 1966, had the company on Stage B for "Ext. Beach" and "Int. Island Lab." [9]

Jock Gaynor, interviewed by Mark Phillips and Frank Garcia, said, "There was always a monster of the week on *Voyage*. Although they offered me the role of Lars, anybody could have done it. It was a paycheck. The costume I wore was rubber. It was made from scuba gear, and under the hot lights I lost about 12 pounds. The series in general was a children's show. High camp. It was not to be taken seriously." [10]

Jock Gaynor (above) in 1960's *The Outlaws* ... and (below) unrecognizable as Lars the amphibian.

Release / Reaction:
(ABC premiere airdate: 2/26/67; network repeat broadcast: 8/27/67)

"Ruby Tuesday," by the Rolling Stones, was the most popular song on the radio. Its flipside, "Let's Spend the Night Together," was banned by many radio programmers due to its sexually suggestive lyric. When the Stones performed the song on *The Ed Sullivan Show*, lead singer Mick Jagger was asked to change the song's hook line to "Let's Spend Some Time Together." You see, *Voyage* wasn't the only series dealing with censorship. Phyllis Diller was the glamor girl on the cover of

505

TV Guide the week "Doomsday Island" first aired on ABC. No one – not "TV Key," not "TV Scout," not *Daily Variety* – bothered to review this turkey. That level of disinterest was reflected in the ratings, too.

A.C. Nielsen ratings report from February 26, 1967: [11]

7 – 7:30 p.m.:	Rating:	Share:
ABC: *Voyage to the Bottom of the Sea*	17.7	no data
CBS: *Lassie*	**22.4**	**no data**
NBC: *Bell Telephone Hour*	9.2	no data

7:30 – 8 p.m.:		
ABC: *Voyage to the Bottom of the Sea*	17.1	28.5%
CBS: *It's About Time*	13.9	21.2%
NBC: "Jack and the Beanstalk"	**29.0**	**44.8%**

The sudden drop in the ratings had more to do with a big event on NBC – "Jack and the Beanstalk" – than any audience distaste for monsters on *Voyage*.

8.8

"The Wax Men" (Episode 82)

(Prod. No. 9224; first aired on Sunday, March 5, 1967)
Written by William Welch
Directed by Harmon Jones
Produced by Irwin Allen and Bruce Fowler, Jr.; Story Editor: Sidney Marshall
Guest Star Michael Dunn

Michael Dunn demonstrates another reason to be afraid of clowns.

From the *Voyage* show files (Irwin Allen papers collection):

An unusual Clown is behind Captain Crane's nightmare of terror when Admiral Nelson and the crew of the Seaview become his waxen enemies. Only by accident does Crane discover how to thwart the plans of the sinister Clown and return the Seaview's crew to normal. [1]

Assessment:

"The Wax Men" is a fun episode, although a bit sluggish in its pacing. At one point the Clown actually tells Captain Crane, "Let's stop wasting any more of your time and mine." We agree! And we can't figure out *why* the guest villain (Michael Dunn as the Clown) wants to take over the Seaview with his army of wax men. Admiral Nelson speculates in the episode's Tag, but neither he nor we can know for sure – the Clown never told anyone. A little scene explaining the Clown's motivation from writer William Welch would have been nice. Dunn's character is clearly inspired by his Dr. Miguelito Loveless persona on *The Wild, Wild, West* (the music cues in "The Wax Men" seem inspired by the Loveless themes featured on *WWW* too), but Welch missed an opportunity to have the Clown do as Loveless always did – brag about his maniacal scheme, which often gave *WWW*'s James West the idea as to how to derail it. This omission mitigates an otherwise enjoyable *Voyage*.

Mike Bailey said, "This episode accomplishes what it strives for – bizarre weirdness. Forget logic – who needs it when one eerie, horrifying thing after another occurs. The clown's humorous appearance and demeanor are counterpoints to the horror of what he's doing – replacing all human life aboard Seaview with soulless wax ciphers. … The real horror is experienced by Crane, who, returning to all of this, discovers one by one that his friends and crew mates have been reduced to wax automatons…. And then, in nightmare fashion, he must 'kill' these lookalikes. Michael Dunn plays the clown to perfect menace. The soundtrack score by composer Robert Drasnin, known for his 1959 album, *Voodoo,* and as musical director for CBS TV (he also worked on *Lost in Space*), adds to the effect. Its off-key percussive punch is a perfect match for the strangeness that plays out on the screen." [2]

Our other resident critic was less impressed. Mark Phillips said, "This one is a colossal shame when you consider that Michael Dunn – an Oscar nominee for *Ship of Fools* (1965), acclaimed for his portrayal of the diabolical Dr. Loveless on *The Wild, Wild West*, and his poignant turn as a stranded Martian in *Norman Corwin Presents* (1972) – has his great talents hidden here by clown makeup and a one-dimensional character." [3]

That "truly bizarre" ending includes the wax men melting. Kudos to director Harmon Jones for suggesting this by having the actors simply go limp and gently collapse, followed by stunning shots of puddles of melted wax, in which the wax oozes from empty uniforms topped with clumps of hair!

Script:

William Welch's writers contract for "The Death Dolls": December 19, 1966.
Welch's treatment, and 1st- and 2nd- draft teleplays approved by Irwin Allen on Dec. 27.
Shooting Final teleplay, "The Wax Men" (pale green paper): December 28.
Page revisions (blue paper): January 3.
Page revisions (green paper): January 10.
Page revisions (yellow paper): January 11.

William Welch returned to his typewriter in better form – better than anything from him in a while. Much credit is owed to David Hedison's performance, the eeriness of the Clown and his waxy-faced zombie followers, and the episode's score. But it all starts with the script.

Since the villain was a clown, and there were no monsters, or Russians, or end-of-the-world scenarios for ABC to fret over, Mary Garbutt of Broadcast Standards and Practices focused her attention elsewhere.

> Pgs 4, 11, 15: [Be sure] various clocks [are] not identifiable as to actual trade/brand names.
>
> Pg 14, Sc 36: Gun not pointed directly into camera.
>
> Pg 35, Sc 139: Please modify [camera] angle of end of this scene so that wax figure does not seem to "walk through" camera.
>
> Pgs 39 & 40: Standard caution on fight – blood to minimum. Scs. 158 thru 160 – Special caution that this sequence is not too shocking or horrifying for family audience.
>
> Pg 51, Sc 200: Please be sure this is not electrocution effect; features not distorted, body not in convulsion – Also not in CU [Close Up] please. Also caution that human scream or cry of pain is not added. [4]

Otherwise, send in the clown! Hmm ... Do you suppose Stephen Sondheim saw this episode before writing "Send in the Clowns" in 1973 for *A Little Night Music*?

Production:

(Filmed January 6 – 12, 1967; 5 days)

Harmon Jones was hired to direct. He was 55 and had received an Oscar nomination for his editing of 1947's *Gentleman's Agreement*. Jones switched from film editing to directing in 1951 with *As Young as You Feel*. After a dozen or so B-films, he made the move to television. He was particularly liked at *Rawhide*, where he directed 13 episodes, and *Death Valley Days*, where he directed 38. This was Jones's only assignment on *Voyage*, but he would work for Irwin Allen one more time, with a 1969 episode of *Land of the Giants*.

Michael Dunn was cast to play the wicked clown, and paid the top guest-star rate of $2,500. He was 32 and already famous for his ongoing role as Dr. Miguelito Loveless in *The Wild, Wild West* (with 10 appearances spanning 1965 through 1969). In 1965, he was nominated for an Oscar for his supporting role in *Ship of Fools*. Two years after this *Voyage*, Dunn had the lead guest role in "Plato's Stepchildren," an episode of *Star Trek*.

Michael Dunn said, "Producers generally are not men of imagination. In a *Voyage to the Bottom of the Sea*, I'm Dr. Loveless again. Same role; big deal." [5]

Robert Conrad faces down Michael Dunn, in Dunn's most noted role: Dr. Miguelito Loveless on **The Wild, Wild West**.

This unique episode required a special score. **Robert Drasnin** was given the task. He was well qualified, having composed music for *The Twilight Zone*, *The Alfred Hitchcock Hour*, *The Man from U.N.C.L.E.*, *Lost in Space*, *The Time Tunnel*, and the 1966 film, *Picture Mommy Dead*. Most importantly, he had scored four episodes of *The Wild, Wild West*, including the one that started it all for Dr. Miguelito Loveless, 1965's "The Night the Wizard Shook the Earth."

Production began on Friday, January 6, 1967 for the first of five days on Stage 10 for this bottle show that required only the standing Seaview sets and the Flying Sub.

The production went off like clockwork, with filming stopping between 5:25 and 6:15 p.m. each day.[6] Furthermore, additional savings were realized in post-production. A memo from Irwin Allen told everyone involved:

> This segment does not require PHOTO EFFECTS and has not been budgeted for any. Under no circumstances is anyone to cause the expenditure of monies for PHOTO EFFECTS in this segment.[7]

Nobody did.

Release / Reaction:
(ABC premiere airdate: 3/5/67; network repeat broadcast: 9/3/67)

Otto Preminger's *Hurry Sundown*, starring Michael Caine and Jane Fonda, was the top movie in most towns and cities across the United States. "Love Is Here and Now You're Gone," by the Supremes, was the new champ on the radio. It was no longer news that the Monkees had the best-selling record album in the country (with *More of the Monkees*), but there was a new album at No. 2 – *Between the Buttons*, by the Rolling Stones. And that pushed the Monkees' first album down to No. 3. There was barely a 12-year-old in America who didn't already own a copy. As for *Voyage*, we got a double dose this week. Within days of the airing of "The Wax Men," the movie version of *Voyage to the Bottom of the Sea* had its television premiere on the NBC Wednesday Night Movie (March 8).

As for the series, "TV Scout" said:

> *Voyage to the Bottom of the Sea* is good science-fiction fun. Seems a cargo of "statues" is taken aboard the Seaview, but one of the crates contains Michael Dunn, who plays his entire role in clown makeup. Dunn is a mad genius who manages to turn everyone aboard the submarine into a waxen image. Then along comes David Hedison, the only live fly in the ointment, and most of the footage is devoted to a fairly suspenseful chase aboard the ship, with Hedison trying to stay alive and everyone, including the wax crew, out to get him. [8]

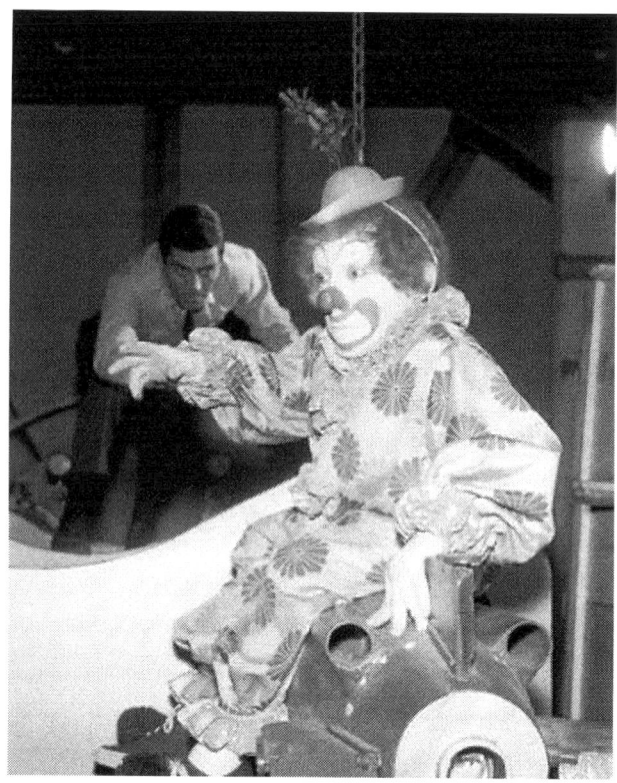

A.C. Nielsen ratings report from March 5, 1967: [9]

7 – 7:30 p.m.:	Rating:	Share:
ABC: *Voyage to the Bottom of the Sea*	16.7	no data
CBS: *Lassie*	**18.5**	**no data**
NBC: *NBC Children's Theatre*	16.7	no data

7:30 – 8 p.m.:		
ABC: *Voyage to the Bottom of the Sea*	17.9	29.0%
CBS: *It's About Time*	16.8	25.9%
NBC: *Walt Disney*	**24.0**	**36.7%**

Even Dr. Loveless couldn't get *Voyage* back to the top of the Nielsens.

8.9

"The Deadly Cloud" (Episode 83)

(Prod. No. 9225; first aired on Sunday, March 12, 1967)
Written by Rik Vollaerts
Directed by Jerry Hopper
Produced by Irwin Allen and Bruce Fowler, Jr.; Story Editor: Sidney Marshall
(with Robert Carson as Jurgenson)

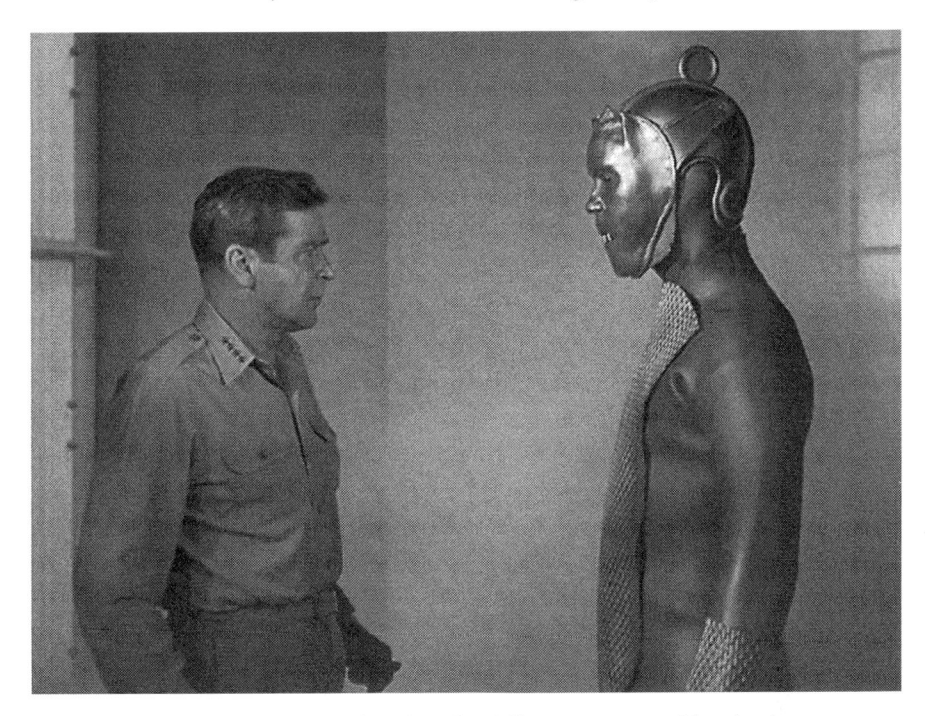

From the *Voyage* show files (Irwin Allen papers collection):

The Seaview is sent to investigate a strange, low-hanging cloud, which has been pin-pointed as the source of appalling world-wide natural disasters. When he learns that the Invaders within the cloud are undermining the Earth's structure by removing all metals for their own use, Admiral Nelson [tries to devise] a plan to destroy the Aliens in order that the world may survive. [1]

Assessment:

We'd seen most of it before. Much was plot points reworked from previous *Voyage*s. Still, we feel "The Deadly Cloud" is fairly compelling viewing.

Yes, it's another aliens-want-to-conquer-the-Earth story. Another episode in which either Admiral Nelson or Captain Crane are possessed (in this case, Lee Crane). Another invulnerable-invaders plot. And there is obvious budget-cutting going on here, with the skeleton crew (this is a "suicide mission," after all). And, of course, there is no point except to entertain.

But consider the pluses:

It's a startling-looking alien (or, if you prefer, stuntman in a silver mask);

These aliens don't care about ruling the Earth; they just want to strip its precious metals, and then vamoose.

David Hedison delivers his usual excellent performance, even if he was asked to portray this sort of thing *ad nauseam*. And they do have fun with the gimmick, with the fake Crane replaced by the real Crane – or is it?

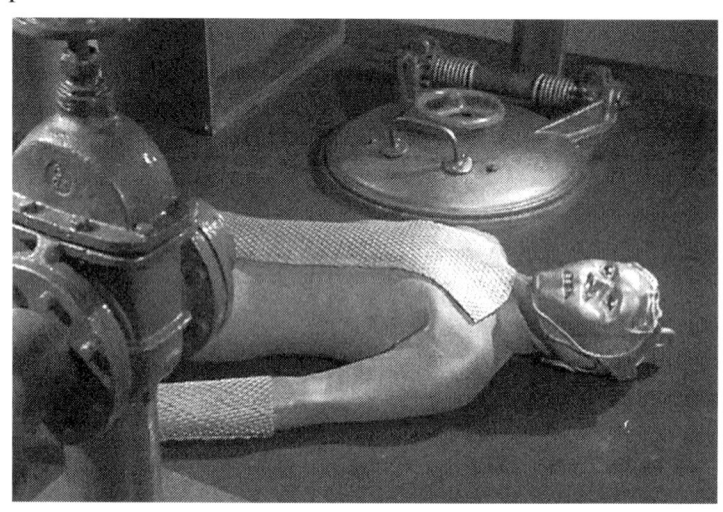

The plot tricks come fast and furious.

We also like how Crane uses his powers to try to torpedo Chief Sharkey in the back with *an actual torpedo*.

On the other hand:

"A horrible episode," said Mike Bailey. "No budget and terribly written. The normally workmanlike Jerry Hopper directs leadenly, and, after taking the money, writer Rik Vollaerts would have been wise to run for the border. When, in the first reel, altogether too-familiar footage of a nuclear blast was used to represent the cloud, I knew we were in big trouble on this outing." [2]

Mark Phillips found it to be a "par for the course third-seasoner." [3]

We'll side with Phillips here. It's worth watching, but hardly worth further discussion.

Script:

Rik Vollaerts' writers contract: December 16, 1966.
Vollaerts' story and 1st- draft teleplay approved by Irwin Allen on December 20.
Vollaerts' 2nd (and final) draft teleplay: December 21.
Shooting Final teleplay (pale green paper): January 5.
Page revisions (blue paper): January 11.
Page revisions (pink paper): January 24.

This would be **Rik Vollaerts'** sixth (and thankfully final) script for *Voyage*. His good fortune was that most of Hollywood had stopped watching, so his reputation survived. He moved on to write four episodes of the boy-and-his-elephant series *Maya*, then got a chance to do a *Star Trek* (the third-season episode "For the World Is Hollow and I Have Touched the Sky"). This came about because Vollaerts knew Gene Roddenberry from when they both wrote scripts for Ziv Productions. Vollaerts asked to be the series story editor; Roddenberry gave him a one-script assignment instead. *Star Trek*'s co-producer, Robert Justman, gave Vollaerts one assignment on his next series, *Then Came Bronson*. Vollaerts also sold a script to *Mannix* in 1969 and one to the sitcom *Julia* in 1970. Then he did a little work in scripting for Saturday-morning cartoons for Hanna-Barbera. He was 56 at that point, and his TV writing career was over. The six substandard scripts he did for *Voyage* may have hurt him after all.

Production:
(Filmed January 16 – 24, 1967; 6 & ½ days)

Jerry Hopper was now on his sixth of 15 *Voyage*s.

Robert Carson (57) played Jurgenson. He was a familiar face (and voice) on television, with more than 200 credits. He was also the narrator of 94 episodes of the 1955-58 series, *Navy Log*, which reenacted true stories from the files of the Defense Department. That qualified him for a cruise on *Voyage*.

Production began on Monday, January 16, 1966, for the first of seven days on Stage 10, with Jerry Hopper directing. It was pretty close to a bottle show, using only standing Seaview sets and the Flying sub … except for two additional sets: "Int. Washington Office" and 'Int. Cloud Room," both of which were built on the same stage. [4]

Release / Reaction:

(ABC premiere airdate: 3/12/67; network repeat broadcast: 7/23/67)

In the movie houses, *How to Succeed in Business Without Really Trying* was doing the best business. Robert Morse and Michele Lee were the stars. "Penny Lane," by the Beatles, was the song being heard the most on the radio. Meanwhile, *Voyage* was serving up leftovers.

"TV Scout," in the *Abilene Reporter News*, said:

> *Voyage to the Bottom of the Sea* runs into cloudy weather – and what a cloud it is, causing as it does tidal waves, earthquakes, storms and alternate bouts of tedium and excitement for the viewer. [5]

A.C. Nielsen ratings report from March 12, 1967: [6]

7 – 7:30 p.m.:	Rating:	Share:
ABC: *Voyage to the Bottom of the Sea*	16.6	no data
CBS: *Lassie*	**20.6**	**no data**
NBC: *Bell Telephone Hour*	6.8	no data
7:30 – 8 p.m.:		
ABC: *Voyage to the Bottom of the Sea*	17.4	30.4%
CBS: *It's About Time*	14.6	24.7%
NBC: *Walt Disney*	**21.0**	**34.8%**

8.10

"Destroy Seaview!" (Episode 84)

(Prod. No. 9226; first aired on Sunday, March 19, 1967)
Written by Donn Mullally
Directed by Justus Addiss
Produced by Irwin Allen and Bruce Fowler, Jr.; Story Editor: Sidney Marshall
Guest Star Arthur Space

From the *Voyage* show files (Irwin Allen papers collection):

> A deposit of a rare element that can provide the power for the ultimate weapon starts the Seaview on a mission that almost ends in tragedy. Brain-washed by agents of an unscrupulous power who want the deposit for their own country, Admiral Nelson turns against his crew. [1]

Assessment:

It's a gas. At least, the part where Admiral Nelson, having had his brains washed by enemy operatives, gasses the entire crew of the Seaview. For the tail end of Season Three, "Destroy Seaview" isn't bad. No monsters, but we return to the espionage format of earlier seasons. Science and logic are on holiday during this outing. Don't ask yourself why the top two officers of the Seaview, along with a guest scientist, would go into the caves of the unstable island by themselves. Or why Morton doesn't seem in a hurry to rescue his Captain when Nelson returns to the ship with tales of a terrible cave-in. Or why the eventual rescue party consists of only two people with a little shovel. Despite this, it's an entertaining tale and a nice change of pace.

"Another great teaser as Nelson seals Crane in a cave," opined Mark Phillips. "But the rest is standard stuff." [2]

Mike Bailey called the script "pedestrian," also noting its surprising lack of urgency. [3]

All true. But you could do worse, and *Voyage* had. Remember – if you dare – episodes like "Monster from the Inferno" and "The Mermaid." This one will do … until a better episode comes along.

Script:

Don Mullally's writers contract: November 7, 1966.
Mullally's story treatment approved by Irwin Allen on November 18.
Mullally's 1st-draft teleplay approved by Allen on December 29.
Mullally's 2nd (and final) draft teleplay approved by Allen on Jan. 10, 1967.
Rev. Shooting Final (blue paper): January 20.
Page revisions (pink paper): January 25.
Page revisions (green paper): January 27.

This was the third and final script **Donn Mullally** wrote for *Voyage*. His others were "Werewolf" and "The Plant Man." Moving on, Mullally landed at *Ironside* for eight assignments, then ten at *Mannix*, followed by numerous assignments at *Kolchak: The Night Stalker*.

Production:

(Filmed January 25 – February 1, 1967; 6 days)

Justus Addiss got the final directing assignment for Season Three. This one had a budget of $177,273 (up from the Season Three per-episode target of $166,485).

Paul Trinka (Patterson) had one of his better paydays on *Voyage*, receiving $1,050 for five days' work.

"Guest Star" **Arthur Space**, as Dr. Land, only received $850. Space was 57 and had been a regular on *National Velvet* (1960-62) and *Lassie* as Doc Weaver (during the 1955-64 seasons). Space worked often in films and TV, with nearly three hundred different appearances on record. Yes, that was his real last name.

Production began on Wednesday, January 25, 1967, for six days of filming. The first three were spent on Stage 10 for all the usual standing Seaview sets, including one not seen in a while, "Int. Air Revitalization Room." The fourth day, also on Stage 10, had the company working on some new, temporary sets: the "Int. Reactor Room & Dogging Wheel" and "Int. Decontamination Room."

The last two days of the production were spent on Stage B, for "Int. Tavern Tunnel" and "Int. Landing Area." The last shot was completed at 7:20 p.m. on Wednesday, February 1, at which point the cast and production company were released for the spring hiatus. The post-production unit would continue working for a few weeks. [4]

Release / Reaction:
(Only ABC broadcast: 3/19/66)

During the week that *Voyage* aired its final new episode for its third season, *In Like Flint*, starring James Coburn, was the most popular movie in America. "Happy Together," by the Turtles, was the song playing the most on the radio. The Monkees would maintain their hold on the No. 1 album spot in the *Billboard* charts for another 12 weeks. Between their first and second album, they had had an impressive seven-month lock on the top spot. The Beatles hadn't released a new album since *Revolver* the previous summer. Pop music was about to change forever, with the coming of the Summer of Love and *Sgt. Pepper's Lonely Hearts Club Band*. When *Voyage* returned in the fall, it would be a whole different world.

"TV Scout" said:

> Richard Basehart has a mission to perform on *Voyage to the Bottom of the Sea*: destroy the Seaview. No monsters this time (and that's a relief), just Basehart brainwashed into

doing THEIR dirty work. First, he kills (or so it seems) David Hedison, then he wipes out the Seaview crew with a knockout gas. Now there are only seconds to spare before the submarine is destroyed. [5]

A.C. Nielsen ratings report from March 19, 1967: [6]

7 – 7:30 p.m.:	Rating:	Share:
ABC: *Voyage to the Bottom of the Sea*	15.6	no data
CBS: *Lassie*	**19.6**	**no data**
NBC: *Bell Telephone Hour*	no data	no data

7:30 – 8 P.M.:		
ABC: *Voyage to the Bottom of the Sea*	17.5	28.5%
CBS: *It's About Time*	13.3	22.5%
NBC: *Walt Disney*	**23.1**	**39.5%**

In less than three months, *Voyage*'s audience share had shrunk from an average of 35% to under 30%, allowing *Lassie* to regain its foothold in the early Sunday nighttime slot. *Disney*, more weeks than not, took top honors.

By the time the ratings could be analyzed for the last several first-run episodes, ABC had already renewed *Voyage* for a fourth season. If the network had delayed making that decision by even a few weeks, the series may have ended with this final episode of Season Three.

Ray Didsbury said, "We all knew, by the fourth year, that *Voyage* had turned into a recurring joke. We didn't even expect to get renewed for a fourth year. Richard [Basehart] would have been happy if it had died sooner. The transition to monster show came about purely for economic reasons. The rubber suits were free – they even gave screen credit to the company who supplied the suits [AMF VOIT]. These were relatively easy to rig up as the monster-of-the-week. That decision hurt the show's morale and affected Richard's caring about the show. There were many arguments about the scripts. Every time we got a new script, it was, 'Well, what are we fighting with this week?' It also hurt us in terms of popularity. The monsters were different, at first, but then they got predictable and boring." [7]

9

Season Four / ABC's Initial Order of 16 – Damage Control

VOYAGE TO THE BOTTOM OF THE SEA -- Richard Basehart, left, and David Hedison straddle the fantastic atomic-powered submarine-of-the-future, the Seaview, as they paddle off on a mission leading to high adventure and danger in producer Irwin Allen's exciting 20th Century-Fox Television series, "Voyage to the Bottom of the Sea" (seen in color each Sunday evening over ABC-TV). Lurking in wait beneath the ship is a contingent of deadly denizens of the deep complemented by a lovely mermaid. Overhead shoots the Seaview's flying submarine at remarkable speeds.

Now that a new season of *Voyage* was assured, there was time to consider its direction. Should there be a change in story emphasis, or perhaps in casting? One thing was a given: Any changes had better not cost very much.

521

One change in the early part of Season Four was an effort to turn the *Voyage* stories away from a monster every week to a monster every *few* weeks, as in the latter part of the second season. A small effort was even made to give the stories a little more explication, in hopes of regaining lost credibility. All concerned, both in Irwin Allen's offices and those at ABC, felt the show had leaned a little too far toward monsters and fantasy storylines. The dropping ratings were an indication of this, as were critical reaction and letters from the fans. Irwin Allen still believed that monsters were a plus for the series, just not in nearly every episode. ABC concurred.

Days before the start of the new season, an article generated by 20th Century-Fox was put out as a newspaper wire story. Its title – an unintended irony – "Authenticity Strong Point of TV Show." The spin doctors told us:

> Irwin Allen's *Voyage to the Bottom of the Sea* series may be viewed by some as a science-fiction program, but, in reality, there is a large percentage of science-fact built into every segment of the 20th Century-Fox Television production. The credit for this authenticity must go to the creator-producer of the show, Irwin Allen. [1]

The article quoted Richard Basehart: "One of the truly remarkable assets of the show is the fact that we are working with equipment whose designs will someday be a reality. After all, the atomic-powered submarine is already a scientific fact. It does not seem so improbable that the concept of the flying submarine that we use on the show might not also be implemented. Because of the authenticity and the detail that has gone into the working sets and props that are used in the show, this series creates its own aura of reality. On our submarine, the Seaview, the lights really light and the machines really run. The difference lies in the fact that the submarine never travels beyond the limits of the sound stage." [2]

Basehart was being a good company man. But did Irwin Allen really think that the verisimilitude of the show's sets would make a difference when the stories themselves were illogical?

Actually, he did.

Another valid concern was the previous years' hash-and-rehash use of the "possessed crewman-of-the-week" theme. Effects shots were repeated, *ad nauseam*, like that sequence of Seaview grazing the ocean floor. As we've seen, Allen had taken to having writers build stories around stock footage. While these practices were great budget savers, how successful were these operations if the patient wasn't revived for a new season? Nevertheless, Allen seemed to think nobody would notice.

ABC's Lew Hunter said, "We rarely cautioned him to be less redundant because we didn't feel we had an intelligent audience to the degree of *Star Trek*. Clearly the audience of that show was more superior to all the television audiences, with the probable exception of *Playhouse 90* and *Studio One*. But we had a child audience. And, if I said to Irwin, 'You've done this before,' I can still hear him say, 'Well? Did it work before? Yes! So, it will work again!'"

Allen had a story rationalizing the repetition-is-good viewpoint. Lew Hunter recalled, "Irwin told a story to me and Harve Bennett one day when we were trying to talk him into doing something a little more literate and less redundant. He said, 'Our audience is like a little boy, who, when his father comes in to read him a bedtime story, and the father says, "I'm going to read you *The Emperor's New Clothes*," and the boy says, "I don't want *The Emperor's New Clothes*, I want *Peter Rabbit*." And the father says, "But I read *Peter Rabbit* for you night in and night out; let's go with *The Emperor's New Clothes*." "No," says the boy, "I want *Peter Rabbit*."' And the father says, "Alright," and then he starts the story, saying, "Mr. McGregor is in the cabbage patch when…" And the boy interrupts and says, "No, no, no. Peter Rabbit is in the cabbage patch and Mr. McGregor comes later."' And that's what Irwin told Harve in relation to some particular point. He was quite satisfied in doing the formula over and over again, and he would point out little quirks in the formula and say, 'See there, see there, that's different!'" [3]

Sadly, not different enough. But the ABC executives felt helpless to change Allen's mind.

Hunter said, "He wouldn't have his shows tested by the network. He said, 'You're hiring me; you're not hiring whoever is sitting in that chair on Sunset Boulevard twisting dials.' If I would say something that he didn't agree with, he'd just say, 'I'm not going to do that.' He was never a profane man. When he'd see me, it was always 'Come on in to the office and have a cup of coffee.' He'd bring out the china and the Danish, and he'd say whatever it was he wanted to deal with me about on that day. And it would take us about ten minutes to eat and drink, and we would have very superficial conversation. Basically, it was about praising him on certain things about the show, and praising Richard Basehart, who he took a lot of pride in the fact that he had cast. But I'd want to get out of the room as quickly as possible because he might say something that I would disagree with, and I was prone *not* to politely agree with anyone at that time who I truly disagreed with. And I preferred to not get thrown off the lot again."

Hunter did get thrown off the lot … more than once. He said, "I remember one time when Irwin and I had some sort of tension, and I remember Harve telling me, in person, 'Lew, I've got to save your ass again.' So, he got in and immediately alleviated whatever dispute we had, which meant caving in to Irwin, I'm sure. But Harve said to me, '*You* can't do this shit; *I* can't do this shit; only Irwin can do his shit, so why try telling him anything that you want to tell him? Just let him do his shit.' And, even then, I couldn't hold back. I still felt I had to do my job, and comment on whatever it was in the memos I wrote." [4]

These memos were, for the most part, ignored.

David Hedison didn't bother with memos. He said, "I was a nice guy, and I did what I was told, and I guess Irwin liked me for that. Except once, I remember, I got a script – I think it was in the third year – and I was always very much of a gentleman, and I held my temper, and one day I was sitting by the pool, and I had just gotten this script for an episode we were going to start shooting the next day. They wrote this damn thing in a hurry, and when I read it, and saw what they were doing to the Captain Crane character, and the way it was written, I just went nuts. I got in my car and went right down to the studio. It was like in a movie – I went crashing into his office and said, 'Goddammit, Irwin, you can't write like this; you can't do this to me!' I went nuts. He was shaking. He said, 'Wait a minute; just wait.' And [he picked up the phone] and called this one, and called that one, and then the whole room was full – it was 50 people! He was terrified; he'd thought I'd gone nuts. Well, I *had* gone nuts. I said, 'The writing's bad sometimes, but *this* is ridiculous!' He said, 'Alright, alright, don't beat a dead horse!' So, finally, they had to rewrite the whole script. Now let's say this is a Wednesday night and we're starting the next morning. So, I got to work at 7 o'clock in the morning and pages were coming in. And finally, about 10 o'clock, Irwin comes onto the set, and he looks at me and he says, 'This is all *your* fault!' I said, 'Yes, but it's a better script.' Anyway, that was my one big argument that I had with dear Irwin." [5]

Despite his disagreements with Allen – and there were many – Lew Hunter said, "I was in the company of one of the greatest characters I'd ever known. He could be frustrating, but I have to admit, I really enjoyed being around him." [6]

Actor Jock Gaynor, who made guest appearances in all of Irwin Allen's 1960s TV series, shared Hunter's sentiments. Gaynor said, "Producer Irwin Allen had a great imagination. He ate, drank and lived show business. He also screamed a lot." [7]

The series rose with Irwin Allen, and would sink under his command, as well. Lew Hunter said, "Irwin never talked very much about his audience. I think that was because *he* was his audience. And I think that's who he was trying to please. And he did an inordinate job of that. He felt that everything he did was wonderful. There was no arguing about it; there was no other point of view. 'Isn't that wonderful, Irwin?' 'Yes, Irwin, it is.' 'Look at the toys and look at Vincent Price,' and stuff like that. He just had a wonderful ego that obviously mimicked Harry Cohn and those people. Irwin would sit in dailies and cheer, and almost have orgasms over some of the things that came on in the dailies. He just loved what he was doing. He really did, probably more than any other producer/director I'd ever seen, with how much he loved his own work." [8]

The only question in the Fall of 1967 was: Did *Voyage* have a full season left … or less? The Nielsen ratings for the first half-dozen episodes would answer that. Until then, ABC ordered 13 episodes of a new Irwin Allen series – *Land of the Giants* – with the understanding that it would be ready in time to serve as a midseason replacement for *Voyage*, if needed.

***

Meanwhile, during the Summer of 1967, as the early episodes of the fourth season were written and filmed, the ratings for the repeating Third Season episodes continued to drop.

The promotional people at 20th Century-Fox were aiming for new spins to rekindle audience interest. Stories about Richard Basehart and David Hedison had been used to hype the start of Seasons Two and Three; now the PR men and women looked to another cast member who had not yet been exploited. Terry Becker was featured in a "TV Key" syndicated story. Entertainment correspondent Harvey Pack said:

> When Terry was first cast, he sat down and wrote a long character analysis of the relatively minor part he had been handed and included many comments on the man's relationship with Basehart, who plays the leader of the expedition. [9]

Becker told Pack, "After a while the role just seemed to get more important. I would even work out things right on the set with Basehart [such as "Terror on Dinosaur Island"]. By proving to everybody that on a naval vessel as important as the 'Seaview,' the logical man with whom the admiral would exchange confidences would be the chief, I succeeded not only in improving my own spot but [made] it easier for the writers to give Basehart's character more substance." [10]

On the day "Fires of Death," the premiere episode of Season Four, first aired, Becker was featured in a syndicated newspaper story by Stan Maays. Becker said, "When I got the part of Chief Sharkey, producer Irwin Allen told me, 'Do what you can with it.' Other than wanting a Ward Bond-type, which he saw in me, he left it open for me to play it any way I felt." [11]

Becker told interviewer Mark Phillips, "Chief Sharkey had an interesting history and that's what I wanted to play. He had an ex-wife, whom he had left 15 years ago, but that storyline couldn't be explored because it didn't feed the nature of the show. *Voyage* was a SF adventure, so there were certain story lines expected of us every week. That meant battling the bad guys and the monsters. Our hopes of dealing with reality stuff ended up going nowhere. I realized that pushing for that kind of story realism ended up as counter-productive. Unless Sharkey's wife is aboard the Seaview and we're threatened by aliens, you're not going to see the chief dealing with his family. Instead, the show fully embraced its adventure concept. As a result, the chief's background related only to the ship and the mission of the week." [12]

Regardless, Becker never shortchanged the show or its audience. He told Jack. E. Anderson for a 1967 article in *The Miami Herald*, "It's a matter of commitment as an actor. I give the role the very best I have. A lot of guys in a series as far out and pure adventure as ours would tend to cop out. You know the type. They sit around talking about how their talent is wasted, the scripts are no good, or the director doesn't know what he's doing. That's not my style. I work hard at making Chief Sharkey believable, a guy the viewer can identify with." [13]

As for Basehart and Hedison, they would continue to do their best, promoting the series and remaining cooperative on the set, despite the diminishing caliber of the scripts and the dimming status of the series.

Al Gail said, "The two leads, fortunately – and unlike some of the other ones in our other series – got along famously. Dave Hedison and Richard Basehart never had a disturbing word between them. *Never*. 'Hey, you got more close-ups than me,' and, 'How come I didn't get this line and you got that?' – there was never that competition, because they were not competitors. David recognized the other one as a fine actor, as an older man, and he never felt competitive. And we made sure that they each had a good role in each episode. So, we never had any trouble on that set. There was more trouble on other sets." [14]

"The cast was great," said George Robotham, who appeared in numerous episodes as a guest player, stuntman, and double. "Richard Basehart was a marvelous guy. David Hedison, who I doubled for, and the other guys, were not only good actors but good people. Irwin Allen was quite a character, so it was never boring. Some episodes were terrific. Others really stretched credibility, but that was okay, it was supposed to be an adventure-fantasy. People wanted the monsters. The production values were usually top-notch and the concept was a good one." [15]

***

The center ring in the mid-to-late 1967 circus environment of 20th Century Fox continued to be the organized chaos of Irwin Allen and his production companies. *The Time Tunnel* had completed its one-season run, but *Land of the Giants* was now the third spoke in Allen's wheel (even though it wouldn't premiere on ABC until the fall of 1968). Irwin Allen Productions was so busy that its "emperor" decided there was a need for a daily newsletter to keep everyone up to speed on the activities of all three series and upcoming pilot films. He called it "I.A. PRODUCTION HOT SHEET." "I.A.," of course, stood for "Irwin Allen," and at the top of each newsletter was the proclamation that it, like the series it tracked, was "CREATED BY IRWIN ALLEN."

Frank La Tourette returned to Allen's camp after a year's leave, now serving as editor of the *Hot Sheet*. The newsletter from October 4, 1967 read:

1. <u>GENERAL</u>:
   (A) The Producer's Meeting will be held at 12:30pm in I.A.'s trailer on the stage.
   (B) All Associate Producers and Story Editors are asked to attend, by 4:00pm each day, any items, re: problems and operations, to be included in the daily "hot sheet."

2. <u>GIANTS</u>:
   (A) The story department read Shelly Stark's rewrite of "On A Clear Night You Can See Earth" with great anticipation. It was a disappointing experience. Dick McDonagh reports that it needs a rewrite from Page 1.
   (B) Charles Bennett is writing the teleplay of "Terror-Go-Round" and expects to complete it by the end of next week.
   (C) Dick McDonagh reports that Lew Hunter of ABC expressed great pleasure when he heard of the changes being incorporated in "The Small War," which Shirl Hendryx is currently rewriting. One suggestion was

passed along from Harve Bennett which Jerry Briskin and Dick McDonagh will discuss with I.A. at the earliest convenient moment.

(D) Bob and Esther Mitchell have delivered the first draft of "The Lost Ones." The story department is now reading it and will deliver a report on it Wednesday morning.

(E) Ellis St. Joseph has completed the first draft of "Underground." All hands are asked to read it as soon as it is available in Xerox, since it may be possible – with minor revisions – to print it and send it to the network this week.

(F) We are anticipating delivery of the first draft of "Ghost Town" from Gil Ralston by Friday, 10/6.

(G) [Director] Harry Harris reports that all is going well as he begins preparation for [filming] "The Weird World."

3. SPACE:

(A) The final status on "Castles in Space": PAGES SHOT: 57-1/8; MINUTES: 53.31.

(B) Peter Packer has delivered the first draft of "Target: Earth."

(C) Because of problems involved with "A Day at The Zoo," which have been solved, both Bill Faralla and Lew Warner have not had time to read "Two Weeks in Space," to determine whether there are any problems that might keep it from going next in the shooting order. They are also urged to read, as soon as possible, "Target: Earth" to determine whether any problems would prevent it from being the backup script to "Two Weeks in Space" in the event the latter might need additional work to make it acceptable for production.

(D) Peter Packer is now rewriting "Space Carnival" [later renamed "Carnival of Space" before being abandoned]; Bill Faralla is urged to impress upon Peter the need for quick delivery of this rewrite because – beyond it – there are, at the moment, no available scripts to move into the shooting order.

(E) Irving Moore starts directing "A Day at the Zoo" today. The usual full cooperation by all hands will be appreciated as an especially warm welcome to a new director on the series.

4. VOYAGE:
   (A) Jus Addiss yesterday completed the additional scenes for "Terror" and "Rescue" with sufficient minutes for both shows.
   (B) Sid Marshall reports that starting with the current show now shooting, there will be FIVE 5-day VOYAGE shows completed within the near future.
   (C) Bruce Fowler reports that Bob Sparr is well prepared as he starts directing "A Time to Die" today. According to Bruce, ABC's report on this script was most flattering. The network considers it one of "our most interesting efforts."
   (D) Another report from the Associate Producer predicts that "The Return of Blackbeard," which finished last night, will be an excellent show.
   (E) The story department is reading Arthur Weiss' first draft of "Savage Jungle." Its report is awaited eagerly.
   (F) Bill Welch will complete "Edge of Doom" today.
   (G) Al Gail is still scheduled to finish the first draft of "The Lobster Man" on Monday, October 6th.

5. CITY BENEATH THE SEA:
   (A) Serge Krizman is expected to make a second presentation of visual concepts for I.A. for his approval by Tuesday, October 10th.

6. THE MAN FROM THE 25TH CENTURY:
   (A) Because of bad weather, which held up the feature on which he is working in the east, Dale Hennesy (Art Director) will not be able to report in on this project until Monday, October 9th. However, he has the script and he is already at work on a visual concept.

7. PROMOTION AND PUBLICITY:
   Henry Goldfarb, VOYAGE stuntman, yesterday made his first test dive at Marineland's big tank preparatory to his attempt at setting an undersea endurance record. The date for the actual attempt has been set by Marineland for November 4, 5 and 6. [16]

It was just another business day in the Fantasy Worlds of Irwin Allen.

The first episode to go into production for *Voyage*'s Season Four was "Man of Many Faces." Indicative of the new mandate to alternate monsters with other science-fiction plotlines and gimmicks, there was not a stuntman in a rubber suit in sight … just a rubber-faced guy with the unbelievable ability to transform himself into a duplicate of whomever he wished. There was also something in the story about the moon being pulled into a collision course with Earth. And an assassination on live TV. *Voyage*'s fourth season was opening with a splash.

9.1

"Man of Many Faces" (Episode 85)

(Prod. No. 1301; first aired Sunday, October 29, 1967)
Written by William Welch
Directed by Harry Harris
Produced by Irwin Allen and Bruce Fowler, Jr.; Story Editor: Sidney Marshall
(with Jock Gaynor as Dr. Randolph Mason)

Richard Basehart as the duplicate Nelson.

From the *Voyage* show files (Irwin Allen Papers Collection):

A young scientist, working on a secret project to harness the tides, crosses the narrow line between genius and madness. When he uses his gift of disguise to embroil Admiral Nelson and Captain Crane in his plot to control the world, and almost destroying it by magnetically pulling the moon out of orbit, it takes all their strength of mind and determination to get the Seaview – and the Earth – on an even keel again. [1]

Assessment:

Mike Bailey said, "This was the big one *Voyage* fans had been waiting for – a return to previous quality. 'Man of Many Faces' is considered to be one of *Voyage*'s best latter-season episodes. It includes much that the series lacked in its last two seasons – location shooting, fun writing, and a creative plot, included. Not another monster-driven sub-bound episode." [2]

The elephant in the room is the idea that Dr. Randolph Mason – the man of many faces – can also be a man of many bodies. Crane and Morton are taller and slimmer than Nelson and Sharkey, besides having different complexions, hair, and eyes. And what about their mannerisms, their voices, their clothing? How does Mason do it, and do it so quickly? At one point, he apparently knocks out (or hypnotizes) Kowalski, then makes him up to look like Sharkey. But, again, they are different body types. Quite a parlor trick.

But if you can roll with this wild concept, and look the other way regarding the lapses in reason and logic, then there is much to appreciate in this episode, which, as Mr. Bailey noted, excels in many areas.

Script:

William Welch's writers contract: April 13, 1967.
Welch's story, plus 1st- and 2nd- draft teleplays approved by Irwin Allen on April 27.
Shooting Final teleplay: April 26.
2nd Rev. Shooting Final teleplay (green paper): June 1, 1967.

William Welch would now be writing every other episode of the series, literally – 13 out of 26. His springboard for this story read:

> When all the world, via satellite TV, sees ADMIRAL NELSON shoot and kill handsome DR. RANDOLPH MASON as he's holding a press conference, among the most interested onlookers is Nelson, himself, in his office with CAPTAIN CRANE. When they try to phone outside to report the real Admiral was nowhere near the TV studio, they find the wires have been cut and [they now] know they are dealing with an organized plot.
>
> What it is, Nelson has some idea: Mason was proposing a technique for supplying the world with limitless energy by harnessing the tides. Nelson, he told his audience, was his enemy in this humanitarian project, and at that moment,

the imposter Nelson shot him. What only he knows, Nelson tells Crane, is that Mason proposed to supply this power by throwing an electro-magnetic field around the moon, and to this end has hidden an electro-magnet of unimaginable size under the ocean. Mason could never see that increasing the power of the tides by harnessing the moon would only draw it close to Earth so that inevitably it must pass a point of no return and fall in on the Earth, destroying it. According to his calculations, says Nelson, they have not much more than a day to find and destroy the magnet.

When CHIEF SHARKEY then arrives to say the police are looking for Nelson, he is told about the imposter and dispatched to prepare Seaview for an immediate trip while Nelson hides and Crane goes to clear his name with the proper authorities. But Crane is followed and kidnapped, and later, when Chief gathers SPARKS, MORTON and KOWALSKI on board to clear the Admiral's name, they watch a newscast interview of Crane on which he's asked if Nelson was with him at the time of the murder. Turning to the audience, Crane says he was <u>not</u>.

The real Crane, meanwhile, manages to escape captivity in the back of a moving van and to make his way to Seaview.

With a police watch on at the loading dock, Nelson contrives to come aboard in a supply crate, and when he and Crane compare notes, they realize they have now both been impersonated on TV.

Seaview, under way, is chased by the Coast Guard, and Crane escapes by submerging, only later to pick up the sound of a pursuing sub, which he eludes masterfully. Meanwhile, he becomes aware when he finds the sub on a wrong course, that the imposter is aboard and, disguised as Morton, tampered with his orders for setting the course. This means that when he and Nelson look at anyone aboard, they won't know if it's the true imposter or not and, worse, they won't even be able to trust each other.[3]

After reading Welch's first-draft teleplay, Irwin Allen wrote a single page of notes, saying, in part:

> Page 13, Scene 29: Chief – his speech to the officers is silly. He would normally ask them what he could do for them? This sequence brings up some questions.
> (1) Why would just 2 police men come (not 10 minutes after the broadcast) to the Nelson Institute expecting to apprehend Admiral Nelson?
> (2) Where did the Television broadcast originate from?
> (3) Was it close enough to Santa Barbara that the police would expect Nelson to have succeeded in getting there before them?...
>
> Pages 18 & 19: This sequence makes Crane look silly. Why would he come to the T.V. station just to announce that Nelson was not with him at the time of the murder?... [4]

Welch hurriedly made minor changes, including emphasizing that Crane was going to the TV station to testify on Nelson's behalf, in hopes of clearing the Admiral. Welch then raced to his next assignment.

Les Warner held his comments until he saw the third-draft script (Sidney Marshall's polish – the April 26 Shooting Final teleplay), then sent Irwin Allen five pages of detailed notes, with cc to all department heads, including Sid Marshall and Al Gail.

> It is difficult to believe that a secretly man-made "electro-magnet" (or any other kind of contrivance) could be strong enough to pull the moon out of its orbit. However, I would believe that this magnet, in tampering with the moon's creation of our tides, could somehow trigger a "cosmic phenomenon" that could do this....
>
> Sc. 173: Nelson's first speech:
> 1. Mason must have used a "latex mask" of his own features to disguise his assistant as himself. So what happened when the police (or morgue) discovered this deception after removing the body?
> 2. Is Nelson making a wild guess or stating a fact that an assistant was used? If it is a fact, then he must have been in communication with the authorities during the preceding DISSOLVE. And, if so, then why wouldn't Crane have known this also?

> 3. Couldn't all this be resolved by having Nelson and Crane discuss a message just received from the authorities in which we learn that Mason's partners (Sc. 25) were apprehended when trying to spirit away the assistant's body after Nelson had alerted the authorities to a deception?...

Wouldn't Mason in the Flying Sub now see the same gigantic moon we have all seen and realize that Nelson's contention was correct; that it is indeed about to destroy the Earth? Or is he slightly insane by this time (his speech in Sc. 158) and doesn't care? Something needs clarifying here.
5

The real problem, as always, was how to make a halfway decent one-hour sci-fi television drama on a budget not much more than what was needed for a half-hour sitcom. Warner addressed these concerns as he counted the various sets, locations, props, and effects.

> The Seaview interior sets are no problem, however, we will need new interior sets:
> 1. The T.V. Studio and Sound Lock
> 2. Nelson's Institute Office
> 3. Rear of Panel Truck
> 4. Crane's Car mock-up.
>
> NOTE: The interior panel truck could ordinarily be a real truck; however, action calls for reverse business inside at the rear doors – which might necessitate building this set.
>
> The Nelson Institute Gates and Ad Building are no problem other than night work as they are existing Studio areas.
>
> The Seaview and Institute Dock is a cost item. Although we are now considering amortizing these costs, I think we will have to consider additional costs for each segment used for possible re-spotting the boat sections and re-furbishing and dressing the Dock. For this episode, these few scenes are also night work.

For the EXT. MOUNTAIN ROADS...This would be one day's work (day-for-night) on local mountain roads.... The only cast involved are Crane and four stunt driver and ride actors.... Due to the action involved in this episode, day for night shooting, and the number of sets to be shot in, I feel that this location could never be plotted within the allotted 6-day schedule. Therefore, it is my belief that this should be planned as a pre-production unit and shot immediately prior to start of principal....

NOTE: The shots involving the Flying Sub and Seaview are specifically requested as new shots; either because we do not have NITE STOCK, or because we need new different angles to augment the Old Stock....

Although I have waved flags at the above items, I realize we are starting this new season with a new attitude, re: costs and scope. With this in mind, but with no average or norm to compare to, I can only hazard a guess that this could now very well be a shootable script – with very little retrenchment, if any. [6]

Production:
(Filmed June 6 – 14, 1967; 7 days)

Harry Harris directed his twelfth episode for *Voyage*. Al Gail said, "In those days, with all the camera tricks and all the opticals and everything that went with it, it was too much of a challenge to the average director. They would say, 'Look, I can get the same money just doing a bedroom parlor and bath [show], I don't need this kind of headache.' So, we would usually stay with a core group [of directors] that we'd use over and over again in all our projects. Now, Harry Harris did *Lost in Space*, *The Time Tunnel* – he did all the shows, because we knew he was dependable." [7]

The budget was set at $167,441.

Jock Gaynor, 33, played Dr. Randolph Mason. As noted earlier, Gaynor was best known for his regular role on the 1960 series *The Outlaws*, as Deputy Marshall Heck Martin. This was his second *Voyage*.

Howard Culver played the moderator of the show on which it appears that Admiral Nelson assassinates Dr. Mason. He was 49, back in the day when 49 looked 59. Producer-director-star Jack Webb loved Culver, and cast him in 18 episodes of *Dragnet*, five for *Adam-12*, three for *Project: U.F.O.*, as well as one time each in a couple other Webb-produced series. Irwin Allen liked Culver too, and brought him out for one episode each of *The Time Tunnel*, *Land of the Giants*, and *Code Red*, plus small roles in the films *The Swarm* and *The Night the Bridge Fell Down*. Away from Webb and Allen, Culver played hotel clerk Howie Uzzell in 48 episodes of *Gunsmoke*. And now you know why he looks familiar.

Production began Tuesday, June 6, 1967, for the first of seven days on Stage 10. It was supposed to be an easy six-day shoot, but director Harris fell behind by a full day, finishing on Wednesday, June 14, at 6:10 p.m.

Besides the standing Seaview sets and the Flying Sub, a handful of temporary sets were arranged for on Stage 10, including "Int. TV Studio" and "Int. Truck."

The exterior of the Fox Administration Building was used by a second-unit team to serve as "Ext. Nelson Institute." This was shot "night for night," finishing at 11:15 p.m. on Friday, the fourth day of the production. A second unit team also filmed sequences on Las Vergennes Road, to pass for "Ext. Mountain Road." They shot the interior of Crane's car at that location.[8]

Release / Reaction:
(ABC premiere airing: 10/29/67; network repeat broadcast: 6/2/68)

VOYAGE TO THE BOTTOM OF THE SEA - Year 4

MAN OF MANY FACES . . . . An imposter disguises himself as Admiral Nelson (Richard Basehart) to assassinate Dr. Randolph Mason (Jock Gaynor) in this exciting scene from the "Man of Many Faces" episode of 20th Century-Fox Television's VOYAGE TO THE BOTTOM OF THE SEA series, seen this (day) at (time) on (channel). #1301/39

This was the week that the rock musical *Hair* premiered in New York City. Also, thousands of people protesting the Vietnam War stormed the Pentagon building. Walt Disney's *The Jungle Book* was doing the most business in the movie houses. The top two best-selling record albums were the Beatles' *Sgt. Pepper's Lonely Hearts Club Band* and *Diana Ross & the Supremes Greatest Hits*. "To Sir, With Love," by Lulu, from the Sidney Poitier movie of the same name, was the song getting the most radio play. On *The New York Times* Best Seller List were *Rosemary's Baby*, *Topaz*, and *The Gabriel Hounds*.

Syndicated "TV Scout," in Texas's *The San Antonio Express and News*, among other newspapers, said:

> *Voyage to the Bottom of the Sea* begins with Richard Basehart committing a cold-blooded murder. Of course, regulars know he wouldn't do such a thing, but before his

impersonator is found, Basehart and David Hedison get to have some good fights and chases. [9]

Nielsen ratings report from October 29, 1967 (full report not available): [10]

	Peak Share:
ABC: *Voyage to the Bottom of the Sea*	28%
CBS: *Lassie / Gentle Ben*	32% / 37%
NBC: *Walt Disney's Wonderful World of Color*	**37%**

9.2

"Time Lock" (Episode 86)

(Prod. No. 1302; first aired Sunday, November 12, 1967)
Written by William Welch
Directed by Jerry Hopper
Produced by Irwin Allen and Bruce Fowler, Jr.; Story Editor: Sidney Marshall
Guest Star John Crawford

TIME LOCK ... (L-R) Alpha (John Crawford) brings Adm. Nelson (Richard Basehart) into the future to add him to his zombified collection of famous military figures in the "Time Lock" episode of 20th Century-Fox Television's VOYAGE TO THE BOTTOM OF THE SEA series, seen this (day) at (time) on (channel). #1302/101

From the *Voyage* show files (used for ABC press release):

> After ADMIRAL NELSON leaves the Seaview lab, a humming sound heralds the appearance of a transparent cylindrical tube. Two metallic clad BEINGS step out and, following Nelson into the Control Room, immobilize the crew while, with an unseen force, propelling Nelson into the tube, a Time Lock, and inform him he's going on a journey in time.

While the crew, recovered, searches the ship, Nelson steps out of a similar tube into a windowless room whose walls are lined with zombie-like military officers. He is greeted by the voice of ALPHA inviting him to enter a passageway and, when he refuses, the officers move in menacingly.

Meanwhile, the sub crew discovers the force field which the Beings have set up outside the lab but are powerless to break through it.

Nelson, ushered into Alpha's office, finds an ordinary looking man wearing dark glasses who, disappointed that Nelson isn't in full dress uniform, informs him he was brought into the future to become an addition to Alpha's collection of officers…. [1]

Assessment:

Mike Bailey and Mark Phillips were bothered by the claustrophobic feel of this episode and found little reason to recommend it. We found several small things to like, and they combine to raise "Time Lock" to above par.

We like how, when the Alpha's silver henchmen board the Seaview in search of Admiral Nelson, the rest of the crew in the Control Room are frozen … except for their eyes, and their minds, which remain active. It gives the scene an eerie feel. We recall a *Star Trek* where the gimmick was used … and a *Wild, Wild West* … and a *Get Smart*.

The Circuitry Room is once again sabotaged (by those silver guys), and the Seaview once again hits bottom, but at least Allen paid to have new footage filmed of this, and it is impressive.

The ideas behind "The Hobby Act" and the five-hour work week are certainly appealing. Sign us up.

The abducted military men from Earth's past are of interest too – and they see and hear all, but have otherwise been turned into numbed zombie goons on display. And that brings us to their collector. Alpha is an interesting character – completely lacking in empathy, remaining focused on his toys. So reprehensible is he that his just end brings with it a degree of satisfaction. Why just shoot him with a gun when Crane can do it with a grenade launcher?!

It's suggested that Alpha's lair may be deep underground. Alpha claims to be typical of his own time period, but Nelson doubts this. "I do believe in the future," he tells Sharkey.

Well, that's as close to a theme as we are about to find. But for an Irwin Allen production, it's a step in the right direction.

Script:
William Welch's writers contract: April 28, 1967.
Welch's story, and 1ˢᵗ- and 2ⁿᵈ- draft teleplays approved by Irwin Allen on May 12.
Shooting Final teleplay: May 16.
2ⁿᵈ Rev. Shooting Final (pink paper): June 13.
Page revisions (green paper): June 14.
Page revisions (yellow paper): June 15.

Demonstrating how a story can change from inception to final screen treatment, **William Welch**'s 13-page story treatment began:

> SEAVIEW is at sea, running submerged on a routine mission, a day's journey out of Santa Barbara. In the Control Room, the ship's clock – a type which resembles an automobile odometer – is at 1048 with the last digit slowly changing from 8 to 9. Suddenly, the entire ship is jolted as though struck by some invisible force. At the same instant, the numbers on the ship's clock begin to accelerate until they are moving forward at bewildering speed. At first, naturally, they believe the clock is malfunctioning. But the other discrepancies begin to

appear on various instrument panels. The depth indicator rises rapidly from four hundred feet below the surface to zero. The speed indicator begins to slow to a stop. The navigational guides similarly spin out of control and all efforts to stabilize the various instruments prove futile.

Crane, at a loss to understand what is going wrong, calls Nelson in his cabin and asks him to come down to inspect the situation. At this point, the engines quit cold and they are at dead stop on the surface. As the crewmen gaze around in helpless wonder, they are startled by the sound of heavy footsteps on the deck above their heads. Then they hear the clang of the main hatch as it is flung open! Before anyone can make a move, a party of men comes swarming down the hatch ladder to the deck. They are all dressed in strange, futuristic clothing, their heavy-soled, silver jack-boots giving them an unmistakable military appearance. And this is reinforced by the fact that every man is armed with a weird and exotic weapon. The weapons are trained on the Control Room crew and they are obviously prisoners! [2]

Regarding the third draft of the script, from May 16, Irwin Allen wrote:

Alpha should not ask the two beings what they propose to do now as he is the one to give orders. He should state a positive reason for having them remain on board so that his decision doesn't sound like a weak excuse for keeping the succeeding Seaview scenes in the script. There are a number of reasons he could use such as the possibility of obtaining Crane or some unusual equipment for his museum collection. There is, of course: his desires to have a full-dress uniform of Nelson's which he asks for much later. In any event, the reason for sabotaging the Seaview should be a good one. [3]

Production Coordinator Les Warner wrote to the staff:

MILITARY CREATURES: Concept is not now clear in the script: In Scene 19 they are described as "out-sized toy soldiers." Aren't these "creatures" real humans that Alpha "shanghaied" out of the past in their original uniforms (the same as the 18th Century British General and "zombie processed"), the same as he hopes to do with Nelson? If so, wouldn't they have authentic period uniforms -- rather than look like toy soldiers? And would they have toy soldier makeup? ...

SCENE 200: If the Military Creatures and the 18th Century British General are really shanghaied humans, who were "zombie processed," is it good story to believe that Nelson would destroy them along with Alpha when he blows up the Future Complex? Nelson's speech: Isn't it confusing that he says: "Alpha was the only human in the entire operation..." when he (and we) know that Alpha's zombie-processed soldiers were also human? [4]

Production:

(Filmed June 15 – 23, 1967; 7 days)
(Added scene filmed August 2, 1967)

This was director **Jerry Hopper**'s tenth of 15 episodes.

William Self approved a budget of $168,610 (higher than the new season's increased per-episode target of $167,441).

John Crawford was paid $1,500 for four days in front of the camera. Crawford was 46 when cast as Alpha, and had already had an amazing career in movies and television, where he would amass over 200 appearances, including very nearly every iconic TV series made during the 1950s, '60s and '70s, and beyond. Among them: *The Twilight Zone*; *Combat!*; *The Fugitive*; *Batman*; *Star Trek*; *Hogan's Heroes*; *Mission: Impossible*; *The Wild, Wild West*; and 14 appearances on *Gunsmoke*. He had worked for Irwin Allen as a supporting guest player in four episodes of *The Time Tunnel* during the 1966-67 TV season. Then, for the 1967-68 season, Allen gave Crawford lead guest roles in an episode of *Lost in Space*, as well as this *Voyage*. Interviewed by

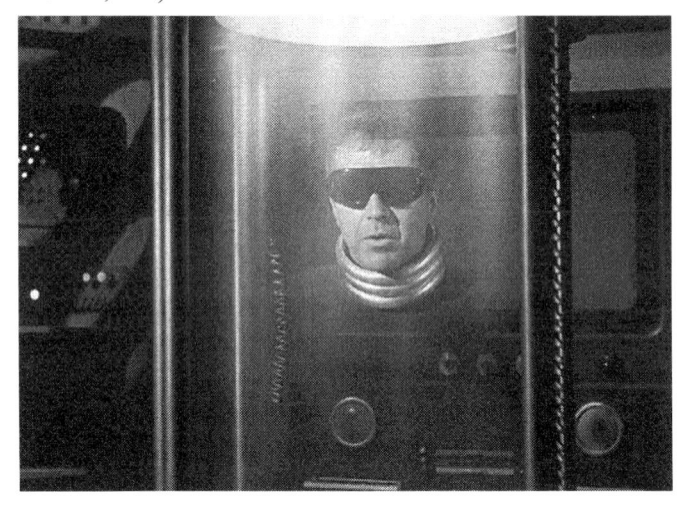

Joel Eisner for *Starlog* magazine, Crawford said, "Irwin Allen was very fussy and had to look at everything and everyone, every detail, costume, wigs, beards, etc."

But Casting Director Larry Stewart at 20th Century-Fox was in a rush and, knowing Crawford was ideal for a supporting role in *The Time Tunnel* episode "The Revenge of Robin Hood," brought the actor in without Allen's approval. Crawford recalled that he was in the middle of filming *The Time Tunnel* when he first met the notorious Irwin Allen. He said, "The director [William Hale] was about two days behind schedule, and we were in the middle of the fourth of what was usually a five-to-six-day shoot. He was really slower than molasses. The usual thing about this is that, with Irwin Allen, you got about three frames behind, he would be down there on the set wanting to know what the hell's going on. For some reason, he let Hale get himself into this big mess. Unbeknownst to me, Irwin Allen, having slipped in through a back door, was standing in the crowd behind the camera. Now, we were in the middle of this take and I was acting up a storm. I was impressed with what I was doing, the way everything was rolling out and how nicely the [English] accent was coming along, so, I suppose, for a little dramatic effect, I thought I could afford a long pause. Well, right in the middle of that pause came a shout, 'All right, cut!' I immediately said, 'No. I'm still acting!' I then went on with the speech and nobody said anything. When I finished, the director said 'cut.' I did not realize at the time that the man who interrupted my scene was Irwin Allen. He just came onto the set and took the job away from the director, just like that. Well, that's how Irwin and I met. The fact that he hadn't rattled me impressed him." [5]

Lennie Hayton provided new music for this, his eighth and final score for *Voyage*.

Production of "Time Lock" began on Thursday, June 15, 1967, for the first of two days on Stage 10 in the Control Room and Missile Room.

Days 3, 4, 5, and part of 6, were spent on Stage B, for sets identified as "Int. Play Room," "Int. Alpha Office," "Int. Future Lab," "Int. Future Corridor," and "Int. Future Cell." At midday, on the that sixth day of filming, they moved back to Stage 10 where a new set had been prepared – "Int. Ship's Lab." Work continued on this set into the seventh day of filming, then, also on Stage 10, "Int. Ventilating Duct." [6]

On Wednesday, August 2, an added scene was filmed in the ship's corridor by Jerry Hopper.

John Crawford said, "During *Voyage*, Richard Basehart had a drinking problem, and he wasn't really with us. I thought he was sort of unfriendly. Years later, I worked with him on *Judgment: The Court Martial of Lt. William Calley*, and we got to be very friendly. This was, of course, after he had given up the booze. He later told me that he was impressed with my work, and the reason why he hadn't been more friendly to me when I appeared on his show. He said, 'Well, I was usually bombed through that whole damned thing.'" [7]

ABC's Lew Hunter said, "We sort of knew about Richard Basehart's three martini lunches, but we didn't really want to know that. I'm sure my reaction was, 'Well, he really needed the drink to go through that dreck that was put on his desk each week.'" [8]

David Hedison said, "He had a tendency to drink too much then, and I think that got in his way. But then, towards the end, he stopped and he got into Zen, and he didn't drink anymore. But those early years of *Voyage* were very, very difficult for him. So, he was in pain, and I'm sure that he had to take *Voyage*;

they were paying him well, and he had lots of alimony with Valentina Cortese, and all of that... and I think that's why he took the job." [9]

Voyage writer Robert Vincent Wright said, "It was a shame that the marvelous acting talents of Richard Basehart were limited to his *Voyage* role. He could have done some great things in film, but his own problems held him back. He was a nice fellow, a little pompous, but really, the whole cast was nice." [10]

Writer Robert Hamner felt differently. He said, "David Hedison was a very nice man, but I didn't care much for Basehart. He was pompous and a bully. He would hide behind Irwin when there was a problem and complain. Irwin would go crazy and yell and scream at whomever Basehart was complaining about. I always felt that was wrong." [11]

Post-Production:

John Crawford said, "['Time Lock' is] one of the few jobs in my entire career that I am really ashamed of, because I had to redub that entire role."

Crawford had to come to the dubbing stage and redo all his lines, a difficult process that often requires multiple takes for each line of dialogue to get the new voice track to match the edited film. Crawford explained, "I had figured if Alpha were a futuristic man who was really all that powerful, he wouldn't have to go around acting or talking tough in a big gruff voice. I thought it would really be even more insidious and frightening if he almost had a kind of genteel voice, and spoke like some of the English performers you've seen. It would have made him unusual, but all the time he was doing these terrible things and capable of doing even worse. I thought it was a hell of an idea and that was my selection.

"When we were shooting the scene, Irwin came down on to the set and he just loved it. Everything was going great."

That is, until somebody put a bug into Allen's ear. Crawford continued: "Well, somebody saw the film – I don't know who it was – and said to Irwin, 'You know, he is speaking so softly and gentle that you have taken away all his power to threaten. He is your antagonist and you have now weakened him with these simpy tones.' ... So, they made me redub it. While we were dubbing it, the soundmen were saying, 'Why in the hell are we dubbing this? This is great stuff.' If it had been done today, or maybe even then but with a different producer and point-of-view, they would have left it alone."

In Crawford's opinion, the looped-in lines ruined his performance. He said, "When you're dubbing a person, even if it's yourself, and they are speaking and elongating the vowels, and you try and play him with a heavy voice, it becomes kind of mechanical because you have to keep it [in] synch with the mouth. Well, it did not quite succeed. They weren't always in synch so therefore when I saw that damned thing on television, I could have died. It was one job I really, truly hated doing, and I hated to watch it because it was almost like a robot's voice. In fact, I wish it had come out like a robot's voice rather than a guy trying to sound tough."

Even so, Crawford continued to work for Irwin Allen, including small roles in *The Poseidon Adventure* and *The Towering Inferno*, followed by a two-part episode for the 1976 series, *Swiss Family Robinson*. He said, "I happen to have liked Irwin Allen. Many people think he was rude, noisy, loud and all this and that. I really enjoyed him, admired him, and while I didn't always agree with his taste, I have to say personally I'd always go along with him. He was a very funny man who spoke in a kind of shorthand. He knew what he wanted and I think many people thought that was rude." [12]

Release / Reaction:
(ABC premiere airdate: 11/12/67; network repeat broadcast: 6/16/68)

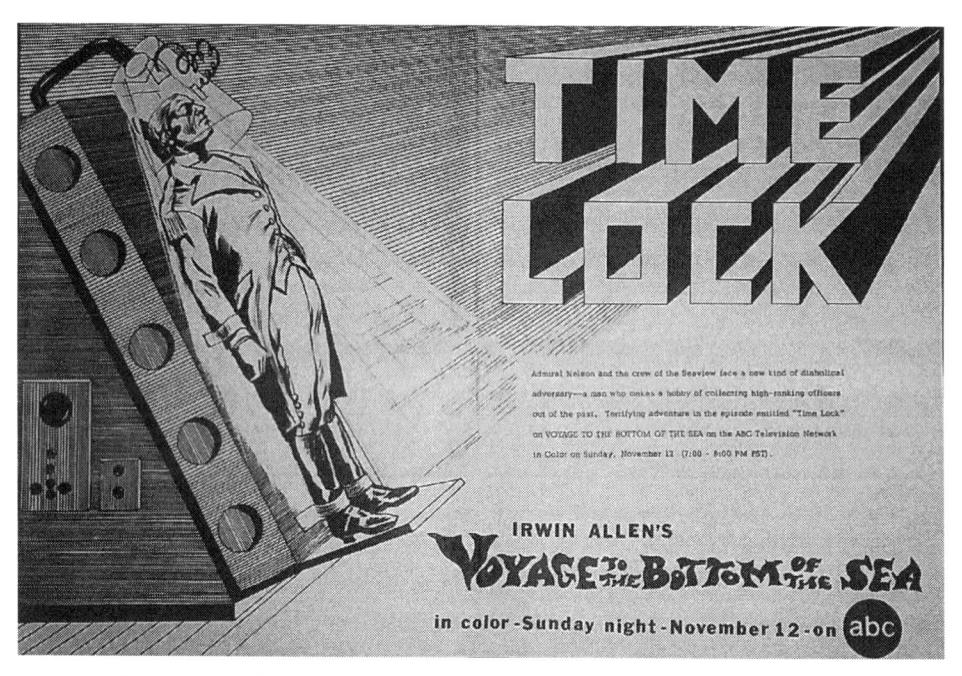

Promotional copy: "Admiral Nelson and the crew of the Seaview face a new kind of diabolical adversary – a man who makes a hobby of collecting high-ranking officers out of the past. Terrifying adventure in the episode entitled 'Time Lock'...."

The week that "Time Lock" first aired on ABC, Surveyor 6 became the first spacecraft to lift off from the surface of the moon. Disney's animated *The*

Jungle Book was top at the movie houses. "To Sir, With Love" was still the most popular song in radioland. The four top-selling albums were *Diana Ross & The Supremes Greatest Hits*, the Beatles' *Sgt. Pepper's Lonely Hearts Club Band*, and two by the Doors, their debut disk and its follow-up, *Strange Days*.

"TV Scout" said:

> *Voyage to the Bottom of the Sea* crosses science-fiction swords with *The Time Tunnel* and *Star Trek*. Two metallic creatures come board the Seaview and kidnap Richard Basehart. He's not taken far away in space, but in time by a man whose hobby is collecting "toy soldiers." The soldiers are real, but turned into robots by a process that removes all their thinking processes. Basehart is the next piece for the collection, as soon as they can get a dress uniform for him from the Seaview. Nothing but the best for our hobbyist. [13]

A.C. Nielsen ratings report from November 12, 1967: [14]

	Peak Share:
ABC: *Voyage to the Bottom of the Sea*	29%
CBS: *Lassie* / *Gentle Ben*	**38% / 33%**
NBC: *Walt Disney's Wonderful World of Color*	33%

9.3

"The Deadly Dolls" (Episode 87)

(Prod. No. 1303; first aired Sunday, October 1, 1967)
Written by Charles Bennett
Directed by Harry Harris
Produced by Irwin Allen and Bruce Fowler, Jr.; Story Editor: Sidney Marshall
Guest Star Vincent Price

Well, this isn't creepy at all ...

From the *Voyage* show files (Irwin Allen Papers Collection):

> An evening of entertainment on board the Seaview turns into a night of terror, as the puppeteer's dolls change into full size replicas of the Seaview's officers and men. When Admiral Nelson and Captain Crane tackle the overwhelming task of a preventing a power from another planet using the Seaview to further its evil designs on the world, they find it takes a journey through an inferno to rid the mighty sub of the horror aboard her. [1]

Assessment:

When American youngsters heard the contemporaneous James & Bobby Purify song "I'm Your Puppet" on the radio, they couldn't have foreseen *this*. But for *Voyage* fans, "The Deadly Dolls" is a delight. It could have been much better, but why nitpick?

Mark Phillips said, "The Nelson puppet is one of the greatest guest characters ever seen in a fantasy show. He pops in and out of view and tries to drive Admiral Nelson nuts with one-liners. The doll has no sense of social etiquette or moral responsibility. He's an 'in-your-face' puppet with attitude, a Muppet gone amok. This episode also benefits from a bizarre sense of humor, the great Vincent Price, a nice working relationship between Nelson and Crane as they team up to battle the nasty dolls, and a rousing special-effects climax. A genuine classic." [2]

"Dolls" is also loaded with violence, not that we're complaining. Punches fly in a couple of prolonged physical confrontations – Crane against several life-size dolls (appearing to be his men), and even Crane against Crane. Crane is beaten to the deck by the fists of a mob who resemble his crew; and he utilizes a flamethrower to blast away two of his opponents – Kowalski and his own replica – reducing them to a blackened stain on the deck. You wouldn't think ABC Broadcast Standards and Practices would let the tikes see this during the family hour in 1967. But here it is, with more ferocity than we recall seeing on the series before. Perhaps worries about violence were outweighed by worries about the plummeting ratings. Regardless, it made for a hot time in the old town tonight.

The direction is top-notch for episodic TV of this era, and Vincent Price is ... well, Vincent Price. And there is a message ... of a completely 1967 sort. As the bumper sticker says, "Be Yourself – Nobody Else Can!"

With all the fun flying our way, the ending seems abrupt. We never see the demise of Professor Multiple. He's there one minute, opposing Crane, then we cut away to Admiral Nelson in the FS1, then return and the not-so-good Professor is nowhere to be seen – just a pile of lifeless puppets (we must assume he's one of them). It seems a careless way to discard a top guest star. The Nelson Puppet gets the last line – "So sad; so sad." (Did we say this episode was wonderfully creepy?)

Script:

Charles Bennett's writers contract: March 16, 1967.
Bennett's story treatment: March 28.
Bennett's 1st-draft teleplay: April 14.
Bennett's 2nd-draft teleplay: April 28.
3rd Rev. Shooting Final teleplay (green paper): June 14.
Page revisions (yellow paper): June 21.
Page revisions (gold paper): July 31.

Charles Bennett was an old-school writer, and had spent his formative writing years collaborating on screenplays for motion pictures, especially those of director Alfred Hitchcock. That meant his story treatments were longer than the average television writer's. During the 1960s, a typical story treatment for an hour TV series would average 12 pages; a more detailed proposal might run as long as 20 pages. Bennett's treatment for "The Deadly Dolls" was 40 pages! The logline – the one-sentence overview – was instead a long paragraph of its own:

> The puppets of a master ventriloquist – a Mr. Multiple – come to life aboard the SEAVIEW. Not only do they come to

life, but they assume human size and human identities; the identities of the Seaview crew and officers. Under the control of Mr. Multiple, who we later learn is himself a man-sized puppet, the Deadly Dolls not only seize control of the Seaview, but are going to employ her scientific devices to condition the world to receive a new life form from Outer Space; Robotic-computer beings will inhabit our planet. Not until Crane and Nelson can fight off the influence of Mr. Multiple and his Deadly Dolls and destroy the headquarters of the master-minding computer does the threat to them and Earth come to an end. [3]

After reading Bennett's first-draft teleplay, Associate Producer Bruce Fowler sent a two-page memo to Irwin Allen, with the expected cc to "Messrs. Sidney Marshall and Al Gail." He said, in part:

> This is a very interesting and entertaining script. I am sure it will make an excellent segment for "VOYAGE." It is well plotted and well executed, with the story moving along throughout.
>
> The characters are well drawn, except for Dr. Multiple. I find that this character changes several times throughout the script. That is, first, he is a man. Second, he is a puppet. Third, he is a puppet, but speaks like a man and, fourth, he is a puppet and speaks like a puppet. I fully realize that we do not want a one-note character, but couldn't Charles [Bennett], perhaps, narrow this range on Dr. Multiple?
>
> On the subject of these puppets – do we need or want any visible differences, for identification, between the real people and the puppet people? Will we have a change in speech pattern for the puppet people? These are questions you will want to resolve. We must decide on a concept of these puppets from a size standpoint. In the beginning of the script – if I read it correctly – the puppets are doll sized. They continue this size when we see their features start to change. Then, in an off screen shot in Sc. 40, Page 14, they become full sized. They are reduced to doll size, once more, when they "die" or are burned. If this is correct, we only have to decide how big is "doll size" for us.

There will be a fair-sized problem for the director on this show. He will have to prepare his shots very carefully for the use of doubles. In the fight scenes, pre-staging should be done with the fight co-coordinator and the director, in order to utilize shooting time fully. The fight at the end of the script, between the real Crane and the Puppet People, reads as too brutal for acceptance by ABC, I think.

To me, the scenes in the Circuitry Room, starting with Sc. 176, on Page 56, where Kowalski (the Puppet Man) is burned, is an exciting and different sequence. However, again I wish to bring up the point of ABC censorship. I hope that we can shoot this just the way it is, but we should be prepared to change it, if necessary. [4]

Production:
(Filmed June 26 through July 5; 7 days)
(Added scene filmed August 1, 1967)

Harry Harris was back in the director's chair for his ninth *Voyage*.

Vincent Price was paid $2,500 for playing Professor Multiple. He was 56, and had worked for Irwin Allen on the big screen with *Dangerous Mission*, *The Story of Mankind*, and *The Big Circus*. The movies that clicked best for Price were horror and science fiction, such as 1953's *House of Wax*, 1958's *The Fly* (co-starring David Hedison), 1959's *House on Haunted Hill*, and 1964's *The Last Man on Earth*. His 1960-1965 participation in several Roger Corman low-budget films "inspired" by the works of Edgar Allan Poe cemented his acting persona as a charmingly evil soul who reveled in sarcastic deviltry.

Price had made several special appearances on TV throughout the 1950s and '60s, including *Alfred Hitchcock Presents*, *The Man from U.N.C.L.E.*, and the villainous Egghead in seven episodes of *Batman*. Right before accepting the role in "The Deadly Dolls," Price starred in a film called *House of 1,000 Dolls*, playing a magician who hypnotizes and kidnaps young girls to be sold to white slave traders.

Paul Trinka was doing well by not being under contract, and took home $1,350 for playing Patterson (for up to six days work).

Arch Whiting, a familiar *Voyage* face, was not under contract but was signed on an as-needed basis. This netted him $1,200 for up to six days, appearing as Sparks.

Harry Geller provided the music. He had written the score for 30 episodes of *The New Phil Silvers Show* (1963-64); 32 episodes of *The Patty Duke Show* (1965-66); 21 episodes of *That Girl* (1966-67); seven episodes of *Cimarron Strip* (1967-68); five for *The Wild, Wild West* (1966-68); and would do eight for *Judd for the Defense* (1968-69); 22 for *The Flying Nun* (1968-69); five for *Daniel Boone* (1968-70); eight for *Gunsmoke* (1965-71); ten for *Arnie* (1970-72); and 11 for *Hawaii Five-O* (1969-1975)! This was Geller's first of four scores for *Voyage*, with four to follow for *Land of the Giants* (1968-69).

Production began on Monday, June 26, 1967 for the first of seven days on Stage 10. It was a bottle show, with only Seaview sets and the Flying Sub needed.

David Hedison said, "I never had any scenes with Vincent Price when we filmed *The Fly* in April of 1958. I talked to him a few times off set and we were at the wrap party together. I only knew him slightly then, as another Fox contract player, having seen him around the lot and in the commissary. Nine years later, he came to Stage 10 as the villain in our 2nd episode [of] the 4th season. The plot was for him and his puppets to take over the *Seaview*. It was a very fun week; we were laughing and joking throughout the filming. I even goosed him once.

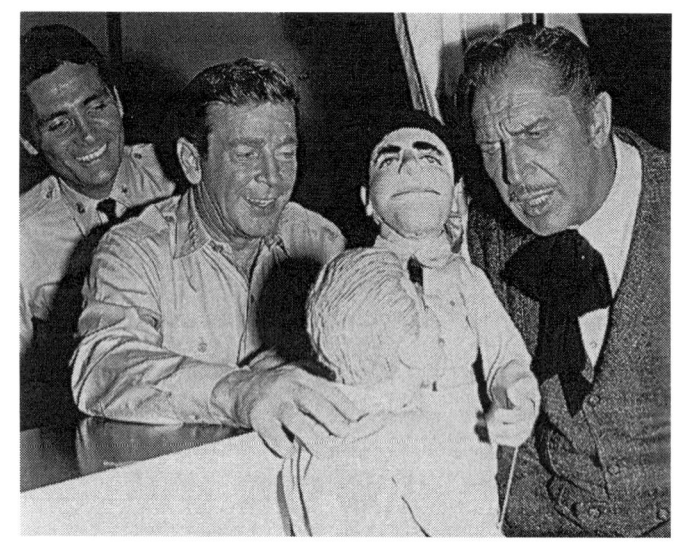

"Vincent pulled me aside and remarked how much I had changed – that I had been so earnest, so serious about my acting on *The Fly*, and now I was so much more relaxed and having such fun with this material. He liked the change." [5]

A partial eighth day of filming was needed when an additional scene was written after the producers watched the rough edit. This was scheduled for August 1, in the afternoon, also on Stage 10, for "Int. Storage Room" and a section of corridor. [6]

Del Monroe told interviewer Mark Phillips, "One of my favorite episodes was 'The Deadly Dolls,' with Vincent Price. What a wonderful actor! He had a résumé as long as my arm, but he was such a humble, down-to-Earth fellow. 'Deadly Dolls' was done in our fourth year and, by that time, our plots were becoming very similar. 'Deadly Dolls' was different. It was a unique idea, and it got us out of the realm of monsters. I'm not belittling *Voyage*, but 'Deadly Dolls' had some class, and it put us into an interesting fantasy world where living puppets that looked like the crew [tried to take over] the submarine." [7]

556

Hedison said, "At the end of the week, Vincent invited me and Richard over to his house for dinner. Richard took his wife, Diana, and I brought my girlfriend. It was a dinner party. Anne Baxter and several other old Fox stars were also there, making it a very lovely evening. To be able to sample Vincent's cuisine was a treat. He was a gourmet chef and the dinner was exquisite. There was also his fabulous art collection to peruse." [8]

Charles Bennett said, "'Deadly Dolls' was good mainly due to my old friend, Vincent Price. He's a wonderful person, but, for him, *Voyage* was simply a quick way to pick up some money for four days' work. *Voyage* did get worse and worse. The stories became fairy tales and pure fantasy. That's all right, there's an audience for that, but I preferred to write more serious stuff." [9]

Release / Reaction:
(ABC premiere airdate: 10/1/67; network repeat broadcast: 4/14/68)

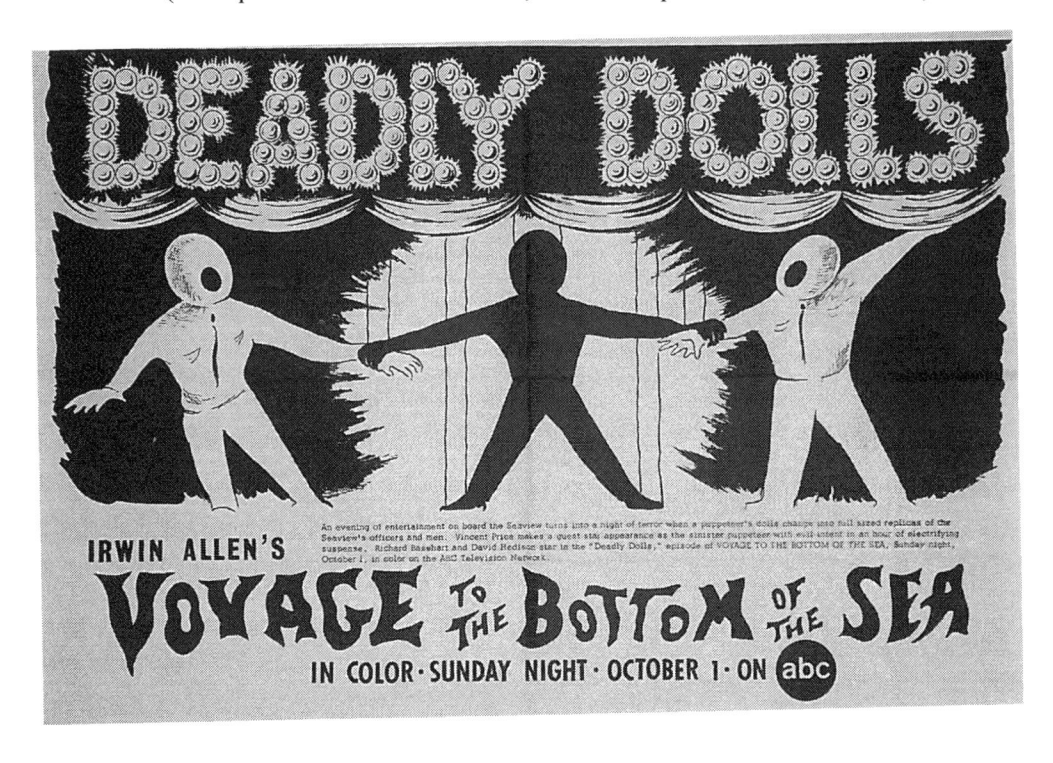

Top song in America this week: "The Letter" by the Box Tops. Lead singer Alex Chilton didn't sound it, but he was only 16. *Bonnie and Clyde* was top movie; its star Warren Beatty was also the film's producer. Of course, the No. 1 album this week, and for 15 other weeks during its initial chart run in 1967, was *Sgt. Pepper*. Montgomery Ward department stores had it on sale for $3.99. Sally

Field, of *The Flying Nun*, had the cover of *TV Guide*. That in itself proved that *Voyage* was not the silliest series on TV.

Voyage was pre-empted by the "Holiday on Ice" on September 24, just one week into the new season. For this reason, Irwin Allen didn't consider "Fires of Death" (aired on September 17) as the true Season Four kickoff. When the series returned on October 1, "The Deadly Dolls" was the big event Allen had wanted to use to launch the new season. With Vincent Price, how could it be anything less?

And then broadcast night came.

"TV Scout" said:

> *Voyage to the Bottom of the Sea* has a good piece of science fiction that would be great if you had never seen science fiction before. Vincent Price is the guest, as the evil Professor Multiple, a puppeteer whose Punch and Judy show is done with puppet replicas of Richard Basehart and David Hedison. Then his dolls become full size replicas of every crew member, and it's up to Basehart and Hedison to escape being captured, while trying to figure out how to get the Seaview back from Multiple's control. [10]

"TV Key" said:

> This far-out episode benefits by the presence of that master of menace, Vincent Price. Seemingly a harmless puppeteer entertaining the crew of the Seaview at first, Professor Multiple's deadly secret is soon let out, and the submariners find themselves replaced by "living" puppets. The weirdo ramifications of the plot may be hard to swallow, but Price is always fun to watch. [11]

A.C. Nielsen ratings report from October 1, 1967: [12]

	Peak Share:
ABC: *Voyage to the Bottom of the Sea*	26%
CBS: *Lassie* / *Gentle Ben*	**34% / 41%**
NBC: *Walt Disney's Wonderful World of Color*	27%

Even Vincent Price couldn't buoy the ratings. *Voyage* was third in its time period and appeared to be sinking fast.

9.4

"Fires of Death" (Episode 88)

(Prod. No. 1304; first aired Sunday, September 17, 1967)
Written by Arthur Weiss
Directed by Jerry Hopper
Produced by Irwin Allen and Bruce Fowler, Jr.; Story Editor: Sidney Marshall
Guest Star Victor Jory

From the *Voyage* show files (Irwin Allen Papers Collection):

On a mission to damp down an erupting volcano which threatens the lives of millions, the Seaview carries, as passenger, Dr. Albert Turner, a volcanologist who claims that this invasion will enable Admiral Nelson and Captain Crane to carry out their task. Not until the Admiral and Dr. Turner have reached a dry cavern within the volcano does the scientist make his claim to immortality known – he's a 500-year-old alchemist – and reveals his plans to use the eruption for his own evil resources before they can prevent the holocaust and complete their mission. [1]

Assessment:

Mark Phillips said, "This episode loads the plate with an indestructible sailor, a doomsday volcano, a golden Chip Morton, an immortal scientist, and magical elixir stones. The results are ... entertaining." [2]

And that's not even mentioning the immortal scientist's android bodyguard. (A foreshadowing of Gene Roddenberry's *Questor*, perhaps?)

Mike Bailey said, "A must-see for Bob Dowdell fans for his 'golden' performance. As noted above, an inane plot carried off with conviction [and] great volcano interior sets. This episode features particularly fine makeup effects under the direction of Ben Nye and some great shots of the full-scale Flying Sub (stern) which appeared in *Voyage*'s final season." [3]

This was among *Voyage*'s most expensive episodes, exceeding its production schedule and budget – but the well-spent money is front and center on the screen.

The clock ticks loudly in this story, for Dr. Turner (Victor Jory), as the sands in his hourglass run down. Sudden aging and death loom in his immediate future. This prompts a plot to induce a massive volcanic explosion, killing millions, and surely all aboard Seaview if they cannot stop him and his golden henchmen (of which Morton is now one).

Okay, we'd seen Morton – and just about everyone else on the Seaview – turned into zombie slaves more times than we'd like to recall, but never laminated in gold! The visual is even more effective than the crew's pasty complexions in Season Three's "The Wax Men." The make-up used on Victor Jory is every bit as stunning. Irwin Allen's people were flexing their creative and technical muscles when it came to the make-up, sets, and effects on display here. In 1967, no one did it better.

Script:

Arthur Weiss's writers contract: March 20, 1967.
Weiss's story treatment: March 29.
Weiss's 1st-draft teleplay: April 4.
Weiss's 2nd (and final) draft teleplay approved by Irwin Allen on April 24.
2nd Rev. Shooting Final (pink paper): June 20.
Page revisions (green paper): June 28.
Page revisions (yellow paper): June 29.
Page revisions (blue paper): July 11.
Page revisions (dark green paper): July 12.

Writer **Arthur Weiss** began his association with *Voyage to the Bottom of the Sea* here. He was 52 and had already served as the story editor on *The Time Tunnel*, handling the rewriting of all episodes except for the pilot. Weiss had been a frequent writer on TV's *Science Fiction Theatre* (1955-56), *Highway Patrol* (1956-57), *Sea Hunt* (1958-61), and *The Fugitive* (1963-65). He also served as associate producer on one of *The Fugitive*'s four seasons. With both *Science Fiction Theatre* and *Sea Hunt* on his résumé, plus a year of service under Irwin Allen on *The Time Tunnel*, Weiss was a perfect choice to become a *Voyage* writer. He followed this with three more scripts for the series, and also wrote four for *Land of the Giants*, then returned to write a pair of TV movies for Irwin Allen: 1977's *Fire!* and the horrid *The Night the Bridge Fell Down*, from 1983.

Weiss's 12-page story treatment for "Fires of Death" began:

> Under the pile driving hammering of seismic shock-waves, the Seaview rocks and pitches, sending the crew sprawling while Nelson and Crane drive the big submarine at flank speed toward their objective: an undersea volcano. Their suicidal mission: to damp the imminent eruption in order to save the lives of thousands of islanders.
>
> Aboard is DR. ALBERT GEBER, volcanologist, whose "damping device" is housed in a 6-foot cylinder. In the privacy of Nelson's Lab, Albert Geber suddenly starts to turn into an ancient man ... his face seems to be on the point of dissolving into dust! [4]

As with most of the Teasers on *Voyage*, the audience was hooked.

After reading Weiss's first-draft script, Bruce Fowler sent four pages of notes to Irwin Allen, with cc to Story Editor Sidney Marshall and Al Gail, saying in part:

> Generally, I find this script most interesting. It possesses qualities that will make it an excellent episode of "VOYAGE." I do think that the story line bogs down a bit in the middle of the script. It becomes very thin and the action is repetitive.
>
> The character of "DR. GEBER" needs clarification. At the very beginning of the script, we should know more about him, why he is aboard the Seaview, and what his background is that makes him so important to this mission. He seems to be

larger than life, and this does not add to his character, but makes him less important.

The dialogue is stiff and awkward in some places.

The use of the two mechanical men is very well handled. They are interesting heavies. There is a problem in their use, however, as the script indicates that they work under water, and also walk, jump or fall into the burning lava. Make-up and wardrobe should be designed with this in mind.

There are several mechanical problems in the script. One is the use of the flying sub -- formerly indicated as the Hydro-Pod in the script -- where it comes up through the burning lava and floats there while our cast boards it. No one in the script reacts to the tremendous heat of the lava, which is prominently featured. Al Gail came up with the solution for this -- a protective spray device, invented by DR. GEBER, which protects the person, or device, from the heat for a certain period of time. This would also give us greater freedom in playing these scenes, as well as a reason for the seeming immunity.

I don't know if it is possible to shoot some of these scenes as indicated -- where, for instance, we see the flying sub diving through the "incandescent jelly-like substance which churns and flashes a thousand blinding colors" -- and the Interior of the Cavern after the first explosion. And it is in this area that I feel the script can be cut down without loss.

The mechanical effects budget on the show will be high, but it contains those elements I feel you were talking about for this new season....[5]

After these general notes, Fowler followed with over two pages of specific, scene-by-scene suggestions for changes in hopes of straight-lining the story, eliminating production problems and tightening up the budget.

Production:

(Filmed July 6 – 14, 1967, plus added scenes on August 2; total of 7 and ¾ days)

Jerry Hopper was selected to direct the fourth-season opener. This was his seventh of 15 *Voyage* assignments.

A budget of $170,194 was approved (higher than the Season Four per-episode goal of $163,205).

As he often did, Bruce Fowler sent Irwin Allen a memo with suggestions for casting the primary guest star. For the role of "Dr. Turner," formerly "Dr. Geber," he suggested, among others, Richard Denning, Kevin Hagen, Liam Sullivan, Ford Rainey, or, in a curious against-type casting, Hugh Beaumont (Ward Cleaver of *Leave it to Beaver*). Allen settled on someone not on Fowler's list.

Victor Jory was paid top guest price of $2,500. He was 65 and had received his star on the Hollywood Walk of Fame in 1960. He had been a respected character actor in Hollywood since the early 1930s, in more than 200 films and TV episodes, often playing heavies. Some of his most notable roles included Injun Joe in 1938's *The Adventures of Tom Sawyer*; Jonas Wilkerson, the overseer of the slaves at Tara, in 1939's *Gone with the Wind*; and Lamont Cranston, aka "The Shadow," in the 1940s filmed serial of *The Shadow*. But forget all that – Jory was one of the leads in the 1953 sci-fi-adventure *Cat-Women of the Moon*.

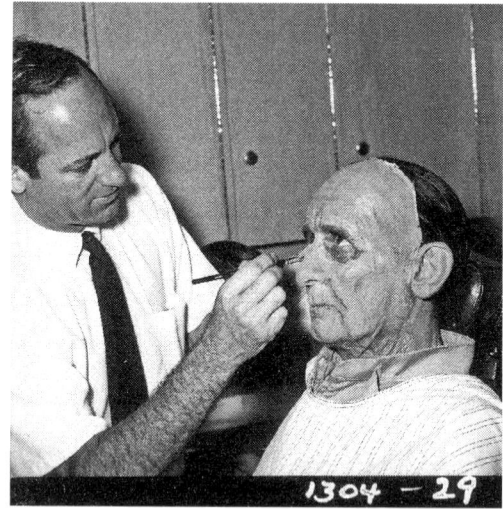

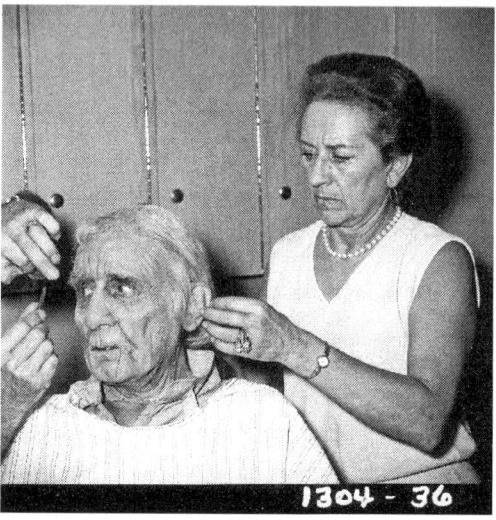

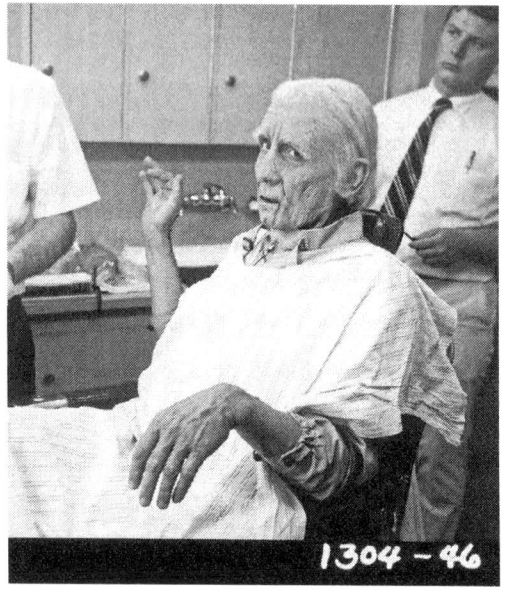

Joe E. Tata was last seen on *Voyage* in the first-season episode, "The Mist of Silence." He played Farrell, the Seaview crewman dragged kicking and screaming from a jail cell to be shot by a firing squad. He was now back for this episode and one other ("Deadly Amphibians") to play small roles, as he already had in several episodes of *Lost in Space* and *The Time Tunnel*.

Tata said, "I returned to *Voyage* in the fourth year, as crewman Brent. I hoped it would lead to a regular role on *Voyage*, but they already had enough regulars." [6]

Production began on Thursday, July 6, 1967 for the first of three days on Stage 10 with the standing Seaview sets, and the Flying Sub. David Hedison took ill and didn't make it in for the third day of filming. The production fell one-half day behind. Hedison would miss a total of four days.

Days 4, 5, and part of 6, were spent on Stage B for the "Int. Volcano Pit" set, and "Ext. Cavern & Beach." [7]

Voyage Art Director Stan Jolley was interviewed for a 20th Century-Fox press release while on the set he built onto Stage B for "Fires of Death." He said, "This is a papier mâché world of creations, and it all begins with an idea conceived in the creative, inventive mind of producer Irwin Allen. When that idea is committed to a script, that's when we take over and the fun begins." [8]

In a press release commissioned by Allen, it was reported:

> Jolley described how one of the first scripts of *Voyage to the Bottom of the Sea* for the new television season called for much action within an active volcano. Producer Allen conceived a spurting hot molten lava interior with spewing

blue gasses, live steam, chambers of glowing, burning rock, and stifling hot ashes falling in the atmosphere.

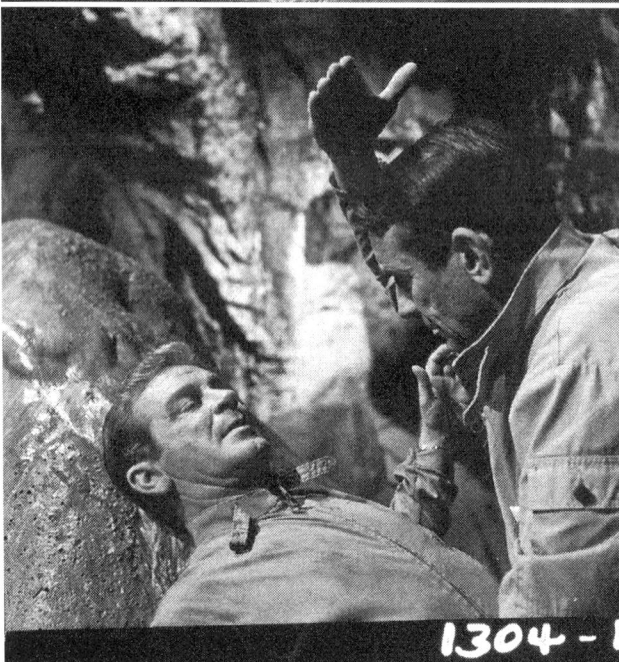

Jolley said, "Not many persons have ever seen the interior of a live volcano and lived to tell about it. So, we immediately started researching the subject. We surveyed all available footage shot around the world at the sites of still active volcanoes. This gave us some idea of what had to be done on our shooting stages. However, we were immediately faced with the problem of shooting in color, because red would be the predominant hue in a confined area inside of a live crater." [9]

The problem was that, in 1967, half the television sets in use across America were still black-and-white. Often, the vivid hues selected for color broadcasts did not translate well to a black-and-white screen. In fact, most cinematographers, when filming on black-and-white film, used blue to portray red. Red would actually appear a dark gray. In the late 1960s, with color television still in its pioneer period, the makers of TV sets had yet to fully adapt their color systems to maintain an industry-wide continuity.

Jolley said, "This is the biggest problem we face week in and week out since color balance for the growing number of color television receivers [is varied]. We began running tests using the myriad of color film available for such problems and came up with the correct combination which afforded us the necessary balances for our purposes." [10]

The PR man wrote:

> Then, from his drawing boards came detailed construction plans which incorporated pools of water soluble liquids which would simulate hot spurting lava when compressed air was fed from beneath its surface; jets of live steam to reflect the intense heat in the atmosphere; ways and means of building huge rock walls that were to form the hades-like interior. Almost overnight, the barren stage on which art director Jolley executed his producer's creation began to take form. And, before the week was out, the shooting crews along with the cast, were recording on color film for posterity, the interior of a real live volcano. When the shooting was completed, Jolley ordered the makeshift structure torn down to make way for a new set for a new script. [11]

Joey Tata told interviewer Mark Phillips, "The volcano set was magnificent. Before filming, Irwin Allen said to me, 'Joey, I know you're very animated, but don't touch the rocks. They're made of foam and they'll bend if you touch them.' When Chuck Couch, who plays the golden man, falls into the lava, you can see his hand hit a rock. The rock sinks in like rubber. Irwin screamed, 'Did you see that! He touched the rock!' I said, 'So? Look at all the rubber rocks floating in the lava.' Irwin said, 'You're not supposed to see those!'" [12]

Tata noted the changes *Voyage* had gone through since his last appearance in the first season. He said, "It's a cult show today. If it had stayed serious, I don't think it would have gotten the audience. People enjoyed the monsters. You either had to choose between the teen audience, which they had, or the middle-aged people. And the special effects were always top of the line. They outdid themselves in 'Fires of Death.' Victor Jory played this immortal living in a volcano. They built this huge set and it was gorgeous. Whenever there was an eruption, Irwin Allen would scream, 'Here goes another eruption!' He would hit a film can with a hammer. The camera would shake like crazy, and we would pretend to fall back and forth. The golden man was played by a high-wire specialist, Chuck Couch. When Chuck fell into the lava, which was made of water and glycerin, he began to sink. The glycerin was pulling him underwater. Three guys jumped in and pulled him out!" [13]

The latter hours of Day 6 were spent back on the Flying Sub set on Stage 10. New scenes had been written to work around the absence of David Hedison.

On the seventh day of production, July 14, Hedison was back and the company worked on Stage 10, with more shooting in the Flying Sub. Additional scenes were shot in the Control Room and Observation Nose, and the Corridor at the Lab door.

The first edit of the episode came in short, so an eighth day of production was scheduled on Wednesday, August 2. With Hedison returned, there was additional shooting in the Control Room, the Missile Room and Sick Bay. Ray Didsbury was burned on his left ankle during an effects shot and had to be treated in the hospital. Jerry Hopper took his last shot at 4 p.m. and "Fires of Death" was finally wrapped. [14]

Release / Reaction:
(ABC premiere airdate: 9/17/67; network repeat broadcast: 4/7/68)

Despite being the fourth episode produced for the fourth season, "Fires of Death" was the first to air, on September 17, 1967. The Summer of Love was just coming to an end, and pop culture had changed greatly since the last new episode of *Voyage* had aired in the

Spring of '67. *Bonnie and Clyde*, starring Warren Beatty and Faye Dunaway (and produced by Beatty) was No. 1 in the movie houses. "Ode to Billie Joe," by Bobbie Gentry, was the top song on the radio, having displaced the Beatles' "All You Need Is Love." The best-selling album in stores across America was *Sgt. Pepper's Lonely Hearts Club Band*, already in its thirteenth week at the top. The second-best seller was the debut release by the Doors, featuring "Light My Fire." Raymond Burr, of *Ironside*, had the cover of *TV Guide*.

Giving a little behind-the-scenes insight from tonight's episode, a filler piece in some newspapers (including the *North Adams Transcript*, in Massachusetts) called "Volcano Recipe." The secret was out:

> Just in case you would like a recipe for making a volcano, here is the one special effects man Stan Jolley used to create a volcano for *Voyage to the Bottom of the Sea*: 3,000 gallons of powdered water soluble, lots of red and yellow food dye mixed together for the lava. Fifty 100-pound bags of red brick dust for the floor surface. Five hundred square yards of aluminum foil for the walls. Fifty-five 25-pound bottles used for steam effect, with 37 steam outlets on the set. [15]

"TV Scout" reviewed the episode:

> *Voyage to the Bottom of the Sea* returns for its fourth season with cast and spectacular scenic effects intact. There's a great looking volcano where much of the action takes place. Seems Victor Jory is aboard the Seaview as a scientist out to stop an impending, deadly eruption. But he's really an alchemist who needs "Elixir Stones" to keep his youth. He's got a robot assistant. Jory takes over Morton (Bob Dowdell) and turns him into a superhuman – and he wouldn't mind doing the same to Richard Basehart. [16]

"Bill," writing for *Variety*, on September 20, 1967, said:

> The big question here is how Richard Basehart and the other feature players have managed to keep a straight face for three seasons. Anyhow, the big atomic sub is cruising into Season Four and the boys are still playing this hour out of the old Saturday matinee serials for real. This type action-adventure is strictly for tots and apparently tot-minded

adults, since Brown & Williamson sees fit to peddle cigs and Bell Telephone princess horns in this frame.

Initialer saw the crew of the Seaview snuffing out an underwater volcano that threatened to blow up half the world. Regular cast played it with the usual grimness, while vet character actor Victor Jory was menacing enough as the baddy. Wandering around the sets with all the standard stuff of pulp sci-fi, Jory was overheard to say, "Don't forget, I'm immortal." Without wincing, Admiral Nelson (Basehart) retorted, "Uh, uh. Only if you take the elixir stones fist." And so on.

Production values are an improvement on those [Saturday matinee] serials of the '30s, but, for text, it's a standoff. [17]

A.C. Nielsen ratings report, September 17, 1967: [18]

7 – 7:30 p.m.:	Peak Share:
ABC: *Voyage to the Bottom of the Sea*	27%
CBS: *Lassie*	**36%**
NBC: *Walt Disney's Wonderful World of Color*	31%

7:30 – 8 p.m.:	
ABC: *Voyage to the Bottom of the Sea*	29.2%
CBS: *Gentle Ben*	**33.8%**
NBC: *Walt Disney's Wonderful World of Color*	27.7%

9.5

"Cave of the Dead" (Episode 89)

(Prod. No. 1305; first aired Sunday, October 8, 1967)
Written by William Welch
Directed by Harry Harris
Produced by Irwin Allen and Bruce Fowler, Jr.; Story Editor: Sidney Marshall
Guest Star Warren Stevens

Voyage prepares fans for Halloween a few weeks early.

From the *Voyage* show files (Irwin Allen Papers Collection):

When Admiral Nelson and Peter Van Wyck, a civilian on a survey mission, spot an uncharted island, the Admiral lands the flying sub in order to explore. The discovery of the skeleton of a murdered man brings down the curse of the Flying Dutchman on them, and starts the Seaview on a terrifying voyage into the past – a voyage that climaxes in a fight between the living and the dead with the lives of all aboard hanging in the balance. [1]

Assessment:

It's another *VTTBOTS* guilty pleasure. The story makes little sense, with the usual holes in the plot. Warren Stevens plays a ghost, and even tells Nelson that he cannot be killed. But the two then get into a physical struggle. A fistfight with a ghost? Regardless, Basehart's old friend Peter Van Wyck (played by Warren Stevens) adds a touch of class to the proceedings.

From the resident critics' couch:

"Lots of creepy scenes, including a dead pirate tangled in a moldy cobweb and living skeletons manning the Seaview's control room. Most interesting are the fantastic shots of the flying sub being battered around by a thunderstorm. The effects people took established shots of the flying sub and superimposed them against a storm. The results are sensational." [2]

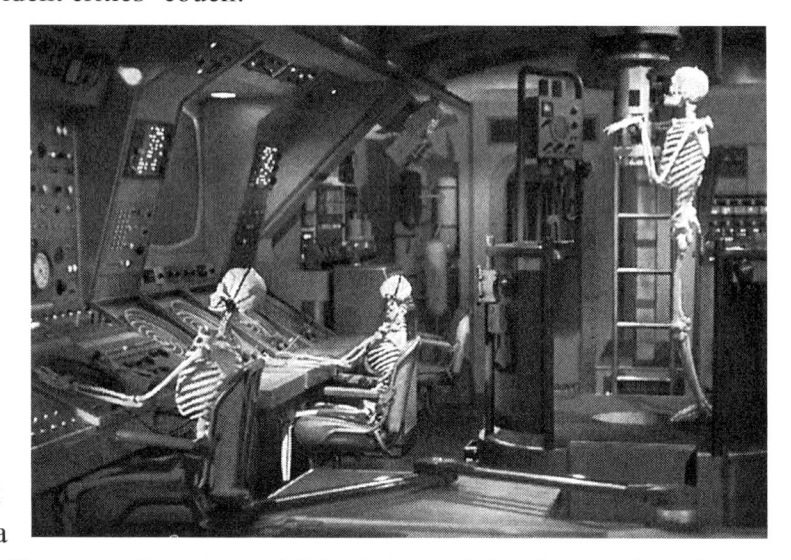

"This episode features one of the rare appearances of the Flying Sub's fourth-year underwater manipulator claws," noted Mark Phillips. "If you look closely through the main FS1 viewports, in some shots, you can see the inner mechanism of the arms where Sharkey and the cockpit would normally be." [3]

You'll encounter something never seen before: Nelson faints! Of course, he *had* just been tapped on the shoulder by a skeleton. Also surprising, and wonderfully effective, is when he returns to consciousness, and sees the face of a skeleton looking down at him ... which then morphs into the face of Captain Crane.

"Cave of the Dead" is wonderful escapism from start to finish.

Script:
William Welch's writers contract: May 15, 1967.
Welch's 1st-draft teleplay: June 1.
Welch's 2nd-draft teleplay: June 6.
Rev. Shooting Final teleplay: June 22.

William Welch loved writing ghost stories ... because, as you've seen, he believed in ghosts. He said, "I believe in God and I believe in the survival of bodily death. Furthermore, I have held these beliefs, which are more like certain convictions than faith, ever since I can remember. What research I may have undertaken in the course has only gone to confirm the things I believed instinctively to start with. Why this should be, I cannot really explain. It is true that my mother subscribed to similar beliefs, but from what I have observed of people, this would ordinarily have tended to drive me away from them, particularly through my teens and twenties. It didn't drive me away. In fact, I read whatever I could get on the subject, finding out by other means everything I could about it, and my already existing convictions were merely confirmed." [4]

After reading Welch's first-draft teleplay, Associate Producer Bruce Fowler wrote to Irwin Allen, with cc to Sidney Marshall and Al Gail. Fowler knew that Allen was extremely fond of Welch and, according to ABC's Lew Hunter, Allen would fight tooth and nail defending Welch's material. So, Fowler began his critique on a careful note:

Any script that Bill Welch writes is interesting. This certainly applies to "THE CAVE OF THE DEAD," but it also contains contradictions that leave me with mixed feelings. It is enjoyable, different and a study in mood. At the same time it goes along on one note, this same mood, it lacks the action and excitement of the normal *Voyage* scripts and it leaves the character of the heavy, Van Wyck, unresolved. These elements all combine to make me feel that this script needs work on it, especially to interject more excitement and physical action.

Bill has succeeded in putting a marvelous quality of impending doom to the Seaview and its crew in this script, and yet it appears to me to be an offstage sort of threat, rather than the more active type I think it requires. I feel cheated when at the end of the Teaser I read that the Flying Sub, with Nelson and Van Wyck aboard, is in terrible trouble, about to crash into the island with no hope of coming out of it. Then at the opening of Act One, Van Wyck, with one line of dialogue, tells Nelson that "... that was the finest emergency landing I've ever seen," and that is all we ever see or hear of it. I think we need the visual picture of the Flying Sub recovering – which, incidentally, we can get out of Stock.

I like the way the script ends. It leaves you wanting more and gives no explanation of how the events took place. I like it, but will our audience?

As a suggestion to open up the show a little, why don't we use process for the Interior of the Flying Sub, when it is on the way to the island. You mentioned that you wanted more process this year, and this would be a good place to make use of it.

The character of Van Wyck needs work. As a suggestion, could there be stronger hints or action on his part to show that he is responsible for the mysterious action before he is revealed as the heavy in the diving bell. I think that Bill [Welch] has deliberately misled us so that the discovery of Van Wyck as the villain would come as more of a shock, yet it doesn't quite come off.

> The script will make a good show for *Voyage*. However, I repeat – may I strongly urge the inclusion of more action sequences. [5]

Production Coordinator Les Warner covered Welch's second-draft teleplay, writing to Allen on June 12. It was a typical memo from Warner, with great attention to the physical challenges of making half a science-fiction movie on a skinny TV budget. Regarding the story being told, he said, in part:

> A good number of questions arise because it is not made clear as to who or what our Van Wyck actually is:
> (1) Is our Van Wyck the ghost of the original Van Wyck, the first mate on the Flying Dutchman? A clue that he is is the act that when he dies he reverts to a skeleton in rags (are these what is left of a first mate's clothes?). But, if so, are we assuming a ghost could materialize and dematerialize the young mortal body he is now "occupying"? And how could the mortal body metamorphose back to the skeleton of the original Van Wyck? He couldn't be a mortal descendent of the original Van Wyck because he has supernatural powers.
> (2) How can killing <u>another</u> man remove the curse the Captain of the Flying Dutchman placed on Van Wyck? And why is it only Nelson whose death can remove the curse? And why didn't Van Wyck kill Nelson at any time he wanted in the sub instead of waiting until in the diving bell? He didn't need the danger to do it because he later starts to kill Nelson with a revolver.
> (3) Why is Van Wyck returning to the cave where (he?) killed the Captain? Was it to get the dagger? If not, what <u>is</u> the secret of the dagger? And why was the Flying Dutchman captain both hanged <u>and</u> stabbed in the heart?
> (4) The VOICE in the cave couldn't be the murdered captain's as the victim certainly wouldn't be placing a curse on anyone who ignored a warning placed at his (the captain's) murder site -- which was no doubt inscribed there by his murderer. If it was the Captain's (or even our Van Wyck's) then why was the Flying Sub supernaturally drawn down to the island cave and then the men cursed for violating the warning not to enter? [6]

Sadly, many of Warner's concerns were *not* addressed in the script polish to come. So – like many Welch stories from the third and fourth seasons – logic and continuity were greatly lacking. Things popped in, things popped out, with little explanation given. But Welch wrote fast, and he wrote to budget, and he understood the show and its characters.

ABC didn't much care for the idea of a skeleton wearing the rags of an ancient uniform. It was too morbid. Mary Garbutt told Irwin Allen:

> Your special care in seeing that sequences with skeleton figures are not too frightening or horrible for family viewing. Can only be approved on film.... Please eliminate "remnants of clothing" on the skeletal figure.... Again, skeletal figure not in uniform or such. [7]

Production:
(Filmed July 17 – 24, 1967; 6 days)

Director **Harry Harris** said, "We used to have a grueling pre-production. We'd have concept meetings. We'd read the script, and we'd sit down and everybody would show up at a concept meeting. And they'd last a long time. And you'd sit down with Irwin and we'd say, 'How are we going to do this? What do you want here? What are you looking for here?' From my standpoint, mainly, because I didn't want to give him something *he* didn't want, I wanted him to tell me what he wants and if I can't give it to him, I have to try and argue him out of it. But the 'How do we do it?' was his first meeting. And we'd go through and take extensive notes on what he wanted, what he would see, what he's looking for. And, then we would proceed with the scheduling of the show, with the art director and all. And then we'd have another meeting. We'd have about four meetings before filming, including our production meeting which would be just before we'd shoot. And we'd have meeting after meeting, and then we'd have subsequent meetings – 'How are we going to build this set?' and 'How are we going to build this prop?' and 'How are we going to do this?,' because it's people answering questions; not easy stuff to do; you're doing something that's unreal. And out of that we would get it done. You'd get into production, and it seems like things went pretty good because nobody had a prop shop like 20th Century-Fox! I mean, Irwin kept that whole prop shop going, and also the miniature department. They wouldn't have had one if it hadn't been for him. And they made great stuff there. They did unbelievable things, in miniature, and in giant stuff. It was unbelievable." [8]

The budget was set at $160,033 (down from the Season Four per-episode target price of $163,205). It helped that **Warren Stevens** was willing to play the role of Van Wyck for $1,750. We last saw him on *Voyage* in "The Saboteur" and "Deadly Invasion."

Filming began on Monday, July 17, 1967 for the first of five-and-a-half days on Stage 10, with the standing Seaview sets, and the Flying Sub. The final day, Monday, July 24, was split between Stage 10 and, for the "Int./Ext. Beach / Cave / Passage" scenes, Stage B. [9]

Release / Reaction:
(ABC premiere airdate: 10/8/67; network repeat broadcast: 4/28/68)

The Beatles' *Sgt. Pepper* continued to dominate record sales, and, one day prior to this broadcast, the group had turned down an offer of $1 million from promoter Sid Bernstein to play a concert in New York. Top songs on the radio: "The Letter," from the Box Tops, followed by "Never My Love," by the Association. *Bonnie and Clyde* was the nation's top-grossing movie. Richard Benjamin, Paula Prentiss, and Jack Cassidy of *He & She* had the cover of *TV Guide*. And *Voyage* had ghosts and skeletons of pirates. The timing seemed perfect – the newest (and most popular) attraction at Disneyland was Pirates of the Caribbean, which had opened earlier in the year.

The promotional copy read: "The curse of the Flying Dutchman plagues Admiral Nelson and the crew of the Seaview in a terrifying voyage into the past. Warren Stevens makes a guest star appearance as Peter Van Wyck, a civilian on a strange exploration of an uncharted island."

"TV Scout" commented:

> If you have been a faithful viewer of *Voyage to the Bottom of the Sea*, "Cave of the Dead" will remind you of several episodes done before. But it's still fun, combining as it does, modern science-fiction with the ancient legend of the Flying Dutchman. Warren Stevens is a guest, as a young naval officer assisting in the search for four ships which have disappeared in the same waters. But he is really much more sinister than that – almost as sinister as a dagger Richard Basehart finds in a cave. [10]

A.C. Nielsen released a report covering the period in which "Cave of the Dead" first aired. Out of 97 network series included in the survey, *Voyage* ranked at No. 63, a big drop from the season before. [11]

A.C. Nielsen ratings report from October 8, 1967 (full report not available): [12]

	Peak Share:
ABC: *Voyage to the Bottom of the Sea*	33%
CBS: *Lassie* / *Gentle Ben*	**37% / 41%**
NBC: *Walt Disney's Wonderful World of Color*	23%

Another report from Nielsen, called the MNA 30-Market Survey, with a focus on large cities, placed *Voyage* much higher. In fact, it placed in the week's twenty top-rated shows.

According to *Variety*, they stacked up as follows: 1) *The Jackie Gleason Show*; 2) *Bewitched*; 3) CBS Friday Night Movie; 4) *The Dean Martin Show*; 5) NBC Tuesday Night Movie; 6) *Green Acres*; 7) *The Beverly Hillbillies*; 8) *The Smothers Brothers Hour*; 9) ABC Wednesday Night Movie; 10) *Bonanza*; 11) CBS Thursday Night Movie; 12) *The Flying Nun*; 13) *The Carol Burnett Show;* 14) The Ice Follies (special); 15) Frank Sinatra special; 16) ***Voyage to the Bottom of the Sea***; 17) *The Jerry Lewis Show*; 18) *The Ed Sullivan Show*; 19) *Family Affair*; 20) *Alice in Wonderland* (special). [13]

9.6

"Sealed Orders" (Episode 90)

(Prod. No. 1306; first aired Sunday, October 22, 1967)
Written by William Welch
Directed by Jerry Hopper
Produced by Irwin Allen and Bruce Fowler, Jr.; Story Editor: Sidney Marshall

From the *Voyage* show files (Irwin Allen Papers Collection):

Seaview, on a secret mission, is carrying an enormously powerful new weapon. Through an accident the weapon begins to leak radiation and before it can be brought under control, members of the crew begin to vanish one by one until at last Admiral Nelson finds himself all alone on the submarine. [1]

Assessment:

Mike Bailey said, "When 'Sealed Orders' came along, it was a great break from the monster-of-the-week shows and the general way-out tone the show had taken on since the beginning of the third season. At last, I thought, something a bit more grounded in reality, even if a hallucinogenic one." [2]

But reality, this episode tells us, lies in your state of mind.

Here was a money-saving concept – all but one member of the ship's complement disappear! Perhaps a better title, and more in the style of Irwin Allen, would have been "The Mysteriously Vanishing Crew."

We'd seen stories about hallucinations before on *Voyage*, but "Sealed Orders" takes the idea to the ultimate level. Music, camera angles, and effects combine by the end of the show to make this *Voyage* a real trip. The crew weren't just seeing sea creatures, or monsters in the corridors, but they mostly *weren't* seeing what was there – each other. It may have been novel for *Voyage*. But we'd seen it elsewhere – in "Where Is Everybody?", the 1959 pilot of *The Twilight Zone*; "The Hour That Never Was," a 1966 episode of *The Avengers*; and we'd see it again, in "The Mark of Gideon," a 1969 episode of *Star Trek*. The premise was handled differently in each, as in "Sealed Orders," but was always eerily effective.

Further, the episode reeks of 1960s Cold War and nuclear paranoia. After watching it, you weren't likely to rest easily – or trust in the wisdom of our government and military leaders. On this series, they were remarkably reckless with their bombs! Was Irwin Allen making a statement? Unlikely. The thinking was probably like this: What could be more dramatic than the end of the world?

Mr. Morton gets the best line in the episode. He is about to be left alone in the Control Room, with no crew to command, when Captain Crane asks if he feels he can "take the conn." Morton replies, "There's nothing to do here but keep from disappearing."

Script:

William Welch's writers contract: June 26, 1967.
Welch's story treatment and 1st- and 2nd-draft teleplays approved by Irwin Allen July 3.
Revised draft of teleplay: July 5.
Shooting Final (pale green paper): July 11.
Page revisions (blue paper): July 24.
Page revisions (pink paper): July 26.
Page revisions (purple paper): July 26.

William Welch was asked to come up with a story that would only require the existing sets built on Stage 10, and no need for guest stars. He was writing to order, but nevertheless came up with a script that made an interesting and entertaining episode.

The neutron bomb is the subject here, the cause of many debates in the 1960s, with prototypes being tested throughout the latter part of the decade and into the 1970s. Officially defined as a type of enhanced-radiation weapon (ERW), the bomb was designed to maximize lethal neutron radiation in the immediate vicinity of the blast while minimizing the physical power of the blast itself. Meaning, kill the people but leave the buildings. By the late 1970s and early 1980s (the time when *Voyage* was supposed to happen), the U.S. had approximately 70 of these type bombs on "active duty" around the world. "Sealed Orders" is the story of one such bomb.

Since this episode deals with a potential nuclear accident, ABC wanted measures taken to prevent its viewers from taking *Voyage to the Bottom of the Sea* as a breaking-news broadcast. It was that troublesome policy that had been in place since the 1938 Orson Welles' *War of the Worlds* radio broadcast panicked America.

Mary Garbutt of the network's Department of Broadcast Standards and Practices told Allen and his staff:

> Pg 1: Please establish future date somewhere in the teaser.
>
> Pg 23, Sc 56: Please modify Nelson's "expectable speech" so that this is Nelson's interpretation of the orders and not a general statement of fact.
>
> Pg 26, etc.: A general caution that the representation of the Fail Safe operation is accurate.
>
> Pgs 27, 51, 53, 54: Of course, the record player, record label, the various clocks not identifiable as to actual trade/brand or company name.
>
> Pgs 29, 36, 39, 41, 48: Standard caution on the various monsters and the "psychedelic" sequences.
>
> Pgs 43, 44: Your usual care in seeing that the moans, the writhing are not over-done. [3]

Perhaps we blinked, but we didn't see the directed futuristic date in the beginning of the episode. Or maybe, like the crew on the Seaview in this tale, we were hallucinating.

Production:

(Filmed July 25 through August 1, 1967; 5 & ½ days)

This was **Jerry Hopper**'s eighth of fifteen directing turns on *Voyage*. His assignment: Shoot empty rooms, and make it interesting. And he did.

Harry Geller provided the new psychedelic music, interwoven with tracked music to comprise the score. This was his second of four *Voyage*s, on the heels of "The Deadly Dolls."

The budget was set at $144,745, which was well below the studio's target price of $163,205 per episode. The savings here, for this bottle show, would help balance the books for the episodes that exceeded the mandatory budget, such as "Fires of Death" and "The Deadly Dolls."

Filming began on Tuesday, July 25, 1967, for what was supposed to be the first of five days on Stage 10, utilizing only the standing Seaview sets and that of the Flying Sub. Director Jerry Hopper fell behind on the fifth day of production. A partial sixth day of filming was needed, with the episode wrapping on Tuesday, August 1, at 1:05 in the afternoon. [4]

Release / Reaction:
(ABC premiere airing: 10/22/67; network repeat broadcast: 7/7/68)

During the week that "Sealed Orders" first aired on ABC, the Vietnam War was escalating, and thousands of anti-war protesters stormed the Pentagon.

Mia Farrow of *Peyton Place* had the cover of *TV Guide*. "To Sir, With Love," by Lulu, had replaced "The Letter," by the Box Tops, as the No. 1 song on the radio. The Supremes' first Greatest Hits package, along with the Doors' debut album, and the Beatles' LSD-influenced *Sgt. Pepper* were the best-selling albums in record stores.

This was a hard episode for ABC to promote. How do you take effective photos of empty rooms, or of crewmembers reacting to empty rooms? So, the network took the brief cameo of Dawson Palmer in a monster get-up to plug the show.

"TV Scout" previewed the trip:

> *Voyage to the Bottom of the Sea* forgets about monsters (except for a few brief scenes) and concentrates on a good mystery. The Seaview is on a top-secret mission, carrying a live warhead, a neutron bomb locked in fail safe position, which can only be activated by the President. That's tough enough, but add these facts: there's a leak from the silo carrying the bomb, and the crew keeps disappearing until there's only two left. [5]

Nielsen ratings report from October 22, 1967: [6]

	Peak Share:
ABC: *Voyage to the Bottom of the Sea*	28%
CBS: *Lassie* / *Gentle Ben*	**38% / 36%**
NBC: *Walt Disney's Wonderful World of Color*	34%

9.7

"Journey with Fear" (Episode 91)

(Prod. No. 1307; first aired Sunday, October 15, 1967)
Written by Arthur Weiss
Directed by Harry Harris
Produced by Irwin Allen and Bruce Fowler, Jr.; Story Editor: Sidney Marshall
(with Eric Matthews as Major Wilson)

From the *Voyage* show files (Irwin Allen papers collection):

A Rocket Capsule, co-piloted by Commander Morton, suddenly disappears while in orbit. Admiral Nelson orders the back-up space craft readied for launching, but while Captain Crane is checking it out, the second capsule also suddenly disappears. Crane learns he has been taken to Venus by

Aliens from the planet Centar, who already hold Morton prisoner. The Aliens, fearing an invasion of their planet, then bring Nelson to Venus, hoping to use his knowledge and abilities for their own end. The officers of the Seaview are forced to the very brink of death by earthquakes before they are able to overcome their captors and return to their ship. [1]

Assessment:

It seemed an odd stretch – from the bottom of the sea to outer space – the sub serving as a launch pad for a space probe. And its executive officer, Chip Morton, we now learn, is a trained astronaut ... as is the sub's captain. Courtesy of another way-out story contrivance, the space trip ends on Venus. But don't dismiss this one too quickly.

"The aliens look impressive, especially those frog eyes (which, alas, don't blink)," Mark Phillips said. "There's also some admirable scientific restraint – Chip Morton reveals that man has landed on the moon but has only landed on Mars via remote controlled vehicle. The aliens, who are not invaders but rather concerned scientists who fear mankind's aggressiveness, explain that they've taken a section of Venus and converted it to an Earth-like atmosphere for interrogation purposes." [2]

Those curious-looking aliens are creepy and silly at the same time. Their thinking process is odd, too. They choose to use Venus as a meeting place – a planet that could not maintain life, so an area of it must be converted in order to do so – which proves temporary at best. And then these aliens have to bring the

Earthmen there. And then they – aliens and Earthmen alike – have to escape from there before the roof falls in on the joint.

But don't write this one off too quickly. While nothing here makes very much sense, "Journey with Fear" is nonetheless entertaining, and visually startling as an artifact of 1960s abstract pop art gone wild. Enjoy.

Script:
Arthur Weiss's story "springboard," "The Venusian Exploration": April 10, 1967.
Weiss's writers contract: April 11, 1967.
Weiss's story treatment, "Venusian Explosion": April 24.
Weiss's revised treatment, now titled "Journey with Fear": May 3.
Weiss's 1st-draft teleplay: May 17.
Weiss's 2nd (and final) draft teleplay approved by Irwin Allen on June 2.
2nd Rev. Shooting Final teleplay (pink paper): August 1.
Page revisions (blue paper): August 1.
Page revisions (green paper): August 3.
Page revisions (gold paper): August 10.

Before a contract was drawn up, **Arthur Weiss** interested Irwin Allen in a story he pitched called "The Venusian Exploration." After the meeting, he wrote up a one-page "springboard":

> Under the supervision of Admiral H.H. Nelson, the Seaview is used as the sea-based launch-pad from which the Venus Excursion Module (VEM) blasts off under the command of Captain Lee Crane. Its mission: to penetrate the obscuring cloud cover of Venus; to land if the physical environment permits; and to bring back specimens. The launch is perfect; escape velocity is attained and outer-space is penetrated on the correct trajectory – And the capsule disappears!
>
> The VEM, contrary to its programming, has been gravitationally attracted; accelerated to the speed of light; and drawn down onto Venus which is in an eternal volcanic and storm-and-lightning convulsion due to the fiery tidal surges of the nearby Sun. It is, in effect, hell in outer space.
>
> Crane's cosmic kidnapping has been accomplished by ANDRO, leader of a humanoid party from Earth's nearest galactic neighbor, Andromeda. Andro's mission: using the natural camouflage of Venus' cloud cover, he is attempting to stop Earth's exploration of the Universe. Andromeda has,

in effect, drawn a line across the cosmos at the Moon, and denies Earth's right to cross it. [3]

It seemed a story more suited to Allen's other series of this period – *Lost in Space*. It was also clearly going to be an expensive production, resulting in a need for more bottle shows to compensate.

By the time Weiss put his story in treatment form, the title had been changed to the generic "Journey with Fear." It opened:

> The tension which stretches like a taut rope throughout the Seaview is tightest in the Missile Room as the count-down to blast-off of a space Module approaches ZERO. CAPTAIN LEE CRANE is the lone occupant of the vehicle. His mission is to: Find and rescue CHIP MORTON whose space capsule disappeared in outer space eleven minutes after yesterday's launch. Blast-off!
>
> With Nelson in the Seaview controlling the operation and Crane in the Module, everything is normal for the first eleven minutes. Then the Module disappears from the control screens! Nelson tries desperately to re-establish contact. Fails!
>
> In the Module, Crane is the dazed prisoner of a glaring white ORB which is in control of the vehicle; cuts communications; accelerates it to almost the speed of light. The Orb engulfs Crane and the Module! [4]

In this story we learn that both Morton and Crane are competent astronauts. When the Seaview's chief is lost, it makes perfect Allen-storytelling sense to send the ship's exec after him in a separate capsule, in hopes that one will stumble across the other. What was left unexplained was how they might actually rescue each other.

Associate Producer Bruce Fowler thought it was remarkable, too:

> I have read this several times now, and I am still in a state of confusion. Confused as to the story line, which seems muddled to me, and confused as to whether it will still make a good show for *Voyage*. I know that we have always bewildered the audience with our fast footwork, as far as science goes, but I think that Arthur has disregarded the

> veneer that makes the whole piece look good. For instance, and to the point – wouldn't the entire world be concerned over the possibility of Venus being hit, and not knowing how it would affect the Earth? Firing a module into space is a complicated procedure. Even in 1972 could our crew do this? Finding a module that is lost in space, and 150 seconds after locating it on an alien planet and communicating with it is quite a task, even for Nelson.
>
> I find a flaw in Arthur's stories and scripts that seems to be of a recurring nature. That is, all of his stories jump around and do not flow at an even pace. There is no build for situations that are dramatic, and there is unnecessary build in other situations. In an attempt to inject pace and action into his stories, he jumps into the middle of sequences. This, for me, anyway, does not increase the tempo, but only leads to confusion. I could understand this technique used effectively in perhaps one story, but it occurs both here and in his previous scripts, so that I begin to think it is a trait of Arthur's, rather than a device.
>
> This story is not my cup of tea. [5]

Allen did not cut the assignment off. Instead, he asked Arthur Weiss to provide a revised treatment for no additional pay. It began on a different note, with perhaps a slightly better justification:

> CHIP MORTON, whose background includes both his experience under Crane and also naval aviation, has been asked by the Space Exploration Agency to co-pilot a probe to Mars which is believed to be a water planet. Hydrographic data will be gathered; Chip is well-qualified for the mission. [6]

In Act 1 of the treatment, Crane blasts off in a "back-up capsule," launched on the "same trajectory in hope of effecting rendezvous with Chip's capsule and rescuing him and the pilot." Regardless, no explanation was given as to how the rescue could be accomplished, or how Crane was qualified for such an assignment. Then, Crane ends up on Venus, running around trying to find Morton, who has been blinded, his co-pilot killed.

As far-fetched and inordinately expensive as it all sounded, Fowler had a change of heart after reading Weiss's first-draft script, delivered on May 17. Or perhaps he merely realized that Irwin Allen was on board with this story, and trusted in Arthur Weiss's ability to pull off the rewriting. Fowler's memo to Allen, with cc to Sidney Marshall and Al Gail, was three pages long, and began:

> This is the best job of writing Arthur has done to date for us. It moves along well, has a definite direction and interesting characters. I like the script and think it can be easily corrected to make a good segment for us.
>
> There are a couple of unfortunate coincidences that must be corrected. They are the use of the "orb" – which is featured so prominently in Charles Bennett's script and the use of the name "Alpha" which Bill Welch used in "Time Lock." The name can be easily changed, but the use of the orb as a device in this story is a bit more difficult.
>
> To get back to the story, I like the roles that Chip and Crane have. They are a bit different and yet very interesting. Do we want any background on why Chip is being sent on the first mission? There should be some explanation as to what or where the mission is that Chip and the Lieutenant are going on. At the present time all we know is that they are being fired into space, seemingly with no rhyme or reason, this is not our procedure. They must have a definite mission to accomplish, this gives importance and purpose to the story. [7]

It shows the sloppiness that abounded in *Voyage*'s latter seasons that Fowler was one of the few to point out problems like this. Neither Sidney Marshall nor Al Gail made any recorded protest. Fowler was being as diplomatic as possible bringing this problem to his boss's attention. Still, it's stunning that no one else had bothered to point out these problems.

Fowler continued:

> While not necessary – I think it might be interesting to the story and for our audience to know that "this is the first firing of a space module from a submarine." "It marks an important and meaningful moment in the history of space exploration" or some such background murmur to increase importance of this event....

> Lieutenant Wilson's death is convenient and that's about the best that I can say for it.
>
> I find that Scene 59 is confusing. The story line jumps back and forth so quickly that you don't know where you are or just what is happening. I know that this can be cleaned up. ...
>
> The indication that Arthur has of water pouring into various sets should be eliminated or our literal-minded crew will have sets and pipes built for this and we will get calls from Martin's office telling us that this is impossible.... [8]

After two more pages of notes, Fowler wrote:

> I am sure that with these corrections this will make a fine script for our show. [9]

Irwin Allen's script notes concerning the revised Shooting Final teleplay were minor, like this:

> Page 13 – Scene 37: Morton drops his pressure suit. In scene 36, page 12 – Both men started to get out of their pressure suits but no mention was made of them carrying the suits in scene 37. Do they have them with them or is this a mistake? [10]

There were more items of this type in Allen's memo. But, as had become standard, no comments about the story itself, or the lack of logic, believability, or theme.

Fortunately, Production Coordinator Les Warner was on the job. Where Allen had sent in a mere half-page of notes, Warner's memo was five pages in length. Some of his points:

> Although the exterior of the capsule is not now indicated, Bruce Fowler advises that there is an Interior and Exterior of a capsule on the lot that could be utilized, with modifications. Otherwise, a very costly item....
>
> The lower section of the Space Rocket in the Missile Room: Although the script indicates this as a "re-dress" (re-vamp) of one of our missile silos, Bruce feels that, to be more logical,

we should explore the possibility of a larger type rocket-base. Either way, this could still be a costly item -- but is necessary to the story as now written....

The "prehensile snake vine" in the jungle clearing: As we all know, this is an expensive, time consuming gimmick. It does not actually pay off and is just added suspense, but we already have enough going for us in these sets. I recommend DELETING this business....

A possible production and cost item with the two Centars, re: concept: They are described as humanoid-type aliens, but with no features on their faces. Not only is this a Wardrobe and/or Makeup (and a convenience-of-wearing) problem, but these Centars (especially #1) do a great deal of talking and I am certain we wouldn't want to see their "masks" moving....Therefore, it is possible we would want to change their concept to aliens with humanoid-type features....

This is an exciting, suspenseful, action-packed story but, by its own elements, a budget problem. Sid Marshall has already greatly reduced the originally alarming production and cost problems; however, I am certain that we are still in trouble and that further retrenchment is mandatory -- not by rewriting (as it already has been written "down") but possibly by directorial confinement as to scope and magnitude of the panic scenes and effects now indicated. [11]

And what did ABC make of all this? The network censors wanted *Voyage* to establish a futuristic date in the early part of the episode. After all, the U.S. had been sending manned missions into space – the last being Gemini 12 with Buzz Aldrin and James Lovell, in November 1966. Apollo 1 never got off the ground – astronauts Gus Grissom, Edward White, and Roger Chaffee perished on January 27, 1967, in a pre-launch cabin fire, which only heightened ABC-TV's concerns over depicting problems with space flights … even such farfetched difficulties as intervention by frog-faced alien creatures. As a result, the date "1981" was superimposed over the start of this *Voyage*.

Production:
(Filmed August 3 – 10, 1967; 6 days)

"Journey with Fear" was **Harry Harris**'s eleventh out of twelve directing assignments.

Gene Dynarski played Centar I. You'll never recognize him here, but, one year before this, he had a prominent role in an early *Star Trek* – "Mudd's Women." This was Dynarski's second *Voyage*, having appeared in Season One's "The Buccaneer," and he would return to Irwin Allen productions to play a prison warden in an episode of *Land of the Giants*.

Gene Dynarski was prominently featured in "Journey with Fear," as the lead alien. But you only heard his voice and his green-colored mouth! Dynarski did better on *Star Trek*, with three appearances (seen here in 1966's "Mudd's Women").

Jim Gosa was cast as Centar II.

And, finally, *Voyage* took a second step to becoming a multiracial series with the casting of a black crewmember. You'll see him briefly in an early scene in the Missile Room.

A budget of $165,465 was approved by William Self, which was just above the studio's target of $163,205 per episode.

Filming began Thursday, August 3, 1967, for the first of three-and-a-half days on Stage B, for sets identified on the schedule as "Int./Ext. Cave," "Ext./Int. Rocky Area," "Ext. T.M.-2 (on Beach)," "Ext. Venusian Landscape," plus an angle of that set which could be combined with a matte shot.

On the fourth day of production, at midday,

the company moved to Stage 10 for filming on the Flying Sub set, as well as a new one: "Int. Rocket Launch Room."

On Wednesday, the fifth day of filming, they remained on Stage 10, with more work in the "Int. Launch Control Room," plus "Int. Space Capsule" and "Int. T.M.-2 Space Capsule."

On the sixth day, still on Stage 10, they filmed on the "Int. Seaview Control Room," as well as the sub's Missile Room set. The last shot was completed at 7:30 p.m. [12]

Enhancing the presentation was 20th Century-Fox library music sweetening the soundtrack. It was lifted from Bernard Herrmann's score for 1959's *Journey to the Center of the Earth*.

This episode had plenty of way-out visuals, and Irwin Allen took advantage of this in extending an invitation to *Jack and Jill* magazine to do a photo story from the set of *Voyage* for a 1968 issue. Richard Basehart could have suggested a few other episodes better suited for promotion. Casting Director Larry Stewart, as quoted in the book *Science Fiction Television Series* by Mark Phillips and Frank Garcia, recalled an incident with Richard Basehart from this time. "One day, network people from Japan visited the set. Through an interpreter, they asked him, 'How do you enjoy the scripts?' Richard replied, 'All I can tell you is that every Friday, someone in Irwin Allen's office flushes a toilet and the script ends up here.' The interpreter tried to explain this to the visitors and they looked totally bewildered." [13]

Release / Reaction:
(ABC premiere airdate: 10/15/67; network repeat broadcast: 5/5/68)

This was the week that the rock musical *Hair* premiered on Broadway. *Bonnie and Clyde* was still the top film in the U.S. "To Sir, With Love" was still the song more radio stations were playing. *Ode to Billie Joe*, by Bobbie Gentry, was the best-selling album across the land. Johnny Carson had the cover of *TV Guide*.

"TV Scout" said:

> *Voyage to the Bottom of the Sea* takes a page from *The Time Tunnel, Star Trek, The Invaders,* and a few pages of its own, and comes up with a wild science-fiction tale youngsters will love. Seems the Seaview is launching a space vehicle from under the sea. Shortly after the launch, the capsule disappears and winds up on Venus, where Centaurs [sic] want to find out just how dangerous we Earth aliens are with our space probes. Lots more "space-napings" before this is over. [14]

"TV Key" said:

> This series usually deals with creatures from the deep, but tonight's adventure finds our heroes thrust into outer space. Youngsters will enjoy the sight of "Centars" from another planet kidnapping a space ship and its occupants from the Seaview. Suspense builds to a climax, for which special effects men can take a well-deserved bow. [15]

A.C. Nielsen ratings report from October 15, 1967: [16]

	Peak Share:
ABC: *Voyage to the Bottom of the Sea*	28%
CBS: *Lassie* / *Gentle Ben*	**36% / 39%**
NBC: *Walt Disney's Wonderful World of Color*	26%

9.8

"Fatal Cargo" (Episode 92)

(Prod. No. 1309; first aired Sunday, November 5, 1967)
Written by William Welch
Directed by Jerry Hopper
Produced by Irwin Allen and Bruce Fowler, Jr.; Story Editor: Sidney Marshall
Guest Star Woodrow Parfrey

Does this episode's "super gorilla" look familiar? It was later used as the Mugato from *Star Trek*'s "A Private Little War," with forehead horn and dorsal spikes added.

From the *Voyage* show files (Irwin Allen papers collection):

A Dr. Blanchard, who claims he can control a super gorilla he has developed, is killed when the giant animal goes berserk. When Admiral Nelson learns of Blanchard's death, he is determined to continue his experiments. Leo Brock, the dead man's assistant, at first protests but finally agrees to help Nelson. The huge gorilla is located aboard the Seaview where it soon becomes apparent that Brock controls the animal and Nelson is destined to be its next victim. Using an electronic device, Brock sends the beast rampaging through the submarine hunting for the Admiral, and the Seaview is threatened with total destruction. [1]

Assessment:

"An energetic, sometimes unsettling episode that is impossible to dislike," Mark Phillips said. [2]

Perhaps. It seems to us that it is also impossible to love. Here's why:

Brock (played by Woodrow Parfrey) is one-dimensional. He's a bad guy – driven by ego, and lacking empathy or any trace of a moral compass. Period. And the ape is a beast, driven by programming. Period. Lip service is given in the episode's Tag scene to explain Brock's motivations. The attempt is brief and ineffective.

Illogic and bad plotting abound. Brock knocks Captain Crane out, then tosses him into a locked compartment. Wouldn't Brock expect that Crane will be discovered and tell who hit him? So, why didn't Brock kill Crane? This ham-handed explanation for Crane's absence was created to give David Hedison a few days off.

The action is redundant. How many times can we watch the crew shoot the gorilla with tranquilizers, only to see him recover and go on another rampage, ripping hatches off their hinges? How many times can we watch Brock lurk in the corridors, performing niggling misdeeds? And no one ever stumbles across him?! All these things make a joke of the security (or lack thereof) on the Seaview. Rather than using his imagination to create new jeopardy, William Welch just hit "replay."

Lastly, do we really need yet another monster smashing up the Circuity Room, leading to the same shot of the Seaview bouncing off the ocean's bottom? And all the rocking of the Seaview, with crewmembers flailing about the Control Room, as sparks fly and alarms sound, was not going to add excitement to this overplayed plot point. After all, we'd seen all that stuff too, *ad nauseum*.

In fact, days after this episode aired, Paul Van Duren wrote in his entertainment column for New Jersey's *Asbury Park Press*:

> Those submariners in *Voyage to the Bottom of the Sea* [need to] make that circuit room secure against monsters and stop all that rocking of the boat! [3]

Well ... there *is* plenty of action in "Fatal Cargo." And the gorilla looks good (for 1967) – so good it was used the next year in the *Star Trek* episode "A Private Little War."

Script:

William Welch's writers contract: June 8, 1967.
Welch's story treatment: June 15.
Welch's 1ˢᵗ- and 2ⁿᵈ-draft teleplays approved by Irwin Allen on August 8.
Shooting Final teleplay (pale green paper): August 8.
Page revisions (pink paper): August 10.
Page revisions (blue paper): August 10.

William Welch's story treatment began:

In the steaming jungles of Equatorial Africa, world-famed anthropologist DR. PIERRE BLANCHARD is in the final stages of a remarkable experiment. It is an attempt to increase, by mutation, the intelligence of the gorilla species. The ultimate idea is to produce an exceptionally strong yet obedient creature capable of following orders and thus able to perform menial tasks requiring unusual strength. Under treatment, his captured specimen has grown to unusual size. All that remains is to test the electronic controls which are designed to transmit orders directly to the creature's brain.

In charge of the electronic control apparatus is Blanchard's assistant, LEO BROCK, a young man with brooding eyes, deep set in a sullen, cadaverous face. Brock has taken a fountain pen and secretly removed its ink cartridge, substituting another cartridge in its place. Having accomplished this without being observed, he gives the innocent-looking pen to Blanchard, who clips it in his breast pocket. They are awaiting the expected arrival of Admiral Nelson, who is on his way in the flying sub to witness the climactic experiment. Suddenly there is a horrific roar as something crashes toward them through the jungle. Brock turns and runs, taking the control box with him and leaving Blanchard to face the terror alone.

As Blanchard, all but frozen in terror, searches frantically for the small electronic control box, the enormous hulk of a gigantic gorilla bursts from the jungle and heads straight for the scientist, its red eyes blazing hatred. The terrible beast looms above Blanchard and attacks, its gargantuan form overwhelming the CAMERA, blacking out the scene. [4]

As we all know by now, ABC would never allow *anything* – much less a big gorilla – to rush toward and overwhelm the camera!

Production:
(Filmed August 11 – 18, 1967; 6 days)

"Fatal Cargo," with a production number of 1309, was planned to be the ninth episode filmed for Season Four. The script meant to precede it ("Terror"; Production Number 1308) was not ready in time, and was pushed back on the production schedule, with "Fatal Cargo" advancing by one position.

Jerry Hopper was at the helm. The budget was set at $160,405, just under the per-season average of $163,205.

Woodrow Parfrey was paid $1,500 to play Brock. Parfrey was 44, and would amass more than 200 appearances in films and on television in a career spanning 1950 to 1984. They especially liked him at *The Man from U.N.C.L.E.*, where he appeared in five episodes (as five different characters), and *Mannix*, where he turned up in nine

Above: Woodrow Parrey, in one of several appearances on *The Man from U.N.C.L.E.* Left: One of Jon Lormer's *Star Trek* appearances.

episodes. But we like him best in a pair of movies from 1973 – as the nervous bank manager in *Charley Varrick* and one of the grimy, toothless prisoners in *Papillon*.

Jon Lormer, who appears briefly as Dr. Blanchard, may also look familiar. Among hundreds of roles in films and on television, he appeared in three episodes of *Star Trek* and four

599

*Twilight Zone*s. At this time, Lormer had a recurring role on *Peyton Place*, in 18 episodes as a judge. He was 61.

Janos Prohaska was a Hungarian immigrant. He was 47, and designed, fabricated, and wore the ape-like suit. Playing apes and bears was his specialty. He appeared as an ape in three episodes of *Gilligan's Island*; he was Bobo the Gorilla in two episodes of *Land of the Giants*; and Darwin the Monkey in "The Sixth Finger," for *The Outer Limits*. His most frequent job was as Cookie Bear on *The Andy Williams Show*.

Production began on Friday, August 11, 1967, for the first of four-and-a-half days on Stage 10, with the standing Seaview sets. Halfway into the fifth day of filming, the company moved to Stage B for

Janos Prohaska, in the same gorilla suit, gets chummy with Lucy.

"Int./Ext. Jungle Camp" and "Ext. Jungle," where they spent the next day and a half. Filming wrapped at 6:15 p.m. on Friday, August 8. [5]

Release / Reaction:

(ABC premiere airdate: 11/5/67; network repeat broadcast: 5/12/68)

This was the week that ATS-3 was launched by the United States to take pictures of the full Earth from space. Also launched was Surveyor 6, which made a soft landing on the moon.

And an unmanned Saturn V was launched to circle the Earth, to test the reentry of an Apollo capsule. NASA was in high gear. So was the U.S. military. Vietnam continued to be the first war fought on TV, with nightly newscasts across America broadcasting color footage of the action and mayhem. The big story this week: U.S. troops conquering Loc Ninh, South Vietnam. *Cool Hand Luke*, starring Paul Newman, was the top film in movie houses. The Supremes, the Beatles, and the Doors had the three best-selling albums in the stores. If you've been reading these little time capsules, you know what they were. You may even own them. And "To Sir, With Love" was *still* the most-played song on the radio. For three of the five weeks that Lulu sat in the top spot, "Soul Man," by Sam and Dave, was stuck at No. 2. Meanwhile, *Voyage* was about to get its best ratings in weeks, thanks to that rampaging white gorilla.

"TV Scout" said:

> A giant white gorilla, whose actions can be controlled by a device in the hands of the week's villain and keeps going berserk. Seems the villain (Woodrow Parfrey) has made the gorilla kill the scientist who perfected the device, and now Richard Basehart has taken man and beast aboard the Seaview for further experiments. But what has happened to David Hedison, who knew Parfrey before? And will the beast completely wreck the Seaview? [6]

A.C. Nielsen ratings report from November 5, 1967: [7]

	Peak Share:
ABC: *Voyage to the Bottom of the Sea*	31%
CBS: *Lassie* / *Gentle Ben*	**35%** / 32%
NBC: *Walt Disney's Wonderful World of Color*	**34%**

ABC was reassured that *Voyage* pulled in a 30-plus share, and picked the series up for the remainder of the season.

9.9

"Rescue" (Episode 93)

(Prod. No. 1310; first aired Sunday, November 19, 1967)
Written by William Welch
Directed by Justus Addiss
Produced by Irwin Allen and Bruce Fowler, Jr.; Story Editor: Sidney Marshall
Guest Star Don Dubbins

From the *Voyage* show files (Irwin Allen papers collection):

> While on a mission to locate a mysterious submarine that has been attacking shipping in the area, Admiral Nelson sends Captain Crane out in the flying submarine to search for a possible underwater submarine base. Crane has just located the base when he is attacked and the flying sub is sent reeling to the bottom. Before the spy aboard the Seaview is identified, both the Admiral and the Captain are brought to the brink of death, and it is only the grim determination of Chief Sharkey and Admiral Nelson that saves the Seaview from a tragic fate. [1]

Assessment:

By this point in the series, the overworked William Welch seemed on cruise control. There's hardly anything here we hadn't seen before. And some things – courtesy of stock footage – we'd seen many times before. An unidentified enemy sub attacking Seaview – *check*; an underwater base needing to be located and taken out – *check*; a spy onboard Seaview – *check*; the Flying Sub knocked to the bottom of the sea – *check*; Captain Crane, in the FS1, running low on oxygen – *check*; a sabotage of the Circuitry Room sending Seaview to the bottom – *check*. With all these recycled concepts, writer Welch *still* couldn't flesh out the story enough for a 51-minute running time. So, he padded. And repeated.

The traitorous C.P.O. Beach (played by Don Dubbins) needed fleshing out, and the script needed tightening. Despite all that doesn't work, "Rescue" offers a much-needed change of pace.

- Crane, on the sunken Flying Sub, is about to give Nelson the coordinates for the enemy submarine den … but, before he can, he passes out. Later, Crane, still on the sunken Flying Sub, is again about to give Nelson the coordinates for the enemy submarine den … but, once more, he passes out.
- C.P.O. Beach – the spy – is told to outfit two divers with scuba tanks containing a special mix of oxygen and helium, to allow the divers to breathe at deeper depths. Morton sends Kowalski to make sure Beach selects the right tanks. But Beach has a confederate switch tanks. Kowalski unwittingly watches Beach provide the wrong tanks. Then Kowalski leaves, satisfied. You may be wondering what the point to all of that was. So did we.
- More padding comes when Admiral Nelson is trapped in the escape hatch, which is filling with water. And, boy, does it take a long time to fill. Poor

Richard Basehart, treading water, was no doubt embarrassed by the sequence. We feel his anguish.

Mark Phillips said, "Richard Basehart tried different ways to liven up his character and here he makes Admiral Nelson incredibly annoyed and grumpy for most of the episode. Even an exasperated Morton rolls his eyes after being chewed out by the Admiral. An exciting story beset by the usual inconsistencies (why is the missile room left unmanned when everyone knows a saboteur is loose aboard ship?)." [2]

This was the first episode broadcast that used Phil Norman's new graphics in the opening credits – the sonar circle freeze-frame. It's a gripping main-title sequence. Sadly, there was very little the effect could do to add excitement to the close of the Teaser for this episode. Torpedoes are fired at the Seaview; it's a near miss; the Seaview is rocking and rolling; Control Room personal are flailing about; FREEZE – Boing, boing, boing into main titles. Future episodes would use the effect to better results.

Script:

William Welch's writers contract: August 11, 1967.
Welch's treatment, and 1ˢᵗ- and 2ⁿᵈ-draft teleplays approved by Irwin Allen on August 17.
Shooting Final teleplay (pale green paper): August 18.
Page revisions (blue paper): August 28.
Page revisions (pink paper): August 28.

This was **William Welch**'s twenty-sixth out of 34 scripts for the series. It was another paint-by-numbers piece. The majority of the recycled shots come from Season Three's "The Lost Bomb." They wouldn't even change the name on the sub – the "Vulcan."

Production:

(Filmed August 21 – 25, 1967; 5 days)
(Additional scenes filmed September 14, 1967)
(Pick up shots taken on October 3, 1967)

"Rescue," Production Number 1310, was planned as the tenth episode to film for Season Four. It advanced forward on the schedule when the script for "Terror" required more rewriting, therefore delaying its filming.

Justus Addiss returned to direct – his twelfth of sixteen.

Don Dubbins was paid $1,250 to play C.P.O. Beach. He was a boyish-looking 39, and worked often in both movies and television. Dubbins was cast in prominent roles in a pair of James Cagney films from 1956 – as Cagney's long-

Don Dubbins (above), as a U.S. astronaut enchanted by a beauty in suspended animation, on *The Twilight Zone*.

lost adopted son in the Western *These Wilder Years*, and as part of a love triangle with Cagney and Irene Papas, in the Western, *Tribute to a Bad Man*. Jack Webb's Drill Instructor character was very punishing of Dubbins in 1957's *The D.I.*, and Webb brought the young actor back for five appearances on the 1960s version of *Dragnet 1967*, including as a Neo-Nazi saboteur in 1967's "The Big Explosion."

Production began Monday, August 21, for the first of five days on Stage 10 for this "bottle show" only requiring standing Seaview sets. But it would take more to complete it.

The episode came in short after the first assembly edit was timed and viewed. Added scenes were written, including sequences for the Flying Sub, now worked into the story, as well as additional scenes written for the Control Room, the corridors, and the Pressure Chamber, sets that were already featured in the original script and production. These new scenes were filmed on Stage 10 on Thursday, September 14, taking a full day of production.[3]

A set photographer covered a rehearsal in the Control Room.

Release / Reaction:
(Only ABC broadcast: 11/19/67)

Little had changed on the pop-culture scene – at least at the top of the various charts. The same movie, single, and record album were in the top positions as during the previous week. The same war news was in the papers and the nightly network-news broadcasts. Casualty reports from U.S. military sources told us that for every American soldier killed, at least five Viet Cong died. And yet the war continued. Family-hour television offered escape from all of that. Tonight's episode of *Voyage*, less so. No monsters for this outing – espionage and betrayal were the themes.

"TV Scout," in the *Madison Capital Times*, from Wisconsin, said:

> When *Voyage to the Bottom of the Sea* has nothing but monsters, you wish they would forget them once in a while. Tonight they have forgotten them, and you wish they hadn't. The Seaview is trying to locate some undersea submarine pens belonging to someone who is unfriendly. David Hedison, in the flying sub, locates them, but is injured as the sub sinks to the bottom and begins to run out of air. And all the efforts of the Seaview to rescue him are hampered by a saboteur aboard. [4]

A.C. Nielsen ratings report from November 19, 1967: [5]

	Peak Share:
ABC: *Voyage to the Bottom of the Sea*	31%
CBS: Lassie / Gentle Ben	**36%** / 31%
NBC: Walt Disney's Wonderful World of Color	**33%**

Voyage pulled in better than a 30-share. Regardless, this episode was passed over for a network repeat broadcast.

9.10

"Terror" (Episode 94)

(Prod. No. 1308; first aired Sunday, November 26, 1967)
Written by Sidney Ellis
Directed by Jerry Hopper
Produced by Irwin Allen and Bruce Fowler, Jr.; Story Editor: Sidney Marshall

From the *Voyage* show files (Irwin Allen papers collection):

> Answering a trouble call from a botanical scientist, Admiral Nelson and Chief Sharkey arrive on the island to find the scientist dying. With his last breath, the man warns them that an Alien Power is planning to take over the world, and they have only eight hours in which to prevent it. Nelson and Sharkey return to the Seaview, taking with them the only "Alien" they can locate – an innocent-looking orchid. Terror strikes when the orchid uses the radio active emanations from the reactor to enable it to multiply rapidly, and takes control of Nelson and most of the Seaview's crew. Not until Captain Crane challenges the Alien's power is the Admiral able to break free and rid his ship, and the world, of the deadly plant. [1]

Assessment:

"Terror" presented yet another story in which one of the series' leads was controlled by an alien, and suddenly turns violent. The uninspired, generic title didn't help. *Voyage* had presented "Terror on Dinosaur Island" in Season Two, and "Night of Terror" in Season Three; now, simply "Terror." A better title might have been "Shoot to Kill!", which is the order given by Admiral Nelson to Captain Crane. If Nelson is taken over again by the alien, Crane must order the crew to shoot him, and make sure he is dead. Crane, after much internal conflict, indeed gives the order. And writer Sidney Ellis uses this sequence to provide some backbone to "Terror" – giving the cast a chance to portray the sort of emotional strife that they were so adept in performing. The otherwise overused premise gets a surprisingly fresh and powerful interpretation.

Standout moments, besides Nelson's determination to save the crew, and Crane's agonizing decision to "Shoot to kill," is Nelson's use of the Flying Sub to attack the Seaview; and his reappearance on the sub, drenching wet and ready to take on the entire crew, with those cold, steely eyes.

Mark Phillips noted, "The plants in this episode are reminiscent of similar dangerous flora in the *Star Trek* episode 'This Side of Paradise' and even more so of those in the original *Outer Limits* episode 'Specimen Unknown.' The threat posed by the deceptively beautiful and seemingly harmless plants makes an interesting counterpoint to rampaging rock beasts." [2]

Just put all those other Nelson-or-Crane-possessed-by-aliens stories out of your mind if you can, and enjoy one of the better treatments of the theme.

Script:
Sidney Ellis's writers contract: March 28, 1967.
Ellis's story treatment: March 5.

Ellis's 1st-draft teleplay approved by Irwin Allen on July 3.
Ellis's 2nd (and final) draft teleplay approved by Allen on August 3.
Shooting Final teleplay (pale green paper): August 3.
Rev. Shooting Final teleplay (on blue paper): August 15.
Page revisions (on pink paper): August 22.
Page revisions (on green paper): August 23.
Page revisions (on yellow paper): August 25.
Page revisions (on gold paper): September 5.
Page revisions (on beige paper): September 6.

Writer **Sidney Ellis** was 48 and a late arrival to *Voyage*, turning in his first of two scripts, of which only "Terror" would be produced. Ellis had a handful of credits as a writer for television (one script each for *Hong Kong* and *Death Valley Days*, and two for *Bonanza*). He was also given a "story by" credit for one episode each of *The Fugitive*, *Combat!*, and *The Outer Limits*. It was a thin resumé for nearly 10 years in the industry. However, by this point in 1967, Irwin Allen was gaining a bad reputation as the maker of series that were not prestigious from a writing standpoint, and therefore were not likely to advance a freelance writer's career. This is why William Welch was writing half the scripts for *Voyage*'s fourth season. Few others may have wanted the job, but Sidney Ellis gave it two shots.

Ellis's treatment began:

> A remote, Pacific island. Nelson, Sharkey and Patterson are seen hacking their way through the jungle, tracking down the source of some mysterious UHF radio signals with the help of a portable RDF. Washington, which has been monitoring the signal ever since they began after a meteorite shower in the area some weeks before, suspects they are Alien in nature and have sent Nelson to investigate.
>
> Following the indicator of the RDF, they come to a clearing. To their intense surprise, it is not a mechanical device that is transmitting the signals, but a flower, a rare and exotic orchid. Even more strange is the fact that Nelson is unable to identify the plant as one native to Earth. Cautious as always when dealing with the unknown, Nelson orders the others to stay clear of the plant, contacts Crane aboard the Seaview by radio to report their find and to request some special equipment to enable them to handle the strange plant safely. Crane replies with disturbing news. Washington has monitored what it takes to be the answers to the original

signals from far out in space and are now concerned that the Earth-based transmitter is guiding an Alien fleet toward this planet. Since appeals for identification and intent broadcast by Washington over the same frequency have been ignored, they must assume the Aliens are hostile. In the interest of security, therefore, they have ordered the transmitter silenced.

While this exchange is taking place, the orchid appears to be watching and listening. It scans all three men, fixes on Nelson, appears to take dead aim at the back of his neck. The corolla constricts, fires a tiny, almost invisible energy-bolt. Nelson reacts as if he'd been bitten by a mosquito, and, commenting wryly on the problem of turning off an orchid, breaks contact with Seaview. Patterson, who is monitoring the RDF, suddenly reports that the orchid has gone dead and that the signals are now emanating from somewhere else close-by. As he tries to get a fix, Nelson snatches the instrument from him, observing caustically that the RDF is obviously out of whack. Patterson protests; offers to prove the device is working properly. When he reaches to take it from Nelson, the Admiral explodes with anger and knocks him brutally to the ground; threatens to kill him if he ever tries to correct him again; then, turning, he swings the RDF viciously against the tree, smashing it and the orchid; harshly orders his two startled crewmen to follow him back to the ship. [3]

So ended the Teaser.

Ellis said, "It was basically a monster show. The trick in winning a writing assignment was to come up with a monster that hadn't been used before. The series was essentially a comic strip. The cast was better than the notes they were given to play, the production values were consistently high, and the special FX, by TV standards, were frequently spectacular. It [just] wasn't a writers' show. Action rather than drama; caricature rather than character; ingenuity rather than creativity; craft rather than art. These were the ingredients demanded of *Voyage*'s writers. This isn't to denigrate the talent and skill of the writers. They possessed both in abundance. They had to, to make the show work." [4]

After reading Ellis's treatment, Producer Bruce Fowler told Story Editor Sidney Marshall:

> I think that there is a good possibility here for a segment of "VOYAGE". I am a bit fretful about a story in which a member of our crew, in this case Nelson, is taken over again by an alien. This story has good potential however.
>
> Several of the present plot developments could stand a re-examination such as: the constant use of a cliff hanger where someone is certainly destroyed, only to find at the start of the next scene that he turns up with a glib line of explanation accounting for his survival. This happens too often in this story.
>
> I think the author throws away a good plot device he uses in the teaser, too quickly. That is – the use of a plant as the source of the radio transmission and the abode of the alien. I might suggest that he consider the possibility of using this ploy thru the first act and then have the takeover come aboard the Seaview. This appeals to me because it is unusual, different and a truly alien threat. That they, our crew, would bring this aboard thinking it poses no threat at all – then to find it for what it is – has an attraction for me.
>
> If this or a similar ploy were used, then perhaps it would still my apprehension in using this type of story. I feel that the physical presence of a threat must be there to bring it home to our audience.
>
> Then Nelson – as Nelson – does nothing. His role is too passive for our lead character. Shouldn't he be always engaged in fighting this possession and isn't he the one that should turn the tables on the alien at the end of the story? The Present end – as you put it – gets off track. It even gets off the whole railroad.
>
> The third act and Tag are the ones that require the most work. A more novel approach to the solution of the problem is required. [5]

Most of Fowler's ideas were incorporated into the script.

Sidney Ellis said, "Writing for *Voyage* wasn't easy. The stories presented no problems, but every movement of every character and every special effect had to be minutely described. Nothing was left to the imagination or to the director's choice. It was to help the production crew schedule and budget the episode more accurately, but I didn't get any artistic satisfaction from virtually directing the show in my script. In fact, I rather resented having to do the director's work for none of his pay!"

Ellis wrote a second *Voyage* script during the series' Fourth Season, called "The Diamond Man." It was held back for the fifth season, which was never to be. Of Irwin Allen, Ellis said, "Fortunately, I never had to work directly with him. I say 'fortunately' because everybody who did was terrified of the man." [6]

Production:
(Filmed August 28 through September 6, 1967; 7 days)
(Added scenes filmed on October 3, 1967)

"Terror" carries Production Number 1308. It was planned to be the eighth episode filmed for Season Four but, to allow more time for script revisions, was pushed back twice in the production sequencing, with "Fatal Cargo" (#1309) and "Rescue (#1310) pulled forward.

The budget was set at $163, 205 (only a couple of hundred dollars under the studio's target per-episode price of $163,364).

Helping matters was that the guest star was a fake plant. Not as helpful was the need for costly animated effects throughout the episode. And numerous highly charged fight sequences.

Production began on Monday, August 28, 1967, on Stage B, for "Ext. Beach and Jungle." They filmed the entire Teaser and the first scenes making up the start of Act I. Worth noting is **Patrick Culliton**, playing Dunlap, the doomed member of the three-man landing party. He gives one hell of a performance as he is possessed, stricken with severe head pain, then tries to kill Nelson and Sharkey … before collapsing to the ground and dying. It was just a tease for what we would get from Richard Basehart a short time later. (Culliton appeared in 12 episodes of *Voyage*, usually as crew members, as well as four turns on *The Time Tunnel* and two on *Land of the Giants*.)

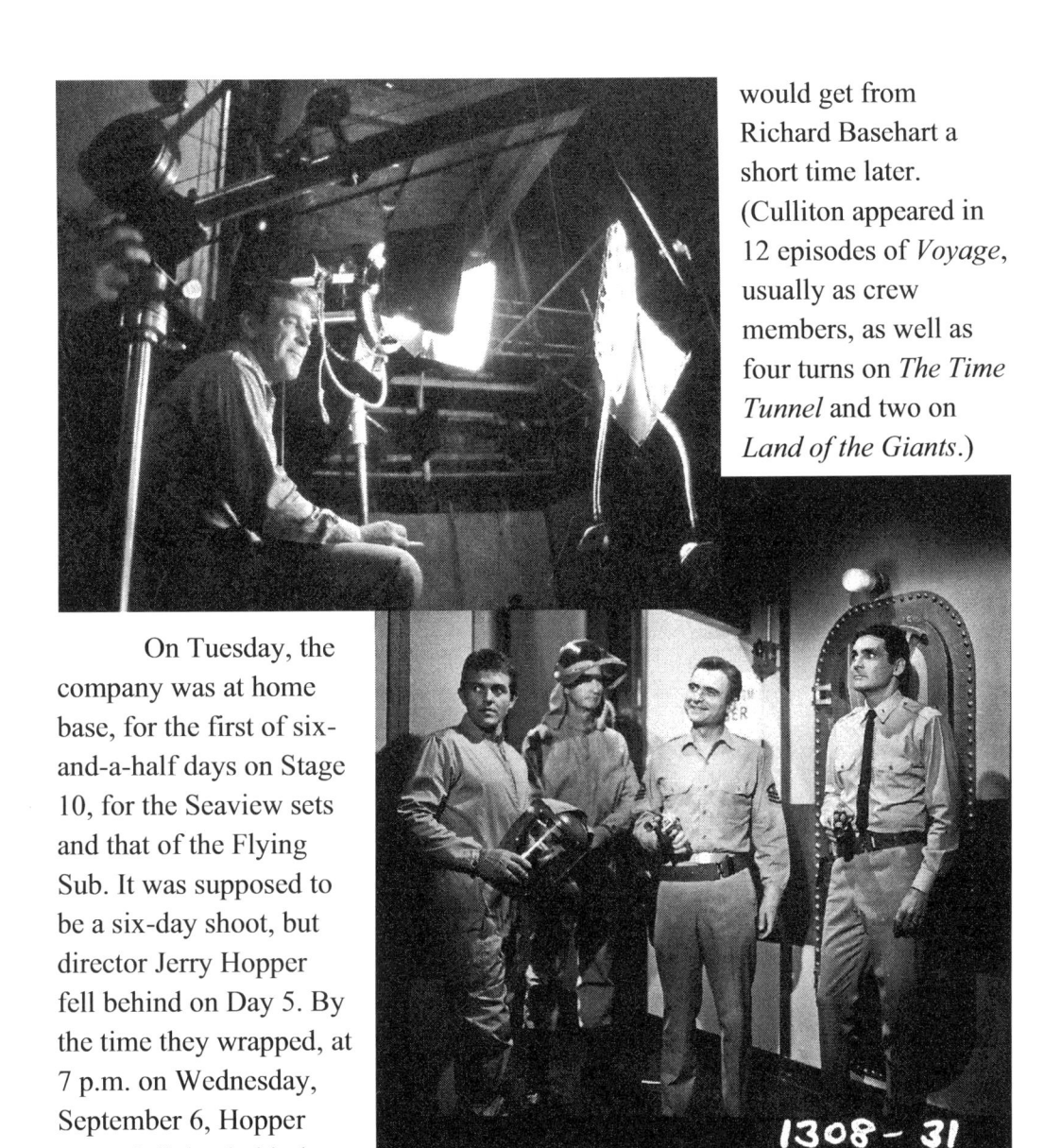

On Tuesday, the company was at home base, for the first of six-and-a-half days on Stage 10, for the Seaview sets and that of the Flying Sub. It was supposed to be a six-day shoot, but director Jerry Hopper fell behind on Day 5. By the time they wrapped, at 7 p.m. on Wednesday, September 6, Hopper was a full day behind. And then the episode timed out short. An additional half day of filming was needed, on Tuesday, October 3, from 9 a.m. to 1:05 p.m. [7]

Release / Reaction:
(ABC premiere airdate: 11/26/67; network repeat broadcast: 6/30/68)

This was the week that Julie Nixon and David Eisenhower announced their engagement. *The Jungle Book* was the top movie across America; the best-selling album in record stores was *Pisces, Aquarius, Capricorn & Jones Ltd.*, by the Monkees; the top song on the radio was "Incense and Peppermint," by

Strawberry Alarm Clock; the cast of *Garrison's Gorillas* had the cover of *TV Guide*; and this week's monster on *Voyage* was an orchid.

"TV Scout," in the *Kenosha News* of Kenosha, Wisconsin, said:

> The Alien-Who-Is-Trying-To-Take-Over-The-Earth-Of-The-Week on *Voyage to the Bottom of the Sea* is a lush orchid. A creature inhabits the exotic plant and pings men in the forehead, and they get vicious and then, sometimes, die. After the plant is brought aboard the Seaview, Richard Basehart gets pinged and in a rational moment he tells David Hedison to kill him. But it's not easy to get rid of either Basehart or the alien force. [8]

A.C. Nielsen ratings report from November 26, 1967: [9]

	Peak Share:
ABC: *Voyage to the Bottom of the Sea*	28%
CBS: *Lassie / Gentle Ben*	**40% / 35%**
NBC: *Walt Disney's Wonderful World of Color*	33%

A Navy family gets a tour of the Seaview and a photo op with Terry Becker and David Hedison during production of "Terror."

9.11

"Blow Up" (Episode 95)

(Prod. No. 1313; first aired Sunday, December 10, 1967)
Written by William Welch
Directed by Justus Addiss
Produced by Irwin Allen and Bruce Fowler, Jr.; Story Editor: Sidney Marshall

From the *Voyage* show files (Irwin Allen Papers Collection):

The Seaview is given secret orders to follow the 11th Fleet during their special maneuvers, in order that the new detection equipment aboard the ships may be thoroughly tested. When a broken fuel line threatens to delay the submarine, Admiral Nelson goes into the small compartment to make the necessary repairs, and is overcome by the fumes. An untested emergency breathing apparatus gives him enough strength to climb out, but is also starts the Seaview on a journey of horror that climaxes in a desperate struggle between Captain Crane and the Admiral, when Nelson prepares to sink the Fleet Admiral's ship. Not until the world has rocked on the edge of disaster is Nelson overcome and given the treatment that removes the noxious gas from his system. [1]

Assessment:

"Blow Up" isn't the first time we've seen Admiral Nelson inflicted with paranoia. It was handled nicely in Season One's "Mutiny." And, since the good Admiral has been either brainwashed or possessed in numerous other episodes, you may wonder how he's able to keep his cool in between.

Still, we like "Blow Up." Richard Basehart's performance is excellent. Further, the anguish projected by the other cast members, David Hedison and Robert Dowdell in particular, is most effective. The conflicts are supercharged, and the handling of these emotional moments have been injected with a sense of realism not always present in the series. Especially intense are the scenes in which Nelson berates Morton in the Control Room; when the Admiral sternly dresses down Chief Sharkey; orders Kowalski to drink steaming-hot coffee; and demands that Crane arrest the Doctor. The interplay between the cast members is superb throughout.

"Blow Up" is compelling drama, and a *tour de force* for the acting talents of very nearly all involved.

Script:

William Welch's writers contract: August 23, 1967.
Welch's 1st- and 2nd-draft teleplays approved by Irwin Allen: August 28, 1967.
Welch's final draft, Shooting Final (pale green paper): August 28, 1967.
Sidney Marshall's page revisions (blue insert pages): September 5, 1967.
Marshall's further page revisions (pink insert pages): September 11, 1967.

William Welch had handled the script polishing for Season One's "Mutiny." Turning out 13 scripts in a single season was taking its toll … especially with all the work he had done for *Voyage* before. Now, Welch, like a true TV hack, was recycling again, including borrowing from "Mutiny" and half a dozen other episodes where Nelson was not quite himself. But this one seemed to jell. The lack of memos regarding the writing of this script, and the only minor script polishing from Sidney Marshall, may indicate the quality present on the written page. Regardless, there was barely a scrap of communication over this teleplay in the show files. The finished product speaks well for itself.

Production:

(Filmed September 7 – 14, 1967; 5 days)

"Blow Up," Production Number 1313, was planned to be the thirteenth episode filmed for Season Four. The two that were supposed to shoot before it, "The Death Clock" (Prod. No. 1311) and "Secret of the Deep" (#1312) were delayed. "Blow Up" therefore advanced two positions on the production roster.

Justus Addis was rushed into the director's chair, without even a final script to break down in pre-production. "Blow Up" wasn't even supposed to be the episode filming during the second week of September 1967. Regardless, his work is measured, confident, and effective.

No guest players were needed. This story was all about the regulars, and the way the cast members play off one another is striking. You can't accuse any of them of going by the numbers. The intensity of their interactions, and their sincerity, is commendable.

Production began on Thursday, September 7, 1967, for the first of five full days on Stage 10, and the standing Seaview sets, for this bottle show. It took an additional hour's work on the morning of Thursday, September 14, to finish the episode, resulting in a fraction of a sixth day of filming. [2]

One thing that slowed down work was a visit to the set of a special V.I.P. – Milton Berle. Promotional pictures were needed by ABC for David Hedison's appearance on *The Hollywood Palace*, with Berle.

Cynthia Lowry, reviewing the "event" for the Associated Press, said:

David Hedison, an actor who neither sings nor dances but does have a television series on ABC, was a guest on Tuesday night's *Hollywood Palace*, also on ABC. So what did he do? He was in a little sketch which satirized his program, *Voyage to the Bottom of the Sea*. Television usually runs into its stormiest weather when it attempts satire, but always seems to find television – from entertainment programs to commercials – its best and easiest target. But by now it has become almost a ritual to use TV stars to kid their own product. It was, as a matter of fact, about time somebody poked a little fun at *Voyage to the*

Visitor Milton Berle is greeted by a starstruck Irwin Allen.

Berle camps it up with David Hedison.

620

Bottom of the Sea and its monster-of-the-week. *Hollywood Palace*'s monster, Rock Man, was not really more ridiculous than some presented seriously in the adventure series. [3]

Regarding his appearance on *Hollywood Palace* and other such appearances, Hedison said, "They sent me out every fall to promote the show while we were on the air. I went to the ABC affiliates in the various cities – places like New York and Miami; Richmond, Virginia; Atlanta; Memphis; Indianapolis; and Columbus, Ohio. I went on the *Merv Griffin Show* once and did a *Hollywood Palace* show with Milton Berle. I basically went wherever the studio picked for me to go. I remember one time they scheduled a hospital visit for me after a very long day of other places I had to be. Those sick little kids waited all day just to see Captain Crane. And when I did finally get there, they lit up and were so happy to meet me. If I doubted that my character was not reaching the viewers, I never did after that visit." [4]

Release / Reaction:
(ABC premiere airdate: 12/10/67; network repeat broadcast: 7/14/68)

This was the week when Jim Morrison, lead singer for the Doors, was arrested onstage during a concert for "disturbing the peace." It wouldn't be the only time. Soul singer Otis Redding died in a plane crash. His song "(Sittin' on) the Dock of the Bay" had been released just weeks earlier and was climbing the pop-music charts. Also killed in the crash were four members of the group the Bar-Kays (Carl Cunningham, Jimmie King, Phalon Jones, and Ronnie Caldwell). They had a Top 5 hit in early 1967 with the instrumental "Soul Finger." Other air and space news: The supersonic airliner prototype, Concorde, was first shown in France, and the U.S. put Pioneer 8 into orbit around the Earth. Science was on the move – this was the week that DNA was first created in a test tube. The top two movies in America were *The Jungle Book* and *Hells Angels on Wheels*. The Monkees' "Daydream Believer" was the top song on the radio, and the group also had the No. 1 album, with *Pisces, Aquarius, Capricorn & Jones Ltd*. Kay Ballard and Eve Arden, of *The Mothers-in-Law*, had the cover of *TV Guide*. And *Voyage*, with a non-monster episode, was about to be pitted against the Peanuts cartoon special, *A Charlie Brown Christmas*.

"TV Scout" said:

> Last season it was David Hedison who lost his mind every week on *Voyage to the Bottom of the Sea*. This season it's

Richard Basehart's turn. Tonight, while trying to repair a malfunction aboard the Seaview, he uses a new Emergency Breathing Apparatus and turns into a paranoiac. Of course, the cause isn't known until final commercial time, but regulars can figure out that something is wrong with the dear old Admiral. Basehart gives a good performance, and that helps. [5]

A.C. Nielsen ratings report from December 10, 1967: [6]

	Peak Share:
ABC: *Voyage to the Bottom of the Sea*	24%
CBS: *Lassie* / *A Charlie Brown Christmas* special	**44% / 51%**
NBC: *Walt Disney's Wonderful World of Color*	29%

9.12

"Deadly Amphibians" (Episode 96)

(Prod. No. 1314; first aired Sunday, December 17, 1967)
Written by Arthur Weiss
Directed by Jerry Hopper
Produced by Irwin Allen and Bruce Fowler, Jr.; Story Editor: Sidney Marshall
Guest Star Don Matheson

From the *Voyage* show files (Irwin Allen Papers Collection):

An amphibious race of creatures from beneath the sea blast a passage through the ocean floor and attack the Seaview, sending her to the bottom. While Admiral Nelson takes stock of the damage and sets repair parties to work, Captain Crane takes off in the flying sub to locate and identify their attackers. The leader of the Amphibians boards the flying sub, and reveals to Crane his plan to use the Seaview's reactor to blast open the ocean floor in order that his people can come forth and take over the oceans of the world. It takes all the Admiral's skill as a scientist and courage as a man to devise a way in which he and Captain Crane can turn the tables on the deadly amphibians. [1]

Assessment:

"One of my favorites," Mark Phillips raved. "It gallops along with new undersea footage, wild costumes (phony looking but so outlandish that they're actually fascinating) and Don Matheson, later star of *Land of the Giants*, has the perfect voice for an arrogant amphibian." [2]

"Okay, I admit it," Mike Bailey confessed, "'The Deadly Amphibians' is kind of fun to watch." [3]

We agree. Does anything else really need to be said about an episode called "Deadly Amphibians"? Watch it and have a blast. But you may not want to admit it.

Script:

Arthur Weiss's writers contract: May 23, 1967.
Weiss's story treatment approved by Irwin Allen on July 5.
Weiss's 1st-draft teleplay approved by Allen on July 14.
Weiss's 2nd (and final) draft teleplay approved by Allen on July 26.
Shooting Final teleplay (on pale green paper): September 6.
Rev. shooting Final teleplay (on blue paper): September 13.
Page revisions (on pink paper): September 14.
Page revisions (on gold paper): September 20.

This was **Arthur Weiss**'s third of four scripts for *Voyage*. We liked "Fires of Death," in which Victor Jory gets really, really old. We almost liked "Journey with Fear" (you know, the one in which Chip Morton gets to be an astronaut, and is abducted to Venus where he is blinded). And now this – just for the fun of it. Weiss's scripts might be becoming sillier, but still worth a peek.

Production:

"Deadly Amphibians," Production No. 1314, was originally slotted as the fourteenth episode to film for Season Four. With "The Death Clock" (Prod. No. 1311) and "Secret of the Deep" (#1312) delayed on the production roster, "Deadly Amphibians" was pulled forward, becoming the twelfth to film.

It was **Jerry Hopper**'s turn again during a season that seemed to rotate him with Justus Addiss and Harry Harris. It had become a monster factory with little or no artistic direction. Terry Becker told interviewer William E. Anchors, Jr., "I have to say that I didn't really admire any of the directors simply because they came in and they left. No one changed anything. They were all nice guys, and they came in and did their job – 'Action' and 'Cut' – and in-between we did our thing." [4]

The budget was set at $158,693 (well under the per-episode average of $163,205)

Don Matheson was paid $1,500 for up to seven days' work, playing the amphibian leader. He was 38 and had already appeared twice on *Lost in Space* (as an alien colonist in "The Sky Is Falling" and as a super android in "Revolt of the Androids"). Irwin Allen had also cast Matheson in the pilot film for *Land of the Giants*. Production on the series was about to begin as this episode of *Voyage* was shooting.

Françoise Ruggieri and Don Matheson in a 1965 episode of *Lost in Space*.

Filming began on Friday, September 15, 1967, for the first of five days on Stage 10 for another bottle show. Only the standing Seaview sets were needed (Control Room, Lab, Missile Room, sections of corridor), as well as the Flying Sub.

Jerry Hopper finished on schedule, but the episode came in short.

On Wednesday, October 18, new scenes were filmed in the Brig, the Sickbay, the Pressure Hatch Room, as well as sections of corridor. The episode *still* timed out short.

Frank La Tourette wrote in the "Hot Sheet" newsletter on October 19:

625

Jerry Hopper got 8:44 minutes yesterday in shooting additional scenes for "Deadly Amphibians." Since the show is 950 feet short, this leaves approximately 3:16 minutes as the minimum to be shot in the green tank on Wednesday, October 25th. [5]

This was actually pushed back by a day, and would take two days with the second-unit team instead of one, in order to come up with the needed minutes of film. Stunt divers Peter Peterson, George Robotham, Norm Bishop, John Lamb, as well as actor Frank Orsatti, worked in the Green Tank on October 26 and 27. [6]

Release / Reaction:
(ABC premiere airdate: 12/17/67; network repeat broadcast: 5/20/68)

During the week "Deadly Amphibians" first aired on ABC-TV, the U.S. reported that 474,300 American soldiers were now deployed in South Vietnam. *Guess Who's Coming to Dinner?*, starring Sidney Poitier, Spencer Tracy, and Katharine Hepburn, was the top-grossing film in movie houses. The Monkees still had the best-selling album in America, with *Pisces, Aquarius, Capricorn & Jones Ltd.*, and the most-played song on radio stations, with "Daydream Believer." Sebastian Cabot, of *Family Affair*, had the cover of *TV Guide*.

Syndicated "TV Scout" said:

> Explosions keep *Voyage to the Bottom of the Sea* full of sound and fury, but, unfortunately, they don't drown out the dialogue. It seems there is not one word in this script that hasn't already been said several times before in the series' long run. The monster of the week is from a race of half-men, half-fish amphibians who want the Seaview's power to drill a hole in the center of the Earth and free more of their kind. Or something like that. [7]

A.C. Nielsen ratings report from December 17, 1967: [8]

	Peak Share:
ABC: *Voyage to the Bottom of the Sea*	23%
CBS: *How the Grinch Stole Christmas* special	**47%**
/ *Gentle Ben*	36%
NBC: *Walt Disney's Wonderful World of Color*	34%

9.13

"The Return of Blackbeard" (Episode 97)

(Prod. No. 1316; first aired Sunday, December 31, 1967)
Written by Al Gail
Directed by Justus Addiss
Produced by Irwin Allen and Bruce Fowler, Jr.
Story Editor: Sidney Marshall
Guest Star Malachi Throne

Blackbeard brings the proverbial sword to the gunfight.

From the *Voyage* show files (Irwin Allen papers collection):

While on a mission to protect a yacht carrying visiting Royalty, the Seaview crew is staggered by the mysterious appearance of "Blackbeard," the notorious pirate of the 18th Century. But the visitation is just the start of a terrifying voyage in which past and present are intermingled, and only Admiral Nelson's quick-witted use of some of the ultra-sophisticated controls aboard the Seaview prevents the Pirate from sinking the Royal yacht and plunging the world into war.[1]

Assessment:

Even diehard *Voyage* fans, like Mark Phillips, had little to say of this episode. Phillips merely commented, "Malachi Throne was fun as Blackbeard but this serio-comical episode runs out of steam and budget by half-time." [2]

Our second resident guest critic, Mike Bailey, added, "There are some fine shots of Seaview under torpedo fire in this episode. Throne is great. Goofy, but fun." [3]

What helps this episode stand out – it was as close as *Voyage* came to doing a comedy. The ever-delightful Malachi Thone, and the obvious pleasure shown by the cast in playing their roles a bit less grim, add to the minor enjoyment. But, despite this walk on the light side, the overly simplistic story, redundant plotting, and general pointlessness on any thematic level keeps this offering a bit under the run-of-the-mill level. And, with the shenanigans running low on steam by the second half, the not-so-big climax can't come soon enough.

Script:

Al Gail's story treatment: August 29, 1967.
Gail's 1st-draft teleplay: September 7.
Gail's 2nd (and final) draft teleplay: September 8.
Shooting Final teleplay (on pale green paper): September 14.
Page revisions (on blue paper): September 19.
Page revisions (on pink paper): September 20.
Page revisions (on dark green paper): September 21.
Page revisions (on yellow paper): September 29.

This story for this episode was hatched at Irwin Allen Productions in the late summer of 1967 – while a screen adaption of a 1965 juvenile novel by Ben Stahl, *Blackbeard's Ghost*, was before the cameras at Disney Studios, starring Dean Jones, Suzanne Pleshette, and, as the buccaneer, Peter Ustinov. It would be in movie houses for Spring 1968. Irwin Allen decided to exploit the pre-release promotion for the film by beating Disney out with his own treatment of the subject. And this meant Al Gail needed to write fast.

"My single greatest recollection is the hysteria that surrounded our efforts to meet omnivorous script deadlines," Al Gail said. "We never missed a deadline, even if it meant Bill Welch, Sid Marshall and I had to rewrite into the dawn hours." [4]

Al Gail's treatment began:

> The Seaview – on a round-the-clock red alert – is patrolling the southwest coast of the United States on one of the most vital assignments of its career.
>
> On the surface – and the skies above – armed-to-the-teeth units of the Navy and Air Force criss-cross the area. The President of the United States has warned all unauthorized shipping to stay clear ... or be blasted out of the water.
>
> The necessity for the RED ALERT becomes evident when we learn that an oceanographic ship is approaching Washington bearing on its deck a space ship from another galaxy ... and within the space ship are emissaries who will meet with most of the world's Chiefs of State.
>
> To protect its emissaries, galactic patrol ships circle our planet in outer space, ready to blast the Earth at the first sign of treachery.
>
> In the Seaview's Control Room there is alert, professional tension as Admiral Nelson and Captain Crane check the electronic eyes and ears of the great sub. Sonar – hydrophones – AMRAC – profile scanner are all clicking away, their red-and-green lights attesting to its untroubled probing at the bottom of the sea.
>
> Sonar calls out. The instrument is emitting sharp, nervous beeps. The sounds are weird – unidentifiable. The hydrophone operator snatches the phones from his ears as a screeching cacophony of sound assaults his eardrums. The AMRAC board goes berserk. The sub-terrestrial scanner

indicates the emanations are coming from an indistinct mass, possibly a weapon bunker.

After a quick conference, Nelson and Crane agree that because of the impending arrival of the oceanographic ship, the only course of action is to retaliate immediately ... to shoot first and ask questions later.

Crane orders Chief Sharkey, in the Missile Room, to prepare to fire a torpedo at the submerged target. The Crewmen move into action. In seconds, the missile is loaded ... and on order ... fired. We see the torpedo cutting through the water. On the sail camera, the men in the Control Room track its course. Suddenly – the shock! The torpedo alters course, swings around as if steered by some unseen hand, and starts to speed back toward the Seaview.

Captain Crane leaps into action, issuing a rapid-fire stream of orders. The Seaview responds nobly, twisting and turning, but the live torpedo hangs grimly on its tail. A violent maneuver causes the missile to miss, but it swings around like it has an intelligence of its own and continues its relentless pursuit. In desperation, Crane swings the Seaview around again, faces the teeth of the powerful missile and blasts it with a laser beam from the observation nose.

A tremendous blast rocks the Seaview. As the lights go to RED, the instruments explode with brilliant flashes – smoke and fire obscure the scene. As the men reel and tumble, Nelson smashes into a bulkhead, falls unconscious. In the midst of the wild confusion, suddenly we hear a musical chord – everyone is frozen in place – and there – standing on the periscope island is a tall, powerful man, his fierce expression heightened by a long, black beard plaited into many black tails. In his hand is a cutlass. His dress is typical of a swashbuckling pirate captain of the early 18th Century. [5]

On that note, Gail ended his Teaser. A dynamite opener like this makes it easy to understand why Irwin Allen always liked to have Cousin Al at his side.
Mary Garbutt of ABC's Department of Standards and Practices wrote:

Pgs 1-8: Please establish future date.

Pg 10, Sc 44: Caution that Nelson's statement about "runaway torpedoes" and World War II is accurate.

Pg 12, 34, 44, 55, 56: Your usual care in seeing that these fights are not unnecessarily brutal or prolonged.

Pg 57: Just a caution that there is no confusion that those are "short range" missiles (otherwise, "Fail Safe"?) [6]

Production:
(Filmed September 22 through October 2, 1967; 7 days)

In order to get "The Return of Blackbeard" (#1316) before the cameras quickly, the two scripts already assigned production numbers, then pushed back in the schedule – "The Death Clock" (#1311) and "Secret of the Deep" (#1312) – were now joined by a third, "The Abominable Snowman" (#1315). "Blackbeard" would film first, as the thirteenth episode produced for Season Four.

Justus Addiss, now a veteran *Voyage* director on his fourteenth cruise, was given a budget of $159,213 (well under the per-episode studio mandate of $163,205).

This was an atypical episode, with a playful antagonist, so it required a score which couldn't be provided entirely from library tracks. **Joseph Mullendore** was therefore engaged to lighten up the music. He had already provided one score for *The Time Tunnel* and was in the process of scoring three episodes of *Lost in Space*. Prior to meeting Irwin Allen, Mullendore had won an Emmy in 1963 for an episode of *The Dick Powell Show*. He had worked often, scoring episodes of *Zane Grey Theater*, *Burke's Law*, and *Honey West*, among other series. He'd also written the score for "The Conscious of the King," a 1966 episode of *Star Trek*. "The Return of Blackbeard" was Mullendore's only assignment for *Voyage*, although Irwin Allen would bring him back to score four episodes of *Land of the Giants*.

Malachi Throne was paid $1,850 to steal the show. This was his third turn on *Voyage*, following a pair of First Season episodes. Throne was a hot guest star on TV at this time, having already been featured on many top series. This included many sci-fi/fantasy genre shows such as *Star Trek*; *Batman*; *The Wild, Wild West*; *The Man from U.N.C.L.E.*; and, closer to home base with Irwin Allen, *The Time Tunnel* and *Lost in Space*, with a *Land of the Giants* on the horizon.

Throne told this author, "I probably had too much fun with that one. I had chewed up the scenery right before that as the 'Thief from Outer Space' [on *Lost in Space*] and was invited to do more of the same. One should always be careful when giving an actor too free of a rein when he's in pirate garb and wielding a cutlass. I really loved doing those shows." [7]

Throne was just weeks away from beginning production on the first season of *It Takes a Thief*, playing his best-known role, Noah Bain.

Robert Wagner and Malachi Throne in *It Takes a Thief* (1968-69).

Production began on Friday, September 22, 1967, for the first of seven days on Stage 10. It was supposed to take six, but director Addiss fell behind on his fourth day of filming and didn't finish until 6:52 p.m. on Monday, October 2. So much for that hoped-for lower-than-average budget. [8]

Frank La Tourette wrote in the Irwin Allen "Hot Sheet" production newsletter:

> [A] report from the Associate Producer [Bruce Fowler] predicts that "The Return of Blackbeard," which finished last night, will be an excellent show. [9]

We'll call it pretty fair.

Release / Reaction:

(ABC premiere airdate: 12/31/67; network repeat broadcast: 6/23/68)

"The Return of Blackbeard" first aired on New Year's Eve, 1967. The infamous "Ice Bowl" was played on this day, when the Green Bay Packers faced off against the Dallas Cowboys for the NFL championship in Green Bay, Wisconsin, with brutal temperatures that dropped as low as minus 13 degrees. Green Bay won, 21-17. The top-grossing movie was *The Graduate*, starring Dustin Hoffman. "Hello, Goodbye," by the Beatles, was getting the most airplay on the radio. The group also had the top-selling album in America, with *Magical Mystery Tour*. Carol Burnett had the cover of *TV Guide*. And Malachi Throne was chewing up the scenery on *Voyage*.

"TV Scout" said:

Malachi Throne has great fun with the avast-ye-land-lubbers role of Blackbeard the Pirate on *Voyage to the Bottom of the Sea*. The script concerns a meeting between a powerful Shah, who has a priceless gold throne on his ship, and the president of the U.S.! Blackbeard wants the throne, and he plans to use the Seaview and its crew to get it. Yes, he does say to Richard Basehart that he "likes the cut of your jib," and yes, David Hedison gets to walk the plank, undersea style. [10]

According to *Variety*'s January 31, 1968 issue, *Voyage* had slipped in the ratings and was again below a 30% audience share (the number typically needed to ensure renewal). Combining all the ratings reports from the start of October through the end of December, the series was averaging a 28% share.

A.C. Nielsen ratings report from December 31, 1967: [11]

	Peak Share:
ABC: *Voyage to the Bottom of the Sea*	23%
CBS: *Lassie* / *Gentle Ben*	**36% / 39%**
NBC: AFL championship Football Game	32%

9.14

"A Time to Die" (Episode 98)

(Prod. No. 1317; first aired Sunday, December 3, 1967)
Written by William Welch
Directed by Robert Sparr
Produced by Irwin Allen and Bruce Fowler, Jr.
Story Editor: Sidney Marshall
Guest Star Henry Jones

From the *Voyage* show files (Irwin Allen papers collection):

Admiral Nelson and Captain Crane are bewildered by some extraordinary happenings aboard the Seaview, until a photograph of the sky convinces them that the giant craft is lost in time. Suddenly, Nelson himself is whirled through time into his own office at the Institute, where Mr. Pem wants the Admiral to help him control the world, and it takes all the ingenuity of the fast-thinking Admiral to outwit the intruder and return his men and his ship to normal. [1]

Assessment:

"A Time to Die" is a marked improvement over many episodes from Seasons Three and Four, partly because it's a bit different. There are no aliens, no monsters, and no mind possessions. This episode is far more original, involving time warps, visions from the past, and a disorienting tumble into that previous time. The techniques used in having Nelson unknowingly step through the portal, taking him from the Seaview to his office at the Nelson Institute, as well as him looking back through the doorway and witnessing past events – taken from "The Thing from Inner Space" – are cleverly handled.

Another reason for the success of "A Time to Die" has to do with the characterization of Mr. Pem. Credit the writing and direction, as well as the performance of Henry Jones, but we also enjoy a delightful chemistry between Jones and Richard Basehart.

William Welch was certainly capable of delivering good scripts, as evidenced by many of his past accomplishments. But Welch was also often a writer in a hurry, with sloppiness in many stories – in the plotting and characterizations. Sometimes important plot points and character elements were skimmed over or left out altogether. This happened here. There are many things concerning Pem – his motivations and his plan; his ability to manipulate time; and his naivety – which are undeveloped. The ending, like many of Welch's recent stories, feels rushed. Regardless, there is much in "A Time to Die" to appreciate.

Director Robert Sparr handles everything with assurance, and there are many subtleties in the performances and his overall direction which benefit the story. Mostly, it's a fresh and interesting premise.

Script:

William Welch's writers contract: September 19, 1967.
Welch's treatment, and 1st- and 2nd-draft teleplays approved by Irwin Allen on Sep. 26.
Shooting Final teleplay (on pale green paper): September 26.
Page revisions (on blue paper): September 28.
Page revisions (on pink paper): October 2.
Added scenes (on gold paper): October 26.

Lover of all things supernatural, **William Welch** sought to include his views on the Fifth Dimension in his script. He said, "The one great stumbling block to the acceptance of what I sincerely believe to be the truth about the nature of existence is the fact that science generally has thought about our *material* universe as being the *entire* universe and not just a small part of a much, much greater whole. Until fairly recently, there was no reason for science to believe anything else. But now, with the work being done on relativity, with the discoveries constantly being made in the area of quantum mechanics, there is beginning to be an excuse for thinking men to raise their sights a little as they realize that Newton did not have all the answers after all." [2]

Welch's beliefs were certainly fervent. And his slightly outré topics also provided an interesting basis for stories. As long as Welch didn't preach a particular belief, Allen was content to accept Welch's sometimes unearthly tales. After all, where else would such out-of-this-world ideas be more at home than in an Irwin Allen production?

Welch's passion could be contagious even when his scripts didn't live up to his ideals and curiosities. "A Time to Die" is one of his success stories.

Production:
(Filmed October 4 – 10, 1967; 5 days)
(Added scenes filmed October 27, 1967; now totaling 6 days)

Director **Robert Sparr** was 52 when assigned his first of five *Voyages*, with a budget of $152, 349 (well under the studio's wish for a per-episode cost of $163,205). Sparr had been nominated for two Emmys, as a film editor, in 1958 and '59 for a pair of *Maverick* episodes. As a TV director, spanning 1959 through 1967, Sparr began with Westerns and had 33 credits on *Lawman*; seven on *Bronco*; eleven on *Cheyenne*; plus one for *Bonanza*. He switched genres to detectives, directing for *Peter Gunn*; *Surfside Six*; *Hawaiian Eye*; and *77 Sunset Strip*. War drama came next, with *The Gallant Men* and *The Rat Patrol*. Sparr also directed for the big screen, with the romantic teen comedy/musical *A Swingin' Summer* (1965). Fantastic TV came next, with five *The Wild, Wild West* assignments, plus two for *Batman* and one *Star Trek*, all before *Voyage*.

Henry Jones was hired to play Mr. Pem, and paid $2,000 for four days' filming. Jones had last

Henry Jones in a 1967 episode of *The Guns of Will Sonnett*.

appeared on *Voyage* in the third season episode "Night of Terror." Allen had also cast him in an episode of *Lost in Space*, as Cousin Smith. Jones would return to play Mr. Pem again in "No Way Back."

It was another atypical episode, and therefore required music not available in the *Voyage* library. **Leith Stevens** provided the new elements of the score heard here. This was the sixth out of nine episodes for which he composed original music.

As with other recent episodes, the production number assigned to "A Time to Die" is not reflective of its sequence in the filming schedule or its broadcast. Designated as Prod. No. 1317, it was actually the fourteenth filmed, not the seventeenth, due to three holdbacks – "The Death Clock" (#1311), "Secret of the Deep" (#1312), and "The Abominable Snowman" (#1315).

Production began on Wednesday, October 4, 1967. For the Irwin Allen "Hot Sheet" production newsletter, Frank La Tourette wrote:

> Bruce Fowler reports that Bob Sparr is well prepared as he starts directing "A Time to Die" today. According to Bruce, ABC's report on this script was most flattering. The network considers it one of "our most interesting efforts." [3]

This was a five-day bottle show, designed to be filmed entirely on Stage 10 with the standing Seaview sets, the Flying Sub, and a set from storage – "Int. Nelson Institute / Admiral's Office" – which the crew would fly in and out, as needed.

Let us take you back in time now, to be a fly on the wall in Stage 10:

As documented by the photos on this page and the next, taken while the on-set photographer roamed the stage, David Hedison and Richard Basehart patiently waited for lighting to be fine-tuned, and an opportunity to rehearse their movements for the camera, while the Script Supervisor timed the scene about to be filmed.

It's a tedious process. The actors have to be prepared to switch on and off, jumping into character and any emotions called for in a particular scene. After the rehearsal, they're told to stand down for five minutes while lights are again adjusted, or a sound issue is tracked down, or they are touched up by make-up, or handed page revisions, cutting or adding lines of dialogue. And then, after cooling off, they are given the command for "Action!", on which they jump back into the heat of the moment.

After the first day of filming, Frank La Tourette reported:

> [W]hile Bob Sparr did very well the first day on pages, he came up a little short on minutes. However, he assures us that in subsequent scenes, he will be more than able to make up this deficiency. Nevertheless, all hands remain alert to make certain we get sufficient minutes out of this picture within the 5-day shooting schedule. [4]

Sparr finished in five days, but the rough edit came in seven minutes short. Two additional scenes were written (for the Reactor Room and a section of corridor), then filmed on Wednesday, October 27. [5]

As a result, Frank La Tourette wrote:

> In the Cost Control Department, all hands are asked to be especially alert and careful in watching and tightening up the costs on all three series. A serious campaign must be launched immediately to control and reduce these costs. In that direction, I.A. asks that no monies be spent without his approval. ...
>
> A minimum of 4 more 5-day VOYAGE shows must be shot before the end of the season. These must be true 5-day shows with varied and endless tippy-toe scenes that will produce minutes in sufficient amount so that a return to the stage to shoot additional scenes will not be necessary. [6]

"Tippy-toe scenes" were what the *Voyage* crew referred to as sequences in which Seaview personnel walked down corridors. These were quickly filmed but could be cut in to extend running time.

Release / Reaction:

(ABC premiere airing: 12/3/67; network repeat broadcast: 5/26/68)

This was the week that the first human heart transplant was performed in South Africa by Dr. Christiaan Barnard. Pediatrician Dr. Benjamin Spock and poet Allen Ginsberg were arrested for protesting against the Vietnam War and the military draft. The biker picture *Hells Angels on Wheels*, starring Adam Roarke and Jack Nicholson, was the top-grossing movie in America. The Monkees had the best-selling album in the U.S., with *Pisces, Aquarius, Capricorn & Jones Ltd.* It was the one with their hit "Pleasant Valley Sunday." And they had the top song on the radio, which wasn't on the album – "Daydream Believer." Danny Thomas and daughter Marlo had the cover of *TV Guide*.

The day "A Time to Die" first aired, David Hedison was the subject of Joan Crosby's syndicated column through NEA (National Editorial Association):

> Three cheers for David Hedison who has maintained his honesty and humor after four years in a television series. As Captain Crane on ABC-TV's *Voyage to the Bottom of the Sea,* David is playing a role that he says he doesn't "think is doing much for me. The true star of a television series like ours is the show itself."
>
> He has even managed to maintain his good nature over the fact that nearly every script seems to have an alien being taking over his mind. [7]

Hedison said, "They don't like Richard Basehart, as the admiral, to go berserk. He's supposed to be the strong-minded one. So, the first one to go is the captain. You know what I would love to do for our final show? A satire on the shows we have done so far, with all the monsters suddenly showing up. I don't think the producer will buy that, though." [8]

In her "TV Scout" syndicated column, Crosby said of "A Time to Die":

> Henry Jones gives *Voyage to the Bottom of the Sea* the little interest it has. He plays Mr. Pem, a smilingly, soft-spoken, sinister man who is such a genius he can control time by virtue of an energy piece that looks like a wrist watch. He transports the Seaview back and ahead and even lets Richard Basehart watch himself in action. It's all pretty confusing, unless you are 6 years old. [9]

A.C. Nielsen ratings report from December 3, 1967: [10]

	Peak Share:
ABC: *Voyage to the Bottom of the Sea*	27%
CBS: *Lassie / Gentle Ben*	**40% / 37%**
NBC: *Walt Disney's Wonderful World of Color*	35%

9.15

"Edge of Doom" (Episode 99)

(Prod. No. 1318; first aired Sunday, March 17, 1968)
Written by William Welch
Directed by Justus Addiss
Produced by Irwin Allen and Bruce Fowler, Jr.
Story Editor: Sidney Marshall

From the *Voyage* show files (Irwin Allen papers collection):

> When he receives orders to deliver a device vital to the country's defense to Pearl Harbor, Admiral Nelson is shocked to learn that the Pentagon suspects that Captain Crane has been replaced by an imposter. During a voyage taut with suspicion and danger, Crane, first puzzled, then infuriated, by the Admiral's manner, fights back and convinces Nelson that the Pentagon had picked on the wrong man. Together, Nelson and Crane unmask the traitor, and complete their mission in good order. [1]

Assessment:

They took the Captain-Crane-or-Admiral-Nelson-acting-out-of-character scenario and turned it on its head. This time, Crane is certainly *in* character. But he's the unwitting target of a conspiracy to test that character by Nelson, Morton, and Sharkey. They're out to convince Crane that he is losing his mind. This raises an intriguing question: Can a man remain sane when the world around him appears to have gone mad? Or, as Rudyard Kipling wrote in his poem "If," can Crane "keep your head when all about you / Are losing theirs and blaming it on you"?

It's handled in a provocative manner. The cast had always been up to this level of dramatic conflict, as was director Justus Addis. The big surprise is who provided the platform for their superior performances – writer William Welch. This time out, it appears that Welch decided to take a little more time, and inject a bit more passion. And what a pleasure it is to see the likes of Richard Basehart, David Hedison, Robert Dowdell, and Terry Becker given material worthy of their talents.

Mark Phillips said, "Many episodes of *Voyage* are distinguished by the cast's acting chemistry. This episode, a taut suspense tale, features several well-played scenes, including an explosive clash between Nelson and Crane." [2]

Script:
William Welch's writers contract: September 27, 1967.
Welch's treatment, and 1st- and 2nd-draft teleplays approved by Irwin Allen on Oct. 9.
Shooting final teleplay (pale green paper): October 6.
Page revisions (blue paper): October 10.
Page revisions (pink paper): October 17.
Page revisions (green paper): November 1.

Voyage to the Bottom of the Sea boasted acting talent as fine as any series on TV, and certainly finer than most. It also had production values which surpassed the vast majority of television productions from this period. And the series premise offered a great range in storytelling. It was just a matter of the writers making proper use of this attributes.

On this occasion, **William Welch** very nearly rose to the challenge. We say "very nearly" because "Edge of Doom" is not without flaws. Despite a hopelessly generic title, Welch was onto something with the story. His one-page "notion" read:

> Nelson receives a request from Washington to conduct a psychological test on Seaview to determine the limits of frustration a sub commander can reach without cracking. The entire crew is to participate without the knowledge of Captain Crane, who is to be the subject of the experiment.

> Nelson's first reaction is an indignant refusal, considering the test as inhuman treatment of an efficient officer. However, the importance of the experiment and the insistence of Washington ultimately convince him to agree.
>
> Before the Seaview sails, a mysterious attack occurs against Chief Sharkey. He apparently escapes the attack and takes his station aboard the sub where, as the experiment begins, he continually reassures the Admiral and several times dissuades him from aborting the test.
>
> Crane, meanwhile, is subjected to a series of frustrations which begin to make him doubt his own reason. The results become more and more perilous until ultimately Crane cracks and the sub is nearly lost. And then, as Nelson attempts to abort the test, he discovers to his horror that forces are at work which have no connection with the experiment. Ultimately, he realizes that Chief Sharkey is an imposter; that the real Sharkey was abducted before sailing and the man everyone assumed was the Chief is actually a saboteur bent on destroying the Seaview. [3]

This germ of a story has great potential. It also has some problems. First, the government comes off as cruel. It's more reminiscent of the CIA's 1950s-60s Project MKUltra mind-control programs than something devised by a near-future government. We don't buy it. Or, at least, we don't want to buy it. Second, it is unclear why, at this very moment, a saboteur would go to such trouble to abduct and impersonate Sharkey. It would be quite an undertaking to find a physical double for a man, all for the purpose of sabotaging the Seaview … when it isn't even on a special mission, as far as the saboteurs know.

Having read Welch's "notion," we can better understand why many of the things Nelson and Morton do to Crane in the episode seem designed to test his tolerance rather than expose a traitor. It is because, originally, no one was trying to expose Crane as a bad guy; just make him a bit crazy. As the story was developed, some on the staff felt that Washington would need a better reason to order Nelson, who then orders Morton, to turn on Crane. So, the idea was introduced that Crane is suspected of being a traitor, and the Seaview is on an important mission in which intelligence believes a traitor has already found a means to get on board, with intent on sabotaging the sub … and the mission. This change helped to better motivate the reason, and all the trouble taken, to get a traitor on board who could pass himself off as a member of the crew. Also introduced at this stage was the enemy sub, and the attack on Seaview.

These additions to the story benefitted the script in all ways except for one – the manner in which Nelson is testing Crane. Originally, it was meant to test Crane's ability to withstand such "torture." Now, with Nelson's instructions being to test Crane's character and loyalty, the dirty tricks played on the Captain come across as sadistic. And this leaves us wanting to see Crane belt Nelson in the mouth at the end of the show.

Perhaps William Welch was in a hurry after all. Regardless, the script makes for compelling drama, flaws and all.

Production:
(Filmed October 11 – 17, 1967; 5 days)
(Added scene filmed on November 8, 1967)

Director **Justus Addiss** wasn't given much to work with, budget-wise. This episode was one of the cheaper ones, set at $148,650 (way down from the studio target per-episode cost of $163,705). Clearly, there was a lot of red ink created by overspending earlier in the season to mop up.

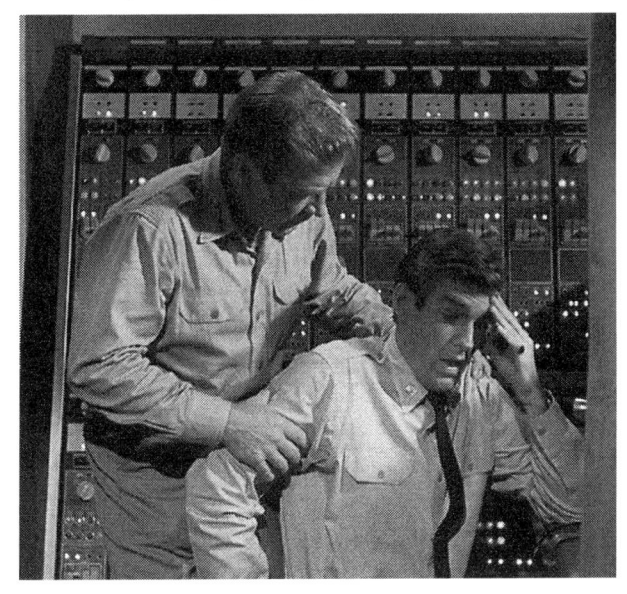

Production began on Wednesday, October 1, 1967 for the first of five days on Stage 10 and the standing Seaview sets, as well as the Flying Sub, and the set for Nelson's office at the Nelson Institute, which they could "fly in" when needed.

After previewing the rough-assembly edit, it was discovered there was a need for additional running time, and a sixth day of production was scheduled for a new scene.

Frank La Tourette wrote in the "Hot Sheet" newsletter on October 20:

> Additional scenes for three VOYAGE shows will be shot next Thursday and Friday, October 27 and 28. The three shows are:

```
A TIME TO DIE:     7 minutes short.
EDGE OF DOOM:      7 minutes short.
BLACKEARD:         1 minute short. [4]
```

It didn't go as planned. Justus Addis returned to direct the added scene on Wednesday, November 8, 1967, for "Int. General's Office," as well as the ship's "Int. Arms Locker" and "Int. Nelson's Cabin," none of which were utilized during the initial five-day production period. [5]

Release / Reaction:
(Only ABC broadcast: 3/17/68)

This was the week Bobby Kennedy announced he was going to run for President. Howard University students, protesting the Vietnam War, seized the school's administration building. *Stay Away, Joe*, starring Elvis Presley, was the top-grossing movie in the U.S. "(Sittin' on) The Dock of the Bay," by the late Otis Redding, was the most played song on the radio. The top-selling record album was *Blooming Hits*, by Paul Mauriat & His Orchestra. The album contained only one hit – "Love Is Blue" – but the cover, featuring a seated woman wearing only body and face paint, was stirring in itself. Sally Field and Alejandro Rey, of *The Flying Nun*, had the cover of *TV Guide*.

Nielsen ratings report from March 17, 1968: [6]
Peak Share:

ABC: *Voyage to the Bottom of the Sea*	24%
CBS: *Lassie / Gentle Ben*	**35% / 36%**
NBC: *Walt Disney's Wonderful World of Color*	33%

"Edge of Doom," despite its improved quality over other run-of-the-mill monster and mental-possession tales on *Voyage*, sunk *Voyage* to new depths in the Nielsens. This convinced both Irwin Allen and ABC that the "Back Ten" episodes would have to be more geared to high-concept, kid-friendly stories. Further, "Edge of Doom" was not given a network repeat airing.

From the Mailbag:

Despite the drop in the ratings, *Voyage* wasn't yet on the chopping block at ABC. To the contrary, just days before "Edge of Doom" aired, Jack Bradford reported in his syndicated "On Hollywood" newspaper column:

Lucky series to win a reprieve and start filming June 1 – *Voyage to the Bottom of the Sea*. David Hedison says, "Every time we add a monster to our show, the ratings go up. We've long since stopped adding girls because the ratings would drop. You figure it out!" [7]

From syndicated "TV Key Mail Bag," March 17, 1968, the day "Edge of Doom" aired:

> Is *Voyage to the Bottom of the Sea* going to be taken off TV? I read an article about the producer, Irwin Allen, and he said something about *Voyage* being in its last year. – M.F. [8]

Steven H. Scheuer replied:

> There is no definite decision about the fate of *Voyage to the Bottom of the Sea*. It may or may not be back next year, as of this writing. However, Allen has a new series in the wings and chances are it will be on the air next season regardless of the fate of *Voyage to the Bottom of the Sea*. The new series is called *Land of the Giants*. [9]

9.16

"Nightmare" (Episode 100)

(Prod. No. 1319; first aired Sunday, January 28, 1968)
Written by Sidney Marshall
Directed by Charles Rondeau
Produced by Irwin Allen and Bruce Fowler, Jr.
Story Editor: Sidney Marshall
Guest Star Paul Mantee

From the *Voyage* show files (Irwin Allen papers collection):

Captain Crane, on a routine flight in the Flying Sub, receives an incomplete message from Admiral Nelson, telling him of great danger aboard the Seaview. Returning to the giant sub, Crane is astounded to find himself seemingly alone on the ship. Suddenly, horror is piled upon horror, culminating in a terrifying moment when Crane offers his life to abort an apparent attack on Washington. Not until the dreadful nightmare is over does Crane learn how his courage and determination turned aside an Alien invasion. [1]

Assessment:

If you can stand still another story in which one or more of the Seaview's crew – Nelson, Morton, Sharkey, and Kowalski this time – behave out of character, seeming to have either gone mad or bad, then "Nightmare" is one of the better ones. This is also another aliens-attempting-to-take-over-the-Earth tale. And it's a budget saver, with approximately half the episode depicting Captain Crane alone, roaming the Seaview, searching for answers, evading capture, dodging bullets and bombs, all of which adds to the redundancy. But, these liabilities aside, it's not a bad show.

David Hedison gives an emotionally charged performance. He evinces a convincing state of betrayal and confusion, balanced effectively by Richard Basehart's detached cold-bloodedness, particularly during the kangaroo-court scene. Robert Dowdy and Terry Becker play it cool too, making for an enthralling passage. The aliens aren't yet invading Earth, but testing the ability of mankind to resist such an attack. The rest of the crew, Nelson included, as we learn, failed the test; Crane is mankind's last hope, and the only card he has left to play is his willingness to make the ultimate sacrifice for his race – to die on their behalf; something the "superior" aliens hadn't comprehended. This element alone, gives the story a theme. What is a hero, after all? One willing to risk, even sacrifice, their life for the good of others.

Mike Bailey said, "A great episode. Well written, directed and downright eerie in spots. David Hedison's scenes with the guesting Paul Mantee are tight and intense. The scene with Nelson and company putting Crane on trial for Patterson's murder truly is a nightmare. An aptly titled and very successful outing." [2]

Script:
Sidney Marshall's writers contract: April 14, 1967.
Marshall's treatment, and 1st- and 2nd-draft teleplays approved on Sept. 28.
Shooting Final teleplay (on pale green paper): October 2.
Page revisions (on blue paper): October 25.
Added scene written (on pink paper): October 25.
Page revisions (on dark green paper): October 25.

Sidney Marshall's two-page springboard read:

> When Lee Crane is attacked underwater by an outlandish, unworldly Creature seemingly out of a bad dream, he manages to return to the Seaview only to find that he has passed through a time warp – and is now in a future, fourth-dimensional world in which all the members of the submarine's crew, INCLUDING A FUTURE CAPTAIN CRANE, are out to destroy the future world!
>
> Cities such as London and Hong Kong are turned to rubble before his eyes as his efforts to prevent this are futile in this fourth-dimensional era. Other attacks are to begin simultaneously on San Francisco, New York and Washington before he is able to resolve the nightmarish mystery in which he is involved. It's a test of human behavior by an Alien Culture to determine how they react to Galactic Stimuli as a prelude to invasion. But Crane's knowledge seemingly comes too late. He's accused by a court aboard his own submarine, HEADED BY CAPTAIN CRANE, of being an enemy spy, and is sentenced to death. [3]

As the story was further developed, the idea of two Cranes was tossed out, replaced by the character Jim Bentley ... and a bigger role for Richard Basehart. It seemed a better idea for Nelson to be the one who put Crane on trial.

Other changes to the story were made at the insistence of ABC. The network did not want a story which depicted several major cities of the world, such as London and Hong Kong, having already been destroyed. The threat of destruction – fine; actual destruction, even if we later learn that this never happened, was pushing the limit. The censors had other concerns.

ABC's Mary Garbutt told Irwin Allen and his staff:

> Pg 1: Noted that future date is supered in Sc. 1. Please indicate same on film for rough cut screening.
>
> Pg 5, 6, 46, 54: Caution that shots of men hit by electrical discharge are not horrible or grotesque to view; Of course, bodies not in convulsion or features distended.
>
> Pgs 9, 11, 13, 18, 25, 26, 31, 39: Your usual care in seeing that fights are not unnecessarily brutal or prolonged; Sc 34: Of course, eyes closed; Sc 43: Caution that we do not see Crane hit by the bullets; Sc 72: Blow with machine gun not in CU;

Scs 77 & 78: If possible, telescope [film from a wide angle]; Sc 92: Nelson's business, more of a shove than a kick; Blood and indications or wound to a minimum in Scs 22 & 49.

Confirming our discussion, re: Bentley-Crane scene and tag: Clarification of "special" alien force or power and Fail Safe. [4]

The future date was now 1982. *Voyage* had sailed from 1973 (the used for early first-season episodes) to 1982, a ten-year span ... in only three seasons.

Production:
(Filmed October 19 – 26, 1967; 6 days)

This was the 100th episode produced for the series.

Charles Rondeau was hired to direct. He was 50 and had solid TV credentials, having directed 14 episodes of the detective series *Surfside 6*; 12 for its sister show, *Hawaiian Eye*; 11 for the World War II drama *The Gallant Men*; 10 for the military comedy *No Time for Sergeants*; and 19 for the Western sitcom *F Troop*. He had also been assigned multiple episodes of *Ben Casey*, *Captain Nice*, *Bourbon Street Beat*, and *Batman*, and he directed one episode of David Hedison's series, *Five Fingers*. This was his first of three *Voyages*.

Paul Mantee played Jim Bentley. He was 36 and had starred in the 1964 cult sci-fi movie *Robinson Crusoe on Mars*. He also appeared once on *The Time Tunnel*.

Production began on Thursday, October 19, 1967, for the first of a planned five days on Stage 10, for this bottle show, utilizing only the standing Seaview sets and that of the Flying Sub.

Frank La Tourette wrote in the "Hot Sheet" newsletter on October 20:

> Since the script on this show is only 51 pages long, Charles Rondeau – the director – must average at least a page a minute. So far, he hasn't and all hands are asked to visit the stage and help him devise and enlarge upon the tippy-toe

scenes already in the script in order to get more minutes. The story department is asked to be prepared to supply additional pages if such will be required before the show is wrapped up. [5]

The "tippy-toe scenes" didn't quite time the episode up to 51 minutes and a partial sixth day of filming took place on October 26 to keep "Nightmare" from becoming a nightmare in the editing room. Rondeau finished with enough footage in the can to make the cut. [6]

Release / Reaction:

(ABC premiere airdate: 1/28/68; network repeat broadcast: 8/4/68)

This was the week the Vietcong launched the devastating Tet Offensive on the U.S. embassy in Saigon, South Vietnam. As a result of statistics coming out of the Pentagon, U.S. citizens had been under the impression that America and South Vietnam were winning the war. The Tet Offensive changed that thinking. Also during the week, former Vice President Richard Nixon announced his candidacy for president. The Western *Firecreek*, starring James Stewart and Henry Fonda, was No. 1 at the box office. The Beatles had the No. 1 album in stores, with *Magical Mystery Tour*. "Green Tambourine," by the Lemon Pipers, was No. 1 on the radio, as well as the best-selling single in America. Elizabeth Montgomery, of *Bewitched*, had the cover of *TV Guide*. And *Voyage* had one of its best episodes so far of Season Four.

"TV Scout" said:

> David Hedison, who has been neglected lately, has the spotlight tonight in a neat piece of science fiction. While in the flying sub, he receives an urgent call to return to the Seaview. He gets there, and can't find anyone, even though he hears voices and sees the controls being operated. Gradually, members of the crew appear, but they're far from normal, since Richard Basehart gives orders to kill Hedison. [7]

A.C. Nielsen ratings report from January 28, 1968: [8]

	Peak Share:
ABC: *Voyage to the Bottom of the Sea*	25%
CBS: *Lassie / Gentle Ben*	**33% / 36%**
NBC: *Walt Disney's Wonderful World of Color*	33%

10

Season Four / ABC's Back Order of 10

As noted on the previous pages, "Nightmare" was the 100th episode filmed for *Voyage to the Bottom of the Sea*. This realization amazed and bemused Richard Basehart. Upon completion of the episode, he commented, "It is hard to believe that we have been working on this show for four years. The living proof came last week, though, when producer Irwin Allen gave the cast and crew a party in honor of the event. The entire submarine was decorated with replicas of all the various monsters and sea creatures that we had encountered during the years of filming.

"After looking around at the display of opposing forces, I began wondering just how the Seaview made it through all its crises in such good shape." [1]

It is remarkable how classically trained actors like Basehart and David Hedison continued to give *Voyage* the best of their thespian talents even when the material didn't merit it. One thing nearly all who worked for, knew, or experienced Irwin Allen agreed on was that knew how to

653

cast his TV series. He managed to find the best performers for the right roles, time and again.

Can you imagine *Voyage to the Bottom of the Sea* without Richard Basehart and David Hedison, or its supporting cast? It's hard to imagine other leads from this time – James Arness, Efrem Zimbalist, Jr., or even Robert Conrad – could have done as well acting opposite Menfish, a Lobster Man, a Mummy, or a Mermaid, and make the viewers take it seriously. Or at least suspend laughter.

So, as we proceed to the final ten episodes of *Voyage to the Bottom of the Sea*, you have ten more opportunities to appreciate the talents of Basehart, Hedison, Dowdell, Becker, Monroe, and Trinka. Cherish it.

10.1

"The Lobster Man" (Episode 101)

(Prod. No. 1320; first aired Sunday, January 21, 1968)
Written by Al Gail
Directed by Justus Addiss
Produced by Irwin Allen and Bruce Fowler, Jr.
Story Editor: Sidney Marshall
Guest Star Victor Lundin

From the *Voyage* show files (Irwin Allen papers collection):

A UFO crashes into the ocean, close to the Seaview, and Admiral Nelson orders it recovered with a magnetic grappler. When the Admiral and Captain Crane examine the torpedo-like alien craft, they fail to find any sign of life, or any way of opening it. Later, however, the UFO is opened from within, and a monstrous Lobster Man emerges. Despite his avowal of peace, the strange Creature causes great havoc aboard the Seaview and Admiral Nelson is forced to take off in the UFO in order to prevent the same havoc being created throughout the world. [1]

Assessment:

Mark Phillips said, "High camp, especially as Lobster Man strolls into the control room and Nelson greets him with a very bored, 'If you come in peace … welcome.' A great line of dialog as Lobster Man prepares to destroy humanity: 'Not even the monkeys will be around to start over again!'" [2]

We liked that line too. But the episode was difficult to get through. In fact, one of us fell to sleep three times while trying to watch it. What makes "The Lobster Man" so soporific? Pointlessness – lack of theme – is one reason. Redundancy is the other. It's like counting sheep, one after another, as your eyes grow heavier and heavier.

We'd seen an uncrackable spaceship Season One's "The Invaders" – with saws, with blow torches, with chemicals. Fortunately, they abbreviated the process here. Come to think of it, the alien in the earlier episode, played by Robert Duvall, also claimed to come in peace … all the while up to mischief. Well, they did it better the first time.

Then we have the repetitious story beats within this episode. Lobster man goes to the nuclear reactor to steal the radioactive rods more than once; the crew shoot him with their .45s more than once, and, despite these weapons proving useless, they still shoot at him, in scene after scene. And they get into punching matches with him, again and again. The Seaview plummets to the ocean floor not once, but twice, courtesy of stock footage both times. We get the Seaview rock and roll more than once. We seem to get everything more than once.

This assessment isn't all negative. Mark Phillips found the whole affair entertainingly camp. We recommend you give it a watch any time you are having trouble falling to sleep. A dose of the Lobster Man may put you out like a switched-off light.

Script:

Al Gail's writers contract: September 29, 1967.
Rev. Shooting final teleplay (on blue paper): October 20.
Page revisions (on pink paper): October 24.
Page revisions (on green paper): October 26.
Page revisions (on yellow paper): December 1.

Defending the tendency to lean toward stories such as "The Lobster Man," and other monster tales (or tails), Al Gail said, "Well, that was also a question of budget. You had to make do with what you had. And Paul Z., who did most of that, was great at improvising. He would pull something from here, something from there, and look around, and there's a monster. For example, there was one show, particularly, 'The Lobster Man,' which was quite popular for its time, and he created this walking lobster outfit – very funny, with the little bells running out of the head, and everything else. It was one of my particularly favorites, because I happened to have written it." [3]

Production:
(Filmed October 30 – November 7, 1967; 7 days)
(Added scenes filmed December 7, for total of 7 and ¾ days)

Director **Justus Addiss** was given a budget of $163,862 to work with, and a lobster man.

Victor Lundin was paid $1,250 to play the crustacean. He was 37, and making his second appearance on *Voyage* (after "The Menfish").

According to writer Mark Phillips, Lundin recalled that Irwin Allen insisted the Lobster Man be presented as a dignified and well-bred crustacean. Lundin reported that Allen told him, "'This is no ordinary Lobster Man. I want people to know he has attended the finest underwater schools.' Irwin Allen

Above: Lighting levels are checked. Below: Basehart and Hedison with director Justus Addiss.

wanted Lobster Man to speak with an English accent. He thought it would provide him with character. But, if you do it too much, it becomes comical. I did just enough to make him happy, and it turned out well." [4]

English accent or not, the idea of working in an episode called "The Lobster Man" didn't fill the recurring cast members with joy. Terry Becker said, "Certainly, as actors, we didn't want to do monsters. Just seeing another guy in a monster suit drove us up the wall." [5]

"Yes, yes, exactly," concurred David Hedison. "The characters were one dimensional and all the emphasis was on photo effects, and, of course, in the fourth year, which drove me crazy, every monster in the world – Fishman, Frogman, Rockman. God, I don't know, it just drove me nuts. And I said this is a sure way of getting cancelled." [6]

Vic Lundin discovered that Richard Basehart had drawn his own battle line in respect to how far he would go in being

Nelson's encounter with the Lobster Man had to be covered by the on-set photographer in two separate promotional photos. Richard Basehart didn't want to open a newspaper and see himself and the crustacean in the same picture.

associated with Irwin Allen's monsters of the week. Lundin said, "Basehart was adamant about never being filmed with a monster. I was near him one day when a publicity photographer stopped to take a picture of the two of us. Basehart went absolutely ballistic on me and the photographer. I really thought he was going to kill us! He didn't want any photos taken of him with 'a monster.' He was a dedicated actor but very difficult to work with. From then on, I stayed away from him and just did my scenes." [7]

Production began on Monday, October 30, 1967 for the first of seven days on Stage 10. It was a bottle show, and planned for six days ... something Irwin Allen considered a leisurely schedule for an episode written for only the standing Seaview sets on Stage 10. But Justus Addiss fell behind on the fourth day of filming and didn't wrap until 6:30 p.m. on Day 7, Tuesday, November 7.

Even with the extra time, the episode timed out short after the first assembly edit. New scenes had to be written and filmed on Thursday, December 7, from 8:27 a.m. to 3:40 p.m. Among the new sequences was a scene in the Officer's Cabin, a set not utilized in the initial production. [8]

Release / Reaction:

(ABC premiere airdate: 1/21/68; network repeat broadcast: 7/28/68)

This was the week that a U.S. bomber with nuclear bombs aboard crashed in Greenland. In Vietnam, the Battle of Khe Sanh began, one of the most-covered battles by the press during the war. And the American intelligence (spy) ship U.S.S. Pueblo, with its crew of 83, was seized in the Sea of Japan by the North Korean Navy. On a lighter note – we certainly needed one – *Rowan & Martin's Laugh-In* premiered on NBC. *The Graduate* was the top-grossing film in movie houses, and the song getting the most play on the radio was, no, not "Mrs. Robinson" from the top-selling album, but "Judy in Disguise (with Glasses)," by John Fred & His Playboy Band. Its title was a riff on the Beatles' "Lucy in the Sky with Diamonds." Speaking of the Beatles, their *Magical Mystery Tour* was *still* the best-selling album in record stores, followed by *Their Satanic Majesties Request*, by the Rolling Stones. And Leif Erickson, Linda Cristal, and Cameron Mitchell, of *The High Chaparral*, had the cover of *TV Guide*. The series featured Mark Slade, who had been a regular on *Voyage*.

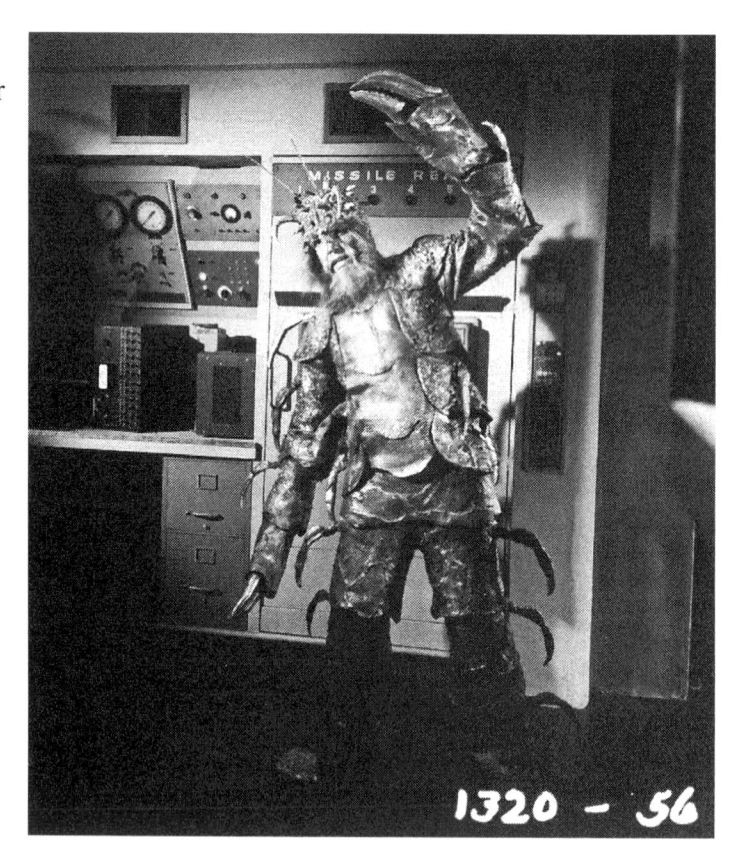

"TV Scout" said:

> A UFO lands right near the Seaview on *Voyage to the Bottom of the Sea*. It's brought aboard where none of the ship's devices can open the thing. But it opens itself and a lobster-

like man emerges, spouting platitudes about peace. Is he really a peaceful sort who only wants a nuclear rod to give his vehicle the power it needs to get back "home," or is he a Trojan horse? [9]

A.C. Nielsen ratings report from January 21, 1968: [10]

	Peak Share:
ABC: *Voyage to the Bottom of the Sea*	25%
CBS: *Lassie* / *Gentle Ben*	**36% / 36%**
NBC: *Walt Disney's Wonderful World of Color*	34%

It had been two weeks since the last episode of *Voyage*, with the series pre-empted one week earlier by a Bing Crosby Golf Tournament. It was back, with a talking crustacean. Ratings like this certainly showed the Lobster Man (and *Voyage*) were in hot water.

10.2

"Terrible Leprechaun" (Episode 102)
(Prod. No. 1321; first aired Sunday, January 7, 1968)
Written by Charles Bennett
Directed by Jerry Hopper
Produced by Irwin Allen and Bruce Fowler, Jr.; Story Editor: Sidney Marshall
Guest Star Walter Burke

From the *Voyage* show files (Irwin Allen papers collection):

While the Seaview is on a mission to inspect a powerful nuclear counter weapon beneath the Irish Sea, Admiral Nelson and Chief Sharkey become involved in a battle for power between two Leprechauns – one on the side of evil, the other on the side of good. Admiral Nelson helps Leprechaun Patrick turn the tables on his evil brother, but, as Commander Morton and Kowalski complete the mission, the Admiral and the Chief decide to keep their adventure with the Little People to themselves. [1]

Assessment:

Sitting through an hour-long marathon of Lucky Charms commercials would be less torturous than watching "The Terrible Leprechaun." General Mills' cereal, introduced in 1964, was at least "magically delicious," and, in 1968, would cost you only 69 cents for two boxes at A&P stores. This *Voyage* cost a lot more, and it lives up to its "terrible" name –don't be conned.

Long-time *Voyage* fan Mike Bailey said, "Charles Bennett was a decent writer – so what happened? Bennett wrote the script of the *Voyage* movie based on a storyline by Irwin Allen. Other writing credits include numerous Hitchcock films (*Sabotage, Secret Agent, Foreign Correspondent, The Man Who Knew Too Much*), as well as other well-known films, including *Reap the Wild Wind*. Incredibly, Bennett went from writing the 1956 *Man Who Knew Too Much* to Irwin Allen's loopy *The Story of Mankind* (1957). Hmmmmm." [2]

Bennett was asked to do what William Welch did – to work scenes from past episodes into the script, to pad the episode without incurring additional production cost. Entire scenes are harvested from past *Voyage*s, taking up several minutes of screen time. We've seen the Flying Sub go through that "bubble storm" before, more than once. You've also seen the sequence with the three Seaview divers encountering an electrical current coming through an undersea cable, which then causes an explosion (more bubbles). This of course leads to the Seaview rock and roll (still more bubbles). Even more blatant, there is the lengthy sequence in which Morton and Kowalski, and a doomed third diver, go into a cave and are trapped between forcefields, as a bomb gets closer to detonation. That came from Season Two's "The Mechanical Man."

Redundancy is prevalent even in the new footage, including seemingly endless shots of the Seaview Control Room rocking and rolling. More of the same in the Flying Sub, as poor David Hedison and Paul Trinka were told to lean this way, then lean that way, over and over, to the accompaniment of shooting sparks. Redundancy also prevails with guest star Walter Burke – two guest stars in one! – as the twin leprechaun brothers yammer away about gold and their sibling feud. At the end of this insipid tale, Admiral Nelson and Chief Sharkey decide not to tell anyone about what they experienced – pretend the whole thing never happened. We wish *we* could.

Script:
Charles Bennett's writers contract: May 16, 1967.
Bennett's story treatment approved by Irwin Allen on June 15.
Bennett's 1st-draft teleplay approved by Allen on August 11.

Bennett's 2nd (and final) draft teleplay approved by Allen on September 28.
Shooting final teleplay (on pale green paper): November 1.
Page revisions (on blue paper): November 9.
Added scene (on pink paper): November 16.

Charles Bennett was on his final *Voyage to the Bottom of the Sea* script assignment. We can be thankful for that. And you can be sure there were fights over substandard scripts such as this final one from Bennett.

Del Monroe said, "Richard [Basehart] told me that when the show was sold to him, it was explained that *Voyage* was going to be a straightforward adventure. We were going to get involved in various political situations around the world. The Seaview would be a method of getting us from one place to another. That's what we did in many of the early segments, and those were some of our best shows…. Ideally, our format allowed for a wide range of stories. But, instead, we got locked into shows where there was a monster loose on the ship. We lost the realism of those first two years. 'The Phantom,' 'The Deadly Dolls,' and 'Return of Blackbeard' were different, but, by the last year, they got too similar. I know Richard and David Hedison had some very heated arguments with Irwin over the storylines." [3]

Charles Bennett would write one more script for Irwin Allen, for *Land of the Giants*, and then find himself out of work … for good. Granted, Bennett was 68 by this time, but, usually, writers write … until their minds go or until they become unemployable due to either personal problems or having laid one too many bombs. "The Terrible Leprechaun" could certainly qualify as that bomb.

Production:

(Filmed November 9 - 16, 1967; 6 days)

Director **Jerry Hopper** was given a budget of $157,632.

Walter Burke was paid $1,500 to appear as both leprechauns, Mickey and Pat. Burke was 60 and of Irish descent. He was a respected character actor in film and TV, best known for his standout role in the Oscar-winning 1949 film *All the King's Men*.

Leith Stevens provided the score.

Production began on Thursday, November 9, 1967, for the first of six days on Stage 10 for this bottle show, featuring only the standing Seaview sets and the Flying Sub. [4]

Actor Pat Culliton, who appeared in numerous episodes of *Voyage* as a crewman, was quoted in the book *Seaview: A 50th Anniversary Tribute*: "'Terrible Leprechaun' was directed by a man named Jerry Hopper. He was a lovely man and a damn good director. I remember what he told me – what to do with this scene where I played a corpsman. I remember him telling me to play it real dry, do Walter Matthau, because I think I was doing triple takes and double takes [reactions]. I have strong recollections about Walter Burke, because he was a legend. He was in *All the King's Men* with Broderick Crawford. He was a marvelous couple leprechauns – the good one and the bad one. That was also a big show for Terry Becker. He was playing an Irishman who kept seeing these leprechauns and nobody would believe him." [5]

Release / Reaction:

(ABC premiere airdate: 1/7/68; network repeat broadcast: 9/15/68)

A different type of ocean voyage aired on television this week – the first of the Jacques Cousteau undersea specials. Meanwhile, in outer space, the unmanned U.S. spacecraft Surveyor 7 made a soft landing on the moon. The Beatles still had the best-selling record album in America, with *Magical Mystery Tour*. They also had the top song on the radio: "Hello, Goodbye." *The Graduate* was the champ in the movie houses. Robert Conrad, of *The Wild, Wild West*, had the cover of *TV Guide*.

Prior to the first broadcast of "The Terrible Leprechaun," 20th Century-Fox issued a press release, carried by newspapers as a filler piece.

When most people think of leprechauns, they think of tiny, elf-like creatures who delight in playing tricks on people.

Producer Irwin Allen took a step toward revising that image recently when "The Terrible Leprechaun" episode of his science-fiction fact adventure series, *Voyage to the Bottom of the Sea* was filmed. Not that Irwin Allen has anything against the little elves. It is just that for the first time they were present in an underwater adventure. Accordingly, instead of their usual little green outfits, the tiny men were fitted with wet suits and scuba gear for their underwater maneuvers. [6]

"TV Scout" said of this episode:

Well, now, me buckos, *Voyage to the Bottom of the Sea* is in the Irish Sea where they run afoul of an evil leprechaun (Walter Burke) whose personal Pot of Gold is in the middle of an atomic reactor. But cheer up, the evil leprechaun has a twin leprechaun, and he's a darlin' boy, a darlin' boy. [7]

A.C. Nielsen ratings report from January 7, 1968: [8]

	Peak Share:
ABC: *Voyage to the Bottom of the Sea*	23%
CBS: *Lassie* / **Gentle Ben**	34% / **37%**
NBC: *Walt Disney's Wonderful World of Color*	**35%**

10.3

"The Abominable Snowman" (Episode 103)

(Prod. No. 1315; first aired Sunday, February 4, 1968)
Written by Robert Hamner
Directed by Robert Sparr
Produced by Irwin Allen and Bruce Fowler, Jr.
Story Editor: Sidney Marshall

From the *Voyage* show files (Irwin Allen papers collection):

> Arriving at a spot less than a hundred miles from the South Pole, Admiral Nelson and Captain Crane are amazed to find that Professor Paulson has turned part of the icy wastes into a tropical paradise. However, it isn't long before those aboard the Seaview learn that the Professor's research has also uncovered a terrifying creature – the Abominable Snowman, who moves through the Seaview leaving death and destruction in its wake. [1]

Assessment:

Robert Sparr's occasionally inspired direction helps. Note when the creature passes in the foreground while the search party walks away in the background. In one of the scenes in the Missile Room, a crane shot lifts us up to reveal the monster on top of a weapons rack, looking down at its hunters. Another plus: An effective monster face and claws compensate for the big, white furry suit. But, at its heart, "The Abominable Snowman" is marred by a pedestrian script. Writer Robert Hamner tells us that the search parties, repeatedly crisscrossing the Seaview, cannot find something this big and horrible (and likely smelly). Even after they see it, they don't believe it! By the time the second half of the "story" comes along, it seems merely a thread for connecting rampaging attacks on crewmen who, no matter how many of their comrades have fallen, continue to venture down corridors on their own in search of the killer. One thing that can't be blamed on the script is the somewhat suspect performance by Dusty Cadis as Rayburn. He was clearly hired for his talent at screaming, not performing dialogue.

Mark Phillips commented, "This episode terrified me as a kid, but flat direction by the usually reliable Bob Sparr robs the monster of much of its menace. The acting of Dusty Cadis in the storage room must be seen to be believed. There's still some creepy, claustrophobic atmosphere and crewman Hawkins' desperate (and doomed) run for his life is chilling." [2]

We differ with Mr. Phillips as to the "flat" direction.

"The Abominable Snowman" is not as bad as the title implies. It's only half bad. And that means it's half good. We'll let you decide which half that is.

Script:

Robert Hamner's story treatment: July 24, 1967.
Hamner's 1st-draft teleplay: August 1.
Hamner's Revised 1st-draft teleplay: September 5.
Hamner's 2nd (and final) draft teleplay approved by Irwin Allen on September 28.
2nd Rev. Shooting Final teleplay (pink paper): November 16.
Page revisions (on green paper): November 24.

Writer **Robert Hamner** returned to the series one final time after a long break of work elsewhere, including *Star Trek*. He said, "The worst thing I ever did to Irwin was to go off to produce *Run for Your Life*. Irwin liked you to be under his thumb and he hated it when I wrote for other shows. We had some enormous fights, but he always needed me, so he would make up. He was a funny guy, a very bright man – an original." [3]

Hamner's story treatment began:

> The Seaview cruises ahead under a treacherously icy sea, just barely missing the razor-sharp submerged jagged edges of the huge icebergs above. They reach their destination and the Seaview surfaces in the middle of the beautiful, warm lagoon of a tropical paradise.
>
> CRANE leads a well-armed landing party ashore and returns with only three survivors of the expedition – PROFESSOR LORENZ PAULSON – a pleasant-faced man in his forties and leader of the expedition; and ARNOLD RAYBURN and DON CHAPMAN, two of his assistants in their late twenties or early thirties – all three men unconscious and in severe shock. Seaview CREWMEN take the three unconscious men to the sickbay as Crane tells NELSON he'd found no other survivors in any of the expedition settlement buildings. But he did find something else that's very interesting and shows Nelson a dried-mud cast he'd made of footprints he'd found all around the settlement.
>
> In the Seaview sickbay, a MEDIC is fixing some medication for Paulson, Rayburn and Chapman who are all still unconscious in their bunks. The camera is now in a closer angle on the Medic as he carefully prepares the medication when a huge shadow suddenly looms over him and he looks up toward it; the terror almost immediately shows on his face. He starts to scream but before he can, a huge, clawed hand reaches into the frame and grabs him around the neck, fiercely cutting off the scream – and his life. [4]

The series had sunk to a new low, despite the man behind the typewriter being capable of much better. Regardless, Hamner was sent to script, then asked for a free rewrite (a Revised 1st draft), before being paid again to polish the material for his second and final draft. Sidney Marshall and Al Gail, under the direction of Irwin Allen, played around with the script a little, then sent it to production.

ABC read the script, and responded:

> Confirming our discussion: Special caution that "the monster" is not too horrible or shocking to view and that the

monster-man struggles do not go, in direction, beyond what is indicated in the script and even telescoped further [with wide angle long-shots], if possible. Also, caution that features of the men, in the struggle, are not "distended" and that bodies in death are not grotesque or "mutilated". Generally, acceptability depends on manner in which it is done and can only be approved on film.

Pg 36, Sc 120, Pg 38, Sc 124: Of course, no effect of monster seeming to move through camera frame. [5]

Production:
(Filmed November 17 - 28, 1967; 7 days)

Robert Sparr was given a budget of $156,512.

Richard Bull was paid $1,000 for four days in front of the camera as the ship's unnamed doctor.

Dusty Cadis was paid $400 for four days work, appearing as Rayburn. We think it was $399 too much. Cadis had played an "Ambulance Attendant" in a 1965 episode of *Lassie*. He did all right there, since all the dialogue was given to the dog. He played a German pilot in an episode of *Combat!*, because he could speak a little German. He played a waiter in two episodes of *Batman*, perhaps having experience in the profession. He played "Arresting Policeman" in a low-budget 1973 movie called *The Mad Bomber*, which bombed. And Irwin Allen, apparently liking Cadis' performance on *Voyage*, brought him back to play a Giant Store Guard in an episode of *Land of the Giants*. Nothing else is known of Cadis, who, hopefully, didn't let these achievements prompt him to quit his day job.

Bruce Mars appeared as a guard who is killed by the snowman in the corridor. His terror resonates right through the TV screen. You can see Mars in a much bigger role from this period, as Kirk's academy nemesis Finnegan, in the 1966 *Star Trek* episode "Shore Leave."

Also good in this episode is **Robert Dowdell** (Chip Morton). Dowdell underplayed his role perfectly. Sadly, he was underplaying a role that was underdeveloped and underwritten. Writer Robert Hamner said of Dowdell, "He was a fine actor and he was so frustrated by that role. He could never get any lines. You had to service all of those guys, but Bob always got left out. Let's face it, it wasn't that interesting a part. I tried to write lines for him, but they got cut." [6]

Production began on Friday, November 17, 1967, for the first of seven days on Stage 10, for this bottle show utilizing only standing Seaview sets. It was supposed to be a six-day production, but director Robert Sparr fell behind on the fourth day of filming and was never able to catch up. [7]

Release / Reaction:
(ABC premiere airdate: 2/4/68; network repeat broadcast: 8/11/68)

ROBERT DOWDELL
20TH CENTURY FOX TELEVISION
"VOYAGE TO THE BOTTOM OF THE SEA"
ABC-TV

In the news this week, police killed three students protesting the Vietnam War at South Carolina State University, and the Dutch Second Chamber condemned the U.S. bombing of North Vietnam. *The Graduate* was the most popular film in the movie houses; "Love Is Blue," by Paul Mauriat, was the song being played the most over the radio; the Beatles' *Magical Mystery Tour* was still the No. 1 album. For only $2.99, at Mason's department stores, you could take a copy home and hear the hits "Penny Lane," "Strawberry Fields Forever," "All You Need Is Love," "Hello, Goodbye," and other radio-friendly songs, like "The Fool on the Hill," and even the strange "I Am the Walrus." Ben Gazzara, of *Run for Your Life*, had the cover of *TV Guide*. And the men of the Seaview were running for their lives ... from a stuntman wrapped in shaggy white carpet ... with a zipper.

Neither "TV Scout" or "TV Key," nor the trades, such as *Variety*, bothered to review this one. The novelty of the parade of monsters on *Voyage* had long since ended.

A.C. Nielsen ratings report from February 4, 1968: [8]

		Peak Share:
ABC:	*Voyage to the Bottom of the Sea*	22%
CBS:	*Lassie / Gentle Ben*	33% / 31%
NBC:	***Walt Disney's Wonderful World of Color***	**37%**

In the days after "The Abominable Snowman" first aired on ABC, "TV Key" Mail Bag column, syndicated to newspapers throughout America, ran the following letter:

> I think *Voyage to the Bottom of the Sea* is getting ridiculous with its plots. Every week we are given a silly mystery rather than a science fiction tale. All those ghosts from the deep and monsters running around the Seaview. The show has degenerated since the first season when it was entertaining without being outrageous. – M.C., West Point, Miss.

Editor Steven H. Scheuer's response:

> *Voyage to the Bottom of the Sea* is science fiction mixed liberally with monsters and other horrors. The kids seem to buy this show in its present state, according to the ratings. The undersea adventure series will continue in its current time slot and date for remainder of this season and probably beyond. [9]

Scheuer apparently hadn't viewed the latest ratings numbers.

10.4

"Man-Beast" (Episode 104)

(Prod. No. 1323; first aired Sunday, February 18, 1968)
Written by William Welch
Directed by Jerry Hopper
Produced by Irwin Allen and Bruce Fowler, Jr.; Story Editor: Sidney Marshall
Guest Star Lawrence Montaigne

From the *Voyage* show files (Irwin Allen papers collection):

In order to test an artificial atmosphere that the inventor, Dr. Kermit Braddock, claims will counteract the tremendous pressure of even the deepest water, Captain Crane is lowered in the diving bell into a trench in the ocean floor. When the bell is raised again, and Crane is back aboard the Seaview, he is unaware that he was unconscious for a time during the ascent. Not until he is alone does he realize that Braddock's artificial air has affected him, and that he is undergoing a strange metamorphosis! While Crane is in his bestial state, a Crewman is murdered, and the Skipper is almost overcome with horror when he finds he cannot remember his actions during that time. Not until Admiral Nelson reaches the Seaview with an antidote is Crane able to free himself so he and the Admiral can confront the real killer, and rid the giant Seaview of the terror aboard her. [1]

Assessment:

A collaboration of good writing, very good direction, excellent make-up, and award-worthy acting from David Hedison, make an episode that stands tall with the best the series had to offer.

Captain Crane, as presented here, is precisely what ABC's Lew Hunter was asking for concerning the Charles Aidman character when they made "Werewolf" during the early portion of Season Three. Now we see the fear and confusion as the man becomes werewolf, and remorse after returning to normal. We didn't quite see all those nuances then, but we do here. David Hedison was given a true opportunity to excel – and he did. The confusion, fear, and remorse Crane experiences register strongly. Also effective are the hyper-energized movements Hedison makes while in make-up as the Man-Beast. No sped-up film here; no technical tricks; it's all in the performance. Notice the jerky motions, the paranoia as he moves down the corridors, and the uninhibited fury when in the presence of others.

One immensely disturbing revelation for Crane is believing that he killed a crewmember. Admiral Nelson tries to comfort him, telling Crane that he was not responsible. But the captain's self-torment remains … until we learn that someone else may have been responsible.

Another big plus is a fresh score. Mike Bailey said, "Leith Stevens' score gives this episode what so many later-season *Voyages* lack – forward drive. Energy oozes from the soundtrack as every filmic element comes together." [2]

Mark Phillips commented, "Lawrence Montaigne brings real pathos to the role of Dr. Braddock. The makeup shots in shadows are effective and the glimpses we get of the dying Montaigne is creepy, as is Crane's 'monster face' during the conclusion in the diving bell." [3]

A *Voyage* classic!

Script:
William Welch's writers contract: November 17, 1967.
Welch's 1st-draft teleplay: November 17.
Rev. Shooting Final teleplay (on blue paper): November 24.
Page revisions (on pink paper): November 29.

William Welch did well with this one, illustrating a curious pattern of hit and miss with his scripts.

Production:
(November 29 – December 6, 1967; 6 days)

Jerry Hopper was given a budget of $161,384.

Lawrence Montaigne was paid $1,350 to play Dr. Braddock. He was 36 and worked often in front of the camera in character parts. He was POW Hayes, in charge of "Diversions," in *The Great Escape*. On TV, he was featured well in episodes of *Dr. Kildare*, *The F.B.I.*, and *The Fugitive*. Montaigne appeared in a pair of *Star Trek* episodes from this period, first as the Romulan war hawk Decius, in "Balance of Terror," then as Stonn, the Vulcan rival for Spock's fiancée, in "Amok Time."

Production began on Wednesday, November 29, 1967, for the first of six days on Stage 10. Besides the standing Seaview and Flying Sub sets, the interior of the diving bell and an office at the Nelson institute were used. [4]

David Hedison told interviewer Mark Phillips, "It was one of my favorite episodes. My stuntman and friend, George Robotham, usually did all of the dangerous stunt work. But I wouldn't let him do anything on 'Man-Beast'! I wanted to do it all. Why? Because I'm an actor and I'm crazy! It was great to play a monster." [5]

Hedison wasn't the only one having a good time on this particular show. Lawrence Montaigne said, "My character was confined to a wheelchair and, between takes, I would ride the wheelchair around. Then Richard Basehart grabbed it and he rode it around. Then some of the crew got hold of it. Let's face it, we were like a bunch of kids." [6]

Release / Reaction:
(ABC premiere airdate: 2/18/68; network repeat broadcast: 9/8/68)

Planet of the Apes, starring Charlton Heston, was the top film in movie houses. The Beatles' *Magical Mystery Tour* was still the best-selling record album in America. On the radio, more requests were coming in for the hauntingly beautiful instrumental "Love Is Blue" than any other song. Efrem Zimbalist Jr. and William Reynolds, of *The FBI*, shared the cover of *TV Guide*. And *Voyage* was about to give us a part-man, part-beast, and a *tour de force* for David Hedison.

"TV Scout" said:

> Handsome David Hedison gets transformed into a hairy beast who goes on rampages. It comes about because he is participating in experiments conducted from the Seaview by a crippled scientist. But don't worry, Richard Basehart is

rushing to the sub with an antidote, if he can only get there in time.[7]

A.C. Nielsen ratings report from February 11, 1968:[8]

	Peak Share:
ABC: *Voyage to the Bottom of the Sea*	24%
CBS: *Lassie* / *Gentle Ben*	**39% / 39%**
NBC: "The Legend of Robin Hood" special	26%

10.5

"Savage Jungle" (Episode 105)
(Prod. No. 1322; first aired Sunday, February 25, 1968)
Written by Arthur Weiss
Directed by Robert Sparr
Produced by Irwin Allen and Bruce Fowler, Jr.
Story Editor: Sidney Marshall
Guest Star Perry Lopez

From the *Voyage* show files (Irwin Allen papers collection):

When it is learned that part of Europe has been enveloped by tropical jungle, Admiral Nelson takes the Seaview on an exploratory mission. Once in the area, the men aboard find tremendous heat, and the jungle starts to take over the Seaview itself. The giant sub is almost destroyed before Admiral Nelson and Captain Crane are able to identify the Aliens aboard, and, by the use of a Gamma Ray Projector, rid their vessel of both the jungle and the Aliens, thus removing the threat overhanging the entire world. [1]

Assessment:

"Savage Jungle" is a visually distinctive episode – unlike any other we had seen before … or would see with what was left to come. The 20th Century-Fox greenery department got a workout with this production. While the premise is as wild as *Voyage* ever got, it somehow holds together – like a tangled web of vines. And it most certainly entertains.

Mark Phillips said, "ABC considered this one of the best episodes of Year Four. Seeing the interior of Seaview consumed by prehistoric plants is interesting." [2]

Mike Bailey said, "The shots of Seaview in the jungle kelp bed are very well done. Perry Lopez as Keeler is effectively troubling, and the dialogue is more intelligent than that in many of the later-season alien invasion episodes." [3]

Script:
Arthur Weiss's writers contract for "The Horrible Neanders": August 29, 1967.
Weiss's story treatment: September 12.
Weiss's 1st-draft teleplay approved by Irwin Allen on October 2.
Weiss's 2nd (and final) draft approved by Allen on October 9.
Rev. Shooting Final (on blue paper): December 1, 1967.
Page revisions (on purple paper): December 15.

Arthur Weiss's story treatment was a remarkable thing to read. Who would come up with such a concept for a 1967-68 TV series? Weiss did. No one could accuse him, or Bruce Fowler, Sidney Marshall, or Irwin Allen of not being open to new ideas. The treatment was called "The Horrible Neanders." It began:

> The SEAVIEW, en route to Gibraltar while carrying a British VIP – the correct and impeccable SIR HENRY WYNDHAM – suddenly goes out of control, its personnel suffocating in broiling HEAT which is somehow being generated within the sub.
>
> The condition is being caused by interference with the sub's nuclear plant by three full-sized, living and breathing NEANDERTHALERS.
>
> There is a partial recurrence of the "heat" crisis as the sub nears the European coast, this time coupled with a weird rise in HUMIDITY, coupled with miasmic vapors which threaten the air-support system. All this is tied somehow into the fact

> that a strange, uncharted underwater jungle threatens to form a barrier barring the Seaview's approach to the coast.
>
> The sub however continues to push and cut its way through the thickening underwater growth which might well entangle its controls.
>
> On board at night there is added to the strange heat and moisture an inchoate terror: it stalks the ship, keeping to the shadows. It is never seen except as a shadow and is heard only as a shuffling noise. Crewmen are killed; others are driven to incoherence by what they have seen. The chase after the shadowy threat apparently costs Sir Henry his life – he disappears.
>
> Crane, chasing one of the shadows into Sir Henry's cabin is all but killed.
>
> We see what has crushed Crane almost to death; and we see why the trail of the shadows was always lost: the Neanderthalers disappear. They become little miniature wooden figures in a small ornate BOX, lined with miniature jungle trees and vines.
>
> But part of the miniature jungle has escaped from the Box. Its tangled VINES have grown into the room, and only a few inches from the unconscious Crane. [4]

So ended Act I. It was perhaps the wildest tale yet considered for production. This was the Summer of Love, when American youth were wreaking changes in society never before imagined. If any shows on TV were keeping up with the explosion of colors, concepts and attitudes – the madness of the times – it was Irwin Allen's TV factory.

Act II began:

> Inside the submarine the jungle growth is soon discovered to have worked its way through air ducts and even through pipes.

Outside the underwater jungle not only becomes impenetrable to forward motion, but is closing in behind, threatening to cut off the Seaview's escape to clear water.

Countermeasures to cut ahead or go back to safety are ineffective. Danger of entrapment of the Seaview threatens.

The next morning the whole sub is invested with strangling vines and tangled undergrowth! The jungle has taken over the sub!

For the primitive monsters this is a perfect environment, and now they show themselves at will, coming out of or going back into their miniature form in the Box. Tropical jungle and humidity have soared to new heights.

Again the Seaview crew try to reverse this trend but this time they fail. The Neanderthalers prevent attempts to lower the temperature, and reduce humidity, to clear the air of swamp fog.

The jungle vines have penetrated the machinery, the electronic panels, the controls. They begin to squeeze and tear at the circuits. The sub begins to go out of control; shorted circuitry fills the fogged air with heat lightning.

Outside the tangled vines wrap themselves around the sub and begin to pull it down toward the bottom, bursting its plates while electrical chaos dooms Seaview from within.

The hoarse, guttural, barking VOICE of the primitive-minded chief Neanderthaler informs the crew of the Seaview that they are doomed. He is an alien. [5]

And that was only the halfway mark in Weiss's treatment.
Frank La Tourette wrote in the "Hot Sheet" newsletter on October 5:

Arthur Weiss is now busily at work on his second draft of "Savage Jungle" which promises to be one of our better and more unique VOYAGE segments. [6]

During the rewrites, the character of Sir Henry Wyndham was tossed out, and the Neanderthals were changed to silver-skinned jungle soldiers.

Production:
(Filmed December 7 – 15, 1967; 6 days)

Robert Sparr was given a budget of $163,057 to work with.

Perry Lopez was paid $1,750 to play Keeler. He was 38, and had starred in a different "jungle" – 1956's *The Steel Jungle*. He played Lt. Esteban Rodriguez in "Shore Leave," a 1966 episode of *Star Trek*. Irwin Allen cast him in a pair of 1966 *The Time Tunnel* episodes. Lopez was best known for the role of Lou Escobar in 1974's *Chinatown* and its 1990 sequel, *The Two Jakes*.

Pat Culliton made $750 for playing the role of Alien #1. He was 23. This was his twelfth episode of *Voyage* (always in small roles, such as a crewman in the Control Room). Irwin Allen also put Culliton in four episodes of *The Time Tunnel*, and two for *Land of the Giants*. Culliton worked steadily for Allen through the 1970s and '80s.

Production began on Thursday, December 7, 1967, for a couple of hours in the late afternoon in the Crew Quarters on Stage 10, with only Del Monroe needed. What followed over the next several days was like nothing seen on the series before.

The first official day of production was Friday, December 8. This was the first of six days on Stage 10 with the standing Seaview sets, both as they normally appeared, and then overgrown with jungle foliage. Also used on Stage 10, the Flying Sub and "Int. Air Support Room." [7]

Pat Culliton, interviewed for *Seaview: A 50th Anniversary Tribute*, said, "I had six days on 'Savage Jungle.' They would paint my hands with silver hair spray and, on my face, they used the famous old Jack Haley technique from the Tin Woodsman. I also remember Nick Dimitri, Scott McFadden and I played the jungle fighters."

The wild premise of this episode, and the Seaview sets stuffed with greenery, no doubt contributed to a sense of levity on the set. Culliton said, "I got into a sword fight with Basehart on the set of 'Savage Jungle.' He was practicing sword fighting for Cyrano De Bergerac and we just started playing around. He was much better than I was. He was more than twice my age and was just making a monkey out of me with these fencing sabers. I don't remember who it was, maybe Robert Sparr, or some assistant, saw an alien sword fighting with the star and yelled, 'Boys, boys, don't do that! You might get hurt, and we're making a movie here!'" [8]

Release / Reaction:

(ABC premiere airdate: 2/25/68; network repeat broadcast: 8/18/68)

This was the week U.S. troops took back the city of Hue, South Vietnam, through a series of bloody battles. War protestors continued to cry for an end of the fighting, but during this week a different breed of protesters gained the attention of the press. After a massive letter-writing campaign by fans of *Star Trek* over the rumored cancellation of the series, along with protesters marching on NBC Burbank and the network's headquarters at Rockefeller Plaza in New York City, NBC made an unprecedented on-air announcement saying that the series would be renewed for a third season. *Planet of the Apes* was still the top film in movie houses. "Love Is Blue," by Paul Mauriat, was in its fifth of six weeks at No. 1 on the *Billboard* chart for single record sales and radio play. Mauriat also had the best-selling album in America, with *Blooming Hits*, having displaced the Beatles' *Magical Mystery Tour*. Joey Bishop had the cover of *TV Guide*. And *Voyage* was about to blow the minds of its viewing audience.

Nielsen ratings report from February 25, 1968: [9]

	Peak Share:
ABC: *Voyage to the Bottom of the Sea*	25%
CBS: *Lassie / Gentle Ben*	**35% / 37%**
NBC: *Walt Disney's Wonderful World of Color*	31%

10.6

"Secret of the Deep" (episode 106)

(Prod. No. 1312; first aired Sunday, February 11, 1968)
Written by William Welch
Directed by Charles Rondeau
Produced by Irwin Allen and Bruce Fowler, Jr.
Story Editor: Sidney Marshall
Guest Star Mark Richman

From the *Voyage* show files (Irwin Allen papers collection):

> Admiral Nelson, acting on secret orders, takes the Seaview out on a hunting mission to locate the source of numerous attacks on the shipping of various nations – attacks with the most sophisticated weapons known – electronic biological mutants – monsters both nuclear and physical such as man has never seen. [1]

"Such as man has never seen," except for the earlier episodes which provided the stock footage seen here.

Assessment:

It was another **William Welch** script written to order, as a means of connecting stock footage and making a new episode from used material.

Mark Phillips said, "One ingenious way to use stock footage of whales, jellyfish and giant fish is to pass them all off as enemy weapons of a foreign power. Lots of action, sharp editing, and Peter Mark Richman is entertaining as Hendrix. It's funny how Hendrix is so inept in his plans to kill Nelson and yet he's always calling up his flunkies over the radio and blaming them for their errors! Also, Hendrix orders his people to clear the area of all 'dangerous denizens' so that he can escape, so why is the monster shark waiting for him?" [2]

This is the flaw in the episode – an antagonist that makes little sense. And all that stock footage, of course. When Hendrix, swimming outside the Seaview, encounters the giant shark, we know what will happen. Just as we know what to expect when the Flying Sub comes near the giant seaweed (or whatever it is) creature. It will grab hold of the FS1. And it will grab hold of the Seaview. Again, we'd seen it all before … literally. So, why watch it again?

Script:

William Welch's writers contract for "Secret of the Abyss": July 19, 1967.
Welch's 2nd-draft teleplay: July 26.
3rd Rev. Shooting Final teleplay (pale green paper): December 13.
Page revisions (on yellow paper): December 13.
Page revisions (on gold paper): December 15.
Page revisions (on beige paper): December 20.
Page revisions (on blue paper): December 27.

The "springboard" for the episode from the *Voyage* show files, called "Secret of the Abyss," read:

> The Seaview is on a special mission which involves the test firing of missiles. Suddenly the great sub is struck by a powerful beam which sends it reeling out of control and threatens its complete destruction. When the beam strikes them a second time, the sub's instruments are able to get a rough fix on the source of the destructive power.
>
> Nelson sets out in the Flying Sub to pinpoint the source of the menacing weapon. The Flying Sub is shot down by the same beam which attacked the Seaview, and Nelson is nearly killed. However, he is rescued and the Flying Sub is brought

> back aboard for repairs. But Nelson has discovered the source of the beam – a laboratory built secretly on the ocean floor. In reporting this extraordinary find to Washington, he is informed the underwater lab is the work of a small group of renegade scientists who were refused government cooperation in a dangerous experiment on the forced mutation of sea creatures. Nelson is asked to try to contact the group and give them the opportunity to call off the experiment, surrendering themselves to Seaview. If they refuse, Nelson is ordered to destroy their lab.
>
> When Seaview again approaches the area, Nelson descends in the diving bell in an effort to contact the lab. The bell is attacked by a monstrous creature on the ocean floor. Escaping, Nelson orders the attack on the creature by the flying sub. The attack is unsuccessful and the flying sub falls into the clutches of the monster – which, of course, is a result of the lab's experiment. [3]

When Welch took his story to teleplay, he added in the villainous Hendrix, a double agent on board the Seaview.

The initial feedback concerning the first-draft teleplay was negative from someone identified only as "J.A.," whose coverage notes were in Irwin Allen's personal files for this episode. From his August 11 memo, J.A. said:

> This seems to be a series of incidents loosely strung together, with the sole purpose of utilizing a great deal of stock film which will almost certainly be recognized by any viewer who sees *Voyage* with any regularity:
> - Distinctive bug-eyed monster – in conjunction with Nelson, Sharkey and diving bell.
> - Seaview belly landing on ledge.
> - Sharkey, Kowalski and the entire sequence of freeing the gate valve in ballast tank.
> - Enormous fish at Seaview viewport.
> - Manta ray hitting Seaview port.
> - Heavy, in the case of Hendrix, eaten by shark.
> - Monster grapples with Flying Sub.
> - Crane shoots laser at monster.
> - Same monster tossing Seaview about.
> - Nelson shoots monster with missile.

- Monster blows up.

The script lacks basic personal conflict. Hendrix, the one character we deal with, disappears from our story just when he is discovered to be the heavy by our principals. Eventually he runs off to be eaten conveniently by shark.

The band of renegades who inhabit the underwater lab are only mentioned in the dialogue. We see only the impersonal lab. [4]

What followed were two pages of specific notes and suggested changes based on individual scenes and elements of dialogue.

Irwin Allen chose to ignore every single one of J.A.'s concerns and suggestions. After all, the whole point of this episode was to make use of that stock footage.

Production:
(Filmed December 18 – 27, 1967; 6 ½ days)

The often-delayed "Secrets of the Deep," the twelfth episode of Season Four to be given a production number (1312), was finally put before the camera as the twenty-first to film.

Following the great success of "Nightmare," **Charles Rondeau** returned to direct his second of three *Voyage*s. He wasn't given much to work with, was he? Considering the amount of stock footage being used, however, the budget wasn't too bad. On paper, anyway, it was set at $163,205.

Mark Richman was paid $2,000 for five days before the camera, playing John Hendrix. This was his second *Voyage*, following the dismal Season Two entry, "The Monster's Web." Irwin Allen would have Richman back for a 1970 episode of *Land of the Giants*.

Production began on Monday, December 18, 1967 for the first of six-and-a-half days on Stage 10, with the standing Seaview sets and the Flying Sub. It was planned as five-and-a-half-day production, with cast and crew due to be released midday on Friday, December 22 to begin the three-day Christmas weekend early. But director Rondeau was one-half day behind when filming stopped Friday afternoon, the 22nd. Filming resumed on Tuesday, December 26, followed by an additional half-day of production on Wednesday, December 27. Rondeau wrapped at 1:10 p.m. [5]

Release / Reaction:
(ABC premiere airdate: 2/11/68; network repeat broadcast: 6/9/68)

This was the week that the first 911 emergency phone system was put into use in the U.S. (in Haleyville, Alabama). *Planet of the Apes* was the top-grossing movie. *Magical Mystery Tour* was top album; "Love Is Blue" the top song on the radio. The Smothers Brothers (Tom and Dick) had the cover of *TV Guide*.

Despite the drop in the ratings, it appeared that ABC was considering taking *Voyage* into a fifth season. At this time, in early February 1968, the only series to get a pink slip was *Batman*, but four others were expected to be cancelled: *The Rat Patrol, Cowboy in Africa*, and *Garrison's Gorillas*. The shows on the "iffy" list were *Peyton Place, N.Y.P.D., The Invaders, The Avengers*, and *The Second Hundred Years*. Surprisingly, with a poor average of only a 22%-to-24% audience share, *Voyage* was being spared getting a notice of dismissal ... so far.

CBS was saying it was undecided about *Lost in Space*, whose numbers were down (although higher than those for *Voyage*). NBC, meanwhile, was being pressured by sci-fi fans to stick with *Star Trek*.

A.C. Nielsen ratings report from February 11, 1968: [6]

	Peak Share:
ABC: *Voyage to the Bottom of the Sea*	22%
CBS: *Lassie / Gentle Ben*	33% / 33%
NBC: *Walt Disney's Wonderful World of Color*	**36%**

10.7

"Flaming Ice" (Episode 107)
(Prod. No. 1324; first aired Sunday, March 3, 1968)
Written by Arthur Browne, Jr.
Directed by Robert Sparr
Produced by Irwin Allen and Bruce Fowler, Jr.
Story Editor: Sidney Marshall
Guest Star Michael Pate

From the *Voyage* show files (Irwin Allen papers collection):

While investigating violent temperature changes around the Polar Ice Cap, the Seaview is trapped in an Ice Grotto by Gelid, leader of the Frost Men, who, in an endeavor to remove all heat from the surroundings, is melting the Ice Cap and threatening to drown the entire world. [1]

Assessment:

Effective make-up, set design, and use of animation help this curious, although convoluted, story. Going by looks alone, this episode is *Voyage* at its best. The imagination of the writers (Arthur Browne, Jr., with Sidney Marshall contributing through script polishing) is certainly displayed in high gear.

The science, of course, is dicey, but you may need to watch the episode more than once to catch its drift. To help unpack the material:

- The aliens – those visually stunning "frost men" – are stranded on Earth, with a spaceship in need of a tune-up (a boost in its nuclear energy). They can't survive temperatures above freezing; a pleasant day at the beach for them is 150 degrees *below* zero. To survive, they have created an environment in a grotto under the polar ice caps. Even this is not cold enough, so they have drilled exhaust shafts through the ice and rock to disperse excess heat. That exhaust causes the flaming ice, like waste gasses venting and burning from a trash pile. But the heat is melting the polar ice cap, and that is causing havoc around the Earth, with severe storms and flooding.
- The Seaview is sent to investigate. The Frost Men perceive the Seaview and crew as "invaders" – warm-blooded creatures whose body temperatures means instant death to them. Upon contact, the aliens melt into puddles of water! It is a fun concept and a terrific visual.
- The aliens want Seaview's nuclear reactor, which will allow them to power up their flying saucer and return home. Admiral Nelson balks; his crew would die without the energy – and heat – provided by the reactor. Gelid – the leader of the aliens – puts it calmly: "What choice do you have – your ship or your world?" If the Frost Men remain on Earth, all life is doomed.
- There is another choice for Nelson – find a way to shut down the alien's equipment, reversing the damage. And this brings about a "this planet isn't big enough for the two of us" scenario.

It is a pleasant change of pace to be presented with aliens that are calm, not screeching and flailing their arms or tentacles while attacking anything that moves. It is also a nice change of pace that these aliens are not trying to take over the Earth, but leave it! Michael Pate, under all that incredible make-up, plays his role with a touch of a calm intelligence.

So much for what works. There are also several things in this story that do not.

- What causes Kowalski's tumble from the flying bridge? The aliens didn't zap him. Kowalski sees them, then off he goes. So, what's up?
- What does the "Doc" do to reverse this condition, causing Kowalski's case of the sweats?
- Why does Kowalski decide to leave the Seaview on his own to go after Nelson and Sharkey? Why does he think he can save them? For that

matter, when it comes to finding and saving Nelson and Sharkey, what is Captain Crane's plan?
- How is it that Kowalski revives Nelson and Sharkey from their frozen state by merely opening the freezer door? Wouldn't Nelson and Sharkey need some resuscitation? After all, they aren't just a couple of pork chops to be taken out of the freezer and let thaw on the kitchen counter.
- Note that the alien equipment is conveniently labeled in English, so that Nelson can easily work it.
- Toward the end of the story, Gelid discovers he doesn't need to remove Seaview's nuclear reactor to get enough power for his spaceship to depart. So, why does he plan to leave the Earth behind as a planet of ice and flame? Mere lack of empathy? To stop mankind from eating popsicles?
- And, if the intent of the aliens was merely to recharge their spaceship and high-tail it out of there, as they say, why do Nelson and Crane feel it is necessary to blow the retreating spaceship out of the sky with a laser beam?

Regardless, this outing is visually distinctive, and is as much fun as going skating on an ice rink. The theme of climate change is eerily prescient. How many of us dreamed in 1968 that such a wacky topic as the melting of polar ice would become a serious concern several decades later?

"Flaming Ice" is worth a look, but you'll need to put all those nagging questions mentioned above out of your mind. In fact, just switch your mind off altogether and enjoy the visuals. Relax and float downstream.

Script:

Arthur Browne, Jr.'s writers contract: March 29, 1967.
Browne's story treatment approved for payment by Irwin Allen on March 29.
Browne's revised treatment, gratis: April 14.
Browne's 1st-draft teleplay approved by Allen on April 27.
Browne's 2nd-draft teleplay approved by Allen on May 29.

Rev. Shooting Final teleplay (blue paper): December 22.
Page revisions (green paper): December 26.
Page revisions (yellow paper): December 28.
Page revisions (gold paper): January 3.

Writer **Arthur Browne, Jr.** was 44; this was his first and only *Voyage*. He had been a frequent writer for series such as *My Friend Flicka*, *The Count of Monte Cristo*, *Fury*, and *The Big Valley*. He wrote 35 episodes of *The Rifleman*.

Browne said of his "Baked Alaska" story, "I had read something about burning ice and story editor Sidney Marshall liked the idea. But the story was a bear to work out. The series, in general, was very well done, with good production values, but I found my episode repetitious. I always did prefer to write westerns, comedy and drama!'" [2]

Browne's revised treatment began with this "Teaser":

> With a thunderous roar, a huge section of the Malaspina Glacier crashes into the sea, CAMERA FOLLOWING it down below the surface TO REVEAL the Seaview following on erratic course through great masses of submerged, threatening ice.
>
> Aboard the ship, sonar and radar readings are being shouted out by the crew with CAPTAIN CRANE evaluating them and giving sharp commands to the help to avoid the ice masses as seen through the bubble nose and monitor. ADMIRAL NELSON and COMMANDER MORTON evaluate sensor readings, revealing that the waters surrounding their position under the Polar Ice Cap are reaching an abnormal, high state and all indications are that something has happened to cause a melting of the polar cap which, in turn, could flood and destroy the world. Monitor scenes reveal tidal waves crashing ashore, engulfing populated areas, and monstrous seas over-riding hapless ships.
>
> Above the Seaview, the ice, hundreds of feet thick, shrieks and groans, with hollow cracking sounds reverberating through the ship. In the bubble nose, Nelson detects an unbelievable sight ahead. Huge chunks of ice, having broken from the cap, are seemingly aflame, the surrounding water having no effect on them. Eerie light shows through the ice

> masses. Sensors report radiation and heat. All indications point to fire ... where fire could not possibly exist.
>
> Crane gives an immediate order to reverse course. It is too late. Like the dying screams of prehistoric monsters, the ice above and about the submarine crumbles, closing in, engulfing the ship.
>
> Inside, the ship is thrown about violently as controls go haywire. Pressure cracks appear and frigid water streams in. The Seaview is obviously doomed, locked in a tomb of ice, sections of which are afire, flaming up and causing more ice to close in.
>
> As the roaring and violent mauling of the ship continues, CAMERA PULLS BACK TO REVEAL the scene framed on a monitor screen in the laboratory of GELID, leader of the Frost Men. He wears a light-weight robe of flaming red which offsets his hands, face and hair which are exposed as he watches the scene, so offset because he is obviously made of pure, white frosted ice. His face is set in a determined, satisfied expression as his hand, gripped about one of two levers marked: IGNITE – EXTINGUISH, depresses the Ignite lever and the Seaview becomes engulfed in more flaming ice.[3]

Browne had a reason for choosing "Gelid" as the name for the leader of the Frost Men. The word means "cold and sluggish."

When Associate Producer Bruce Fowler saw Browne's first-draft script, he wrote to Irwin Allen:

> I am impressed by the fact that this is a first draft teleplay, and a first by Arthur for our series, and the fact that he has captured the feeling of our show so well. This script – as in any first draft, requires some work. Then it will turn out to be an exciting segment of *Voyage*. It is a bit slow in the action lines, and needs tightening, especially in the Teaser.
>
> I like the Frost Men as heavies, but do feel that Gelid should be in the main line of story more, especially toward the ending.

> The character of Nelson has an unusually passive role in this show – it seems every time he is about to get started doing something – Zap – and he gets frozen again. I would suggest that this be re-examined. ...
>
> The effects on this show are going to have to be examined with great care. The number of times the Snow Men are melted, and the number of times our people are frozen, as well as their equipment, are quite chilling. I do think that this is an item that can be reduced, not only for the cost factor involved, but also for additional dramatic impact, when it does happen. There are a large number of burn-ins in the show, also, which must be examined.
>
> Mechanical Effects on this show are going to prove a problem. Their importance to the story is such that I would urge every effort be made to retain them even in the present amount. They are used with effect, and add to the story. This is one of our earliest shows, and will add to the overall production values.
>
> These things fall into their proper perspective against the picture as a whole, when you realize what a different, exciting *Voyage* this will make. [4]

Fowler continued with two pages of notes regarding specific dialogue, scenes, and sequences throughout the script. In conclusion, he wrote:

> I have a question – if Gelid and crew want to get rid of all the heat in the ice, as being dangerous to them – how come they do it by burning the ice and making it hotter? I feel like a fool asking this – knowing that SCIENCE and SID [Marshall] and AL [Gail] have this answer at the tip of their cigarette lighters, but would you be kind enough to illuminate me – with cold light, or course. [5]

Fowler was a clever producer. He could have called the writer, or asked Sidney Marshal or Al Gail. But, instead, he put the question to Irwin Allen, forcing Allen to justify this silly plot point. Burning ice, sure – but *how? Why?* Fowler diplomatically pointed out this seeming fallacy without challenging or criticizing Allen. That's how one stays employed in Hollywood ... in 1967 ... and today.

Production:
(Filmed December 27, 1967 through January 5, 1968; 7 days)

Robert Sparr was given a budget of $166,320.

Michael Pate was paid $1,650 to play Gelid. This was Pate's third *Voyage*, having played the Colonel in "Long Live the King" and Hamid in "The Traitor," both from the first season.

Michael Pate, seen before the make-up (above) and after (right).

Continuing to respond to criticism that the episodes of *Voyage* had taken on a "sameness," Irwin Allen pulled out all the stops to distinguish the latest from those before, including storytelling, set design, make-up, and, in the final stages, a fresh score. **Alexander Courage** was given the assignment, his sixth and final for *Voyage*. Courage would work for Allen again, providing the score for two episodes of *Land of the Giants*.

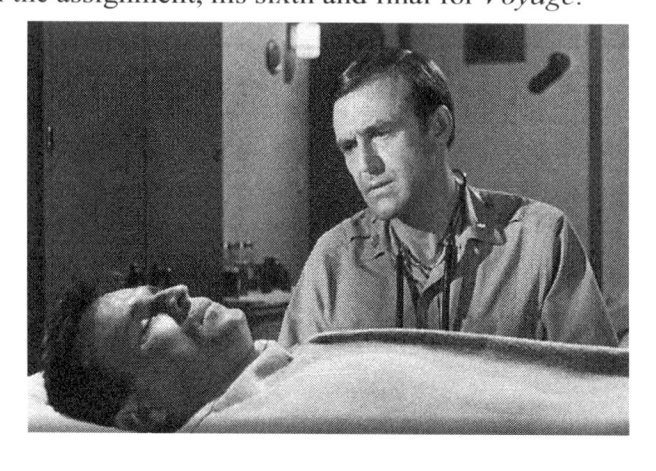

Filming began on Wednesday, December 27, 1967, for the first of three days on Stage 10 and the standing Seaview sets, including the "Int. Reactor Room."

The next four days (4-7) were spent on Stage B, for "Int. Gelid's Lab," "Int. Tunnel" and "Int./Ext. Ice Grotto." [6]

Michael Pate told interviewer Mark Phillips, "It was a unique story and, as actors, we came off looking not too badly. The episode was very true to the genre. The makeup was uncomfortable and it could have been better had they spent more pre-production time on it, but time is always money. The sets were top class and director Robert Sparr gave me freedom with the part."

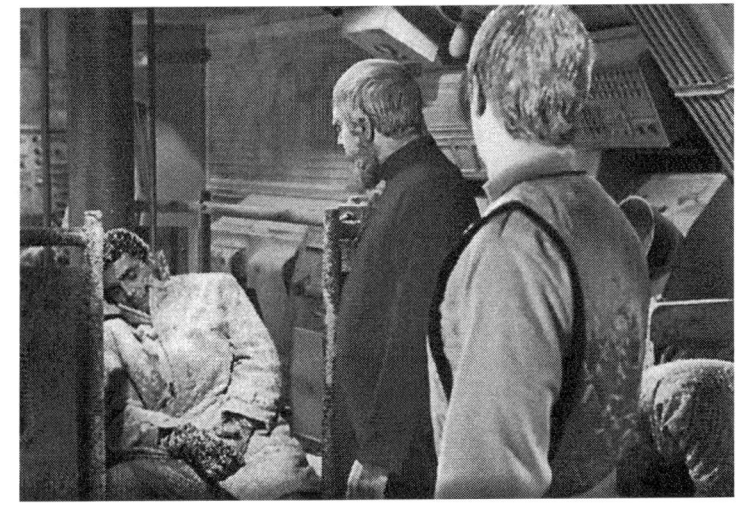

Regarding Richard Basehart, Pate said, "He was a lovely man and a great actor. I did three *Voyage* episodes and, after finishing on Friday nights, Richard and I would sit and have a drink in his dressing room. Dick spent the weekends going over the scripts and preparing himself for the endless struggle to make the work meet his high standards. I know the show was tough on him. You would have had to be Rambo to survive that 1960s jungle production factory, especially when you're the lead, working forty weeks a year." [7]

Release / Reaction:
(ABC premiere airdate: 3/3/68; network repeat broadcast: 9/1/68)

The Western *Day of the Evil Gun*, starring Glenn Ford, was the movie doing the best business at the box office. Paul Mauriat still had the top song and album in America. David Canary and Lorne Greene of *Bonanza* had the cover of *TV Guide*.

Nothing was written in stone yet, but according to the Doan Report in this week's *TV Guide*, *Land of the Giants* was "penciled in to replace *Voyage to the Bottom of the Sea.*" It was the first indication that *Voyage* was on the "iffy" list for renewal.

As for the other sci-fi series, ABC had come to a decision and was cancelling *The Invaders*. CBS was jettisoning *Lost in Space*. But NBC would retain *Star Trek*, which had been averaging a 27% audience share in its Friday-night time slot. Even though it was falling short of pulling a 30 share, *Trek* was nonetheless NBC's top-rated series of the night.

"TV Scout," by way of the *Edwardsville Intelligencer* in Illinois, said:

> Some good scenic effects as the Seaview is held in the icy grip of a grotto which manages to have walls of flame. Forget the plot – once again it's about aliens who need the Seaview's nuclear reactor to get home – and enjoy the special effects. [8]

A.C. Nielsen ratings report from March 3, 1968: [9]

		Peak Share:
ABC:	*Voyage to the Bottom of the Sea*	23%
CBS:	***Lassie / Gentle Ben***	**32% / 34%**
NBC:	*Walt Disney's Wonderful World of Color*	33%

10.8

"Attack!" (Episode 108)

(Prod. No. 1325; first aired Sunday, March 10, 1968)
Written by William Welch
Directed by Jerry Hopper
Produced by Irwin Allen and Bruce Fowler, Jr.
Story Editor: Sidney Marshall
Guest Stars Skip Homeier and Kevin Hagen

From the *Voyage* show files (Irwin Allen papers collection):

While trying to locate the underwater base of a UFO which has attacked an American fleet, Admiral Nelson and Kowalski are taken prisoners by the Aliens who operate the base. Worried by their mysterious disappearance, Captain Crane makes a rescue attempt, but the Seaview is damaged and sent to the bottom by a strange wall of flame. While repairs are being made, an Alien, Robek, is discovered aboard the submarine, and, despite his mistrust, Crane is forced to accept the Alien's aid. [1]

Assessment:

You certainly can't say that this episode is a one-topic show. Among the story elements are:

- An alien invasion fleet;
- An antigravity chamber under the sea;
- A possessed Kowalski;
- An underwater heat wave (with flames, no less!);
- An unseen assassin aboard Seaview;
- A peacenik alien;
- A jungle chase (on an island that exists within that underwater antigravity chamber; sunshine included!).

Mark Phillips said, "The idea of Robek being a peace-loving alien reflected the division over the Vietnam war at the time – a nation torn between the hawks (military proponents) and the doves (hippies and university students opposed to war). Unfortunately, Robek and his philosophy are not very well developed. There's a fantastic shot of a fleet of flying saucers hovering in a giant cavern. This semi-animated matte painting was originally created for Irwin Allen's unsold pilot, 'Man from the 25th Century.'" [2]

Mike Bailey added, "Note to wardrobe – enemy space-aliens never to be garbed in purple again!" [3]

Amen.

William Welch's script is chockful of interesting concepts and plot turns. Just when you think you know what will happen, Welch does the opposite – something his scripts had lacked in the last year. But the individual elements of this story don't always gel, and some of the plot points and characters, as noted by Mr. Phillips, could have used further development.

Nitpicking aside, "Attack!," like "Savage Jungle" and "Flaming Ice," offers a much-needed change of pace. It may speed through its cluttered and convoluted story, but it never bores, almost always entertains, and often surprises. We may even watch this one again!

Script:

William Welch's writers contract for "Alien World," parts 1 and 2: March 14, 1967.
Welch's revised contract, for "Attack," formerly "The Alien World, Part 2": March 14.
Welch's treatment, plus 1ˢᵗ-and 2ⁿᵈ-draft teleplays approved by Irwin Allen on April 13.
Welch's revised final-draft teleplay: December 12.
Rev. Shooting final teleplay (blue paper): January 2, 1968.

Page revisions (pink paper): January 5.
Page revisions (green paper): January 15.

William Welch struck again with his thirty-third script for *Voyage*.

The story began as "Alien World," planned as a two-part episode, explaining why "Attack!" has enough story for two. The idea was to get a leg up in the network ratings wars by airing Part 1 of "Alien World" one week prior to the kickoff of the 1967-68 TV season, then, with the audience hooked, air Part 2 during the official Fall Premiere Week when CBS and NBC would be starting their new seasons of first-run episodes. (You will recall that the fourth season of *Voyage* did indeed start a week before the official Fall TV season, with the airing of "Fires of Death" on September 17, 1967. This was followed by a pre-emption, then the episode Allen really wanted to kickoff with, "The Deadly Dolls," on October 1. These two episodes took the place of what might have been "Alien World, Parts 1 and 2.")

On March 14, 1967, a contract was drawn up between 20th Century-Fox and William Welch for the two-parter. By the end of the day, the first contract was replaced with a second, now calling for Part 2 as a separate property, with the title "Attack!" Regardless, the two scripts would be tied together, and Welch was still considering it a two-part story. [4]

Welch's treatment, delivered in late March, was called "City of Doom, Parts 1 and 2." It began:

> A strangely monstrous thing moves through the dark, murky waters of the ocean depths, coming directly toward CAMERA. Two baleful eyes stare straight ahead. Another angle reveals the thing to be Seaview's new underwater exploration vehicle "SEAPOD-1." Inside, manning the controls, are Kowalski and Patterson. They report back to Seaview that they have located the object on the ocean floor which is obviously the source of the electronic impulses they have been receiving. The object seems to be some sort of remote control radar station. Crane, from the Seaview, orders them to retrieve the object and bring it back aboard for study. Crane then excitedly reports to Nelson this may be the clue they are looking for to pin point the course of the secret attack that destroyed a whole fleet. And, undersea, mechanical arms are now extended from the Seapod and the arms grope for the installation on the bottom. Just as the

> weird "arms" take hold of the object, the men inside react in startled surprise at something they see through the viewport.
>
> Aboard Seaview, Crane hears the call of alarm from Seapod's radio and tries to learn what has happened. But now all communication is abruptly ended. At the same moment, Sonar reports all contact with the craft has been lost. To all intents and purposes, the small exploratory craft and its two crew members have vanished without a trace from the ocean bottom!
>
> Crane orders Seaview ahead to the Seapod's last reported position, then waits tensely as the great submarine inches forward. All at once there is a great and violent upheaval as what appears to be a sheet of flame erupts directly in front of the glass-nosed sub. The searing of a thermal wave strikes Seaview with such intensity that many of its delicate instruments are fused and the vessel reels back, completely out of control! [5]

What followed, in treatment form, was a total of 16 pages for Part 1 and another 14 for Part 2. Irwin Allen was not pleased by what he read. He typed up four pages of notes on March 27, sending them to William Welch.

> The overwhelming production costs and the difficult story problems involved makes it impractical to do this two-parter. Episode I seems to be a big and unexciting stall to introduce Episode II. Perhaps this is the basic problem. There is only enough story for one episode.
>
> The Seapod is a waste! Instead of the two-parter being built around it, the Pod is used unimportantly, unspectacularly and only incidentally.
>
> We had agreed to lean more heavily on Crane this year. This two-parter does the opposite, especially in Episode II.
>
> Why has Sharkey been eliminated?
>
> I believe that Hedison and Basehart will be deeply disappointed. Neither one of them can come off well.

> I really don't know what the story is all about and is it worth all this to tell it?
>
> The Buck Rogers overtones (in Episode II) come off old-fashioned and will play very stilted.
>
> The teaser of Episode I won't work. It's less than a half page long. There's no build up. [6]

More specifically, Allen wrote:

> ... The character of Robek and the story he tells about the city beneath the sea seems to be treated as a throw-away. Robek never pays off and the city beneath the sea, which is supposed to be the subject matter of the two-parter, is never seen till the tag of Episode I, which brings us to the embarrassing question – What is the big, exciting, overwhelming hook in the following week in order that our ratings not suffer by the premiere week of the other two networks? If we haven't accomplished this goal, then the whole project is really pointless. ...
>
> The top of Pg. 5: Robek refuses to tell who is behind the building of the secret city. What is Robek trying to accomplish? Either he tells Nelson what he knows or he doesn't....
>
> On the bottom of Pg. 6 and the top of Pg. 7: it says that Robek spends most of his time closeted with the Admiral. I'm terribly concerned this will lead to long talk sessions and no action. Because of the above, we must determine if Robek is a prisoner, held against his will, or a willing ally who, for either the sake of mankind or for reasons of his own, is willing to take the Seaview to the hidden city.
>
> Morton, whose one of our best actors and was badly used last season, is here again not used at all. ...
>
> Pg. 13: How do we show the miniature flying sub in the ocean surrounded by a roaring wall of flames?

Pg. 14: The transfer from the Flying Sub to the Seapod and the reason for it is pretty lame indeed. Also, from a production stand-point almost impossible to show. How do I show on 1 frame the Flying Sub, the Seapod and the swimmers crossing from one to the other?

Where do you propose to shoot "the jungle of flowered tears?"

In Episode II, Act I, Pg. 2: It speaks of the flying saucer landing close by with the hatch opening and several figures emerging. This would be the most expensive undertaking that VOYAGE ever tried. We can't possibly build a full-sized spaceship. ...

On Pg. 3: "A dazzling and imposing building." How can I afford to build this, or what do you have in mind?

Pg 3: Why is Malenk ancient and wasted? ...

Pg. 4 is filled with inconsistencies and confusing. I don't know what the colonists are doing on Earth. "Observing and studying" is not enough of an answer unless you explain to what end. (And here I'm concerned that you will be too close to my CBS project – THE MAN FROM THE 25TH CENTURY).

Pg. 4: The idea that Nelson would become the Governor of the new colony is kind of silly. He certainly would not give up his own life and career to head a colony of invaders from another planet. The request on the part of Malenk is ridiculous and any thought that Nelson would consider this is even more silly. The audience will be disturbed with us. ...

Pg. 12: It seems impossible that Malenk would contrive to have all of his people killed – just because revolutionaries within his own group would attempt to fire missiles against the people of Earth. Right or wrong, his people are his people.

On the top of Pg. 12 you speak of a wild battle beginning? How wild is it and how expensive?

Pg. 14: in the tag the flying sub and the flying saucer are fighting. It sounds good on paper, but how can we afford to photograph it? [7]

Welch's assignment was cut to just one script, primarily the story as it picked up in what was to be the second of the two parts. In other words, nearly a complete rewrite.

Considering Allen's harsh notes, and the sloppiness of the script he was reading, it is remarkable he didn't cut the assignment completely – and cut the writer while he was at it. Instead, the script went forward. Its writer, Mr. Welch, would be given a total of 13 assignments during the fourth season.

Production:
(Filmed January 8 – 16, 1968; 6 ½ days)

The budget given to director **Jerry Hopper** was $163,205. It was something to shoot for, even though there was no way this episode. Hopper was now on his last of 15 directing assignments for *Voyage*.

Skip Homeier was 37 and making his third appearance on *Voyage*, following "The Amphibians" and "The Day the World Ended." He was paid $1,500 for up to six days' work.

Kevin Hagen played the alien leader, Komal. He was a favorite with Irwin Allen, and was on his second *Voyage* (the first was Season Two's "The Shape of Doom"). He also made one stopover at *Lost in Space* and four on *The Time Tunnel*. He would soon be cast in the recurring role of Lt. Dobbs Kobick for nine episodes of *Land of the Giants*.

Irwin Allen continued to spend extra money in the final days of the series, again commissioning a composer to provide new music, at a time when most series cruised on tracked scores. **Irving Gertz** got the job, his only assignment for *Voyage*, although he was paid to score an early episode of *Land of the Giants* at the same time. Gertz had a long list of B-movies to his credit, including a 20th Century Fox film that co-starred David Hedison (1961's *Marines, Let's Go!*). Often employed by Fox,

Gertz had also scored episodes of numerous TV series at the studio, such as *Adventures in Paradise, Follow the Sun, Peyton Place,* and *Daniel Boone.*

Production began Monday, January 8, 1967, for the first of five days on Stage 10, with the standing Seaview sets (Int. Sick Bay, Int. Control Room & Nose, Int. Crane's Cabin, Int. Circuitry Room, Int. Corridors, Int. Reactor Room & Corridor, as well as the Flying Sub, "Int. Power Complex," and a "Limbo" set. On the sixth day, planned as the last, the company moved to Stage B for "Ext. Jungle Area" and "Ext. Jungle Shore." Half of a seventh day was needed for newly written scenes to be filmed back on Stage 10, in the Missile Room and Sickbay, with wrap time coming at 3:54 p.m.[8]

Release / Reaction:
(ABC premiere airdate: 3/10/68; network repeat broadcast: 7/21/68)

Stay Away, Joe starring Elvis Presley was the big movie at the theaters; "(Sittin' on) The Dock of the Bay," by the late Otis Redding, was the most-played song on the radio; *Blooming Hits*, by Paul Mauriat, the top-selling album.

The day "Attack!" aired on ABC, Skip Homeier was profiled in a filler piece syndicated to newspapers, including the *Wichita Falls Times*, of Texas. It told how Homeier began his theatrical career as a bad boy of Hitler's Youth Movement in the stage production of *Tomorrow the World*, then reprised the role for the 1944 film version. He was so closely identified with the role that much of his future, on stage and screen, would be playing villains. But not on this night's episode of *Voyage*.

Homeier said, "Happily, casting directors don't have as long a memory. At least they haven't been always casting me as a bad guy." [9]

Some did. The same week this episode of *Voyage* aired, Homeier again wore a Nazi military uniform in "Patterns of Force," an episode of *Star Trek*.

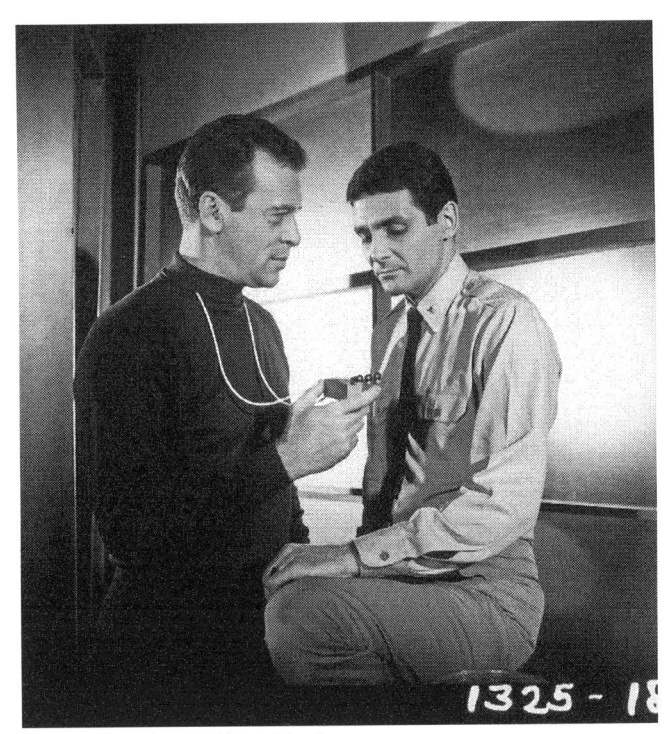

Of the *Voyage* episode, he said. "I play Robek, an alien from another planet with a peace message. I'm not totally bad and not totally good. Despite that recommendation, Robek is killed saving the Seaview and Earth from total destruction. I guess until I get more lionhearted, I'll have to keep playing a good-bad guy." [10]

"TV Scout," by way of the *Abilene Reporter-News*, in Texas, wrote:

> *Voyage to the Bottom of the Sea* is another opportunity for scenic designers to demonstrate that they can often be far more important to a TV series than the story. This plot is about aliens who plan to destroy the Earth and have set up a base on the ocean bottom to go about their grisly business. Enough? [11]

It wasn't enough to boost *Voyage* above third place in its time period, and a disappointing audience share of only 23%.

A.C. Nielsen ratings report from March 10, 1968: [12]

	Peak Share:
ABC: *Voyage to the Bottom of the Sea*	23%
CBS: *Lassie* / *Gentle Ben*	**33% / 35%**
NBC: *Walt Disney's Wonderful World of Color*	33%

10.9

"No Way Back" (Episode 109)

(Prod. No. 1326; first aired Sunday, March 31, 1968)
Written by William Welch
Directed by Robert Sparr
Produced by Irwin Allen and Bruce Fowler, Jr.
Story Editor: Sidney Marshall
Guest Star Henry Jones

Synopsis:

From the *Voyage* show files (Irwin Allen papers collection):

Admiral Nelson is amazed when Mr. Pem, the Time Traveler who was supposedly killed aboard the Seaview by an electrical discharge, appears in his office at the Institute. Before he can question his visitor, the Admiral receives the tragic news that Seaview and all aboard her have been destroyed by an explosion at sea. Stricken, Nelson turns to the man who claims to control time and makes a deal. Pem can make a new Time Device in Nelson's Lab – if he uses it to take Nelson back in time to before the explosion aboard the submarine so that Nelson can try to prevent it! Once back in time aboard the Seaview, he is horrified to learn that Mr. Pem's plan is to change the course of the American Revolution in such a way as to make himself the most powerful individual of the 20th century! Their backs to the wall, Admiral Nelson and Captain Crane have to call upon all the resources at their command to outwit the wily Mr. Pem, locate the explosive device he had hidden aboard the mighty sub, destroy it and bring the Seaview safely home. [1]

And, in the course of the story, they meet Major General Benedict Arnold!

Assessment:

"No Way Out" is an imaginative and entertaining episode. It's another welcome break from the sameness that many third- and fourth-season *Voyage* episodes had fallen into. It's dramatic and humorous by turns. And it delivers a first in television history with a wallop, as the regulars of a TV series are killed off within the opening minutes (when Seaview is blown to bits). *Star Trek: The Next Generation* would later do the same thing in their 1992 episode "Cause and Effect."

There is poetic justice at the end, as Mr. Pem suffers a fate he'd threatened on Admiral Nelson, to have to relive some final horrible minutes. You'll likely enjoy all the minutes in this taunt, daring episode.

Script:
William Welch's writers contract: December 5, 1967.
Welch's story, and 1st- and 2nd-draft teleplay approved by Irwin Allen on January 2.
Shooting Final teleplay (pale green paper): January 9.
Page revisions (blue paper): January 11.

This was **William Welch**'s thirty-fourth – drum roll and heavy sigh, please – and *final* script for the series. The results are above average, but the strain of writing every other show during the fourth season (and quite a few before that) had taken its toll. Welch later said, "By 1967, I was writing an average of an hour television show every week for Irwin Allen at 20th Century-Fox. It was a pace that was nearly impossible to maintain. I soon found out how true that was when, in early 1968, I suffered a stroke that was very nearly fatal. I had no choice then but to slow down and get my bearings once more." [2]

The slowdown came too late. Welch wrote his last four scripts in 1975, for Irwin Allen's *Swiss Family Robinson*.

Voyage writer Robert Vincent Wright said, "William Welch was a workaholic and he died of a heart attack that everybody felt was due to stress." [3]

Production:
(Filmed January 16 – 24, 1968; 6 and ¼ days)

Director **Robert Sparr** checked out of *Voyage* with this episode. For the following season, he went over to *Voyage*'s Sunday-evening competitor *Lassie*, with three directing assignments, then straight into B-films, with 1969's *More Dead Than Alive* and *Once You Kiss a Stranger*…. While scouting locations for a third film, *Barquero*, Sparr was killed in a plane crash in Colorado.

Henry Jones was paid $2,500 for a second turn playing Mr. Pem. This was his third *Voyage*. He wouldn't work for Irwin Allen again. But this wasn't the last we'd see of Jones. He would appear in more than 30 movies after this, as well as guest appearances on over 60 TV series, and as a regular on seven other series, most notable in 48 episodes of *Phyllis* (1975-77).

Barry Atwater was paid $750 to play Gen. Benedict Arnold. He was on his second *Voyage* (following Season One's "The Buccaneer"). One year after this, Atwater would play "Surak" in the 1969 *Star Trek* episode, "The Savage Curtain." He may be best known as Janos Skorzeny, the titular vampire in the 1971 TV Movie, *The Night Stalker*.

William Beckley was paid $750 to play Major John Andre. He had appeared in a 1966 episode of *The Time Tunnel*. Poignancy is added to the story when Nelson must return Andre – a man all on the Seaview liked – to the sad fate in store for him.

Production began on Tuesday, January 16, 1968 at 3:50 p.m., right after the last shot had been taken for the previous episode, "Attack!" They were on the Control Room set. It was the first of seven days on the stage, with the standing Seaview sets. On the next to last day, they even flew in the Ext. Flying Bridge set … and, for the final day of filming, Wednesday, January 24, 1968, Admiral Nelson's office at the Nelson Institute. They finished at 4:30 p.m., too late to begin work on the next episode, so the cast was dismissed while the crew prepared for the next day's filming – the first shot to be taken for "The Death Clock." [4]

Release / Reaction:

(Only ABC broadcast: 3/31/68)

On the day the final new episode of *Voyage to the Bottom of the Sea* aired, Mel Brooks's *The Producers* was the top film in movie houses. The soundtrack to *The Graduate* was the best-selling record album. "(Sittin' on) The Dock of the Bay," by Otis Redding, was the top song on the radio. President Lyndon B. Johnson addressed the American public about the Vietnam War and its effects on the nation. Johnson announced he would order a partial halt of bombing missions over North Vietnam, and then propose peace talks. In closing, the solemn-faced President shocked the nation: "I shall not seek, and I will not accept, the nomination of my party for another term as your president." Days later, civil-rights activist Martin Luther King, Jr. was assassinated in Memphis, Tennessee.

"No Way Back" was the second-to-last episode of *Voyage* to film … and the very last new episode to air.

"TV Scout" said of this episode:

> Henry Jones as diabolical Mr. Pem, the man with the pocket watch time machine, returns for the last new show of the series…. The episode is fun -- the Seaview blows up and all hands are lost. Admiral Nelson, back at the institute, makes a deal with Mr. Pem to return them to a period before the destruction of the sub, so they can prevent it. But once aboard, Mr. Pem has his own ideas, and they involve changing the course of history as it pertains to people like Benedict Arnold and Major Andre. [5]

A.C. Nielsen ratings report from March 31, 1968: [6]

	Peak Share:
ABC: *Voyage to the Bottom of the Sea*	22%
CBS: *Lassie* / ***Gentle Ben***	31% / **36%**
NBC: *Walt Disney's Wonderful World of Color*	**34%**

10.10

"The Death Clock" (Episode 110)
(Prod. No. 1311; first aired Sunday, March 24, 1968)
Written by Sidney Marshall
Directed by Charles Rondeau
Produced by Irwin Allen and Bruce Fowler, Jr.
Story Editor: Sidney Marshall
Guest Star Chris Robinson

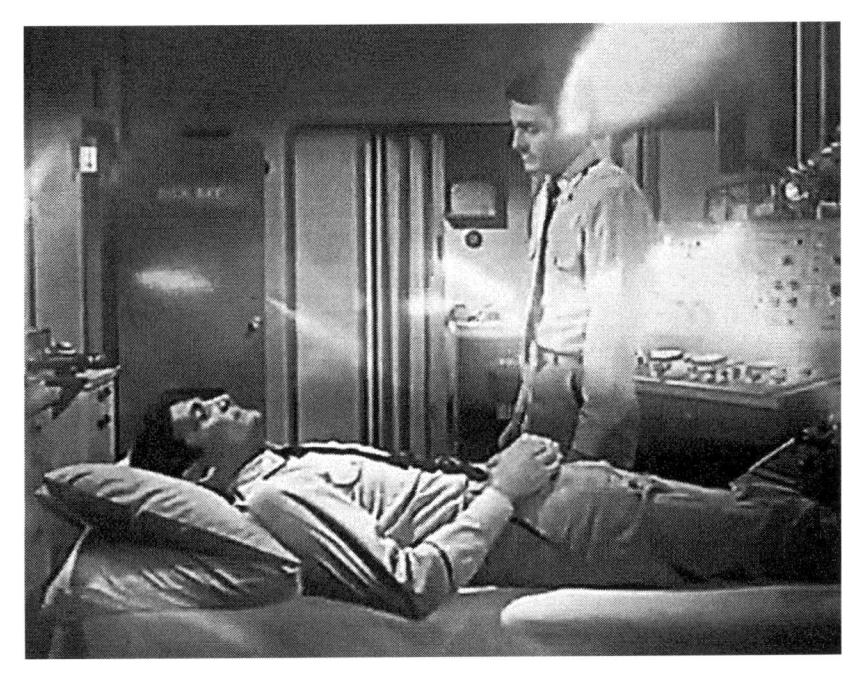

From the *Voyage* show files (Irwin Allen papers collection):

Captain Crane, recovering consciousness after an explosion in the Reactor Room, finds himself under arrest for the murder of Admiral Nelson. Confused and bewildered, he escapes from his guards and takes refuge in Sick Bay, where he finds a strange being from the Fourth Dimension awaiting him. The Alien, amused at the Captain's panic, tells him that he used the Captain's form for the murderous attack upon the Admiral. He is, in fact, using the men aboard the Seaview as guinea pigs for his time machine experiments. However, the murder will not take place until the following day, so the Captain has a sporting chance to beat the clock, which is ticking away the seconds. Searching desperately for a way to save his ship and those aboard her, Crane finds an ally in Chief Sharkey, whose belief in his Captain transcends the evidence of his own eyes. [1]

Assessment:

"The Death Clock" features an idea seen in the previous episode filmed, "No Way Out" – a man (or men) fighting against time to keep horrible events of the future from occurring. We'd also seen a double of Captain Crane, a possessed Crane, or a deranged Crane try to kill Admiral Nelson before. Despite this, "The Death Clock" is wonderfully executed. Its writing, direction, acting, music, and effects, both physical and animated, place it among the very best episodes in the series.

Mark Phillips said, "Another episode with a wealth of photographic tricks that effectively depict a nightmarish world where everyone seems against Captain Crane." [2]

Mike Bailey shared the sentiment: "Dang it, yet another Year Four episode that has me wishing there had been a fifth year of this series. If you like 'em way-out, this is the outing for you." [3]

Following the buildup of quality present in "Man-Beast," "Savage Jungle," "Flaming Ice," "Attack!", and "No Way Back," *Voyage* was going out in style. "The Death Clock" may be the best of the recent lot. It *is* among *Voyage*'s finest hours.

Script:

Sidney Marshall's writers contract: December 18, 1967.
Marshall's story, and 1st- and 2nd-draft teleplay approved by Irwin Allen Jan. 17, 1968.
Shooting Final teleplay (pale green pages): January 18.
Page revisions (blue paper): January 23.

After writing this episode, **Sidney Marshall** didn't skip a beat. He moved from being story editor and rewrite man on *Voyage* to story consultant on the first season of *Hawaii Five-O* (1968-69). For the latter part of that year, he served as producer. Then he was back working for Irwin Allen, with a pair of script assignments on *Land of the Giants*, then again as associate producer on Allen's 1971 TV movie and pilot film *City Beneath the Sea*. During 1971-72, Marshall served as executive story consultant on *Bonanza*, then back to Allen's side again as associate producer on 1972's blockbuster *The Poseidon Adventure*, and the biggest movie of 1974 and '75, *The Towering Inferno*. Marshall's last job was as a production executive on Allen's 1978 exploitation film *The Swarm*. Marshall didn't live to see that movie bomb; he passed away in December, 1977, at age 67.

Production:
(Filmed January 25 through February 2, 1968; 5 and ¾ days)

"The Death Clock" was intended to go into production before the other time-travel story, "No Way Out," but Sidney Marshall didn't have *time* to finish his script, focusing instead on rewriting all the other scripts scheduled for production. Therefore, this Production Number 1311 was not the eleventh episode to film for the Fourth Season, but the twenty-sixth.

Director **Charles Rondeau** was given a budget of $163,205 for his, and the series', final voyage. He left Irwin Allen's employ to direct episodes for the last seasons of *The Wild, Wild West* and *Get Smart*, then on to *Mission: Impossible* and *The Partridge Family*, among other series.

Irwin Allen again splurged to have a new score for this late-season entry. **Harry Geller** was given the challenge, and met it head on with his inspired mood music. Geller had scored three other fourth-season episodes of *Voyage* ("The Deadly Dolls," "Sealed Orders" and "Savage Jungle"). He would go on to handle an equal number of episodes for *Land of the Giants*. If you are familiar with *The Wild, Wild West*, and some of its horror-themed and surreal episodes, the music heard here may remind you of that series. There is a reason – Geller had scored five *WWW* episodes.

Chris Robinson was paid $1,750 to play Corpsman Mallory. He was 29 and had been a regular on *12 O'Clock High* (as Sgt. Sandy Komansky in 47 episodes), as well as a guest performer on multiple episodes each for *The Virginian, The Detectives*, The *Alfred Hitchcock Hour*, and *Wagon Train. Photoplay* magazine nominated him as Most Promising New Star in 1966. Robinson stayed busy in the soaps during the 1980s, '90s, and beyond (with *General Hospital, The Bold and the Beautiful* and *Another World*) and would receive a Soap Digest award nomination for the latter, as "Outstanding Villain," for *Another World.* He's pretty villainous here, as well.

Production began on Thursday, January 25, 1968, for the first of five-and-a-half days on Stage 10 with the standing Seaview sets, and that of the Flying Sub. On midday of the sixth day of production, the company moved to Stage B to film the "Ext. Seaview Deck" and "Ext. Section of Jungle 1, 5, 6 and 7." By this point, director Charles Rondeau had fallen behind, and a seventh day was needed to finish on Stage B, with

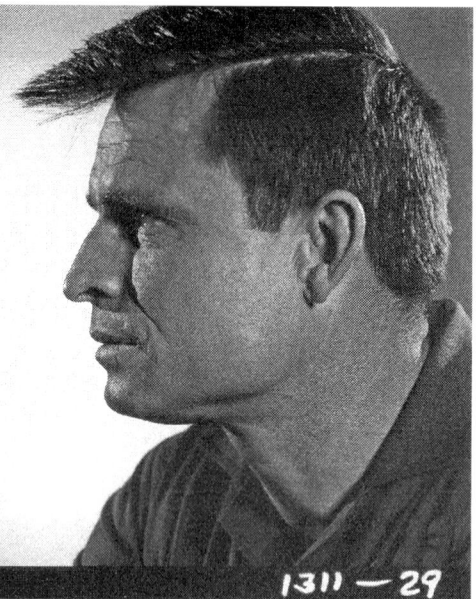

While filming this final episode for Season Four, and expecting it would be the last for the series, the set photographer took portrait shots of supporting cast members Robert Dowdell, Del Monroe, and Paul Trinka, for use in promoting the syndicated rerun package. Also taken from the same sessions was a portrait shot of guest star Chris Robinson (previous page).

"Ext. Section of Jungle 2, 3 and 4," and "Int. Limbo Optical" set. Rondeau took his last shot at 3:38 p.m. Then it was all over. [4]

As cast and crew left the wrap party that day, most suspected they would not be returning for another season. ABC made it official before this episode aired.

Release / Reaction:
(ABC premiere airdate: 3/24/68; network repeat broadcast: 8/25/68)

No Way to Treat a Lady, starring Rod Steiger, Lee Remick, and George Segal, was No. 1 in the movie houses. The average movie ticket was $1.50. And gas would cost you 34 cents a gallon to and from the theater. While driving, you could switch on the radio and hear the late Otis Redding, who still had the top song, with "(Sittin' on) The Dock of the Bay." Paul Mauriat & His Orchestra continued to have the top album in the stores – you know, the one with "Love Is Blue." Bill Cosby and Robert Culp, of *I Spy*, had the cover of *TV Guide* ... for the third time.

"TV Scout," by means of the *Edwardsville Intelligencer* in Illinois, said:

> One of the slicker science-fiction episodes is shown, even if it does get pretty confusing before it's all over. David Hedison, in sick bay after a radiation explosion, runs into a corpsman with a strange machine -- something to do with the Fourth Dimension. So Hedison rises from himself, gets a gun and kills Richard Basehart. The trick: it's today in sick bay and tomorrow on the rest of the ship. [5]

Nielsen ratings report from March 24, 1968: [6]

	Peak Share:
ABC: *Voyage to the Bottom of the Sea*	22%
CBS: *Lassie / Gentle Ben*	35% / 34%
NBC: *Walt Disney's Wonderful World of Color*	**36%**

From the Mail Bag:

From "TV Key Mail Bag," July 6, 1968 column:

> David Hedison is so handsome and such a good leading-man type. I wish he would make some movies. I'm tired of seeing him play in the juvenile series *Voyage to the Bottom of the Sea*. – M.E.F., San Antonio, Tex.

Editor Steven H. Scheuer answered:

> You needn't worry about seeing David Hedison in *Voyage to the Bottom of the Sea* anymore after the summer reruns. The

adventure series has been cancelled. Hedison will probably make some films now that he is free from his weekly TV duties. [7]

11

Submarine Down – The End of the Voyage

"The Death Clock" was the final episode to film. It was also the last time David Hedison and Richard Basehart worked together.

At a 1993 convention appearance, Hedison was asked about working with Richard Basehart. He responded, "What it was like was fantastic! I was a very lucky actor to be working with him…. He was a wonderful man. He taught me an awful lot, because I don't think I was as good an actor at that first year as I was when the series ended. I think I learned a lot from him and I'm grateful. And I love you, Richard!" [1]

"Death Clock" was Richard Bull's twenty-seventh episode of *Voyage*. When asked how he liked working for Irwin Allen, Bull said, "Fine, but in four years time, I never really knew him. Never was even formally introduced. Strange man." [2]

Richard Basehart would continue working till his last day on Earth. He was even heard for a few years after that, in new episodes of the TV series *Knight*

719

Rider, narrating the opening title sequence. Standout roles were still ahead of him, on the big screen, with 1972's *Rage*, in which he took second bill under George C. Scott; 1976's horror-thriller *Mansion of the Doomed*, for which he had the lead; 1978's comedy heist caper, *The Great Bank Hoax*, in another lead role; and 1980's *Being There*, with a special guest appearance opposite Peter Sellers. On the small screen, Basehart worked often in TV movies, such as his co-starring role opposite Eleanor Parker in 1969's *Hans Brinker*; 1970's *Sole Survivor* and *The Andersonville Trail* (both co-starring William Shatner); 1972's *Assignment: Munich*, co-starring with Roy Schneider; 1973's *... And Millions Die!*, top-billed with Susan Strasberg; and the lead as George Washington in 1975's *Valley Forge*. Basehart also had top guest-star turns on popular series such as *Ironside*, *Gunsmoke*, *Hawaii Five-0*, and *Columbo*. In the latter, he and Honor Blackman played the guest murderers. And Basehart worked again for Irwin Allen, in the 1971 TV movie/pilot, *City Beneath the Sea*; the 1976 TV movie/pilot *Time Travelers*; and the 1976 TV movie *Flood!*

David Hedison was never short of work. He had the lead in the 1971 TV movie, *A Kiss Is Just a Kiss*, billed above Keir Dullea; played Felix Leiter, the CIA contact for James Bond, in 1973's *Live and Let Die* and 1989's *License to Kill*; starred opposite Meredith Baxter in the 1973 TV movie horror film, *The Cat Creature*; had the lead in the 1974 TV movie, *The Compliment*; second billing under Robert Stack in Irwin Allen's 1975 TV movie/pilot, *Adventures of the Queen*; to name a few. He guest-starred in dozens of prime-time TV series. As late as the new millennium, he was a regular on the daytime soap *The Young and the Restless*. But Hedison didn't transcend *Voyage* to the degree that Richard Basehart did; the bulk of his roles came with third, fourth, or fifth billing. Regardless, he worked often, with over 100 appearances post-*Voyage*.

Robert Dowdell had close to 40 screen appearances after *Voyage*, including turns for Irwin Allen, in a 1969 episode of *Land of the Giants*; the 1971 TV movie *City Beneath the Sea*; and the 1986 TV movie *Outrage!* He made guest appearances on popular series of the day such as *McMillan & Wife*, *The F.B.I.*, *Adam-12*, *S.W.A.T.*, *Buck Rogers in the 25th Century*, *CHiPs*, *Hart to Hart*, *Fame*, and *Dynasty*. Most were moderate roles.

Del Monroe had over 50 post-*Voyage* screen appearances. Most, however, were minor roles.

Terry Becker chose to move behind the camera after *Voyage* ended, with one-off directing jobs for *Mod Squad*; *Love, American Style*; *The Courtship of Eddie's Father*; *The Brady Bunch*; *Mission: Impossible*; and *M*A*S*H*. He stayed longer at *Room 222*, with eight assignments. Mostly, Becker busied himself as a producer, with 1977's no-big-deal feature film *The Banana*

Company, and several TV movies, including 1977's *The Last Hurrah*, starring his production-company partner, Carroll O'Connor. Becker returned to acting in the new millennium with several screen appearances.

Paul Trinka took two acting jobs from Irwin Allen, in a pair of *Land of the Giants*, and popped up in a 1970 episode of *The Bold Ones*, and one in 1971 for *Night Gallery*. Sadly, Trinka passed away in 1973 from brain cancer. He was only 42.

Arch Whiting (Sparks) also appeared in a *Land of the Giants*, one of 23 acting jobs after *Voyage*. Thirteen of those were in his own short-lived series, *Run, Joe, Run* (1974-75). He played second to a police dog named Joe.

Richard Bull (Doc) had his greatest success ahead of him, as Nels Oleson, in 146 episodes of *Little House on the Prairie*, plus three reunion TV movies. Bull worked all around the dial, appearing several times each in series as diverse as *Family Affair*; *Mission: Impossible*; *Nichols*; *The F.B.I.*; *Mannix*; *The Streets of San Francisco*; *Barnaby Jones*; *Mary Hartman, Mary Hartman*; and *Highway to Heaven*.

But no one worked more, and harder, than Irwin Allen. Del Monroe said, "Many people were afraid of Irwin because he was always yelling and shouting, but underneath that he was a generous, nice, warm guy. He gave me four years' work, and I could have had more. He wanted me for a recurring role on *Land of the Giants*, but I turned it down. I didn't want to be identified as a SF actor." [3]

No one seemed more surprised at *Voyage*'s cancellation than Irwin Allen. He commented to the press that he believed it should have continued for at least a few more years. Perhaps he had stopped reading the ratings reports that consistently placed the series in third position as its fourth season progressed … although this is unlikely. He meticulously collected survey reports and kept them among his personal papers.

David Hedison said, "[Irwin] just loved all, as I say, the 'heavy stuff,' and the grimness and the monsters and all that sort of stuff. *Voyage to the Bottom of the Sea* was on the air for four years; had wonderful actors; it could have been on for seven or for eight. And I think he ruined it in the last year or two, bringing in the Fossil Man, the Rock Man, the Lobster Man, the *This* Man or *That* Man. It was ludicrous. I mean, the show was bound to go off the air. And towards the end, I thought, you know, 'This is going to be the end.' And sure enough – boom, we were off." [4]

Mike Bailey was watching when "No Way Back," the last new episode of *Voyage* to air, had its ABC broadcast on March 31, 1968. He said, "Back in 1968, viewing the final first-run episode of *Voyage* was very hard for me. The fact is, I was one of those kids from a broken family who had latched onto Seaview's crew as family, and Nelson as father-figure. Corny perhaps; perhaps maudlin, but I don't apologize for it. In spite of my indignation over script quality and monster-of-the-week orientation toward the end, *Voyage* was a wonderful and important part of my life. Hats off to Irwin for being such a kid, albeit a mean one on occasion, and hats off to Richard Basehart for being such a great dad to boys like me, although he was apparently never even aware of that role. My one regret is that, in later life, I never attempted to write a letter to him saying thanks. I was always afraid I would come off sounding like some kind of weirdo or geek, which of course, may not be far from the truth. And then there's the talented and gracious David Hedison. Along with Del Monroe, Paul Trinka, Terry Becker, Bob Dowdell and, back in Season One, Henry Kulky and Paul Carr. They weren't too shabby either. Last but not least, I must remember to tip my cap to internet friend Ray Didsbury, who was along for almost all of the 110 episodes of *Voyage to the Bottom of the Sea*." [5]

In return, we'll tip our own fan beanies to the late Mike Bailey.

By the time *Voyage* left the ABC network, *The Time Tunnel* had likewise exited, one year earlier. And *Lost in Space* had been grounded by CBS. It too was sent into syndicated rerun-land. But Irwin Allen was *not* finished sharing his fantasy worlds on American television in the 1960s. As discussed, he had a new series launching: *Land of the Giants*. Ever the workaholic, Allen was also preparing a new pilot called *City Beneath the Sea* (borrowing a title from an episode of *Voyage to the Bottom of the Sea*). It also recycled stock-film footage from *Voyage*, including one substantial prop: the Flying Sub.

Allen targeted NBC with his "new" concept, hoping to replace *Star Trek* as the sole science-fiction series on the Peacock Network. Although the project began in 1969 with an eleven-minute filmed presentation, Allen's made-for-TV movie of *City Beneath the Sea* didn't air until January 25, 1971. It had a big "all-star" cast, with Stuart Whitman in the lead, supported by Rosemary Forsyth and Robert Colbert, late of *The Time Tunnel*. Also giving support and star power, two other *Time Tunnel* alumni: James Darren and Whit Bissell. In addition, there were "special guest appearances" by Joseph Cotton, Edward G. Robinson, Sugar Ray Robinson, Robert Wagner, and even Richard Basehart and Robert Dowdell. Allen found himself a former *Star Trek* writer, director, and producer – John Meredyth Lucas – to write the script (based on a story by Irwin Allen, ensuring "the emperor" his "created by" credit).

Allen, of course, directed and produced.

The pilot did not sell. In the early 1970s, television was in a state of abrupt change. America's period of fantastic television was winding down. That's series such as *Star Trek*, *The Wild, Wild West*, *The Man from U.N.C.L.E.*, *Batman*, *I*

Dream of Jeannie, Bewitched, The Munsters, The Addams Family, Gilligan's Island, and others, including those produced by Irwin Allen, and imported series, such as *The Avengers*. TV violence was under attack by the Federal Communications Commission and consumer groups. The mood of the nation had changed from the pop-art explosions of Andy Warhol, Peter Max, the Beatles, and Irwin Allen, to the kinder, gentler "adult" themes of *Marcus Welby, M.D.*, *Medical Center*, and *Then Came Bronson*.

    Allen would shift back to the big screen, becoming known as the "Master of Disaster," with his early 1970s big-screen mega-hits *The Poseidon Adventure* and *The Towering Inferno*. He kept his presence felt on television with big-event TV movies, such as *Flood!* and *Fire!* He would attempt to make another undersea voyage on television with *The Amazing Captain Nemo*, and another time-travel tale, with *Time Travelers*. He would keep the family Robinson earthbound for one season on ABC, with *Swiss Family Robinson*. Man Against Man and Man Against Nature remained the themes. All-star casts provided one of the attractions; state-of-the-art special effects and relentless action-adventure the others. It was a format that had worked well for Allen before. But, as with all trends, it eventually fell out of favor.

    As Allen's popularity declined in the late 1970s and throughout the 1980s, so did his health. He had lived to work. As his work lost luster with the public, his physical state also seemed to decline.

    But for nearly half a decade, Irwin Allen was front and center at 20th Century-Fox and on American TV, spinning fantasy tales for mass consumption. The kids ate them up. Many adults did, too. His second-most-popular series was *Lost in Space*. We have taken an in-depth look at that program, as well as a further study of its creator and maker, in a three-volume book series. And *Space* has experienced a renaissance, via a big-budget remake for Netflix.

    The owners of *Voyage to the Bottom of the Sea* have wanted to remake Irwin Allen's formative first series as well. It may happen one day, but we don't expect it. *Voyage* may be best served by allowing it to stand as it is, a curious artifact of a bygone era – the 1960s. We should simply treasure the wild imagination of Irwin Allen, encouraged by a TV network focused on harmless entertainment and ratings; a superbly talented cast; and the special-effects might of 20th Century-Fox studios. These ingredients, including their sometimes-opposing agendas, which made *Voyage* unique and special. Even when the material, or the restrictive budget, cheapened the show, there was always something to admire. Even the lesser *Voyage*s have merit. They are good fun. Sometimes good fun is good enough.

The Fantasy Worlds of Irwin Allen haven't yet ended. In the hearts of those who've not lost their sense of childlike wonder … they never will.

David Hedison in early 1968, on his way into *Voyage*'s home port – 20th Century-Fox Stage 10. Bon voyage, good friend.

Appendices

Appendix A:
Voyage to the Toy Store

This section is a sampling of the merchandising tie-ins for the *Voyage to the Bottom of the Sea* series during its 1964-1968 run.

No one loved – or collected – the merchandising more than Irwin Allen. And it wasn't just an egotistical display (though, as we know, Allen was not deficient in that regard). No – part of his personality remained childlike, and he delighted in each crop of toys. The fact that they were licensed gave him an excuse to have them around.

"His office was like a toy store," Allan Hunt said. "He had the models of the Seaview and the Flying Sub; the games; the trading cards; everything! There were spaceships and planes hanging on strings from the ceiling; things on his desk, on shelves. It was all quite an eyeful." [1]

No one was more dazzled by the inner sanctum of Allen's office than Billy Mumy, who was playing Will Robinson in *Lost in Space*. Interviewed for

Above, L-R: The 1961 film novelization; the same book repackaged with series photo. On the following page: Paul Fairman's 1965 original paperback tie-in.

727

this book, Mumy recalled, "I used to go into his office, and he would have piles of merchandise, including *Lost in Space* merchandise. And he would always say, 'Billy, you can have *one*.' So, I would get a box of cards, or a game board, or a model or something. But only one at a time, because I could only have *one*. So, I made it a point of going into his office as often as I could. And he would again say, 'Billy, you can have *one*.' And I'd take another!

"I think Irwin was childlike in his own sense of what he liked, because if you look at the projects he made – dinosaur movies, circus movies, a television series going undersea, then one into space, then back in time – they were all the areas that are so easy for a child to let his imagination run wild in. Those were the areas he chose to play in." [2]

In conjunction with the original film, Pyramid Books released a novelization by sci-fi author Theodore Sturgeon, who later wrote for the series *Star Trek*, *Tales of Tomorrow*, and *The Invaders*. The same movie novelization was rereleased in 1965, repackaged with photos from the TV series.

In 1965, Pyramid Books released an original paperback tie-in, *City Under the Sea*, by genre author Paul W. Fairman.

In 1964, famous sports-card manufacturer Donruss added to their media line with a set of 66 cards of *Voyage* images. The card fronts, in black-and-white, featured various images of the cast. To fill the roster, minor cast members like

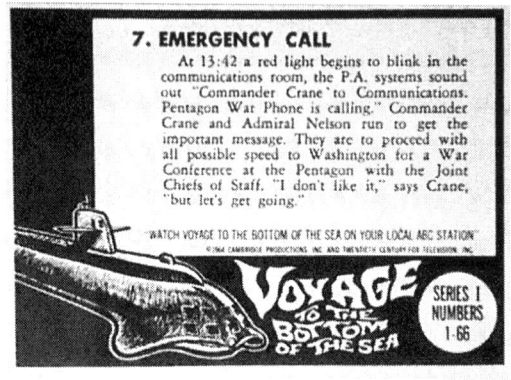

"Curly" Jones, Sparks, Kowalski, and others appeared. The card backs were printed in blue ink, serializing the episode "Eleven Days to Zero."

Milton Bradley's *Voyage* board game (above) and (below) card-matching game.

Milton Bradley licensed two games tied into the *Voyage* franchise. The first, released in 1964, was a two-player board game. You navigated a Go-like grid to maneuver your plastic subs against your opponent. Each player had eight subs (black or white) with which to approach and destroy the other. You could get it at Associated Hardware in Uniontown, PA., for only 88 cents!

In 1965 MB released a *Voyage* card game. It had a pair-matching format, much like Crazy Eights. The cards featured images of the Seaview printed in green, red, or blue, each numbered 1-13.

MB released two "Junior Jigsaw" puzzles of scenes from "Eleven Days to Zero," as well as a tray puzzle (frogmen battling a shark) for younger fans.

Whitman's coloring book (left) and juvenile novel (right).

Whitman Publishing issued two tie-in books in 1965. For little brother or sister, there was a 128-page coloring book. For the older fry, Whitman released a juvenile novel. It was written by sci-fi author Raymond E. Jones (*This Island Earth*), and related the Seaview's encounter with a long-lost colony of Minoans. These Mediterranean folks fled into underwater caves around 1100 BC, but since then have developed their own hi-tech civilization. The undersea government is undergoing a revolution, with Nelson and crew caught in the middle – before a seaquake nearly dooms them all.

Aurora released two model kits tied into the show. The first was the Seaview, in 1965. (This kit was rereleased by Polar Lights in 2002.)

Top image: The Flying Sub model kit from Aurora. Middle image and below: Competing 3-D offerings: Tru-Vue and View-Master.

In 1966, the Flying Sub was introduced, as featured in *Voyage*'s second season. The Flying Sub's bright-yellow manta-ray shape took glorious advantage of the new season's color format. The kit has been rereleased several times by Monogram.

Voyage images were also licensed in 1966 to a now-forgotten company, Tru-Vue. Unlike View-Master's more familiar system, the Tru-Vue "Magic Eyes" 3-D apparatus fed a card of two side-by-side images into a viewer which processed them vertically.

The more common View-Master slide set, also released in 1966, contained scenes from "Deadly Creature Below!"

Nothing was cooler in the 1960s for a young fan of

731

adventure than seeing images come alive in the 3-D View-Master effect. These weren't film trims from the show. A photographer from View-Master would visit the set and shoot the rehearsals with the 3-D process. For this reason, the View-Master scene didn't always match what we saw onscreen. That made it all the more special. Macy's had the View-Master set on sale in Christmas 1966 for only $1.75!

PLAY BOTH ON LAND AND IN WATER REMCO

VOYAGE TO THE BOTTOM OF THE SEA SEAVIEW SUBMARINE SET
AS SEEN ON T.V.

DIVES • STEERS • SURFACES
FIRES TORPEDOES
ELASTIC MOTOR PROPULSION

Remco offered several "playsets" featuring plastic figures of the Seaview; two crewmen in diving suits; a minisled; a domed sea crawler; and some critters to square off against.

Aladdin's 1967 lunch set.

Of course there was a *Voyage to the Bottom of the Sea* lunchbox and Thermos, but waiting for it tried young fans' patience. Aladdin Industries came late to the game with its 1967 *Voyage* metal lunchbox and Thermos.

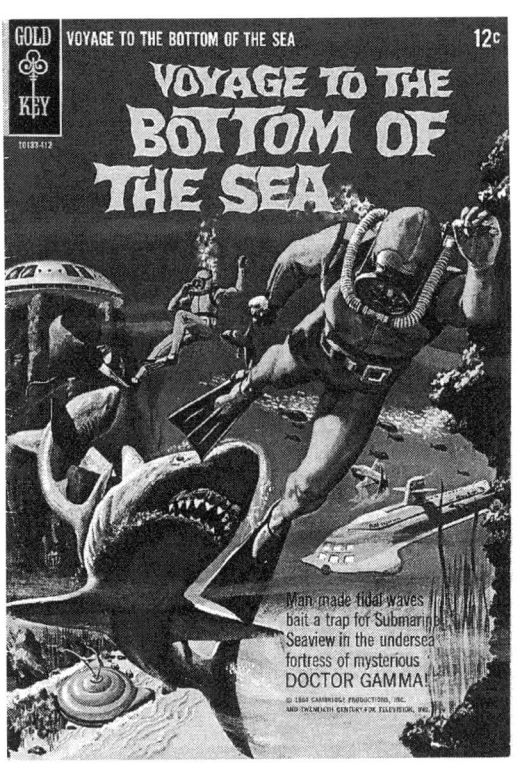

In the sixties, you may recall, nearly every grocery store, drugstore, and ten-cent store had one or more metal comic-book spinners offering dozens of titles. From 1964-68, one of those offerings was probably Gold Key's *Voyage* comic. Typical of Gold Key's TV tie-in titles – some others were *The Man from U.N.C.L.E.* and *The Twilight Zone* – front covers were luscious paintings of action scenes which didn't necessarily appear in the story. In ludicrous contrast to the comics' covers, the interior art often bore minimal resemblance to the Seaview interiors or cast members. Storylines were about what you'd expect from a comic aimed at grade-schoolers: sea creatures mutating into monsters; undersea giants; lost civilizations; and other "high-concept" adventures.

Issue 1 (above), from December 1964, contained the story "The Last Survivor," featuring Dr. Gamma, who was seen in the *Voyage* pilot, and, at that time, was planned to be a recurring villain in the tradition of Blofeld in the James Bond stories. For this story, the crew of the Seaview investigate a mysterious tidal-wave disaster and search for the lone survivor.

Issue 2 (right), published in early 1965, had a story in which "a mysterious fluid from the center of the Earth threatens to turn all ocean life into monsters!"

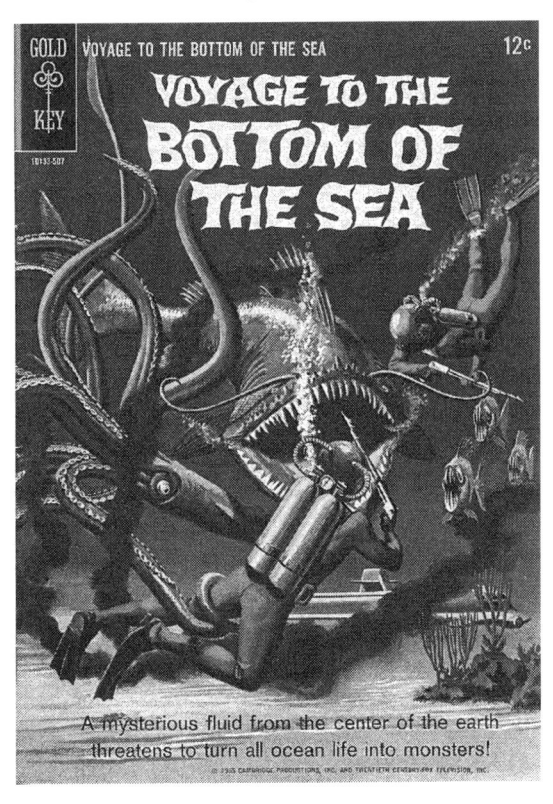

The third issue (next page, top left) was cover-dated October 1965, in time for the start of the second season. The tease on the cover: "Like a man possessed, Admiral Nelson sets the Seaview on the ill-fated course of a phantom ship!"

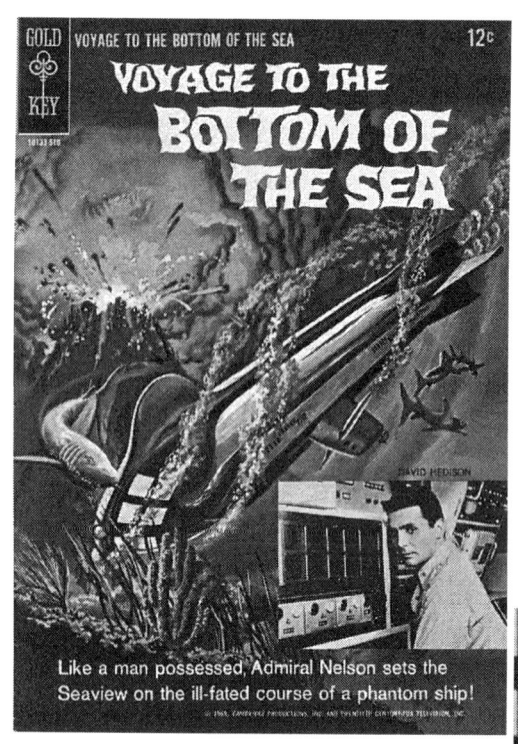

Issue 4 (below) hit drugstore comic-book racks for May 1966. The tease: "The Seaview becomes a helpless toy in the hands of an UNDERSEA GIANT!" It was the type story that could only be told in print ... until recent advances in CGI ... or, the previous November, when a giant wrestled with the Seaview in the episode "Leviathan."

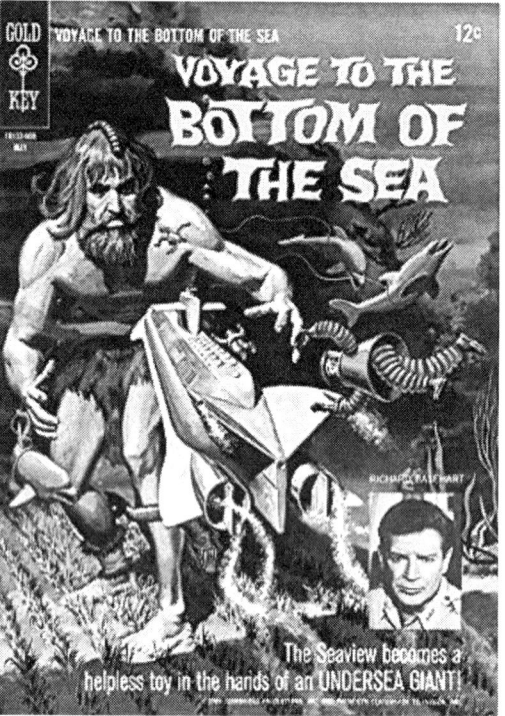

Issue 5 (below) was perhaps in your collection come August 1966.

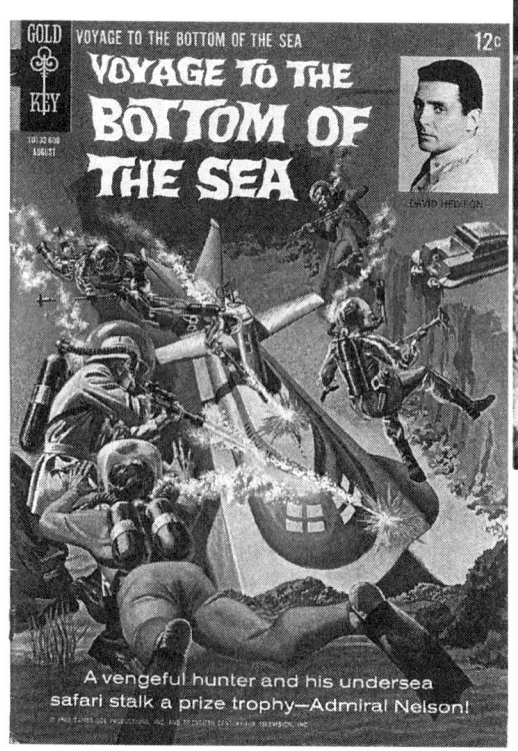

The promise of excitement on the cover: "A vengeful hunter and his undersea safari stalk a prize trophy – Admiral Nelson!"

Issue 6 (next page, top left), from November 1966, presented a story we weren't likely to see on TV: "Land-locked, the Seaview becomes an open target as it battles its way to water!"

Vol. 7 (below) was available in February 1967. The logline on the front: "The Seaview nets the frantic leader of a living city on the ocean's floor!" And doesn't that city on the ocean's floor look a bit like Atlantis?

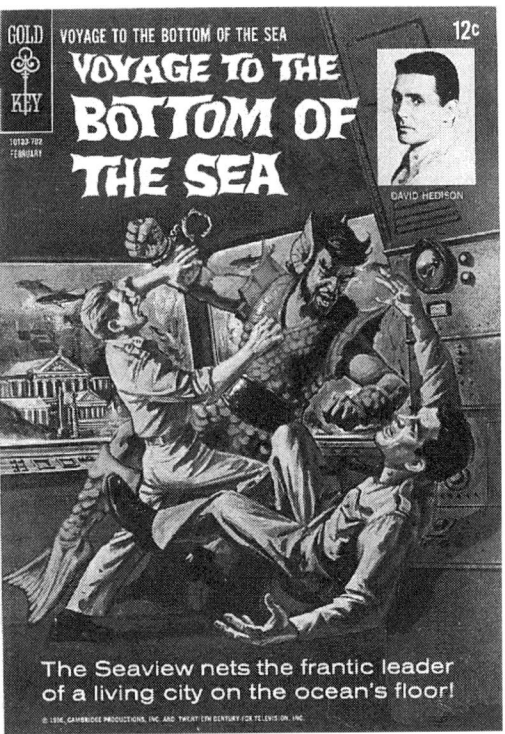

The eighth issue (below), out  for May 1967, boasted: "From the frozen wastes of time, a million-year-old beast comes to life aboard the Seaview!" Don't you *hate* it when that happens?

Issue 9 (next page, top left), for August 1967, continued the trend of showing what Irwin Allen would have liked to do with the TV series ... if

735

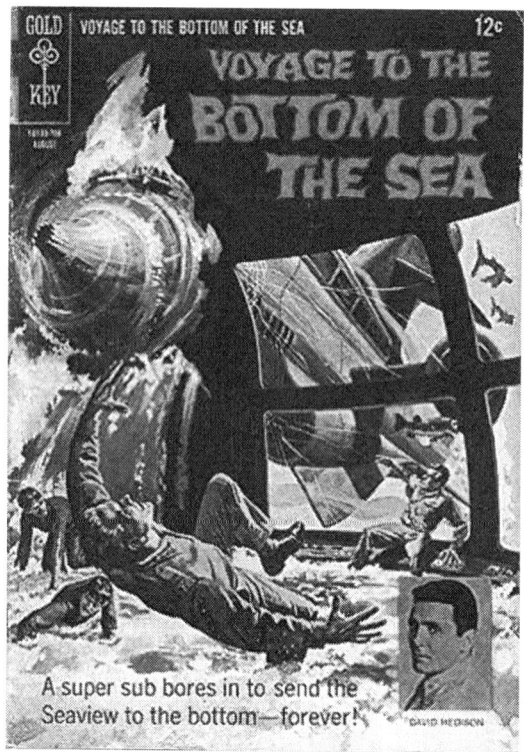

only he had a big enough budget. The logline on the cover proclaimed: "A super sub bores in to send the Seaview to the bottom – forever!"

Issue 10 (below), bore the cover pitch, "Admiral Nelson struggles to save his crew from madness – and the Seaview from Davy Jones' locker!" It was cover-dated November 1967.

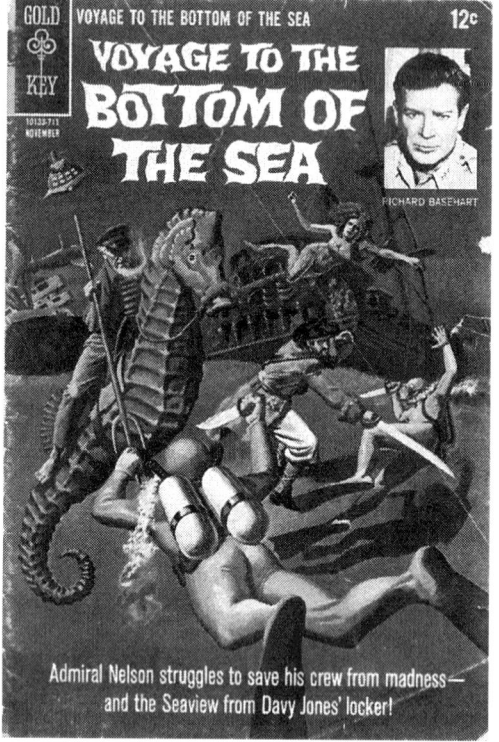

Hmm. 1967. Davy Jones was with the Monkees, right?

Issue 11 (left), out in February 1968, as the last episode of the TV series was filming, had an explosive cover … and an intriguing concept: "The Seaview takes on a life of its own and runs amuck!"

In May, 1968, as ABC ran summer repeats from *Voyage*'s fourth season, Gold Key comic #12 hit the stands.

The image is to the left; the hook on the cover: "The sea creatures declare war on mankind – and make Seaview the prime target for all-out assault!"

No. 13 (below), from August 1968, a month before *Voyage* left the ABC network, again went where the TV series could never afford to go, with a giant bug battling our intrepid crew. "Blasted into the depths of time, the Seaview is menaced by mutant monstrosities!"

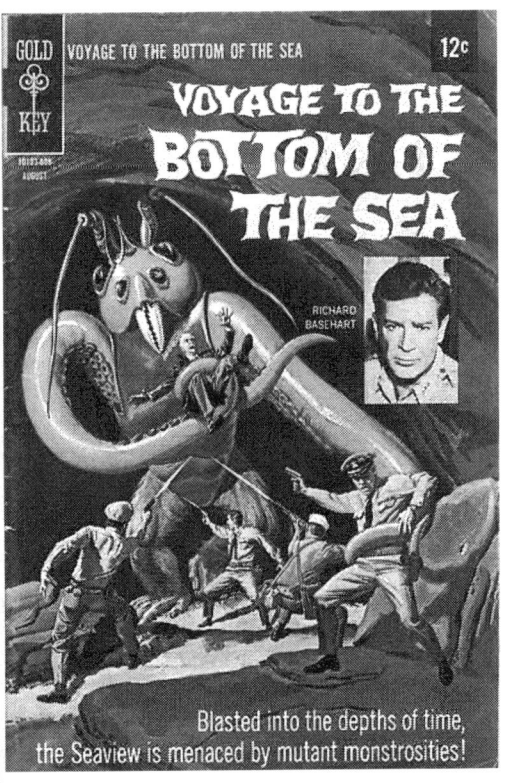

The price had gone up by three cents for issue 14 (left), out in November 1968, as the 110 syndicated episodes of *Voyage* began to play on TV stations across America. It had the wackiest cover yet, and a crazy premise to go with it: "The Seaview becomes a living creature and tries to devour her crew!" You can only imagine what the ABC censors would have made of this one.

Issues # 15 and 16 recycled covers and storylines from earlier editions.

In 2009, Hermes Press reprinted the 14 issues (minus the final two reprint issues) of the Gold Key comic-book series in two volumes. These full-color reproductions included the issues' original front painted covers and the rear "pin-up" photo covers.

This chapter covers only *some* of the licensed *Voyage* products which appeared during the show's run. (Did you know that Paul Sawtell's series theme was issued as sheet music?) Over the intervening decades, many new items have appeared, along with reissues of model kits, soundtracks, and video releases. The continuing market for these "treasures from below" is an enduring tribute to Irwin Allen's talent for catching the imaginations of the young and adventurous. We wish you happy hunting, online or at garage sales or thrift shops, for your own collection of mementos.

Appendix B:
Episode Lists

Season One, Production Order (Volume 1):

Prod.	#	Title:	Prod. Dates
1	6008	Eleven Days to Zero	(11/18 – 12/4/63)
2	7202	The Village of Guilt	(6/15 – 6/24/64)
3	7203	The Mist of Silence	(6/24 – 7/3/64)
4	7204	The City Beneath the Sea	(7/6 – 7/14/64)
5	7205	Turn Back the Clock	(7/15 – 7/22/64)
6	7206	Hail to the Chief	(7/23 – 7/31/64)
7	7207	The Fear-Makers	(8/3 – 8/10/64)
8	7208	Hot Line	(8/11 – 8/18/64)
9	7209	The Sky Is Falling	(8/20 – 8/28/64)
10	7210	The Price of Doom	(8/31 – 9/8/64)
11	7211	Long Live the King	(9/9 – 9/16/64)
12	7212	Submarine Sunk Here	(9/17 – 9/25/64)
13	7213	The Magnus Beam	(10/8 – 10/16/64)
14	7214	No Way Out	(10/19 – 10/27/64)
15	7215	The Blizzard Makers	(10/28 – 11/4/64)
16	7216	The Ghost of Moby Dick	(11/5 - 11/12/64)
17	7217	Doomsday	(11/13 – 11/20/64)
18	7219	Mutiny	(11/23 – 12/1/64)
19	7220	The Last Battle	(12/2 – 12/9/64)
20	7221	The Invaders	(12/10 – 12/18/64)
21	7223	The Indestructible Man	(12/21 – 12/31/64)
22	7223	The Buccaneer	(12/31/64 – 1/13/65)
23	7224	The Human Computer	(1/13 – 1/25/65)
24	7226	The Saboteur	(1/26 – 2/3/65)
25	7227	Cradle of the Deep	(2/4 – 2/12/65)
26	7228	The Exile	(2/15 – 2/23/65)
27	7229	The Amphibians	(2/15 – 2/22/65)
28	7230	The Creature	(2/23 – 3/3/65)
29	7231	The Enemies	(3/3 – 3/11/65)
30	7218	The Condemned	(3/22 – 3/29/65)
31	7232	The Secret of the Loch	(3/11 – 3/19/65)
32	7225	The Traitor	(3/30 – 4/6/65)

Season One, Broadcast Order (Volume 1):

Air #	Prod. #	Air date:	Title:
1-01	6008	9/14/64	Eleven Days to Zero
1-02	7204	9/21/64	The City Beneath the Sea
1-03	7207	9/28/64	The Fear-Makers

1-04	7203	10/05/64	The Mist of Silence
1-05	7210	10/12/64	The Price of Doom
1-06	7209	10/19/64	The Sky Is Falling
1-07	7205	10/26/64	Turn Back the Clock
1-08	7202	11/02/64	The Village of Guilt
1-09	7208	11/09/64	Hot Line
1-10	7212	11/16/64	Submarine Sunk Here
1-11	7213	11/23/64	The Magnus Beam
1-12	7214	11/30/64	No Way Out
1-13	7215	12/07/64	The Blizzard Makers
1-14	7216	12/14/64	The Ghost of Moby Dick
1-15	7211	12/21/64	Long Live the King
1-16	7206	12/28/64	Hail to the Chief
1-17	7220	01/04/65	The Last Battle
1-18	7219	01/11/65	Mutiny
1-19	7217	01/18/65	Doomsday
1-20	7221	01/25/65	The Invaders
1-21	7223	02/01/65	The Indestructible Man
1-22	7223	02/08/65	The Buccaneer
1-23	7224	02/15/65	The Human Computer
1-24	7226	02/22/65	The Saboteur
1-25	7227	03/01/65	Cradle of the Deep
1-26	7229	03/08/65	The Amphibians
1-27	7228	03/15/65	The Exile
1-28	7230	03/22/65	The Creature
1-29	7231	03/29/65	The Enemies
1-30	7232	04/05/65	The Secret of the Loch
1-31	7218	04/12/65	The Condemned
1-32	7225	04/19/65	The Traitor
Repeat	-	04/26/65	(The Price of Doom)
Repeat	-	05/03/65	(The Sky Is Falling)
Pre-emption		05/10/65	(*"Saga of Western Man" special*)
Repeat	-	05/17/65	(Village of Guilt)
Repeat	-	05/24/65	(Submarine Sunk Here)
Repeat	-	05/31/65	(No Way Out)
Repeat	-	06/07/65	(The Ghost of Moby Dick)
Repeat	-	06/14/65	(The Invaders)
Repeat	-	06/21/65	(Mutiny)
Repeat	-	06/28/65	(Doomsday)
Repeat	-	07/05/65	(The Indestructible Man)
Repeat	-	07/12/65	(The Creature)
Repeat	-	07/19/65	(Hot Line)
Repeat	-	07/26/65	(The Saboteur)
Repeat	-	08/02/65	(The Amphibians)
Repeat	-	08/09/65	(The Exile)
Repeat	-	08/16/65	(The Enemies)
Repeat	-	08/23/65	(The Condemned)
Repeat	-	08/30/65	(The Fear-Makers)

Repeat - 09/06.65 (The City Beneath the Sea)

Season Two, Production Order:

Prod.	#	Title:	Prod. Dates
33	8201	Jonah and the Whale	(6/24 – 7/6/66)
34	8202	... And Five of Us Are Left	(7/8 – 7/15/65)
35	8203	Time Bomb	(7/16 – 7/23/65)
36	8204	Escape from Venice	(7/26 – 8/2/65)
37	8205	The Cyborg	(8/3 – 8/12/65)
38	8206	The Deadliest Game	(8/12 – 8/20/65)
39	8207	The Left-Handed Man	(8/23 – 8/30/65)
40	8209	The Silent Saboteurs	(8/31 – 9/7/65)
41	8210	The Death Ship	(9/10 – 9/17/65)
42	8211	Leviathan	(9/20 – 9/28/65)
43	8212	The Peacemaker	(9/29 – 10/6/65)
44	8213	The Monster from Outer Space	(10/7 – 10/14 + 11/10 – 11/11/65)
45	8214	The X Factor	(10/15 – 10/25/65)
46	8215	The Machines Strike Back	(10/25 – 11/2/65)
47	8216	Killers of the Deep	(11/3 – 11/10/65)
48	8217	Terror on Dinosaur Island	(11/12 – 11/22/65)
49	8218	Deadly Creature Below!	(11/22 – 12/2/65)
50	8219	The Phantom Strikes	(12/3 – 12/14/65)
51	8220	The Sky's on Fire	(12/16 – 12/27/65)
52	8221	Graveyard of Fear	(12/27/65 – 1/5/66)
53	8222	The Shape of Doom	(1/5 – 1/12/66)
54	8223	Dead Men's Doubloons	(1/13 – 1/21/66)
55	8224	The Monster's Web	(1/24 – 2/3/66)
56	8225	The Menfish	(2/4 – 2/11/66)
57	8226	The Mechanical Man	(2/14 – 2/22/66)
58	8227	The Return of the Phantom	(2/22 – 3/4/66)

Season Two, Broadcast Order:

Air #	Prod. #	Air date:	Title:
2-01	8201	09/19/65	Jonah and the Whale
2-02	8203	09/26/65	Time Bomb
2-03	8202	10/03/65	... And Five of Us Are Left
2-04	8205	10/10/65	The Cyborg
2-05	8204	10/17//65	Escape from Venice
2-06	8207	10/24//65	The Left-Handed Man
2-07	8206	10/31/65	The Deadliest Game
2-08	8211	11/07/65	Leviathan
2-09	8212	11/14/65	The Peacemaker
2-10	8209	11/21/65	The Silent Saboteurs
Pre-emption		11/28/65	(*"The Dangerous Christmas of Red Riding Hood"*)
2-11	8214	12/05/65	The X Factor

2-12	8215	12/12/65	The Machines Strike Back
2-13	8213	12/19/65	The Monster from Outer Space
2-14	8217	12/26/65	Terror on Dinosaur Island
2-15	8216	01/02/66	Killers of the Deep
2-16	8218	01/09/66	Deadly Creature Below!
2-17	8219	01/16/66	The Phantom Strikes
2-18	8220	01/23/66	The Sky's on Fire
2-19	8221	01/30/66	Graveyard of Fear
2-20	8222	02/06/66	The Shape of Doom
2-21	8223	02/13/66	Dead Men's Doubloons
2-22	8210	02/20/66	The Death Ship
2-23	8224	02/27/66	The Monster's Web
2-24	8225	03/06/66	The Menfish
2-25	8226	03/13/66	The Mechanical Man
2-26	8227	03/20/66	The Return of the Phantom
Repeat	-	03/27/66	(The Cyborg)
Repeat	-	04/02/66	(Terror on Dinosaur Island)
Repeat	-	04/10/66	(Killers of the Deep)
Repeat	-	04/17/66	(Jonah and the Whale)
Repeat	-	04/24/66	(... And Five of Us Are Left)
Repeat	-	05/01/66	(The Monster from Outer Space)
Repeat	-	05/08/66	(The Death Ship)
Repeat	-	05/14/66	(Dead Men's Doubloons)
Repeat	-	05/22/66	(The Sky's on fire)
Repeat	-	05/29/66	(The Deadliest Games)
Repeat	-	06/05/66	(The Machine Strikes Back)
Repeat	-	06/12/66	(The Peacemaker)
Pre-emption		06/19/66	(*U.S. Open sports special*)
Repeat	-	06/26/66	(Deadly Creature Below)
Repeat	-	07/03/66	(The Mechanical Man)
Repeat	-	07/10/66	(The Left-Handed Man)
Repeat	-	07/17/66	(The Shape of Doom)
Repeat	-	07/24.66	(The X Factor)
Repeat	-	07/31/66	(The Phantom Strikes)
Repeat	-	08/07/66	(The Menfish)
Repeat	-	08/14/66	(Leviathan)
Repeat	-	08/21/66	(Escape from Venice)
Repeat	-	08/28/66	(The Return of the Phantom)
Repeat	-	09/04/66	(Time Bomb)
Repeat	-	09/11/66	(Graveyard of Fear)

Season Three, Production Order:

Prod.	#	Title:	Prod. Dates
59	9201	Monster from the Inferno	(6/20 – 6/28/66)
60	9202	Werewolf	(6/29 – 7/8/66)
61	9203	Day of Evil	(7/11 – 7/18/66)
62	9204	Night of Terror	(7/19 – 7/26/66)
63	9205	The Day the World Ended	(7/27 – 8/3/66)
64	9206	The Terrible Toys	(8/4 – 8/11/66)
65	9207	Deadly Waters	(8/12 – 8/19/67)
66	9208	The Thing from Inner Space	(8/22 – 8/29/66)
67	9210	The Death Watch	(8/30 – 9/6/66)
68	9209	Deadly Invaders	(9/7 – 9/14/66)
69	9211	The Lost Bomb	(9/15 – 9/22/66)
70	9213	The Brand of the Beast	(9/23 – 9/30/66)
71	9212	The Plant Monster	(10/3 – 10/10/66)
72	9214	The Creature	(10/11 – 10/18/66)
73	9215	The Haunted Submarine	(10/19 – 10/25/66)
74	9216	Death from the Past	(10/26 – 11/3/66)
75	9217	The Heat Monster	(11/4 – 11/11/66)
76	9218	The Fossil Men	(11/14 – 11/21/66)
77	9219	The Mermaid	(11/22 – 11/29/66)
78	9220	The Mummy	(11/30 – 12/6/66)
79	9221	The Shadowman	(12/7 – 12/15/66)
80	9222	No Escape from Death	(12/16 – 12/23/66)
81	9223	Doomsday Island	(12/27/66 – 1/4/67)
82	9224	The Wax Men	(1/6 – 1/12/67)
83	9225	Deadly Cloud	(1/16 – 1/24/67)
84	9226	Destroy Seaview!	(1/25 – 2/1/66)

Season Three, Broadcast Order:

Air #	Prod. #	Air date:	Title:
3-01	9201	09/18/66	Monster from the Inferno
3-02	9202	09/25/66	Werewolf
3-03	9205	10/02/66	The Day the World Ended
3-04	9204	10/09/66	Night of Terror
3-05	9206	10/16/66	The Terrible Toys
3-06	9203	10/23/66	Day of Evil
3-07	9207	10/30/66	Deadly Waters
3-08	9208	11/06/66	Thing from Inner Space

3-09	9210	11/13/66	The Death Watch
3-10	9209	11/20/66	Deadly Invasion
3-11	9215	11/27/66	The Haunted Submarine
3-12	9212	12/04/66	The Plant Man
3-13	9211	12/11/66	The Lost Bomb
3-14	9213	12/18/66	The Brand of the Beast
Pre-emption		12/25/66	("*The Dangerous Christmas of Red Riding Hood*")
3-15	9214	01/01/67	The Creature
3-16	9216	01/08/67	Death from the Past
3-17	9217	01/15/67	The Heat Monster
3-18	9218	01/22/67	The Fossil Men
3-19	9219	01/29/67	The Mermaid
3-20	9220	02/05/67	The Mummy
3-21	9221	02/12/67	Shadowman
3-22	9222	02/19/67	No Escape from Death
3-23	9223	02/26/67	Doomsday Island
3-24	9224	03/05/67	The Wax Men
3-25	9225	03/12/67	Deadly Cloud
3-26	9226	03/19/67	Destroy Seaview!
Pre-emption		03/26/67	("*The Robe*" Sunday Night Movie)
Repeat	-	04/02/67	(The Terrible Toys)
Repeat	-	04/08/67	(Night of Terror)
Repeat	-	04/16/67	(The Plant Monster)
Pre-emption		04/23/67	(*"Go!!!"* variety special)
Repeat	-	05/01/67	(Werewolf)
Repeat	-	05/07/67	(Day of Evil)
Repeat	-	05/14/67	(The Thing from Inner Space)
Repeat	-	05/21/67	(The Heat Monster)
Repeat	-	05/28/67	(The Day the World Ended)
Repeat	-	06/04/67	(Deadly Invasion)
Repeat	-	06/11/67	(The Haunted Submarine)
Repeat	-	06/18/67	(The Monster from the Inferno)
Repeat	-	06/25/67	(The Shadowman)
Repeat	-	07/02/67	(Deadly Waters)
Repeat	-	07/09/67	(The Creature)
Repeat	-	07/16/67	(Death from the Past)
Repeat	-	07/23/67	(The Deadly Cloud)
Repeat	-	07/30/67	(The Fossil Men)
Repeat	-	08/06/67	(The Mermaid)
Repeat	-	08/13/67	(The Mummy)
Repeat	-	08/20/67	(No Escape from Death)
Repeat	-	08/27/67	(Doomsday Island)
Repeat	-	09/03/67	(The Wax Men)
Pre-emption		09/10/67	(*"Africa"* special)

Season Four, Production Order:

Prod.	#	Title:	Prod. Dates
85	1301	Man of Many Faces	(6/6 – 6/17/67)
86	1302	Time Lock	(6/15 – 6/23/67)
87	1303	The Deadly Dolls	(6/26 – 7/5/67)
88	1304	Fires of Death	(7/6 – 7/14/67 + 8/2/67)
89	1305	Cave of the Dead	(7/17 – 7/24/67)
90	1306	Sealed Orders	(7/25 – 8/1/67)
91	1307	Journey with Fear	(8/3 – 8/10/67)
92	1309	Fatal Cargo	(8/11 – 8/18/67)
93	1310	Rescue	(8/21 – 8/25/67 + 9/14 + 10/3/67)
94	1308	Terror	(8/28 – 9/6/67 + 10/3/67)
95	1313	Blow Up	(9/7 – 9/14/67)
96	1314	Deadly Amphibians	(9/15 – 9/21/67 + 10/18/67)
97	1316	The Return of Blackbeard	(9/22 – 10/2/67)
98	1317	A Time to Die	(10/7 – 10/10/67 + 10/27/67)
99	1318	Edge of Doom	(10/11 – 10/17/67 + 11/8/67)
100	1319	Nightmare	(10/19 – 10/26/67)
101	1320	The Lobster Man	(10/30 – 11/7/67 + 12/7/67)
102	1321	Terrible Leprechaun	(11/9 – 11/16/67)
103	1315	The Abominable Snowman	(11/17 – 11/28/67)
104	1323	Man-Beast	(11/29 – 12/6/67)
105	1322	Savage Jungle	(12/7 – 12/15/67)
106	1311	Secret of the Deep	(12/18 – 12/27/67)
107	1324	Flaming Ice	(12/27/67 – 1/5/68)
108	1325	Attack!	(1/8 – 1/16/68)
109	1326	No Way Back	(1/16 – 1/24/68)
110	1312	The Death Clock	(1/25 – 2/2/68)

Season Four, Broadcast Order:

Air #	Prod. #	Air date:	Title:
4-01	1304	09/17/67	Fires of Death
Pre-emption		09/24/67	(*"Holiday On Ice" special*)
4-02	1303	10/01/67	The Deadly Dolls
4-03	1305	10/08/67	Cave of the Dead
4-04	1307	10/15/67	Journey with Fear
4-05	1306	10/22/67	Sealed Orders
4-06	1301	10/29/67	Man of Many Faces
4-07	1309	11/05/67	Fatal Cargo
4-08	1302	11/12/67	Time Lock
4-09	1310	11/19/67	Rescue
4-10	1308	11/26/67	Terror
4-11	1317	12/03/67	A Time to Die

4-12	1313	12/10/67	Blow Up
4-13	1314	12/17/67	Deadly Amphibians
Pre-emption		12/24/67	(*"Nativity Story" Christmas special*)
4-14	1316	12/31/67	The Return of Blackbeard
4-15	1321	01/07/68	Terrible Leprechaun
Pre-emption		01/14/68	(*"Bing Crosby Golf" special*)
4-16	1320	01/21/68	The Lobster Man
4-17	1319	01/28/68	Nightmare
4-18	1315	02/04/68	The Abominable Snowman
4-19	1311	02/11/68	Secret of the Deep
4-20	1323	02/18/68	Man-Beast
4-21	1322	02/25/68	Savage Jungle
4-22	1324	03/03/68	Flaming Ice
4-23	1325	03/10/68	Attack!
4-24	1318	03/17/68	Edge of Doom
4-25	1311	03/24/68	The Death Clock
4-26	1326	03/31/68	No Way Back
Repeat	-	04/07/68	(Fires of Death)
Repeat	-	04/14/68	(The Deadly Dolls)
Pre-emption		04/21/68	(*"Romp!" entertainment special*)
Repeat	-	04/28/68	(Cave of Death)
Repeat	-	05/05/68	(Journey with Fear)
Repeat	-	05/12/68	(Fatal Cargo)
Repeat	-	05/20/68	(Deadly Amphibians)
Repeat	-	05/26/68	(A Time to Die)
Repeat	-	06/02/68	(Man of Many Faces)
Repeat	-	06/09/68	(Secret of the Deep)
Repeat	-	06/16/68	(Time Lock)
Repeat	-	06/23/68	(The Return of Blackbeard)
Repeat	-	06/30/68	(Terror)
Repeat	-	07/07/68	(Sealed Orders)
Repeat	-	07/14/68	(Blow Up)
Repeat	-	07/21/68	(Attack!)
Repeat	-	07/28/68	(The Lobster Man)
Repeat	-	08/04/68	(Nightmare)
Repeat	-	08/11/68	(The Abominable Snowman)
Repeat	-	08/18/68	(Savage Jungle)
Repeat	-	08/25/68	(The Death Clock)
Repeat	-	09/01/68	(Flaming Ice)
Repeat	-	09/08/68	(Man-Beast)
Repeat	-	09/15/68	(Terrible Leprechaun)

Appendix C:
Bibliography

WEBSITES:

cinemaretro.com
classicfilmtvcafe.com
cultbox.co.uk
diaboliquemagazine.com
iann.net
latimes.com
newspapers.com
popcultureaddict.com
sci-fi-online.com
thunderchild.com
variety.com
vttbots.com

BOOKS:

Abbott, Jon. *Irwin Allen Television Productions, 1964-1970: A Critical History*. McFarland & Company, Inc., 2006.

Abbott, L.B. *Special Effects: Wire, Tape and Rubber Band Style*. ASC Press, 1984.

Anchors, William E., Jr., editor. *Irwin Allen Scrapbook, Volume Two*, Alpha Control Press, 1992.

Anchors, William E., Jr., and Frederick Barr. *Seaview: A 50th Anniversary Tribute to Voyage to the Bottom of the Sea*. Alpha Control Press, 2012.

Bennet, Charles. *Hitchcock's Partner in Suspense: The Life of Screenwriter Charles Bennett*. The University Press of Kentucky, 2014.

Brooks, Tim, and Earle Marsh. *The Complete Directory to Prime Time Network TV Shows 1946-Present*. Ballantine Books, 1979.

Colliver, Timothy L. *Seaview: The Making of Voyage to the Bottom of the Sea*. Star Tech, 1992.

Phillips, Mark, and Frank Garcia. *Science Fiction Television Series, Volume 1*. McFarland & Company, Inc., 1994.

Phillips, Mark, and Frank Garcia. *Science Fiction Television Series, Volume 2*. McFarland & Company, Inc., 1996.

Welch, William. *Talks with the Dead*. Pinnacle Books, 1975.

Whitburn, Joel, editor. *Billboard Hot 100 Charts*. Record Research, Inc., 1990.

Whitburn, Joel, editor. *Billboard Pop Album Charts*. Record Research, Inc., 1993.

End Notes

Chapter 1: Fathoming Irwin Allen

1. D'Agosta, Joe (2020). Personal interview.
2. Harris, Harry (1995). Interviewed by Kevin Burns (used by permission).
3. D'Agosta, Joe (2020). Personal interview.
4. Hunter, Lew (2015). Personal interview.
5. *ibid.*
6. Gail, Al (1995). Interviewed by Kevin Burns (used by permission).
7. Allen, Sheila Mathews (1995). Interviewed by Kevin Burns (used by permission).
8. Gail, Al (1995). Interviewed by Kevin Burns (used by permission).
9. Allen, Michael (2015). Personal interview.
10. Gail, Al (1995). Interviewed by Kevin Burns (used by permission).
11. Mosby, Aline. "Scientists in 14 Countries Took Pictures for Hollywood Film, *The Sea Around Us*." *The Lubbock Avalanche-Journal* [TX], February 15, 1953.
12. "Hollywood's Newest Stars Made Entirely of Rubber." *The Logansport Pharos-Tribune* [IN], April 27, 1955.
13. Thomas, Bob. "Story of Man Being Filmed." *The Ithaca Journal* [NY], November 26, 1956.
14. Clark, Mike. "Designing Man." *Starlog* #187, February 1993.
15. Zastupnevich, Paul (1995). Interviewed by Kevin Burns (used by permission).
16. Marcus, Vitina (2015). Personal interview.
17. Hedison, David (2017). Interviewed by Mike Clark (used by permission).
18. Chartrand, Harvey. "Interview: David Hedison." *Diabolique Magazine*, August 12, 2013. https://diaboliquemagazine.com/interview-david-hedison/
19. Hedison, David (2017). Interviewed by Mike Clark (used by permission).
20. Hedison, David. Audio Commentary. *Voyage to the Bottom of the Sea - The Complete Collection*. 20th Century Fox, 2007.
21. Marcus, Vitina (2015). Personal interview.
22. Hunter, Lew (2015). Personal interview.
23. *ibid.*
24. D'Agosta, Joe (2020). Personal interview.
25. Hunter, Lew (2015). Personal interview.
26. D'Agosta, Joe (2020). Personal interview.
27. Hunter, Lew (2015). Personal interview.
28. D'Agosta, Joe (2020). Personal interview.
29. Hunter, Lew (2015). Personal interview.

Chapter 2: Casting Off for Season Two

1. Martin, William. "David Hedison (James Bond, 'Voyage to the Bottom of the Sea') interview." *Cultbox*, July 4, 2012. https://cultbox.co.uk/interviews/exclusives/david-hedison-james-bond-voyage-to-the-bottom-of-the-sea-interview
2. Phillips, Mark. "Giant Jellyfish & Time-Lost Dinosaurs, Part One." *Starlog* #181, August 1992.
3. Anchors, William E., Jr., and Frederick Barr. *Seaview: A 50th Anniversary Tribute to Voyage to the Bottom of the Sea*. Alpha Control Press, 2012.
4. Hunt, Allan (2020). Personal interview.
5. Phillips, Mark. "The Life of Riley." *Starlog* #196, November 1993.
6. Hunt, Allan (2020). Personal interview.
7. *ibid.*

Chapter 3: Fall 1965

1. "1965-66 Networks' Checkerboard (First Draft)." *Variety*, February 10, 1965.
2. "Teenagers Set TV Tastes." *Variety*, June 9, 1965.
3. 20th Century-Fox press release. *Ames Daily Tribune* [IA], September 11, 1965.
4. "Daku." "Telepic Followup." *Daily Variety*, February 24, 1965.
5. *Variety*, March 3, 1965.

6. Phillips, Mark. "Charting a Voyage to the Bottom of the Sea!" *Filmfax* #81/82, October 2000/January 2001.
7. MacMinn, Aleene. "Smooth Sailing for David Hedison." *The Los Angeles Times*, July 4, 1965.
8. Allen, Irwin, memo to Bob Suhosky, April 26, 1965. (Courtesy Synthesis Entertainment, assisted by Ron Hamill).
9. Kaufman, Dave. *Daily Variety*, June 17, 1965.
10. Kaufman, Dave. "Allen's 1997 Space Shot 1st Primetime Cliffhanger." *Daily Variety*, June 17, 1965.
11. 20th Century-Fox press release, 1965.
12. Dern, Marian. "Well, Of Course, It Isn't Exactly *Hamlet*…" *TV Guide*, June 19, 1965.
13. ibid.
14. ibid.

Chapter 4: Season Two / ABC's Initial Order of 16

1. "This Season, Boys and Girls … Mostly." *Dayton Daily News* [OH], February 19, 1966.

Chapter 4.1: "Jonah and the Whale"

1. Irwin Allen papers collection (Courtesy Synthesis Entertainment, assisted by Ron Hamill).
2. Graham, Glen. "Miggie Covers TV Invitation." *Argus-Courier* [Petaluma, CA], n.d.
3. "*Voyage* Predicts Teen Jargon of '75." *Waterloo Daily Courier* [IA] December 5, 1965.
4. Clark, Mike. "Misplaced Among the Stars." *Starlog* #159, October 1990.
5. Gunston, David. "The Man Who Was Jonah." *The Age* [Melbourne, Australia], May 4, 1960.
6. King, Susan. "David Hedison Looks Back on Periscope Days." *The Los Angeles Times*, January 30, 2011.
7. Samish, Adrian. Memo to Irwin Allen, January 20, 1965, UCLA Special Collections Library.
8. ibid.
9. Hunter, Lew (2015). Personal interview.
10. Samish, Adrian. Memo to Irwin Allen, January 20, 1965, UCLA Special Collections Library.
11. Allen, Irwin. Memo, "General Notes," January 30, 1965. UCLA Special Collections Library.
12. Allen, Irwin. Memo, "Jonah," April 26, 1965. UCLA Special Collections Library.
13. Garbutt, Mary. Continuity and Acceptance Department memo, "Jonah," May 19, 1965.
14. Wincelberg, Shimon. Memo to Irwin Allen, June 17, 1965, UCLA Special Collections Library.
15. Show file for "Jonah and the Whale," casting/salaries, UCLA Special Collections Library.
16. Show file for "Jonah and the Whale," Daily Production Report, UCLA Special Collections Library.
17. "Fish Swallows Man in *Voyage* Sequence." *Fort Lauderdale News* [FL], July 30, 1965.
18. Wickman, Sven. "Cradle of the Deep." *Mike's Voyage to the Bottom of the Sea Zone*. http://www.vttbots.com/episode_guide_year_1q.html
19. "While Strolling Through the Whale One Day…" *TV Guide*, October 9, 1965.
20. Phillips, Mark. "Charting a Voyage to the Bottom of the Sea!" See Chapter 3, note 6.
21. Phillips, Mark. "The Life of Riley." See Chapter 2, note 6.
22. ibid.
23. Show file for "Jonah and the Whale," budget, UCLA Special Collections Library. "Call the Plumber," *The Sydney Morning Herald* [New South Wales, Australia], February 21, 1966.
24. "Irwin Allen Has Huge Water Bill." *The Indianapolis Star* [IN], April 10, 1966.
25. Clark, Mike. "Misplaced Among the Stars." See Chapter 4.1, note 4.
26. Crosby, Joan. "TV Scout." *The News-Herald* [Franklin, PA], September 18, 1965.
27. Scheuer, Steven H. "TV Key." *Lima News* [OH], September 19, 1965.
28. "Daku." Review of "Jonah and the Whale." *Daily Variety*, September 21, 1965.
29. McIntyre, Tom. Review of "Jonah and the Whale." *Gaston Gazette* [Gastonia, NC], September 21, 1965.
30. Irwin Allen papers collection (Courtesy Synthesis Entertainment, assisted by Ron Hamill).

Chapter 4.2: "… And Five of Us Are Left"

1. Irwin Allen papers collection (Courtesy Synthesis Entertainment, assisted by Ron Hamill).
2. Phillips, Mark. "Giant Jellyfish & Time-Lost Dinosaurs, Part Two." *Starlog* #182, September 1992.
3. ibid.
4. ibid.
5. Hedison, David. Audio Commentary. *Voyage to the Bottom of the Sea - The Complete Collection*. 20th Century Fox, 2007.

6. Phillips, Mark. "Giant Jellyfish & Time-Lost Dinosaurs, Part Two." See note 2.
7. Harris, Harry (1995). Interviewed by Kevin Burns (used by permission).
8. *ibid.*
9. Phillips, Mark, and Mike Bailey. "And Five of Us Are Left." *Mike's Voyage to the Bottom of the Sea Zone*. http://www.vttbots.com/ep_guide_season2_2.html
10. *ibid.*
11. Harris, Harry (1995). Interviewed by Kevin Burns (used by permission).
12. "$15,000 Quake on *Voyage*." *Hartford Courant* [CT], October 3, 1965.
13. Phillips, Mark. "Charting a Voyage to the Bottom of the Sea!" See Chapter 3, note 6.
14. Scheuer, Steven H. "TV Key." *San Antonio Light* [TX], October 3, 1965.
15. Crosby, Joan. "TV Scout." *San Antonio Express* [TX], October 3, 1965.
16. "Bill." Review of "… And Five of Us Are Left." *Variety*, October 6, 1965.
17. McIntyre, Tom. Review of "… And Five of Us Are Left." *Gaston Gazette* [Gastonia, NC], September 21, 1965.
18. Shiels, Bob. Review of "… And Five of Us Are Left." *Calgary Herald* [Alberta, Canada], January 24, 1966.
19. Irwin Allen papers collection (Courtesy Synthesis Entertainment, assisted by Ron Hamill).
20. Phillips, Mark. "Giant Jellyfish & Time-Lost Dinosaurs, Part Two." See note 2.
21. Harris, Harry (1995). Interviewed by Kevin Burns (used by permission).

Chapter 4.3: "Time Bomb"

1. Irwin Allen papers collection (Courtesy Synthesis Entertainment, assisted by Ron Hamill).
2. Phillips, Mark, and Mike Bailey. "Time Bomb." *Mike's Voyage to the Bottom of the Sea Zone*. http://www.vttbots.com/ep_guide_season2_1.html#bomb
3. *ibid.*
4. Phillips, Mark. "Giant Jellyfish & Time-Lost Dinosaurs, Part Two." See Chapter 4.2, note 2.
5. Garbutt, Mary. Continuity & Acceptance Department memo, "Time Bomb," July 8, 1965, UCLA Special Collections Library.
6. *ibid.*
7. Johnson, Erskine. "Meet David Hedison: Never Gets Girl on the Screen." *Philadelphia Daily News* [PA], May 23, 1965.
8. Archerd, Army. "Just for Variety." *Daily Variety*, May 28, 1965.
9. MacMinn, Aleene. "Smooth Sailing for David Hedison." See Chapter 3, note 7.
10. Lewis, Dan. "More of Bard, Basehart Asks." *The Record* [Hackensack, NJ], September 30, 1965.
11. Phillips, Mark. "Giant Jellyfish & Time-Lost Dinosaurs, Part Two." See Chapter 4.2, note 2.
12. Anchors and Barr, *Seaview: A 50th Anniversary Tribute to Voyage to the Bottom of the Sea*.
13. *ibid.*
14. "Balin Role Expanded to Five Episodes." *The Los Angeles Times*, August 18, 1965.
15. Show file for "Time Bomb," Daily Production Report, UCLA Special Collections Library.
16. Show file for "Time Bomb," budget, UCLA Special Collections Library.
17. Thompson, Ruth. "Basehart Pleased by Colorful Additions to *Voyage*." *The Sentinel* [Carlisle, PA], November 13, 1965.
18. Scheuer, Steven H. "TV Key." *Battle Creek Enquirer* [MI], September 26, 1965.
19. Crosby, Joan. "TV Scout." *Abilene Reporter-News* [TX], September 26, 1965.
20. Stephen, Andy. *Times Colonist* [Victoria, British Columbia, Canada], October 1, 1965.
21. Irwin Allen papers collection (Courtesy Synthesis Entertainment, assisted by Ron Hamill).

Chapter 4.4: "Escape from Venice"

1. Irwin Allen papers collection (Courtesy Synthesis Entertainment, assisted by Ron Hamill).
2. Phillips, Mark, and Mike Bailey. "Escape from Venice." *Mike's Voyage to the Bottom of the Sea Zone*. http://www.vttbots.com/ep_guide_season2_8.html
3. *ibid.*
4. Johnson, Erskine. "Meet David Hedison: Never Gets Girl on the Screen." See Chapter 4.3, note 7.
5. Garbutt, Mary. ABC Continuity and Acceptance Department memo, "Escape from Venice," July 8, 1965, UCLA Special Collections Library.
6. Crosby, Joan. "Hedison Can't Find Girl to Love." *Fort Lauderdale News* [FL], November 5, 1965.
7. Phillips, Mark. "The Life of Riley." See Chapter 2, note 6.

8. Show file for "Escape from Venice," Daily Production Report, UCLA Special Collections Library.
9. Show file for "Escape from Venice," budget, UCLA Special Collections Library.
10. "TV Scout." *Abilene Reporter-News* [TX], October 17, 1965.
11. Irwin Allen papers collection (Courtesy Synthesis Entertainment, assisted by Ron Hamill).
12. La Tourette, Frank. Undated memo to staff, UCLA Special Collections Library.

Chapter 4.5: "The Cyborg"

1. Irwin Allen papers collection (Courtesy Synthesis Entertainment, assisted by Ron Hamill).
2. Phillips, Mark, and Mike Bailey. "The Cyborg." *Mike's Voyage to the Bottom of the Sea Zone*. http://www.vttbots.com/ep_guide_season2_3.html
3. Garbutt, Mary. ABC Continuity and Acceptance Department memo, "The Cyborg," July 21, 1965, UCLA Special Collections Library.
4. *ibid.*
5. *ibid.*
6. Phillips, Mark. "Giant Jellyfish & Time-Lost Dinosaurs, Part One." See Chapter 2, note 2.
7. Show file for "The Cyborg," Daily Production Report, UCLA Special Collections Library.
8. *ibid.*
9. Show file for "The Cyborg," budget, UCLA Special Collections Library.
10. "Will Success – Or Wide Screen – Spoil Vic Buono?" *Janesville Daily Gazette* [WI], October 1, 1965.
11. "There, At the Bottom of the Sea, Is…" *Hagerstown Daily Mail* [MD], October 9, 1965.
12. *ibid.*
13. *ibid.*
14. *ibid.*
15. "TV Scout." *Abilene Reporter-News* [TX], October 10, 1965.
16. Scheuer, Steven H. "TV Key." *Gazette Mail* [Charleston, WV], October 10, 1965.
17. McIntyre, Tom. "Profile Richard Basehart." *Gaston Gazette* [Gastonia, NC], March 13, 1966.
18. Irwin Allen papers collection (Courtesy Synthesis Entertainment, assisted by Ron Hamill).

Chapter 4.6: "The Deadliest Game"

1. Irwin Allen papers collection (Courtesy Synthesis Entertainment, assisted by Ron Hamill).
2. Phillips, Mark, and Mike Bailey. "The Deadliest Game." *Mike's Voyage to the Bottom of the Sea Zone*. http://www.vttbots.com/ep_guide_season2_15.html
3. *ibid.*
4. Allen, Irwin. Undated memo on "The Deadliest Game,", UCLA Special Collections Library.
5. Phillips, Mark. "Giant Jellyfish & Time-Lost Dinosaurs, Part One." See Chapter 2, note 2.
6. Anchors and Barr, *Seaview: A 50th Anniversary Tribute to Voyage to the Bottom of the Sea*.
7. *ibid.*
8. Show file for "The Deadliest Game," Daily Production Report, UCLA Special Collections Library.
9. Show file for "The Deadliest Game," budget, UCLA Special Collections Library.
10. *The Indianapolis Star* (Indiana), October 31, 1965.
11. Scheuer, Steven H. "TV Key." *San Antonio Light* [TX], October 31, 1965.
12. "TV Scout." *Kenosha News* [WI], October 30, 1965.
13. Irwin Allen papers collection (Courtesy Synthesis Entertainment, assisted by Ron Hamill).

Chapter 4.7: "The Left-Handed Man"

1. Irwin Allen papers collection (Courtesy Synthesis Entertainment, assisted by Ron Hamill).
2. Phillips, Mark, and Mike Bailey. "The Left-Handed Man." *Mike's Voyage to the Bottom of the Sea Zone*. http://www.vttbots.com/ep_guide_season2_16.html
3. *ibid.*
4. Phillips, Mark. "Giant Jellyfish & Time-Lost Dinosaurs, Part Two." See Chapter 4.2, note 2.
5. Allen, Irwin. Memo on "The Left-Handed Man," August 10, 1965, UCLA Special Collections Library.
6. Brown, Dorothy. ABC Continuity and Acceptance Department memo, "The Left-Handed Man," July 8, 1965, UCLA Special Collections Library.
7. Show file for "The Left-Handed Man," Daily Production Report, UCLA Special Collections Library.
8. Show file for "The Left-Handed Man," budget, UCLA Special Collections Library.

9. *The Sacramento Bee* [CA], October 24, 1965.
10. Scheuer, Steven H. "TV Key." *The Fresno Bee* (California), October 24, 1965.
11. Newton, Dwight. "Fox Comic Book Culture." *The San Francisco Examiner* [CA], October 25, 1965.
12. *ibid.*
14. Irwin Allen papers collection (Courtesy Synthesis Entertainment, assisted by Ron Hamill).

Chapter 4.8: "The Death Ship"

1. Irwin Allen papers collection (Courtesy Synthesis Entertainment, assisted by Ron Hamill).
2. Phillips, Mark, and Mike Bailey. "The Death Ship." *Mike's Voyage to the Bottom of the Sea Zone.* http://www.vttbots.com/ep_guide_season2_9.html
3. *ibid.*
4. La Tourette, Frank. Undated memo on "One by One," UCLA Special Collections Library.
5. Welch, William. Undated memo on "One by One," UCLA Special Collections Library.
6. La Tourette, Frank. Undated memo on "One by One," UCLA Special Collections Library.
7. Allen, Irwin. Memo, August 24, 1965, "One by One," UCLA Special Collections Library.
8. La Tourette, Frank. Undated memo on "One by One," UCLA Special Collections Library.
9. Welch, William. Undated memo on "One by One," UCLA Special Collections Library.
10. Allen, Irwin. Memo, August 24, 1965, "One by One," UCLA Special Collections Library.
11. La Tourette, Frank. Undated memo on "One by One," UCLA Special Collections Library.
12. Allen, Irwin. Memo, August 24, 1965, "One by One," UCLA Special Collections Library.
13. La Tourette, Frank. Undated memo on "One by One," UCLA Special Collections Library.
14. Allen, Irwin. Memo, August 24, 1965, "One by One," UCLA Special Collections Library.
15. La Tourette, Frank. Undated memo on "One by One," UCLA Special Collections Library.
16. Allen, Irwin. Memo, August 24, 1965, "One by One," UCLA Special Collections Library.
17. La Tourette, Frank. Undated memo on "One by One," UCLA Special Collections Library.
18. Allen, Irwin. Memo, August 24, 1965, "One by One," UCLA Special Collections Library.
19. Welch, William. Undated memo on "One by One," UCLA Special Collections Library.
20. La Tourette, Frank. Undated memo on "One by One," UCLA Special Collections Library.
21. Brown, Dorothy. ABC Continuity and Acceptance Department memo, "The Death Ship," August 24, 1965, UCLA Special Collections Library.
22. *ibid.*
23. *ibid.*
24. Continuity Acceptance Requirements memo, "The Death Ship," July 25, 1965, UCLA Special Collections Library.
25. Show file for "The Death Ship," Daily Production Report, UCLA Special Collections Library.
26. Phillips, Mark. "Giant Jellyfish & Time-Lost Dinosaurs, Part One." See Chapter 2, note 2.
27. Anchors and Barr, *Seaview: A 50th Anniversary Tribute to Voyage to the Bottom of the Sea.*
28. Perry, Elizabeth. Vttbots.com, courtesy Mark Phillips and Mike Bailey.
29. Show file for "The Death Ship," budget, UCLA Special Collections Library.
30. "TV Scout." *Abilene Reporter-News* [TX], February 20, 1966.
31. Irwin Allen papers collection (Courtesy Synthesis Entertainment, assisted by Ron Hamill).

Chapter 4.9: "The Silent Saboteurs"

1. Irwin Allen papers collection (Courtesy Synthesis Entertainment, assisted by Ron Hamill).
2. Phillips, Mark, and Mike Bailey. "The Silent Saboteurs." *Mike's Voyage to the Bottom of the Sea Zone.* http://www.vttbots.com/ep_guide_season2_22.html
3. *ibid.*
4. Garbutt, Mary. ABC Continuity and Acceptance Department memo, "The Silent Saboteurs," August 23, 1965, UCLA Special Collections Library.
5. Allen, Irwin. Memo on "The Silent Saboteurs," September 4, 1965,
6. *ibid.*
7. Show file for "The Silent Saboteurs," Daily Production Report, UCLA Special Collections Library.
8. Show file for "The Silent Saboteurs," budget, UCLA Special Collections Library.
9. "TV Scout." *Daily Kennebec Journal* [Augusta, ME], November 20, 1965.
10. Irwin Allen papers collection (Courtesy Synthesis Entertainment, assisted by Ron Hamill).

Chapter 4.10: "Leviathan"

1. Irwin Allen papers collection (Courtesy Synthesis Entertainment, assisted by Ron Hamill).
2. Phillips, Mark, and Mike Bailey. "Leviathan." *Mike's Voyage to the Bottom of the Sea Zone.* http://www.vttbots.com/ep_guide_season2_4.html
3. *ibid.*
4. Phillips, Mark. "Giant Jellyfish & Alien Invaders, Part Three." *Starlog* #183, October 1992.
5. Allen, Irwin. Memo on "Leviathan," August 25, 1965, UCLA Special Collections Library.
6. *ibid.*
7. *ibid.*
8. Garbutt, Mary. ABC Continuity and Acceptance Department memo, "Leviathan," August 30, 1965, UCLA Special Collections Library.
9. Show file for "Leviathan," Daily Production Report, UCLA Special Collections Library.
10. Phillips, Mark. "The Life of Riley." See Chapter 2, note 6.
11. Phillips, Mark, and Frank Garcia. *Science Fiction Television Series, Volume 2*. McFarland & Company, Inc., 1996.
12. Harris, Harry (1995). Interviewed by Kevin Burns (used by permission).
13. *ibid.*
14. Show file for "Leviathan," budget, UCLA Special Collections Library.
15. "Sexy Feet?" *Syracuse Post Standard* [NY], November 7, 1965.
16. "TV Scout." *Abilene Reporter-News* [TX], November 7, 1965.
17. Scheuer, Steven H. "TV Key." *San Antonio Light* [TX], November 7, 1965.
18. McIntyre, Tom. Review of "Leviathan." *Gaston Gazette* [Gastonia, NC].
19. Irwin Allen papers collection (Courtesy Synthesis Entertainment, assisted by Ron Hamill).

Chapter 4.11: "The Peacemaker"

1. Irwin Allen papers collection (Courtesy Synthesis Entertainment, assisted by Ron Hamill).
2. Phillips, Mark, and Mike Bailey. "The Peacemaker." *Mike's Voyage to the Bottom of the Sea Zone.* http://www.vttbots.com/ep_guide_season2_18.html
3. *ibid.*
4. Phillips, Mark. "Giant Jellyfish & Time-Lost Dinosaurs, Part One." See Chapter 2, note 2.
5. La Tourette, Frank. Undated notes on "The Peacemaker."
6. Garbutt, Mary. ABC Continuity and Acceptance Department memo, "The Peacemaker," September 21, 1965, UCLA Special Collections Library.
7. D'Agosta, Joe (2015). Personal interview.
8. Show file for "The Peacemaker," Daily Production Report, UCLA Special Collections Library.
9. Hunt, Allan (2020). Personal interview.
10. D'Agosta, Joe (2015). Personal interview.
11. Phillips, Mark. "The Life of Riley." See Chapter 2, note 6.
12. Show file for "The Peacemaker," Daily Production Report, UCLA Special Collections Library.
13. Show file for "The Peacemaker," Budget, UCLA Special Collections Library.
14. "TV Scout." *Daily Kennebec Journal* (Augusta, Maine), November 13, 1965.
15. Irwin Allen papers collection (Courtesy Synthesis Entertainment, assisted by Ron Hamill).

Chapter 4.12: "The Monster from Outer Space"

1. Irwin Allen papers collection (Courtesy Synthesis Entertainment, assisted by Ron Hamill).
2. Phillips, Mark, and Mike Bailey. "The Monster from Outer Space." *Mike's Voyage to the Bottom of the Sea Zone.* http://www.vttbots.com/ep_guide_season2_23.html
3. *ibid.*
4. Brown, Dorothy. ABC Continuity and Acceptance Department memo, "The Migrants," October 4, 1965, UCLA Special Collections Library.
5. Phillips and Garcia. *Science Fiction Television Series, Volume 2*. See Chapter 4.10, note 11.
6. Show file for "The Monster from Outer Space," Daily Production Report, UCLA Special Collections Library.
7. Show file for "The Monster from Outer Space," Budget, UCLA Special Collections Library.
8. Phillips, Mark, and Mike Bailey. "The Monster from Outer Space." See note 2.
9. Phillips, Mark. "Giant Jellyfish & Time-Lost Dinosaurs, Part Two." See Chapter 4.2, note 2.

10. Lowry, Cynthia. "Television Show Proves Exciting." *Joplin News Herald* [MO], December 20, 1965.
11. Irwin Allen papers collection (Courtesy Synthesis Entertainment, assisted by Ron Hamill).

Chapter 4.13: "The X Factor"

1. Irwin Allen papers collection (Courtesy Synthesis Entertainment, assisted by Ron Hamill).
2. Phillips, Mark, and Mike Bailey. "The X Factor." *Mike's Voyage to the Bottom of the Sea Zone*. http://www.vttbots.com/ep_guide_season2_20.html
3. *ibid.*
4. Garbutt, Mary. ABC Continuity and Acceptance Department memo, "The X Factor," October 14, 1965, UCLA Special Collections Library.
5. Hunt, Allan (2020). Personal interview.
6. Show file for "The X Factor," Daily Production Report, UCLA Special Collections Library.
7. Show file for "The X Factor," Budget, UCLA Special Collections Library.
8. "TV Scout." *Oneonta Star* [NY], December 4, 1965.
9. Irwin Allen papers collection (Courtesy Synthesis Entertainment, assisted by Ron Hamill).

Chapter 4.14: "The Machines Strike Back"

1. Irwin Allen papers collection (Courtesy Synthesis Entertainment, assisted by Ron Hamill).
2. Phillips, Mark, and Mike Bailey. "The Machines Strike Back." *Mike's Voyage to the Bottom of the Sea Zone*. http://www.vttbots.com/ep_guide_season2_17.html
3. *ibid.*
4. Carmel, Roger C. (1982). Personal interview.
5. Phillips, Mark. "Giant Jellyfish & Time-Lost Dinosaurs, Part Two." See Chapter 4.2, note 2.
6. Allen, Irwin. Memo on "The Machines Strike Back," October 28, 1965, UCLA Special Collections Library.
7. Phillips, Mark. "Charting a Voyage to the Bottom of the Sea!" See Chapter 3, note 6.
8. Anchors and Barr, *Seaview: A 50th Anniversary Tribute to Voyage to the Bottom of the Sea*.
9. Show file for "The Machines Strike Back," Daily Production Report, UCLA Special Collections Library.
10. Show file for "The Machines Strike Back," Budget, UCLA Special Collections Library.
11. Stern, Harold. "Basehart Doing TV Series Basically for Money." *Arizona Republic* [Phoenix], December 9, 1965.
12. *ibid.*
13. Crosby, Joan. "TV Scout." *Daily Kennebec Journal* [Augusta, ME], December 11, 1965.
14. Scheuer, Steven H. "TV Key." *Gazette Mail* [Charleston, WV], December 12, 1965.
15. Irwin Allen papers collection (Courtesy Synthesis Entertainment, assisted by Ron Hamill).

Chapter 4.15: "Killers of the Deep"

1. Irwin Allen papers collection (Courtesy Synthesis Entertainment, assisted by Ron Hamill).
2. Phillips, Mark, and Mike Bailey. "Killers of the Deep." *Mike's Voyage to the Bottom of the Sea Zone*. http://www.vttbots.com/ep_guide_season2_12.html
3. *ibid.*
4. Phillips, Mark. "Giant Jellyfish & Time-Lost Dinosaurs, Part Two." See Chapter 4.2, note 2.
5. Harris, Harry (1995). Interviewed by Kevin Burns (special arrangement with Jacobs/Brown).
6. Show file for "Killers of the Deep," Daily Production Report and Budget, UCLA Special Collections Library.
7. Phillips, Mark. "Giant Jellyfish & Time-Lost Dinosaurs, Part Two." See Chapter 4.2, note 2.
8. "TV Scout." *Abilene Reporter-News* [TX], January 2, 1966.
9. Irwin Allen papers collection (Courtesy Synthesis Entertainment, assisted by Ron Hamill).
10. Aukerman, Charles. "Speaking of *Voyage* – It Really Isn't That Bad!" *Medina County Gazette* [OH], January 4, 1966.

Chapter 4.16: "Terror on Dinosaur Island"

1. Irwin Allen papers collection (Courtesy Synthesis Entertainment, assisted by Ron Hamill).
2. Phillips, Mark, and Mike Bailey. "Terror on Dinosaur Island." *Mike's Voyage to the Bottom of the Sea Zone*. http://www.vttbots.com/ep_guide_season2_5.html

3. *ibid.*
4. *ibid.*
5. Phillips, Mark. "Do You Remember…" *The TV Collector* #96, February 1999.
6. Garbutt, Mary. ABC Continuity and Acceptance Department memo, "Terror on Dinosaur Island," November 5, 1965, UCLA Special Collections Library.
7. Hunt, Allan (2020). Personal interview.
8. Phillips, Mark. "Do You Remember…" See note 5.
9. Anchors and Barr, *Seaview: A 50th Anniversary Tribute to Voyage to the Bottom of the Sea*.
10. Show file for "Terror on Dinosaur Island," Daily Production Report and Budget, UCLA Special Collections Library.
11. Hunter, Lew (2015). Personal interview.
12. "TV Scout." *Daily Kennebec Journal* [Augusta, ME], December 24, 1965.
13. Irwin Allen papers collection (Courtesy Synthesis Entertainment, assisted by Ron Hamill).
14. La Tourette, Frank. Undated memo to Irwin Allen.

Chapter 5: Season Two / ABC's Back Order of 10

1. Horowitz, Murray. "Execution Papers Tentatively Drawn for 30% of Web Programs." *Variety*, December 8, 1965.

Chapter 5.1: "Deadly Creature Below!"

1. Irwin Allen papers collection (Courtesy Synthesis Entertainment, assisted by Ron Hamill).
2. Phillips, Mark, and Mike Bailey. "Deadly Creature Below." *Mike's Voyage to the Bottom of the Sea Zone*. http://www.vttbots.com/ep_guide_season2_7.html
3. *ibid.*
4. Allen, Irwin. Memo on "Escape," November 8, 1965, UCLA Special Collections Library.
5. Garbutt, Mary. ABC Continuity and Acceptance Department memo, "Escape," November 5, 1965, UCLA Special Collections Library.
6. Garbutt, Mary. ABC Continuity and Acceptance Department memo, "Escape," November 15, 1965, UCLA Special Collections Library.
7. Comi, Paul (2013). Personal interview.
8. "TV Mail." *The Daily Oklahoma*, March 6, 1966.
9. Show file for "Deadly Creature Below," Daily Production Report and Budget, UCLA Special Collections Library.
10. "TV Scout." *Abilene Reporter-News* [TX], January 9, 1966.
11. Irwin Allen papers collection (Courtesy Synthesis Entertainment, assisted by Ron Hamill).
12. *Variety*, January 11, 1966.

Chapter 5.2: "The Phantom Strikes"

1. Irwin Allen papers collection (Courtesy Synthesis Entertainment, assisted by Ron Hamill).
2. Phillips, Mark, and Mike Bailey. "The Phantom Strikes." *Mike's Voyage to the Bottom of the Sea Zone*. http://www.vttbots.com/ep_guide_season2_6.html
3. Welch, William. *Talks with the Dead* (Pinnacle Books, 1975).
4. Allen, Irwin. Memo on "The Ghost Ship," November 21, 1965, UCLA Special Collections Library.
5. *ibid.*
6. *ibid.*
7. Phillips, Mark. "The Life of Riley." See Chapter 2, note 6.
8. Anchors and Barr, *Seaview: A 50th Anniversary Tribute to Voyage to the Bottom of the Sea*.
9. Phillips and Garcia. *Science Fiction Television Series, Volume 2*. See Chapter 4.10, note 11.
10. Phillips, Mark. "The Life of Riley." See Chapter 2, note 6.
11. Show file for "The Phantom Strikes," Daily Production Report and Budget, UCLA Special Collections Library.
12. "Alfred Ryder a Specialist in Sinister Characters." *Pasadena Independent Star-News* [CA], January 16, 1966.
13. *ibid.*
14. "TV Key." *Oneonta Star* [NY], January 15, 1966.
15. Irwin Allen papers collection (Courtesy Synthesis Entertainment, assisted by Ron Hamill).

16. Phillips, Mark. "Man Down Under." *Starlog Yearbook*, February 2003.
17. Anchors and Barr, *Seaview: A 50th Anniversary Tribute to Voyage to the Bottom of the Sea*.
18. *ibid*.
19. Phillips and Garcia. *Science Fiction Television Series, Volume 2*. See Chapter 4.10, note 11.

Chapter 5.3: "The Sky's on Fire"

1. Irwin Allen papers collection (Courtesy Synthesis Entertainment, assisted by Ron Hamill).
2. Phillips, Mark, and Mike Bailey. "The Sky's on Fire" *Mike's Voyage to the Bottom of the Sea Zone*. http://www.vttbots.com/ep_guide_season2_11.html
3. Kelly, Kevin. "Producer's Nightmare Science-Fiction Epic." *The Boston Globe*, June 14, 1961.
4. Allen, Irwin. Memo on "The Sky's on Fire" first draft, November 28, 1965, UCLA Special Collections Library.
5. *ibid*.
6. *ibid*.
7. *ibid*.
8. Garbutt, Mary. ABC Continuity and Acceptance Department memo, "The Sky's on Fire," December 9, 1965, UCLA Special Collections Library.
9. *ibid*.
10. Phillips, Mark. "Charting a Voyage to the Bottom of the Sea!" See Chapter 3, note 6.
11. Anchors and Barr, *Seaview: A 50th Anniversary Tribute to Voyage to the Bottom of the Sea*.
12. Show file for "The Sky's on Fire," Daily Production Report and Budget, UCLA Special Collections Library.
13. Irwin Allen papers collection (Courtesy Synthesis Entertainment, assisted by Ron Hamill).

Chapter 5.4: "Graveyard of Fear"

1. Irwin Allen papers collection (Courtesy Synthesis Entertainment, assisted by Ron Hamill).
2. Phillips, Mark, and Mike Bailey. "Graveyard of Fear." *Mike's Voyage to the Bottom of the Sea Zone*. http://www.vttbots.com/ep_guide_season2_21.html
3. *ibid*.
4. Phillips, Mark. "Giant Jellyfish & Time-Lost Dinosaurs, Part Two." See Chapter 4.2, note 2.
5. Garbutt, Mary. ABC Continuity and Acceptance Department memo, "Graveyard of Fear," December 9, 1965, UCLA Special Collections Library.
6. Allen, Irwin. Memo on "Graveyard of Fear," December 18, 1965, UCLA Special Collections Library.
7. Phillips, Mark. "Giant Jellyfish & Time-Lost Dinosaurs, Part Two." See Chapter 4.2, note 2.
8. Phillips, Mark. "Charting a Voyage to the Bottom of the Sea!" See Chapter 3, note 6.
9. Show file for "Graveyard of Fear," Daily Production Report and Budget, UCLA Special Collections Library.
10. "TV Scout." *San Antonio Light* [TX], January 30, 1966.
11. Scheuer, Steven H. "TV Key." *Wisconsin State Journal* [Madison], January 30, 1966.
12. Irwin Allen papers collection (Courtesy Synthesis Entertainment, assisted by Ron Hamill).
13. La Tourette, Frank. Undated memo to Irwin Allen. Irwin Allen papers collection (Courtesy Synthesis Entertainment, assisted by Ron Hamill).
14. *ibid*.
15. "TV Group Rates Kiddie Programs." *Gazette Mail* [Charleston, WV], January 31, 1966.
16. Irwin Allen papers collection (Courtesy Synthesis Entertainment, assisted by Ron Hamill).

Chapter 5.5: "The Shape of Doom"

1. Irwin Allen papers collection (Courtesy Synthesis Entertainment, assisted by Ron Hamill).
2. Phillips, Mark, and Mike Bailey. "The Shape of Doom." *Mike's Voyage to the Bottom of the Sea Zone*. http://www.vttbots.com/ep_guide_season2_19.html
3. *ibid*.
4. Allen, Irwin. Memo on "Denizen of Doom," January 4, 1966, UCLA Special Collections Library.
5. Garbutt, Mary. ABC Continuity and Acceptance Department memo, "Denizen of Doom," January 5, 1966, UCLA Special Collections Library.
6. Show file for "The Shape of Doom," Daily Production Report and Budget, UCLA Special Collections Library.
7. McIntyre, Tom. "Profile Richard Basehart." See Chapter 4.5, note 17.

8. "TV Scout." *Abilene Reporter-News* [TX], February 6, 1966.
9. Irwin Allen papers collection (Courtesy Synthesis Entertainment, assisted by Ron Hamill).

Chapter 5.6: "Dead Men's Doubloons"

1. Irwin Allen papers collection (Courtesy Synthesis Entertainment, assisted by Ron Hamill).
2. Phillips, Mark, and Mike Bailey. "Dead Men's Doubloons." *Mike's Voyage to the Bottom of the Sea Zone*. http://www.vttbots.com/ep_guide_season2_14.html
3. Phillips and Garcia. *Science Fiction Television Series, Volume 2*. See Chapter 4.10, note 11.
4. Show file for "The Shape of Doom," Daily Production Report and Budget, UCLA Special Collections Library.
5. Scheuer, Steven H. "TV Key." *San Antonio Light* [TX], February 13, 1966.
6. Irwin Allen papers collection (Courtesy Synthesis Entertainment, assisted by Ron Hamill).

Chapter 5.7: "The Monster's Web"

1. Irwin Allen papers collection (Courtesy Synthesis Entertainment, assisted by Ron Hamill).
2. Phillips, Mark, and Mike Bailey. "The Monster's Web." *Mike's Voyage to the Bottom of the Sea Zone*. http://www.vttbots.com/ep_guide_season2_10.html
3. *ibid*.
4. Hunt, Allan (2020). Personal interview.
5. Allen, Irwin. Memo on "Web of Destruction," January 16, 1966, UCLA Special Collections Library.
6. La Tourette, Frank. Undated memo on "Web of Destruction" to Irwin Allen. Irwin Allen papers collection (Courtesy Synthesis Entertainment, assisted by Ron Hamill).
7. McIntyre, Tom. "Profile Richard Basehart." See Chapter 4.5, note 17.
8. Phillips, Mark. "The Life of Riley." See Chapter 2, note 6.
9. Phillips and Garcia. *Science Fiction Television Series, Volume 2*. See Chapter 4.10, note 11.
10. Show file for "The Monster's Web," Daily Production Report and Budget, UCLA Special Collections Library.
11. "TV Scout." *Abilene Reporter* [TX], February 27, 1966.
12. Irwin Allen papers collection (Courtesy Synthesis Entertainment, assisted by Ron Hamill).

Chapter 5.8: "The Menfish"

1. Irwin Allen papers collection (Courtesy Synthesis Entertainment, assisted by Ron Hamill).
2. Phillips, Mark, and Mike Bailey. "The Menfish." *Mike's Voyage to the Bottom of the Sea Zone*. http://www.vttbots.com/ep_guide_season2_13.html
3. *ibid*.
4. *ibid*.
5. Phillips, Mark. "Giant Jellyfish & Time-Lost Dinosaurs, Part One." See Chapter 2, note 2.
6. Phillips, Mark. "The Life of Riley." See Chapter 2, note 6.
7. Phillips, Mark. "Giant Jellyfish & Time-Lost Dinosaurs, Part One." See Chapter 2, note 2.
8. Allen, Irwin. Memo on "'The Menfish' or 'Sea Demons'," Second Draft, January 30, 1966, UCLA Special Collections Library.
9. La Tourette, Frank. Undated notes on "The Menfish," UCLA Special Collections Library.
10. Garbutt, Mary. ABC Continuity and Acceptance Department memo, "The Menfish," January 28, 1966, UCLA Special Collections Library.
11. Phillips, Mark. "Giant Jellyfish & Time-Lost Dinosaurs, Part One." See Chapter 2, note 2.
12. Anchors and Barr, *Seaview: A 50th Anniversary Tribute to Voyage to the Bottom of the Sea*.
13. Phillips, Mark. "Giant Jellyfish & Time-Lost Dinosaurs, Part One." See Chapter 2, note 2.
14. Anchors and Barr, *Seaview: A 50th Anniversary Tribute to Voyage to the Bottom of the Sea*.
15. La Tourette, Frank. Undated production Notes on "The Menfish," UCLA Special Collections Library.
16. Witbeck, Charles. "Monsters Figure in Ratings Battle." *The Winona Daily News* [MN], April 10, 1966.
17. Zastupnevich, Paul (1995). Interviewed by Kevin Burns (used by permission).
18. Phillips, Mark, and Mike Bailey. "The Menfish." See note 2.
19. Phillips and Garcia. *Science Fiction Television Series, Volume 2*. See Chapter 4.10, note 11.
20. Show file for "The Menfish," Daily Production Report and Budget, UCLA Special Collections Library.
21. "TV Scout." *Abilene Reporter-News* [TX], March 6, 1966.

22. Irwin Allen papers collection (Courtesy Synthesis Entertainment, assisted by Ron Hamill).

Chapter 5.9: "The Mechanical Man"

1. Irwin Allen papers collection (Courtesy Synthesis Entertainment, assisted by Ron Hamill).
2. Phillips, Mark, and Mike Bailey. "The Mechanical Man." *Mike's Voyage to the Bottom of the Sea Zone*. http://www.vttbots.com/ep_guide_season2_13.html#mechanical
3. *ibid.*
4. Marshall, Sidney. Memo on "Final Warning," December 27, 1965, UCLA Special Collections Library.
5. Show file for "The Mechanical Man," Daily Production Report and Budget, UCLA Special Collections Library.
6. "Heart Throb Turns Heavy." *Hutchinson News* [KS], March 12, 1966.
7. *ibid.*
8. "TV Scout." *Abilene Reporter-News* [TX], March 13, 1966.
9. Irwin Allen papers collection (Courtesy Synthesis Entertainment, assisted by Ron Hamill).

Chapter 5.10: "The Return of the Phantom"

1. Irwin Allen papers collection (Courtesy Synthesis Entertainment, assisted by Ron Hamill).
2. Phillips, Mark, and Mike Bailey. "Return of the Phantom." *Mike's Voyage to the Bottom of the Sea Zone*. http://www.vttbots.com/ep_guide_return_phantom.html
3. *ibid.*
4. Bailey, Michael. "David Hedison interview, 2005." *Mike's Voyage to the Bottom of the Sea Zone*. http://vttbots.com/hedison_interview_2005.html
5. Marcus, Vitina (2015). Personal interview.
6. *ibid.*
7. Show file for "The Mechanical Man," Daily Production Report, UCLA Special Collections Library.
8. Hedison, David. Audio Commentary. *Voyage to the Bottom of the Sea - The Complete Collection*. 20th Century Fox, 2007.
9. Marcus, Vitina (2015). Personal interview.
10. Phillips and Garcia. *Science Fiction Television Series, Volume 2*. See Chapter 4.10, note 11.
11. Bailey, Michael. "David Hedison interview, 2005." See note 4.
12. McIntyre, Tom. "Profile Richard Basehart." See Chapter 4.5, note 17.
13. *ibid.*
14. *ibid.*
15. Hedison, David. Audio Commentary. *Voyage to the Bottom of the Sea - The Complete Collection*. 20th Century Fox, 2007.
16. "TV Scout." *San Antonio Express and News* [TX], March 20, 1966.
17. Scheuer, Steven H. "TV Key." *Lima News* [OH], March 20, 1966.
18. Irwin Allen papers collection (Courtesy Synthesis Entertainment, assisted by Ron Hamill).

Chapter 6: Fall 1966: Welcome to the Monster Mash

1. Hunt, Allan (2020). Personal interview.
2. Gail, Al. Interviewed by Kevin Burns, 1995 (used by special arrangement with Jacobs/Brown).
3. *ibid.*
4. Hunter, Lew (2015). Personal interview.
5. *ibid.*
6. *ibid.*
7. "David Hedison: Torpedoed by Success." *TV Guide*, July 16, 1966.
8. *ibid.*
9. *ibid.*
10. Kaufman, Dave. "Beasts Bot Beauts in Sea." *Daily Variety*, August 3, 1966.
11. *ibid.*
12. Rush, Herman (2015). Personal interview.
13. Anchors and Barr, *Seaview: A 50th Anniversary Tribute to Voyage to the Bottom of the Sea*.
14. Kaufman, Dave. "Beasts Bot Beauts in Sea." See note 10.
15. Hunt, Allan (2020). Personal interview.

16. Phillips, Mark. "The Life of Riley." See Chapter 2, note 6.
17. *ibid.*
18. Mumy, Bill (2015). Personal interview.

Chapter 7: Season Three: ABC's Initial Order of 16

1. Gail, Al (1995). Interviewed by Kevin Burns (used by permission).

Chapter 7.1: "Monster from the Inferno"

1. Irwin Allen papers collection (Courtesy Synthesis Entertainment, assisted by Ron Hamill).
2. Phillips, Mark, and Mike Bailey. "Monster from the Inferno." *Mike's Voyage to the Bottom of the Sea Zone*. http://www.vttbots.com/epi_guide_season3_1.html
3. *ibid.*
4. Allen, Irwin. Memo on "Monster from the Inferno," April 18 draft, April 18, 1966, UCLA Special Collections Library.
5. Ward, Calvin. ABC Department of Broadcast Standards and Practices memo, "Monster from the Inferno," April 29, 1966, UCLA Special Collections Library.
6. Allen, Irwin. Memos on "Monster from the Inferno," 3rd draft, May 6 & 8, 1966, UCLA Special Collections Library.
7. Allen, Irwin. Memo on "Monster from the Inferno," 4th draft, May 15, 1966. UCLA Special Collections Library.
8. Show file for "Monster from the Inferno," Daily Production Report and Budget, UCLA Special Collections Library.
9. Harris, Harry (1995). Interviewed by Kevin Burns (special arrangement with Jacobs/Brown).
10. Strout, Dick. "Hollywood Profiles," 1966.
11. Harris, Harry (1995). Interviewed by Kevin Burns (used by permission).
12. Strout, Dick. "Hollywood Profiles," 1966.
13. *ibid.*
14. "TV Scout." *Abilene Reporter-News* [TX], September 18, 1966.
15. Scheuer, Steven H. "TV Key." *Lima News* [OH], September 18, 1966.
16. "Pit." Review of "Monster from the Inferno." *Variety*, September 21, 1966.
17. Daku. Review of "Monster from the Inferno." *Daily Variety*, September 20, 1966.
18. Irwin Allen papers collection (Courtesy Synthesis Entertainment, assisted by Ron Hamill).

Chapter 7.2: "Werewolf"

1. Irwin Allen papers collection (Courtesy Synthesis Entertainment, assisted by Ron Hamill).
2. Phillips, Mark, and Mike Bailey. "Werewolf." *Mike's Voyage to the Bottom of the Sea Zone*. http://www.vttbots.com/epi_guide_season3_2.html
3. Allen, Irwin. Memo on "Werewolf" revised draft, May 15, 1966, UCLA Special Collections Library.
4. Garbutt, Mary. ABC Department of Broadcast Standards and Practices memo, "Werewolf," May 30, 1966, UCLA Special Collections Library.
5. Hunter, Lew. Letter to Sid Marshall, May 31, 1966, re "Werewolf," UCLA Special Collections Library.
6. Hunter, Lew (2015). Personal interview.
7. Phillips and Garcia. *Science Fiction Television Series, Volume 2*. See Chapter 4.10, note 11.
8. *ibid.*
9. Show file for "Werewolf," Daily Production Report and Budget, UCLA Special Collections Library.
10. Kleiner, Dick. "Show Boat." *Pulaski Southwest Times* [VA], September 25, 1966.
11. Allen, Irwin. *Daily Variety*, September 29, 1966.
12. "TV Scout." *Edwardsville Intelligencer* [IL], September 29, 1966.
13. Murphy, Ken. "No Pip Squeak Problems on Voyage Expedition." *Waterloo Daily Courier* [IA], October 9, 1966.
14. Irwin Allen papers collection (Courtesy Synthesis Entertainment, assisted by Ron Hamill).
15. *Broadcasting*, October 17, 1966.

Chapter 7.3: "Day of Evil"

1. Irwin Allen papers collection (Courtesy Synthesis Entertainment, assisted by Ron Hamill).
2. Phillips, Mark, and Mike Bailey. "Day of Evil." *Mike's Voyage to the Bottom of the Sea Zone*. http://www.vttbots.com/epi_guide_season3_7.html
3. *ibid.*
4. Allen, Irwin. Memo on "Day of Evil," 2nd draft, April 30, 1966, UCLA Special Collections Library.
5. Garbutt, Mary. ABC Department of Broadcast Standards and Practices memo, "Day of Evil," June 2, 1966, UCLA Special Collections Library.
6. Bennett, Harve. Letter to Irwin Allen, June 8, 1966, UCLA Special Collections Library.
7. Bennett, Harve. Letter to Irwin Allen, June 9, 1966, UCLA Special Collections Library.
8. Hunter, Lew (2015). Personal interview.
9. King, Susan. "David Hedison Looks Back on Periscope Days." See Chapter 4.1, note 6.
10. "TV Scout." *Abilene Reporter-News* [TX], May 7, 1967.
11. Irwin Allen papers collection (Courtesy Synthesis Entertainment, assisted by Ron Hamill).

Chapter 7.4: "Night of Terror"

1. Irwin Allen papers collection (Courtesy Synthesis Entertainment, assisted by Ron Hamill).
2. Phillips, Mark, and Mike Bailey. "Night of Terror." *Mike's Voyage to the Bottom of the Sea Zone*. http://www.vttbots.com/epi_guide_season3_4.html
3. *ibid.*
4. Phillips, Mark. "Giant Jellyfish & Alien Invaders, Part Three." See Chapter 4.10, note 4.
5. Marshall, Sid. Undated memo to Irwin Allen on "Spanish Gold," UCLA Special Collections Library.
6. Hunter, Lew. Letter to Sid Marshall on "Spanish Gold," June 20, 1966, UCLA Special Collections Library.
7. Allen, Irwin. Undated memo on "Spanish Gold," aka "The Real and the Unreal," UCLA Special Collections Library.
8. Garbutt, Mary. ABC Department of Broadcast Standards and Practices memos, "Spanish Gold," 1st & 2nd drafts, June 15 & 27, 1966, UCLA Special Collections Library.
9. Show file for "Night of Terror," Daily Production Report and Budget, UCLA Special Collections Library.
10. Hedison, David. Audio Commentary. *Voyage to the Bottom of the Sea - The Complete Collection*. 20th Century Fox, 2007.
11. Irwin Allen papers collection (Courtesy Synthesis Entertainment, assisted by Ron Hamill).

Chapter 7.5: "The Day the World Ended"

1. Irwin Allen papers collection (Courtesy Synthesis Entertainment, assisted by Ron Hamill).
2. Phillips, Mark, and Mike Bailey. "The Day the World Ended." *Mike's Voyage to the Bottom of the Sea Zone*. http://www.vttbots.com/epi_guide_season3_3.html
3. *ibid.*
4. Welch, William. "The Day the World Ended" notion, UCLA Special Collections Library.
5. Garbutt, Mary. ABC Department of Broadcast Standards and Practices memo, "The Day the World Ended," 1st draft, July 13, 1966, UCLA Special Collections Library.
6. Show file for "The Day the World Ended," Daily Production Report and Budget, UCLA Special Collections Library.
7. "TV Scout." *Edwardsville Intelligencer* [IL], September 30, 1966, preview.
8. Irwin Allen papers collection (Courtesy Synthesis Entertainment, assisted by Ron Hamill).
9. Summers, Bill. "*Voyage* All You Want in Escapism." *Orlando Evening Star* [FL], October 3, 1966,
10. Shiels, Bill. *Calgary Herald* [Alberta, Canada], October 7, 1966.

Chapter 7.6: "The Terrible Toys"

1. Irwin Allen papers collection (Courtesy Synthesis Entertainment, assisted by Ron Hamill).
2. Phillips, Mark, and Mike Bailey. The Terrible Toys." *Mike's Voyage to the Bottom of the Sea Zone*. http://www.vttbots.com/epi_guide_season3_5.html
3. Phillips, Mark. "Giant Jellyfish & Time-Lost Dinosaurs, Part Two." See Chapter 4.2, note 2.
4. Undated Story Premise, "The Terrible Toys," UCLA Special Collections Library.
5. Wright, Robert Vincent. Undated treatment, "The Terrible Toys," UCLA Special Collections Library.

6. Phillips, Mark. "Giant Jellyfish & Time-Lost Dinosaurs, Part Two." See Chapter 4.2, note 2.
7. Show file for "The Terrible Toys," Daily Production Report and Budget, UCLA Special Collections Library.
8. Hunter, Lew (2015). Personal interview.
9. Crosby, Joan. "TV Scout." *Abilene Reporter-News* [TX], October 16, 1966.
10. Irwin Allen papers collection (Courtesy Synthesis Entertainment, assisted by Ron Hamill).

Chapter 7.7: "Deadly Waters"

1. Irwin Allen papers collection (Courtesy Synthesis Entertainment, assisted by Ron Hamill).
2. Phillips, Mark, and Mike Bailey. "Deadly Waters." *Mike's Voyage to the Bottom of the Sea Zone.* http://www.vttbots.com/epi_guide_season3_6.html
3. ibid.
4. Phillips, Mark. "Giant Jellyfish & Time-Lost Dinosaurs, Part Two." See Chapter 4.2, note 2.
5. Wright, Robert Vincent. Undated treatment for "Deadly Waters," UCLA Special Collections Library.
6. Allen, Irwin. Memo on "Deadly Waters," script draft dated June 15, 1966, UCLA Special Collections Library.
7. Phillips, Mark. "Giant Jellyfish & Time-Lost Dinosaurs, Part Two." See Chapter 4.2, note 2.
8. "Acting Breeds Complexity, Star Asserts." *Ogden Standard Examiner* [UTY], October 30, 1966.
9. "TV Scout." *Abilene Reporter-News* [TX], October 30, 1966.
10. Scheuer, Steven H. "TV Key." *Lima News* [OH], October 30, 1966.
11. Irwin Allen papers collection (Courtesy Synthesis Entertainment, assisted by Ron Hamill).

Chapter 7.8: "Thing from Inner Space"

1. Irwin Allen papers collection (Courtesy Synthesis Entertainment, assisted by Ron Hamill).
2. Phillips, Mark, and Mike Bailey. "Thing from Inner Space." *Mike's Voyage to the Bottom of the Sea Zone.* http://www.vttbots.com/epi_guide_season3_11.html
3. ibid.
4. Welch, William. Treatment, "Thing from Inner Space," June 29, 1966 draft, UCLA Special Collections Library.
5. Allen, Irwin. Memo on "Thing from Outer [sic] Space," August 5, 1966, UCLA Special Collections Library.
6. Ward, Calvin. ABC Department of Broadcast Standards and Practices memo, "The Thing from Inner Space," August 15, 1966, UCLA Special Collections Library.
7. Hunter, Lew (2015). Personal interview.
8. Show file for "Thing from Inner Space," Daily Production Report and Budget, UCLA Special Collections Library.
9. Scheuer, Steven H. "TV Key." *Albuquerque Journal* [NM], November 6, 1966.
10. Irwin Allen papers collection (Courtesy Synthesis Entertainment, assisted by Ron Hamill).

Chapter 7.9: "The Death Watch"

1. Irwin Allen papers collection (Courtesy Synthesis Entertainment, assisted by Ron Hamill).
2. Phillips, Mark, and Mike Bailey. "The Death Watch." *Mike's Voyage to the Bottom of the Sea Zone.* http://www.vttbots.com/epi_guide_season3_9.html
3. Gail, Al (1995). Interviewed by Kevin Burns (used by permission).
4. Anchors and Barr, *Seaview: A 50th Anniversary Tribute to Voyage to the Bottom of the Sea*.
5. "TV Scout." *San Antonio Express and Mail* [TX], November 13, 1966.
6. Daku. Review of "The Death Watch." *Daily Variety*, November 15, 1966.
7. Irwin Allen papers collection (Courtesy Synthesis Entertainment, assisted by Ron Hamill).

Chapter 7.10: "Deadly Invasion"

1. Irwin Allen papers collection (Courtesy Synthesis Entertainment, assisted by Ron Hamill).
2. Phillips, Mark, and Mike Bailey. "Deadly Invasion." *Mike's Voyage to the Bottom of the Sea Zone.* http://www.vttbots.com/epi_guide_season3_12.html
3. Allen, Irwin. Notes on "Deadly Invasion," 1st-draft script, May 5, 1966; additional notes, May 9, 1966; 2nd-draft script, May 16, 1966; 4th-draft script, September 2, 1966, UCLA Special Collections Library.

4. Garbutt, Mary. ABC Department of Broadcast Standards and Practices memo, "Deadly Invasion," July 13 and August 22, 1966, UCLA Special Collections Library.
5. Phillips, Mark. "Do You Remember..." See Chapter 4.16, note 5.
6. Show file for "Deadly Invasion," Daily Production Report and Budget, UCLA Special Collections Library.
7. "TV Scout." *Abilene Reporter-News* [TX], November 20, 1966.
8. Scheuer, Steven H. "TV Key." *Oneonta Star* [NY], June 3, 1967.
9. Irwin Allen papers collection (Courtesy Synthesis Entertainment, assisted by Ron Hamill).

Chapter 7.11: "The Lost Bomb"

1. *TV Guide*, December 10, 1966.
2. Phillips, Mark, and Mike Bailey. "The Lost Bomb." *Mike's Voyage to the Bottom of the Sea Zone*. http://www.vttbots.com/epi_guide_season3_17.html
3. *ibid.*
4. Phillips, Mark, and Mike Bailey. "The Lost Bomb." See note 2.
5. Allen, Irwin. Notes on "The Lost Bomb," May 27, 1966; on 2nd draft, June 23, 1966, UCLA Special Collections Library.
6. Phillips and Garcia. *Science Fiction Television Series, Volume 2*. See Chapter 4.10, note 11..
7. Phillips, Mark. "Do You Remember..." See Chapter 4.16, note 5.
8. Show file for "The Lost Bomb," Daily Production Report and Budget, UCLA Special Collections Library.
9. "Mohr's 'Heavy.'" *Syracuse Herald-Journal* [NY], December 11, 1966.
10. *ibid.*
11. Scheuer, Steven H. "TV Key." *San Antonio Light* [TX], December 11, 1966.
12. Colliver, *Seaview: The Making of Voyage to the Bottom of the Sea*.

Chapter 7.12: "The Brand of the Beast"

1. *TV Guide*, December 17, 1966.
2. Phillips, Mark, and Mike Bailey. "The Brand of the Beast." *Mike's Voyage to the Bottom of the Sea Zone*. http://www.vttbots.com/epi_guide_season3_20.html
3. *ibid.*
4. Welch, William. Undated story idea, "The Mark of the Beast," UCLA Special Collections Library.
5. *ibid.*
6. Garbutt, Mary. ABC Department of Broadcast Standards and Practices memo, "The Brand of the Beast," September 22, 1966, UCLA Special Collections Library.
7. Show file for "The Brand of the Beast," Daily Production Report and Budget, UCLA Special Collections Library.
8. "TV Scout." *Abilene Reporter-News* [TX], December 18, 1966.
9. Steven H. Scheuer. "TV Key." *Oneonta Star* [NY], December 17, 1966.
10. Irwin Allen papers collection (Courtesy Synthesis Entertainment, assisted by Ron Hamill).

Chapter 7.13: "The Plant Man"

1. *TV Guide*, December 3, 1966.
2. Phillips, Mark, and Mike Bailey. "The Plant Man." *Mike's Voyage to the Bottom of the Sea Zone*. http://www.vttbots.com/epi_guide_season3_21.html
3. *ibid.*
4. Mullally, Donn. Undated story springboard, "The Plant Man," UCLA Special Collections Library.
5. Allen, Irwin. Notes on 2nd-draft script, July 19, 1966 UCLA Special Collections Library.
6. *ibid.*
7. Warner, Les. Memo to Irwin Allen, June 27, 1966, UCLA Special Collections Library.
8. Fowler, Bruce. Memo to Sidney Marshall, June 28, 1966, UCLA Special Collections Library.
9. Harris, Harry (1995). Interviewed by Kevin Burns (used by permission).
10. Phillips, Mark. "Do You Remember..." See Chapter 4.16, note 5.
11. Show file for "The Plant Man," Daily Production Report and Budget, UCLA Special Collections Library.
12. Phillips, Mark. "Do You Remember..." See Chapter 4.16, note 5.
13. Phillips, Mark. "Giant Jellyfish & Alien Invaders, Part Three." See Chapter 4.10, note 4.
14. Scheuer, Steven H. "TV Key." *Albuquerque Journal* [NM], December 4, 1966.

15. "TV Scout." *San Antonio Express and Mail* [TX], December 4, 1966.
16. Irwin Allen papers collection (Courtesy Synthesis Entertainment, assisted by Ron Hamill).

Chapter 7.14: "The Creature"

1. Irwin Allen papers collection (Courtesy Synthesis Entertainment, assisted by Ron Hamill).
2. Phillips, Mark, and Mike Bailey. "The Creature." *Mike's Voyage to the Bottom of the Sea Zone*. http://www.vttbots.com/epi_guide_season3_13.html
3. *ibid.*
4. Warner, Les. Memo to Irwin Allen, August 19, 1966, UCLA Special Collections Library.
5. Warner, Les. Memo to Irwin Allen, September 1, 1966, UCLA Special Collections Library.
6. Gail, Al (1995). Interviewed by Kevin Burns (used by special arrangement with Jacobs/Brown).
7. Phillips, Mark, and Mike Bailey. "The Creature." See note 2.
8. Phillips, Mark. "Charting a Voyage to the Bottom of the Sea!" See Chapter 3, note 6.
9. Crosby, Joan. "TV Scout." *The Kenosha News* [WI], July 8, 1967.
10. Durpham, Karen P. "TV Week / You Are the Critic." *Daily Review* [Galveston, TX], December 25, 1966.
11. Irwin Allen papers collection (Courtesy Synthesis Entertainment, assisted by Ron Hamill).

Chapter 7.15: "The Haunted Submarine"

1. Irwin Allen papers collection (Courtesy Synthesis Entertainment, assisted by Ron Hamill).
2. Phillips, Mark, and Mike Bailey. "The Haunted Submarine." *Mike's Voyage to the Bottom of the Sea Zone*. http://www.vttbots.com/epi_guide_season3_10.html
3. Phillips, Mark. "Giant Jellyfish & Time-Lost Dinosaurs, Part Two." See Chapter 4.2, note 2.
4. Welch, William. Undated Notion/Springboard for "The Haunted Submarine," UCLA Special Collections Library.
5. Show file for "The Haunted Submarine," Daily Production Report and Budget, UCLA Special Collections Library.
6. Phillips, Mark. "Charting a Voyage to the Bottom of the Sea!" See Chapter 3, note 6.
7. Strout, Dick. "Hollywood Profiles," 1966.
8. "TV Scout." *The Kenosha News* [WI], July 8, 1967.
9. Irwin Allen papers collection (Courtesy Synthesis Entertainment, assisted by Ron Hamill).

Chapter 7.16: "Death from the Past"

1. Irwin Allen papers collection (Courtesy Synthesis Entertainment, assisted by Ron Hamill).
2. Phillips, Mark, and Mike Bailey. "Death from the Past." *Mike's Voyage to the Bottom of the Sea Zone*. http://www.vttbots.com/epi_guide_season3_16.html
3. *ibid.*
4. Warner, Les. Memo to Irwin Allen, September 28, 1966, UCLA Special Collections Library.
5. Warner, Les. Memo to Irwin Allen, October 17, 1966, UCLA Special Collections Library.
6. *ibid.*
7. Show file for "Death from the Past," Daily Production Report and Budget, UCLA Special Collections Library.
8. Strout, Dick. "Hollywood Profiles," 1966.
9. "TV Scout." *Madison Capital News* [WI], July 15, 1967.
10. Irwin Allen papers collection (Courtesy Synthesis Entertainment, assisted by Ron Hamill).

Chapter 8.1: "The Heat Monster"

1. Irwin Allen papers collection (Courtesy Synthesis Entertainment, assisted by Ron Hamill).
2. Phillips, Mark, and Mike Bailey. "The Heat Monster." *Mike's Voyage to the Bottom of the Sea Zone*. http://www.vttbots.com/epi_guide_season3_23.html
3. *ibid.*
4. Bennett, Charles. "Hell's Hinges Are Hot" treatment, September 10, 1966, UCLA Special Collections Library.
5. *ibid.*
6. *ibid.*

7. Fowler, Bruce. Memo to Sidney Marshall, October 11, 1966, UCLA Special Collections Library.
8. *ibid.*
9. *ibid.*
10. *ibid.*
11. *ibid.*
12. Warner, Les. Memo to Irwin Allen, October 28, 1966, UCLA Special Collections Library.
13. Phillips, Mark, and Mike Bailey. "The Heat Monster." See note 2.
14. Strout, Dick. "Hollywood Profiles," 1966.
15. "TV Scout." *Madison Capital Times* [WI], May 20, 1967.
16. Irwin Allen papers collection (Courtesy Synthesis Entertainment, assisted by Ron Hamill).

Chapter 8.2: "The Fossil Men"

1. Irwin Allen papers collection (Courtesy Synthesis Entertainment, assisted by Ron Hamill).
2. Phillips, Mark, and Mike Bailey. "The Fossil Men." *Mike's Voyage to the Bottom of the Sea Zone*. http://www.vttbots.com/epi_guide_season3_18.html
3. *ibid.*
4. Phillips, Mark, and Mike Bailey. "The Fossil Men." See note 2.
5. Garbutt, Mary. ABC Department of Broadcast Standards and Practices memo, "The Fossil Men," November 9, 1966, UCLA Special Collections Library.
6. Fowler, Bruce. Memo to Irwin Allen, November 8, 1966, UCLA Special Collections Library.
7. Anchors and Barr, *Seaview: A 50th Anniversary Tribute to Voyage to the Bottom of the Sea*.
8. Show file for "The Fossil Men," Daily Production Report and Budget, UCLA Special Collections Library.
9. *Kingston Gleaner* (Jamaica), January 22, 1967, "Monster Adventure on JBC-TV," no writer listed.
10. "Monster Adventure on JBC-TV." *Kingston Gleaner* (Jamaica), January 22, 1967.
11. *ibid.*
12. "TV Scout." *Edwardsville Intelligencer* [IL], January 21, 1967.
13. Irwin Allen papers collection (Courtesy Synthesis Entertainment, assisted by Ron Hamill).

Chapter 8.3: "The Mermaid"

1. Irwin Allen papers collection (Courtesy Synthesis Entertainment, assisted by Ron Hamill).
2. Phillips, Mark, and Mike Bailey. "The Mermaid." *Mike's Voyage to the Bottom of the Sea Zone*. http://www.vttbots.com/epi_guide_season3_15.html
3. *ibid.*
4. Hunter, Lew (2015). Personal interview.
5. Garbutt, Mary. ABC Department of Broadcast Standards and Practices memo, "The Mermaid," November 18, 1966, Revised Shooting Final, UCLA Special Collections Library.
6. Meads, Mike. ABC Department of Broadcast Standards and Practices memo, "The Mermaid," November 18, 1966, Revised Shooting Final, UCLA Special Collections Library.
7. Show file for "The Mermaid," Daily Production Report and Budget, UCLA Special Collections Library.
8. "Two Stars to Open in Hi Life Club." *Bakersfield Californian*, January 20, 1967.
9. "TV Scout." *Madison Capital Times* [WI], August 5, 1967.
10. Irwin Allen papers collection (Courtesy Synthesis Entertainment, assisted by Ron Hamill).

Chapter 8.4: "The Mummy"

1. Irwin Allen papers collection (Courtesy Synthesis Entertainment, assisted by Ron Hamill).
2. Phillips, Mark, and Mike Bailey. "The Mummy." *Mike's Voyage to the Bottom of the Sea Zone*. http://www.vttbots.com/epi_guide_season3_14.html
3. *ibid.*
4. Garbutt, Mary. ABC Department of Broadcast Standards and Practices memo, "The Mummy," November 28, 1966, UCLA Special Collections Library.
5. Harris, Harry (1995). Interviewed by Kevin Burns (used by permission).
6. Show file for "The Mummy," Daily Production Report and Budget, UCLA Special Collections Library.
7. "2,000-Year-Old Mummy Role Makes Problem." *Bakersfield Californian*, December 10, 1966.
8. "TV Scout." *Madison Capital Times* [WI], August 12, 1967.
9. Irwin Allen papers collection (Courtesy Synthesis Entertainment, assisted by Ron Hamill).

Chapter 8.5: "Shadowman"

1. Irwin Allen papers collection (Courtesy Synthesis Entertainment, assisted by Ron Hamill).
2. Phillips, Mark, and Mike Bailey. "Shadowman." *Mike's Voyage to the Bottom of the Sea Zone*. http://www.vttbots.com/epi_guide_season3_24.html
3. *ibid.*
4. *ibid.*
5. Warner, Les. Memo to Irwin Allen, October 5, 1966, UCLA Special Collections Library.
6. Warner, Les. Memo to Irwin Allen, October 18, 1966, UCLA Special Collections Library.
7. Allen, Irwin. Notes on "Shadowman," November 10, 1966, UCLA Special Collections Library.
8. *ibid.*
9. Show file for "The Shadowman," Daily Production Report and Budget, UCLA Special Collections Library.
10. "TV Scout." *Madison Capital Times* [WI], June 24, 1967.
11. Irwin Allen papers collection (Courtesy Synthesis Entertainment, assisted by Ron Hamill).
12. "Mail Bag." *Hutchinson News* [KS], February 18, 1967,

Chapter 8.6: "No Escape from Death"

1. Irwin Allen papers collection (Courtesy Synthesis Entertainment, assisted by Ron Hamill).
2. Phillips, Mark, and Mike Bailey. "No Escape from Death." *Mike's Voyage to the Bottom of the Sea Zone*. http://www.vttbots.com/epi_guide_season3_22.html
3. *ibid.*
4. Show file for "No Escape from Death," Daily Production Report and Budget, UCLA Special Collections Library.
5. Harris, Harry (1995). Interviewed by Kevin Burns (used by permission).
6. Crosby, Joan. "TV Scout." *San Antonio Express and News* [TX], February 19, 1967.
7. Irwin Allen papers collection (Courtesy Synthesis Entertainment, assisted by Ron Hamill).

Chapter 8.7: "Doomsday Island"

1. Irwin Allen papers collection (Courtesy Synthesis Entertainment, assisted by Ron Hamill).
2. Phillips, Mark, and Mike Bailey. "Doomsday Island." *Mike's Voyage to the Bottom of the Sea Zone*. hhttp://www.vttbots.com/epi_guide_season3_26.html
3. *ibid.*
4. Allen, Irwin. Notes on "Doomsday Island," June 26, 1966, UCLA Special Collections Library.
5. Fowler, Bruce. Memo to Sidney Marshall, June 29, 1966, UCLA Special Collections Library.
6. *ibid.*
7. *ibid.*
8. Warner, Les. Memo to Irwin Allen, July 1, 1966, UCLA Special Collections Library.
9. Show file for "Doomsday Island," Daily Production Report and Budget, UCLA Special Collections Library.
10. Phillips and Garcia. *Science Fiction Television Series, Volume 2*. See Chapter 4.10, note 11.
11. Irwin Allen papers collection (Courtesy Synthesis Entertainment, assisted by Ron Hamill).

Chapter 8.8: "The Wax Men"

1. Irwin Allen papers collection (Courtesy Synthesis Entertainment, assisted by Ron Hamill).
2. Phillips, Mark, and Mike Bailey. "The Wax Men." *Mike's Voyage to the Bottom of the Sea Zone*. http://www.vttbots.com/epi_guide_season3_8.html
3. *ibid.*
4. Garbutt, Mary. ABC Department of Broadcast Standards and Practices memo, "The Wax Men," January 3, 1967, UCLA Special Collections Library.
5. Maays, Stan. "Michael Dunn's Just Getting Started." *Waterloo Daily Courier* [IA], July 23, 1967.
6. Show file for "The Wax Men," Daily Production Report and Budget, UCLA Special Collections Library.
7. Allen, Irwin. Undated memo "To All Concerned, re: Photo Effects Budget," UCLA Special Collections Library.
8. "TV Scout." *North Adams Transcript* [MA], March 4, 1967.
9. Irwin Allen papers collection (Courtesy Synthesis Entertainment, assisted by Ron Hamill).

Chapter 8.9: "The Deadly Cloud"

1. Irwin Allen papers collection (Courtesy Synthesis Entertainment, assisted by Ron Hamill).
2. Phillips, Mark, and Mike Bailey. "The Deadly Cloud." *Mike's Voyage to the Bottom of the Sea Zone*. http://www.vttbots.com/epi_guide_season3_19.html
3. *ibid.*
4. Show file for "The Deadly Cloud," Daily Production Report and Budget, UCLA Special Collections Library.
5. "TV Scout." *Abilene Reporter-News* [TX], July 23, 1967.
6. Irwin Allen papers collection (Courtesy Synthesis Entertainment, assisted by Ron Hamill).

Chapter 8.10: "Destroy Seaview!"

1. Irwin Allen papers collection (Courtesy Synthesis Entertainment, assisted by Ron Hamill).
2. Phillips, Mark, and Mike Bailey. "Destroy Seaview!" *Mike's Voyage to the Bottom of the Sea Zone*. http://www.vttbots.com/epi_guide_season3_25.html
3. *ibid.*
4. Show file for "Destroy Seaview," Daily Production Report and Budget, UCLA Special Collections Library.
5. "TV Scout." *Madison Capital Times* [WI], March 18, 1967.
6. Irwin Allen papers collection (Courtesy Synthesis Entertainment, assisted by Ron Hamill).
7. Phillips, Mark. "Charting a Voyage to the Bottom of the Sea!" See Chapter 3, note 6.

Chapter 9: Season Four / ABC's Initial Order of 16 – Damage Control

1. "Authenticity Strong Point of TV Show." *Express and News* [San Antonio, Tx], August 27, 1967.
2. *ibid.*
3. Hunter, Lew (2015). Personal interview.
4. *ibid.*
5. Hedison, David. Audio Commentary. *Voyage to the Bottom of the Sea - The Complete Collection*. 20th Century Fox, 2007.
6. Hunter, Lew (2015). Personal interview.
7. Phillips and Garcia. *Science Fiction Television Series*, Volume 2. See Chapter 4.10, note 11.
8. Hunter, Lew (2015). Personal interview.
9. Pack, Harvey. "He Likes Series Role." *The Arizona Republic* [Phoenix], July 2, 1967.
10. *ibid.*
11. Maays, Stan. "Role of Sharkey Is Means to End." *The North Adams Transcript* [MA], September 23, 1967.
12. Phillips, Mark. "Do You Remember…" See Chapter 4.16, note 5.
13. Anderson, Jack E. "*Voyage* Actor Visiting Here." *The Miami Herald* [FL], May 26, 1967.
14. Gail, Al (1995). Interviewed by Kevin Burns (used by special arrangement with Jacobs/Brown).
15. Phillips, Mark. "Do You Remember…" See Chapter 4.16, note 5.
16. La Tourette, Frank. I.A. Productions *Hot Sheet,* October 4, 1968, Irwin Allen papers collection (Courtesy Synthesis Entertainment, assisted by Ron Hamill).

Chapter 9.1: "Man of Many Faces"

1. Irwin Allen papers collection (Courtesy Synthesis Entertainment, assisted by Ron Hamill).
2. Phillips, Mark, and Mike Bailey. "Man of Many Faces." *Mike's Voyage to the Bottom of the Sea Zone*. http://www.vttbots.com/episode_guide_year4_b.html#man
3. Welch, William. Undated "Man of Many Faces" springboard, UCLA Special Collections Library.
4. Allen, Irwin. Undated memo on "Man of Many Faces," UCLA Special Collections Library.
5. Warner, Les. Memo to Irwin Allen, April 27, 1967, UCLA Special Collections Library.
6. *ibid.*
7. Gail, Al (1995). Interviewed by Kevin Burns (used by special arrangement with Jacobs/Brown).
8. Show file for "Man of Many Faces," Daily Production Report and Budget, UCLA Special Collections Library.
9. "TV Scout." *Express and News* [San Antonio, TX], June 2, 1968.
10. Colliver, *Seaview: The Making of Voyage to the Bottom of the Sea*.

Chapter 9.2: "Time Lock"

1. Irwin Allen papers collection (Courtesy Synthesis Entertainment, assisted by Ron Hamill).
2. Welch, William. Undated treatment for "Time Lock," UCLA Special Collections Library.
3. Allen, Irwin. Notes on "Time Lock," June 7, 1967, UCLA Special Collections Library.
4. Warner, Les. Memo to Irwin Allen, May 17, 1967, UCLA Special Collections Library.
5. Eisner, Joel. "Merchant of Menace." *Starlog* #223, February 1996.
6. Show file for "Time Lock," Daily Production Report and Budget, UCLA Special Collections Library.
7. Eisner, Joel. "Merchant of Menace." See note 5.
8. Hunter, Lew (2015). Personal interview.
9. Hedison, David. Audio Commentary. *Voyage to the Bottom of the Sea - The Complete Collection.* 20th Century Fox, 2007.
10. Phillips, Mark. "Giant Jellyfish & Time-Lost Dinosaurs, Part Two." See Chapter 4.2, note 2.
11. *ibid.*
12. Eisner, Joel. "Merchant of Menace." See note 5.
13. "TV Scout." *Hagerstown Daily Mail* [MD], November 11, 1967.
14. Colliver, *Seaview: The Making of Voyage to the Bottom of the Sea.*

Chapter 9.3: "The Deadly Dolls"

1. Irwin Allen papers collection (Courtesy Synthesis Entertainment, assisted by Ron Hamill).
2. Phillips, Mark, and Mike Bailey. "The Deadly Dolls." *Mike's Voyage to the Bottom of the Sea Zone.* http://www.vttbots.com/episode_guide_year_4a.html#dolls
3. Bennett, Charles. "The Deadly Dolls" treatment, March 28, 1967, UCLA Special Collections Library.
4. Fowler, Bruce. Memo to Irwin Allen, April 17, 1967, UCLA Special Collections Library.
5. Hedison, David. "The Deadly Dolls." *David Hedison.* http://www.davidhedison.net/hedison/galleries/vtbots/voyagedvd/season04/deadly%20dolls/deadly_dolls.htm
6. Show file for "The Deadly Dolls," Daily Production Report and Budget, UCLA Special Collections Library.
7. Phillips, Mark. "Man Down Under." See Chapter 5.2, note 16.
8. Hedison, David. "The Deadly Dolls." See note 5.
9. Phillips, Mark. "Giant Jellyfish & Alien Invaders, Part Three." See Chapter 4.10, note 4.
10. "TV Scout." *Edwardsville Intelligencer* [IL], September 30, 1967.
11. Scheuer, Steven H. "TV Key." *Lima News* [OH], October 1, 1967.
12. Colliver, *Seaview: The Making of Voyage to the Bottom of the Sea.*

Chapter 9.4: "Fires of Death"

1. Irwin Allen papers collection (Courtesy Synthesis Entertainment, assisted by Ron Hamill).
2. Phillips, Mark, and Mike Bailey. "Fires of Death." *Mike's Voyage to the Bottom of the Sea Zone.* http://www.vttbots.com/episode_guide_year_4a.html#fires
3. *ibid.*
4. Weiss, Arthur. "Fires of Death" treatment, March 29, 1967, UCLA Special Collections Library.
5. Fowler, Bruce. Memo to Irwin Allen, April 12, 1967, UCLA Special Collections Library.
6. Phillips, Mark. "Do You Remember…" See Chapter 4.16, note 5.
7. Show file for "Fires of Death," Daily Production Report and Budget, UCLA Special Collections Library.
8. 20th Century-Fox Press Release, 1967. Stan Jolley. Irwin Allen papers collection (Courtesy Synthesis Entertainment, assisted by Ron Hamill).
9. *ibid.*
10. *ibid*
11. *ibid*
12. Phillips and Garcia. *Science Fiction Television Series*, Volume 2. See Chapter 4.10, note 11.
13. Phillips, Mark. "Do You Remember…" See Chapter 4.16, note 5.
14. Show file for "Fires of Death," Daily Production Report and Budget, UCLA Special Collections Library.
15. "Volcano Recipe." *North Adams Transcript* [MA], October 7, 1967.
16. "TV Scout." *Edwardsville Intelligencer* [IL], September 16, 1967.
17. Bill. Review of "Fires of Death." *Variety*, September 20, 1967.
18. Irwin Allen papers collection (Courtesy Synthesis Entertainment, assisted by Ron Hamill).

Chapter 9.5: "Cave of the Dead"

1. Irwin Allen papers collection (Courtesy Synthesis Entertainment, assisted by Ron Hamill).
2. Phillips, Mark, and Mike Bailey. "Cave of the Dead." *Mike's Voyage to the Bottom of the Sea Zone*. http://www.vttbots.com/episode_guide_year_4a.html#cave
3. *ibid.*
4. Welch. *Talks with the Dead.*
5. Fowler, Bruce. Memo to Irwin Allen, June 2, 1967, UCLA Special Collections Library.
6. Warner, Les. Memo to Irwin Allen, June 12, 1967, UCLA Special Collections Library.
7. Garbutt, Mary. ABC Department of Broadcast Standards and Practices memo, "Cave of the Dead," July 10, 1967, UCLA Special Collections Library.
8. Harris, Harry (1995). Interviewed by Kevin Burns (used by permission).
9. Show file for "Cave of the Dead," Daily Production Report and Budget, UCLA Special Collections Library.
10. "TV Scout." *Madison Capital Times* [WI], October 7, 1967.
11. *Variety*, October 25, 1967.
12. Colliver, *Seaview: The Making of Voyage to the Bottom of the Sea.*
13. *Variety*, October 25, 1967, TV ratings.

Chapter 9.6: "Sealed Orders"

1. Irwin Allen papers collection (Courtesy Synthesis Entertainment, assisted by Ron Hamill).
2. Phillips, Mark, and Mike Bailey. "Sealed Orders." *Mike's Voyage to the Bottom of the Sea Zone*. http://www.vttbots.com/episode_guide_year4_b.html#sealed
3. Garbutt, Mary. ABC Department of Broadcast Standards and Practices memo, "Sealed Orders," July 13, 1967, UCLA Special Collections Library.
4. Show file for "Sealed Orders," Daily Production Report and Budget, UCLA Special Collections Library.
5. "TV Scout." *Kenosha News* [WI], October 21, 1967.
6. Colliver, *Seaview: The Making of Voyage to the Bottom of the Sea.*

Chapter 9.7: "Journey with Fear"

1. Irwin Allen papers collection (Courtesy Synthesis Entertainment, assisted by Ron Hamill).
2. Phillips, Mark, and Mike Bailey. "Journey with Fear." *Mike's Voyage to the Bottom of the Sea Zone*. http://www.vttbots.com/episode_guide_year_4a.html#journey
3. Weiss, Arthur. "The Venusian Exploration" springboard, April 10, 1967, UCLA Special Collections Library.
4. Weiss, Arthur. "Journey with Fear" treatment, April 24, 1967, UCLA Special Collections Library.
5. Fowler, Bruce. Memo to Sid Marshall and Al Gail, May 3, 1967, UCLA Special Collections Library.
6. Weiss, Arthur. "Journey with Fear" treatment, May 3, 1967, UCLA Special Collections Library.
7. Fowler, Bruce. Memo to Irwin Allen, May 18, 1967, UCLA Special Collections Library.
8. *ibid.*
9. *ibid.*
10. Allen, Irwin. Undated notes on "Journey with Fear," UCLA Special Collections Library.
11. Warner, Les. Memo to Irwin Allen, Pre-Production Analysis for "Journey with Fear," June 29, 1967, UCLA Special Collections Library.
12. Show file for "Journey with Fear," Daily Production Report and Budget, UCLA Special Collections Library.
13. Phillips and Garcia. *Science Fiction Television Series, Volume 2.* See Chapter 4.10, note 11.
14. "TV Scout." *Edwardsville Intelligencer* [IL], October 14, 1967.
15. Scheuer, Steven H. "TV Key." *Kokomo Tribune* [IN], October 15, 1967.
16. Colliver, *Seaview: The Making of Voyage to the Bottom of the Sea.*

Chapter 9.8: "Fatal Cargo"

1. Irwin Allen papers collection (Courtesy Synthesis Entertainment, assisted by Ron Hamill).
2. Phillips, Mark, and Mike Bailey. "Fatal Cargo." *Mike's Voyage to the Bottom of the Sea Zone*. http://www.vttbots.com/episode_guide_year4_b.html#fatal
3. Van Duren, Paul. *Asbury Park Press* [NJ], November 8, 1967.
4. Welch, William. "Fatal Cargo" treatment dated June 15, 1967, UCLA Special Collections Library.
5. Show file for "Fatal Cargo," Daily Production Report and Budget, UCLA Special Collections Library.

6. "TV Scout." *Edwardsville Intelligencer* [IL], October 14, 1967.
7. Colliver, *Seaview: The Making of Voyage to the Bottom of the Sea*.

Chapter 9.9: "Rescue"

1. Irwin Allen papers collection (Courtesy Synthesis Entertainment, assisted by Ron Hamill).
2. Phillips, Mark, and Mike Bailey. "Rescue." *Mike's Voyage to the Bottom of the Sea Zone*. http://www.vttbots.com/episode_guide_year_4c.html#rescue
3. Show file for "Rescue," Daily Production Report and Budget, UCLA Special Collections Library.
4. "TV Scout." *Madison Capital Times* [WI], October 7, 1967.
5. Colliver, *Seaview: The Making of Voyage to the Bottom of the Sea*.

Chapter 9.10: "Terror"

1. Irwin Allen papers collection (Courtesy Synthesis Entertainment, assisted by Ron Hamill).
2. Phillips, Mark, and Mike Bailey. "Terror." *Mike's Voyage to the Bottom of the Sea Zone*. http://www.vttbots.com/episode_guide_year_4c.html#terror
3. Ellis, Sidney. "Terror" treatment, dated May 5, 1967, UCLA Special Collections Library.
4. Phillips, Mark. "Giant Jellyfish & Alien Invaders, Part Three." See Chapter 4.1, note 4.
5. Fowler, Bruce. Memo to Sid Marshall, May 9, 1967, UCLA Special Collections Library.
6. Phillips, Mark. "Giant Jellyfish & Alien Invaders, Part Three." See Chapter 4.10, note 4.
7. Show file for "Terror," Daily Production Report and Budget, UCLA Special Collections Library.
8. "TV Scout." *Kenosha News* [WI], October 21, 1967.
9. Colliver, *Seaview: The Making of Voyage to the Bottom of the Sea*.

Chapter 9.11: "Blow Up"

1. Irwin Allen papers collection (Courtesy Synthesis Entertainment, assisted by Ron Hamill).
2. Show file for "Blow Up!", Daily Production Report and Budget, UCLA Special Collections Library.
3. Lowry, Cynthia. "Always Satirize Shows." *Fond Du Lac Commonwealth Reporter* [WI], September 20, 1967.
4. Anchors and Barr, *Seaview: A 50th Anniversary Tribute to Voyage to the Bottom of the Sea*.
5. "TV Scout." *Kenosha News* [WI], December 9, 1967.
6. Colliver, *Seaview: The Making of Voyage to the Bottom of the Sea*.

Chapter 9.12: "Deadly Amphibians"

1. Irwin Allen papers collection (Courtesy Synthesis Entertainment, assisted by Ron Hamill).
2. Phillips, Mark, and Mike Bailey. "Deadly Amphibians." *Mike's Voyage to the Bottom of the Sea Zone*. http://www.vttbots.com/episode_guide_year_4d.html#deadly
3. *ibid*.
4. Anchors and Barr, *Seaview: A 50th Anniversary Tribute to Voyage to the Bottom of the Sea*.
5. I.A. Productions *Hot Sheet*, Vol. 1, No. 48, October 19, 1967, Irwin Allen papers collection (Courtesy Synthesis Entertainment, assisted by Ron Hamill).
6. Show file for "Deadly Amphibians," Daily Production Report and Budget, UCLA Special Collections Library.
7. "TV Scout." *San Antonio Express* [TX], December 17, 1967.
8. Colliver, *Seaview: The Making of Voyage to the Bottom of the Sea*.

Chapter 9.13: "The Return of Blackbeard"

1. Irwin Allen papers collection (Courtesy Synthesis Entertainment, assisted by Ron Hamill).
2. Phillips, Mark, and Mike Bailey. "The Return of Blackbeard." *Mike's Voyage to the Bottom of the Sea Zone*. http://www.vttbots.com/episode_guide_year_4d.html#return
3. *ibid*.
4. Clark, Mike. "The Master of Disaster." *Starlog* #176, March 1992.
5. Gail, Al. Treatment of "The Return of Blackbeard," dated August 29, 1966, UCLA Special Collections Library.

6. Garbutt, Mary. ABC Department of Broadcast Standards and Practices memo, "The Return of Blackbeard," July 13, 1967, UCLA Special Collections Library.
7. Throne, Malachi. Author interview, 2012.
8. Show file for "The Return of Blackbeard," Daily Production Report and Budget, UCLA Special Collections Library.
9. I.A. Productions *Hot Sheet,* Vol. 1, No. 39, October 4, 1967, Irwin Allen papers collection (Courtesy Synthesis Entertainment, assisted by Ron Hamill).
10. "TV Scout." *Express and News* [San Antonio, TX], December 31, 1967.
11. Colliver, *Seaview: The Making of Voyage to the Bottom of the Sea.*

Chapter 9.14: "A Time to Die"

1. Irwin Allen papers collection (Courtesy Synthesis Entertainment, assisted by Ron Hamill).
2. Welch. *Talks with the Dead.*
3. I.A. Productions *Hot Sheet,* Vol. 1, No. 39, October 4, 1967, Irwin Allen papers collection (Courtesy Synthesis Entertainment, assisted by Ron Hamill).
4. I.A. Productions *Hot Sheet,* Vol. 1, No. 40, October 5, 1967, Irwin Allen papers collection (Courtesy Synthesis Entertainment, assisted by Ron Hamill).
5. Show file for "A Time to Die," Daily Production Report and Budget, UCLA Special Collections Library.
6. I.A. Productions *Hot Sheet,* Vol. 1, No. 49, October 20, 1967, Irwin Allen papers collection (Courtesy Synthesis Entertainment, assisted by Ron Hamill).
7. Crosby, Joan. *The Courier-News* [Bridgewater, NJ], November 22, 1967.
8. *ibid.*
9. Crosby, Joan. "TV Scout." *Madison Capital Times* [WI], October 7, 1967.
10. Colliver, *Seaview: The Making of Voyage to the Bottom of the Sea.*

Chapter 9.15: "Edge of Doom"

1. Irwin Allen papers collection (Courtesy Synthesis Entertainment, assisted by Ron Hamill).
2. Phillips, Mark, and Mike Bailey. "Edge of Doom." *Mike's Voyage to the Bottom of the Sea Zone.* http://www.vttbots.com/episode_guide_year_4f.html#edge
3. Welch, William. Undated "The Edge of Doom" story notion, UCLA Special Collections Library.
4. I.A. Productions *Hot Sheet,* Vol. 1, No. 49, October 20, 1967, Irwin Allen papers collection (Courtesy Synthesis Entertainment, assisted by Ron Hamill).
5. Show file for "Edge of Doom," Daily Production Report and Budget, UCLA Special Collections Library.
6. Colliver, *Seaview: The Making of Voyage to the Bottom of the Sea.*
7. Bradford, Jack. "Jack Bradford on Hollywood." *The Missoulian* [MT], March 10, 1967.
8. Scheuer, Steven H. "TV Mail Bag." *The Ogden Standard-Examiner* [UT], March 17, 1968.
9. *ibid.*

Chapter 9.16: "Nightmare"

1. Irwin Allen papers collection (Courtesy Synthesis Entertainment, assisted by Ron Hamill).
2. Phillips, Mark, and Mike Bailey. "Nightmare." *Mike's Voyage to the Bottom of the Sea Zone.* http://www.vttbots.com/episode_guide_year_4e.html#nightmare
3. Marshall, Sidney. Undated "Nightmare" springboard, UCLA Special Collections Library.
4. Garbutt, Mary. ABC Department of Broadcast Standards and Practices memo, "Nightmare," October 6, 1967, UCLA Special Collections Library.
5. I.A. Productions *Hot Sheet,* Vol. 1, No. 49, October 20, 1967, Irwin Allen papers collection (Courtesy Synthesis Entertainment, assisted by Ron Hamill).
6. Show file for "Nightmare," Daily Production Report and Budget, UCLA Special Collections Library.
7. "TV Scout." *Edwardsville Intelligencer* [IL], January 27, 1967.
8. Colliver, *Seaview: The Making of Voyage to the Bottom of the Sea.*

Chapter 10: Season Four / ABC's Back Order of 10

1. "Party for Cast, Crew as Show Passes Milestone." *Sioux City Journal* [IA], October 29, 1967.

Chapter 10.1: "The Lobster Man"

1. Irwin Allen papers collection (Courtesy Synthesis Entertainment, assisted by Ron Hamill).
2. Phillips, Mark, and Mike Bailey. "The Lobster Man." *Mike's Voyage to the Bottom of the Sea Zone*. http://www.vttbots.com/episode_guide_year_4d.html#lobster
3. Gail, Al. Interviewed by Kevin Burns, 1995 (used by special arrangement with Jacobs/Brown).
4. Phillips and Garcia. *Science Fiction Television Series, Volume 2*. See Chapter 4.10, note 11.
5. *ibid.*
6. Anchors and Barr, *Seaview: A 50th Anniversary Tribute to Voyage to the Bottom of the Sea*.
7. Phillips and Garcia. *Science Fiction Television Series, Volume 2*. See Chapter 4.10, note 11.
8. Show file for "The Lobster Man," Daily Production Report and Budget, UCLA Special Collections Library.
9. "TV Scout." *Madison Capital Times* [WI], January 20, 1967.
10. Colliver, *Seaview: The Making of Voyage to the Bottom of the Sea*.

Chapter 10.2: "Terrible Leprechaun"

1. Irwin Allen papers collection (Courtesy Synthesis Entertainment, assisted by Ron Hamill).
2. Phillips, Mark, and Mike Bailey. "Terrible Leprechaun." *Mike's Voyage to the Bottom of the Sea Zone*. http://www.vttbots.com/episode_guide_year_4d.html#terrible
3. Phillips, Mark. "Man Down Under." See Chapter 5.2, note 16.
4. Show file for "Terrible Leprechaun," Daily Production Report and Budget, UCLA Special Collections Library.
5. Anchors and Barr, *Seaview: A 50th Anniversary Tribute to Voyage to the Bottom of the Sea*.
6. "Little Elves Take to Water." *The Odessa American* [TX], December 2, 1967.
7. "TV Scout." *Herald-Mail* [Hagerstown, MD], January 6, 1968.
8. Colliver, *Seaview: The Making of Voyage to the Bottom of the Sea*.

Chapter 10.3: "The Abominable Snowman"

1. Irwin Allen papers collection (Courtesy Synthesis Entertainment, assisted by Ron Hamill).
2. Phillips, Mark, and Mike Bailey. "The Abominable Snowman." *Mike's Voyage to the Bottom of the Sea Zone*. http://www.vttbots.com/episode_guide_year_4e.html#abominable
3. Phillips, Mark. "Giant Jellyfish & Alien Invaders, Part Three." See Chapter 4.10, note 4.
4. Hamner, Robert. "The Abominable Snowman" treatment, July 24, 1967, UCLA Special Collections Library.
5. Garbutt, Mary. ABC Department of Broadcast Standards and Practices memo, "The Abominable Snowman," November 15, 1967, UCLA Special Collections Library.
6. Phillips, Mark. "Giant Jellyfish & Alien Invaders, Part Three." See Chapter 4.10, note 4.
7. Show file for "The Abominable Snowman," Daily Production Report and Budget, UCLA Special Collections Library.
8. Colliver, *Seaview: The Making of Voyage to the Bottom of the Sea*.
9. Scheuer, Steven H. "Television Q's, A's." *News-Journal* [Mansfield, OH], February 10, 1968.

Chapter 10.4: "Man-Beast"

1. Irwin Allen papers collection (Courtesy Synthesis Entertainment, assisted by Ron Hamill).
2. Phillips, Mark, and Mike Bailey. "Man-Beast." *Mike's Voyage to the Bottom of the Sea Zone*. http://www.vttbots.com/episode_guide_year_4e.html#man
3. *ibid.*
4. Show file for "Man-Beast," Daily Production Report and Budget, UCLA Special Collections Library.
5. Phillips and Garcia. *Science Fiction Television Series, Volume 2*. See Chapter 4.10, note 11
6. *ibid.*
7. "TV Scout." *Edwardsville Intelligencer* [IL], January 27, 1967.
8. Colliver, *Seaview: The Making of Voyage to the Bottom of the Sea*.

Chapter 10.5: "Savage Jungle"

1. Irwin Allen papers collection (Courtesy Synthesis Entertainment, assisted by Ron Hamill).

2. Phillips, Mark, and Mike Bailey. "Savage Jungle." *Mike's Voyage to the Bottom of the Sea Zone*. http://www.vttbots.com/episode_guide_year_4f.html#savage
3. *ibid.*
4. Weiss, Arthur. "The Horrible Neanders" treatment, September 12, 1967, UCLA Special Collections Library.
5. *ibid.*
6. I.A. Productions *Hot Sheet*, Vol. 1, No. 40, October 5, 1967, Irwin Allen papers collection (Courtesy Synthesis Entertainment, assisted by Ron Hamill).
7. Show file for "Savage Jungle," Daily Production Report and Budget, UCLA Special Collections Library.
8. Anchors and Barr, *Seaview: A 50th Anniversary Tribute to Voyage to the Bottom of the Sea*.
9. Colliver, *Seaview: The Making of Voyage to the Bottom of the Sea*.

Chapter 10.6: "Secret of the Deep"

1. Irwin Allen papers collection (Courtesy Synthesis Entertainment, assisted by Ron Hamill).
2. Phillips, Mark, and Mike Bailey. "Secret of the Deep." *Mike's Voyage to the Bottom of the Sea Zone*. http://www.vttbots.com/episode_guide_year_4e.html#secret
3. Welch, William. Undated "Secret of the Abyss" springboard, UCLA Special Collections Library.
4. "J.A." Script notes on "Secret of the Deep," August 30, 1967, UCLA Special Collections Library.
5. Show file for "Secret of the Deep," Daily Production Report and Budget, UCLA Special Collections Library.
6. Colliver, *Seaview: The Making of Voyage to the Bottom of the Sea*.

Chapter 10.7: "Flaming Ice"

1. Irwin Allen papers collection (Courtesy Synthesis Entertainment, assisted by Ron Hamill).
2. Phillips, Mark. "Do You Remember…" See Chapter 4.16, note 5.
3. Browne, Arthur. "The Flaming Ice" revised treatment, undated, UCLA Special Collections Library.
4. Fowler, Bruce. Memo to Sid Marshall and Al Gail, May 1, 1967, UCLA Special Collections Library.
5. *ibid.*
6. Show file for "Flaming Ice," Daily Production Report and Budget, UCLA Special Collections Library.
7. Phillips, Mark. "Do You Remember…" See Chapter 4.16, note 5.
8. "TV Scout." *Edwardsville Intelligencer* [IL], January 27, 1967.
9. Colliver, *Seaview: The Making of Voyage to the Bottom of the Sea*.

Chapter 10.8: "Attack!"

1. Irwin Allen papers collection (Courtesy Synthesis Entertainment, assisted by Ron Hamill).
2. Phillips, Mark, and Mike Bailey. "Attack!" *Mike's Voyage to the Bottom of the Sea Zone*. http://www.vttbots.com/episode_guide_year_4f.html#attack
3. *ibid.*
4. Show file for "Attack!" Daily Production Report and Budget, UCLA Special Collections Library.
5. Welch, William. Undated "City of Doom, Parts 1 and 2" treatment, UCLA Special Collections Library.
6. Allen, Irwin. Notes on "City of Doom," March 27, 1967, UCLA Special Collections Library.
7. *ibid.*
8. Show file for "Attack!" Daily Production Report and Budget, UCLA Special Collections Library.
9. "Skip Started as Mean Brat." *Wichita Falls Times* [TX], March 10, 1968.
10. *ibid.*
11. "TV Scout." *Abilene Reporter-News* [TX], July 21, 1968.
12. Colliver, *Seaview: The Making of Voyage to the Bottom of the Sea*.

Chapter 10.9: "No Way Back"

1. Irwin Allen papers collection (Courtesy Synthesis Entertainment, assisted by Ron Hamill).
2. Welch. *Talks with the Dead*.
3. Phillips, Mark. "Giant Jellyfish & Time-Lost Dinosaurs, Part One." See Chapter 2, note 2.
4. Show file for "No Way Back," Daily Production Report and Budget, UCLA Special Collections Library.
5. "TV Scout." *Edwardsville Intelligencer* [IL], March 29, 1968.
6. Colliver, *Seaview: The Making of Voyage to the Bottom of the Sea*.

Chapter 10.10: "The Death Clock"

1. Irwin Allen papers collection (Courtesy Synthesis Entertainment, assisted by Ron Hamill).
2. Phillips, Mark, and Mike Bailey. "The Death Clock." *Mike's Voyage to the Bottom of the Sea Zone*. http://www.vttbots.com/episode_guide_year_4j.html#death
3. *ibid.*
4. Show file for "The Death Clock," Daily Production Report and Budget, UCLA Special Collections Library.
5. "TV Scout." *Edwardsville Intelligencer* [IL], August 8, 1968.
6. *Seaview: The Making of Voyage to the Bottom of the Sea, by Tim Colliver* (1992, Timothy L. Colliver).
7. Scheuer, Steven H. "TV Key Mail Bag," *News-Journal* [Mansfield, OH], July 6, 1968.

Chapter 11: Submarine Down – The End of the Voyage

1. Anchors and Barr, *Seaview: A 50th Anniversary Tribute to Voyage to the Bottom of the Sea*.
2. *ibid.*
3. Phillips, Mark. "Man Down Under." See Chapter 5.2, note 16.
4. Hedison, David. Audio Commentary. *Voyage to the Bottom of the Sea - The Complete Collection*. 20th Century Fox, 2007.
5. Phillips, Mark, and Mike Bailey. "No Way Back." *Mike's Voyage to the Bottom of the Sea Zone*. http://www.vttbots.com/episode_guide_year_4j.html#noway

Appendix A: Voyage to the Toy Store

1. Hunt, Allan (2020). Personal interview.
2. Mumy, Bill (2015). Personal interview.

You may also enjoy these books from Jacobs/Brown Press:

Beaming Up and Getting Off: Life Before and After Star Trek
by Walter Koenig

Previously on X-Men: The Making of an Animated Series
by Eric Lewald

Mary: The Mary Tyler Moore Story
by Herbie J Pilato

The Show Runner: An Insider's Guide to Successful TV Production
by Cy Chermak

Swords, Starships and Superheroes: From Star Trek to Xena to Hercules, A TV Writer's Life Scripting the Stories of Heroes
by Paul Robert Coyle

These Are the Voyages – Star Trek: The Original Series
in three volumes, by Marc Cushman with Susan Osborn

These Are the Voyages – Gene Roddenberry and Star Trek in the 1970s
in three volumes, by Marc Cushman:
Volume 1 (1970-75) / Volume 2 (1975-77) Volume 3 (1977-1980)

Irwin Allen's Voyage to the Bottom of the Sea: The Authorized Biography of a Classic Sci-Fi Series
in two volumes, by Marc Cushman and Mark Alfred

Irwin Allen's Lost in Space: The Authorized Biography of a Classic Sci-Fi Series
in three volumes, by Marc Cushman

Long Distance Voyagers: The Story of the Moody Blues – Volume One (1965-1979)
by Marc Cushman

Jacobs/Brown Media Group, LLC
Jacobs/Brown Press

Printed in Great Britain
by Amazon